Hiking Trails, Eastern United States

REFERENCE--NOT TO BE
TAKEN FROM THIS ROOM

Hiking Trails, Eastern United States

Address, Phone Number and Distances for 5000 Trails, with Indexing of Over 200 Guidebooks

by STEVE RAJTAR

McFarland & Company, Inc., Publishers
Jefferson, North Carolina, and London

British Library Cataloguing-in-Publication data are available

Library of Congress Cataloguing-in-Publication Data

Rajtar, Steve, 1951–
    Hiking trails, eastern United States : address, phone number and distances for 5000 trails, with indexing of over 200 guidebooks / by Steve Rajtar.
    p. cm.
    Includes bibliographical references (p.) and index. ∞
    ISBN 0-7864-0142-7 (sewn softcover : 50# alk. paper)
    1. Hiking—United States—East—Guidebooks. 2. Trails—United States—East—Guidebooks. 3. Trails—United States—East—Directories. 4. East (U.S.)—Guidebooks. I. Title.
GV199.42.E19R35   1995
917.4′04—dc20
                        95-17296
                             CIP

©1995 Steve Rajtar. All rights reserved

Manufactured in the United States of America

McFarland & Company, Inc., Publishers
  Box 611, Jefferson, North Carolina 28640

This is dedicated to my parents,
Steve and Rose,
who started me off on the right trail

Table of Contents

Preface	1	New Hampshire	135
Alabama	5	*Index*	142
Index	8	New Jersey	144
Connecticut	10	*Index*	152
Index	15	New York	154
Delaware	17	*Index*	178
Index	18	North Carolina	184
District of Columbia	19	*Index*	197
Florida	20	Ohio	200
Index	35	*Index*	209
Georgia	39	Pennsylvania	213
Index	47	*Index*	233
Illinois	50	Rhode Island	239
Index	59	*Index*	241
Indiana	63	South Carolina	242
Index	69	*Index*	250
Kentucky	71	Tennessee	253
Index	79	*Index*	263
Louisiana	82	Vermont	267
Index	84	*Index*	271
Maine	86	Virginia	273
Index	92	*Index*	299
Maryland	94	West Virginia	303
Index	100	*Index*	315
Massachusetts	102	Wisconsin	317
Index	111	*Index*	329
Michigan	115	Interstate Trails	335
Index	126	*List of Sources Used*	337
Mississippi	130		
Index	133		

PREFACE

There are areas of the North American continent where it is still possible—if not especially advisable—to create one's own hiking trail by drawing two dots on a map and connecting them with a line. With luck one might be able to follow that line and make a successful hike; if, on the other hand, luck did not hold, the hapless pioneer could easily drown, fall off a cliff, walk into an unanticipated building or stray into the path of an oncoming bus.

For practical purposes, then, hikers generally rely on established trails and the experience of those who have gone before. All over North America there are plotted routes that allow one to see the landscape's rivers, cliffs, trees, wildlife, buildings and buses. Researching the trails in a particular area makes it possible to plan a hiking trip with some degree of confidence; one can know what basic conditions to expect and select a trail and hiking gear accordingly. Certain kinds of information are important in planning any trip on foot. Is the area a park or national forest? Is there a campground? What are the general facts about each particular trail? Hikers want to know, for obvious reasons, the length of the trail, its location, its proximity to stores and medical facilities, and various other details that reduce the possibility of unpleasant surprises.

This information is usually available; the difficulty has always been in finding it. There are hundreds of books about trails, but their very abundance is part of the problem. Because these books are either not comprehensive or geographically narrow, there has been no single source that one might consult for information on *any* trail in North America. The present work is intended to fill that gap, providing concise information on every trail that I could discover and serving as a link to the people and organizations that one should contact for detailed, up-to-the-minute information. I strongly recommend that anyone planning a trip should make use of the addresses and telephone numbers provided to learn everything possible about the intended destination. Conditions can change rapidly, and often trails must be closed temporarily as a result of heavy rain or strong winds that erode pathways or topple trees and render the trails impassable. No book can substitute for a park ranger's voice over the telephone in relaying this kind of information.

Nor, I fear, can any book exhaustively list every trail and park in existence at any given moment, because changes are always occurring. While researching the material for this book I became aware that several brand new trails had been established, and that some had just closed. And the literature has always been fragmentary: for instance I was surprised, after checking 100 sources, that the 101st had data on dozens of trails that were not even hinted at in the first 100. That happened again after the 200th source, with the 201st being one of the most information-filled books I had seen on the subject. Then, after I decided to stop at 250 sources, I happened to see one more book that, amazingly, contained information on 500 more trails. This book represents my best attempt to present a comprehensive listing of books available on trails as of the end of 1994, the date I established as a cutoff.

The book is organized into serially numbered entries, each of which constitutes either a specific trail or an area whose publicity identifies hiking as an offered activity. The material presented varies, depending upon what is available in print or from the entity involved. The following examples show the forms that entries may take.

Example 1—Single Trail

461   **Orlando Historic Trail**, Corb Sarchet, 132 Waverley Pl., Orlando, FL 32806, (407) 648-9636 or (407) 422-8285. 5.5 miles loop. Awards available. (SAR 1994)

Following the name of the trail is the name, address and telephone number of its sponsor or contact person, who should be contacted for further information. The total distance of the trail is shown, and reference to it as a "loop" indicates that the start is also the endpoint. By contrast, a "straight" trail is not one that has no curves, but simply one that connects two different points rather than returning the hiker to the starting point. When hiking on a straight trail, one should double the listed distance for an accurate measure of the total hike, or else have a vehicle waiting at the endpoint. The reference to awards means that patches, medals or other memorabilia may be purchased from the sponsor. The final item, "(SAR 1994)," indicates that the author (hence the initials) most recently hiked the trail in 1994, confirming the information to be correct at that time.

Example 2—Public Park

460   **O'Leno State Park**, Rt. 2, Box 307, High Springs, FL 32643, (904) 454-1853. Named trails: Limestone 0.5(s), Pareners Branch 3.5(l), River Rise (Natural Bridge) 13.0(l), River Sink 1.0(s). (SAR 1993)

This entry lists multiple trails, each of which is located (at least in part) within the same park. Rather than list each trail separately, they have been grouped together. Please note that the words "Trail" (in the name of nearly every hiking route) and "miles" (in the length, where available) have been omitted for efficient use of space. In this example, the first trail listed should be read as the Limestone Trail, a straight trail with a length of one-half mile. The second is Pareners Branch Trail, a loop of 3.5 miles. If the route is named anything other than "trail" (such as path, walk, road, trek, etc.), or if the available measurement is other than in miles (such as kilometers, feet, minutes or hours), that information is included.

Example 3 — Public Park

463   Orlando Wilderness Park, Wheeler Rd., Christmas, FL 32709, (407) 246-2348; or Orlando Recreation Bureau, 649 W. Livingston St., Orlando, FL 32801, (407) 246-2649. (AA 1993)

This entry has no separate trails listed, which may occur for any of three reasons: (1) the area has no established trails, but is appropriate for striking off on one's own for miles through the wilderness; (2) the trails are not named, but might be separately marked with different colored blazes or numbers; or (3) no previously published work lists trail names, and as of press time they could not be obtained directly from the park. In Example 3 the reference to "(AA 1993)" indicates that the information provided in entry 463 was contained in a book, pamphlet or letter which came from the "above address" (the one listed in the entry) in 1993.

Example 4 — Commercial Campground

457   Ocala Springs RV Park, Rt. 1, Box 1305, Anthony, FL 32167, (904) 236-9918. (CFC)

This entry describes one of many private camping areas which advertise hiking as an available activity. The reference to "(CFC)" indicates that the information came from the book listed with that three-letter designation in the final chapter of this directory. Often, entries have a string of such designations, indicating numerous works where at least a mention of the hiking opportunities for this location may be found. They are listed in reverse chronological order of publication, the most recent first, rather than in any order corresponding to their breadth or accuracy of information.

There are dozens of books that devote entire chapters to single trails, enticing the hiker to get out there and start walking. But at the end of the description, instead of an address there may be only a vague direction such as "The trailhead is just a few miles down the dirt road from Pork Junction, near the store at the base of the mountain." The reader is left with no means of finding further information. Such directions are not found in this book. Generally their usefulness is slight at best, and the broad scope of this book imposes certain space limitations. To find out more about a particular trail or area, a reader may instead call or write the persons listed as contacts and receive clearer and more complete directions.

Information on awards associated with various trails is included in part because the Boy Scouts and other outdoor-oriented youth organizations are among the foremost groups involved in hiking, and are the biggest source of patches and medals for hikers who complete specified trails. Most of the youths involved with these groups are award-oriented and are eager to take hikes whose completion may entitle them to a medal or patch.

These patches and medals are generally available to all hikers, whether or not they are affiliated with the sponsoring organization. When an entry indicates "Awards available," at least one type (patch, medal, pin, etc.) is offered for sale by the sponsor—but as with other information, it is wise to verify the currency of these items in advance.

An index by city follows the entries for each state. Because of this organization, the hiker can scan the index to determine what trails are nearby in a home state, a neighboring state or a visit destination.

Any readers who have information about established trails that are not listed in this book are encouraged to send it to me, in care of the publisher, so that I can incorporate it into any future edition. The same applies to corrections of the material I have written, especially since the facts always continue to change.

Alabama

Alligator Trail see entry 40.
1 **Anniston Museum of Natural History**, 4301 McClellan Blvd., Anniston, AL 36201, (205) 237-6766 or (205) 237-6776. (ATA; MSE)
2 **Azalea Trail**, Mobile Chamber of Commerce, 451 Government St., Mobile, AL 36602. (GFA)
3 **Bankhead National Forest**, P.O. Box 278, S. Main St., Double Springs, AL 35553, (205) 832-4470; or Forest Supervisor, 1765 Highland Ave., Montgomery, AL 36107. 23.0 miles total. Named trails: Bee Branch 1.0. (EGH; WCD; GOP; GFC; MSE; FGU; WPS; GNF)
4 **Bashi Creek**, Corps of Engineers, Mobile District, P.O. Box 2288, Mobile, AL 33628. (GFC)
Bee Branch Trail see entry 3.
5 **Bill Dannelly Reservoir**, Corps of Engineers, Mobile District, P.O. Box 2288, Mobile, AL 33628. (GFC)
6 **Birmingham Botanical Gardens Wildflower Trail**, 2612 Lane Park Rd., Birmingham, AL 35223. (GFA)
7 **Blue Pond**, SR 137, Andalusia, AL 36420. (ATA)
8 **Brushy Lake**, FR 245, Moulton, AL 35650. (ATA)
9 **Buck's Pocket State Park**, Rt. 1, Box 36, Grove Oak, AL 35975, (205) 659-2000. (AOB; ATA; MSE)
10 **Burritt Museum and Park**, 3101 Burritt Dr., Huntsville, AL 35801, (205) 536-2882. (MSE; GFA)
11 **Camp Alaflo**, Alabama-Florida Council, BSA, P.O. Box 2028, Dothan, AL 36301, (334) 793-7882; or Camp Alaflo, Rt. 2, Box 185, New Brockton, AL 36351, (334) 894-6621. (SFC)
12 **Camp Mawbila**, Mobile Area Council, BSA, 2587 Government Blvd., Mobile, AL 36606, (334) 476-4600; or Camp Mawbila, Jackson, AL 36545, (334) 246-4974. (SFC)
Cave Creek Trail see entry 88.
13 **Cheaha State Park**, Rt. 1, Box 79-A, Lineville, AL 36266, (205) 488-5111. (WCD; ATA; MSE)
14 **Chewacla State Park**, P.O. Box 447, Shell Toomer Pkwy., Auburn, AL 36830, (334) 887-5621. (WCD; ATA; MSE)
15 **Chickasaw State Park**, US 43, Linden, AL 36748. (ATA)
16 **Chicksabogue County Park**, 760 Aldock Rd., Mobile, AL 36613, (334) 452-8496. (WCD)
17 **Chief Ladiga Trail**, Tommy Allison, City of Piedmont, P.O. Box 112, Piedmont, AL 36272, (205) 447-9007. 21.0 miles planned; current as to 3.0 miles (1993). (GRT)
18 **Chilatchee Creek Park**, CR 29, Alberta, AL 36720, (334) 682-4244. (WCD)
Chinnabee Lake Shore Trail see entry 88.
19 **Chinnabee Silent Trail**, Moran Colburn, 304 Dabney St., Talladega, AL 35160; or Talladega School for Deaf & Blind, P.O. Box 698, Talladega, AL 35160. 6.0 miles loop. Awards available. (AA 1989)
20 **Claiborne Lake**, Public Affairs Officer, U.S. Army Engineer District, Mobile, P.O. Box 2288, Mobile, AL 36328. (LRA)
21 **Clarkson Covered Bridge**, CR 11, Cullman, AL 35055. (AOB)
22 **Cloudmont Ski and Golf Resort**, CR 89, Mentone, AL 35984, (205) 634-3841. (AOB)
23 **Coffeeville Lake**, Corps of Engineers,

Mobile District, P.O. Box 2288, Mobile, AL 33628. (GFC)
24 Coleman Lake, FR 5004, Heflin, AL 36264. (ATA)
25 Conecuh National Forest, P.O. Box 310, 1100 S. 3-Notch St., Andalusia, AL 36420, (334) 222-2555. Named trails: Conecuh 20.0(l). (EGH; ATA; MSE; FGU)
Conecuh Trail see entry 25.
26 Confederate Memorial Park, US 31, Clanton, AL 35045, (334) 755-1990. (ATA; MSE)
27 Cornwall Furnace Park, CR 92, Cedar Bluff, AL 35959, (205) 927-8455. (AOB)
28 Deerlick Creek, CR 89, Tuscaloosa, AL 35406, (205) 759-1591. (WCD)
29 DeSoto Caverns Park, Rt. 1, Box 265, Childersburg, AL 35044, (205) 378-7252. (WCD; ATA; MSE)
30 DeSoto Scout Trail, C.M.T. Sawyer, II, P.O. Box 71, Ft. Payne, AL 35967; or Choccolocco Council, BSA, P.O. Box 4549, Anniston, AL 36204-4549, (205) 237-1777. 16.0 miles straight. Awards available. (AA 1989)
31 DeSoto State Park, Rt. 1, Box 210, Fort Payne, AL 35967, (205) 843-0051 or (205) 845-5075. 20.0 miles. (AOB; EGH; WCD; ATA; MSE; OTB)
32 Discovery Trail, Walter E. Whitacre, 301 Belvedere Rd., S.E., Huntsville, AL 35803. 11.2 miles. (HTA)
33 Dismals Garden Trail, SR 43, Phil Campbell, AL 35581. 1.0 mile. (OTB)
34 Escatawpa Hollow Campground, US 98, Wilmer, AL 36587, (334) 649-4233. (WCD)
35 Eufala National Wildlife Refuge, Rt. 2, Box 97-B, Eufala, AL 36027, (205) 687-4065. 13.0 miles. (GFA; GNW)
36 Florence Alabama Historical Trail, Boy Scout Troop 217, P.O. Box 823, Tuscumbia, AL 35674; or Tennessee Valley Council, BSA, 2211 Drake Ave., S.W., Huntsville, AL 35805, (205) 883-7071. 7.0 miles loop. Awards available. (AA 1992)
37 Fort Gaines Campground, Bienville Blvd., Dauphin Island, AL 36528, (334) 861-2742. (WCD; MSE)

38 Fort Morgan State Historic Park, SR 180, Gulf Shores, AL 36542. (OTB)
39 Fort Toulouse-Jackson Park, US 231, Wetumpka, AL 36092, (334) 567-3002. (WCD; GFA; OTB)
40 Gulf State Park, SR 182, Gulf Shores, AL 36542, (334) 968-6353. Named trails: Alligator, Lakes. (WCD; ATA; MSE; OTB)
41 Gunter Hill Park, CR 7, Benton, AL 36785, (334) 269-1053. (WCD)
42 Haines Island, Corps of Engineers, Mobile District, P.O. Box 2288, Mobile, AL 33628. (GFC)
43 Holt Lake, Resource Manager, Holt Lake, P.O. Box 520, Demopolis, AL 36732. (LRA)
44 Horseshoe Bend Historic Trail, Tukabatchee Area Council, BSA, 3067 Carter Hill Rd., P.O. Box 3115, Montgomery, AL 36111. 10.0 miles straight. Awards available. (AA 1992)
45 Horseshoe Bend National Military Park, Rt. 1, Box 103, Daviston, AL 36256, (205) 234-7111. 13.0 miles. Named trails: Battlefield 5.0, Ecology 6.0. Awards available. (AA 1992)
46 Isaac Creek Park, CR 17, Monroeville, AL 36460, (334) 282-4489. (WCD)
47 Joe Wheeler State Park, Park Rd., Rogersville, AL 35652, (205) 247-1184. (WCD; ATA; MSE)
48 KOA-Sequoia Caverns, US 11, Valley Head, AL 35989, (205) 635-6423. (WCD)
49 Lake Chinnabee, SR 42, Tuscaloosa, AL 35401. (ATA)
50 Lake Guntersville State Park, Star Route 63, Box 224, Guntersville, AL 35976, (205) 582-3666. 20.0 miles. (AOB; ATA; MSE)
51 Lake Lurleen State Park, CR 21, Tuscaloosa, AL 35401, (205) 339-1558. (WCD; ATA)
52 Lakepoint Resort State Park, US 431, Eufala, AL 36027, (205) 687-6676. (AOB; WCD; ATA; MSE)
Lakes Trail see entry 40.
53 Landmark Park, US 431N, Dothan, AL 36302, (334) 794-3452. (AOB; MSE)
54 Lewis Smith Lake, CR 22, Russellville, AL 35653. (ATA)

ALABAMA

55 **Little River Canyon Mouth County Park**, CR 275, Leesburg, AL 35983. (WCD)
56 **Little River Canyon Trail**, SR 275, Fort Payne, AL 35967, (205) 845-0051. 6.0 miles. (GFA)
57 **Lookout Mountain Trail**, Noccalula Falls and Park, 1400 Noccalula Rd., Gadsden, AL 35901, (205) 546-5848 or (800) ALABAMA. 125 miles. (FTS)
58 **Madison County Nature Trail**, S. Shawdee Rd., Huntsville, AL 35803, (205) 883-9501. 2.0 miles. (MSE; OTB)
59 **Mallard Creek**, Wheeler Lake, Spring Creek Rd., Decatur, AL 35603. (WCD)
60 **Maxwell Historical Trail**, Wing Commander's Youth Representative, Bldg. 853, Maxwell AFB, AL 36112-5712, (334) 285-7330. 8.5 miles loop. Awards available. (AA 1992)
61 **Monte Sano Railway Trail**, Rebecca Bergquist, Huntsville Land Trust, P.O. Box 43, Huntsville, AL 35804, (205) 534-5263. 2.0 miles. (GRT)
62 **Monte Sano State Park**, 5105 Nolen Ave., Huntsville, AL 35801, (205) 534-3757. (WCD; ATA; MSE)
63 **Mound State Monument**, SR 69, Moundville, AL 35474, (205) 371-2572. (WCD; ATA; MSE)
64 **Natchez Trace National Scenic Trail** (see separate entry **4954** in interstate section).
65 **Noccalula Falls City Park**, Noccalula Rd., Gadsden, AL 35901, (205) 543-7412. (AOB; WCD; MSE)
Nubbin Creek Trail see entry 88.
66 **Oak Mountain State Park**, P.O. Box 278, Pelham, AL 35124, (205) 663-6771. 30.0 miles. (EGH; WCD; ATA)
67 **Odum Scout Trail**, Talladega Chamber of Commerce, P.O. Drawer A, Talladega, AL 35160, (205) 362-9075. 10.0 miles straight. Awards available. (AA 1989)
Odum Trail see entry 88.
68 **Open Pond**, SR 137, Andalusia, AL 36420. (ATA)
69 **Ozark Camper Park**, US 231, Ozark, AL 36360, (334) 774-3219. (ATA; MSE)
70 **Paul M. Grist State Park**, Rt. 7, Box 28, Selma, AL 36701, (334) 872-5846. (ATA; MSE)
71 **Payne Lake**, SR 25, Greensboro, AL 36744. (ATA)
72 **Pine Glen**, FR 500, Heflin, AL 36264. (ATA)
73 **Pinhoti Trail**, Talladega National Forest, District Ranger, 1001 North St., Talladega, AL 35160-2503; or U.S. Forest Service, 450 SR 46, Heflin, AL 36264; (for patch, contact Mrs. Lucille Morgan, Cleburn County Library, P.O. Box 428, Heflin, AL 36264). 100 miles. Awards available for 62.8 miles section. (AA 1990)
74 **Point Mallard City Park**, 8th St. SE, Decatur, AL 35601, (205) 351-7772. (AOB; WCD; ATA; MSE)
75 **Prairie Creek Park**, CR 29, Lowndesboro, AL 36752, (334) 872-9554. (WCD)
76 **Rickwood Caverns State Park**, Rt. 3, Box 340, Warrior, AL 35180, (205) 647-9692. (ATA; MSE)
77 **River Mont Cave Historic Trail**, P.O. Box 122, Bridgeport, AL 35740; or Bobby Hill, 711 Diamond Ave., Bridgeport, AL 35740, (205) 495-3941. 12.0 miles straight. Awards available for hiking and trail clearing. (SAR 1992)
78 **Riverside Campground & Lodge**, CR 48, Fairhope, AL 36532, (334) 947-3953. (WCD)
79 **Rock Bridge Canyon Trail**, SR 19, Red Bay, AL 35582. (OTB)
80 **Ruffner Mountain Nature Center**, 1214 S. 81st St., Birmingham, AL 35206, (205) 933-4104 or (205) 933-4124. (ATA; MSE)
81 **Russell Cave Trail**, Russell Cave National Monument, Rt. 1, Box 175, Bridgeport, AL 35740, (205) 495-2672. 0.8 mile. (AOB; ATA; NPS; NPV; OTB; CGA)
82 **S.W. Taylor State Recreation Area**, SR 39, Gainesville, AL 35464. (ATA)
83 **Sherling Lake City Park**, CR 185/263, Greenville, AL 36037, (334) 382-3638. (WCD; ATA)
84 **Silver Creek Park**, Corps of Engineers, Mobile District, P.O. Box 2288, Mobile, AL 33628. (GFC)

85 **Sipsey River**, FR 26, Haleyville, AL 35565. (ATA)
86 **Sleepy Holler RV Campground**, US 78, Jasper, AL 35501, (205) 489-5111. (WCD)
87 **Space Walk Scenic Trail**, Troop 364, BSA, 301 Belvedere Rd. SE., Huntsville, AL 35803. 11.0 miles. Awards available. (HTA)
88 **Talladega National Forest**, Forest Supervisor, 1765 Highland Ave., Montgomery, AL 36107, (334) 832-4470; or District Ranger, 1001 North St., Talladega, AL 35160-2503, (205) 362-2909. Named trails: Cave Creek 4.0(s), Chinnabee Lake Shore 2.0(l), Nubbin Creek 4.0(s), Odum 4.7(s), Pinhoti 100(s), Skyway Loop 6.0(s). (AA 1994)
89 **Tannehill Historical State Park**, Eastern Valley Rd., Bessemer, AL 35020, (205) 477-5711. (WCD; MSE)
90 **Tannehill Scout Trail**, Tannehill State Park, Rt. 1, Box 124, 12632 Confederate Pkwy., McCalla, AL 35111, (205) 477-6571. 12.6 miles straight. Awards available. (AA 1989)
91 **Thomas Mill Creek Park**, SR 97, Abbeville, AL 36310, (334) 255-5816. (WCD)
92 **Thunder Canyon Campground**, Thunder Canyon Rd., Ider, AL 35981, (205) 632-2103. (WCD)
93 **Thunderbird Scout Trail**, Choccolocco Council, BSA, P.O. Box 4599, Anniston, AL 36204, (205) 237-1777; or Comer Scout Reservation, Rt. 1, Mentone, AL 35984, (205) 634-3445. Awards available. (AA 1989)
94 **Tuscumbia Historical Trek**, Boy Scout Troop 217, P.O. Box 823, Tuscumbia, AL 35674; or Tennessee Valley Council, BSA, 2211 Drake Ave., Huntsville, AL 35805, (205) 883-7071. 2.0 miles loop. Awards available. (AA 1992)
95 **Tuskegee Institute Trail**, US 29S, Tuskegee, AL 36088, (334) 727-3200 or (334) 727-2652. 8.5 miles. (FTS)
96 **Tuskegee National Forest**, Rt. 1, Box 204AA, Tuskegee, AL 36088, (334) 727-2652. (MSE; OTB; FGU)
97 **USS Alabama Historical Trail**, 5860 College Pkwy., Mobile, AL 36613, (334) 675-7037; or A.F. Palmer, 200 Rapier St., Mobile, AL 36604. 11.0 miles loop. Awards available. (SAR 1990)
98 **Warpath Ridge Trail**, Troop 304, BSA, 601 Monte Sano Blvd., Huntsville, AL 35801. 12.0 miles. Awards available. (HTA)
99 **Warrior Caverns State Park**, Warrior, AL 35180, (205) 647-9692. (WCD)
100 **Wheeler National Wildlife Refuge**, P.O. Box 1643, Decatur, AL 35602, (205) 353-7243. 100 miles. (ATA; GNW)
101 **Wilson Dam/Rockpile**, SR 133/TVA Reservation Rd., Muscle Shoals, AL 35661. (WCD)
102 **Wind Creek State Park**, Rt. 2, Box 145, Alexander City, AL 35010, (205) 329-0845 or (205) 234-2101. (ATA; MSE)
103 **Woodhaven**, Rt. 2, Box 10A, Lowry Rd., Valley Head, AL 35989, (205) 635-6438. (AOB)

Generally:
Commissioner, Department of Conservation and Natural Resources, 64 N. Union St., Montgomery, AL 36130, (334) 261-3486. (SFC)
National Forests in Alabama, 1765 Highland Ave., Montgomery, AL 36107, (334) 832-7630. (EGH)

Index (by city)

Abbeville: Thomas Mill Creek Park 91
Alberta: Chilatchee Creek Park 18
Alexander City: Wind Creek State Park 102
Andalusia: Blue Pond 7; Conecuh National Forest 25; Open Pond 68
Anniston: Anniston Museum of Natural History 1
Auburn: Chewacla State Park 14
Benton: Gunter Hill Park 41
Bessemer: Tannehill Historical State Park 89

ALABAMA

Birmingham: Birmingham Botanical Gardens Wildflower Trail 6; Ruffner Mountain Nature Center 80
Bridgeport: River Mont Cave Historic Trail 77; Russell Cave Trail 81
Camden: Bill Dannelly Reservoir 5
Cedar Bluff: Cornwall Furnace Park 27
Childersburg: DeSoto Caverns Park 29
Claiborne: Haines Island 42
Clanton: Confederate Memorial Park 26
Cullman: Clarkson Covered Bridge 21
Dauphin Island: Fort Gaines Campground 37
Daviston: Horseshoe Bend Historic Trail 44; Horseshoe Bend National Military Park 45
Decatur: Mallard Creek 59; Point Mallard City Park 74; Wheeler National Wildlife Refuge 100
Demopolis: Holt Lake 43
Dothan: Landmark Park 53
Double Springs: Bankhead National Forest 3
Eufala: Eufala National Wildlife Refuge 35; Lakepoint Resort State Park 52
Fairhope: Riverside Campground & Lodge 78
Florence: Florence Alabama Historical Trail 36
Ft. Payne: DeSoto State Park 31; Little River Canyon Trail 56
Gadsden: Lookout Mountain Trail 57; Noccalula Falls City Park 65
Gainesville: S.W. Taylor State Recreation Area 82
Gilbertown: Coffeeville Lake 23
Greensboro: Payne Lake 71
Greenville: Sherling Lake City Park 83
Grove Oak: Buck's Pocket State Park 9
Gulf Shores: DeSoto Scout Trail 30; Fort Morgan State Historic Park 38; Gulf State Park 40; Thunderbird Scout Trail 93
Guntersville: Lake Guntersville State Park 50
Haleyville: Sipsey River 85
Heflin: Coleman Lake 24; Pine Glen 72; Pinhoti Trail 73
Huntsville: Burritt Museum and Park 10; Discovery Trail 32; Madison County Nature Trail 58; Monte Sano Railway Trail 61; Space Walk Scenic Trail 87; Warpath Ridge Trail 98
Ider: Thunder Canyon Campground 92
Jackson: Camp Mawbila 12
Jasper: Sleepy Holler RV Campground 86
Leesburg: Little River Canyon Mouth County Park 55
Linden: Chickasaw State Park 15
Lineville: Cheaha State Park 13
Lowndesboro: Prairie Creek Park 75
Maxwell AFB: Maxwell Historical Trail 60
McCalla: Tannehill Scout Trail 90
Mentone: Cloudmont Ski and Golf Resort 22
Mobile: Azalea Trail 2; Chicksabogue County Park 16; Claiborne Lake 20; USS Alabama Historical Trail 97
Monroeville: Isaac Creek Park 46
Montgomery: Talladega National Forest 88
Moulton: Brushy Lake 8
Moundville: Mound State Monument 63
Muscle Shoals: Wilson Dam/Rockpile 101
New Brockton: Camp Alaflo 11
Ozark: Ozark Camper Park 69
Pelham: Oak Mountain State Park 66
Phil Campbell: Dismals Garden Trail 33
Piedmont: Chief Ladiga Trail 17
Red Bay: Rock Bridge Canyon Trail 79
Rogersville: Joe Wheeler State Park 47
Russellville: Lewis Smith Lake 54
Selma: Paul M. Grist State Park 70
Talladega: Chinnabee Silent Trail 19; Odum Scout Trail 67; Talladega National Forest 88
Tuscaloosa: Deerlick Creek 28; Lake Chinnabee 49; Lake Lurleen State Park 51
Tuscumbia: Tuscumbia Historical Trek 94
Tuskegee: Tuskegee Institute Trail 95
Valley Head: KOA-Sequoia Caverns 48; Woodhaven 103
Warrior: Rickwood Caverns State Park 76; Warrior Caverns State Park 99
Wetumpka: Fort Toulouse-Jackson Park 39
Wilmer: Escatawpa Hollow Campground 34

Connecticut

104 **Airline Hiking Trail**, Connecticut Office of State Parks and Recreation, 165 Capitol Ave., Hartford, CT 06106, (203) 566-2304. 3.66 miles. (HTN)
105 **Airline State Park Trail**, (Northern) John Folsom, Mashamoquet Brook State Park, Pomfret Center, CT 06259, (203) 928-6121; or (Southern) Joe Hickey, Bureau of Outdoor Recreation, Department of Environmental Protection, 165 Capitol Ave., Hartford, CT 06106, (203) 566-2304. Northern section 26.8 miles straight; Southern section 22.7 miles straight. (GRT)
106 **Algonquin State Forest**, SR 8, Colebrook, CT 06021. (SNE; GNA)
107 **Altschul Trails**, Mrs. Edward Hughes, Altschul Preserve Committee, Carrington Dr., Greenwich, CT 06830, (203) 622-1700 or (203) 629-2916. (NNY)
   Ambler Trail *see* entry 135.
108 **American Legion State Forest**, SR 20, Riverton, CT 06065. Named trails: Henry Buck 1.5. (GNA; HTN)
109 **Ansonia Nature & Recreation Center**, 10 Deerfield Ln., Ansonia, CT 06401. 2.0 miles. (GFA)
110 **Appalachian Side Trails** (not listed elsewhere), Appalachian Trail Conference, Washington and Jackson Sts., P.O. Box 807, Harpers Ferry, WV 25425-0807, (304) 535-6331; or Appalachian Mountain Club, Pinkham Notch Camp, Gorham, NH 03581, (604) 466-2727. Named trails: Bald Peak 3.2, Breadloaf Mountain 0.3, Lion's Head 0.2, Mohawk, Paradise Lane 2.1, Prospect Mountain 0.5, Undermountain 1.9. (BMG; ATG #3)
111 **Appalachian Trail** (see separate entry 4948 in interstate section).
112 **Audubon Center in Greenwich**, 613 Riverside Rd., Greenwich, CT 06830, (203) 869-5272. 8.0 miles. (MNE; SNE; NNY; GNA)
   Bald Peak Trail *see* entry 110.
113 **Bantam Lake**, Bantam Lake AYH-Hostel, East Shore Rd., Lakeside, CT 06758, (203) 567-9258. (AYH)
114 **Barn Island Wildlife Management Area**, Department of Environmental Protection, Eastern District, Wildlife Bureau, 209 Hebron Rd., Marlborough, CT 06447, (203) 295-9525. (SNE; GNA)
115 **Barnes Memorial Nature Center**, 175 Shrub Rd., Bristol, CT 06010, (203) 589-6082. (MNE)
116 **Bartlett Arboretum**, University of Connecticut, 151 Brookdale Rd., Stamford, CT 06903, (203) 322-6971. (MNE; GFA; NNY)
117 **Bigelow Hollow State Park**, SR 190, Stafford, CT 06075. (SNE; GNA)
118 **Birdcraft Trail**, Birdcraft Museum, 314 Unquowa Rd., Fairfield, CT 06430, (203) 259-0416. (NNY)
119 **Black Rock State Park**, US 6, Thomaston, CT 06787. (GNA)
120 **Bluff Point Coastal Reserve**, Connecticut Office of State Parks and Recreation, 165 Capitol Ave., Hartford, CT 06106, (203) 566-2304. (SNE; GNA)
   Breadloaf Mountain Trail *see* entry 110.
121 **Burr Pond State Park**, SR 8, Torrington, CT 06790. (MNE; GNA)
   Butterfly Trail *see* entry 181.
122 **Byrum River Trail**, Mrs. Gerrish Milliken, Byrum River Gorge Committee, 39 Pierson Dr., Greenwich, CT 06830, (203) 869-7969; or New York-New Jersey Trail Commission, 232 Madison Ave., Rm. 908, New York, NY 10116, (212) 685-9699. 5.3 miles straight. (NYW)

CONNECTICUT

123 **Caldwell Area,** Mr. Joseph Zeranski, Greenwich Audubon Society, 163 Fieldpoint Rd., Greenwich, CT 06830, (203) 661-9607. 1.25 miles. Named trails: Loop. (NNY)
124 **Calf Island,** Greenwich YMCA, Calf Island Branch, 50 E. Putnam Ave., Greenwich, CT 06830, (203) 869-1630. (NNY)
125 **Camp Deer Lake,** Quinnipiac Council, BSA, 1861 Whitney Ave., Hamden, CT 06517, (203) 288-6211. (SFC)
126 **Camp Housatonic,** Housatonic Council, BSA, Plaza-on-the-Green, 90 Minerva St., Derby, CT 06401, (203) 734-3329. (SFC)
127 **Camp Sequassen,** Quinnipiac Council, BSA, 1861 Whitney Ave., Hamden, CT 06517, (203) 288-6211. (SFC)
128 **Campbell Falls State Park,** SR 272, Norfolk, CT 06058. (MNE; SNE)
   Canonicus Trail *see* entry 191.
   Castle Trail *see* entry 191.
129 **Charles Hubbard Memorial Trail,** Bernard N. Kane, 138 State St., Guilford, CT 06437. 2.5 miles. (HTN)
   Charles Pack Trail *see* entry 195.
130 **Chatfield Hollow State Park,** N. Branford Rd., Killinworth, CT 06419, (203) 663-2030. (MNE; SNE; GNA)
   Chatfield Trail *see* entry 131.
131 **Cockaponset State Forest,** SR 9, Haddam, CT 06438. Named trails: Chatfield 4.5, Cockaponset 10.0(l). (GNA; HTN)
   Cockaponset Trail *see* entry 131.
132 **Connecticut Audubon Center,** Roy and Margot Larsen Sanctuary, 2325 Burr St., Fairfield, CT 06430, (203) 259-6305. 6.5 miles. (MNE; SNE; GFA; NNY)
   Deer Knoll Trail *see* entry 135.
133 **Denison Pequotsepos Nature Center,** Pequotsepos Rd., Stonington, CT 06378, (203) 536-1216. 5.0 miles. (MNE)
134 **Dennis Hill State Park,** SR 272, Norfolk, CT 06058. (MNE)
135 **Devil's Den Preserve,** P.O. Box 1162, Weston, CT 06883, (203) 266-4991. 20.0 miles. Named trails: Ambler, Deer Knoll, Great Ledge. (EGH; SNE; NNY; GNA)
136 **Devil's Hopyard State Park,** SR 82, Salem, CT 06420. 15.0 miles. (SNE; GNA)
137 **East Rock Park,** East Rock Rd., New Haven, CT 06511, (203) 787-8021. (FNE; MNE)
   Elliot Bronson Trail *see* entry 191.
138 **Ellithorpe Flood Control Area,** Department of Environmental Protection, Eastern District, Wildlife Bureau, 209 Hebron Rd., Marlborough, CT 06447, (203) 295-9525. (SNE)
139 **Enders State Forest,** Connecticut Office of State Parks and Recreation, 165 Capitol Ave., Hartford, CT 06106, (203) 566-2304. (GNA)
140 **Farmington Canal Line State Park Trail,** Dick Hartlem, Cheshire Department of Parks and Recreation, 559 S. Main St., Cheshire, CT 06410, (203) 272-2743. 6.8 miles straight. (GRT)
141 **Farmington River Fishing Access Area Trail,** Daniel Dickinson, Park and Recreation Supervisor, Farmington Headquarters, 178 Scott Swamp Rd., Farmington, CT 06032, (203) 677-1819. 3.5 miles straight. (GRT)
142 **Flanders Nature Center,** Flanders Rd., Woodbury, CT 06798, (203) 263-3711. (MNE; GFA)
143 **Franklin Swamp Wildlife Management Area,** Department of Environmental Protection, Eastern District, Wildlife Bureau, 209 Hebron Rd., Marlborough, CT 06447, (203) 295-9525. (SNE)
144 **Gay City State Park,** SR 85, Andover, CT 06232. (SNE; GNA)
145 **Gillette Castle State Park,** SR 82, East Haddam, CT 06423. (MNE; NET)
   Great Gulf Trail *see* entry 174.
   Great Ledge Trail *see* entry 135.
   Green Trail *see* entry 165.
146 **Hancock Brook-Lion Head Trail,** Connecticut Forest and Park Association, 1010 Main St., East Hartford, CT 06106. 3.0 miles loop. (HTN)
147 **Haystack Mountain State Park,** SR 272, Norfolk, CT 06058. (MNE)
   Henry Buck Trail *see* entry 108.
   High Woods Trail *see* entry 181.
148 **Hop River State Park Trail,** Joe Hickey, Bureau of Outdoor Recreation, Department of Environmental Protection, 165 Capitol Ave., Hartford, CT

06106, (203) 566-2304. 19.6 miles straight. (GRT)
149 **Hopeville Pond State Park**, SR 201, Voluntown, CT 06384. Named trails: Nehantic. (SNE; GNA)
150 **Housatonic Meadows State Park**, US 7, Cornwall Bridge, CT 06754. Named trails: Pine Knob Loop 2.5(l). (GFC; SNE; NET; GNA)
151 **Housatonic Range Trail**, New York-New Jersey Trail Conference, 232 Madison Ave., Rm. 908, New York, NY 10116, (212) 685-9699. 8.0 miles. (HFI; NYW)
152 **Housatonic State Forest**, US 7, Falls Village, CT 06031. (SNE; GNA)
153 **Hubbard Park**, W. Main St., Meriden, CT 06450, (203) 634-0003 ext. 410. (GFA)
154 **Hungerford Outdoor Center**, 191 Farmington Ave., Kensington, CT 06037, (203) 827-9064. (MNE)
155 **Hurd State Park**, SR 151, Middle Haddam, CT 06456. (SNE; GNA)
156 **James L. Goodwin State Forest**, Connecticut Office of State Parks and Recreation, 165 Capitol Ave., Hartford, CT 06106, (203) 566-2304. (SNE; GNA)
157 **Jericho Trail**, Connecticut Forest and Park Association, 1010 Main St., East Hartford, CT 06108. 3.0 miles. (HTN)
Jesse Girard Trail see entry 195.
158 **John A. Minnelto State Park**, Connecticut Office of State Parks and Recreation, 165 Capitol Ave., Hartford, CT 06106, (203) 566-2304. (SNE)
159 **Kent Falls State Park**, US 7, Kent, CT 06757, (203) 927-3238. (MNE; GFC; NET)
160 **Kettletown State Park**, SR 172, Southbury, CT 96488. (GFC; MNE; SNE)
161 **Lake Waramaug State Park**, Lake Waramaug Rd., Kent, CT 06757. (MNE)
162 **Larkin Bridle Trail**, Tim O'Donoghue, Supervisor, Southford Falls State Park, Quaker Farms Rd., Southbury, CT 06488, (203) 264-5169. 10.7 miles straight. (GRT)
163 **Lee Memorial Garden**, New Canaan Garden Center, P.O. Box 4, New Canaan, CT 06840, (203) 966-2120. 0.75 mile. (NNY)

Lillian Wadsworth Trail see entry 181.
Lion's Head Trail see entry 110.
164 **Lone Pine Trail**, Connecticut Forest and Park Association, 1010 Main St., East Hartford, CT 06108. 3.0 miles. (HTN)
Loop Trail see entry 124.
165 **Macedonia Brook State Park**, Macedonia Brook Rd., Kent, CT 06757, (203) 927-3238. Named trails: Green 0.5, Pine Hill 1.2, Red 0.3, Yellow Offshoot 1.1. (MNE; SNE; NET; GNA; HTN)
166 **Mansfield Hollow State Park**, SR 89, Mansfield Center, CT 06250. (SNE; GNA)
167 **Mashamoquet Brook State Park**, US 44, Abington, CT 06230. (SNE; GNA)
168 **Mattabesett Trail**, Connecticut Forest and Park Association, 16 Meriden Rd., Middletown, CT 06457, (203) 346-2372. 52.0 miles. (SNE; GNA)
169 **Mattatuck State Forest**, SR 8, Plymouth, CT 06782. (SNE; GNA)
170 **Mattatuck Trail**, Connecticut Forest and Park Association, 1010 Main St., East Hartford, CT 06108; or Connecticut Office of State Parks and Recreation, 165 Capitol Ave., Hartford, CT 06106, (203) 566-2304. 35.0 miles. (DGW; GNA; BHT; HTN)
171 **Meshomasic State Forest**, SR 2, Marlborough, CT 06447. (SNE; GNA)
172 **Metacomet-Monadnock Trail** (see separate entry **4952** in interstate section).
173 **Mine Hill Preserve**, Southbury, CT 06448, (203) 264-5678. (ANI)
174 **Mohawk State Forest**, SR 4, Cornwall, CT 06753. Named trails: Great Gulf 1.0(l). (SNE; GNA)
Mohawk Trail see entry 110.
175 **Montgomery Pinetum**, Bible St., Cos Cob, CT 06807, (203) 622-7823. (NNY)
176 **Moosup Valley State Park Trail**, Mike Reid, Park and Recreation Supervisor, Pachaug State Forest Headquarters, P.O. Box 5, Voluntown, CT 06384, (203) 346-2920. 8.1 miles straight. (GRT)
177 **Morgan R. Chaney Sanctuary**, Connecticut Audubon Society, 2325 Burr St., Fairfield, CT 06439, (203) 259-6305. (SNE)

CONNECTICUT

178 **Mystic River Walk**, Mystic Seaport Museum, Greenmanville Ave., Mystic, CT 06355, (203) 572-0711. 5.5 miles. (AGW)
Narragansett Trail see entry 191.
179 **Nassahegon State Forest**, SR 4, Burlington, CT 06013. (SNE)
180 **Natchaug State Forest**, US 44, Abington, CT 06230. 55.0 miles. Named trails: Natchaug 12.0. (SNE; GNA)
Natchaug Trail see entry 180.
181 **Nature Center for Environmental Activities**, P.O. Box 165, 10 Woodside Ln., Westport, CT 06881, (203) 227-7253. Named trails: Butterfly, High Woods, Lillian Wadsworth, Sensitivity, Swamp Loop. (MNE; DGW; NNY)
182 **Naugatuck Trail**, Connecticut Forest and Park Association, 1010 Main St., East Hartford, CT 06108. 4.8 miles. (HTN)
183 **Nehantic State Forest**, SR 11, East Lyme, CT 06333. (SNE; GNA)
Nehantic Trail see entries 149 and 191.
184 **Nepaug State Forest**, US 202, Collinsville, CT 06022. (SNE)
185 **New Canaan Nature Center**, 144 Oenoke Rd., New Canaan, CT 06840, (203) 966-9577. (MNE; GFA; NNY)
186 **Nipmuck State Forest**, SR 190, Stafford, CT 06075. (SNE; GNA)
187 **Nipmuck Trail**, Connecticut Forest and Park Association, 1010 Main St., East Hartford, CT 06108; or Connecticut Office of State Parks and Recreation, 165 Capitol Ave., Hartford, CT 06106, (203) 566-2304. 21.5 miles. (GNA; BHT; HTN)
188 **Northeast Audubon Center**, SR 4, Sharon, CT 06069, (203) 364-0520. 11.0 miles. (MNE; SNE)
189 **Northwest Park**, SR 75, Windsor, CT 06095, (203) 683-0774. 6.5 miles. (MNE)
190 **Oak Grove Nature Center**, Oak Grove St., Manchester, CT 06040, (203) 643-0949. (MNE; GFA)
191 **Pachaug State Forest**, SR 138, Voluntown, CT 06384. Named trails: Canonicus 2.5, Castle 1.5, Narragansett 20.0, Nehantic 14.0, Pachaug 15.0, Quinebaugh 9.7, Rhododendron Sanctuary 2.0. (EGH; SNE; WON; GNA; BHT)
Pachaug Trail see entry 191.

Paradise Lane Trail see entry 110.
192 **Paugussett Trail**, Connecticut Forest and Park Association, 1010 Main St., East Hartford, CT 06108. 4.4 miles. (BHT; HTN)
193 **Pawling Nature Preserve**, Connecticut Office of State Parks and Recreation, 165 Capitol Ave., Hartford, CT 06106, (203) 566-2304. (ANI)
194 **Penwood State Park**, Connecticut Office of State Parks and Recreation, 165 Capitol Ave., Hartford, CT 06106, (203) 566-2304. (SNE; GNA)
195 **Peoples State Forest**, SR 20, Riverton, CT 06065. Named trails: Charles Pack 1.9, Elliot Bronson 1.5, Jesse Girard 1.3, Robert Ross 2.0. (SNE; GNA; HTN)
Pine Hill Trail see entry 165.
Pine Knob Loop Trail see entry 150.
196 **Pomperang Trail**, Connecticut Forest and Park Association, 1010 Main St., East Hartford, CT 06108. 5.3 miles. (BHT; HTN)
Prospect Mountain Trail see entry 110.
197 **Putnam Memorial State Park**, SR 107, Danbury, CT 06810, (203) 938-2285. (MNE; NNY)
198 **Quaddick State Forest and State Park**, SR 193, Thompson, CT 06277. (SNE)
199 **Quinebaug River Wildlife Management Area**, Department of Environmental Protection, Eastern District, Wildlife Bureau, 209 Hebron Rd., Marlborough, CT 06447, (203) 295-9525. (SNE)
Quinebaugh Trail see entry 191.
200 **Quinnipiac Trail**, Connecticut Forest and Park Association, 1010 Main St., East Hartford, CT 06108. 21.0 miles. (BHT; HTN)
Red Trail see entry 165.
201 **Regicides Trail**, West Rock Nature Recreation Center, Wintergreen Ave., New Haven, CT 06515, (203) 787-8016. 0.75 mile. (DGW)
Rhododendron Sanctuary Trail see entry 191.
202 **Roaring Brook Nature Center**, US 44, Canton, CT 06019, (203) 693-0263. Named trails: Tunxis 8.0. (MNE; DGW)

Robert Ross Trail *see* entry 191.
203 **Rocky Neck State Park**, East Lyme, CT 06333, (203) 739-5471. 4.0 miles. (MNE; SNE)
204 **Salmon River State Forest**, SR 2, Marlborough, CT 06447. Named trails: Salmon River. (SNE; GNA)
   Salmon River Trail *see* entry 204.
   Sensitivity Trail *see* entry 181.
205 **Shade Swamp Sanctuary**, Connecticut Office of State Parks and Recreation, 165 Capitol Ave., Hartford, CT 06106, (203) 566-2304. Named trails: Blue 2.0(l), White 1.75(l). (SNE; GNA)
206 **Sharon Audubon Center**, Sharon, CT 06069, (203) 364-5825. 11.0 miles. (GNA)
207 **Shenipsit State Forest**, SR 190, Somers, CT 06071. (SNE; GNA)
208 **Shenipsit Trail**, Connecticut Forest and Park Association, 1010 Main St., East Hartford, CT 06108; or Connecticut Office of State Parks and Recreation, 165 Capitol Ave., Hartford, CT 06106, (203) 566-2304. 30.0 miles. (SNE; GNA; HTN)
209 **Simsbury Farms**, Old Farms Rd., Simsbury, CT 06070, (203) 658-0864 or (203) 651-3751. (MNE)
210 **Sleeping Giant State Park**, SR 10, Mt. Carmel, CT 06518. 28.0 miles. Named trails: Green 2.0, Orange 2.4, Tower 1.6, Violet 3.2, White 2.8, Yellow 2.2. (EGH; SNE; NET; GNA; HTN)
211 **Southford Falls State Park**, Quaker Farms Rd., Southbury, CT 06488, (203) 264-5169. (MNE; OTB)
212 **Squantz Pond State Park**, SR 37, New Fairfield, CT 06812, (203) 797-4165. (MNE)
213 **Stamford Nature Center**, 39 Scofieldtown Rd., Stamford, CT 06903, (203) 322-1646. 3.0 miles. (MNE; NNY; NEO)
214 **Stratton Brook Park/Town Forest Trail**, Dan Dickinson, Supervisor, Stratton Brook State Park, 194 Stratton Brook Rd., Simsbury, CT 06070, (203) 242-1158; or Gerald G. Toner, Director, Department of Culture, Parks and Recreation, 933 Hopmeadow St., Simsbury, CT 06070, (203) 651-3751. 2.5 miles straight. (GRT)

Swamp Loop *see* entry 181.
215 **Talcott Mountain State Park**, SR 185, Simsbury, CT 06070, (203) 677-0662. Named trails: Talcott Mountain 1.25, Tower. (MNE; OTB; NET; GNA)
   Talcott Mountain Trail *see* entry 215.
216 **Topsmead State Park**, SR 118, Litchfield, CT 06759. (MNE)
   Tower Trail *see* entry 215.
217 **Tunxis State Forest**, SR 181, West Hartland, CT 06091. Named trails: Tunxis 59.0. (EGH; SNE; GNA)
   Tunxis Trail *see* entry 217.
   Undermountain Trail *see* entry 110.
218 **Wadsworth Falls State Park**, SR 157, Middletown, CT 06457, (203) 344-2950. (MNE)
219 **Weir Preserve**, The Nature Conservancy, Connecticut Chapter, Science Tower, P.O. Box MMM, Wesleyan Station, Middletown, CT 06457, (203) 344-0716. (NNY)
220 **West Rock Nature Recreation Center**, Wintergreen Ave., New Haven, CT 06515, (203) 787-8016. (MNE)
221 **West Thompson Area**, Corps of Engineers, New England Division, 424 Trapelo Rd., Waltham, MA 02254. (GFC)
222 **Westwoods**, Guilford Land Conservation Trust, P.O. Box 200, Guilford, CT 06437. 40.0 miles. (EGH)
223 **Wharton Brook State Park**, 200 Mount Carmel Ave., Hamden, CT 06514. (ANI)
224 **White Memorial Conservation Center**, US 202, Litchfield, CT 06759, (203) 567-0857 or (203) 567-0015. 35.0 miles. (FRN; MNE; SNE; NET; ANI; GNA)
   Yellow Offshoot Trail *see* entry 165.

Generally:
Connecticut Forest and Park Association, 1010 Main St., East Hartford, CT 06108. (HTN)
Connecticut Office of State Parks and Recreation, 165 Capitol Ave., Hartford, CT 06106, (203) 566-2304. (EGH)
Corps of Engineers, New England Division, 424 Trapelo Rd., Waltham, MA 02254. (GFC)

Index (by city)

Abington: Mashamoquet Brook State Park 167; Natchaug State Forest 180
Andover: Gay City State Park 144
Ansonia: Ansonia Nature & Recreation Center 109
Bristol: Barnes Memorial Nature Center 115
Burlington: Nassahegon State Forest 179
Canton: Roaring Brook Nature Center 202
Cheshire: Farmington Canal Line State Park Trail 140; Farmington River Fishing Access Area Trail 141
Colebrook: Algonquin State Forest 106
Collinsville: Nepaug State Forest 184
Cornwall: Mohawk State Forest 174
Cornwall Bridge: Housatonic Meadows State Park 150
Cos Cob: Montgomery Pinetum 175
Danbury: Putnam Memorial State Park 197
Derby: Camp Housatonic 126
East Haddam: Gillette Castle State Park 145
East Hartford: Hancock Brook-Lion Head Trail 146; Jericho Trail 157; Lone Pine Trail 164; Naugatuck Trail 182; Paugussett Trail 192; Pomperang Trail 196
East Lyme: Nehantic State Forest 183
Fairfield: Birdcraft Trail 118; Connecticut Audubon Center 132; Morgan B. Chaney Sanctuary 177
Falls Village: Housatonic State Forest 152; Mattatuck Trail 170
Greenwich: Altschul Trails 107; Audubon Center in Greenwich 112; Byrum River Trail 122; Caldwell Area 123; Calf Island 124
Guilford: Charles Hubbard Memorial Trail 129; Westwoods 222
Haddam: Cockaponset State Forest 131
Hamden: Camp Deer Lake 125; Camp Sequassen 127; Quinnipiac Trail 200; Wharton Brook State Park 223
Hartford: Airline Hiking Trail 104; Enders State Forest 139; Hop River State Park Trail 148; James L. Goodwin State Forest 156; John A. Minnelto State Park 158; Pawling Nature Preserve 193; Penwood State Park 194; Shade Swamp Sanctuary 205

Kensington: Hungerford Outdoor Center 154
Kent: Kent Falls State Park 159; Lake Waramaug State Park 161; Macedonia Brook State Park 165
Killinworth: Chatfield Hollow State Park 130
Lakeside: Bantam Lake 113
Litchfield: Topsmead State Park 216; White Memorial Conservation Center 224
Manchester: Oak Grove Nature Center 190
Mansfield Center: Mansfield Hollow State Park 166
Marlborough: Barn Island Wildlife Management Area 114; Ellithorpe Flood Control Area 138; Meshomasic State Forest 171; Quinebaug River Wildlife Management Area 199; Salmon River State Forest 204
Meriden: Hubbard Park 153
Middle Haddam: Hurd State Park 155
Middletown: Mattabessett Trail 168; Wadsworth Falls State Park 218; Weir Preserve 219
Mt. Carmel: Sleeping Giant State Park 210
Mystic: Mystic River Walk 178
New Canaan: Lee Memorial Garden 163; New Canaan Nature Center 185
New Fairfield: Squantz Pond State Park 212
New Haven: East Rock Park 137; Regicides Trail 201; West Rock Nature Recreation Center 220
Norfolk: Campbell Falls State Park 128; Dennis Hill State Park 134; Haystack Mountain State Park 147
Plymouth: Mattatuck State Forest 169
Pomfret Center: Airline State Park Trail 105
Poquonock: Bluff Point Coastal Reserve 120
Riverton: American Legion State Forest 108; Franklin Swamp Wildlife Management Area 143; Peoples State Forest 195
Salem: Devil's Hopyard State Park 136
Sharon: Northeast Audubon Center 188; Sharon Audubon Center 206

Simsbury: Simsbury Farms 209; Stratton Brook Park/Town Forest Trail 214; Talcott Mountain State Park 215
Somers: Shenipsit State Forest 207
Southbury: Kettletown State Park 160; Larkin Bridle Trail 162; Mine Hill Preserve 173; Southford Falls State Park 211
Stafford: Bigelow Hollow State Park 117; Nipmuck State Forest 186
Stamford: Bartlett Arboretum 116; Stamford Nature Center 213
Stonington: Denison Pequotsepos Nature Center 133
Thomaston: Black Rock State Park 119
Thompson: Quaddick State Forest and State Park 198
Torrington: Burr Pond State Park 121
Voluntown: Hopeville Pond State Park 149; Moosup Valley State Park Trail 176; Pachaug State Forest 191
Waltham: West Thompson Area 221
West Cornwall: Housatonic Range Trail 151
West Hartland: Tunxis State Forest 217
Weston: Devil's Den Preserve 135
Westport: Nature Center for Environmental Activities 181
Willimantic: Nipmuck Trail 187
Windsor: Northwest Park 189; Shenipsit Trail 208
Woodbury: Flanders Nature Center 142

Delaware

225 **Ashland Nature Center**, P.O. Box 700, Hockessin, DE 19707. 2.0 miles. (DMV)
226 **Assawoman Wildlife Area**, Division of Fish and Wildlife, Department of Natural Resources and Environmental Control, Edward Tatnall Bldg., Dover, DE 19901, (302) 678-4401. (GNA)
227 **Bellevue State Park**, Marsh Rd., Wilmington, DE 19810, (302) 571-3390. (ATM; MMA)
228 **Blackbird State Forest**, US 13, Clayton, DE 19938. 54.0 miles. (GFC)
229 **Bombay Hook National Wildlife Refuge**, Rt. 1, Box 147, Smyrna, DE 19977, (302) 653-9345 or (302) 653-6872. (AMI; DMP; MMA; DBV; OTB; AMC; GNA; GNW)
230 **Brandywine Creek State Park**, P.O. Box 3782, Greenville, DE 19807, (302) 678-4506. Named trails: Brandywine 37.5. (ATM; MMA; AMI; GNA)
  Brandywine Trail *see* entry 230.
231 **Caesar Rodney Historic Trail**, Del-Mar-Va Council, BSA, 8th and Washington Sts., Wilmington, DE 19801-1597, (302) 652-3741 or (800) 766-SCOUT or fax (302) 652-3899. 11.0 miles straight. Awards available. (SAR 1993)
232 **Cape Henlopen State Park**, US 9, Lewes, DE 19958, (302) 645-8983. Named trails: Pinelands Nature 2.0(l). (WCD; ATM; MMA; DBV; DMA; AMC; GNA)
233 **Chesapeake and Delaware Canal Trail**, Del-Mar-Va Council, BSA, 8th and Washington Sts., Wilmington, DE 19801-1597, (302) 652-3741. 7.25 miles. (DMV)
234 **Delaware Seashore State Park**, Rt. 2, Box 850, Rehoboth Beach, DE 19971, (302) 227-2800. (WCD; GNA)
235 **Dover Heritage Trail**, P.O. Box 1628, 408 S. State St., Dover, DE 19901, (302) 678-2040. 2 hours. (DMP; MMA; RTH; CBP)
236 **Ellendale State Forest**, SR 113, Ellendale, DE 19941. 50.0 miles. (GFC)
237 **Fort Delaware State Park**, Pea Patch Island, Delaware City, DE 19706, (302) 834-7941. (ATM)
238 **Fort Dupont Park and Activity Center**, Minnesota Ave. & Randle Cir., SE, Washington, DC 20019, (202) 426-7723. (CGA)
239 **Holly Lake Campsites**, SR 24, Rehoboth Beach, DE 19971, (302) 945-3410. (WCD)
240 **Iron Hill Trail**, Del-Mar-Va Council, BSA, 8th and Washington Sts., Wilmington, DE 19801-1597, (302) 652-3741. 2.0 miles. (DMV)
241 **Killins Pond State Park**, Paradise Alley Rd., Felton, DE 19943, (302) 284-3412. (WCD; ATM; MMA)
242 **Little Creek Wildlife Area**, SR 9, Little Creek, DE 19961. (AMC; GNA)
243 **Lums Pond State Park**, Howell School Rd., Glasgow, DE 19713, (302) 368-6989. (WCD; ATM; MMA)
244 **Nanticoke Wildlife Area**, Division of Fish and Wildlife, Department of Natural Resources and Environmental Control, Tatnall Bldg., Dover, DE 19901, (302) 678-4431. (AMC; GNA)
245 **Norman G. Wilder Wildlife Area**, Division of Parks and Recreation, Edward Tatnall Bldg., Dover, DE 19901, (302) 678-4401. 10.0 miles. (DMV; AMC)
  Pinelands Nature Trail *see* entry 232.
246 **Prime Hook National Wildlife Refuge**, Rt. 1, Box 195, Milton, DE 19968, (302) 684-8419. (AMC; GNA; GNW)

247 **Redden State Forest**, US 113, Georgetown, DE 19947. (GFC)
248 **Trap Pond State Park**, Rt. 2, Box 331, Laurel, DE 19956, (302) 875-5153. (WCD; ATM; MMA; DMA; OTB; AMC; GNA)
249 **Walter S. Carpenter, Jr. State Park**, SR 896, Newark, DE 19711, (302) 731-1310. (ATM; MMA; OTB)
250 **Winterthur Gardens Trail**, Winterthur Museum and Gardens, SR 52, Winterthur, DE 19735, (302) 888-4600 or (800) 448-3883. 2.5 miles. (DMP; DBV; AGW; CBP)
251 **Woodland Beach Wildlife Area**, SR 6, Woodland Beach, DE 19977. (GNA)

Generally:
Department of Natural Resources and Environmental Control, 89 Kings Hwy., P.O. Box 1401, Dover, DE 19903, (302) 736-4702. (SFC)
Division of Fish and Wildlife, Department of Natural Resources and Environmental Control, Edward Tatnall Bldg., Dover, DE 19901, (302) 678-4401. (GNA)
Forestry Section, Department of Agriculture, 2320 S. Dupont Hwy., Dover, DE 19903, (302) 736-4811. (GFC)

Index (by city)

Clayton: Blackbird State Forest 228
Delaware City: Fort Delaware State Park 237
Dover: Assawoman Wildlife Area 226; Caesar Rodney Historic Trail 231; Dover Heritage Trail 235; Nanticoke Wildlife Area 244; Norman G. Wilder Wildlife Area 245
Ellendale: Ellendale State Forest 236
Felton: Killins Pond State Park 241
Georgetown: Redden State Forest 247
Glasgow: Lums Pond State Park 243
Greenville: Brandywine Creek State Park 230
Hockessin: Ashland Nature Center 225
Laurel: Trap Pond State Park 248
Lewes: Cape Henlopen State Park 232; Chesapeake and Delaware Canal Trail 233
Little Creek: Little Creek Wildlife Area 242
Milton: Prime Hook National Wildlife Refuge 246
Newark: Iron Hill Trail 240; Walter S. Carpenter, Jr. State Park 249
Rehoboth Beach: Delaware Seashore State Park 234; Holly Lake Campsites 239
Smyrna: Bombay Hook National Wildlife Refuge 229
Washington, DC: Fort Dupont Park and Activity Center 238
Wilmington: Bellevue State Park 227
Winterthur: Winterthur Gardens Trail 250
Woodland Beach: Woodland Beach Wildlife Area 251

DISTRICT OF COLUMBIA

Constitution Gardens Trail *see* entry 261.

East Potomac Park Trail *see* entry 261.

252 **Fort Circle Parks National Recreation Trail**, National Park Service, U.S. Department of the Interior, Washington, DC 20240. 8.0 miles. (NFG)

253 **Lady Bird Johnson Park and Lyndon Baines Johnson Memorial Grove Trail**, George Washington Memorial Pkwy., Turkey Run Park, McLean, VA 22101, (703) 557-8991. 1.0 mile. (CGA; NWA; ANP)

254 **Lincoln Pilgrimage Trail**, American Historical Trails, Inc., P.O. Box 769, Monroe, NC 28110, (704) 289-1604. 7.5-11.5 miles straight. Awards available. (SAR 1991)

255 **National Arboretum**, Public Information Officer, U.S. National Arboretum, Washington, DC 20002, (202) 399-5400 or (202) 472-9100. 9.0 miles. (NAT; NWA)

256 **National Capital Bicentennial Trail of Freedom**, American Historical Trails, Inc., P.O. Box 769, Monroe, NC 28110, (704) 289-1604. 6.5-9.5 miles straight. Awards available. (SAR 1991)

257 **National Capital Lincoln Trail**, National Capital Area Council, BSA, 9190 Wisconsin Ave., Bethesda, MD 20814-3897, (301) 530-9360. 14.0 miles straight. Awards available. (SAR 1991)

258 **National Children's Island**, 1025 15th St., N.W., Suite 700, Washington, DC 20005, (202) 727-3045. (NWA)

259 **National Zoological Park**, Public Information Specialist, National Zoological Park, Smithsonian Institution, Washington, DC 20008, (202) 381-7300 or (202) 387-7400. 6 trails 0.25-0.8 miles each. (SAR 1991)

260 **Potomac Heritage Trail** (*see* separate entry 4957 in interstate section).

261 **Potomac Park**, Public Information Officer, National Capital Region, National Park Service, 1100 Ohio Dr., S.W., Washington, DC 20242, (202) 426-6700. Named trails: Constitution Gardens 3.0, East Potomac Park 5.0(l), Tidal Basin 1.0(l). (NWA)

262 **The President's Trail**, American Historical Trails, Inc., P.O. Box 769, Monroe, NC 28110, (704) 289-1604. 8.0-11.0 miles straight. Awards available. (SAR 1991)

263 **Rambling Through Georgetown Walking Tour**, 3039 Albemarle St., Washington, DC 20008; or 710 Warren Dr., Annapolis, MD 21403. (RTH)

264 **Rock Creek Park**, 5000 Glover Rd., N.W., Washington, DC 20015, (202) 426-6834. 15.0 miles. (SAR 1991)

265 **Theodore Roosevelt Island**, Superintendent, George Washington Memorial Pkwy., Turkey Run Park, McLean, VA 22101, (703) 557-8991 or (202) 426-6922. 3.5 miles. (WCD; NAT; NPE; CGA; GPW; AMI; NWA; ANP; NPG)

Tidal Basin Trail *see* entry 261.

Generally:
Director, Department of Environmental Services, 415 12th St., NW, Washington, DC 20004, (202) 727-5748. (SFC)
Public Information Officer, National Park Service, U.S. Department of the Interior, National Capital Region, 1100 Ohio Dr., S.W., Washington, DC 20242, (202) 426-6700. (NWA)

FLORIDA

266 **Alderman's Ford County Park Trail**, Hillsborough County Parks, 1101 East River Cove Ave., Tampa, FL 33604-3200, (813) 272-5840. 2.0 miles. (PTG; SFL; GCN)
   Allan Cruikshank Memorial Trail see entry 444.
267 **Allen Mill Pond**, Rt. 3, Box 64, Live Oak, FL 32060, (904) 362-1001. 2.0 miles. (SFL)
   Alligator Creek Trail see entry 349.
268 **Amelia Island State Recreation Area**, 12157 Heckscher Dr., Ft. George Island, FL 32226, (904) 251-3231. (SFL)
269 **Ancient Dunes Trail**, Anastasia State Recreation Area, 5 Anastasia Park Dr., St. Augustine, FL 32085, (904) 461-2033. 0.6 mile. (SAR 1993)
270 **Andrew Jackson Historic Trail** (a/k/a Jackson Red Ground Trail), John Steiger, 8100 Monticello Dr., Pensacola, FL 32514, (904) 477-0122; or Blackwater River State Forest, Rt. 1, Box 77, Milton, FL 32570. 22.0 miles straight. Awards available. (AA 1990)
271 **Andrews Wildlife Management Area**, Florida Game and Fresh Water Fish Commission, 620 South Meridian St., Tallahassee, FL 32399, (904) 488-1960. (SFL)
   Anhinga Trail see entry 349.
272 **Apalachicola Bluffs and Ravines Preserve Trail**, The Nature Conservancy, Northwest Florida Land Steward, 515A N. Adams St., Tallahassee, FL 32301, (904) 222-0199. 3.5 miles. (SFL)
   Apalachicola Bluffs Trail see entry 538.
273 **Apalachicola National Forest**, USFS, Apalachicola District, P.O. Box 578, Bristol, FL 32321, (904) 643-2282; or Forest Supervisor, 2586 Seagate Dr., Tallahassee, FL 32301. 66.0 miles. Named trails: Apalachicola 29.0, Camel Lake Loop 9.4, Discovery 0.1, Silver Lake 1.0, Vinzant Riding. (SFL; HBF; MSE; FTA; GCN; FIF; GTF; FGU; GNA; NFG)
   Apalachicola Trail see entry 273.
274 **Arbuckle State Forest**, Division of Forestry, Lakeland District, 5745 S. Florida Ave., Lakeland, FL 33803, (813) 648-3160. (SFL)
275 **Arbuckle Wildlife Management Area**, Florida Game and Fresh Water Fish Commission, South Region, 3900 Drane Field Rd., Lakeland, FL 33803, (813) 644-9269. (SFL)
276 **Archbold Nature Trail**, P.O. Box 2057, Lake Placid, FL 33852, (813) 465-2571. (AIF)
277 **Archie Carr National Wildlife Refuge**, Merritt Island National Wildlife Refuge, P.O. Box 6504, Titusville, FL 32782, (407) 867-0667. (SFL)
278 **Aucilla Wildlife Management Area**, Florida Game and Fresh Water Fish Commission, Northeast Region, Rt. 7, Box 440, Lake City, FL 32055, (904) 758-0525. (SFL)
279 **Avon Park Air Force Range**, Natural Resources Manager, 56 CSS/DEN, Avon Park, FL 33825, (813) 452-4119. Named trails: Lake Arbuckle 16.0(l), Sandy Point Wildlife Refuge. (SFL; AIF; GCN; GTF; GNA)
280 **Babson Park/Audubon Center**, P.O. Box 148, Babson Park, FL 33827, (813) 638-1355. (PTG; MCW)
281 **Bahia Honda Nature Trail**, Rt. 1, Box 782, Big Pine Key, FL 33043, (305) 872-2353. (AA 1990)
282 **Barley Barber Swamp Trail**, Florida

Power & Light, (407) 640-2089. 1.0 mile. (GCN)

Barrier Dune Trail *see* entry 498.
Bayshore Loop Trail *see* entry 349.
Beach Trail *see* entry 311.
Bear Lake Trail *see* entry 349.
Bear Paw Trail *see* entry 427.
Beech-Magnolia Nature Trail *see* entry 358.

283 **Big Cypress National Preserve Trail**, Star Route, Box 110, Ochopee, FL 33943, (813) 695-2000; or Big Cypress National Preserve, P.O. Box 1247, Naples, FL 33939, (813) 262-1066. 29.0 miles. (HBF; FTA; GTF; GNA)

Big Cypress South Trail *see* entry 349.

284 **Big Lagoon State Recreation Area**, 12301 Gulf Beach Hwy., Pensacola, FL 32507, (904) 492-1595. (SAR 1990)

285 **Big Shoals State Forest**, Florida Game and Fresh Water Fish Commission, Northwest Region, 6938 SR 2321, Panama City, FL 32409, (904) 265-3676. (SFL)

Big Stump Trail *see* entry 427.

286 **Big Talbot Island State Park**, Florida Department of Natural Resources, Office of Communications, Marjory Stoneman Douglas Bldg., 3900 Commonwealth Blvd., Tallahassee, FL 32399, (904) 488-6327. (SFL)

287 **Biscayne National Park**, P.O. Box 1369, Homestead, FL 33090, (305) 230-7275. Named trails: Boardwalk, Elliot Key 8.0, Self-guiding Nature, Spite Highway 14.0(s). (ATF; SFL; HBF; MCW; RTR; GCN; NPV; GTF; NPE; OTB; CGA; GNA)

288 **Bivens Arm Nature Park**, 3650 S. Main St., Gainesville, FL 32601, (904) 374-2056. Named trails: Gator Gap Loop, North Bridge, Tumblin Creek Path. (MCW; FIF; OCT)

Black Point Wildlife Drive *see* entry 444.

289 **Blackwater River State Forest**, Rt. 1, Box 77, Milton, FL 32570, (904) 957-4111. 26.0 miles. Named trails: Jackson Red Ground 21.0, Sweetwater 1.5. (AA 1990)

290 **Blanchard Park**, 2451 N. Dean Rd., Union Park, FL 32817, (407) 521-3352. (OCS; PTG)

291 **Blowing Rocks Preserve**, P.O. Box 3795, Tequesta, FL 33469, (407) 575-2297 or (407) 747-3113. (SFL)

292 **Blue Spring State Park**, 2100 W. French Ave., Orange City, FL 32763, (904) 775-3663. 8.0 miles. (SAR 1992)

Blueberry Trail *see* entry 448.
Boardwalk Trail *see* entry 287.
Bobcat Trail *see* entry 349.

293 **Boca Grande Bike Path**, Bicycle Coordinator, Lee County Department of Transportation, 2022 Hendry St., Fort Myers, FL 33901, (813) 335-2220. 6.5 miles straight. (GRT)

Bolen Bluff Trail *see* entry 472.

294 **Boyd Hill Nature Park**, 1101 Country Club Way S., St. Petersburg, FL 33705, (813) 893-7326. Named trails: Field Mouse, Gator Loop, Lake Maggiore, Main, Oak-Pine Hammock, Pine Flatwoods, Scrub Island, Swamp Woodlands, Willow Marsh. (SAR 1992)

295 **Bradwell Bay Federal Wilderness Area**, National Forests in Florida, P.O. Box 13548, Tallahassee, FL 32308, (904) 878-1131. (GCN)

296 **Brevard Museum of History and Natural Science**, 2201 Michigan Ave., Cocoa, FL 32926, (407) 632-1830 or (407) 632-1920. (PTG; HFL)

297 **Bull Creek Wildlife Management Area**, Florida Game and Fresh Water Fish Commission, Central Region, 1239 SW 10th St., Ocala, FL 32674, (904) 732-1225. (SFL)

298 **Bulow Ruins Nature Trail**, Bulow Plantation Ruins State Historic Site, P.O. Box 655, Bunnell, FL 32110, (904) 439-2219. (CFC; GFA)

299 **Bulow Woods Trail**, Bulow Creek State Park, P.O. Box 653, Bunnell, FL 32010, (904) 439-2219. 6.2 miles. (SFL; AIF; FTA)

Buster Island Loop Trail *see* entry 417.

300 **C.B. Smith Park**, Flamingo Rd. & Hollywood Blvd., Pembroke Pines, FL 33084. (ATF)

301 **Cady Way to Fashion Square Greenway**, Mrs. Pat Hopkins, City of Orlando, 1414 N. Orange Ave., Orlando, FL 32804, (407) 246-2011. 4.0 miles straight. (ORL; GRT)

302 **Caladesi Island Trail**, Caladesi Island State Park, #1 Causeway Blvd., Dunedin, FL 33528, (813) 443-5903. (AA 1990)

Camel Lake Loop Trail see entry 273.

303 **Camp Blanding Wildlife Management Area**, Florida Game and Fresh Water Fish Commission, Northeast Region, Rt. 7, Box 440, Lake City, FL 32055, (904) 758-0525. (SFL)

304 **Camp Brorein**, Gulf Ridge Council, BSA, P.O. Box 24077, 4410 Boy Scout Blvd., Tampa, FL 33623, (813) 872-2691 or fax (813) 875-2775; or Camp Brorein, 277 Boy Scout Rd., Odessa, FL 33556. (SFC)

305 **Camp Flaming Arrow**, Gulf Ridge Council, BSA, P.O. Box 24077, 4410 Boy Scout Blvd., Tampa, FL 33623, (813) 872-2691 or fax (813) 875-2775; or Camp Flaming Arrow, 1201 Boy Scout Rd., Lake Wales, FL 33853, (813) 696-1116. (SFC)

306 **Camp Frank E. Gannett**, Southwest Florida Council, BSA, 8600 S. Tamiami Trail, Fort Myers, FL 33907, (813) 936-8072; or Camp Frank E. Gannett, Rt. A, Box 58, Punta Gorda, FL 33950, (813) 639-4800. (SFC)

307 **Camp Mitchell Nature Trail**, Central Florida Council, BSA, P.O. Box 531084, 1215 E. Nebraska St., Orlando, FL 32853, (407) 896-4801. (CFC)

308 **Camp Sawyer**, South Florida Council, BSA, 2960 Coral Way, Miami, FL 33145, (305) 446-8431; or Camp Sawyer, Big Pine Key, FL 33043. (SFC)

309 **Camp Seminole**, South Florida Council, BSA, 2960 Coral Way, Miami, FL 33245, (305) 446-8431; or Camp Seminole, Davie, FL 33314, (904) 726-1745. (SFC)

310 **Camp Soule**, West Central Florida Council, BSA, P.O. Box 3408, Seminole, FL 33342, (813) 391-0171; or Camp Soule, 2201 Soule Rd., Clearwater, FL 33519, (813) 726-3102. (SFC)

311 **Canaveral National Seashore**, District Ranger's Office, P.O. Box 6447, Titusville, FL 32782, (407) 867-4675. Named trails: Beach 24.0(s), Castle Windy 0.5, Dike Road to Target Rock 2.5, Eldora Hammock 0.5, Max Hoeck Creek Wildlife Drive 4.3, Old Eldora 0.5, Old Hammock, Sand Road 13.0(s), Turtle Mound 0.25. (SFL; HBF; MCW; NPV; DIF; GTF; NPE; CGA; GNA)

312 **Cape Florida Trail**, Bill Baggs Cape Florida State Recreation Area, 1200 S. Crandon Blvd., Key Biscayne, FL 33149, (305) 361-5811. (AA 1990)

313 **Cape St. George Island**, Apalachicola National Estuarine Research Reserve, 261 7th St., Apalachicola, FL 32320, (904) 653-8063. (SFL)

314 **Cary State Forest**, Division of Forestry, 8719 W. Beaver St., Marietta, FL 32205, (904) 781-1434 or (904) 266-9349. 18.0 miles. (SAR 1994)

315 **Castello Hammock**, 22301 SW 162nd Ave., Goulds, FL 33170, (305) 245-4321. (GFA 1989)

Castle Windy Trail see entry 311.

Cateye Trail see entry 427.

316 **Cayo Costa State Park**, P.O. Box 1150, Boca Grande, FL 33921, (813) 964-0375. (AA 1990)

317 **Cedar Key Scrub State Reserve**, c/o Waccasassa Bay State Preserve, P.O. Box 187, Cedar Key, FL 32625, (904) 543-5567. (SFL; NGC)

318 **Central Florida Zoological Park Nature Trail**, Central Florida Zoological Park, 3755 US 17-92, P.O. Box 309, Lake Monroe, FL 32747, (407) 323-4450. (SAR 1989)

Chacala Trail see entry 472.

319 **Charles Deering Estate**, 16701 SW 72nd Ave., Miami, FL 33157, (305) 235-1668. (SFL)

320 **Chekika Trail**, Chekika State Recreation Area, P.O. Box 1313, Homestead, FL 33030, (305) 253-0950. (AA 1990)

Christian Point Trail see entry 349.

321 **Christian Tract, Suwannee River**, Suwannee River Water Management District, Rt. 3, Box 64, Live Oak, FL 32060, (904) 362-1001. (SFL)

Citrus Hiking Trail see entry 557.

Citrus Horse Trail *see* entry 557.
Clay Trail *see* entry 439.
Clearwater Trail *see* entry 456.
Coastal Prairie Trail *see* entry 349.
322 **Collier-Seminole Trail**, Collier-Seminole State Park, Marco, FL 33937, (813) 394-3397; or Collier-Seminole State Park, Rt. 4, Box 848, Naples, FL 33961. 6.1 miles. (SFL)
Colonel Robins Trail *see* entry 557.
Cone's Dike Trail *see* entry 472.
323 **Conservancy Nature Center**, 1450 Merrihue Dr., Naples, FL 33942, (813) 262-0304. (FOB; MCW; GFA; FIF)
324 **Coon's Creek Recreation Area**, MacDill AFB, Bayshore Blvd., Tampa, FL 33611, (813) 830-4982. (WCD)
Coquina Trail *see* entry 332.
325 **Corkscrew Swamp Trail**, Chief Naturalist, Corkscrew Swamp Wildlife Sanctuary, Rt. 6, Box 1875-A, Naples, FL 33964, (813) 657-3771. 1.75 miles. (ATF; SFL; FOB; MCW; GDN; DIF; GTF; OTB; FEI; GNA)
Cow Camp Trail *see* entry 417.
326 **Crandon Park**, Dade County Parks and Recreation, 50 S.W. 32nd Rd., Miami, FL 33129, (305) 638-6414. (GCN)
327 **Crews Lake Park**, 16735 Crews Lake Dr., P.O. Box 11327, Spring Hill, FL 34610, (813) 847-8118 ext. 8828. 2.0 miles. (SFL)
Croom Hiking Trail *see* entry 557.
328 **Crystal River State Archaeological Site**, 3400 N. Museum Point, Crystal River, FL 32629, (904) 795-3817. (MCW; SSI)
Cypress Creek Trail *see* entry 356.
329 **Dade Battlefield Trail**, Dade Battlefield State Historic Site, P.O. Box 938, Bushnell, FL 33513, (904) 793-4781. 0.5 mile. (AA 1990)
330 **Dead Lakes Trail**, Dead Lakes State Recreation Area, P.O. Box 989, Wewahitchka, FL 32465, (904) 639-2702. 1.0 mile. (AA 1990)
331 **Dead River Youth Camp**, Hillsborough County Parks Department, 1101 E. River Cove Ave., Tampa, FL 33604-3200, (813) 272-5840. (CFC)

Deep Creek Trail *see* entry 500.
332 **Deerfield Island Park**, Deerfield Beach, FL 33441, (305) 480-4423. Named trails: Coquina, Mangrove 1550'. (HFL)
333 **DeLand KOA**, Park Manager, 1440 E. Minnesota Ave., Orange City, FL 32763, (904) 775-3996. (CFC)
334 **DeLeon Springs Trail**, DeLeon Springs State Recreation Area, P.O. Box 1338, DeLeon Springs, FL 32028, (904) 985-4212. 1.0 mile. (SAR 1991)
335 **Dent Smith Trail**, Florida Institute of Technology, 150 W. University Blvd., Melbourne, FL 32901, (407) 768-8000. 1.0 mile. (HFL; MCW; SAR 1969)
336 **DeSoto National Memorial Trail**, P.O. Box 14871, Bradenton, FL 34280, (813) 792-0458. 0.8 mile. (PTG; CGA; YNP; ANP)
337 **DeSoto Trail**, Florida Department of Natural Resources, Office of Communications, Marjory Stoneman Douglas Bldg., 3900 Commonwealth Blvd., Tallahassee, FL 32399, (904) 488-6327. (AA 1989)
338 **Devil's Millhopper Trail**, Devil's Millhopper State Geological Site, 4732 N.W. 53rd Ave., Gainesville, FL 32601, (904) 377-5935. 1.0 mile. (SAR 1990)
Dike Road to Target Rock Trail *see* entry 311.
Dinosaur Trail *see* entry 454.
Discovery Trail *see* entry 273.
339 **Donald McDonald Park Trail**, Vero Beach Work Center, Division of Forestry, 4330 4th St., Vero Beach, FL 32960, (407) 562-2079. (GCN)
340 **Downtown Tallahassee Historic Trail**, R.A. Gray Bldg., Museum of Florida History Gift Shop, 500 S. Bronough St., Tallahassee, FL 32399, (904) 488-1484. 8.0 miles loop. (AA 1992)
341 **DuPuis Reserve Wildlife and Environmental Area**, Florida Game and Fresh Water Fish Commission, 551 N. Military Tr., West Palm Beach, FL 33415, (305) 640-6100; or South Florida Water Management District, P.O. Box 24680, 3301 Gun Club Rd., West Palm Beach, FL 33416, (407) 686-8800. 38.1 miles. (FWM; SFL)

342 **Easterlin Park Trail**, 1000 NW 38th St., Oakland Park, FL 33334, (305) 938-0610. (GCN)
Echo Pond Trail see entry 349.
343 **Edward Ball Wakulla Springs State Park**, One Spring Dr., Wakulla Springs, FL 32305, (904) 222-7279. (SFL)
344 **Eglin Air Force Base**, Natural Resources Branch, 3200 SPTW/DEMN, Eglin AFB, FL 32542, (904) 882-4164. (SFL)
345 **Egmont Key Historic Trail**, Bruce W. Dietch, Troop 27, 4120 12th Ave. W., Bradenton, FL 34205, (813) 746-2053. 2.0 miles loop. Awards available. (SAR 1993)
346 **Egmont Key State Park and National Wildlife Refuge**, Slip 656, 4801 37th St. S., St. Petersburg, FL 33711, (813) 894-6577. (SAR 1993)
Eldora Hammock Trail see entry 311.
Elliott Key Trail see entry 287.
347 **Erna Nixon County Park Trail**, 600 Evans Rd., West Melbourne, FL 32904, (407) 952-4525. (GCN)
348 **Eureka Springs Trail**, Eureka Springs Park, 6400 Eureka Springs Rd., Tampa, FL 33610, (813) 626-7994. (PTG)
349 **Everglades National Park**, P.O. Box 279, Homestead, FL 33030, (305) 247-6211. Named trails: Alligator Creek 14.6, Anhinga 5.0, Bayshore Loop, Bear Lake 4.0(l), Big Cypress South 27.0(l), Bobcat, Christian Point 4.0, Coastal Prairie 12.0, Echo Pond, Gumbo Limbo 5.0, Long Pine Key 3.0- 14.0, Loop 3.0-5.0, Mahogany Hammock 5.0, Old Ingram Highway 11.0, Pa-hay-okee Overlook 0.25, Pineland 5.0, Rowdy Bend 5.0, Shark Valley 15.0, Slash Pine 7.0, Snake Bight 4.0, Tram Road 15.0, West Lake 5.0. (LGU; EAN; HFL; FTG; HBF; HFK; MCW; GCN; GNP; NPV; GTF; NPE; CGA; NPG)
350 **Everglades Water Conservation Areas**, South Florida Water Management District, P.O. Box 24680, 3301 Gun Club Rd., West Palm Beach, FL 33416, (407) 686-8800. (SFL)
Experiment Trail see entry 450.

351 **Fakahatchee Strand Trail**, Fakahatchee Strand State Preserve, P.O. Box 548, Copeland, FL 33926. 10.0 miles straight. (SFL; GTF)
352 **Falling Waters Trail**, Falling Waters State Recreation Area, Rt. 5, Box 660, Chipley, FL 32428, (904) 638-4030. 0.5 mile. (AA 1990)
353 **FAMCAMP-Eglin AFB**, John Sims Pkwy., Valparaiso, FL 32580, (904) 882-5058. (WCD)
354 **Faver-Dykes Trail**, Faver-Dykes State Park, 1000 Faver-Dykes Rd., St. Augustine, FL 32086, (904) 794-0997. 0.25 mile. (SAR 1990)
355 **Felix Lake Nature Trail**, Morale, Welfare and Recreation, Department of the Air Force, Tyndall Air Force Base, FL 32403-5000. 3.0 miles. (GTF)
Fence Trail see entry 439.
356 **Fern Forest Nature Center**, Pompano Beach, FL 33060. Named trails: Cypress Creek 0.5, Maple Walk 0.3, Prairie Overlook 1.0. (HFL)
Fern Loop Trail see entry 448.
Field Mouse Trail see entry 294.
357 **Flagler Beach Trail**, Flagler Beach State Recreation Area, 3100 S. SR A1A, Flagler Beach, FL 32036, (904) 439-2474. 0.5 mile. (SAR 1990)
Flood Plain Horse Trail see entry 358.
Floodplain Nature Trail see entry 358.
358 **Florida Caverns State Park**, Marianna, FL 32446, (904) 482-9598. Named trails: Beech-Magnolia Nature, Flood Plain Horse, Floodplain Nature, Pine Island Nature. (SAR 1993)
359 **Florida Historic Trails 100 Mile Hiking Award**, Milledge Murphey, Ph.D., 1815 N.W. 7th Pl., Gainesville, FL 32603, (904) 373-9234. Awards available to hikers who accumulate 100 miles on Ft. Clinch Historic Trail, Ft. Clinch Environmental Trail, St. Augustine Historic Trail, Ft. Matanzas Historic Trail, Osceola-Olustee Historic Trail, and Ft. Caroline Historic Trail. (AA 1993)
360 **Florida Keys National Wildlife Refuges**, P.O. Box 510, Big Pine Key, FL 33043, (305) 872-2239. (GNA; GNW)

361 **Florida National Scenic Trail**, Florida Trail Association, Inc., P.O. Box 13708, 115 N.E. 7th Ave., Gainesville, FL 32604, (904) 378-8823. Working toward completion of 1300 miles continuous trail. Sections entirely on public land are listed individually, the rest are: Everglades—Okeechobee West 41.5, Everglades—Okeechobee East 62.5, Corbett Wildlife Management Area 14.0, Highlands—Okeechobee 9.1, Green Swamp 19.3, Bull Creek 17.0, Lake Jessup 27.4, Cassia 25.8, Rice Creek 35.0, Gold Head Branch 29.0, Osceola National Forest 35.0, Suwannee River 48.8, Champion 12.9, Gilman—Buckeye 26.0, Buckeye 23.5, Aucilla River 17.3, St. Marks National Wildlife Refuge 43.4, Apalachicola National Forest-East 32.6, Apalachicola National Forest-West 33.4, Pine Log—St. Joe 29.0. (BPM; NPF; FTA)

362 **Flying Eagle**, c/o Southwest Florida Water Management District, 2379 Broad St., Brooksville, FL 346009, (904) 796-7211. (SFL)

Fork Trail see entry 439.

363 **Ft. Caroline Historic Trail**, Milledge Murphey, Ph.D., 1815 N.W. 7th Pl., Gainesville, FL 32603, (904) 373-9234. 5.37 miles loop (includes trail to fort 0.25, Old French Trail 1.0, walk along road to Ribault Memorial 1.4, Two Ponds Trail and part of Willie Browne Trail 2.72). Awards available. (SAR 1991)

364 **Ft. Clinch Environmental Trail**, Milledge Murphey, Ph.D., 1815 N.W. 7th Pl., Gainesville, FL 32603, (904) 373-9234. 5.0 miles loop. Awards available. (SAR 1994)

365 **Ft. Clinch Historic Trail**, Milledge Murphey, Ph.D., 1815 N.W. 7th Pl., Gainesville, FL 32603, (904) 373-9234. 16.0 miles loop. Awards available. (SAR 1994)

366 **Ft. Clinch State Park**, 2601 Atlantic Ave., Fernandina Beach, FL 32034, (904) 261-4211. Named trails: Magnolia Loop, Willow Pond Nature 1.0(l). (SAR 1994)

367 **Fort Cooper Trail**, Fort Cooper State Park, 3100 S. Old Floral City Rd., Inverness, FL 32650, (904) 726-0315. (AA 1990)

368 **Fort DeSoto County Park**, P.O. Box 3, Tierra Verde, FL 33715, (813) 866-2484; or Pinellas County Parks, 407 S. Garden Ave., Clearwater, FL 33516, (813) 866-2662. (SAR 1993)

369 **Fort Foster Nature Trail**, Hillsborough River State Park, 15402 US 301N, Thonotosassa, FL 33592, (813) 986-1020. (SAR 1993)

370 **Fort Gadsden State Historic Site**, US 98, Apalachicola, FL 32320, (904) 670-8988. (MCW)

371 **Fort George Island**, Florida Department of Natural Resources, Office of Communications, Marjory Stoneman Douglas Bldg., 3900 Commonwealth Blvd., Tallahassee, FL 32399, (904) 488-6327. (SFL)

372 **Ft. Matanzas Historic Trail**, Milledge Murphey, Ph.D., 1815 N.W. 7th Pl., Gainesville, FL 32603, (904) 373-9234; or Fort Matanzas National Monument, 1 Castillo Dr., St. Augustine, FL 32084, (904) 829-6506. 0.6 mile plus ferry ride to historic fort. Awards available. (SAR 1993)

373 **Fort McCoy Wildlife Management Area**, Florida Game and Fresh Water Fish Commission, 620 S. Meridian St., Tallahassee, FL 32304, (904) 488-4676. (GNA)

374 **Fort Pickens Historical Trail**, Michael M. Sams, Troop 3, Cokesbury United Methodist Church, 5725 N. 9th Ave., Pensacola, FL 32504, (904) 477-0852. 5.0 miles loop. Awards available. (SAR 1990)

375 **Fort Pierce Inlet State Recreation Area**, North Beach, 2200 Atlantic Blvd., Fort Pierce, FL 33449, (407) 468-3985. 5.2 miles. (AA 1990)

376 **G.U. Parker Wildlife Management Area**, Florida Game and Fresh Water Fish Commission, 620 S. Meridian St., Tallahassee, FL 32304, (904) 488-4676. (GNA)

377 **Gainesville-Hawthorne State Trail**, Jack Gillen, Park Manager, Paynes Prairie State Preserve, Rt. 2, Box 41, Micanopy, FL 32667, (904) 466-3397. 14.0 miles straight. (GRT)

Gator Gap Loop Trail see entry 288.

Gator Lake Nature Trail *see* entry 495.

Gator Loop Trail *see* entry 294.

378 **General James A. Van Fleet State Trail**, Robert Seifer, Park Programs Development Specialist, Division of Parks and Recreation, Florida Department of Natural Resources, 12549 State Park Dr., Clermont, FL 34711, (904) 394-2280. 28.5 miles straight. (GRT; ORL)

379 **Ginnie Springs**, 2300 N.E. Ginnie Springs Rd., High Springs, FL 32643, (904) 454-2202. (ATF; CFC)

Gobbler Ridge Trail *see* entry 417.

380 **Gold Head Branch Trail**, Gold Head Branch State Park, 6239 SR 21, Keystone Heights, FL 32656, (904) 473-4701. 3.0 miles. (FTA)

Graveyard Trail *see* entry 439.

381 **Grayton Beach Trail**, Grayton Beach State Recreation Area, Rt. 2, Box 790-1, Santa Rosa Beach, FL 32459, (904) 231-4210. 1.0 mile. (AA 1990)

382 **Green Swamp Wildlife Management Area**, Southwest Florida Water Management District, 2379 Broad St., Brooksville, FL 34609, (904) 796-7211. 19.0 miles. (SFL; HFL)

383 **Guana River State Park**, S. Ponte Vedra Blvd., Ponte Vedra Beach, FL 32082, (904) 825-5071. (SFL)

384 **Guana River Wildlife Management Area**, Florida Game and Fresh Water Fish Commission, Central Region, 1239 SW 10th St., Ocala, FL 32674, (904) 732-1225. (SFL)

385 **Gulf Hammock Wildlife Management Area**, Florida Game and Fresh Water Fish Commission, Northeast Region, Rt. 7, Box 440, Lake City, FL 32055, (904) 758-0525. (SFL)

386 **Gulf Islands National Seashore**, P.O. Box 100, 1801 Gulf Breeze Pkwy., Gulf Breeze, FL 32561, (904) 934-2600. (SFL; MCW; NPV)

Gumbo Limbo Trail *see* entry 349.

387 **Hagens Cove**, Florida Game and Fresh Water Fish Commission, Northeast Region, Rt. 7, Box 440, Lake City, FL 32055, (904) 758-0525. (SFL)

Half-Dry Nature Trail *see* entry 531.

388 **Hanna Park**, 500 Wonderland Dr., Atlantic Beach, FL 32233, (904) 249-2316. (ATF; CFC; MCW; GCN)

Hardwood Trail *see* entry 439.

389 **Hickory Mound Unit**, Big Bend Wildlife Management Area, Florida Game and Fresh Water Fish Commission, Northeast Region, Rt. 7, Box 440, Lake City, FL 32055, (904) 758-0525. (SFL)

390 **Highlands Hammock Trail**, Highlands Hammock State Park, Rt. 1, Box 310, 5931 Hammock Rd., Sebring, FL 33870, (813) 385-0011. 4.0 miles. (AA 1990)

391 **Hillsborough River State Park**, 15402 US 301N, Thonotosassa, FL 33592, (813) 986-1020. 3.2 miles. (SAR 1990)

392 **Hobe Sound National Wildlife Refuge**, P.O. Box 645, Hobe Sound, FL 33475, (407) 546-6141; or South Florida Refuges, P.O. Box 510, Big Pine Key, FL 33043, (407) 546-6141. Named trails: Sand Pine Scrub Nature. (SFL; MCW; GCN)

393 **Honeymoon Island Nature Trail**, Honeymoon Island State Recreation Area, #1 Causeway Blvd., Dunedin, FL 32528, (813) 734-4255. (AA 1990)

394 **Hontoon Island Trail**, Hontoon Island State Park, 2309 River Ridge Rd., DeLand, FL 32720, (904) 736-5309. 2.0 miles. (SAR 1991)

Hornet Trail *see* entry 439.

395 **Hugh Taylor Birch Trail**, Hugh Taylor Birch State Recreation Area, 3109 E. Sunrise Blvd., Fort Lauderdale, FL 33304, (305) 564-4521. (AA 1990)

Hydrowatch Trail *see* entry 427.

396 **Ichetucknee Springs Nature Trail**, Ichetucknee Springs State Park, Rt. 2, Box 108, Fort White, FL 32038, (904) 497-2511. (SAR 1991)

397 **Indian Key Trail**, Park Manager, Long Key State Recreation Area, P.O. Box 776, Long Key, FL 33001, (305) 664-4815. (AA 1990)

Indian Relic Trail *see* entry 538.

Indigo Trail *see* entry 400.

398 **Island Hiking Trail**, Little Talbot Island State Park, 12157 Heckscher Dr.,

FLORIDA 27

Fort George, FL 32226, (904) 251-3231. 4.1 miles loop. (SAR 1989)

399 **J.B. Starkey Wilderness Park**, Southwest Florida Water Management District, 2379 Broad St., Brooksville, FL 34609, (904) 796-7211. (SFL)

400 **J.N. "Ding" Darling National Wildlife Refuge**, P.O. Drawer B, Sanibel, FL 33957, (813) 472-1100. 8.0 miles. Named trails: Indigo 2.0, Shell Mound, South Dike. (SFL; AIF; FEI; GNA; FIF; GNW)

401 **J.W. Corbett Wildlife Management Area**, Florida Game and Fresh Water Fish Commission, Everglades Region, 551 N. Military Trail, West Palm Beach, FL 33415, (407) 640-6100. (SFL)

Jackson Red Ground Trail see entries 270 and entry 289.

402 **Jena Unit**, Big Bend Wildlife Management Area, Florida Game and Fresh Water Fish Commission, Northeast Region, Rt. 7, Box 440, Lake City, FL 32055, (904) 758-0525. (SFL)

403 **Joe Budd Wildlife Management Area**, Florida Game and Fresh Water Fish Commission, Northwest Region, 6938 SR 2321, Panama City, FL 32409, (904) 265-3676. (SFL)

404 **John Chestnut, Sr. County Park Trail**, East Lake Rd., Palm Harbor, FL 34683, (813) 784-4686. (GCN)

405 **John D. MacArthur Beach State Park**, 10900 SR 703, North Palm Beach, FL 33408, (407) 624-6950 or (407) 624-6952. (SFL)

406 **John Pennekamp Park Trail**, John Pennekamp Coral Reef State Park, P.O. Box 487, Key Largo, FL 33037, (305) 451-1202. (AA 1990)

407 **John Prince County Park**, Campground Reservations, Palm Beach County Parks and Recreation Department, 2700 6th Ave., Lake Worth, FL 33461, (407) 582-7992. (GCN)

408 **Jonathan Dickinson State Park**, 16450 S.E. Federal Hwy., Hobe Sound, FL 33455, (407) 546-2771. Named trails: Kitching Creek, Wilson Creek. (SAR 1990)

409 **Junior Museum of Bay County**, 1731 Jenks Ave., Panama City, FL 32405, (904) 769-6128. (MCW)

Juniper Springs Trail see entry 456.

410 **Kelly Park**, 400 E. Kelly Park Rd., Apopka, FL 32712, (407) 889-4179. (SAR 1993)

411 **Key Deer Refuge**, P.O. Box 510, Big Pine Key, FL 33043, (305) 872-2353 or (305) 872-2239. Named trails: Key Deer Refuge, Pinewoods Nature. (MCW; GCN)

Key Deer Refuge Trail see entry 411.

412 **Kicco Wildlife Management Area**, Florida Game and Fresh Water Fish Commission, South Region, 3900 Drane Field Rd., Lakeland, FL 33803, (813) 644-9269. (SFL)

413 **Kissimmee River Trail**, South Florida Water Management District, P.O. Box 24680, 3301 Gun Club Rd., West Palm Beach, FL 33416, (407) 686-8800. 36.0 miles. (SFL)

Kitching Creek Trail see entry 408.

414 **Koreshan Trail**, Koreshan State Historic Site, P.O. Box 7, Estero, FL 33928, (813) 992-0311. 0.5 mile. (AA 1990)

LaChua Trail see entry 472.

Lake Arbuckle Trail see entry 279.

415 **Lake Cane-Marsha Park**, 7300 Conroy Rd., Orlando, FL 32825, (407) 296-5191. (OCS)

416 **Lake Griffin State Recreation Area**, 103 US 441-27, Fruitland Park, FL 32731, (904) 787-7402. (AA 1990)

417 **Lake Kissimmee State Park**, Rt. 4, Box 243, Lake Wales, FL 33853, (813) 696-1112. Named trails: Buster Island Loop 6.4(l), Cow Camp 1.75(s), Gobbler Ridge 4.2, North Loop 6.1(l). (SAR 1989)

418 **Lake Louisa State Park**, 12549 State Park Dr., Clermont, FL 34711, (904) 394-3969. (SFL)

Lake Maggiore Trail see entry 294.

419 **Lake Manatee State Recreation Area**, 20007 SR 64, Bradenton, FL 34202, (813) 741-3028. (CFC; SFL)

420 **Lake Mills County Park**, Tropical Ave., Chuluota, FL 32766, (407) 323-9615. (SAR 1992)

Lake Norris Aquatic Trail see entry 427.

421 **Lake Ocklawaha**, U.S. Army Corps of Engineers, P.O. Box 4970, Jacksonville,

FL 32210; or Ranger, Lake Ocklawaha, P.O. Box 1317, Palatka, FL 32277, (904) 328-2737. (ATF; GNA)

422 **Lake Okeechobee Trail**, U.S. Army Corps of Engineers, Natural Resources Office, 525 Ridgelawn Rd., Clewiston, FL 33440, (813) 983-3335. 110 miles loop. (SFL)

423 **Lake Seminole**, U.S. Army Corps of Engineers, P.O. Box 96, Chattahoochee, FL 32324, (904) 663-2291. (SFL)

424 **Lake Talquin Trail**, Lake Talquin State Recreation Area, Star Route 1, Box 2222, Tallahassee, FL 32310, (904) 576-8233. (SFL; GCN)

425 **Lake Woodruff National Wildlife Refuge**, P.O. Box 488, DeLeon Springs, FL 32028, (904) 985-4673. (SFL; GNW)

426 **Lakes Park**, Six Mile Cypress Pkwy., Fort Myers, FL 33912. (ATF)

Lakeside Nature Trail see entry 531.

427 **LaNoChe Scout Reservation**, P.O. Box 323, Paisley, FL 32767, (904) 669-2225; or Central Florida Council, BSA, P.O. Box 531084, 1215 E. Nebraska St., Orlando, FL 32553-1084, (407) 896-4801. Named trails: Bear Paw, Big Stump, Cateye, Hydrowatch, Lake Norris Aquatic, Perimeter 8.0(l), Sulphur Springs, Trapper Creek Nature. (SAR 1993)

428 **Larry and Penny Thompson Memorial Park Trail**, 12541 SW 184th St., Miami, FL 33177, (305) 233-8231. 5.0 miles. (GCN; GTF)

Laurel Oaks Trail see entry 512.

Layton Nature Trail see entry 430.

429 **Lettuce Lake County Park**, 6920 E. Fletcher Ave., Tampa, FL 33637, (813) 985-7845. (PTG; SFL)

430 **Lignumvitae Key State Botanical Area**, P.O. Box 1052, Islamorada, FL 33036, (305) 664-4815. Named trails: Layton Nature. (SFL; HFK)

Limestone Trail see entry 460.
Limpkin Trail see entry 513.

431 **Little Manatee River State Recreation Area Trail**, 215 Lightfoot Rd., Wimauma, FL 33598, (813) 634-4781. 6.5 miles loop. (SFL; GCN)

432 **Lochloosa Wildlife Management Area**, Florida Game and Fresh Water Fish Commission, 620 S. Meridian St., Tallahassee, FL 32304, (904) 488-4676. (GNA)

433 **Long Key Trail**, Long Key State Recreation Area, P.O. Box 776, Long Key, FL 33001, (305) 664-4815. 0.75 mile. (AA 1990)

Long Pine Key Trail see entry 349.
Loop Trail see entry 349.
Loop Trail see entry 439.

434 **Lower Suwannee and Cedar Key National Wildlife Refuge**, Rt. 1, Box 1193C, Chiefland, FL 32626, (904) 493-0238; or Cedar Key National Wildlife Refuge, Rt. 2, Box 44, Homossassa, FL 32646, (904) 628-2201. 45.0 miles. (SFL; NGC)

435 **Lower Wekiva River State Reserve**, 8300 SR 46, Sanford, FL 32711, (407) 330-6728. (SFL)

436 **Loxahatchee National Wildlife Refuge**, Rt. 1, Box 278, Boynton Beach, FL 33437, (305) 732-3684; or P.O. Box 2737, Delray Beach, FL 33437-2737. 60.0 miles. Named trails: Marsh Nature 3.2(l). (ATF; SFL; MCW; GFA; GTF; GNA; GNW)

437 **Maclay State Gardens Nature Trail**, Alfred B. Maclay State Gardens, 3540 Thomasville Rd., Tallahassee, FL 32303, (904) 385-4232. (AA 1990)

Magnolia Loop Trail see entry 366.

438 **Magnolia Park**, Ocoee-Apopka Rd., Winter Garden, FL 34787, (407) 886-4231. (SAR 1994)

Magnolia Trail see entry 513.
Mahogany Hammock Trail see entry 349.
Main Trail see entry 294.

439 **Manatee Springs State Park**, Rt. 2, Box 617, Chiefland, FL 32626, (904) 493-4288. Named trails: Clay 0.95(s), Fence 2.73(s), Fork 0.22(s), Graveyard 0.21(s), Hardwood 0.82(s), Hornet 0.53(s), Loop 0.49(s), Scenic 0.85(s), Shacklefoot 1.75(s), Sink 0.61(l). (SAR 1993)

Mangrove Trail see entry 332.
Maple Walk see entry 356.
Marsh Nature Trail see entry 436.
Marsh Rabbit Run Trail see entry 499.

440 **Matheson Hammock Park**, Old

Cutler Rd., Coral Gables, FL 33156. (SAR 1991)

441 **Mattair Spring Tract**, Suwannee River Water Management District, Rt. 3, Box 64, Live Oak, FL 32060, (904) 362-1001. (SFL)

Max Hoeck Creek Wildlife Drive see entry 311.

442 **McGregor Smith Scout Reservation**, South Florida Council, BSA, 2960 Coral Way, Miami, FL 33145, (305) 446-8431; or McGregor Smith Scout Reservation, P.O. Box 1553, Inverness, FL 32650, (904) 726-4426. (SFC)

McKethan Lake Nature Trail see entry 557.

443 **Medard County Park Trail**, 5726 Panther Loop, Plant City, FL 33567, (813) 681-8862. (GCN)

444 **Merritt Island National Wildlife Refuge**, P.O. Box 6447, Titusville, FL 32782, (407) 267-1110; or Merritt Island National Wildlife Refuge, P.O. Box 6504, Merritt Island, FL 32782, (407) 867-0667. Named trails: Allan Cruikshank Memorial 5.0, Black Point Wildlife Drive 7.0, Oak Hammock 1.2, Palm Hammock 2.0. (SAR 1995)

445 **Mike Machek Trail**, Gulf Stream Council, BSA, 2935 Australian Ave., West Palm Beach, FL 33407, (305) 844-0279; or Tanah Keeta Scout Reservation, Boy Scout Rd., Tequesta, FL 33469, (305) 746-8749. 5.2 miles loop. Awards available. (SAR 1994)

446 **Moccasin Lake Nature Park**, 2750 Park Lake Trail Ln., P.O. Box 4748, Clearwater, FL 34619-5601, (813) 462-6024. (ATF; PTG; MCW)

447 **Morikami Trail**, Morikami Museum of Japanese Culture, 4000 Morikami Park Rd., Delray Beach, FL 33445, (407) 499-0631. 1.5 miles. (ATF; FTG; MCW; GFA; HFL)

448 **Morningside Nature Center**, 3540 E. University Ave., Gainesville, FL 32601, (904) 374-2170. Named trails: Blueberry, Fern Loop, Tupelo. (GFA; FIF; ODT)

449 **Moss Park**, Moss Park Rd., Orlando, FL 32832, (407) 273-2327. (SAR 1992)

Mounds Pool Trail see entry 500.

450 **Museum of Science and Industry**, 4801 E. Fowler Ave., Tampa, FL 33617-2099, (813) 985-5531. Named trails: Experiment, Naturalist, Pathfinders. (ATF; PTG)

451 **Myakka River Trail**, Myakka River State Park, Myakka City, FL 33551; or Myakka River State Park, 13207 SR 72, Sarasota, FL 34241-9542, (813) 924-1027. 38.0 miles. (FWM; SFL; FTA; GCN; GTF)

452 **Nassau Wildlife Management Area**, Florida Game and Fresh Water Fish Commission, 620 S. Meridian St., Tallahassee, FL 32304, (904) 488-4676. (GNA)

Naturalist Trail see entry 450.

453 **Nature Center and Planetarium of Lee County**, Ortiz Ave., Fort Myers, FL 33905, (813) 275-3435. (MCW)

New River Trail see entry 512.

454 **New Smyrna Sugar Mill Ruins State Historic Site**, P.O. Box 861, New Smyrna Beach, FL 32069, (904) 428-2126. Named trails: Dinosaur. (MCW; GFA; ODT)

North Bridge Trail see entry 288.

North Loop Trail see entry 417.

455 **North Peninsula State Recreation Area**, c/o Flagler Beach State Recreation Area, 3100 S. SR A1A, Flagler Beach, FL 32036, (904) 439-2474. (SFL)

Oak Hammock Trail see entry 444.

Oak-Pine Hammock Trail see entry 294.

456 **Ocala National Forest**, United States Department of Agriculture, Forest Service, Seminole Ranger District, 1551 Umatilla Rd., Eustis, FL 32726, (904) 367-3721; or Lake George Ranger District, 17147 E. Silver Springs St., Silver Springs, FL 32688, (904) 625-2520. Named trails: Clearwater 1.0, Juniper Springs 0.7, Ocala One-Hundred Mile Horse 100, Ocala 66.0, St. Francis Interpretive, Timucuan Indian 1.1. (SAR 1993)

Ocala One-Hundred Mile Horse Trail see entry 456.

457 **Ocala Springs RV Park**, Rt. 1, Box 1305, Anthony, FL 32167, (904) 236-9918. (CFC)

Ocala Trail see entry 456.

Ochlockonee River Nature Trail see entry 458.

458 **Ochlockonee River State Park**, P.O. Box 5, Sopchoppy, FL 32358, (904) 962-2771. Named trails: Ochlockonee River Nature 1.0, River 0.6. (AA 1990)

459 **Old Cutler Historic Trail**, South Florida Council, BSA, 15255 NW 82nd Ave., Miami Lakes, FL 33016, (305) 364-0020. 13.0 miles straight. Annual hike in early December. Awards available. (SAR 1991)

Old Eldora Trail see entry 311.

Old French Trail see entry 363.

Old Hammock Trail see entry 311.

Old Ingram Highway see entry 349.

460 **O'Leno State Park**, Rt. 2, Box 307, High Springs, FL 32643, (904) 454-1853. Named trails: Limestone 0.5(s), Pareners Branch 3.5(l), River Rise (Natural Bridge) 13.0(l), River Sink 1.0(s). (SAR 1993)

461 **Orlando Historic Trail**, Corb Sarchet, 132 Waverley Pl., Orlando, FL 32806, (407) 648-9636 or (407) 422-8285. 5.5 miles loop. Awards available. (SAR 1994)

462 **Orlando Ten Commandments Hike**, Central Florida Council, BSA, P.O. Box 531084, Orlando, FL 32553-1084, (407) 896-4801. Mileage varies (annual event). Awards available. (SAR 1995)

463 **Orlando Wilderness Park**, Wheeler Rd., Christmas, FL 32709, (407) 246-2348; or Orlando Recreation Bureau, 649 W. Livingston St., Orlando, FL 32801, (407) 246-2649. (AA 1993)

464 **Orlo Vista Park**, Nowell Ave., Orlando, FL 32835, (407) 299-6124. (OCS)

Ornamental Gardens Trail see entry 550.

465 **Oscar Scherer Trail**, Oscar Scherer State Recreation Area, P.O. Box 398, Osprey, FL 33559, (813) 966-3154. 0.8 mile. (SAR 1990)

466 **Osceola District Schools Environmental Study Center**, 4300 S. Poinciana Blvd., Kissimmee, FL 32758, (407) 870-0551. (PTG)

467 **Osceola National Forest**, USDA Forest Service, 227 N. Bronough St., Suite 4061, Tallahassee, FL 32301, (904) 681-7265; or District Ranger, US 90, P.O. Box 70, Lake City, FL 32072, (904) 752-0331. (SAR 1990)

468 **Osceola-Olustee Historic Trail**, Milledge Murphey, Ph.D., 1815 N.W. 7th Pl., Gainesville, FL 32603, (904) 373-9234. Includes Olustee Battlefield Trail. 22.4 miles straight. Awards available. (SAR 1994)

Osprey Trail see entry 513.

469 **Otter Lake**, Refuge Manager, St. Marks National Wildlife Refuge, P.O. Box 68, St. Marks, FL 32355, (904) 925-6280. Named trails: Otter Lake Loop 7.9, Ridge 4.6(s). (GTF)

Otter Lake Loop Trail see entry 469.

Pa-hay-okee Overlook Trail see entry 349.

Palm Hammock Trail see entry 444.

470 **Palm Island Nature Trail**, Palm Island Park, Mount Dora, FL 32757, (904) 383-2165. 1.0 mile. (PTG; FTG)

Pareners Branch Trail see entry 460.

Pathfinders Trail see entry 450.

471 **Paynes Creek Trail**, Paynes Creek State Historic Site, P.O. Box 547, Bowling Green, FL 33834, (813) 375-4717. 1.0 mile. (AA 1990)

472 **Payne's Prairie State Preserve**, Rt. 2, Box 41, Micanopy, FL 32667, (904) 466-3397. Named trails: Bolen Bluff 1.0, Chacala 10.0, Cone's Dike 5.0, LaChua Trail 2.0, Wacahoota 0.25(l). (SAR 1990)

473 **Pelican Path**, Chamber of Commerce, Old Mallory Square, Key West, FL 33040. (FIF; AGW)

474 **Pensacola Historical Trail**, John Steiger, 8100 Monticello Dr., Pensacola, FL 32514, (904) 477-0122. 4.0 miles loop. Awards available. (SAR 1990)

475 **Pensacola Naval Air Station Historical Trail**, John Steiger, 8100 Monticello Dr., Pensacola, FL 32514, (904) 477-0122. 10.0 miles straight. Awards available. (SAR 1990)

476 **Pensacola Walking Tour**, Visitor Information Center, 1401 E. Gregory St., Pensacola, FL 32501, (904) 434-1234; or (800) 343-4321 (in FL); or (800) 874-1234 (in rest of U.S.). (FIF)

477 **Perdido Key State Recreation Area**,

c/o Big Lagoon State Recreation Area, 12301 Gulf Beach Hwy., Pensacola, FL 32507, (904) 492-1595. (SFL)

Perimeter Trail *see* entry 427.

Pine Flatwoods Trail *see* entry 294.

Pine Island Nature Trail *see* entry 358.

478 Pine Log Trail, District Forester, Pine Log State Forest, 715 W. 15th St., Panama City, FL 32401, (904) 763-6589. 3.0 miles. (SFL; AIF; GCN; GTF)

Pineland Trail *see* entry 349.

479 Pinellas Trail, Jerry Cummings, Pinellas Trail Park Ranger, Pinellas County Parks Department, 631 Chestnut St., Clearwater, FL 34616, (813) 581-2953. 47.0 miles straight. (GRT)

Pinewoods Nature Trail *see* entry 411.

480 Pioneer Park, Hardee County B.O.C.C. Park Manager, 412 W. Orange St., Rm. A-204, Wauchula, FL 33873, (813) 735-0330. (CFC)

Plum Orchard Trail *see* entry 500.

481 Point Washington Wildlife Management Area, Florida Game and Fresh Water Fish Commission, 620 S. Meridian St., Tallahassee, FL 32304, (904) 488-4676. (GNA)

482 Polk County Rail Trail, P.O. Box 45, Winter Haven, FL 33882. 28.5 miles straight. (SFL)

483 Ponce de Leon Park, W. Marion Ave., Punta Gorda, FL 33950, (813) 639-3505. (MCW)

484 Ponce de Leon Springs State Recreation Area, Rt. 5, Box 660, Chipley, FL 32428, (904) 638-6130. (SFL; MCW)

485 Potts Preserve, Southwest Florida Water Management District, 2379 Broad St., Brooksville, FL 34609, (904) 796-7211. (SFL)

Prairie Overlook Trail *see* entry 356.

486 Prairie-Lakes State Preserve, P.O. Box 220, Kenansville, FL 32739, (305) 436-1626. 5.5 and 5.7 miles loops, plus 24.0 miles straight. (GCN; FTA)

487 Ravine Gardens Trail, Ravine State Gardens, P.O. Box 1096, 1600 Twigg St., Palatka, FL 32078, (904) 328-4366. 1.8 miles loop. (AA 1990)

Red Cedar Nature Trail *see* entry 491.

488 Rice Creek Trail, Hudson Pulp and Paper Company, P.O. Box 1040, Palatka, FL 32077. 3.0 miles loop. (GTF; GNA)

Richloam Hiking Trail *see* entry 557.

Ridge Trail *see* entry 469.

River Rise Trail *see* entry 460.

River Sink Trail *see* entry 460.

River Trail *see* entry 458.

489 Robert Brent Wildlife Management Area, Florida Game and Fresh Water Fish Commission, 620 S. Meridian St., Tallahassee, FL 32304, (904) 488-4676. (GNA)

490 Rock Springs Run Trail, Rock Springs Run State Reserve, Rt. 1, Box 365D, Sorrento, FL 32776, (904) 383-3311. 10.0 miles. (AA 1990)

Rocky Bayou Nature Trail *see* entry 491.

491 Rocky Bayou State Recreation Area, Rt. 1, Box 597, Niceville, FL 32578, (904) 897-3222. Named trails: Red Cedar Nature 0.5, Rocky Bayou Nature 0.7, Sand Pine Nature 1.3. (AA 1990)

492 Rookery Bay National Estuarine Sanctuary, 401 Shell Island Rd., Naples, FL 33942, (813) 775-8569. (SFL)

Rowdy Bend Trail *see* entry 349.

493 Ruth Springs Tract, Suwannee River Water Management District, Rt. 3, Box 64, Live Oak, FL 32060, (904) 362-1001. 6.3 miles. (SFL)

494 Saddle Creek Park Trail, P.O. Box 60, Bartow, FL 33860, (813) 665-2283. 1.5 miles. (CFC; SFL)

St. Andrews Nature Trail *see* entry 495.

495 St. Andrews State Recreation Area, 4415 Thomas Dr., Panama City, FL 32407, (904) 234-2522. Named trails: Gator Lake Nature 0.3, St. Andrews Nature 0.4. (AA 1990)

496 St. Augustine Historic Trail, Milledge Murphey, Ph.D., 1815 N.W. 7th Pl., Gainesville, FL 32603, (904) 373-9234. 8.0 miles loop. Awards available. (SAR 1993)

St. Francis Interpretive Trail *see* entry 456.

497 **St. George Island State Park**, Dr. Julian G. Bruce, St. George Island State Park, P.O. Box 62, Eastport, FL 32328, (904) 670-2111. 9.0 miles. (AA 1990)
  St. Joseph Bay Trail *see* entry 498.
498 **St. Joseph Peninsula State Park**, T.H. Stone Memorial St. Joseph Peninsula State Park, Star Route 1, Box 200, Port St. Joe, FL 32456, (904) 227-1327. Named trails: Barrier Dune, St. Joseph Bay. (AA 1990)
499 **St. Lucie Inlet State Preserve**, c/o Jonathan Dickinson State Park, 16450 SE Federal Hwy., Hobe Sound, FL 33455, (407) 744-7603. Named trails: Marsh Rabbit Run 4.0, Sand Pine Scrub Nature 0.5. (HFL; GCN)
500 **St. Marks National Wildlife Refuge**, P.O. Box 68, St. Marks, FL 32355, (904) 925-6280. 60.0 miles. Named trails: Deep Creek 12.0(s), Mounds Pool, Plum Orchard, Stoney Bayou. (EGH; FWM; AIF; GOP; MCW; GFA; GTF; GNA; GNW)
501 **St. Vincent National Wildlife Refuge**, P.O. Box 447, Apalachicola, FL 32320, (904) 653-8808. 96.0 miles. (EGH; GTF; GNA; GNW)
502 **San Felasco Hammock Trail**, San Felasco Hammock State Preserve, c/o Devil's Millhopper State Geological Site, 4732 N.W. 53rd Ave., Gainesville, FL 32601, (904) 336-2008. (AA 1990)
503 **San Luis Archaeological and Historical Site**, Mission Rd., Tallahassee, FL 32304, (904) 487-3711. (ATF)
504 **San Marcos de Apalache Trail**, San Marcos de Apalache State Historic Site, P.O. Box 27, St. Marks, FL 32355, (904) 925-6216. (AA 1990)
505 **Sand Hill Scout Reservation**, West Central Florida Council, BSA, P.O. Box 3408, Seminole, FL 34642, (813) 391-0171. (CFC)
  Sand Pine Nature Trail *see* entry 491.
  Sand Pine Scrub Nature Trail *see* entries 392 and 499.
  Sand Road Trail *see* entry 311.
  Sandhills Trail *see* entry 524.
  Sandy Point Wildlife Refuge Trail *see* entry 279.

506 **Sanibel-Captiva Trail**, Sanibel-Captiva Conservation Foundation, Sanibel Island, FL 33957. 4.15 miles loop. (GTF)
507 **Sanlan Ranch Nature Trail**, Sanlan Ranch Campground, 3929 US 98S, Lakeland, FL 33813, (813) 665-1726. (CFC)
508 **Savanna Recreational Area Park**, 1400 E. Midway Rd., Ft. Pierce, FL 33482, (407) 464-7855. (GCN)
509 **Sawgrass Lake Trail**, Sawgrass Lake Park, 7400 25th St. N., St. Petersburg, FL 33702, (813) 527-3814. 5,732'. (PTG; SFL)
  Scenic Trail *see* entry 439.
510 **Science Center of Pinellas County**, 7701 22nd Ave. N., St. Petersburg, FL 33710, (813) 384-0027. (MCW)
  Scrub Island Trail *see* entry 294.
511 **Scrub Plum Nature Trail**, Dr. David LaHart, Region 3 Environmental Education Service Project, (407) 783-0300; or Jan Zerbe, Region 4 Environmental Education Service Project, (800) 392-2209. (FWM)
512 **Secret Woods Nature Center**, 2701 W. SR 84, Fort Lauderdale, FL 33312, (305) 791-1030. Named trails: Laurel Oaks 1,216', New River 3,200'. (HFL; GCN)
  Self-guiding Nature Trail *see* entry 287.
513 **Seminole County Environmental Studies Center**, 2985 Osprey Tr., Longwood, FL 32750, (407) 321-0452. Named trails: Limpkin, Magnolia, Osprey, Super Mud Walk. (SAR 1989)
514 **Seminole Ranch Wildlife Management Area**, Florida Game and Fresh Water Fish Commission, Central Region, 1239 SW Tenth St., Ocala, FL 32674, (904) 732-1225. (SAR 1989)
  Shacklefoot Trail *see* entry 439.
  Shark Valley Trail *see* entry 349.
  Shell Mound Trail *see* entry 400.
  Silver Lake Trail *see* entry 273.
  Sink Trail *see* entry 439.
  Slash Pine Trail *see* entry 349.
  Snake Bight Trail *see* entry 349.
515 **Snyder Park**, SW 4th Ave., Fort Lauderdale, FL 33315. (MCW)
516 **Soldiers Creek Park**, Big Tree Park/

FLORIDA

Soldiers Creek Park, 3000A Southgate Rd., Sanford, FL 32773, (407) 323-9615. 3.0 miles loop. (SFL)

517 **South Depot Avenue Bike Route**, Bicycle Coordinator, Traffic and Engineering Department, Mail Station 28, P.O. Box 490, Gainesville, FL 32602, (904) 334-2130. 1.0 mile straight. (GRT)

South Dike Trail see entry 400.

518 **South Lido Park**, 2201 Benjamin Franklin Dr., Lido Key, FL 34236, (813) 951-5572. (PTG)

519 **Spanish Trail Scout Reservation**, Gulf Coast Council, BSA, 9440 University Pkwy., Pensacola, FL 32514, (904) 476-6336; or Spanish Trail Scout Reservation, Rt. 5, Box 227, Defuniak Springs, FL 32433, (904) 892-5312. (SFC)

520 **Spirit of the Suwannee County Park**, Rt. 1, Box 98, Live Oak, FL 32060, (904) 364-1683. (GCN)

Spite Highway see entry 287.

521 **Spring Creek Unit**, Big Bend Wildlife Management Area, Florida Game and Fresh Water Fish Commission, Northwest Region, Rt. 7, Box 440, Lake City, FL 32055, (904) 758-0525. (SFL)

522 **Starkey Wilderness**, Southeast Florida Water Management District, 5060 US 41S, Brooksville, FL 33572-9712, (904) 796-7211. (GCN)

523 **Steinhatchee Wildlife Management Area**, Florida Game and Fresh Water Fish Commission, 620 S. Meridian St., Tallahassee, FL 32304, (904) 488-4676. (GNA)

Sulphur Springs Trail see entry 427.

Super Mud Walk see entry 513.

524 **Suwannee River State Park**, Rt. 8, Box 297, Live Oak, FL 32060, (904) 362-2746. Named trails: Sandhills 0.3, Suwannee River 0.3. (AA 1990)

Suwannee River Trail see entry 524.

Swamp Woodlands Trail see entry 294.

Sweetwater Trail see entry 289.

525 **Tallahassee Museum of History and Natural Science**, Lake Bradford, Tallahassee, FL 32304, (904) 576-1636. (ATF)

526 **Tallahassee-St. Marks Historic Railroad State Trail**, Clifton Maxwell, Trail Manager, Division of Parks and Recreation, Florida Department of Natural Resources, 1022 Desoto Park Dr., Tallahassee, FL 32301, (904) 922-6007. 16.0 miles straight. (GRT; SFL; GCN)

527 **Talquin Wildlife Management Area**, Florida Game and Freshwater Fish Commission, Northwest Region, 6938 SR 2321, Panama City, FL 32409, (904) 265-3676. (SFL)

528 **10 Commandments Hike**, Tequesta District Executive, South Florida Council, BSA, 15255 NW 82nd Ave., Miami Lakes, FL 33016, (305) 364-0020. 6.2 miles. Annual hike on the day before Palm Sunday. (SAR 1993)

529 **Tenoroc State Reserve**, 3829 Tenoroc Mine Rd., Lakeland, FL 33805, (813) 499-2422. (SFL)

530 **Three Lakes Wildlife Management Area**, Florida Game and Fresh Water Fish Commission, Central Region, 1239 SW Tenth St., Ocala, FL 32674, (904) 732-1225. (SFL)

531 **Three Rivers State Recreation Area**, Rt. 1, Box 15-A, Sneads, FL 32460, (904) 593-6565. Named trails: Half-Dry Nature 0.3, Lakeside Nature 1.5. (AA 1990)

532 **Tibet-Butler Nature Preserve**, Winter Garden-Vineland Rd., Orlando, FL 32836, (407) 876-6696. (OCS)

533 **Tide Swamp Unit**, Big Bend Wildlife Management Area, Florida Game and Fresh Water Fish Commission, 620 S. Meridian St., Tallahassee, FL 32304, (904) 488-4676. (SFL; GNA)

534 **Tiger Bay Wildlife Management Area**, Florida Game and Fresh Water Fish Commission, Central Region, 1239 SW Tenth St., Ocala, FL 32674, (904) 732-1225. (SFL)

535 **Tiger Creek Preserve**, Lake Wales Office, The Nature Conservancy, P.O. Box 1319, Lake Wales, FL 33859, (813) 678-1551. (SFL)

Timucuan Indian Trail see entry 456.

536 **Tomoka Trail**, Tomoka State Park, 2099 N. Beach St., Ormond Beach, FL 32074, (904) 677-3931. 0.5 mile. (SAR 1992)

537 **Topeekeegee Yugnee Park**, Hollywood, FL 33022. (ATF)
538 **Torreya State Park**, Rt. 2, Box 70, Bristol, FL 32321, (904) 643-2674. Named trails: Apalachicola Bluffs 0.4(s), Indian Relic 0.4(s), Torreya 7.0(l), Weeping Ridge. (SAR 1993)
Torreya Trail see entry 538.
539 **Tosohatchee State Reserve**, 3365 Taylor Creek Rd., Christmas, FL 32709, (407) 568-5893. 15.9 miles loop plus 16.9 miles straight. (AA 1990)
540 **Tradewinds Park**, 4400 N.W. 39th Ave., Pompano Beach, FL 33073. (ATF)
Tram Road Trail see entry 349.
Trapper Creek Nature Trail see entry 427.
541 **Tree Tops Park**, 3900 S.W. 10th Ave., Davie, FL 33329. (ATF)
542 **Trimble Park Nature Trail**, Earlwood Ave., Tangerine, FL 32777, (904) 383-1993. (SAR 1990)
Tumblin Creek Path see entry 288.
Tupelo Trail see entry 448.
543 **Turkey Lake Park**, 3401 Hiawassee Rd., Orlando, FL 32811, (407) 299-5594. 7.0 miles. (HFL; MCW; GTF)
Turtle Mound Trail see entry 311.
Two Ponds Trail see entry 363.
544 **University of Central Florida**, Dr. Hank Whittier, 4000 Central Florida Blvd., Orlando, FL 32765, (407) 823-2978. (SAR 1992)
545 **University of North Florida**, P.O. Box 17074, Jacksonville, FL 32318. 12.0 miles. (GTF)
546 **Upper Hillsborough River**, Southwest Florida Water Management District, 2379 Broad St., Brooksville, FL 34609-6899, (800) 423-1476. (CFC)
547 **Upper Tampa Bay County Park**, 8001 Double Branch Rd., Tampa, FL 33615, (813) 855-1765. (SFL)
Vinzant Riding Trail see entry 273.
Wacahoota Trail see entry 472.
548 **Waldo Road Trail**, Bicycle Coordinator, Traffic and Engineering Department, Mail Station 28, P.O. Box 490, Gainesville, FL 32602, (904) 334-2107. 3.0 miles straight. (GRT)
549 **Wallwood Scout Reservation**, Suwannee River Area Council, BSA, P.O. Box 306, Tallahassee, FL 32302, (904) 576-4146; or Wallwood Scout Reservation, Rt. 3, Box 201, Quincy, FL 32351, (904) 627-3269. (SFC)
Washington Oaks Nature Trail see entry 550.
550 **Washington Oaks State Gardens**, 6400 N. Oceanshore Blvd., Palm Coast, FL 32037, (904) 445-3161. Named trails: Ornamental Gardens Walk 0.8, Washington Oaks Nature 0.3. (AA 1990)
Weeping Ridge Trail see entry 538.
551 **Wekiwa Springs State Park**, 1800 Wekiwa Cir., Apopka, FL 32712, (407) 884-2009. Named trails: Wekiwa Springs 13.0. (SAR 1994)
Wekiwa Springs Trail see entry 551.
West Lake Trail see entry 349.
552 **West Orange Greenway**, Robert Seifer, Park Programs Development Specialist, Division of Parks and Recreation, Florida Department of Natural Resources, 12549 State Park Dr., Clermont, FL 34711, (904) 394-2280. 33.0 miles straight. (ORL)
553 **Whispering Pines Trail**, Whispering Pines Park, 1700 Forest Dr., Inverness, FL 32650. 2.5 miles. (PTG)
554 **Wickham Park Nature Trail**, 2500 Parkway Dr., Melbourne, FL 32935, (407) 255-4307. (SAR 1988)
555 **Wilderness Park**, Parks and Recreation Department, 1101 E. River Cove St., Tampa, FL 33604, (813) 272-5840. (SFL)
Willie Browne Trail see entry 363.
Willow Marsh Trail see entry 294.
Willow Pond Nature Trail see entry 366.
Wilson Creek Trail see entry 408.
556 **Withlacoochee River Park**, Pasco County Parks and Recreation Department, 6520 Ridge Rd., Port Richey, FL 34668, (813) 847-8118. (SFL)
557 **Withlacoochee State Forest**, Division of Forestry, Withlacoochee Forest Center, 15019 Broad St., Brooksville, FL 34601, (904) 796-5650. Named trails: Citrus Hiking 40.6(l), Citrus Horse, Colonel Robins 3.2(l), Croom Hiking 22.3(l),

McKethan Lake Nature 2.5(l), Richloam Hiking 25.3(l). (AA 1989)
558 **Withlacoochee State Trail**, Robert Seifer, Park Programs Development Specialist, Division of Parks and Recreation, Florida Department of Natural Resources, 12549 State Park Dr., Clermont, FL 34711, (904) 394-2280. 47.0 miles straight. (GRT)
559 **Woodlands Nature Trail**, Woodlands Lutheran Camp, 15749 SR 455, Montverde, FL 34756, (407) 469-2792. (CFC)

Generally:
Florida Department of Natural Resources, Office of Communications, Marjory Stoneman Douglas Bldg., 3900 Commonwealth Blvd., Tallahassee, FL 32389, (904) 488-6327. (DNR)
National Forests in Florida, 227 N. Bronough St., Suite 4061, Tallahassee, FL 32301, (904) 681-7265. (EGH)
Sierra Club, c/o Beth Ann Brick, 462 Fernwood, Key Biscayne, FL 33149. (EGH)
U.S. Army Corps of Engineers, P.O. Box 4970, Jacksonville, FL 32210. (GNA)

Index (by city)

Anthony: Ocala Springs RV Park 457
Apalachicola: Cape St. George Island 313; Fort Gadsden State Historic Site 370; St. Vincent National Wildlife Refuge 501
Apopka: Kelly Park 410; Wekiwa Springs State Park 551
Atlantic Beach: Hanna Park 388
Avon Park: Avon Park Air Force Range 279
Babson Park: Babson Park/Audubon Center 280
Baldwin: Cary State Forest 314
Bartow: Saddle Creek Park Trail 494
Big Pine Key: Bahia Honda Nature Trail 281; Camp Sawyer 308; Florida Keys National Wildlife Refuges 360; Key Deer Refuge 411
Boca Grande: Cayo Costa State Park 316
Bowling Green: Paynes Creek Trail 471
Boynton Beach: Loxahatchee National Wildlife Refuge 436
Bradenton: DeSoto National Memorial Trail 336; Lake Manatee State Recreation Area 419
Branford: Ruth Springs Tract 493
Bristol: Apalachicola National Forest 273; Torreya State Park 538
Brooksville: Starkey Wilderness 522; Upper Hillsborough River 546; Withlacoochee State Forest 557
Bunnell: Bulow Ruins Nature Trail 298; Bulow Woods Trail 299
Bushnell: Dade Battlefield Trail 329
Cedar Key: Cedar Key Scrub State Reserve 317
Chattahoochee: Lake Seminole 423
Chiefland: Lower Suwannee and Cedar Key National Wildlife Refuge 434; Manatee Springs State Park 439
Chipley: Falling Waters Trail 352; Ponce de Leon Springs State Management Area 484
Christmas: Orlando Wilderness Park 463; Seminole Ranch Wildlife Management Area 514; Tosohatchee State Reserve 539
Chuluota: Lake Mills County Park 420
Clearwater: Camp Soule 310; Moccasin Lake Nature Park 446; Pinellas Trail 479
Clermont: General James A. Van Fleet State Trail 378; Lake Louisa State Park 418; West Orange Greenway 552; Withlacoochee State Trail 558
Clewiston: Lake Okeechobee Trail 422
Cocoa: Brevard Museum of History and Natural Science 296
Copeland: Fakahatchee Strand Trail 351
Coral Gables: Matheson Hammock Park 440; 10 Commandments Hike 528
Crystal River: Crystal River State Archaeological Site 328
Dade City: Withlacoochee River Park 556
Davie: Camp Seminole 309; Tree Tops Park 541
Daytona Beach: Tiger Bay Wildlife Management Area 534

Defuniak Springs: Spanish Trail Scout Reservation 519
DeLand: Hontoon Island Trail 394
DeLeon Springs: DeLeon Springs Trail 334; Lake Woodruff National Wildlife Refuge 425
Delray Beach: Morikami Trail 447
Dowling Park: Christian Tract, Suwannee River 321
Dunedin: Caladesi Island Trail 302; Honeymoon Island Nature Trail 393
Eastport: St. George Island State Park 497
Eglin AFB: Eglin Air Force Base 344
Egmont Key: Egmont Key Historic Trail 345; Egmont Key State Park and National Wildlife Refuge 346
Estero: Koreshan Trail 414
Fanning Springs: Andrews Wildlife Management Area 271
Fernandina Beach: Ft. Clinch Environmental Trail 364; Ft. Clinch Historic Trail 365; Ft. Clinch State Park 366
Flagler Beach: Flagler Beach Trail 357; North Peninsula State Recreation Area 455
Fort George: Island Hiking Trail 398
Fort Lauderdale: Hugh Taylor Birch Trail 395; Secret Woods Nature Center 512; Snyder Park 515
Fort McCoy: Fort McCoy Wildlife Management Area 373
Fort Myers: Boca Grande Bike Path 293; Lakes Park 426; Nature Center and Planetarium of Lee County 453
Fort Pierce: Fort Pierce Inlet State Recreation Area 375; Savanna Recreational Area Park 508
Fort White: Ichetucknee Springs Nature Trail 396
Frostproof: Arbuckle State Forest 274; Arbuckle Wildlife Management Area 275
Fruitland Park: Lake Griffin State Recreation Area 416
Gainesville: Bivens Arm Nature Park 288; Devil's Millhopper Trail 338; Florida National Scenic Trail 361; Gainesville-Hawthorne State Trail 377; Morningside Nature Center 448; San Felasco Hammock Trail 502; South Depot Avenue Bike Route 517; Waldo Road Trail 548

Goulds: Castello Hammock 315
Gulf Breeze: Gulf Islands National Seashore 386
High Springs: Ginnie Springs 379; O'Leno State Park 460
Hobe Sound: Hobe Sound National Wildlife Refuge 392; Jonathan Dickinson State Park 408; St. Lucie Inlet State Preserve 499
Hollywood: Topeekeegee Yugnee Park 537
Holopaw: Bull Creek Wildlife Management Area 297
Homestead: Biscayne National Park 287; Chekika Trail 320; Everglades National Park 349; Everglades Water Conservation Areas 350
Indiantown: DuPuis Reserve Wildlife and Environmental Area 341
Inverness: Flying Eagle 362; Fort Cooper Trail 367; McGregor Smith Scout Reservation 442; Potts Preserve 485; Whispering Pines Trail 553
Islamorada: Lignumvitae Key State Botanical Area 430
Jacksonville: Amelia Island State Recreation Area 268; Ft. Caroline Historic Trail 363; Fort George Island 371; University of North Florida 545
Jacksonville Beach: Big Talbot Island State Park 286
Kenansville: Prairie-Lakes State Preserve 486; Three Lakes Wildlife Management Area 530
Key Biscayne: Cape Florida Trail 312
Key Largo: John Pennekamp Park Trail 406
Key West: Pelican Path 473
Keystone Heights: Gold Head Branch Trail 380
Kissimmee: Osceola District Schools Environmental Study Center 466
Lake City: Aucilla Wildlife Management Area 278; Osceola National Forest 467
Lake Monroe: Central Florida Zoologial Park Nature Trail 318
Lake Ocklawaha: Lake Ocklawaha 421
Lake Placid: Archbold Nature Trail 276
Lake Wales: Camp Flaming Arrow 305; Lake Kissimmee State Park 417; Tiger Creek Preserve 535
Lake Worth: John Prince County Park 407

FLORIDA   *Index*   37

Lakeland: Green Swamp Wildlife Management Area 382; Sanlan Ranch Nature Trail 507; Tenoroc State Reserve 529
Lebanon Station: Gulf Hammock Wildlife Management Area 385
Lido Key: South Lido Park 518
Lithia: Alderman's Ford County Park Trail 266
Live Oak: Allen Mill Pond 267; Mattair Spring Tract 441; Spirit of the Suwannee County Park 520
Long Key: Indian Key Trail 397; Long Key Trail 433
Longwood: Seminole County Environmental Studies Center 513
Marco: Collier-Seminole Trail 322
Marianna: Florida Caverns State Park 358
Melbourne: Dent Smith Trail 335; Scrub Plum Nature Trail 511; Wickham Park Nature Trail 554
Miami: Charles Deering Estate 319; Crandon Park 326; Larry and Penny Thompson Memorial Park Trail 428; Old Cutler Historic Trail 459
Micanopy: Payne's Prairie State Preserve 472
Milton: Blackwater River State Forest 289
Montverde: Woodlands Nature Trail 559
Mt. Dora: Palm Island Nature Trail 470
Munson: Andrew Jackson Historic Trail 270
Myakka City: Myakka River Trail 451
Naples: Conservancy Nature Center 323; Corkscrew Swamp Trail 325; Rookery Bay National Estuarine Sanctuary 492
New Smyrna Beach: New Smyrna Sugar Mill Ruins State Historic Site 454
Niceville: Rocky Bayou State Recreation Area 491
North Palm Beach: J.W. Corbett Wildlife Management Area 401; John D. MacArthur Beach State Park 405
Oakland Park: Easterlin Park Trail 342
Oasis: Kicco Wildlife Management Area 412; Kissimmee River Trail 413
Ochopee: Big Cypress National Preserve Trail 283
Odessa: Camp Brorein 304
Okeechobee: Barley Barber Swamp Trail 282
Olustee: Olustee Battlefield Trail 468; Osceola-Olustee Historic Trail 468

Orange City: Blue Spring State Park 292; DeLand KOA 333
Orlando: Cady Way to Fashion Square Greenway 301; Camp Mitchell Nature Trail 307; Lake Cane-Marsha Park 415; Moss Park 449; Orlando Historic Trail 461; Orlando Ten Commandments Hike 462; Orlo Vista Park 464; Tibet-Butler Nature Preserve 532; Turkey Lake Park 543; University of Central Florida 544
Ormond Beach: Tomoka Trail 536
Osprey: Oscar Scherer Trail 465
Paisley: LaNoChe Scout Reservation 427
Palatka: Ravine Gardens Trail 487; Rice Creek Trail 488
Palm Coast: Washington Oaks State Gardens 550
Palm Harbor: John Chestnut, Sr. County Park Trail 404
Panacea: Bradwell Bay Federal Wilderness Area 295
Panama City: Junior Museum of Bay County 409; Pine Log Trail 478; St. Andrews State Recreation Area 495
Pembroke Pines: C.B. Smith Park 300
Pensacola: Big Lagoon State Recreation Area 284; Fort Pickens Historical Trail 374; Pensacola Historical Trail 474; Pensacola Naval Air Station Historical Trail 475; Pensacola Walking Tour 476; Perdido Key State Recreation Area 477
Perry: Hagens Cove 387; Hickory Mound Unit 389; Spring Creek Unit 521
Plant City: Medard County Park Trail 443
Point Washington: Point Washington Wildlife Management Area 481
Pompano Beach: Fern Forest Nature Center 356; Tradewinds Park 540
Ponte Vedra Beach: Guana River State Park 383
Port Richey: J.B. Starkey Wilderness Park 399
Port St. Joe: St. Joseph Peninsula State Park 498
Punta Gorda: Camp Frank E. Gannett 306; Ponce de Leon Park 483
Quincy: Wallwood Scout Reservation 549
St. Augustine: Ancient Dunes Trail 269; Faver-Dykes Trail 354; Ft. Matanzas Historic Trail 372; Guana River Wildlife

Management Area 384; St. Augustine Historic Trail 496
St. Marks: Otter Lake 469; St. Marks National Wildlife Refuge 500; San Marcos de Apalache Trail 504; Tallahassee-St. Marks Historic Railroad State Trail 526
St. Petersburg: Boyd Hill Nature Park 294; Sawgrass Lake Trail 509; Science Center of Pinellas County 510
Sanford: Lower Wekiva River State Reserve 435; Soldiers Creek Park 516
Sanibel: J.N. "Ding" Darling National Wildlife Refuge 400; Sanibel-Captiva Trail 506
Santa Rosa Beach: Grayton Beach Trail 381
Sebring: Highlands Hammock Trail 390
Seminole: Sand Hill Scout Reservation 505
Silver Springs: Ocala National Forest 456
Sneads: Three Rivers State Recreation Area 531
Sorrento: Rock Springs Run Trail 490
Spring Hill: Crews Lake Park 327
Starke: Camp Blanding Wildlife Management Area 303
Steinhatchee: Jena Unit 402; Steinhatchee Wildlife Management Area 523; Tide Swamp Unit 533
Tallahassee: Apalachicola Bluffs and Ravines Preserve Trail 272; DeSoto Trail 337; Downtown Tallahassee Historic Trail 340; G.U. Parker Wildlife Management Area 376; Joe Budd Wildlife Management Area 403; Lake Talquin Trail 424; Lochloosa Wildlife Management Area 432; Maclay State Gardens Nature Trail 437; Nassau Wildlife Management Area 452; Robert Brent Wildlife Management Area 489; San Luis Archaeological and Historical Site 503; Tallahassee Museum of History and Natural Science 525; Talquin Wildlife Management Area 527
Tampa: Coon's Creek Recreation Area 324; Dead River Youth Camp 331; Eureka Springs Trail 348; Lettuce Lake County Park 429; Museum of Science and Industry 450; Upper Tampa Bay County Park 547; Wilderness Park 555
Tangerine: Trimble Park Nature Trail 542
Tequesta: Blowing Rocks Preserve 291; Mike Machek Trail 445
Thonotosassa: Fort Foster Nature Trail 369; Hillsborough River State Park 391
Tierra Verde: Fort DeSoto County Park 368
Titusville: Archie Carr National Wildlife Refuge 277; Canaveral National Seashore 311; Merritt Island National Wildlife Refuge 444
Tyndall AFB: Felix Lake Nature Trail 355
Union Park: Blanchard Park 290
Valparaiso: FAMCAMP-Eglin AFB 353
Vero Beach: Donald McDonald Park Trail 339
Wakulla Springs: Edward Ball Wakulla Springs State Park 343
Wauchula: Pioneer Park 480
West Melbourne: Erna Nixon County Park Trail 347
Wewahitchka: Dead Lakes Trail 330
Wimauma: Little Manatee River State Recreation Area Trail 431
Winter Garden: Magnolia Park 438
Winter Haven: Polk County Rail Trail 482

GEORGIA

Ada-Hi Falls Nature Trail *see* entry 577.
560 **Alexander H. Stephens State Park**, SR 47, Crawfordsville, GA 30631, (706) 456-2221. (ATN; MSE)
561 **Allatoona Campground Beach Marina**, Allatoona Rd., Cartersville, GA 30120, (404) 974-3182. (WCD)
562 **Allatoona Lake**, Reservoir Manager, P.O. Box 487, Cartersville, GA 30120, (404) 382-4700 and (404) 382-4708. (ATN; MSE; GNA; LRA)
563 **Amicalola Falls State Park**, Star Route, Box 213, Dawsonville, GA 30534, (706) 265-2885. 3.5 miles. Named trails: Trail to Base of Amicalola Falls 0.3(s), West Ridge Loop 0.8(l). (ATN; AAC; MSE; NAT; GFA; GOB; TNG; GNA)
564 **Amity Park**, Corps of Engineers—West Point Lake, New State Line Rd., West Point, GA 31833, (205) 499-2404. (WCD)
565 **Andersonville National Historical Site Trail**, Rt. 1, Box 85, Andersonville, GA 31711. 75.0 miles. (PGF)
566 **Andersonville Prison Historical Trail**, Boy Scout Troop 217, P.O. Box 823, 102 Valley View Dr., Tuscumbia, AL 35674. 3.0 miles straight. Awards available. (SAR 1993)
Andrews Cove Trail *see* entry 591.
Anna Ruby Falls National Recreation Trail *see* entry 591.
567 **Appalachian Camper Park**, US 441/23, Clarksville, GA 30523, (706) 754-9319. (WCD)
568 **Appalachian Trail** (see separate entry **4948** in interstate section).
569 **Approach Trail**, Appalachian Trail Conference, P.O. Box 807, Harpers Ferry, WV 24525-0807; or Toccoa Ranger District, E. Main St., P.O. Box 1839, Blue Ridge, GA 30513, (706) 632-3031. 8.7 miles straight. (GMG; ATG #10; TNG)
570 **Arabi Campsites**, Deep Creek Rd., Arabi, GA 31712, (912) 273-6464. (WCD)
Arkquah National Recreation Trail *see* entry 591.
571 **Atlanta Botanical Garden Trail**, 1345 Piedmont Ave. at the Prado, P.O. Box 77246, Atlanta, GA 30357, (404) 876-5858 or (404) 876-5859. (LGU; ATN; AAC)
572 **Atlanta History Center-Buckhead**, 3101 Andres Dr., N.W., Atlanta, GA 30305, (404) 261-1837. Named trails: Swan Woods 0.5. (AAC)
Azalea Trail *see* entry 584.
573 **Bartram Trail** (see separate entry **4949** in interstate section).
Bear Creek Trail *see* entry 591.
Bear Hair Gap Trail *see* entry 722.
574 **Bear Hollow Wildlife Trail**, 293 Gran Ellen Dr., Athens, GA 30601, (706) 357-6060. 20 minutes. (AAC)
Beech Bottom Trail *see* entry 591.
575 **Benton MacKaye Trail** (see separate entry **4950** in interstate section).
Big Acorn Nature Walk/Burnt Acorn Nature Walk *see* entry 586.
Big Rock Nature Trail *see* entry 617.
576 **Big Rock Trail**, Camp Rainey Mountain, Northeast Georgia Council, BSA, P.O. Box 6049, Athens, GA 30604, (706) 548-5293. 1.0 mile loop. Awards available. (SAR 1991)
577 **Black Rock Mountain State Park**, Mountain City, GA 30562, (706) 746-2141. Named trails: Ada-Hi Falls Nature 0.2(s), James E. Edmonds Backcountry 6.5(l), Tennessee Rock Loop 2.2(l). (WCD; ATN; GFA; GOB; TNG; GNA)

578 **Blackbeard Island National Wildlife Refuge**, The Savannah Coastal Refuges Office, P.O. Box 8487, Savannah, GA 31412, (912) 232-4321 ext. 415. 20.0 miles. (AA 1993)
579 **Blackburn Park**, Old SR 9E, Dahlonega, GA 30533, (706) 864-4050. (WCD)
580 **Blanton Creek Park**, Lick Skillet Rd., Columbus, GA 31908, (706) 643-7737. (WCD)
   Blood Mountain Spur Trail see entry 591.
   Bluff Trail see entry 666.
581 **Blythe Island Regional Park**, SR 303, Brunswick, GA 31525, (912) 267-9200. (WCD)
582 **Bobby Brown State Park**, Bobby Brown Park Rd., Elberton, GA 30635, (706) 213-2046. (WCD; ATN)
   Bottoms Loop Trail see entry 720.
   Bragg Hike see entry 594.
   Brasstown Bald Trail see entry 591.
   Brickhill Trail see entry 602.
   Broad River Trail see entry 591.
   Bunkley Trail see entry 602.
583 **Bush Mountain Outdoor Activity Center**, 1442 Richland Rd., S.W., Atlanta, GA 30310, (404) 752-5385. 3.0 miles. (AAC)
   Byron Reece Nature Trail see entry 722.
584 **Callaway Gardens**, Pine Mountain, GA 31822, (800) 282-8181. Named trails: Azalea, Rhododendron, Wildflower. (AAC)
585 **Camp Pine Mountain**, George H. Lanier Council, BSA, P.O. Box 392, West Point, GA 31833, (706) 645-1682; or Camp Pine Mountain, West Point, GA 31833, (404) 645-2536. (SFC)
   Cannon Hike see entry 594.
   Canyon Rim Trail see entry 689.
586 **Carters Lake**, U.S. Army Corps of Engineers, Resource Manager, P.O. Box 86, Oakman, GA 30732-9999, (706) 334-2248. Named trails: Big Acorn Nature Walk/Burnt Oak Nature Walk 0.5(l), Hidden Pond 0.6(l), Tumbling Waters Nature 1.2(l). (ATN; GFC; MSE; TNG)
587 **Cedar Mountain Camping & Fish**ing, Blairsville, GA 30512, (706) 745-5853. (WCD)
588 **Chattahoochee National Recreation Area**, 1978 Island Ford Pkwy., Dunwoody, GA 30350, (404) 394-7912 or (404) 394-8335 or (404) 952-4419. (ATN; AAC; NAT)
589 **Chattahoochee Nature Center**, 9135 Willeo Rd., Roswell, GA 30075, (404) 992-2055. (ATN; AAC; NAT)
590 **Chattahoochee Trail**, Rick Gordon, Director, Columbus Parks and Recreation Department, P.O. Box 1340, Columbus, GA 31993, (706) 571-4785. 11.5 miles straight planned, current as to 1.0 mile. (GRT)
591 **Chattahoochee-Oconee National Forest**, 508 Oak St. NW, Gainesville, GA 30501, (706) 536-0541; or Chattahoochee River National Recreation Area, 1900 Northridge Rd., Dunwoody, GA 30338, (404) 394-7912; or Forest Supervisor, 601 Broad St., SW, Gainesville, GA 30501; or Chattooga Ranger District, P.O. Box 196, Burton Rd., Clarkesville, GA 30523, (706) 754-6221; or Brasstown Ranger District, US 19/129S, P.O. Box 216, Blairsville, GA 30512, (706) 745-6928; or Cohutta Ranger District, 401 Old Ellijay Rd., Chatsworth, GA 30705, (706) 695-6736; or Tallulah Ranger District, P.O. Box 438, Chechero/Savannah St., Clayton, GA 30525, (706) 782-3320; or Chestatee Ranger District, P.O. Box 2080, 200 W. Main, Bank of Dahlonega Bldg., Dahlonega, GA 30533, (706) 864-6173; or Armuchee Ranger District, P.O. Box 465, 706 Foster Blvd., LaFayette, GA 30728, (706) 638-1085; or Oconee National Forest, SR 212, Eatonton, GA 31024, (706) 468-2244; or Toccoa Ranger District, E. Main St., P.O. Box 1839, Blue Ridge, GA 30513, (706) 632-3031. 400 miles. Named trails: Andrews Cove 1.8(s), Anna Ruby Falls National Recreation 0.5(s), Arkquah National Recreation 5.4(s), Bear Creek 0.8(s), Beech Bottom 4.0(s), Blood Mountain Spur 0.7(s), Brasstown Bald 0.5(s), Broad River 4.1(s), Chattooga River 10.7(s), Chestnut Lead 1.8(s), Chickamauga 6.2, Coleman River 0.9(s), Conasauga River

13.1(s), DeSoto Falls 1.6(s), Dockery Lake 3.4(s), Dukes Creek Falls 0.8(s), Duncan Ridge National Recreation 35.0(l), Emery Creek 3.2(s), Fall Branch 0.2(s), Grassy Mountain Tower 2.0(s), Helton Creek Falls 0.1(s), Hemp Top 2.1(s), Hickory Creek 8.6(s), Hickory Ridge 3.5(s), High Shoals 1.2(s), Holcomb Creek 0.6(s), Horse Trough Falls 0.3(s), Horseshoe Bend 3.0(s), Jack's Knob National Recreation 4.5, Jack's River 16.7(s), Jarrard Gap 1.2(s), Johns Mountain 3.1(l), Keown Falls Loop 2.0(l), Lake Blue Ridge 0.6(l), Lake Russell 3.3(s), Lakeshore 0.5(l), Logan Turnpike 1.9(s), Mill Shoals 2.4(s), Mills Creek Falls 0.5(s), Mountaintown Creek 5.6(s), Panther Creek 4.0(s), Park Nature 2.0, Penitentiary Branch 3.5(s), Pine Mountain 25.0, The Pocket 2.5, Rabun Bald 2.9(s), Rabun Beach 0.9(s), Raven Cliffs 2.5(s), Raven Rocks 0.8(s), Rice Camp 3.9(s), Rich Mountain 8.8(s), Rough Ridge 7.0(s), Slaughter Creek 2.7(s), Smith Creek 4.5(s), Songbird 0.5(s), Sosobee Cove 0.6(s), Sugar Cove 2.2(s), Sutton Hole 0.3(s), Tearbritches 3.4(s), Three Forks 1.2(s), Warwoman Dell Interpretive 0.4(l), Yellow Mountain 3.1(s). (EGH; WCD; ATN; AAC; GFC; GMG; MSE; NAT; GOB; ATG #10; TNG; BGG; CGA; FGU; GNA; WPS; BHT; SAP)

592 **Chattanooga West Diagonal Lookout Mtn.-KOA**, Slygo Rd., Trenton, GA 30752, (706) 657-6815. (WCD)

Chattooga River Trail see entry 591.

593 **Chehaw Park**, SR 91, Albany, GA 31706, (912) 430-5275. (MSE)

Cherokee Trail see entry 708.

Chestnut Lead Trail see entry 591.

594 **Chickamauga National Battlefield**, Rossville Kiwanis Club, P.O. Box 488, Rossville, GA 30741, (706) 255-9025 or (706) 756-0333. Named trails: Bragg Hike 7.0(l), Cannon Hike 14.0(l), Confederate Line 6.0(l), Historical Battlefield 14.0(l), Memorial 12.0(l), Nature 5.0(l), Perimeter 20.0(l). (SAR 1992)

Chickamauga Trail see entry 591.

Cistern Trail see entry 699.

595 **Clarks Hill Lake**, U.S. Army Corps of Engineers, South Atlantic Division, 510 Title Bldg., 30 Pryor St., SW, Atlanta, GA 30335-6801. (GFC)

Cloudland Backcountry Trail see entry 596.

596 **Cloudland Canyon State Park**, Rt. 2, Rising Fawn, GA 30738, (706) 657-4050. Named trails: Cloudland Backcountry 5.4(l), Rimrock Nature, Waterfall 0.6(s), West Rim Loop 4.9(l). (WCD; ATN; OTB; TNG; BGG; GNA)

Coleman River Trail see entry 591.

Conasauga River Trail see entry 591.

Confederate Line Trail see entry 594.

Coosa Backcountry Trail see entry 722.

597 **Cotton Hill Park**, Corps of Engineers—Walter F. George Lake, SR 39, Fort Gaines, GA 30643, (912) 768-2516. (WCD)

598 **Covecrest Christian Renewal Center**, Bridge Creek Rd., Clayton, GA 30525, (800) 782-2683. (WCD)

599 **Crockford-Pigeon Mountain Wildlife Management Area**, Georgia Department of Natural Resources, Game and Fish, Game Management, Rt. 1, Floyd Springs Rd., Armuchee, GA 30105, (706) 295-6041. Named trails: Pocket 6.2(l), Rocktown 1.1(s). (TNG)

600 **Crooked River State Park**, 3092 SR 40 Spur, St. Marys, GA 31558, (912) 882-5256. Named trails: Hiking 1.5, Sempervirens Nature 0.5. (WCD; ATN; MSE; GGC)

601 **Cumberland Island Historic Trail**, Al Pearson, Troop 222, P.O. Box 222, 657 Wright St., St. Marys, GA 31558, (912) 882-3551. 6.0 miles loop. Awards available. (SAR 1994)

602 **Cumberland Island National Seashore**, P.O. Box 806, St. Marys, GA 31558, (912) 882-4337; or (912) 882-4335 to reserve a seat on the ferry. Named trails: Brickhill, Bunkley, Duck House, Dungeness, Kings Bottom, River, Roller Coaster, South Point, Tar Kiln, Terrapin Point, Willow Pond, Yankee Paradise. (SAR 1994)

DeSoto Falls Trail see entry 591.

Dike System Circuit Walk see entry 618.

603 **Dillard's Resort**, US 23/441, Dillard, GA 30537, (706) 746-2714. (WCD)
Dockery Lake Trail see entry 591.
604 **Doll Mountain Campground**, SR 282, Ellijay, GA 30540, (706) 334-2248. (WCD)
Duck House Trail see entry 602.
Dukes Creek Falls Trail see entry 591.
Duncan Ridge National Recreation Trail see entry 591.
Dungeness Trail see entry 602.
605 **Earl May Boat Basin and Park**, W. Shotwell St., Bainbridge, GA 31717. (ATN)
606 **Earth Day Nature Trail**, Georgia Department of Natural Resources, One Conservation Way, Brunswick, GA 31523, (912) 264-7218. (BGI)
Easy Effort Trail see entry 610.
607 **Elachee Nature Science Center**, 2125 Elachee Dr., Gainesville, GA 30504, (706) 532-1976. (GOP)
608 **Elijah Clark State Park**, US 378, Lincolnton, GA 30817, (706) 359-3458. (WCD; ATN; MSE)
Emery Creek Trail see entry 591.
609 **Eufala National Wildlife Refuge**, P.O. Box 258, Eufala, AL 36027, (205) 687-4065. Named trails: Eufala Nature 0.5. (GNA)
Eufala Nature Trail see entry 609.
Fall Branch Trail see entry 591.
610 **Fernbank Science Center**, 156 Heaton Park Dr., N.E., Atlanta, GA 30307, (404) 378-4311. Named trails: Easy Effort. (AAC; MSE; NAT; GFA)
611 **Flat Creek Ranch Campground**, Mountville Rd., Hogansville, GA 30230, (706) 637-4862. (WCD)
612 **Fort Benning Historic Trail**, Chattahoochee Council, BSA, 1710 Buena Vista Rd., P.O. Box 5425, Columbus, GA 31906-0425, (706) 327-2634. 1.0-13.0 miles straight. Awards available. (AA 1994)
613 **Fort Fredrica National Monument**, Rt. 4, Box 286-C, St. Simons Island, GA 31522, (912) 638-3639. (YNP; ANP; NPG)
614 **Fort Gordon Recreation Area**, Ray Owens Rd., Leah, GA 30802, (706) 541-0338. (WCD)

615 **Fort King George**, Georgia Department of Natural Resources, P.O. Box 711, Darien, GA 31305, (912) 437-4770. 1.0 mile. (GGC)
616 **Fort McAllister State Historic Park**, SR 144 Spur, Richmond Hill, GA 31324, (912) 727-2339. (WCD)
617 **Fort Mountain State Park**, Rt. 7, Box 1-K, Chatsworth, GA 30705, (706) 695-2621. Named trails: Big Rock Nature 0.5(s), Gahuti Backcountry 8.2(l), Goldmine Branch 0.7(s), Lake 1.2(l), Old Fort 1.8(s). (WCD; ATN; GMG; MSE; GFA; TNG; BRM; GNA)
618 **Fort Pulaski National Monument**, P.O. Box 98, Savannah Beach, GA 31328, (912) 786-5787. Named trails: Dike System Circuit Walk, Island 0.25, Nature 0.5. (ATN; MSE; NPV; NPE; GGC; CGA; YNP; ANP)
619 **Fort Yargo State Park**, SR 81, Winder, GA 30680, (404) 867-3489. (WCD; ATN; MSE)
620 **Franklin D. Roosevelt State Park**, Pine Mountain, GA 31822, (706) 633-4858. (WCD; ATN; MSE; GNA)
Gahuti Backcountry Trail see entry 617.
621 **General Coffee State Park**, SR 32, Douglas, GA 31533, (912) 384-7082. (WCD; ATN; MSE; GNA)
622 **George L. Smith State Park**, SR 23, Twin City, GA 30471, (912) 763-2759. (WCD)
623 **George T. Bagby State Park**, SR 39, Fort Gaines, GA 31751. (ATN)
624 **Georgia Mountain County Park**, US 76, Hiawassee, GA 30546, (706) 896-4191. (WCD)
625 **Golden Isles Vacation Park**, SR 303, Brunswick, GA 31525, (912) 265-5429. (WCD)
Goldmine Branch Trail see entry 617.
626 **Goose Creek Campground**, US 129/19/180, Blairsville, GA 30512, (706) 745-5111. (WCD)
Grassy Mountain Tower Trail see entry 591.
627 **Grassy Pond Recreation Area**, Loch Laurel Rd., Lake Park, GA 31636, (912) 559-5840. (WCD)

GEORGIA

628 **The G.R.I.T.S. Trail**, Gary Jenkins, President, Georgia Rails Into Trails Society, P.O. Box 371, Lithia Springs, GA 30057, (404) 920-2881. 35.0 miles. (GRT)

629 **Hamburg State Park**, Hamburg Rd., Warthen, GA 31094, (912) 552-2393. (WCD)

630 **Hard Labor Creek State Park**, US 278, Rutledge, GA 30663, (706) 557-2863. (WCD; ATN; GNA)

631 **Harris Neck National Wildlife Refuge**, Savannah National Wildlife Refuges Complex, P.O. Box 8487, Savannah, GA 31412, (912) 232-4321 ext. 415. (GNA)

632 **Hart State Park**, US 29/SR 8, Hartwell, GA 30643, (706) 376-8756. (WCD)

633 **Hartwell Lake Reservoir and Dam**, US 29, Hartwell, GA 30643, (706) 376-4788. (GFA)

Helton Creek Falls Trail see entry 591.

Hemp Top Trail see entry 591.

634 **Heritage Park Trail**, Tim Banks, Assistant Director, Rome-Floyd County Parks and Recreation Authority, 300 W. Third St., Rome, GA 30165, (706) 291-0766. 1.5 miles straight. (GRT)

Hickory Creek Trail see entry 591.

Hickory Ridge Trail see entry 591.

Hidden Pond Trail see entry 586.

635 **High Falls State Park**, Rt. 5, Box 108, Jackson, GA 30233, (912) 994-1080. (WCD; ATN; GOB; GNA)

High Shoals Trail see entry 591.

Hiking Trail see entry 600.

636 **Historic Augusta Trail**, Georgia-Carolina Council, BSA, 1252 Gordon Park Rd., Augusta, GA 30901, (706) 826-4471. 6.0 miles straight. Awards available. (SAR 1993)

637 **Historic Downtown Decatur, A Walking Tour**, DeKalb Historical Society, Old Courthouse on the Square, Decatur, GA 30030, (404) 373-1088 or (404) 373-3076. (AAC)

638 **Historic Marietta Walking/Driving Tour**, Marietta Welcome Center, No. 4 Depot St., Marietta, GA 30060, (404) 499-1115. (AAC)

639 **Historic Roswell Tour**, Roswell Historic Society, Inc., 227 S. Atlanta St., Roswell, GA 30075, (706) 992-1665. (AAC; GFA)

Historical Battlefield Trail see entry 594.

640 **Hofwyl-Broadfield Plantation Historic Site**, US 17, Darien, GA 31305, (912) 264-9263. (MSE)

Holcomb Creek Trail see entry 591.

641 **Holiday Park**, Corps of Engineers—West Point Lake, SR 109, La Grange, GA 30240, (706) 884-6818. (WCD)

Homestead Loop Trail see entry 691.

Horse Trough Falls Trail see entry 591.

Horseshoe Bend Trail see entry 591.

642 **Hostel in the Forest**, P.O. Box 1496, Brunswick, GA 31521, (912) 264-9738 or (912) 638-2623. (LGU; AYH)

643 **Indian Springs State Park**, Indian Springs, GA 30231, (404) 775-7241. (WCD; ATN; MSE; GOB)

Island Trail see entry 618.

644 **J. Strom Thurmond Dam and Lake**, SR 43, Clark's Hill, SC 29821, (706) 722-3770 or (803) 333-2476. (ATN; MSE)

Jack's Knob National Recreation Trail see entry 591.

Jack's River Trail see entry 591.

Jackson Gap Trail see entry 666.

James E. Edmonds Backcountry Trail see entry 577.

Jarrard Gap Trail see entry 591.

645 **Jekyll Island Campground**, Beach View Dr., Jekyll Island, GA 31520, (912) 635-3021. (WCD)

646 **Jim Woodruff Dam**, Reservoir Manager, Lake Seminole, P.O. Box 96, Chattahoochee, FL 32324. (LRA)

John Smart Trail see entry 666.

647 **John Tanner State Park**, SR 16, Carrollton, GA 30117, (404) 832-7545. (WCD; ATN)

Johns Mountain Trail see entry 591.

648 **Kennesaw Mountain Historical Trails**, Kemo Trails, c/o BSA Troop 116, P.O. Box 512, Acworth, GA 30101. 5.0, 10.0 and 16.0 mile loops. Awards available. (SAR 1993)

649 **Kennesaw Mountain National Battlefield Park**, P.O. Box 1167, 900 Kennesaw

Mountain Dr., Kennesaw, GA 30144-4854, (404) 427-4686. 15.0 miles. (SAR 1993)

Keown Falls Loop Trail see entry 591.

Kings Bottom Trail see entry 602.

650 **KOA-Atlanta South**, SR 351, McDonough, GA 30253, (404) 957-2610. (WCD)

651 **KOA-Calhoun**, SR 156, Calhoun, GA 30701, (706) 629-7511. (WCD)

652 **KOA-Cartersville**, Cassville Rd., Cartersville, GA 30120, (404) 382-7330. (WCD)

653 **KOA-Smoke Rise**, US 441, Commerce, GA 30529, (706) 335-5535. (WCD)

654 **Kolomoki Mounds State Park**, US 27, Blakely, GA 31723, (912) 723-5296. (WCD; ATN; MSE; OTB)

655 **L & D RV Campground**, SR 18, Forsyth, GA 31029, (912) 994-6237. (WCD)

Lake Blue Ridge Trail see entry 591.

Lake Russell Trail see entry 591.

656 **Lake Sinclair**, US 441, Milledgeville, GA 31061. (ATN)

657 **Lake Sydney Lanier**, U.S. Army Corps of Engineers, South Atlantic Division, 510 Title Bldg., 30 Pryor St., SW, Atlanta, GA 30335-6801. (ATN; GFC)

658 **Lake Tobesofkee**, SR 74, Macon, GA 31210, (912) 474-8770. (MSE)

Lake Trail see entry 617.

659 **Lake Walter F. George**, SR 39, Fort Gaines, GA 31751. (ATN)

660 **Lake Winfield Scott**, SR 180, Suches, GA 30572. (ATN)

Lakeshore Trail see entry 591.

661 **Laura S. Walker State Park**, SR 177, Waycross, GA 31501, (912) 287-4900. (WCD)

662 **Laurel Lodge & Campground**, Laurel Lodge Rd., Clarkesville, GA 30523, (706) 947-3241. (WCD)

663 **LeConte-Woodmanston Plantation**, P.O. Box 356, Hinesville, GA 31313, (912) 884-5837 or (912) 368-7002. (GGC)

664 **Leisure Time Family Campground**, Westmoreland Rd., Cleveland, GA 30528, (706) 865-6466. (WCD)

665 **Little Ocmulgee State Park**, US 441/319, McRae, GA 31055, (912) 868-2832. (WCD; ATN; OTB)

Logan Turnpike Trail see entry 591.

666 **Lookout Mountain**, Chickamauga and Chattanooga National Military Park, P.O. Box 2128, Fort Oglethorpe, GA 30742, (706) 866-9241. Named trails: Bluff, Jackson Gap, John Smart, Lower Truck, Skyuka, Southend, Upper Truck. (SAR 1992)

Lower Truck Trail see entry 666.

667 **Magnolia Springs State Park**, US 25, Millen, GA 30442, (912) 982-1660. Named trails: Woodpecker Woods Nature. (WCD; ATN; OTB)

668 **Marine Extension Center**, University of Georgia Marine Extension Service, P.O. Box 13687, Savannah, GA 31416, (912) 356-2496. (GGC)

669 **Marshall Forest**, Horseley Creek Rd., Rome, GA 30161, (706) 291-0766; or c/o P.O. Box 11, Shorter College, Rome, GA 30161, (706) 235-4869 or (706) 232-2463; or Ms. Dana Edgens, Horseshoe Bend, Rome, GA 30161, (706) 235-5821. Named trails: Marshall Forest Braille. (ATN; MSE; GNA)

Marshall Forest Braille Trail see entry 669.

670 **Martin's-Glebe Plantation Campground**, US 84/SR 38, Midway, GA 31320, (912) 884-5218. (AA 1993)

671 **McIntosh Lake Campground**, SR 57, Euloma, GA 31304, (912) 832-6215. (WCD)

672 **McQueen Island Historic Scenic Multipurpose Trail**, Jim Golden, Director, Chatham County Parks, Recreation and Cultural Affairs Department, P.O. Box 1746, Savannah, GA 31402, (912) 352-0032. 6.0 miles straight planned, current as to 3.0 miles. (GRT)

Memorial Trail see entry 594.

Microwatershed Trail see entry 684.

Mill Shoals Trail see entry 591.

Mills Creek Falls Trail see entry 591.

673 **Mistletoe State Park**, Appling, GA 30502, (706) 541-0321. 5.0 miles. (WCD; ATN; GOB)

674 **Moccasin Creek State Park**, SR 197, Clarkesville, GA 30523, (706) 947-3194. (WCD; ATN)

675 **Mt. View Campground**, US 129/9, Cleveland, GA 30528, (706) 865-3877. (WCD)
676 **Mountain View Campground**, Swallow Creek Rd., Hiawassee, GA 30546, (706) 896-4589. (WCD)
   Mountaintown Creek Trail *see* entry 591.
677 **Museum of Arts and Sciences**, 4182 Forsyth Rd., Macon, GA 31210, (912) 477-3232. (ATN)
   Nature Trail *see* entry 594.
   Nature Trail *see* entry 618.
678 **Neals Landing**, U.S. Army Corps of Engineers, South Atlantic Division, 510 Title Bldg., 30 Pryor St., SW, Atlanta, GA 30335-6801. (GFC)
   North Pocket Trail *see* entry 686.
679 **Nottely River Campground**, US 19/129, Blairsville, GA 30512, (706) 745-5124. (WCD)
680 **Oatland Island Education Center**, Island Expy., Savannah, GA 31402, (912) 233-6651. (GFA)
681 **Ocmulgee National Monument**, 1207 Emery Hwy., Macon, GA 31201, (912) 742-0447. 3.5 miles. Named trails: Opelofa Nature 1.0. (MSE; NPV; NPE; CGA; YNP; ANP; NPG)
682 **Okefenokee National Wildlife Refuge**, P.O. Box 117, Waycross, GA 31501, (912) 496-7836. (CFA; WTW; OTB; CTD; GNW)
683 **Okefenokee Swamp Park**, Waycross, GA 31501, (912) 283-0583. (GGC)
   Old Fort Trail *see* entry 617.
   Opelofa Nature Trail *see* entry 681.
684 **Panola Mountain State Conservation Park**, Rt. 1, Box 364-B, 2600 SR 155, S.W., Stockbridge, GA 30281, (404) 474-2914. Named trails: Microwatershed 1.25, Rock Outcrop 0.75. (ATN; AAC; GFA; GOB; GNA)
   Panther Creek Trail *see* entry 591.
   Park Nature Trail *see* entry 591.
   Penitentiary Branch Trail *see* entry 591.
   Perimeter Trail *see* entry 594.
685 **Piedmont National Wildlife Refuge**, Round Oak, GA 31080, (912) 986-5441 or (912) 986-3651. (GFA; GNA; GNW)

686 **Pigeon Mountain**, Game and Fish Division, Georgia Department of Natural Resources, Rt. 1, Armuchee, GA 30105, (706) 295-6041. 5.0 miles. Named trails: North Pocket, South Pocket. (BGG; GNA)
687 **Pine Lake Campground**, Gardi Rd., Jesup, GA 31545, (912) 427-3664. (WCD)
688 **Pine Lake RV Campground**, SR 186, Bishop, GA 30621, (706) 769-5486. (WCD)
   Pine Mountain Trail *see* entry 591.
   Pocket Trail *see* entry 599.
   The Pocket Trail *see* entry 591.
689 **Providence Canyon State Park**, Rt. 2A, Box 54A, Lumpkin, GA 31815, (912) 838-6414. Named trails: Canyon Rim 2.0. (ATN; MSE; GFA; OTB; GNA)
690 **R. Shaefer Heard Area**, Corps of Engineers—West Point Lake, US 29, West Point, GA 31833, (706) 645-2404. (WCD)
   Rabun Bald Trail *see* entry 591.
   Rabun Beach Trail *see* entry 591.
   Raven Cliffs Trail *see* entry 591.
   Raven Rocks Trail *see* entry 591.
691 **Red Top Mountain State Park**, 781 Red Top Mountain Rd., S.E., Cartersville, GA 30120, (404) 974-5182 or (404) 975-4203. Named trails: Homestead Loop 5.8(l), Sweetgum Nature 0.6(l). (WCD; ATN; AAC; TNG)
692 **Reed Bingham State Park**, P.O. Box 459, Adel, GA 31620, (912) 324-2286 or (912) 896-7788. 3.0 miles. (WCD; ATN; MSE; GDC)
   Rhododendron Trail *see* entry 584.
   Rice Camp Trail *see* entry 591.
   Rich Mountain Trail *see* entry 591.
   Rimrock Nature Trail *see* entry 596.
   River Trail *see* entry 602.
693 **River's End Campground**, Polk St., Tybee Island, GA 31328, (800) 786-1016. (WCD)
   Rock Outcrop Trail *see* entry 684.
   Rocktown Trail *see* entry 599.
694 **Rocky Creek**, Laurel Rd., Milledgeville, GA 31061. (ATN)
   Roller Coaster Trail *see* entry 602.
695 **Rome-Floyd County Park**, Lock & Dam Rd., Rome, GA 30161, (706) 234-5001. (WCD)

GEORGIA

Rough Ridge Trail *see* entry 591.
Sandpiper Trail *see* entry 701.
696 **Sandy Creek Nature Center**, Old Commerce Rd., Athens, GA 30601, (706) 354-2930. (ATN; MSE)
697 **Sandy Creek Park**, US 441, Athens, GA 30601, (706) 354-2935. (ATN; MSE)
698 **Satilla River Vacationland**, Rt. 1, Box 210B, Waynesville, GA 31566, (912) 778-4671. (WCD)
699 **Savannah National Wildlife Refuge**, The Savannah Coastal Refuges Office, P.O. Box 8487, Savannah, GA 31402, (912) 944-4415. 40.0 miles. Named trails: Cistern. (AA 1993)
700 **Savannah Science Museum's Ogeechee River Property**, Savannah Science Museum, 4405 Paulsen St., Savannah, GA 31405, (912) 355-6705. (GGC)
Sempervirens Trail *see* entry 600.
701 **Skidaway Island State Park**, Waters Ave., Savannah, GA 31404, (912) 356-2523. Named trails: Sandpiper. (WCD; ATN; GGC)
Skyuka Trail *see* entry 666.
Slaughter Creek Trail *see* entry 591.
702 **Sleepy Hollow Campground**, SR 255, Sautee, GA 30571, (706) 878-2618. (WCD)
Smith Creek Trail *see* entry 591.
Songbird Trail *see* entry 591.
Sosobee Cove Trail *see* entry 591.
South Pocket Trail *see* entry 686.
South Point Trail *see* entry 602.
Southend Trail *see* entry 666.
703 **Southern Forest World**, N. Augusta Ave., Waycross, GA 31501, (912) 285-4056. (MSE)
704 **State Botanical Gardens of Georgia**, 2450 S. Milledge Ave., Athens, GA 30601, (706) 542-1244. 5.0 miles. (ATN; AAC; NAT)
705 **Stateline Park**, Corps of Engineers— West Point Lake, US 27, La Grange, GA 30240. (WCD)
706 **Stephen C. Foster State Park**, SR 177, Fargo, GA 31631, (912) 637-5274. (WCD; ATN; MSE; GFA; GNA)
707 **Stone Mountain Historical Trail**, Cherokee Trail and Campsites, P.O. Box 708, Tucker, GA 30084. 8.0 miles loop. Awards available. (SAR 1993)
708 **Stone Mountain Park**, P.O. Box 778, Stone Mountain, GA 30086, (404) 498-5600 or (404) 498-5690. Named trails: Cherokee, Wildlife. (SAR 1993)
Sugar Cove Trail *see* entry 591.
709 **Sunbury Historic Site**, Rt. 1, Box 236, Midway, GA 31320, (912) 884-5999. (GGC)
710 **Sunset Campground**, SR 17, Lavonia, GA 30553, (706) 356-8932. (WCD)
Sutton Hole Trail *see* entry 591.
711 **Suwannee Canal Recreation Area**, SR 23/121, Folkston, GA 31537, (912) 496-7836. (ATN; MSE; GFA; OTB)
Swan Woods Trail *see* entry 572.
Sweetgum Nature Trail *see* entry 691.
712 **Sweetwater Creek State Park**, Rt. 1, Box 816, Mt. Vernon Rd., Lithia Springs, GA 30057, (404) 944-1700. 5.0 miles. (ATN; AAC; NAT; GFA; GNA)
713 **Talisman RV Resort**, US 441/129, Madison, GA 30650, (706) 342-1799. (WCD)
714 **Tallulah Gorge Park**, Tallulah Falls, GA 30573, (706) 754-5103. (ATN)
Tar Kiln Trail *see* entry 602.
Tearbritches Trail *see* entry 591.
Terrapin Point Trail *see* entry 602.
715 **Terrora Park**, US 441/23, Tallulah Falls, GA 30573. (GFA)
Three Forks Trail *see* entry 591.
716 **Trackrock Campground**, Track Rock Creek Rd., Blairsville, GA 30512, (706) 745-2420. (WCD)
717 **Trail of Tears** (see separate entry 4958 in interstate section).
Trail to Base of Amicalola Falls *see* entry 563.
718 **Tugaloo State Park**, Rt. 1, Lavonia, GA 30553, (706) 356-4362. (ATN; GOB)
Tumbling Waters Nature Trail *see* entry 586.
719 **Turner Campsite**, US 19, Cleveland, GA 30528, (706) 865-4757. (WCD)
Unicoi Lake Trail *see* entry 720.
720 **Unicoi State Park**, P.O. Box 849, Helen, GA 30545, (706) 878-2201. 12.0 miles. Named trails: Bottoms Loop 2.1(l), Unicoi Lake 2.4(l). (WCD; ATN; AAC; GMG; MSE; GOB; TNG; GNA)

Upper Truck Trail *see* entry 666.
Victoria Bryant Perimeter Trail *see* entry 721.
721 **Victoria Bryant State Park**, Rt. 1, Box 257, Royston, GA 30662, (706) 245-6270. Named trails: Victoria Bryant Perimeter 1.3(s), Victoria Path Nature 0.5(l). (WCD; ATN; GOB; TNG)
Victoria Path Nature Trail *see* entry 721.
722 **Vogel State Park**, Rt. 1, Box 1230, Blairsville, GA 30512, (706) 745-2628. Named trails: Bear Hair Gap 3.6(l), Byron Reece Nature 0.4(l), Coosa Backcountry 12.4(s). (WCD; ATN; GMG; GOB; TNG; BRM; GNA)
723 **W.H. Reynolds Memorial Nature Preserve**, 5665 Reynolds Rd., Morrow, GA 30260. 4.0 miles. (AAC)
Warwoman Dell Interpretive Trail *see* entry 591.
724 **Wassau Island National Wildlife Refuge**, The Savannah Coastal Refuges Office, P.O. Box 8487, Savannah, GA 31412, (912) 232-4321 ext. 415. (AA 1993)
Waterfall Trail *see* entry 596.
725 **Watson Mill Bridge State Park**, SR 22, Comer, GA 30629, (706) 783-5349. (WCD; ATN)
726 **West Point Lake**, Resource Manager, P.O. Box 574, West Point, GA 31833, (706) 645-2937. 20.0 miles. (ATN; GNA; LRA)
West Ridge Loop Trail *see* entry 563.
West Rim Loop Trail *see* entry 596.
727 **Whispering Pines Campground**, US 41, Acworth, GA 30101, (404) 974-7380. (WCD)

728 **Whitetail Ridge**, Corps of Engineers—West Point Lake, SR 109, La Grange, GA 30240, (706) 884-8972. (WCD)
Wildflower Trail *see* entry 584.
Wildlife Trails *see* entry 708.
729 **Wildwood Park**, SR 104, Appling, GA 30802, (706) 541-0586. (WCD)
Willow Pond Trail *see* entry 602.
730 **Wilwood County Park**, SR 104, Evans, GA 30809, (706) 541-0586. (WCD)
Woodpecker Woods Nature Trail *see* entry 667.
731 **Woodring Branch Public Use Area**, US 411, Chatsworth, GA 30705, (706) 334-2248. (WCD)
732 **Wormsloe Historic Site**, Georgia Department of Natural Resources, 7601 Skidaway Rd., Savannah, GA 31406, (912) 352-2548. (GGC)
Yankee Paradise Trail *see* entry 602.
Yellow Mountain Trail *see* entry 591.
733 **Yellow River Game Ranch**, 4525 US 78, Lilburn, GA 30247, (404) 972-6643. (ATN; AAC; NAT)
734 **Yogi Bear's Jellystone Park Atlanta South**, Highfalls Rd., Barnesville, GA 30204, (404) 358-2205. (WCD)

Generally:
Commissioner, Department of Natural Resources, 270 Washington St., SW, Atlanta, GA 30334, (404) 656-3500 (SFC); or Rt. 1, Floyd Spgs. Rd., Armuchee, GA 30105, (706) 295-6041. (TNG)
U.S. Army Corps of Engineers, South Atlantic Division, 510 Title Bldg., 30 Pryor St., SW, Atlanta, GA 30325-6801. (GFC)

Index (by city)

Acworth: Whispering Pines Campground 727
Adel: Reed Bingham State Park 692
Albany: Chehaw Park 593
Andersonville: Andersonville National Historical Site Trail 565; Andersonville Prison Historical Trail 566

Appling: Mistletoe State Park 673; Wildwood Park 729
Arabi: Arabi Campsites 570
Armuchee: Crockford-Pigeon Mountain Wildlife Management Area 599; Pigeon Mountain 686
Athens: Bear Hollow Wildlife Trail 574;

Sandy Creek Nature Center 696; Sandy Creek Park 697; State Botanical Gardens of Georgia 704

Atlanta: Atlanta Botanical Garden Trail 571; Atlanta History Center-Buckhead 572; Bush Mountain Outdoor Activity Center 583; Clarks Hill Lake 595; Fernbank Science Center 610; Lake Sydney Lanier 657; Neals Landing 678

Augusta: Historic Augusta Trail 636

Bainbridge: Earl May Boat Basin and Park 605

Barnesville: Yogi Bear's Jellystone Park Atlanta South 734

Bishop: Pine Lake RV Campground 688

Blairsville: Cedar Mountain Camping & Fishing 587; Chattahoochee-Oconee National Forest 591; Goose Creek Campground 626; Nottely River Campground 679; Trackrock Campground 716; Vogel State Park 722

Blakely: Kolomoki Mounds State Park 654

Blue Ridge: Approach Trail 569; Chattahoochee-Oconee National Forest 591

Brunswick: Blythe Island Regional Park 581; Earth Day Nature Trail 606; Golden Isles Vacation Park 625; Hostel in the Forest 642

Calhoun: KOA-Calhoun 651

Carrollton: John Tanner State Park 647

Cartersville: Allatoona Campground Beach Marina 561; Allatoona Lake 562; KOA-Cartersville 652; Red Top Mountain State Park 691

Chatsworth: Chattahoochee-Oconee National Forest 591; Fort Mountain State Park 617; Woodring Branch Public Use Area 731

Chattahoochee, FL: Jim Woodruff Dam 646

Clarkesville: Appalachian Camper Park 567; Chattahoochee-Oconee National Forest 591; Laurel Lodge & Campground 662; Moccasin Creek State Park 674

Clark's Hill: J. Strom Thurmond Dam and Lake 644

Clayton: Big Rock Trail 576; Chattahoochee-Oconee National Forest 591; Covecrest Christian Renewal Center 598

Cleveland: Leisure Time Family Campground 664; Mt. View Campground 675; Turner Campsite 719

Columbus: Blanton Creek Park 580; Chattahoochee Trail 590; Fort Benning Historic Trail 612

Comer: Watson Mill Bridge State Park 725

Commerce: KOA-Smoke Rise 653

Crawfordsville: Alexander H. Stephens State Park 560

Dahlonega: Blackburn Park 579; Chattahoochee-Oconee National Forest 591

Darien: Fort King George 615; Hofwyl-Broadfield Plantation Historic Site 640

Dawsonville: Amicalola Falls State Park 563

Decatur: Historic Downtown Decatur, A Walking Tour 637

Dillard: Dillard's Resort 603

Douglas: General Coffee State Park 621

Dunwoody: Chattahoochee National Recreation Area 588; Chattahoochee-Oconee National Forest 591

Eatonton: Chattahoochee-Oconee National Forest 591

Elberton: Bobby Brown State Park 582

Ellijay: Doll Mountain Campground 604

Eufala: Eufala National Wildlife Refuge 609

Euloma: McIntosh Lake Campground 671

Evans: Wilwood County Park 730

Fargo: Stephen C. Foster State Park 706

Folkston: Suwannee Canal Recreation Area 711

Forsyth: L & D RV Campground 655

Fort Gaines: Cotton Hill Park 597; George T. Bagby State Park 623; Lake Walter F. George 659

Fort Oglethorpe: Chickamauga National Battlefield 594; Lookout Mountain 666

Gainesville: Chattahoochee-Oconee National Forest 591; Elachee Nature Science Center 607

Hartwell: Hart State Park 632; Hartwell Lake Reservoir and Dam 633

Helen: Unicoi State Park 720

Hiawassee: Georgia Mountain County Park 624; Mountain View Campground 676

Hinesville: LeConte-Woodmanston Plantation 663

Hogansville: Flat Creek Ranch Campground 611

Indian Springs: Indian Springs State Park 643
Jackson: High Falls State Park 635
Jekyll Island: Jekyll Island Campground 645
Jesup: Pine Lake Campground 687
Kennesaw: Kennesaw Mountain Historical Trails 648; Kennesaw Mountain National Battlefield Park 649
La Grange: Holiday Park 641; Stateline Park 705; Whitetail Ridge 728
LaFayette: Chattahoochee-Oconee National Forest 591
Lake Park: Grassy Pond Recreation Area 627
Lavonia: Sunset Campground 710; Tugaloo State Park 718
Leah: Fort Gordon Recreation Area 614
Lilburn: Yellow River Game Ranch 733
Lincolnton: Elijah Clark State Park 608
Lithia Springs: The G.R.I.T.S. Trail 628; Sweetwater Creek State Park 712
Lumpkin: Providence Canyon State Park 689
Macon: Lake Tobesofkee 658; Museum of Arts and Sciences 677; Ocmulgee National Monument 681
Madison: Talisman RV Resort 713
Marietta: Historic Marietta Walking/Driving Tour 638
McDonough: KOA-Atlanta South 650
McRae: Little Ocmulgee State Park 665
Midway: Martin's-Glebe Plantation Campground 670; Sunbury Historic Site 709
Milledgeville: Lake Sinclair 656; Rocky Creek 694
Millen: Magnolia Springs State Park 667
Morrow: W.H. Reynolds Memorial Nature Preserve 723
Mountain City: Black Rock Mountain State Park 577
Oakman: Carters Lake 586
Pine Mountain: Callaway Gardens 584; Franklin D. Roosevelt State Park 620
Richmond Hill: Fort McAllister State Historic Park 616
Rising Fawn: Cloudland Canyon State Park 596
Rome: Heritage Park Trail 634; Marshall Forest 669; Rome-Floyd County Park 695
Roswell: Chattahoochee Nature Center 589; Historic Roswell Tour 639
Round Oak: Piedmont National Wildlife Refuge 685
Royston: Victoria Bryant State Park 721
Rutledge: Hard Labor Creek State Park 630
St. Marys: Crooked River State Park 600; Cumberland Island Historic Trail 601; Cumberland Island National Seashore 602
St. Simons Island: Fort Fredrica National Monument 613
Sautee: Sleepy Hollow Campground 702
Savannah: Blackbeard Island National Wildlife Refuge 578; Harris Neck National Wildlife Refuge 631; Marine Extension Center 668; McQueen Island Historic Scenic Multipurpose Trail 672; Oatland Island Education Center 680; Savannah National Wildlife Refuge 699; Savannah Science Museum's Ogeechee River Property 700; Skidaway Island State Park 701; Wassau Island National Wildlife Refuge 724; Wormsloe Historic Site 732
Savannah Beach: Fort Pulaski National Monument 618
Stockbridge: Panola Mountain State Conservation Park 684
Stone Mountain: Stone Mountain Historical Trail 707; Stone Mountain Park 708
Suches: Lake Winfield Scott 660
Tallulah Falls: Terrora Park 715
Trenton: Chattanooga West Diagonal Lookout Mtn.-KOA 592
Twin City: George L. Smith State Park 622
Tybee Island: River's End Campground 693
Warthen: Hamburg State Park 629
Waycross: Laura S. Walker State Park 661; Okefenokee National Wildlife Refuge 682; Okefenokee Swamp Park 683; Southern Forest World 703
Waynesville: Satilla River Vactionland 698
West Point: Amity Park 564; Camp Pine Mountain 585; R. Shaefer Heard Area 690; West Point Lake 726
Winder: Fort Yargo State Park 619

Illinois

735 **Abraham Lincoln Trail**, Abraham Lincoln Council, BSA, 1911 W. Monroe, Fairhills Mall, Springfield, IL 62704. 20.0 miles. Awards available. (AA 1994)

736 **Adventurer Award**, Forest Preserve District of DuPage County, Oak Brook, IL 60301, (708) 790-4900 ext. 243. Hikes in various parks near Oak Park. Awards available. (AA 1994)

737 **Algonquin Woods Nature Trail**, Karl Lindahl, 8705 W. Sunset Rd., Niles, IL 60714, (708) 692-2065. 5.5 miles loop. Awards available. (AA 1992)

738 **Apple River Canyon State Park**, SR 78, Stockton, IL 61085, (815) 745-3302. (WCD; ATI; OTB)

739 **Argyle Lake State Park**, Rt. 1, Colchester, IL 62326, (618) 776-3422. (ATI; MGL)

Ausaganash Trail see entry 830.

740 **Bail's Timberline Lake Campground**, P.O. Box 241, St. Elmo, IL 62458, (618) 829-3383. (WCD)

741 **Bayou Bluffs Campground**, CR 800E, Cornell, IL 61319, (815) 358-2537. (WCD)

742 **Beall Woods State Park**, Rt. 2, Mount Carmel, IL 62863, (618) 298-2442. (NAT; IPB)

743 **Beat the Bounds Trail**, Robert Burns, 1416 Noyes St., Evanston, IL 60201. 15.0 miles. Awards available. (HTA)

744 **Beaver Dam State Park**, Carlinville, IL 62626. (ATI)

Beech Grove Handicapped Trail see entry 793.

Beech Loop Trail see entry 793.

745 **Belleville Historical Trail**, Troop 83, St. Clair District, Okaw Valley Council, BSA, 4100 W. Main St., Belleville, IL 62223. (NHT)

Belvidere/Caledonia Route see entry 752.

746 **Big Foot Trail**, Indian Portage Trails, 11140 S. Trumbull, Chicago, IL 60655-3530. 13.0 miles loop. Awards available. (AA 1992)

747 **Big Quarry Trail**, Sauk-Thorn Creek Trail, Inc., P.O. Box 273, Dolton, IL 60419; or c/o Chas. L. Deegan, 14066 Lincoln, Dolton, IL 60419. 10.0 miles. Awards available. (HTA)

748 **Big River State Forest**, Oquawka-Keithsburg Rd., Oquawka, IL 61469, (309) 374-2496. (WCD; ATI)

Big Rock Trail see entry 875.

Big Woods Trail see entry 793.

749 **Bird Haven-Robert Ridgway Memorial**, East St., Olney, IL 62450, (618) 395-7302. (MGL)

750 **Black Hawk State Park**, 1510 46th Ave., Rock Island, IL 61201, (309) 788-0177. (ATI; MGL; OTB)

751 **Blackhawk Trail**, Blackhawk Area Council, BSA, P.O. Box 4085, 1800 Seventh Ave., Rockford, IL 61110-0585, (815) 397-0210. 20.0 miles loop. Awards available. (AA 1992)

Blaine/State Line Route see entry 752.

Bluff Trail see entry 943.

752 **Boone County Historical Trail**, Boone County Conservation District, (815) 547-7935. Named routes: Belvidere/Caledonia Route 30.0, Blaine/State Line Route 30.0, Piscasaw Route 30.0, South Prairie Route 30.0. (IOB)

753 **Breezewood Campground**, SR 96, Nauvoo, IL 62354, (217) 453-6420. (WCD)

754 **Buffalo Rock State Park**, P.O. Box 39, US 5, Ottawa, IL 61350, (815) 433-2220. (MGL)

ILLINOIS

755 **Burnidge Forest Preserve**, Coombs Rd., Elgin, IL 60123, (708) 741-4833. (NAT)

756 **Cahokia Mounds State Historic Site**, Bus. US 40, Cahokia, IL 62206, (618) 344-5268. (MGL)

757 **Cahokia Pilgrimage Trail**, 1400 N. 81st St., East St. Louis, IL 62203. 19.0 miles. Awards available. (HTA)

758 **Camp Cherokee Hills**, Piankeshaw Council, BSA, 704 N. Hazel St., Danville, IL 61832, (217) 442-0869; or Camp Cherokee Hills, Rt. 1, Georgetown, IL 61846, (217) 662-6223. (SFC)

759 **Camp Rainbow**, Rainbow Council, BSA, 2600 N. Winterbottom Rd., Morris, IL 60450, (815) 942-4450. (SFC)

760 **Cantigny Park**, 1S151 Winfield Rd., Wheaton, IL 60187, (708) 260-8167 or fax (708) 668-7898. (AA 1994)

761 **Carlyle Lake**, Corps of Engineers, North Central District, 536 Clark St., Chicago, IL 60605; or Eldon Hazlett & South Shore State Parks, 1351 Ridge St., Carlyle, IL 62231. (ATI; GFC; LRA)

762 **Castle Rock State Park**, SR 2, Oregon, IL 61061, (815) 732-7329. (MGL)

763 **Cave-in-Rock State Park**, P.O. Box 338, Cave-in-Rock, IL 62919, (618) 289-4325. (WCD; ATI; IOB; TOV)

764 **Cedar Lake Ranch**, US 45, Vienna, IL 62995, (618) 695-2600. (WCD)

Cedarhurst Braille Trail see entry 870.

765 **Chain O'Lakes State Park**, 39947 N. State Park Rd., Spring Grove, IL 60081, (312) 587-5512. 2.0 miles. (WCD; ATI; MGL; NAT)

Chamnestown School Trail see entry 778.

766 **Chautauqua National Wildlife Refuge**, Rt. 2, Manito Rd., Havana, IL 62644, (309) 535-2290. (ATI; NAT; GFA)

767 **Chicago Botanic Gardens**, Lake-Cook Rd., Glencoe, IL 60022, (708) 835-5440. (NAT)

768 **Chicago Lincoln Ave. Trail**, Troop 881, BSA, c/o Bill LaFleur, Irving Park Baptist Church, 4401 W. Irving Park Rd., Chicago, IL 60641; or Bryan Albro, 1107 E. Juniper Ln., Mt. Prospect, IL 60056, (708) 255-6635. 7.0 miles. Awards available. (AA 1992)

769 **Chicago Portage National Historic Site Trail**, Sauk-Thorn Creek Trail, Inc., P.O. Box 273, Dolton, IL 60419. 5.0 miles. Awards available. (HTA)

770 **Chief Chicagou Trail**, Sauk-Thorn Creek Trail, Inc., P.O. Box 273, Dolton, IL 60419. 14.0 miles. Awards available. (HTA)

771 **Chief Sauganash Trail**, Sauk-Thorn Creek Trail, Inc., P.O. Box 273, Dolton, IL 60419. 11.0 miles. Awards available. (HTA)

772 **Chief Shabbona Trail**, Snyder Watson, 1515 Burry Ave., Joliet, IL 60435, (815) 727-7054. 16.5 miles. Awards available. (AA 1992)

773 **Clark County Park**, Clarksville Rd., Marshall, IL 62441, (217) 889-3601. (WCD)

774 **Clinton Lake**, Clinton Lake-Mascoutin State Recreation Complex, CR 14, DeWitt, IL 61735, (217) 935-8722. (WCD)

775 **Comlara County Park**, Comlara Park Rd., Hudson, IL 61748, (309) 726-2022. (WCD)

776 **Community Lake Campground**, SR 4, Percy, IL 62272, (618) 497-2942. (WCD)

777 **Constitution Trail**, Keith Rich, Director, Bloomington Parks and Recreation Department, 109 E. Olive St., Bloomington, IL 61701, (309) 823-4260. 5.3 miles planned, current as to 4.3 miles. (GRT)

778 **Crab Orchard National Wildlife Refuge**, P.O. Box J, Carterville, IL 62918, (618) 997-3344. Named trails: Chamnestown School. (MGL; IOB; OTB; GNW)

Crab Tree Trail see entry 793.

779 **Dam West Recreation Area**, Corps of Engineers—Lake Carlyle, SR 127, Carlyle, IL 62231, (618) 594-4410. (WCD)

780 **Decatur Historic Trail**, John Washburn, 2051 S. Gate Dr., Decatur, IL 62521. 12.0 miles. Awards available. (HTA)

Deer Meadow Trail see entry 793.

781 **Delabar State Park**, Keithsburg Rd., Oquawka, IL 61469, (309) 374-2496. (WCD; ATI; OTB)

782 **Delyte Morris Bikeway**, Anna Schonlau, Assistant Recreation Director, Recreation Department, Southern Illinois University at Edwardsville, P.O. Box 1057, Edwardsville, IL 62026, (618) 692-3235. 2.6 miles straight. (GRT)

783 **Dickson Mounds Nature Trail**, Dickson Mounds Museum, Lewistown, IL 61542. (GFA)

784 **Discovery '76 Trail**, Troop 881, BSA, c/o Bill LaFleur, Irving Park Baptist Church, 4401 W. Irving Park Rd., Chicago, IL 60641; or Bryan Albro, 1107 E. Juniper Ln., Mt. Prospect, IL 60056, (708) 255-6635. 10.0 miles. Awards available. (AA 1992)

785 **Dixon Springs State Park Trail**, Rt. 1, Brownfield, IL 62911, (618) 949-3394. 1.7 miles. (WCD; ATI; IOB)

786 **Dolan Lake County Park**, SR 14, McLeansboro, IL 62859. (ATI)

787 **Eagle Creek State Park**, SR 128, Findlay, IL 62534, (217) 756-8260. (WCD; ATI)

788 **Eagle Trail**, Okaw Valley Council, BSA, 1801 N. 17th St., Belleville, IL 62223, (618) 236-3320. 8.0 miles loop. Awards available. (AA 1994)

East Woods Trail see entry 875.

789 **Eldon Hazlett State Park**, 1351 Ridge St., Carlyle, IL 62231, (618) 594-3015. (WCD; ATI; MGL)

Evergreen Trail see entry 875.

790 **Fern Rocks Trail**, Site Superintendent, Fern Rocks Nature Preserve, Giant City State Park, Rt. 1, Makanda, IL 62958, (618) 457-4836. (IOB)

791 **Ferne Clyffe State Park**, P.O. Box 120, SR 37, Goreville, IL 62939, (618) 995-2411. (WCD; ATI; MGL)

792 **Fitzpatrick's Yogi Bear Jellystone Camp-Resort**, 8574 Millbrook Rd., P.O. Box 306, Millbrook, IL 60536, (708) 553-5172. (WCD)

793 **Forest Glen Preserve County Park**, CR 5, Westville, IL 61883, (217) 662-2142; or Vermillion County Conservation District, Rt. 1, Box 495A, Westville, IL 61883, (217) 662-6284. Named trails: Beech Grove Handicapped, Beech Loop, Big Woods, Crab Tree, Deer Meadow, Hawk Hill, Hickory Ridge, Old Barn, Primitive Loop, Spring Crest, Tall Tree, Willow Creek. (AA 1992)

794 **Forest Lakes Resort**, CR 1995E, Staunton, IL 62088, (618) 635-2644. (WCD)

795 **Forest Park Nature Center**, 5809 Forest Park Dr., Peoria, IL 61614, (309) 688-6413. 6.0 miles. (MGL)

Forest Trail see entry 875.

796 **Forest W. Bo Woods Recreation Area**, Corps of Engineers—Lake Shelbyville, SR 32, Sullivan, IL 61951, (217) 774-3951. (WCD)

797 **Fort Dearborn Massacre Trail**, Troop 881, BSA, c/o Bill La Fleur, Irving Park Baptist Church, 4401 W. Irving Park Rd., Chicago, IL 60641; or Brian Albro, 1107 E. Juniper Ln., Mt. Prospect, IL 60056, (708) 255-6635. 2.0 miles straight. Awards available. (AA 1992)

798 **Fort Dearborn Trails**, Chicago Area Council, BSA, Camping Service, 300 W. Adams St., Chicago, IL 60606. 5 trails totalling 77.0 miles. Awards available. (AA 1992)

799 **Fort Kaskaskia State Historic Site**, Fort Kaskaskia Rd., Chester, IL 62233, (618) 859-3741. (WCD)

800 **Fort Massac State Park**, US 45, Metropolis, IL 62960, (618) 524-4712. (WCD; ATI)

801 **Fox Ridge State Park**, Rt. 1, Box 234, SR 130, Charleston, IL 61920, (217) 345-6416. (WCD; ATI; MGL)

802 **Fox River Recreation RV Park**, SR 173, Antioch, IL 60002, (708) 395-6090. (WCD)

803 **Fox River Trail**, Jon Duerr, Superintendent, Kane County Forest Preserve, 719 Batavia Ave., Geneva, IL 60134, (708) 232-5981; or Charles E. Hoscheit, Director, Fox Valley Park District, 712 S. River St., Aurora, IL 60506, (708) 897-0516. 33.0 miles straight. (GRT)

Fragrance Garden Trail see entry 875.

804 **Francis City Park**, US 34, Kewanee, IL 61443, (309) 852-0511. (WCD)

805 **Frank Lloyd Wright Heritage Trail**, Thatcher Woods Area Council, BSA, 855

ILLINOIS

W. Madison St., Oak Park, IL 60302, (312) 386-8108. 6.2 miles straight. Awards available. (AA 1994)

806 **Friends Creek Regional Park**, County Rd., Argenta, IL 62501, (217) 795-4421. (WCD; MGL)

807 **Fullersburg Woods Environmental Center**, 3609 Spring Rd., Oak Brook, IL 60521, (312) 790-4912. Named trails: Which-a-Way. (MGL)

808 **Fulton County Conservation Area**, P.O. Box 464, St. David, IL 61563, (309) 668-2931. (AA 1992)

Garden of the Gods Trail see entry 931.

Gau-Nash-Ke Trail see entry 830.

809 **Gebhard Woods State Park**, P.O. Box 272, Morris, IL 60450, (815) 942-0796. Named trails: I&M Canal State. (ATI; GFC; MGL; NAT)

810 **Geneseo Campground**, Rt. 5, Box 14, SR 82N, Geneseo, IL 61254, (309) 944-6465. (WCD)

Geographic Trail see entry 875.

811 **Giant City State Park**, P.O. Box 70, Makanda, IL 62958, (618) 457-4836. 20.0 miles. Named trails: Red Cedar Hiking 20. (EGH; ATI; MGL)

812 **Glenwood The Camping Resort**, US 6, Marseilles, IL 61341, (815) 795-2195. (WCD)

813 **Great River Trail**, Patrick Marsh, Bi-State Regional Commission, 1504 Third Ave., Rock Island, IL 61201, (309) 793-6300. 65.0 miles straight planned, current as to 27.0 miles straight. (GRT)

814 **Great Western Trail**, Jon Duerr, Superintendent, Kane County Forest Preserve, 719 Batavia Ave., Geneva, IL 60134, (708) 232-5981; or Terry Hannan, Superintendent, Dekalb County Forest Preserve, 110 E. Sycamore St., Sycamore, IL 60178, (815) 895-7191. 18.0 miles straight. (GRT)

815 **Great Western Trail (DuPage Parkway Section)**, Charles Tokarski, Chief of Traffic Planning and Programming, DuPage County Division of Transportation, 130 N. County Farm Rd., Wheaton, IL 60189, (708) 682-7318. 12.0 miles straight. (GRT)

816 **Green Bay Trail**, Larry King, Superintendent, Highland Park Forestry Department, 1150 Half Day Rd., Highland Park, IL 60035, (708) 432-0800 ext. 282; or John Houde, Village of Glencoe, 675 Village Ct., Glencoe, IL 60022, (708) 835-4111; or Dan Newport, Director, Winnetka Park District, 510 Green Bay Rd., Winnetka, IL 60093, (708) 501-2040; or Bill Lambrecht, Wilmette Park District, 1200 Wilmette Ave., Wilmette, IL 60091, (708) 256-6100. 9.5 miles straight. (GRT; HTM)

817 **Greene Valley Forest Preserve**, Woodridge, IL 60517, (312) 790-4900 ext. 243. Named trails: Tricky Tree-Key. (AA 1994)

818 **The Grove National Historic Landmark**, 1421 Milwaukee Ave., Glenview, IL 60025, (312) 299-6096. (MGL)

Hawk Hill Trail see entry 793.

819 **Hebron Hills Camping**, Rt. 2, Box 35, Oakland, IL 61943, (217) 346-3385. (WCD)

820 **Henderson County State Conservation Area**, SR 164, Oquawka, IL 61469, (309) 374-2496. (WCD)

821 **Hennepin Canal Parkway State Park**, SR 88, Sheffield, IL 61361, (815) 454-2328. (ATI; IOB)

Heritage Trail see entry 931.

822 **Heron Pond-Little Black Slough Nature Preserve**, US 45, Vienna, IL 62995. (OTB)

Hickory Ridge Trail see entry 793.

823 **Hidden Springs State Forest**, SR 32, Shelbyville, IL 62565, (217) 644-3091. (WCD; ATI)

824 **Hide-A-Way Lakes**, 8045 Van Emmon Rd., Yorkville, IL 60560, (708) 553-6323. (WCD)

825 **Horseshoe Lake State Park**, P.O. Box 1307, Granite City, IL 62040, (618) 931-0270. 4.0 miles. (WCD; ATI; NAT)

I&M Canal State Trail see entry 809.

826 **Illini State Park**, Rt. 1, Box 60, US 6, Marseilles, IL 61341, (815) 795-2448. (WCD; ATI; NAT)

827 **Illinois Beach State Park**, Sheridan Rd., Zion, IL 60099, (708) 662-4811. (WCD; ATI; NAT)

ILLINOIS

828 **Illinois Prairie Path National Recreation Trail**, P.O. Box 1086, 616 Delles Rd., Wheaton, IL 60187, (312) 665-5310; or William Nemec, Rt. 3, Box 1517, St. Charles, IL 60174; or Jean Mooring, P.O. Box 1086, Wheaton, IL 60189, (708) 665-5310; or Charles Tokarski, DuPage County Division of Transportation, 130 N. County Farm Rd., Wheaton, IL 60187, (708) 682-7318; or Charles E. Hoscheit, Director, Fox Valley Park District, P.O. Box 818, Aurora, IL 60507, (708) 897-0516. 55.0 miles. (GRT; EGH; NAT; IOB; NFG; HTM)

Illinois Trees Nature Trails *see* entry 875.

829 **Indian Butterfield Trail**, Ken Curtis, 647 S. Washington St., Paxton, IL 60957. 26.0 miles. Awards available. (HTA)

830 **Indian Portage Trails**, 11140 S. Turnbull, Chicago, IL 60655-3530. Named trails: Ausaganash 15.0, Gau-Nash-Ke 17.3-26.0, Sheshikmaos Sepe 17.3. Awards available. (AA 1992)

Interior Canyon Trail *see* entry 943.

831 **Johnson 1910 Farm**, US 6, Geneseo, IL 61254. (MGL)

832 **Johnson Sauk Trail State Park**, SR 78, Kewanee, IL 61443, (309) 853-5589. (WCD; ATI)

Joy Path *see* entry 875.

833 **Jubilee College State Park**, Rt. 2, Box 72, Brimfield, IL 61571, (309) 243-7683. (WCD; ATI; MGL)

Juniper Ridge Trail *see* entry 870.

834 **Kankakee River State Park**, Rt. 1, Bourbonnais, IL 60914, (815) 933-1383. (WCD; ATI; MGL; IOB)

835 **Kennekuk Cove Park**, Danville, IL 61832. (ATI)

836 **Kickapoo State Park**, Rt. 1, Box 374, Oakwood, IL 61858, (217) 442-4915. (WCD; NAT)

837 **Kishwankee Scout Reservation**, Calumet Council, BSA, P.O. Box 3230, Munster, IL 46321, (312) 474-6212; or Kishwankee Scout Reservation, Kirkland, IL 60146, (815) 522-6200. (SFC)

838 **Ladd Arboretum**, 2024 McCormick Blvd., Evanston, IL 60201, (708) 864-5181. (NAT)

839 **Lake Le-Aqua-Na State Park**, Lake Park Rd., Lena, IL 61048, (815) 369-4282. (WCD; ATI)

840 **Lake Murphysboro State Park**, SR 149, Murphysboro, IL 62966, (618) 684-2867. (WCD)

841 **Lake Shelbyville**, Lake Manager, P.O. Box 26, Shelbyville, IL 62565. (ATI; LRA)

842 **Lakeland Park**, Lakeland Park Dr., Canton, IL 61520, (309) 647-4702. (AA 1992)

843 **Lakewood Resort**, 10070 Mill Hollow Rd., Savanna, IL 61074, (815) 273-2898. (WCD)

Landscape Display Paths *see* entry 875.

844 **Lazy Days Campground**, SR 16, Litchfield, IL 62056, (217) 324-3233. (WCD)

845 **Lewis & Clark Trail** (a/k/a E. Frank Hutchinson Memorial Trail), Lewis & Clark Trail Association, P.O. Box 385, Wood River, IL 62095. 13.5 miles straight. Awards available. (AA 1992)

846 **Libertyville Trail**, Steve Magmusen, Director of Public Works, 200 E. Cook Ave., Libertyville, IL 60048, (708) 362-2430. 3.0 miles straight. (GRT)

847 **Lincoln Circuit Trail**, Arrowhead Council, BSA, 1 Henson Pl., Champaign, IL 61820-7805, (217) 356-7291. 20.0 miles. Awards available. (NHT; MVC; HTA)

848 **Lincoln Heritage Trail** (a/k/a Lincolnland Cub Heritage Trail), Abraham Lincoln Council, BSA, Fairhills Mall, Springfield, IL 62704, (217) 546-5570. 2.0 miles. Awards available. (AA 1992)

849 **Lincoln Homesite Trail**, John Washburn, 2051 S. Gate Dr., Decatur, IL 62521. 10.0-20.0 miles. Awards available. (NHT; HTA)

850 **Lincoln Memorial Garden and Nature Center**, 2031 E. Lake Shore Dr., Springfield, IL 62707, (217) 529-1111. 5.0 miles. (MGL; GFA)

851 **Lincoln Trail Homestead State Park**, P.O. Box 705, Mt. Zion, IL 62549, (217) 963-2729. (MGL)

852 **Lincoln Trail State Park**, Rt. 1, Box 117, Marshall, IL 62441, (217) 826-2222. (WCD; ATI; MGL)

853 Lincoln's New Salem State Park, SR 97, Petersburg, IL 62659, (217) 632-7953. (WCD; MGL)
   Little Grand Canyon Trail *see* entry 931.
854 Little Woodsman Nature Trails, Sauk-Thorn Creek Trail, Inc., P.O. Box 273, Dolton, IL 60419. 6 hikes. Awards available. (HTA)
855 Lone Point Access Area, Corps of Engineers—Lake Shelbyville, Findlay, IL 62534, (217) 774-3851. (WCD)
856 Long Prairie Trail, Boone County Conservation District, 7600 Appleton Rd., Belvidere, IL 61008, (815) 547-7935. 6.5 miles straight. (GRT)
857 Lowden Memorial State Park, P.O. Box 403, E. River Rd., Oregon, IL 61061, (815) 732-6828. (WCD; ATI; MGL)
858 Lowell Parkway Bicycle Path, Dave Zinnen, Director of Administration and Recreation, or Debra Carey, Naturalist, Dixon Park District, 804 Palmyra Ave., Dixon, IL 61021, (815) 284-3306. 3.0 miles straight. (GRT)
859 Madison County Nature Trail, George Arnold, Madison County Trail Volunteers, 1306 St. Louis St., Edwardsville, IL 62025, (618) 656-3994. 6.3 miles straight planned, current as to 3.0 miles. (GRT)
860 Maple Grove Forest Preserve, Downers Grove, IL 60515, (312) 790-4900 ext. 243. (AA 1994)
861 Maple Leaf Park, Greenbrier St., Earlville, IL 60518, (815) 246-8751. (WCD)
862 Marshall State Fish & Wildlife Area, Rt. 1, Box 238, Lacon, IL 61540, (309) 246-8351. (WCD; ATI; NAT)
863 Martyrdom Trail, Orville Hale, Martyrdom Trail Committee, P.O. Box 223, Rt. 1, Box 57, Nauvoo, IL 62345, (217) 453-6543. 23.0 miles straight. Awards available. (AA 1992)
864 Matthiessen State Park, P.O. Box 381, Utica, IL 61373, (815) 667-4868. (ATI; MGL; NAT; GFA)
865 McHenry County Prairie Trail, Steve Weller, Executive Director, McHenry County Conservation District, 6512 Harts Rd., Ringwood, IL 60072, (815) 678-4431. 12.0 miles. (GRT)
866 Mendota Hills Campground, 642 US 52, Amboy, IL 61310, (815) 849-5930. (WCD)
867 Mick's Lake & Recreational Campground, CR 530, Highland, IL 62249, (618) 644-5855. (WCD)
868 Middle Fork State Park, US 74, Oakwood, IL 61858. (ATI)
869 Mississippi Palisades State Park, 4577 US 84N, Savanna, IL 61074, (815) 273-2731. 12.0 miles. (WCD; ATI; MGL; IOB; OTB)
870 Mitchell Museum, Richview Rd., Mt. Vernon, IL 62864, (618) 242-1236. (MGL)
871 Mitigwaki Trail, Sauk-Thorn Creek Trail, Inc., P.O. Box 273, Dolton, IL 60419. 13.0 miles. Awards available. (HTA)
872 Moraine Hills State Park, 914 S. River Rd., McHenry, IL 60050, (815) 385-1624. 11.0 miles. Named trails: Pike Marsh Nature 0.5. (ATI; NAT; IOB)
873 Moraine View State Park, Leroy-Levington Rd., Leroy, IL 61752, (309) 724-8032. (WCD; ATI)
874 Morrison-Rockwood State Park, SR 78, Morrison, IL 61270, (815) 772-4708. (WCD; ATI)
875 Morton Arboretum, Lisle, IL 60532, (708) 968-0074. Named trails: Big Rock 0.9, East Woods 1.1, Evergreen 0.9, Forest 0.7, Fragrance Garden, Geographic 0.9, Illinois Trees Nature 1, Illinois Trees Nature 2&3 2.3(l), Joy Path, Landscape Display Paths, Outpost Wild Garden, Ozark Area 0.5, Prairie 0.7, Thornhill. (AA 1992)
   Nature Treasure Hunt Trail *see* entry 860.
876 Nauvoo State Park, P.O. Box 337, Nauvoo, IL 62354, (217) 453-2512. (WCD; ATI; MGL)
877 North Shore Bike Trail, Martin G. Buehler, Director of Transportation, Lake County Division of Transportation, 600 W. Winchester Rd., Libertyville, IL 60048, (708) 362-3950. 14.7 miles straight planned, current as to 14.0 miles. (GRT)

ILLINOIS

878 **O'Connell's Yogi Bear's Jellystone Park Camp-Resort**, P.O. Box 175, Greenwing Rd., Amboy, IL 61310, (815) 857-3860. (WCD)
   Old Barn Trail see entry 793.
879 **Old Nauvoo Trail**, Cynthia B. House, 716 E. Oakton St., Arlington Heights, IL 60004. 7 hours loop (by car). Awards available. (AA 1992)
   Outpost Wild Garden Trail see entry 875.
880 **Oxpojke Trail**, Bishop Hill Heritage Association, P.O. Box 1853, Bishop Hill, IL 61419, (309) 927-3504 or (309) 927-3513. 11.0 miles loop. Awards available. (AA 1992)
   Ozark Area Trail see entry 875.
881 **Ozark Shawnee Trail**, Egyptian Council, BSA, 803 E. Herrin St., Herrin, IL 62948. Awards available. (HTA)
882 **Palatine Trail**, Fred P. Hall, Director of Parks and Recreation, Palatine Park District, 250 E. Wood St., Palatine, IL 60067, (708) 991-0333. 28.0 miles straight. (GRT)
883 **Palos Pioneer Trail**, Sauk-Thorn Creek Trail, Inc., P.O. Box 273, Dolton, IL 60419. 15.0 miles. Awards available. (HTA)
884 **Pecatonica Prairie Path**, Dave Derwent, President, Pecatonica Prairie Path, Inc., 248 W. Horner St., P.O. Box 534, Pecatonica, IL 61063, (815) 239-2180. 21.0 miles straight. Awards available. (AA 1992)
885 **Pere Marquette State Park**, P.O. Box 325, Grafton, IL 62037, (618) 786-3323. 15.0 miles. (WCD; ATI; NAT; IOB)
886 **Piasa Red Bird Trail**, Trails Unlimited, Inc., P.O. Box 166, East Alton, IL 62024. Awards available. (MVC)
887 **Pierce Lake Trail**, 1705 Paradise Blvd., Rockford, IL 61103. 12.0 miles. Awards available. (HTA)
   Pike Marsh Nature Trail see entry 872.
888 **Pilcher Park**, US 30, Joliet, IL 60436, (815) 726-2207. (MGL)
889 **Pimiteoui Bike Trail**, Carol Hallock, President, Pimiteoui Trail Association, 3016 N. Western Ave., Peoria, IL 61604, (309) 688-1165; or George M. Burrier, 213 N. Oklahoma Ave., Morton, IL 61550, (309) 266-5085. 2.0 miles straight. (GRT)
890 **Pine Lakes Resort**, Pittsfield/New Salem Rd., Pittsfield, IL 62363, (217) 285-6719. (WCD)
891 **Pine View Campground**, Sleepy Hollow Rd., Amboy, IL 61310, (815) 857-3964. (WCD)
   Piscasaw Route see entry 752.
892 **Pleasant Creek Campground**, Deer Park Rd., Utica, IL 61373, (815) 433-5875. (WCD)
893 **Potawatomi Trail**, John & Betty Yentes, 2216 Sunset Dr., Pekin, IL 61554. 10.0 miles. Awards available. (HTA)
   Prairie Trail see entry 875.
   Primitive Loop Trail see entry 793.
894 **Prophetstown State Park**, SR 78, Prophetstown, IL 61277, (815) 537-2926. (WCD; ATI)
895 **Pyramid State Park**, SR 127/13, Pinckneyville, IL 62274, (618) 357-2574. (WCD; ATI)
896 **Quincy Campground/Valley View**, US 24, Quincy, IL 62301, (217) 222-7229. (WCD)
897 **Raccoon Lakes Campground**, Rt. 1, Box 208, Airport Rd., Mapleton, IL 61547, (309) 697-2616. (WCD)
898 **Rainmaker Campground**, CR 650E, Litchfield, IL 62056, (217) 532-6370. (WCD)
899 **Ramsey Lake State Park**, US 51, Ramsey, IL 62080, (618) 423-2215. (WCD; ATI)
900 **Randolph County State Fish & Wildlife Area**, CR DD, Chester, IL 62233, (618) 826-2706. (WCD; ATI)
901 **Rapatuck Trail**, Prairie Council, BSA, 607 Bondi Bldg., Galesburg, IL 61401, (309) 343-1145. 5.0-16.0 miles loop. Awards available. (AA 1992)
902 **Red Caboose Trail**, Three Fires Council, BSA, 415 N. Second St., St. Charles, IL 60174, (708) 584-9250. 11.36 miles straight. Awards available. (AA 1992)
   Red Cedar Hiking Trail see entry 811.
903 **Red Hills State Park**, Rt. 4, Sumner, IL 62466, (618) 936-2469. (ATI; IOB)

ILLINOIS

904 **Rend Lake**, Corps of Engineers, North Central Region, 536 Clark St., Chicago, IL 60605; or Wayne Fitzgerald State Park, P.O. Box D, Benton, IL 62812, (618) 724-2493. (ATI; GFC; MGL; LRA)
Rim Rock Nature Trail see entry 931.
905 **River Ridge Back Pack Trail**, Piankeshaw Council, BSA, 704 N. Hazel, Danville, IL 61832; or Forest Glen Preserve, Rt. 1, Box 495A, Westville, IL 61883, (217) 662-6284. 11.0 miles. Awards available. (AA 1992)
906 **River Road Camping & Marina**, River Rd., Oregon, IL 61061, (815) 234-5383. (WCD)
River Trail see entry 943.
907 **River Trail Nature Center**, 3120 N. Milwaukee Ave., Northbrook, IL 60062, (312) 824-8360. 1.5 miles. (MGL)
908 **River Trail of Illinois**, Jim Coutts, Director, Fon du Lac Park District, 201 Veterans Dr., East Peoria, IL 61611, (309) 699-3923. 9.0 miles straight planned, current as to 5.3 miles. (GRT)
909 **River-to-River Trail**, US 45, Vienna, IL 62995; or Shawnee National Forest, 901 S. Commercial St., Harrisburg, IL 62946, (618) 253-7114. 47.0 miles. (EGH; IOB; FGU)
910 **Robin Hood Woods**, SR 16, Shelbyville, IL 62565, (217) 774-4222. (WCD)
911 **Rock Cut State Park**, 7318 Harlem Rd., Caledonia, IL 61011, (815) 885-3311. (ATI; NAT)
912 **Rock Cut Trail**, 1705 Paradise Blvd., Rockford, IL 61103. 5.0 miles. Awards available. (HTA)
913 **Rock Island Arsenal Trail**, Troop 664—BSA, P.O. Box 15504, Davenport, IA 52806-0504. 10.0 miles. Awards available. (HTA)
914 **Rock Island Trail**, Paul Oltman, Trail Ranger, Rock Island Trail State Park, P.O. Box 64, Wyoming, IL 61491, (309) 695-2228; or George M. Barrier, 213 N. Oklahoma Ave., Morton, IL 61550, (309) 266-5085. 28.0 miles straight. (GRT)
915 **Rock River Recreation Path**, Vance Barrie, Marketing Coordinator, Rockford Park District, 1401 N. Second St., Rockford, IL 61107-3086, (815) 987-8694. 3.3 miles straight. (GRT)
916 **Rock Springs Center for Environmental Discovery**, Rock Springs Rd., Decatur, IL 62522, (217) 423-7708. 12.0 miles. (MGL; GFA)
917 **Ronald J. Foster Heritage Trail**, Glen Carbon Village Hall, P.O. Box 757, Glen Carbon, IL 62034, (618) 288-1200. 3.2 miles straight. (GRT)
918 **Running Deer Trail**, John & Betty Yentes, 2216 Sunset Dr., Pekin, IL 61554. 4.0-6.0 miles. Awards available. (HTA)
919 **Sac-Fox Trail**, Troop 109, P.O. Box 232, Moline, IL 61265. 15.0 miles. Awards available. (AA 1992)
920 **Saline County Park**, Equality, IL 62934. (ATI)
921 **Sam Dale Lake State Conservation Area**, SR 161, Cisne, IL 62823, (618) 835-2292. (WCD)
922 **Sam Parr State Park**, SR 130, Newton, IL 62448, (618) 783-2661. (WCD)
923 **Sam Vadalabene Bike Trail**, Ron Tedesco, Illinois Department of Transportation, 1100 Eastport Plaza Dr., P.O. Box 988, Collinsville, IL 62234-6198, (618) 346-3100. 14.2 miles straight. (GRT)
924 **Sand Ridge State Park**, Manito Rd., Havana, IL 62644. (ATI)
925 **Sangamon Acres Campground**, Cisco Rd., Monticello, IL 61856, (217) 669-2233. (WCD)
926 **Sangchris Lake State Park**, SR 29, Rochester, IL 62563, (217) 498-9208. (WCD)
927 **Saukenauk Scout Reservation**, Saukee Area Council, BSA, 2336 Oak St., Quincy, IL 62301, (217) 224-0204; or Saukenauk Scout Reservation, Rt. 2, Mendon, IL 62315, (217) 985-3735. (SFC)
928 **Sauk-Thorn Creek Trail**, P.O. Box 273, Dolton, IL 60419. 18.5 miles. Awards available. (HTA)
Sentinel Rock Trail see entry 931.
929 **Shabbona Lake State Park**, Rt. 1, Box 120, Shabbona, IL 60550, (815) 824-2106. (IOB)
930 **Shabbona Lake State Recreation Area**, Preserve Rd., Shabbona, IL 60550, (815) 824-2565. (WCD)

Shawnee Hiking Trail *see* entry 931.
931 **Shawnee National Forest**, 901 S. Commercial St., Harrisburg, IL 62946, (618) 253-7114. Named trails: Garden of the Gods 6.0, Heritage 9.0, Little Grand Canyon, Rim Rock Nature, Sentinel Rock, Shawnee Hiking 120.0. (EGH; WCD; ATI; GFC; NAT; IOB; FGU; TOV; GTB; NFG)
932 **She-Ka-Gong Trail**, P.O. Box 273, Dolton, IL 60419. 12.0 miles. Awards available. (HTA)
933 **Shelbyville Fish and Wildlife Area**, Rt. 1, Box 42-A, Bethany, IL 61914, (217) 665-3112. (NAT)
934 **Sherwood Camping Resort**, SR 37, Ina, IL 62846, (618) 437-5530. (WCD)
935 **Sherwood Forest City Park**, CR 1275N, Hillsboro, IL 62049, (217) 532-5211. (WCD)
936 **Sherwood Forest Recreation**, CR 400E, Casey, IL 62420, (217) 382-6632. (WCD)
Sheskikmaos Sepe Trail *see* entry 830.
937 **Siloam Springs State Park**, Kellerville Rd., Quincy, IL 62301, (217) 894-6205. (WCD; ATI)
938 **Silver Springs Fish and Wildlife Area**, Rt. 1, Box 318, Yorkville, IL 60560, (708) 553-6297. 10.5 miles. (NAT)
939 **South Marcum Recreation Area**, Corps of Engineers—Rend Lake, Petroff Rd., Benton, IL 62812. (WCD)
South Prairie Route *see* entry 752.
940 **Spokes on the Wheel Auto Tour**, Cynthia B. House, 716 E. Oakton St., Arlington Heights, IL 60004. Awards available. (AA 1992)
941 **Spoon River Valley Trail**, Spoon River Scenic Committee, P.O. Box 59, Ellisville, IL 61431. 55.0 miles. Awards available. (AA 1992)
Spring Crest Trail *see* entry 793.
942 **Spring Lake State Conservation Area**, Rt. 1, Box 248, Manito, IL 61546, (309) 968-7135. (WCD; MGL; IOB)
943 **Starved Rock State Park**, P.O. Box 116, SR 178, Utica, IL 61373, (815) 667-4926. 20.0 miles. Named trails: Bluff, Interior Canyon, River. (WCD; ATI; MGL; NAT; IOB; OTB)
944 **Stephen A. Forbes State Fish and Wildlife Area**, Rt. 1, Kinmundy, IL 62865, (618) 547-3381. (WCD; ATI; MGL; NAT; IOB)
945 **Stephenson County Blackhawk Trail**, Lena Community Park District, 609 N. Schuyler St., Lena, IL 61048, (815) 369-5351. 12.0 miles. Awards available. (NHT; HTA)
946 **Sun Singer Trail**, Sun Singer Trail Committee, P.O. Box 50, Monticello, IL 61856. 19.0 and 28.0 miles. Awards available. (AA 1992)
Tall Tree Trail *see* entry 793.
947 **Tallgrass Nature Trail**, Goose Lake Prairie State Park, 5010 N. Jugtown Rd., Morris, IL 60450, (815) 942-2899. 1.5 miles. (IOB)
948 **Thomson Causeway Area**, Corps of Engineers—Lock & Dam 13, Lewis Ave., Thomson, IL 61285, (815) 589-3229. (WCD; ATI)
Thornhill Trail *see* entry 875.
949 **Thunderhead Resort Kamp**, Loud Thunder Rd., Illinois City, IL 61259, (309) 791-0215. (WCD)
950 **Timber Trails Campground**, Mulberry Grove, IL 62262, (618) 326-8264. (WCD)
951 **Trail of Tears State Forest**, Rt. 3, Wolf Lake, IL 62998, (618) 833-4910. 36.0 miles. (IOB)
952 **Trail of the Fu Dogs**, Sun Singer Trail Committee, P.O. Box 50, Monticello, IL 61856. 11.0 and 20.0 miles. Awards available. (AA 1992)
953 **Trail of the Lagoons**, Sauk-Thorn Creek Trail, Inc., P.O. Box 273, Dolton, IL 60419; or Charles L. Deegan, 14066 Lincoln, Dolton, IL 60419. 14.0 miles. Awards available. (HTA)
Tricky Tree-Key Trail *see* entry 817.
954 **Tyler Creek Forest Preserve**, Elgin, IL 60120, (708) 741-5082. (NAT)
955 **Virgil Gilman Nature Trail**, Charles E. Hoscheit, Director, Fox Valley Park District, P.O. Box 818, Aurora, IL 60507, (708) 897-0516. 12.0 miles straight. (GRT)

ILLINOIS

956 **Volo Bog State Natural Area**, 28478 Brandenburg Rd., Ingleside, IL 60041, (815) 344-1294. (NAT; OTB)
957 **Wacca Lake Trail**, Boy Scout Troop 127, Bob Schaltenbrand, P.O. Box 269, 833 S. Mill St., Nashville, IL 62263, (618) 327-8522. 9.0 miles loop. Awards available. (AA 1992)
958 **Walcamp Outdoor Ministry Center**, Five Points Rd., Kingston, IL 60145, (815) 784-5141. (WCD)
959 **Walnut Point State Fish and Wildlife Area**, SR 133, Oakland, IL 61943, (217) 346-3336. (WCD; ATI; NAT)
960 **Washington County Lake Conservation Area**, SR 127, Nashville, IL 62263, (618) 327-3137. 14.0 miles. (WCD; ATI; IOB)
961 **Wayne Fitzgerrell State Park**, SR 154, Sesser, IL 62884, (618) 629-2320. (WCD; ATI)
962 **Weinberg-King State Park**, SR 101, Augusta, IL 62311, (217) 392-2345. (WCD; ATI)
963 **Weldon Springs State Park**, US 51, Clinton, IL 61727, (217) 935-2644. (WCD; ATI; MGL)
 Which-a-Way Trail *see* entry 807.
964 **White Pines Forest State Park**, Pines Rd., Oregon, IL 61061, (815) 946-3717. (WCD; ATI; MGL)
965 **Wildlife Prairie Park**, Taylor Rd., Peoria, IL 61607, (309) 676-0998. (MGL)
 Willow Creek Trail *see* entry 793.
966 **Wolf Creek State Park**, SR 32, Windsor, IL 61957, (217) 459-2831. (WCD; ATI)
967 **Wolf Lake Trail**, Sauk-Thorn Creek Trail, Inc., P.O. Box 273, Dolton, IL 60419. 8.5 miles. Awards available. (HTA)

Generally:
Director, Department of Conservation, Lincoln Tower Plaza, 524 S. Second St., Springfield, IL 62706, (217) 782-6302. (SFC)
Sierra Club, 506 S. Wabash, Rm. 525, Chicago, IL 60605. (EGH)
U.S. Army Corps of Engineers, North Central District, 536 Clark St., Chicago, IL 60605. (GFC)

Index (by city)

Amboy: Mendota Hills Campground 866; O'Connell's Yogi Bear's Jellystone Park Camp-Resort 878; Pine View Campground 891
Andalusia: Sac-Fox Trail 919
Antioch: Fox River Recreation RV Park 802
Argenta: Friends Creek Regional Park 806
Augusta: Weinberg-King State Park 962
Aurora: Illinois Prairie Path National Recreation Trail 828; Virgil Gilman Nature Trail 955
Belleville: Belleville Historical Trail 745
Belvidere: Boone County Historical Trail 752; Long Prairie Trail 856
Benton: South Marcum Recreation Area 939
Bethany: Shelbyville Fish and Wildlife Area 933
Bishop Hill: Oxpojke Trail 880
Bloomington: Constitution Trail 777
Bourbonnais: Kankakee River State Park 834
Brimfield: Jubilee College College State Park 833
Brownfield: Dixon Springs State Park 785
Cahokia: Cahokia Mounds State Historic Site 756
Caledonia: Rock Cut State Park 911
Canton: Lakeland Park 842
Carlinville: Beaver Dam State Park 744
Carlyle: Carlyle Lake 761; Dam West Recreation Area 779; Eldon Hazlett State Park 789
Carterville: Crab Orchard National Wildlife Refuge 778
Casey: Sherwood Forest Recreation 936
Cave-in-Rock: Cave-in-Rock State Park 763
Champaign: Lincoln Circuit Trail 847
Channahon: Chief Shabbona Trail 772
Charleston: Fox Ridge State Park 801
Chester: Fort Kaskaskia State Historic Site

799; Randolph County State Fish & Wildlife Area 900
Chicago: Big Foot Trail 746; Chicago Lincoln Ave. Trail 768; Discovery '76 Trail 784; Fort Dearborn Massacre Trail 797; Fort Dearborn Trails 798; Indian Portage Trails 830; Rend Lake 904
Cisne: Sam Dale Lake State Conservation Area 921
Clinton: Weldon Springs State Park 963
Colchester: Argyle Lake State Park 739
Collinsville: Sam Vadalabene Bike Trail 923
Cornell: Bayou Bluffs Campground 741
Danville: Kennekuk Cove Park 835
Davenport, IA: Rock Island Arsenal Trail 913
Decatur: Decatur Historic Trail 780; Lincoln Homesite Trail 849; Rock Springs Center 916
Des Plaines: Algonquin Woods Nature Trail 737
DeWitt: Clinton Lake 774
Dixon: Lowell Parkway Bicycle Path 858
Dolton: Big Quarry Trail 747; Chicago Portage National Historic Site Trail 769; Chief Chicagou Trail 770; Chief Sauganash Trail 771; Little Woodsman Nature Trails 854; Mitigwaki Trail 871; Palos Pioneer Trail 883; Sauk-Thorn Creek Trail 928; She-Ka-Gong Trail 932; Trail of the Lagoons 953; Wolf Lake Trail 967
Downers Grove: Maple Grove Forest Preserve 860
Earlville: Maple Leaf Park 861
East Alton: Piasa Red Bird Trail 886
East Peoria: River Trail of Illinois 908
East St. Louis: Cahokia Pilgrimage Trail 757
Edwardsville: Delyte Morris Bikeway 782; Madison County Nature Trail 859
Elgin: Burnidge Forest Preserve 755; Tyler Creek Forest Preserve 954
Ellisville: Spoon River Valley Trail 941
Equality: Saline County Park 920
Evanston: Beat the Bounds Trail 743; Ladd Arboretum 838
Findlay: Eagle Creek State Park 787; Lone Point Access Area 855
Geneseo: Geneseo Campground 810; Johnson 1910 Farm 831

Geneva: Fox River Trail 803; Great Western Trail 814
Georgetown: Camp Cherokee Hills 758
Glen Carbon: Ronald J. Foster Heritage Trail 917
Glencoe: Chicago Botanic Gardens 767; Green Bay Trail 816
Glenview: The Grove National Historic Landmark 818
Goreville: Ferne Clyffe State Park 791
Grafton: Pere Marquette State Park 885
Granite City: Horseshoe Lake State Park 825
Harrisburg: Shawnee National Forest 931
Havana: Chautauqua National Wildlife Refuge 766; Sand Ridge State Park 924
Herrin: Ozark Shawnee Trail 881
Highland: Mick's Lake & Recreational Campground 867
Highland Park: Green Bay Trail 816
Hillsboro: Sherwood Forest City Park 935
Hudson: Comlara County Park 775
Illinois City: Thunderhead Resort Kamp 949
Ina: Sherwood Camping Resort 934
Ingleside: Volo Bog State Natural Area 956
Joliet: Pilcher Park 888
Kewanee: Francis City Park 804; Johnson Sauk Trail State Park 832
Kingston: Walcamp Outdoor Ministry Center 958
Kinmundy: Stephen A. Forbes State Fish and Wildlife Area 944
Kirkland: Kishwankee Scout Reservation 837
Knoxville: Rapatuck Trail 901
Lacon: Marshall State Fish & Wildlife Area 862
Lena: Lake Le-Aqua-Na State Park 839; Stephenson County Blackhawk Trail 945
Leroy: Moraine View State Park 873
Lewistown: Dickson Mounds Nature Trail 783
Libertyville: Libertyville Trail 846; North Shore Bike Trail 877
Lisle: Morton Arboretum 875
Litchfield: Lazy Days Campground 844; Rainmaker Campground 898
Makanda: Fern Rocks Trail 790; Giant City State Park 811

Manito: Spring Lake State Conservation Area 942
Mapleton: Raccoon Lakes Campground 897
Marseilles: Glenwood The Camping Resort 812; Illini State Park 826
Marshall: Clark County Park 773; Lincoln Trail State Park 852
McHenry: Moraine Hills State Park 872
McLeansboro: Dolan Lake County Park 786
Mendon: Saukenauk Scout Reservation 927
Metropolis: Fort Massac State Park 800
Millbrook: Fitzpatrick's Yogi Bear Jellystone Camp-Resort 792
Monticello: Sangamon Acres Campground 925; Sun Singer Trail 946; Trail of the Fu Dogs 952
Morris: Camp Rainbow 759; Gebhard Woods State Park 809; Tallgrass Nature Trail 947
Morrison: Morrison-Rockwood State Park 874
Mount Carmel: Beall Woods State Park 742
Mt. Vernon: Mitchell Museum 870
Mt. Zion: Lincoln Trail Homestead State Park 851
Mulberry Grove: Timber Trails Campground 950
Murphysboro: Lake Murphysboro State Park 840
Nashville: Wacca Lake Trail 957; Washington County Lake Conservation Area Trail 960
Nauvoo: Breezewood Campground 753; Martyrdom Trail 863; Nauvoo State Park 876; Old Nauvoo Trail 879; Spokes on the Wheel Auto Tour 940
Newton: Sam Parr State Park 922
Northbrook: River Trail Nature Center 907
Oak Brook: Adventurer Award 736; Fullersburg Woods Environmental Center 807
Oak Park: Frank Lloyd Wright Heritage Trail 805
Oakland: Hebron Hills Camping 819; Walnut Point State Fish and Wildlife Area 959
Oakwood: Kickapoo State Park 836; Middle Fork State Park 868
Olney: Bird Haven-Robert Ridgway Memorial 749
Oquawka: Big River State Forest 748; Delabar State Park 781; Henderson County State Conservation Area 820
Oregon: Blackhawk Trail 751; Castle Rock State Park 762; Lowden Memorial State Park 857; River Road Camping & Marina 906; White Pines Forest State Park 964
Ottawa: Buffalo Rock State Park 754
Palatine: Palatine Trail 882
Paxton: Indian Butterfield Trail 829
Pecatonica: Pecatonica Prairie Path 884
Pekin: Potawatomi Trail 893; Running Deer Trail 918
Peoria: Forest Park Nature Center 795; Pimiteoui Bike Trail 889; Wildlife Prairie Park 965
Percy: Community Lake Campground 776
Petersburg: Lincoln's New Salem State Park 853
Pinckneyville: Pyramid State Park 895
Pittsfield: Pine Lakes Resort 890
Prophetstown: Prophetstown State Park 894
Quincy: Quincy Campground/Valley View 896; Siloam Springs State Park 937
Ramsey: Ramsey Lake State Park 899
Ringwood: McHenry County Prairie Trail 865
Rochester: Sangchris Lake State Park 926
Rock Island: Black Hawk State Park 750; Great River Trail 813
Rockford: Pierce Lake Trail 887; Rock Cut Trail 912; Rock River Recreation Path 915
St. Charles: Illinois Prairie Path National Recreation Trail 828; Red Caboose Trail 902
St. David: Fulton County Conservation Area 808
St. Elmo: Bail's Timberline Lake Campground 740
Savanna: Lakewood Resort 843; Mississippi Palisades State Park 869
Sesser: Wayne Fitzgerrell State Park 961
Shabbona: Shabbona Lake State Park 929; Shabbona Lake State Recreation Area 930
Sheffield: Hennepin Canal Parkway State Park 821
Shelbyville: Hidden Springs State Forest 823; Lake Shelbyville 841; Robin Hood Woods 910
Spring Grove: Chain O'Lakes State Park 765

Springfield: Abraham Lincoln Trail 735; Lincoln Heritage Trail 848
Staunton: Forest Lakes Resort 794
Stockton: Apple River Canyon State Park 738
Sullivan: Forest W. Bo Woods Recreation Area 796
Sumner: Red Hills State Park 903
Thomson: Thomson Causeway 948
Utica: Matthiessen State Park 864; Pleasant Creek Campground 892; Starved Rock State Park 943
Vienna: Cedar Lake Ranch 764; Heron Pond-Little Black Slough Nature Preserve 822; River-to-River Trail 909
Waterloo: Eagle Trail 788
Westville: Forest Glen Preserve County Park 793; River Ridge Back Pack Trail 905
Wheaton: Cantigny Park 760; Great Western Trail 815; Illinois Prairie Path National Recreation Trail 828
Wilmette: Green Bay Trail 816
Windsor: Wolf Creek State Park 966
Winnetka: Green Bay Trail 816
Wolf Lake: Trail of Tears State Forest 951
Wood River: Lewis & Clark Trail 845
Woodridge: Greene Valley Forest Preserve 817
Wyoming: Rock Island Trail 914
Yorkville: Hide-A-Way Lakes 824; Silver Springs Fish and Wildlife Area 938
Zion: Illinois Beach State Park 827

INDIANA

Adventure Trail *see* entry 1015.
968 **Al White Trail**, Crossroads of America Council, BSA, 1900 N. Meridian St., Indianapolis, IN 46202, (317) 925-1900. 8.0 miles. Awards available. (SAR 1989)
969 **American Heritage Trail**, Trail Headquarters, Bear Wallow Hill, Rt. 4, Box 88, Nashville, IN 47448-9451. 12.1 miles loop. Awards available. (AA 1993)
970 **Angel Mounds State Historic Site**, 8215 Pollack Ave., Evansville, IN 47715, (812) 853-3956. (ATI)
971 **Anthony Wayne Trail**, Pokagon-Kekionga Trails, Inc., P.O. Box 10353, Ft. Wayne, IN 46851, (219) 744-5444 or (219) 749-0152. Named segments: Fort Wayne 10.0, Kekionga 25.0, Wayne Trace 38.0. Awards available. (AA 1994)
972 **Auburn to Waterloo Bike Trail**, Andy Jagoda, Parks and Recreation Superintendent, Auburn Parks Department, P.O. Box 506, Auburn, IN 46706, (219) 925-8245. 4.0 miles straight. (GRT)
Bailly-Chellberg Trail *see* entry 1029.
973 **Bears of Blue River Trail**, Bears of Blue River Historical Society, SR 9, Shelbyville, IN 46176. 14.8 miles. Awards available. (HTA)
974 **Bendix Woods Park**, SR 2, South Bend, IN 46624, (219) 654-3155. (MGL)
975 **Bixler Lake City Park**, SR 6, Kendallville, IN 46755, (219) 347-1064. (WCD; ATI)
976 **Bloomington Rail Trail**, Leslie Clark, Bloomington Parks and Recreation Department, 349 S. Walnut St., Bloomington, IN 47401, (812) 332-9668. 6.2 miles straight. (GRT)
977 **Bonneyville Mill Park**, CR 131, Bristol, IN 46507, (219) 533-6121. (ATI; MGL; GFA; OTB)

978 **Brookville State Lake**, SR 101, Brookville, IN 47012, (317) 647-6557. (WCD)
979 **Brown County Bike Trail**, Trail Headquarters, Bear Wallow Hill, Rt. 4, Box 88, Nashville, IN 47448-9451. 25.8 miles. Awards available. (HTA)
980 **Brown County State Park**, P.O. Box 116, Nashville, IN 47448, (812) 988-6406. 27.0 miles. (WCD; ATI; MGL; IBP)
Calumet Trail *see* entry 1029.
981 **Camp Arthur**, Buffalo Trace Council, BSA, P.O. Box 3245, 1050 Bayard Park Dr., Evansville, IN 47731, (812) 423-5246; or Camp Arthur, Rt. 1, Bruceville, IN 47631, (812) 324-2242. (SFC)
982 **Camp Buffalo**, Sagamore Council, BSA, 410 N. Main St., Kokomo, IN 46901, (317) 452-8253; or Camp Buffalo, Rt. 4, Box 214, Monticello, IN 47960, (219) 278-7114. (SFC)
983 **Camp Cary**, Sagamore Council, BSA, 410 N. Main St., Kokomo, IN 46901, (317) 452-8253; or Camp Cary, 6286 SR 26E, Lafayette, IN 47905, (317) 447-1990. (SFC)
984 **Camp Louis Ernst**, Hoosier Trails Council, BSA, 2307 E. Second St., Bloomington, IN 47401, (812) 273-6809; or Camp Louis Ernst, Rt. 1, Dupont, IN 47231, (812) 273-3052. (SFC)
985 **Cass County Park**, US 24, Logansport, IN 46947, (219) 753-2928. (WCD)
986 **Chain O'Lakes State Park**, SR 9, Albion, IN 46701, (219) 636-2654. (WCD; ATI; OTB)
987 **Chain O'Lakes Trail**, Pokagon-Kekionga Trails, Inc., P.O. Box 10353, Ft. Wayne, IN 46851, (219) 744-5444 or (219) 749-0152. 10.0 miles. Awards available. (AA 1994)
988 **Chief Little Turtle Trail**, Pokagon-

Kekionga Trails, Inc., P.O. Box 10353, Ft. Wayne, IN 46851, (219) 744-5444 or (219) 749-0152. 10.0 miles. Awards available. (AA 1994)

989 **Clark State Forest**, P.O. Box 119, Henryville, IN 47126, (812) 294-4306. Named trails: Clark State Forest 20.0(l), Resource 0.1(l), White Oak Nature 0.9(l). (AA 1994)

Clark State Forest Trail see entry 989.

990 **Clark's Advance Trail**, Larry Benson, 148 Pine View Dr., Vincennes, IN 47591. 10.2 miles. Awards available. (AA 1993)

991 **Clegg Botanical Garden**, CR 400E, Lafayette, IN 47901, (317) 742-0325. (MGL)

Cliffside Trail see entry 1024.

992 **Clifty Falls State Park**, SR 62, Madison, IN 47250, (812) 265-1331. (WCD; ATI; MGL; OTB)

993 **Covered Bridge Trail**, Mike Market, Rt. 1, Box 17, Montezuma, IN 47862; or T.W. Thomas, P.O. Box 255, Montezuma, IN 47862; or Paul K. Bartlow, 420 Madison, Montezuma, IN 47862. 18.5-22.5 miles. Awards available. (MVC; HTA)

994 **Crossland Scout Reservation**, Sagamore Council, BSA, 410 N. Main St., Kokomo, IN 46901, (317) 452-8253; or Crossland Scout Reservation, Rt. 1, Box 45, Larwill, IN 46764, (219) 327-3472. (SFC)

Crystal Palace Tour see entry 1048.

995 **Deer Hollow Trek**, Pokagon-Kekionga Trails, Inc., P.O. Box 10353, Ft. Wayne, IN 46851, (219) 744-5444 or (219) 749-0152. 5.0 miles. Awards available. (AA 1994)

996 **Delaware Lake Campground**, Ft. Benjamin Harrison, Shafter Rd., Indianapolis, IN 46216, (317) 542-4862. (WCD)

997 **Dobbs Park & Nature Center**, SR 46, Terre Haute, IN 47802, (812) 877-1095. 4.0 miles. (MGL)

998 **Donna Jo Recreation Area**, 1255 S. CR 350E, Kouts, IN 46347, (219) 766-2186. (WCD)

999 **Dream Lake State Forest Recreation Area**, SR 60, Hamburg, IN 47172, (812) 246-5421. (WCD; ATI)

Dripstone Trail see entry 1048.

1000 **Eagle Creek Park**, 7840 W. 56th St., Indianapolis, IN 46254, (317) 293-4827. (ATI; MGL)

1001 **East Bank Trail**, Karl Stevens, South Bend Parks Department, 301 S. St. Louis Blvd., South Bend, IN 46617, (219) 284-9401. 0.5 mile straight. (GRT)

1002 **Erie Trail Linear Park**, Donald E. Thomas, City Planner, Department of Planning, City of Hammond, 649 Conkey, Hammond, IN 46324, (219) 853-6398. 3.75 miles straight. (GRT)

1003 **Ferdinand State Forest**, SR 264, Ferdinand, IN 47532, (812) 367-1524. (WCD; ATI)

1004 **Flags of the Nations Trail**, Trail Headquarters, Bear Wallow Hill, Rt. 4, Box 88, Nashville, IN 47448-9451, (812) 988-2636. 13.0 miles loop. Awards available. (AA 1993)

1005 **Forest Park**, SR 19, Noblesville, IN 46060, (317) 773-0007. (MGL)

Fort Wayne Segment see entry 971.

1006 **Foster Park Trail**, Pokagon-Kekionga Trails, Inc., P.O. Box 10353, Ft. Wayne, IN 46851, (219) 744-5444 or (219) 749-0152. 6.5 miles. Awards available. (AA 1994)

1007 **Fowler County Park**, US 24, Logansport, IN 46947, (219) 753-2928. (MGL)

1008 **France Park**, US 24, Logansport, IN 46947. (ATI)

1009 **Franke Park Trek**, Pokagon-Kekionga Trails, Inc., P.O. Box 10353, Ft. Wayne, IN 46851, (219) 744-5444 or (219) 749-0152. 1.5 miles. Awards available. (AA 1994)

1010 **Free Spirit Campground**, SR 446, Bedford, IN 47421, (812) 834-6361. (WCD)

1011 **Gordon's Camping**, SR 3, Kendallville, IN 46755, (219) 351-3383. (WCD)

1012 **Greene-Sullivan State Forest**, SR 159, Dugger, IN 47848, (812) 648-2810. (WCD; ATI)

1013 **Hardy State Lake**, SR 203, Scottsburg, IN 47170, (812) 794-3800. (WCD; ATI)

1014 **Harmonie State Park**, Harmonie Pkwy., New Harmony, IN 47631, (812) 682-4821. (WCD; MGL)

INDIANA

1015 **Harrison-Crawford State Forest**, 7240 Old Forest Rd., Corydon, IN 47112, (812) 738-8232. Named trails: Adventure 35.0. (EGH; WCD; ATI; IBP)

1016 **Hawthorn County Park**, Stop 10 Rd., Terre Haute, IN 47803, (812) 238-8225. (WCD)

1017 **Hayes Regional Arboretum**, 801 Elks Rd., Richmond, IN 47374, (317) 962-3745. 10.0 miles. (ATI; MGL; IBP)

1018 **Hayswood Nature Reserve**, SR 135, Corydon, IN 47112. (ATI)

1019 **Hickory Grove Lakes Campground**, CR 173, Portland, IN 47371, (219) 335-2639. (WCD)

1020 **Hickory Hills Campground**, CR 400S, Knox, IN 46534, (219) 772-4817. (WCD)

1021 **Hickory Hills Campground**, S. Cataract Rd., Spencer, IN 47460, (317) 795-6079. (WCD)

1022 **Hidden Lake Campground**, SR 37, Fairmount, IN 46928, (317) 948-4862. (WCD)

1023 **Hindostan Falls Trail**, Fred King, P.O. Box 15, Huron, IN 47437; or Trail Committee, 307 Riley St., Loogootee, IN 47553. 16.0 miles. Awards available. (MVC; HTA)

1024 **Hoosier National Forest**, 811 Constitution Ave., Bedford, IN 47421, (812) 275-5987. 75.0 miles. Named trails: Cliffside 0.75, Mogan Ridge 21.0(l), Two Lakes 12.0(l). (EGH; WCD; ATI; MGL; TOV)

1025 **Hovey Lake State Fish & Wildlife Area**, SR 69, Mt. Vernon, IN 47620, (812) 838-2928. (GFC)

1026 **Huntington Reservoir**, Indiana Department of Natural Resources, Division of State Parks, 616 State Office Bldg., Indianapolis, IN 46204. (GFC)

1027 **Huntington State Lake**, SR 5, Huntington, IN 46750, (219) 468-2125. (WCD; ATI)

1028 **Indian Head Lake & Campground**, US 41/SR 28, Attica, IN 47918, (317) 762-2195. (WCD)

1029 **Indiana Dunes National Lakeshore**, 1100 N. Mineral Springs Rd., Porter, IN 46304, (219) 926-7561; or Indiana Dunes State Park, 1600 N. 25E, Chesterton, IN 46304, (219) 926-4520. Named trails: Bailly-Chellberg 2.0, Calumet Dune 0.5, Indiana Dunes 0.5, Ly-co-ki-we, Mt. Tom 3.0, Old Sauk. (WCD; ATI; MGL; NAT; NPV; NPE; AGW; CGA; IBP; YNP; ANP)

Indiana Dunes Trail see entry 1029.

1030 **Indiana Lincoln Trail Hike**, Buffalo Trace Council, BSA, P.O. Box 3245, 1050 Bayard Park Dr., Evansville, IN 47731-3245. 17.2 miles. Awards available. (AA 1992)

1031 **Jackson-Washington State Forest**, SR 250, Brownstown, IN 47220, (812) 358-2160. Named trails: Knobstone 58.0. (EGH; WCD; OTB)

1032 **Jasper-Pulaski State Forest**, SR 143, Medaryville, IN 47957, (219) 843-4841. (WCD; ATI)

1033 **Johnny Appleseed Trek**, Pokagon-Kekionga Trails, Inc., P.O. Box 10353, Ft. Wayne, IN 46851, (219) 744-5444 or (219) 749-0152. 8.0 miles. Awards available. (AA 1994)

Kekionga Segment see entry 971.

1034 **Kekionga Trail**, Pokagon-Kekionga Trails, Inc., P.O. Box 10353, Ft. Wayne, IN 46851, (219) 744-5444 or (219) 749-0152. 10.0 miles. Awards available. (AA 1994)

1035 **Kil-So-Quah Trail**, Pokagon-Kekionga Trails, Inc., P.O. Box 10353, Ft. Wayne, IN 46851, (219) 744-5444 or (219) 749-0152. 10.0 miles. Awards available. (AA 1994)

1036 **Kingsbury Fish & Wildlife Area**, Indiana Department of Natural Resources, Division of Fish and Wildlife, 608 State Office Bldg., Indianapolis, IN 46204, (219) 393-3612. (GFC; MGL)

Knobstone Trail see entry 1031.

1037 **KOA-Columbus**, 8855 S. 300W, Columbus, IN 47201, (812) 342-6229. (WCD)

1038 **KOA-Richmond Kampground**, 3101 Cart Rd., Richmond, IN 47374, (317) 962-1219. (WCD)

1039 **Lake Lemon Park**, Tunnel Rd., Bloomington, IN 47408. (ATI)

1040 **Larry L. Ayers Memorial Trail**, Jack P. Taylor, 28 Washington St., Shelburn, IN 47879. 11.0-15.0 miles. Awards available. (MVC; HTA)

1041 **Laughery Creek Trail**, Lloyd Martin, 6442 Louesse Ln., Cincinnati, OH 45248, (513) 574-3864. 36.0 miles. Awards available. (AA 1991)

1042 **Lemon Lake County Park**, SR 55, Merrillville, IN 46410, (219) 769-PARK or (219) 663-8170. Named trails: Touchstone. (MGL)

1043 **Lickford Valley Family Campground**, Rt. 1, Mauckport, IN 47142, (812) 732-4947. (WCD)

1044 **Lieber State Recreation Area**, SR 243, Cloverdale, IN 46120, (317) 795-4576. (WCD)

1045 **Lincoln Boyhood National Monument**, Lincoln City, IN 47553, (812) 937-4757. Named trails: Lincoln Historical, Memorial, Trail of Twelve Stones. (CGA)

1046 **Lincoln Boyhood Trail**, Ron Alstadt, 20 Ornament Ln., Santa Claus, IN 47579. 1.0 mile. Awards available. (HTA)

Lincoln Historical Trail see entry 1045.

1047 **Lincoln State Park**, US 231, Dale, IN 47523, (812) 937-4710. (WCD; ATI; MGL)

Ly-ko-ki-we Trail see entry 1029.

1048 **Marengo Cave Park**, P.O. Box 217, Marengo, IN 47140, (812) 365-2705. Named trails: Crystal Palace Tour 0.3, Dripstone 1.0. (WCD; ATI; MGL; IBP)

1049 **Martin State Forest**, P.O. Box K, US 50, Shoals, IN 47581, (812) 247-3491. Named trails: Tank Spring 3.0. (WCD; ATI; IBP)

1050 **Mary Gray Bird Sanctuary**, Rt. 6, Box 165, CR 350S, Connersville, IN 47331, (317) 825-9788. (ATI; MGL; IBP)

1051 **Mastodon Trek**, Pokagon-Kekionga Trails, Inc., P.O. Box 10353, Ft. Wayne, IN 46851, (219) 744-5444 or (219) 749-0152. 5.0 miles. Awards available. (AA 1994)

1052 **Maumee Scout Reservation**, Hoosier Trails Council, BSA, 2307 E. Second St., Bloomington, IN 47401, (812) 273-6809; or Maumee Scout Reservation, Rt. 1, Norman, IN 47264, (812) 995-3272. (SFC)

1053 **McCormick's Creek State Park**, SR 46, Spencer, IN 47401, (812) 829-2235. (WCD; ATI; MGL)

Memorial Trail see entry 1045.

1054 **Menefee's Camp Sack-In**, CR 40-S, Angola, IN 46704, (219) 665-5166. (WCD)

1055 **Merry Lea Environmental Learning Center**, SR 109, Goshen, IN 46526, (219) 533-3161. (MGL)

1056 **Miami Indian Historical Site**, CR 600N and 300W, Marion, IN 46952. (ATI)

1057 **Mississinewa State Lake**, CR 500S, Peru, IN 46970, (317) 473-6528. (WCD; ATI)

1058 **Mississinewa Trail**, Pokagon-Kekionga Trails, Inc., P.O. Box 10353, Ft. Wayne, IN 46851, (219) 744-5444 or (219) 749-0152. 10.0 miles. Awards available. (AA 1994)

Mogan Ridge Trail see entry 1024.

1059 **Monroe Lake State Recreation Area**, Wayne-Hoosier National Forest, 1615 J St., Bedford, IN 47421, (812) 837-9546. (WCD; LRA)

1060 **Morgan-Monroe State Forest**, 6220 Forest Rd., Martinsville, IN 46151, (317) 342-4026. (WCD; ATI; IBP)

1061 **Mounds State Park**, SR 232, Anderson, IN 46017, (317) 642-6627. (WCD; ATI; MGL)

Mt. Tom Trail see entry 1029.

1062 **Muscatatuck National Wildlife Refuge**, P.O. Box 631, Seymour, IN 47274, (812) 522-4352. (GNW)

1063 **Muskhogen Trail**, Troop 301, BSA, 2109 Lincoln Ave., Evansville, IN 47714; or Vivian Taylor, 435 S. Spring St., Evansville, IN 47714, (812) 477-6777. 6.75 miles. Awards available. (AA 1992)

1064 **North Country Trail** (see separate entry **4955** in interstate section).

1065 **Old Evansville Walking Tour**, Evansville, IN 47708, (812) 425-8147. (GFA)

1066 **The Old Overdorf Lake**, Main St., Acadia, IN 46030, (317) 984-5955. (WCD)

Old Sauk Trail see entry 1029.

1067 **Ouabache Trail & Trek**, Pokagon-Kekionga Trails, Inc., P.O. Box 10353, Ft. Wayne, IN 46851, (219) 744-5444 or (219) 749-0152. 10.0 and 2.8 miles. Awards available. (AA 1992)

1068 **Oubache Trails County Park**, Fort

Knox Rd., Vincennes, IN 47591, (812) 882-4316. (WCD; ATI)

1069 **Owen-Putnam State Forest**, Fish Creek Rd., Spencer, IN 47460, (812) 829-2462. (WCD; ATI)

1070 **Oxbow Park**, US 33, Goshen, IL 46526, (219) 534-3541. (ATI; MGL)

1071 **Patoka Lake State Recreation Area**, SR 164, Wickliffe, IN 47116, (812) 685-2464. (WCD; ATI)

1072 **Pike State Forest**, SR 364, Winslow, IN 47598, (812) 789-5251. (WCD; ATI)

1073 **Pit Lake Trek**, Pokagon-Kekionga Trails, Inc., P.O. Box 10353, Ft. Wayne, IN 46851, (219) 744-5444 or (219) 749-0152. 5.0 miles. Awards available. (AA 1994)

1074 **Pokagon State Park**, SR 127, Rt. 2, Box 29C, Angola, IN 46703, (219) 833-2012. Named trails: Potawatomi State Nature Preserve. (WCD; ATI; MGL; IBP)

1075 **Pokagon Trail & Trek**, Pokagon-Kekionga Trails, Inc., P.O. Box 10353, Ft. Wayne, IN 46851, (219) 744-5444 or (219) 749-0152. 8.0 and 3.5 miles. Awards available. (AA 1994)

1076 **Possum Trot Vineyards**, 8310 N. Possum Trot Rd., Nashville, IN 47448, (812) 988-2694. (MGL)

1077 **Potato Creek State Park**, SR 4, Lakeville, IN 46536, (219) 656-8186. (WCD; ATI; MGL)

Potawatomi State Nature Preserve Trail *see* entry 1074.

1078 **Potawatomi Trail Hike**, Calumet Council, BSA, 8751 Calumet Ave., Munster, IN 46321. 10.0 miles. Awards available. (HTA)

1079 **Pow Wow Ridge Kampground**, Smyrna Rd., Richmond, IN 47374, (317) 962-1487. (WCD)

1080 **Prairie-Duneland Trail**, Carl Fisher, Superintendent, Portage Parks and Recreation Department, 2100 Willowcreek Rd., Portage, IN 46368, (219) 762-1675. 6.0 miles straight planned, current as to 1.5 miles. (GRT)

1081 **Raccoon State Recreation Area**, US 36, Rockville, IN 47872, (317) 344-1412. (WCD)

1082 **Redbrush Park**, SR 258, Seymour, IN 47274, (812) 497-2480. (WCD)

Resource Trail *see* entry 989.

1083 **Riddle Point City Park**, Tunnel Rd., Bedford, IN 47421, (812) 332-5220. (WCD)

1084 **Riley Trail**, Randall Shepherd, c/o Hancock County Historical Society, 7859 E. 200S, P.O. Box 375, Greenfield, IN 46140. 12.0 miles. Awards available. (AA 1992)

1085 **Riley Trail**, Indianapolis City Information Center, Pan American Plaza, Capitol Ave., Indianapolis, IN 46204. 20.0 miles. (AA 1989)

1086 **River City Campground & Music Park**, River Rd., South Whitley, IN 46787, (219) 723-4444. (WCD)

1087 **Rolling Timbers**, SR 2, Rolling Prairie, IN 46371, (219) 778-2498. (WCD)

1088 **St. Patrick's Park**, US 31, South Bend, IN 46614, (219) 277-4828. (MGL)

1089 **Salamonie State Lake**, Manager, Salamonie Reservoir, Rt. 7, Box 99, Huntington, IN 46750, (219) 468-2125. (WCD; ATI; MGL; LRA)

1090 **Salamonie Trail**, Pokagon-Kekionga Trails, Inc., P.O. Box 10353, Ft. Wayne, IN 46851, (219) 744-5444 or (219) 749-0152. 8.0 miles. Awards available. (AA 1994)

1091 **Sand Creek Campground**, 1000 N. 350 E., Chesterton, IN 46304, (219) 926-7482. (WCD)

1092 **Shades State Park**, SR 234, Waveland, IN 47989, (317) 435-2810. 15.0 miles. (WCD; ATI; MGL; OTB)

1093 **Shakamak State Park**, SR 48, Jasonville, IN 47438, (812) 665-2158. (WCD; MGL)

1094 **Soldiers Memorial Park**, La Porte, IN 46350. (ATI)

1095 **South Harrison Park**, SR 11, Elizabeth, IN 47117. (ATI)

1096 **Spring Mill State Park**, P.O. Box 376, SR 60, Mitchell, IN 47446, (812) 849-4129. (WCD; ATI; MGL; IBP)

1097 **Starve Hollow Lake State Forest**, CR 250, Vallonia, IN 47281, (812) 358-3464. (WCD; ATI)

1098 **Sullivan County Park**, Foley St., Sullivan, IN 47882, (812) 268-5537. (WCD)

1099 **Summit Lake State Park**, Messick Rd., New Castle, IN 47362, (317) 766-5873. (WCD; ATI)
1100 **T.C. Steele State Historic Site**, T.C. Steele Rd., Belmont, IN 47448, (812) 998-2785. (ATI; MGL; GFA)
  Tank Spring Trail see entry 1049.
1101 **Ten O'Clock Line Trail**, Trail Headquarters, Bear Wallow Hill, Rt. 4, Box 88, Nashville, IN 47448-9451, (812) 988-2636. 16.0 miles. Awards available. (AA 1993)
1102 **Thrasher's Woods**, SR 16, Monon, IN 47959, (219) 253-8224. (WCD)
1103 **Tippicanoe Battlefield Scenic Trail**, Tippicanoe Battlefield State Memorial, P.O. Box 1811, Battle Ground, IN 47920, (317) 463-1600 or (317) 567-2147. (ATI; IBP)
1104 **Tippicanoe River State Park**, US 35, Winamac, IN 46996, (219) 946-3213. (WCD; ATI; MGL; OTB)
  Touchstone Trail see entry 1042.
  Trail of Twelve Stones see entry 1045.
1105 **Tulip Tree Trace**, Trail Headquarters, Bear Wallow Hill, Rt. 4, Box 88, Nashville, IN 47448-9451. 18.0 miles. Awards available. (AA 1993)
1106 **Turkey Run State Park**, SR 47, Marshall, IN 47859, (317) 597-2635. (WCD; ATI; MGL)
1107 **Twin Mills Camping Resort**, 1675 W. SR 120, Howe, IN 46746, (219) 562-3212. (WCD)
  Two Lakes Trail see entry 1024.
1108 **Versailles State Park**, US 50, Versailles, IN 47042, (812) 689-6424. (WCD; ATI)
1109 **Wabash Heritage Trail**, P.O. Box 366, Battle Ground, IN 47920, (317) 567-2147. 6.5 miles. Awards available. (AA 1994)
1110 **Washington Park**, Franklin St., Michigan City, IN 46360, (219) 873-1506. (ATI)
1111 **Wawasee Lake Park**, SR 13, Fort Wayne, IN 46802. (ATI)
  Wayne Trace Segment see entry 971.
1112 **Wesselman Park**, 551 N. Boeke Rd., Evansville, IN 47711, (812) 479-0771. (ATI; IBP)
1113 **Westwood Park**, CR 275W, New Castle, IN 47362, (317) 987-1232. (WCD; ATI)
  White Oak Nature Trail see entry 989.
1114 **Whitewater Canal State Historic Site**, US 52, Metamora, IN 47030, (317) 647-6512. (ATI; MGL)
1115 **Whitewater Canal Trail**, Mike Martin, Streams and Trails Specialist, Indiana Department of Natural Resources, 402 W. Washington, Rm. 271, Indianapolis, IN 46204, (317) 232-4070. 8.0 miles straight planned, current as to 2.0 miles. (GRT)
1116 **Whitewater Canal Trail**, Trail Headquarters, Bear Wallow Hill, Rt. 4, Box 88, Nashville, IN 47448-9451, (812) 988-2636. 11.7 miles loop. Awards available. (AA 1993)
1117 **Whitewater Memorial State Park**, SR 101, Liberty, IN 47353, (317) 458-5565. (WCD; MGL)
1118 **Willow Slough State Fish & Wildlife Area**, CR 275S, Morocco, IN 47362, (317) 285-2704. (WCD)
1119 **Wyandotte Cave Walk**, Wyandotte Caves, Rt. 1, Box 60A, Leavenworth, IN 47137, (812) 738-2782. 1.5 miles. (IBP)
1120 **Wyandotte Trail**, 641 Rawlings St., Louisville, KY 40217. 14.3 miles. Awards available. (HTA)
1121 **Wyandotte Woods State Forest**, SR 462, Corydon, IN 47112, (812) 738-8232. (WCD)
1122 **Yellowwood State Forest**, SR 46, Pierceton, IN 46562, (219) 594-2124. (WCD; ATI; MGL)
1123 **Yellowwood Trail**, Trail Headquarters, Bear Wallow Hill, Rt. 4, Box 88, Nashville, IN 47448-9451, (812) 988-2636. 11.5-20.2 miles. Awards available. (WCD; ATI; MGL)
1124 **Yogi Bear's Jellystone Park Camp-Resort**, Rt. 1, Pierceton, IN 46562, (219) 594-2124. (WCD)

Generally:
Indiana Department of Natural Resources, Division of State Parks, 616 State Office Bldg., Indianapolis, IN 46204, (317) 232-4124. (EGH)

INDIANA

Indiana Department of Natural Resources, 402 W. Washington, Rm. 271, Indianapolis, IN 46204, (317) 232-4070. (GRT)

U.S. Army Corps of Engineers, North Central District, 536 Clark St., Chicago, IL 60605. (GFC)

Index (by city)

Acadia: The Old Overdorf Lake 1066
Albion: Chain O'Lakes State Park 986
Anderson: Mounds State Park 1061
Angola: Menefee's Camp Sack-In 1054; Pokagon State Park 1074; Pokagon Trail and Trek 1075
Attica: Indian Head Lake & Campground 1028
Auburn: Auburn to Waterloo Bike Trail 972
Aurora: Laughery Creek Trail 1041
Battle Ground: Tippicanoe Battlefield State Memorial 1103; Wabash Heritage Trail 1109
Bedford: Free Spirit Campground 1010; Hoosier National Forest 1024; Monroe Lake State Recreation Area 1059; Riddle Point City Park 1083
Belmont: T.C. Steele State Historic Site 1100
Bloomington: Bloomington Rail Trail 976; Lake Lemon Park 1039
Bluffton: Ouabache Trail and Trek 1067
Bristol: Bonneyville Mill Park 977
Brookville: Brookville State Lake 978
Brownstown: Jackson-Washington State Forest 1031
Bruceville: Camp Arthur 981
Chesterton: Sand Creek Campground 1091
Cloverdale: Lieber State Recreation Area 1044
Columbus: KOA-Columbus 1037
Connersville: Mary Gray Bird Sanctuary 1050
Corydon: Harrison-Crawford State Forest 1015; Hayswood Nature Reserve 1018; Wyandotte Woods State Forest 1121
Dale: Lincoln State Park 1047
Dugger: Greene-Sullivan State Forest 1012
Dupont: Camp Louis Ernst 984
Elizabeth: South Harrison Park 1095
Evansville: Angel Mounds State Historic Site 970; Muskhogen Trail 1063; Old Evansville Walking Tour 1065; Wesselman Park 1112
Fairmount: Hidden Lake Campground 1022
Ferdinand: Ferdinand State Forest 1003
Ft. Wayne: Anthony Wayne Trail 971; Chain O'Lakes Trail 987; Chief Little Turtle Trail 988; Deer Hollow Trek 995; Foster Park Trail 1006; Franke Park Trek 1009; Johnny Appleseed Trek 1033; Kekionga Trail 1034; Mastodon Trek 1051; Pit Lake Trek 1073; Wawasee Lake Park 1111
Goshen: Merry Lea Environmental Learning Center 1055; Oxbow Park 1070
Hamburg: Dream Lake State Forest Recreation Area 999
Hammond: Erie Trail Linear Park 1002
Henryville: Clark State Forest Trail 989
Howe: Twin Mills Camping Resort 1107
Huntington: Huntington Reservoir 1026; Kil-So-Quah Trail 1035; Salamonie State Lake 1089
Huron: Hindostan Falls Trail 1023
Indianapolis: Al White Trail 968; Delaware Lake Campground 996; Eagle Creek Park 1000; Riley Trail 1085; Whitewater Canal Trail 1115
Jasonville: Shakamak State Park 1093
Kendallville: Bixler Lake City Park 975; Gordon's Camping 1011
Kingsbury: Kingsbury Fish & Wildlife Area 1036
Knox: Hickory Hills Campground 1020
Kouts: Donna Jo Recreation Area 998
La Porte: Soldiers Memorial Park 1094
Lafayette: Camp Cary 983; Clegg Botanical Garden 991
LaGro: Salamonie Trail 1090
Lakeville: Potato Creek State Park 1077
Larwill: Crossland Scout Reservation 994
Laurel: Whitewater Canal Trail 1116
Leavenworth: Wyandotte Cave Walk 1119

Liberty: Whitewater Memorial State Park 1117
Lincoln City: Indiana Lincoln Trail 1030; Lincoln Boyhood National Monument 1045
Logansport: Cass County Park 985; Fowler County Park 1007; France Park 1008
Louisville, KY: Wyandotte Trail 1120
Madison: Clifty Falls State Park 992
Marengo: Marengo Cave Park 1048
Marion: Miami Indian Historical Site 1056
Marshall: Turkey Run State Park 1106
Martinsville: Morgan-Monroe State Forest 1060
Mauckport: Lickford Valley Family Campground 1043
Maxwell: Riley Trail 1084
Medaryville: Jasper-Pulaski State Forest 1032
Merrillville: Lemon Lake County Park 1042
Metamore: Whitewater Canal State Historic Site 1114
Michigan City: Washington Park 1110
Mitchell: Spring Mill State Park 1096
Monon: Thrasher's Woods 1102
Montezuma: Covered Bridge Trail 993
Monticello: Camp Buffalo 982
Morocco: Willow Slough State Fish & Wildlife Area 1118
Mt. Vernon: Hovey Lake State Fish & Wildlife Area 1025
Munster: American Heritage Trail 969; Brown County Bike Trail 979; Brown County State Park 980; Flags of the Nations Trail 1004; Possum Trot Vineyards 1076; Ten O'Clock Line Trail 1101; Tulip Tree Trace 1105; Yellowwood Trail 1123
New Castle: Summit Lake State Park 1099; Westwood Park 1113
New Harmony: Harmonie State Park 1014
Noblesville: Forest Park 1005
Norman: Maumee Scout Reservation 1052

Peru: Mississinewa State Lake 1057; Mississinewa Trail 1058
Pierceton: Yellowwood State Forest 1122; Yogi Bear's Jellystone Park Camp-Resort 1124
Portage: Prairie-Duneland Trail 1080
Porter: Indiana Dunes National Lakeshore 1029
Portland: Hickory Grove Lakes Campground 1019
Richmond: Hayes Regional Arboretum 1017; KOA-Richmond Kampground 1038; Pow Wow Ridge Kampground 1079
Rockville: Raccoon State Recreation Area 1081
Rolling Prairie: Rolling Timbers 1087
Santa Claus: Lincoln Boyhood Trail 1046
Scottsburg: Hardy State Lake 1013
Seymour: Muscatatuck National Wildlife Refuge 1062; Redbrush Park 1082
Shelburn: Larry L. Ayers Memorial Trail 1040
Shelbyville: Bears of Blue River Trail 973
Shoals: Martin State Forest 1049
South Bend: Bendix Woods Park 974; East Bank Trail 1001; St. Patrick's Park 1088
South Whitley: River City Campground & Music Park 1086
Spencer: Hickory Hills Campground 1021; McCormick's Creek State Park 1053; Owen-Putnam State Forest 1069
Sullivan: Sullivan County Park 1098
Terre Haute: Dobbs Park & Nature Center 997; Hawthorn County Park 1016
Vallonia: Starve Hollow Lake State Forest 1097
Versailles: Versailles State Park 1108
Vincennes: Clark's Advance Trail 990; Oubache Trails County Park 1068
Waveland: Shades State Park 1092
Wickliffe: Patoka Lake State Recreation Area 1071
Winamac: Tippicanoe River State Park 1104
Winslow: Pike State Forest 1072

Kentucky

1125 **Abraham Lincoln Birthplace National Historic Site**, Rt. 1, Hodgenville, KY 42748, (502) 358-3874. (NPV; NPE; OTB; CGA)
    Anchor Trek *see* entry 1151.
    Angel Windows Trail *see* entry 1156.
    Artillery Trail *see* entry 1194.
    Audubon Trail *see* entry 1174.
    Auxier Branch Trail *see* entry 1156.
    Auxier Ridge Trail *see* entry 1156.
    Back Country Trail *see* entry 1174.
1126 **Bailey's Point Campground**, Corps of Engineers—Barren River Lake, SR 517, Scottsville, KY 42164, (602) 622-6959. (WCD)
    Baker Hollow Trail *see* entry 1132.
1127 **Ballard County Wildlife Management Area**, US 51/60/62, Wickliffe, KY 42087, (502) 224-2244. (MSE)
    Bark Camp Creek Trail *see* entry 1156.
    Barkley Trail *see* entry 1194.
1128 **Barren River Lake State Resort Park**, US 31E, Glasgow, KY 42141, (502) 646-2151. (WCD; ATK; MSE)
    Barton (West Pinnacle) Trail *see* entry 1132.
    Basin Mountain Trail *see* entry 1132.
    Beaver Creek Loop Trail *see* entry 1156.
1129 **Beaver Creek Wilderness**, US 27, Somerset, KY 42501, (606) 679-2010. (MSE)
    Becky Branch Trail *see* entry 1156.
    Bee Rock Nature Trail *see* entry 1156.
1130 **Beech Bend Park**, Beech Bend Park Rd., Bowling Green, KY 42101. (ATK)
1131 **Ben Hawes State Park**, US 60, Owensboro, KY 42301, (502) 684-9808. (MSE)

    Bent Twig Nature Trail *see* entry 1133.
1132 **Berea College Forest**, Office of the Business Vice-President, College P.O. Box 3204, Berea College, Berea, KY 40404, (606) 986-9341 or (606) 986-4336. 19.2 miles. Named trails: Baker Hollow 4.3, Barton (West Pinnacle) 1.0, Basin Mountain 2.8, Boy Scout (Robe Mountain) 2.4, Buzzard Roost 0.6, Chestnut Hollow 0.4, Eagles Nest, East Pinnacle 0.7, Fat Man's Misery 0.7, Indian Fort 2.2, Main Dome 1.4, Narrow Gap 1.2, Shadow 1.2. (GBD; GKO)
1133 **Bernheim Forest Arboretum and Nature Center**, SR 245, Clermont, KY 40110, (502) 543-2451. 23.5 miles. Named trails: Bent Twig Nature 1.0, Big Rock Horse, Double Cabin Hollow 4.0, Fern Valley 7.0, High Point 0.5, Iron Ore Hill 2.0, Jackson Overlook 2.0, Knob Top 0.5(l), Overalls Fork 3.0, Pauls Point Loop, Poplar Flats 0.75(l), Rocky Run 0.75(l), Sun and Shade 0.5, Tower 0.5. (ATK; MSE; GFA; OTB; GBD; GKO)
1134 **Big Bone Lick State Park**, SR 338, Walton, KY 41094, (606) 384-3522. Named trails: Big Bone Lick 1.0. (WCD; ATK; MSE; OTB)
    Big Bone Lick Trail *see* entry 1134.
    Big Everidge Trail *see* entry 1198.
    Big Limestone Trail *see* entry 1156.
    Big Rock Horse Trail *see* entry 1133.
    Big Spring Trail *see* entry 1205.
    Black Oak Loop Trail *see* entry 1194.
1135 **Blue Licks Battlefield State Park**, Blue Lick Springs, KY 40311. (ATK)
    Blue Trail *see* entry 1145.
    Blue Trail *see* entry 1217.
    Blue-Gray Trail *see* entry 1194.

KENTUCKY

Bluff Campsite Spur Trail see entry 1150.
Boone's Trace see entry 1197.
Boswell Trail see entry 1194.
Boy Scout (Robe Mountain) Trail see entry 1132.
Boy Scout Trail see entry 1194.
1136 **Breaks Interstate Park**, P.O. Box 100, Breaks, VA 24607, (703) 865-4413. 10.0 miles. Named trails: Center Creek, Chestnut Ridge, Cold Spring, Geological, Grassy, Grassy Overlook, Laurel Branch, Loop, Nature, Overlook, Prospector's, Ridge, River, Towers. (ATK; MSE; GBD; GKO)
Buck Branch Trail see entry 1156.
Buck Trail see entry 1156.
1137 **Buckhorn Lake State Resort Park**, SR 15/28, Hazard, KY 41701, (606) 398-7510. 2.0 miles. Named trails: Leatherwood, Moonshiner's Hollow. (MSE; OTB; GBD)
Buckingham Hollow Trail see entry 1194.
1138 **Buena Vista Trail**, Audubon Council, BSA, P.O. Box 280, 330 Allen St., Owensboro, KY 42302; or John James Audubon State Park, Henderson, KY 42420, (502) 826-2247. 9.0 miles loop. Awards available. (AA 1992)
Buffalo Canyon Trail see entry 1156.
1139 **Buffalo Trace Trail**, Scioto Area Council, BSA, P.O. Box 1305, 612 Masonic Bldg., Portsmouth, OH 45662. 28.0 miles. Awards available. (AA 1993)
1140 **Buffalo Trail**, Wah-La-Ha—Buffalo Trail, Inc., 420 Ewing St., Frankfort, KY 40601. 5.5 miles straight. Awards available. (AA 1992)
Buzzard Roost Trail see entry 1132.
1141 **Cadiz Railroad Trail**, Stan White, Cadiz Railroad Trail Committee, P.O. Drawer B, Cadiz, KY 42211, (502) 522-8483. 1.5 miles straight. (GRT)
Camp Energy Trail see entry 1194.
1142 **Camp Wildcat Hollow**, Audubon Council, BSA, P.O. Box 280, Owensboro, KY 42302, (502) 684-9272; or Camp Wildcat Hollow, Rt. 4, Russellville, KY 42301, (502) 726-9546. (SFC)
Canal Loop Trail see entry 1194.

1143 **Canal Recreation Area**, Corps of Engineers—Lake Barkley, The Trace, Grand Rivers, KY 42045, (502) 362-4840. (WCD)
Cane Creek Trail see entry 1156.
1144 **Capitol View Trail**, 512 Mohegan Tr., Frankfort, KY 40601, (502) 695-1098. 15.0 miles straight. Awards available. (AA 1992)
Cardinal Trail see entry 1174.
Carrington Rock Trail see entry 1156.
1145 **Carter Caves State Resort Park**, SR 182, Olive Hill, KY 41164, (606) 286-4411. 7.75 miles. Named trails: Blue, Green, Natural Bridge, Red, Yellow. (WCD; ATK; GBD)
Cave Island Nature Trail see entry 1205.
1146 **Cave Run Lake**, Morehead Ranger District, P.O. Box 10, Rodburn Hollow, Morehead, KY 40351, (606) 784-5624. (MSE)
Cave Run Trail see entry 1156.
1147 **Caveland Trail**, So-Ky Trails, Inc., P.O. Box 404, Bowling Green, KY 42101-0404. 10.0 miles loop. (AA 1992)
Cedar Bluffs Trail see entry 1194.
Cedar Cliffs Trail see entry 1156.
1148 **Cedar Hills Campground**, P.O. Box 305, Park City, KY 42160, (502) 749-2891. (WCD)
Center Creek Trail see entry 1136.
Center Furnace Trail see entry 1194.
Chadwell Gap Trail see entry 1155.
Chained Rock Trail see entry 1222.
Chalk Bluff Trail see entry 1151.
Chestnut Hollow Trail see entry 1132.
Chestnut Loop Trail see entry 1194.
Chestnut Ridge Trail see entry 1136.
Chimney Top Rock Overlook Trail see entry 1156.
Cliffside Trail see entry 1156.
1149 **Clyde E. Buckley Wildlife Sanctuary**, Rt. 3, Frankfort, KY 40601, (606) 873-5711. 4.0 miles. Named trails: White. (GBD; GKO)
Cold Spring Trail see entry 1136.
Collie Ridge Campsite Spur Trail see entry 1150.

KENTUCKY

1150 **Collie Ridge Composite Trail**, So-Ky Trails, Inc., P.O. Box 404, Bowling Green, KY 42101-0404. 11.9 miles loop. Includes following trails: Bluff Campsite Spur, Collie Ridge Campsite Spur, Good Spring Church, Jaggers Cemetery, Liberty School, Turnhole Ridge Horseback Spur, Waterfall Campsite Spur, Wet Prong, Wildcat Hollow. Awards available. (AA 1992)
    Collie Ridge Trail *see* entry 1205.

1151 **Columbus-Belmont Battlefield State Park**, SR 58, Columbus, KY 42032, (502) 677-2327. 11.5 miles. Named trails: Anchor Trek 3.5, Chalk Bluff 8.0. (ATK; MSE; GBD)

1152 **Conley Bottom Resort**, Conley Bottom Rd., Monticello, KY 42633, (606) 348-6351. (WCD)
    Connecting Trail *see* entry 1194.
    Connecting Trail *see* entry 1205.
    Cottage Meadow Trail *see* entry 1190.
    Courthouse Rock Trail *see* entry 1156.

1153 **Cradle of Forestry in America Interpretive Trails**, National Scenic Byway, Salt Lick, KY 40371, (606) 784-7788. (WCD)
    Cross Trail *see* entry 1194.
    Cross-Over Trail *see* entry 1156.

1154 **Cumberland Falls State Resort Park**, SR 90, Corbin, KY 40701, (606) 528-4121 or (800) 325-0063. 15.0 miles. (ATK; MSE; GKO)

1155 **Cumberland Gap National Historical Park**, P.O. Box 1848, Middlesboro, KY 40965, (606) 248-2817. 50.0 miles. Named trails: Chadwell Gap 2.3, Ewing 3.9, Gibson Gap 5.0(s), Green Leaf Nature 0.75, Hemlock Nature 0.2, Honey Spur Tree Nature 1.1, Lewis Hollow a/k/a Skylight Cave 1.68(s), Little Yellow Creek 1.6, Mischa Mokwa 22.0, Ridge 16.0(s), Sugar Run 2.25, Sugar Run Nature 0.3, Tri-State 3.5, Wilderness Road 0.5, Woodson Gap 3.0(s). (EGH; PGF; WCD; ATK; GFC; GNM; MSE; NPE; OTB; CGA; WPS; YNP; GBD; ANP; IFT)
    Daniel Boone Hut Trail *see* entry 1156.

1156 **Daniel Boone National Forest**, 100 Vaught Rd., Winchester, KY 40391, (606) 745-3100; or Stanton Ranger District, SR 15, Stanton, KY 40380, (606) 663-2852; or Berea Ranger District, Berea, KY 40403, (606) 986-8434; or Somerset Ranger District, Rt. 2, Box 507, Somerset, KY 42501, (606) 679-2018; or London Ranger District, P.O. Box G, London, KY 40741, (606) 864-4163; or Stearns Ranger District, P.O. Box 459, Whitley City, KY 42653, (606) 376-5323; or Redbird Ranger District, P.O. Box 1, Big Creek, KY 40914, (606) 598-2192. 500 miles. Named trails: Angel Windows 0.3, Auxier Branch 0.8, Auxier Ridge 1.1, Bark Camp Creek 3.0, Beaver Creek Loop 0.2, Becky Branch 1.0, Bee Rock Nature 0.5, Big Limestone 6.0, Buck 1.5, Buck Branch 1.25, Buffalo Canyon 5.0, Cane Creek 2.0, Carrington Rock 2.5, Cave Run 5.0, Cedar Cliffs, Chimney Top Rock Overlook 0.2, Cliffside 2.5, Courthouse Rock 2.4, Cross-Over 1.5, Daniel Boone Hut 0.7, Dog Slaughter 4.0, Double Arch 1.0, Grays Arch 0.3, Gulf Bottom 1.2, Hidden Arch 1.0, Hog Pen 3.0, Hughes Fork 3.0, Koomer Ridge 5.3, Lakeside North 2.9, Lakeside South 6.0, Lakeside 2.0, Laurel Creek 2.5, Lick Creek 3.2, Mark Branch 2.4, Martins Branch 1.0, Moonbow 12.0, Natural Arch 1.2, Ned Branch 1.7, Parker Mountain 4.0, Peter Branch 1.7, Pinch-Em Tight 1.8, Princess Arch 0.2, Red River Gorge National Recreation 36.0, Redbird Crest 66.0, Renfro Creek 2.2, Roaring Rocks 0.2, Rock Bridge 1.3, Rockcastle Narrows 1.4, Rough 8.7, Rush Ridge 1.0, Scuttle Hole 1.1, Shawnee Nature, Silvermine Arch 1.0, Sky Bridge Loop 0.9, Skyline 0.4, Sugar Tree Hollow 1.7, Swift Camp Creek 6.7, Three Forks of Beaver Creek Overlook 1.0, Tower 0.4, Tunnel Ridge, Twin Branch 1.1, Whistling Arch 0.2, Whittleton Arch 0.2, Whittleton Branch 1.9, Wildcat 2.0, Winding Stair Gap 1.7, Yahoo Arch 1.8, Yahoo Falls 10.0, Yamacraw 6.0. (EGH; WCD; ATK; GFC; MSE; OTB; FGU; GBD; GKO; LRA; NFG)
    Dennison Ferry Trail *see* entry 1205.

Devil's Backbone Trail *see* entry 1194.
1157 **Dewey Lake**, Corps of Engineers, Louisville District, P.O. Box 59, Louisville, KY 40201; or Jenny Wiley State Resort Park, Prestonburg, KY 41653. (GFC; LRA)
Dog Slaughter Trail *see* entry 1156.
Dogwood Loop Trail *see* entry 1194.
Double Arch Trail *see* entry 1156.
Double Cabin Hollow Trail *see* entry 1133.
Dry Canteen Trail *see* entry 1221.
Dug Road March *see* entry 1221.
1158 **Eagle Valley Camping Resort**, SR 36, Sanders, KY 41083, (502) 347-9361. (WCD)
Eagles Nest Trail *see* entry 1132.
East Pinnacle Trail *see* entry 1132.
Echo River Trail *see* entry 1205.
Ewing Trail *see* entry 1155.
Fat Man's Misery Trail *see* entry 1132.
Fern Garden Trail *see* entry 1222.
1159 **Fern Lake Campground**, SR 305, Paducah, KY 42003, (502) 444-7939. (WCD)
Fern Valley Trail *see* entry 1133.
First Creek Lake Trail *see* entry 1205.
1160 **Fishtrap Lake**, Corps of Engineers, Louisville District, P.O. Box 59, Louisville, KY 40201. (ATK; GFC)
Fort Henry Trail System *see* entry 1194.
Fraziers Knob Trail *see* entry 1197.
Frozen Niagara Tour *see* entry 1205.
1161 **Gays Creek Campground**, Corps of Engineers—Buckhorn Lake, SR 1833, Buckhorn, KY 41721, (606) 398-7496. (WCD)
1162 **General Butler State Resort Park**, SR 227, Carrollton, KY 41008, (502) 732-4384. (WCD; ATK; MSE)
Geological Trail *see* entry 1136.
Gibson Gap Trail *see* entry 1155.
Good Spring Church Trail *see* entry 1150.
Good Spring Loop Trail *see* entry 1205.
Grassy Overlook Trail *see* entry 1136.

Grassy Trail *see* entry 1136.
Grays Arch Trail *see* entry 1156.
1163 **Grayson Lake**, Corps of Engineers, SR 7, Grayson, KY 41143. (ATK)
Green Leaf Nature Trail *see* entry 1155.
Green River Bluffs Trail *see* entry 1205.
1164 **Green River Lake**, SR 55, Campbellsville, KY 42718. (ATK)
Green Trail *see* entry 1145.
1165 **Greenbo Lake State Resort Park**, HC 60, Box 562, Greenup, KY 41144, (606) 473-7324. (ATK; MSE; TOV)
Gulf Bottom Trail *see* entry 1156.
Half-Day Tour *see* entry 1205.
Hematite Trail *see* entry 1194.
Hemlock Garden Trail *see* entry 1222.
Hemlock Nature Trail *see* entry 1155.
Heritage Trail *see* entry 1205.
Hidden Arch Trail *see* entry 1156.
High Point Trail *see* entry 1133.
High Trail *see* entry 1194.
Hillman Heritage National Recreation Trail *see* entry 1194.
Hillman Trail *see* entry 1194.
Historic Tour *see* entry 1205.
Hog Pen Trail *see* entry 1156.
1166 **Holiday Campground**, SR 90, Corbin, KY 40701, (606) 376-2732. (WCD)
1167 **Holiday Hills Campground**, Rt. 1, Box 406, SR 93S, Eddyville, KY 42038, (502) 388-7236. (WCD)
1168 **Holmes Bend Recreation Area**, Corps of Engineers—Green River Lake, Holmes Bend Rd., Campbellsville, KY 42718, (502) 384-4623. (WCD)
1169 **Holt's Campground & Fishing Lake**, 2351 Templin Ave., Bardstown, KY 40004, (502) 348-6717. (WCD)
Honey Spur Tree Nature Trail *see* entry 1155.
Honeymoon Falls Trail *see* entry 1222.
Honker Trail *see* entry 1194.
1170 **Horine Memorial Trail**, Zit-Kala-Sha Hiking Trails, P.O. Box 14102, Louisville, KY 40214, (502) 361-2624; or P.O. Box 1924, Louisville, KY 40201.

KENTUCKY

10.7 miles. Awards available. (NHT; HTA)

Hughes Fork Trail *see* entry 1156.

Indian Fort Trail *see* entry 1132.

Interstate Trail *see* entry 1194.

1171 **Iron Furnace Trail**, Rt. 5, Box 496A, Irvine, KY 40336. (NHT)

Iron Ore Hill Trail *see* entry 1133.

Jackson Overlook Trail *see* entry 1133.

Jaggers Cemetery Trail *see* entry 1150.

1172 **Jefferson Forest Loop Trail**, Wilderness Jefferson Co., 117 Freeman Ave., Louisville, KY 40214. 5.0-10.0 miles. Awards available. (HTA)

Jenny Wiley Trail *see* entry 1173.

1173 **Jenny Wiley Trails**, Jenny Wiley Trail Conference, c/o Brian Mattingly, Trail Director, P.O. Box 636, Catlettsburg, KY 41129, (606) 739-5191; or Kentucky Department of Parks, 12th Floor, Capital Plaza Tower, Frankfort, KY 40601, (502) 564-5410. Named trails: Jenny Wiley 180, Lozier, Michael Tygart 24.0, Simon Kenton 9.0. (EGH; ATK; TOV; GBD)

1174 **John James Audubon State Park**, P.O. Box 576, US 41N, Henderson, KY 42420, (502) 826-2247. 15.75 miles. Named trails: Audubon, Back Country, Cardinal, Kentucky Coffee Tree, King Benson 2,000', Lake Overlooks, Museum 1,200'(l), Wilderness Lake 1.75(l), Woodpecker. (WCD; ATK; MSE; OTB; GBD; GKO)

1175 **Kendall Recreation Area**, US 127, Jamestown, KY 42629, (606) 679-6337. (WCD)

Kentucky Coffee Tree Trail *see* entry 1174.

1176 **Kentucky Dam Village State Resort Park**, US 62/641, Gilbertsville, KY 42044, (502) 362-4271. (ATK; MSE)

1177 **Kentucky Foothills Travel Ways**, Recreation, Tourism & Convention Commission, P.O. Box 66, Morehead, KY 40351. 6 loops 16.0-117 miles each. (HTA)

1178 **Kentucky Lincoln Trail**, Zit-Kala-Sha Hiking Trails, P.O. Box 14102, Louisville, KY 40214; or Old Kentucky Home Council, BSA, P.O. Box 36273, Louisville, KY 40233, (502) 361-2624. 33.0 miles. Awards available. (NHT; MVC; HTA)

1179 **Kentucky Zollicoffer Trail**, Bluegrass Council, BSA, 975 Liberty Rd., Lexington, KY 40505. Awards available. (MVC)

1180 **Kincaid Lake State Park**, US 27, Williamstown, KY 41097, (606) 654-3531. (ATK; MSE)

King Benson Trail *see* entry 1174.

Knob Top Trail *see* entry 1133.

1181 **KOA-Bowling Green**, SR 884, Bowling Green, KY 42101, (502) 843-1919. (WCD)

1182 **KOA-Cincinnati South**, US 25, Crittenden, KY 41010, (606) 428-2000. (WCD)

1183 **KOA-Green River Lake**, SR 55, Campbellsville, KY 42718, (502) 465-3916. (WCD)

1184 **KOA-Horse Cave**, SR 218, Horse Cave, KY 42749, (502) 786-2819. (WCD)

1185 **KOA-Indian Hills**, 1440 SR 1383, Russell Springs, KY 42642, (502) 866-5616. (WCD)

1186 **KOA-KY Lakes/Paducah**, US 62, Calvert City, KY 42029, (502) 395-5841. (WCD)

1187 **KOA-Laurel River**, Rt. 11, Box 241, Corbin, KY 40701, (606) 528-1534. (WCD)

1188 **KOA-Louisville South**, 2433 SR 44E, Shepherdsville, KY 40165, (502) 543-2041. (WCD)

1189 **KOA-Renfro Valley**, SR 25, Renfro Valley, KY 40473, (606) 256-2474. (WCD)

Koomer Ridge Trail *see* entry 1156.

1190 **Lake Barkley State Resort Park**, SR 1489, Cadiz, KY 42211, (502) 924-1131. 6.0 miles. Named trails: Cottage Meadow 0.5, Lena Madesin Phillips 0.75(l), Wagon Wheel 0.2, Wilderness 2.0(l). (WCD; ATK; MSE; GBD; LRA)

1191 **Lake Cumberland State Resort Park**, US 127, Jamestown, KY 42629, (502) 343-3111; or Corps of Engineers, Louisville District, P.O. Box 59, Louisville, KY 40201. 4.0 miles. Named trails: Pumpkin Creek Nature. (WCD; ATK; GFC; MSE; CTD; GBD)

KENTUCKY

1192 **Lake Malone State Park,** SR 973, Dunmore, KY 42339, (502) 657-2111. (MSE)
   Lake Overlooks Trail *see* entry 1174.
1193 **Lake Shelby Park,** Burks Branch Rd., Shelbyville, KY 40065. (ATK)
   Lakeside North Trail *see* entry 1156.
   Lakeside South Trail *see* entry 1156.
   Lakeside Trail *see* entry 1156.
1194 **Land Between the Lakes,** Golden Pond, KY 42231, (502) 924-5602. 125 miles. Named trails: Artillery, Barkley, Black Oak Loop, Blue-Gray 1.0, Boswell, Boy Scout 6.0, Buckingham Hollow, Camp Energy 12.0, Canal Loop 14.2, Cedar Bluffs 1,500', Center Furnace 0.3, Chestnut Loop, Connecting, Cross, Devil's Backbone, Dogwood Loop, Fort Henry System 26.0, Hematite 2.75, High, Hillman 4.0, Hillman Heritage National Recreation, Honker 2.25(s), Interstate 6.5(l), Long Creek National Recreation 0.25, Low, Motor Resource Tour, North-South 14.0, Paw Paw Path 1,500', Peripheral, Peytona, Picket Loop, Piney Hike 'n Bike 2.75, Rushing Creek 8.0, Short Leaf Pine, Songbird Walk, Telegraph, Trail of These Hills 1.25, Woodland Walk 0.75(l). (AA 1992)
1195 **Land Between the Lakes Trail,** Four Rivers Council, BSA, P.O. Box 7033, Paducah, KY 42001-7033. 16.0 miles. Awards available. (MVC; HTA)
   Lantern Tour *see* entry 1205.
   Laurel Branch Trail *see* entry 1136.
   Laurel Cove Trail *see* entry 1222.
   Laurel Creek Trail *see* entry 1156.
1196 **Laurel River Lake,** Corps of Engineers, Resource Manager, 1433 Laurel Lake Rd., London, KY 40741, (606) 864-6412. (MSE)
   Leatherwood Trail *see* entry 1137.
   Lena Madesin Phillips Trail *see* entry 1190.
1197 **Levi Jackson Wilderness Road State Park,** US 25, London, KY 40741, (606) 864-5108. 9.0 miles. Named trails: Boone's Trace 3.0, Fraziers Knob 6.0, Wilderness Road 3.0. (WCD; ATK; MSE; GBD)
   Lewis Hollow Trail *see* entry 1155.
   Liberty School Trail *see* entry 1150.
   Lick Creek Trail *see* entry 1156.
1198 **Lilley Cornett Woods,** P.O. Box 78, Skyline, KY 41851, (606) 633-5828. 6.0 miles. Named trails: Big Everidge 4.0, Shop Hollow 2.0. (GBD; GKO)
1199 **Lincoln Memorial Trail,** Zit-Kala-Sha Hiking Trails, P.O. Box 14102, Louisville, KY 40214. 14.0 miles. Awards available. (NHT; HTA)
1200 **Little Shepherd Trail,** Little Shepherd Arts and Crafts Corporation, P.O. Box 806, Whitesburg, KY 41858, (606) 633-7503. 46.0 miles straight. (ATK; GBD)
   Little Yellow Creek Trail *see* entry 1155.
   Living Stairway Trail *see* entry 1222.
1201 **Lloyd Wildlife Management Area,** Gardnersville Rd., Williamstown, KY 41097, (606) 428-2262. (MSE)
   Long Creek National Recreation Trail *see* entry 1194.
1202 **Long Hunter's Trek,** Trail Blazers-BSA, P.O. Box 43059, Middletown, KY 40243. 13.1 miles. Awards available. (HTA)
   Loop Trail *see* entry 1136.
   Lost Trail *see* entry 1222.
1203 **Louisville Heritage Trail,** Metro Kiwanis Club, 310 W. Kentucky, Suite 715, Louisville, KY 40202. 10.0-12.0 miles. Awards available. (HTA)
   Low Trail *see* entry 1194.
   Lozier Trail *see* entry 1173.
   Main Dome Trail *see* entry 1132.
1204 **Mammoth Cave Jellystone Park Camp Resort,** 1002 Mammoth Cave Rd., Cave City, KY 42127, (502) 773-3840. (WCD)
1205 **Mammoth Cave National Park,** Mammoth Cave, KY 42259, (502) 758-2328. Named surface trails: Big Spring 1.0, Cave Island Nature 0.9, Collie Ridge 5.0, Connecting, Dennison Ferry 3.5, Echo River 2.25, First Creek Lake 2.3, Good Spring Loop 7.7, Green River Bluffs 0.9, Heritage, Sunset Point 0.25, Turnhole Ridge 3.2, West Prong of the Buffalo 3.0. Named underground trails: Frozen Niagara Tour 0.5 mile, 1.5 hrs.,

KENTUCKY

Half-Day Tour 4.0 miles, 4.5 hrs., Historic Tour 2.0 miles, 2.0 hrs., Lantern Tour 3.0 miles, 3.0 hrs., Physically Handicapped Tour, Wild Cave Tour 5.0 miles, 6.0 hrs. (LGU; EGH; WCD; ATK; FFV; MSE; GNP; NPV; NPE; OTB; AGW; CGA; GBD; GKO)

1206 **Mammoth Cave Trail**, So-Ky Trails, Inc., P.O. Box 404, Bowling Green, KY 42101-0404. 13.0 miles. (AA 1992)

Mark Branch Trail see entry 1156.

Martins Branch Trail see entry 1156.

1207 **Massacre Trail**, Historic Middletown, Inc., P.O. Box 43013, Middletown, KY 40253-0013; or Bill Hockensmith, 11104 Finchley Rd., Louisville, KY 40243. 12.0 miles. Awards available. (AA 1992)

Michael Tygart Trail see entry 1173.

1208 **Mill Springs State Park**, SR 90, Monticello, IL 61856. (OTB)

1209 **Mischa-Mokwa Adventure Trail**, Bluegrass Council, BSA, 975 Liberty Rd., Lexington, KY 40505, (606) 231-7811. 21.0 miles. Awards available. (NHT; MVC; HTA)

Mischa Mokwa Trail see entry 1155.

Moonbow Trail see entry 1156.

Moonshiner's Hollow Trail see entry 1137.

Motor Resource Tour see entry 1194.

1210 **Moutardier Area**, Corps of Engineers—Nolin River Lake, SR 259, Leitchfield, KY 42754, (502) 286-4230. (WCD)

1211 **Munfordville Battlefield Trek**, P.O. Box 636, Munfordville, KY 42765. 6.0-10.0 miles. Awards available. (HTA)

Museum Trail see entry 1174.

1212 **My Old Kentucky Home State Park**, US 150, Bardstown, KY 40004, (502) 348-3502. (ATK)

Narrow Gap Trail see entry 1132.

Natural Arch Trail see entry 1156.

1213 **Natural Bridge State Resort Park**, Mountain Pkwy., Slade, KY 40376, (606) 663-2214 or (800) 325-1710. 9.75 miles. (WCD; ATK; MSE; GBD; GKO)

Natural Bridge Trail see entry 1145.

Nature Trail see entry 1136.

Ned Branch Trail see entry 1156.

North-South Trail see entry 1194.

1214 **Oak Creek Campground**, P.O. Box 161, Walton, KY 41094, (606) 485-9131. (WCD)

1215 **Ohio County Park**, SR 69, Hartford, KY 42347, (502) 298-9761. (WCD)

1216 **Ohio River Trail**, Ohio River Trail Corporation, P.O. Box 567, Brandenburg, KY 40108. 14.0-20.4 miles. Awards available. (AA 1992)

1217 **Otter Creek City Park**, 850 Otter Creek Rd., Rt. 1, Vine Grove, KY 40175, (502) 583-3577. 9.7 miles. Named trails: Blue 4.5, Red 2.5(l), White 0.75, Yellow 2.0. (WCD; ATK; GBD)

Overalls Fork Trail see entry 1133.

Overlook Trail see entry 1136.

1218 **Ox Cart Trail**, 8929 Brown Austin Rd., Fairdale, KY 40118. 18.6 miles. Awards available. (MVC; HTA)

Parker Mountain Trail see entry 1156.

Pauls Point Loop Trail see entry 1133.

Paw Paw Path see entry 1194.

1219 **Pennyrile Forest State Resort Park**, SR 109, Madisonville, KY 42431, (502) 797-3421. (ATK; MSE; OTB; GKO)

Peripheral Trail see entry 1194.

1220 **Perryville Battlefield**, Perryville, KY 40468. (ATK)

1221 **Perryville Pilgrimage Trek**, Donnie Leonard, Rt. 1, Box 54B, Perryville, KY 40468. Named trails: Dry Canteen 15.0, Dug Road March 15.0. Awards available. (HTA)

Peter Branch Trail see entry 1156.

Peytona Trail see entry 1194.

Physically Handicapped Tour see entry 1205.

Picket Loop Trail see entry 1194.

Pinch-Em Tight Trail see entry 1156.

1222 **Pine Mountain State Resort Park**, Pineville, KY 40977, (606) 337-3066. 6.8 miles. Named trails: Chained Rock, Fern Garden 1.0(l), Hemlock Garden, Honeymoon Falls, Laurel Cove 1.3, Living Stairway 0.5(l), Lost 0.5(l), Rock Hotel 1.0. (WCD; ATK; GKO)

Piney Hike 'n Bike Trail see entry 1194.

1223 **Pioneer Mt. Trail**, Bluegrass Council, BSA, 975 Liberty Rd., Lexington, KY 40505. Awards available. (MVC; HTA)

1224 **Pioneer Playhouse Trailer Park**, US 150, Danville, KY 40422, (606) 236-2747. (WCD)

1225 **Pippa Passes Home Hostel**, P.O. Box 15, Pippa Passes, KY 41844, (606) 368-2753. (AYH)

Poplar Flats Trail *see* entry 1133.
Princess Arch Trail *see* entry 1156.
Prospector's Trail *see* entry 1136.

1226 **Pulaski Park**, SR 80, Somerset, KY 42501. (ATK)

Pumpkin Creek Nature Trail *see* entry 1191.
Red River Gorge National Recreation Trail *see* entry 1156.
Red Trail *see* entry 1145.
Red Trail *see* entry 1217.
Redbird Crest Trail *see* entry 1156.

1227 **Reelfoot National Wildlife Refuge**, P.O. Box 98, Samburg, TN 38254. (WTW)

Renfro Creek Trail *see* entry 1156.
Ridge Trail *see* entry 1136.
Ridge Trail *see* entry 1155.
River Trail *see* entry 1136.

1228 **Road Runner Trail**, Ms. Sandy Blake, 10906 Holsclaw Hill Rd., Fairdale, KY 40118. 5.0-10.0 miles. Awards available. (HTA)

Roaring Rocks Trail *see* entry 1156.
Rock Bridge Trail *see* entry 1156.
Rock Hotel Trail *see* entry 1222.
Rockcastle Narrows Trail *see* entry 1156.
Rocky Run Trail *see* entry 1133.

1229 **Rough River Dam State Resort Park**, SR 79, Falls of Rough, KY 40119, (502) 257-2311 or (800) 325-1713. (WCD; ATK; MSE; LRA)

Rough Trail *see* entry 1156.
Rush Ridge Trail *see* entry 1156.
Rushing Creek Trail *see* entry 1194.
Scuttle Hole Trail *see* entry 1156.
Shadow Trail *see* entry 1132.

1230 **Shaker Trail**, So-Ky Trails, Inc., P.O. Box 404, Bowling Green, KY 42101-0404. 10.0 miles. (AA 1992)

Shawnee Nature Trail *see* entry 1156.

1231 **Sheltowee Trace National Preservation Trail**, Daniel Boone National Forest, P.O. Box 727, 100 Vaught Rd., Winchester, KY 40391, (606) 745-3100. 257 miles. (EGH; MVC; PTD; OTB; MSO; FGU; HTA; GBD)

Shop Hollow Trail *see* entry 1198.
Short Leaf Pine Trail *see* entry 1194.

1232 **Siltstone Trail**, Wilderness Jefferson Co., 117 Freeman Ave., Louisville, KY 40214. 6.5 miles. Awards available. (HTA)

Silvermine Arch Trail *see* entry 1156.
Simon Kenton Trail *see* entry 1173.
Sky Bridge Loop Trail *see* entry 1156.
Skylight Cave Trail *see* entry 1155.
Skyline Trail *see* entry 1156.
Songbird Walk *see* entry 1194.

1233 **Spencer-Morton Preserve**, c/o Director, Division of Wild Areas, Eastern Kentucky University, Richmond, KY 40475, (606) 622-3122. (GKO)

1234 **Still Waters Campground**, US 127, Frankfort, KY 40601, (502) 223-8896. (WCD)

Sugar Run Nature Trail *see* entry 1155.
Sugar Run Trail *see* entry 1155.
Sugar Tree Hollow Trail *see* entry 1156.

1235 **Sulphur Creek Resort**, SR 485, Burkesville, KY 42717, (502) 433-7200. (WCD)

Sun and Shade Trail *see* entry 1133.

1236 **Sunrock Farm**, 103 Gibson Ln., Wilder, KY 41076, (606) 781-5502. (GOP)

Sunset Point Trail *see* entry 1205.
Swift Camp Creek Trail *see* entry 1156.
Telegraph Trail *see* entry 1194.
Three Forks of Beaver Creek Overlook Trail *see* entry 1156.
Tower Trail *see* entry 1133.
Tower Trail *see* entry 1156.
Towers Trail *see* entry 1136.
Trail of These Hills *see* entry 1194.

1237 **Triple Arch Trail**, Trail Blazers-BSA, P.O. Box 43059, Middletown, KY 40243. 14.4 miles. Awards available. (HTA)

Tri-State Trail *see* entry 1155.
Tunnel Ridge Trail *see* entry 1156.
Turnhole Ridge Horseback Spur Trail *see* entry 1150.

Turnhole Ridge Trail *see* entry 1205.
Twin Branch Trail *see* entry 1156.
Wagon Wheel Trail *see* entry 1190.
1238 Wah-La-Ha Trail, Wah-La-Ha—Buffalo Trail, Inc., 420 Ewing St., Frankfort, KY 40601. 7.0 miles straight. Awards available. (AA 1992)
1239 Walnut Mead Campground, SR 21, Berea, KY 40403, (606) 986-4951. (WCD)
Waterfall Campsite Spur Trail *see* entry 1150.
West Prong of the Buffalo Trail *see* entry 1205.
Wet Prong Trail *see* entry 1150.
Whistling Arch Trail *see* entry 1156.
1240 White Acres Campground, US 62W, Bardstown, KY 40004, (502) 348-9677. (WCD)
White Trail *see* entry 1149.
White Trail *see* Otter Creek C.P. 1217.
Whittleton Arch Trail *see* entry 1156.
Whittleton Branch Trail *see* entry 1156.
Wild Cave Tour *see* entry 1205.
Wildcat Hollow Trail *see* entry 1150.
Wildcat Trail *see* entry 1156.
Wilderness Lake Trail *see* entry 1174.
Wilderness Road Trail *see* entry 1155.
Wilderness Road Trail *see* entry 1197.
Wilderness Trail *see* entry 1190.
Winding Stair Gap Trail *see* entry 1156.
Woodland Walk *see* entry 1194.
Woodpecker Trail *see* entry 1174.
Woodson Gap Trail *see* entry 1155.
Yahoo Arch Trail *see* entry 1156.
Yahoo Falls Trail *see* entry 1156.
Yamacraw Trail *see* entry 1156.
Yellow Trail *see* entry 1145.
Yellow Trail *see* entry 1217.
1241 Zollicoffer Trail, Trail Blazers-BSA, P.O. Box 43059, Middletown, KY 40243. 18.0 miles. Awards available. (HTA)

Generally:
Kentucky Department of Parks, 12th Floor, Capital Plaza Tower, Frankfort, KY 40601, (502) 564-5410 or (800) 255-PARK. (ATK)
Recreation, Tourism & Convention Commission, P.O. Box 66, Morehead, KY 40351. (HTA)
U.S. Army Corps of Engineers, Louisville District, P.O. Box 59, Louisville, KY 40201. (GFC)

Index (by city)

Bardstown: Holt's Campground & Fishing Lake 1169; My Old Kentucky Home State Park 1212; White Acres Campground 1240
Berea: Berea College Forest 1132; Daniel Boone National Forest 1156; Walnut Mead Campground 1239
Big Creek: Daniel Boone National Forest 1156
Blue Lick Springs: Blue Licks Battlefield State Park 1135
Bowling Green: Beech Bend Park 1130; KOA-Bowling Green 1181; Shaker Trail 1230
Brandenburg: Ohio River Trail 1216
Breaks: Breaks Interstate Park 1136
Buckhorn: Gays Creek Campground 1161
Burkesville: Sulphur Creek Resort 1235
Cadiz: Cadiz Railroad Trail 1141; Lake Barkley State Resort Park 1190
Calvert City: KOA-KY Lakes/Paducah 1186
Campbellsville: Green River Lake 1164; Holmes Bend Recreation Area 1168; KOA-Green River Lake 1183
Carrollton: General Butler State Resort Park 1162
Catlettsburg: Jenny Wiley Trails 1173
Cave City: Mammoth Cave Jellystone Park Camp Resort 1204
Clermont: Bernheim Forest Arboretum and Nature Center 1133

Columbus: Columbus-Belmont Battlefield State Park 1151
Corbin: Cumberland Falls State Resort Park 1154; Holiday Campground 1166; KOA-Laurel River 1187
Crittenden: KOA-Cincinnati South 1182
Danville: Pioneer Playhouse Trailer Park 1224
Dunmore: Lake Malone State Park 1192
Eddyville: Holiday Hills Campground 1167
Fairdale: Ox Cart Trail 1218; Road Runner Trail 1228
Falls of Rough: Rough River Dam State Resort Park 1229
Frankfort: Buffalo Trail 1140; Capitol View Trail 1144; Clyde E. Buckley Wildlife Sanctuary 1149; Still Waters Campground 1234; Wah-La-Ha Trail 1238
Gilbertsville: Kentucky Dam Village State Resort Park 1176
Glasgow: Barren River Lake State Resort Park 1128
Golden Pond: Land Between the Lakes 1194
Grand Rivers: Canal Recreation Area 1143
Grayson: Grayson Lake 1163
Greenup: Greenbo Lake State Resort Park 1165
Hartford: Ohio County Park 1215
Hazard: Buckhorn Lake State Resort Park 1137
Henderson: John James Audubon State Park 1174
Hodgenville: Abraham Lincoln Birthplace National Historic Site 1125
Horse Cave: KOA-Horse Cave 1184
Irvine: Iron Furnace Trail 1171
Jamestown: Kendall Recreation Area 1175; Lake Cumberland State Resort Park 1191
Leitchfield: Moutardier Area 1210
Lexington: Kentucky Zollicoffer Trail 1179; Mischa-Mokwa Adventure Trail 1209; Pioneer Mt. Trail 1223
London: Daniel Boone National Forest 1156; Laurel River Lake 1196; Levi Jackson Wilderness Road State Park 1197
Louisville: Dewey Lake 1157; Fishtrap Lake 1160; Horine Memorial Trail 1170; Jefferson Forest Loop Trail 1172; Kentucky Lincoln Trail 1178; Lincoln Memorial Trail 1199; Louisville Heritage Trail 1199; Siltstone Trail 1232
Madisonville: Pennyrile Forest State Resort Park 1219
Mammoth Cave: Caveland Trail 1147; Collie Ridge Composite Trail 1150; Mammoth Cave National Park 1205; Mammoth Cave Trail 1206
Maysville: Buffalo Trace Trail 1139
Middlesboro: Cumberland Gap National Historical Park 1155
Middletown: Long Hunter's Trek 1202; Massacre Trail 1207; Triple Arch Trail 1237; Zollicoffer Trail 1241
Monticello, IL: Mill Springs State Park 1208
Monticello, KY: Conley Bottom Resort 1152
Morehead: Cave Run Lake 1146; Kentucky Foothills Travel Ways 1177
Munfordville: Munfordville Battlefield Trek 1211
Olive Hill: Carter Caves State Resort Park 1145
Owensboro: Ben Hawes State Park 1131; Buena Vista Trail 1138
Paducah: Fern Lake Campground 1159; Land Between the Lakes Trail 1195
Park City: Cedar Hills Campground 1148
Perryville: Perryville Battlefield 1220; Perryville Pilgrimage Trek 1221
Pineville: Pine Mountain State Resort Park 1222
Pippa Passes: Pippa Passes Home Hostel 1225
Renfro Valley: KOA-Renfro Valley 1189
Richmond: Spencer-Morton Preserve 1233
Russell Springs: KOA-Indian Hills 1185
Russellville: Camp Wildcat Hollow 1142
Salt Lick: Cradle of Forestry in America Interpretive Trails 1153
Samburg: Reelfoot National Wildlife Refuge 1227
Sanders: Eagle Valley Camping Resort 1158
Scottsville: Bailey's Point Campground 1126
Shelbyville: Lake Shelby Park 1193
Shepherdsville: KOA-Louisville South 1188
Skyline: Lilley Cornett Woods 1198
Slade: Natural Bridge State Resort Park 1213
Somerset: Beaver Creek Wilderness 1129;

KENTUCKY

Daniel Boone National Forest 1156; Pulaski Park 1226
Stanton: Daniel Boone National Forest 1156
Vine Grove: Otter Creek City Park 1217
Walton: Big Bone Lick State Park 1134; Oak Creek Campground 1214
Whitesburg: Little Shepherd Trail 1200
Whitley City: Daniel Boone National Forest 1156

Wickliffe: Ballard County Wildlife Management Area 1127
Wilder: Sunrock Farm 1236
Williamstown: Kincaid Lake State Park 1180; Lloyd Wildlife Management Area 1201
Winchester: Daniel Boone National Forest 1156; Sheltowee Trace National Preservation Trail 1231

LOUISIANA

1242 **Acadiana City Park**, 1021 E. Alexander St., Lafayette, LA 70501, (504) 261-8388. (LGU; WCD; NAT; GFA)

1243 **Alexander State Forest**, US 169, Woodworth, LA 71485, (318) 487-5058. (WCD)

1244 **Audubon State Commemorative Area**, SR 956, St. Francisville, LA 70775, (504) 635-3739. (ATA)

1245 **Bayou Barn**, P.O. Box 313-H, Crown Point, LA 70072, (504) 689-2663. (WCD)

Bayou Coquille Trail *see* entry 1278.

1246 **Bayou Segnette State Park**, US 90, Westwego, LA 70094. (ATA)

1247 **Bienville Trail**, R.J. Daret, 1312 Broadway, New Orleans, LA 70118, (504) 861-8611. 4.8 miles straight. Awards available. (SAR 1990)

1248 **Buhlow Lake**, US 71, Pineville, LA 71360. (ATA)

1249 **Cajun Campground**, US 190, Eunice, LA 70535, (318) 457-5753. (WCD)

1250 **Camp Avondale**, Istrouma Area Council, BSA, 1000 Scenic Hwy., Baton Rouge, LA 70802, (504) 344-0305; or Camp Avondale, Rt. 2, Box 91, Clinton, LA 70722. (SFC)

1251 **Camp Mt. Bayou**, Evangeline Area Council, BSA, 116 Bertrand Dr., Lafayette, LA 70506, (318) 235-8551; or Camp Mt. Bayou, St. Landry, LA 71367, (318) 461-2922. (SFC)

1252 **Caney Lakes Recreation Area**, SR 159, Minden, LA 71055, (318) 745-3503. (MSW)

1253 **Capitol Historical Trail**, Louisiana Hiking Trails, Inc., 1833 Cloverdale Ave., Baton Rouge, LA 70808, (504) 344-4287. 7.0 miles straight or 10.0 miles loop. Awards available. (SAR 1990)

1254 **Capri Court**, 101 Capri Ct., Houma, LA 70364, (504) 879-4288. (WCD)

1255 **Carrollton Historical Trail**, R.J. Daret, 1312 Broadway, New Orleans, LA 70118, (504) 861-8611. 5.2 miles straight. Awards available. (SAR 1990)

1256 **Carruth Historic Trails**, West Baton Rouge Historical Association-Trails, 845 N. Jefferson, Port Allen, LA 70767. 2.0 and 10.0 miles loops. Awards available. (SAR 1990)

1257 **Catahoula National Wildlife Refuge**, P.O. Drawer LL, Jena, LA 71342, (318) 992-5261. (GNW)

1258 **Chalmette Historical Trail**, P.O. Box 70, Arabi, LA 70032. 7.0 and 16.4 miles. Awards available. (AA 1991)

1259 **Chemin-a-Haut State Park**, SR 139, Bastrop, LA 71220, (318) 283-0812. (MSW; WCD; ATA)

1260 **Cherokee Beach and Campgrounds**, SR 442, Tickfaw, LA 70466. (OTB)

1261 **Chicot State Park**, SR 3042, Ville Platte, LA 70586, (318) 363-2403. (MSW; WCD; ATA)

1262 **Christien Campground**, US 84, Whitehall, LA 71322, (318) 992-6695. (WCD)

1263 **Cotile Reservoir**, SR 1 N200, Alexandria, LA 71301. (ATA)

1264 **Creole Nature Trail**, SR 27 & 82, Sulphur, LA 70663; or Southwest Louisiana Convention & Visitors Bureau, 1211 N. Lakeshore Dr., P.O. Box 1912, Lake Charles, LA 70602, (318) 436-9588 or (318) 436-9863. 1.5 miles. (MSW; GFA)

1265 **Cypress Black Bayou Recreation Area**, SR 162, Benton, LA 71006. (OTB)

1266 **D'Arbonne National Wildlife Ref-**

LOUISIANA

uge, P.O. Box 3065, Monroe, LA 71201, (318) 325-1735. (GNW)
1267 Fairview-Riverside State Park, SR 22, Madisonville, LA 70447. (ATA)
1268 Fountainebleau State Park, US 190, Mandeville, LA 70448, (504) 624-4443. (WCD; ATA)
1269 Frenchman's Wilderness, SR 3177, Henderson, LA 70517, (318) 228-2616. (WCD)
1270 Harahan Historic Trail, P.O. Box 727, Laplace, LA 70069-0727. 12.0 miles. Awards available. (HTA)
1271 Harahan Levee Hike, P.O. Box 727, Laplace, LA 70069-0727. 6.5 miles. Awards available. (HTA)
1272 Hidden Oaks Campground, US 190, Hammond, LA 70401, (800) 359-0940. (WCD)
1273 Home Place Acres Park, Rt. 1, Box 200, Athens, LA 71003, (318) 258-4943. (WCD)
 Honey Island Swamp Nature Trail *see* entry 1296.
1274 Indian Creek Campground, Fontano Rd., Independence, LA 70443, (504) 878-6567. (WCD)
1275 Indian Creek Reservoir, US 71, Alexandria, LA 71301. (WCD)
1276 Istrouma Trail, Istrouma Area Council, BSA, P.O. Box 66676, Baton Rouge, LA 70896, (504) 926-2697. 11.0 miles loop. Awards available. (AA 1990)
1277 Jacobs Nature Park, Blanchard-Furrh Rd., Blanchard, LA 71009. (GFA)
1278 Jean Lafitte National Historical Park, 423 Canal St., Rm. 206, New Orleans, LA 70116. Named trails: Bayou Coquille, Ring Levee. (PGF; NAT; CGA)
1279 Kemper Wilderness Park, Cotton Rd., Morgan City, LA 70380. (MSW)
1280 Kincaid Reservoir, SR 28, Gardner, LA 71431. (ATA)
1281 Kisatchie National Forest, P.O. Box 479, Homer, LA 71040; or Kisatchie National Forest, P.O. Box 5500, 2500 Shreveport Hwy., Pineville, LA 71360, (318) 473-7160. Named trails: Longleaf, Sugar Cane National Recreation 7.5, Wild Azalea National Recreation 31.0.

(EGH; MSW; WCD; ATA; GFC; OTB; FGU; CTD; LRA)
1282 KOA-Alexandria West/Kincaid Lake, 64 Kisatchie Ln., Boyce, LA 71409, (318) 445-5227. (WCD)
1283 KOA-Vinton/Lake Charles, 1514 Azema, Vinton, LA 70668, (318) 589-2300. (WCD)
1284 Lacassine National Wildlife Refuge, Rt. 1, Box 186, Lake Arthur, LA 70549, (318) 774-2750. (GNW)
1285 Lafayette Natural History Museum, 637 Girard Park Dr., Lafayette, LA 70503, (318) 268-5544. (NAT)
1286 Lake Bistineau State Park, SR 163, Doyline, LA 71023, (318) 745-3503. (WCD; ATA)
1287 Lake Claiborne State Park, SR 146, Homer, LA 71040. (ATA)
1288 Lake Fausse Point, 500 Main St., Jeanerette, LA 70544, (318) 276-4293. (ATA; NAT)
1289 Lake Vista Nature Preserve Trail, 214 Arkansas, Bogalusa, LA 70427, (504) 732-3666. 1.0 mile. (NAT)
1290 Little Red Church Historic Trail, BSA Troop 267, c/o Craig N. Melancon, 10 Horse Shoe Ln., St. Rose, LA 70087-9656. 10.0 miles. Awards available. (AA 1994)
 Longleaf Trail *see* entry 1281.
1291 Los Adaes State Commemorative Area, Rt. 6, Robeline, LA 71469. (GFA)
1292 Louisiana Nature and Science Center, 11000 Lake Forest Blvd., P.O. Box 870610, New Orleans, LA 70187-0610, (504) 246-5672. (GOP; LGU; ATA; NAT)
1293 Louisiana State Arboretum, Ville Platte, LA 70586, (318) 363-2503. 4.0 miles. (FTS; GFA; OTB)
1294 Mansfield Commemorative Trail, SR 84, Mansfield, LA 71052. 0.25 mile. (OTB)
1295 North Toledo Bend State Park, SR 3229, Zwolle, LA 71486. (ATA)
1296 Pearl River Management Area, P.O. Box 14526, Baton Rouge, LA 70898, (504) 863-7042. Named trails: Honey Island Swamp Nature. (NAT)
1297 Port Hudson State Commemorative

Area, US 61, Port Hudson, LA 70791. (GFA)
1298 **Poverty Point State Commemorative Area,** SR 577, Epps, LA 71237. (ATA)
Ring Levee Trail *see* entry 1278.
1299 **Riverton Lake Campground,** US 165, Columbia, LA 71418, (318) 649-5707. (WCD)
1300 **Sabine National Wildlife Refuge,** M.R.H. Box 107, Hackberry, LA 70645, (318) 762-5135. (GNW)
1301 **St. Bernard State Park,** SR 39, New Orleans, LA 70122. (ATA)
1302 **Sam Houston Jones State Park,** Rt. 4, Box 294, State Park Rd., Lake Charles, LA 70609, (318) 855-2665. (MSW; WCD; ATA; OTB)
1303 **Spanish Fort Trail,** BSA Troop 269, P.O. Box 6245, Metarie, LA 70009. 7.0-9.5 miles straight. Awards available. (AA 1989)

Sugar Cane National Recreation Trail *see* entry 1281.
1304 **Sweetwater Ranch & Campground,** Cooper Rd., Loranger, LA 70446, (504) 878-6853. (WCD)
1305 **Valentine Lake,** SR 28, Gardner, LA 71431. (ATA)
Wild Azalea National Recreation Trail *see* entry 1281.
1306 **Yogi Bear's Jellystone New Orleans-Hammond,** SR 445, Hammond, LA 70401, (504) 542-1507. (WCD)
1307 **Zemurray Gardens,** SR 40, Loranger, LA 70446. (OTB)

Generally:
Department of Natural Resources, P.O. Box 94396, Baton Rouge, LA 70804, (504) 342-4500. (SFC)
Louisiana Office of State Parks, P.O. Box 44426, Baton Rouge, LA 70804, (504) 342-8111. (EGH)

Index (by city)

Alexandria: Cotile Reservoir 1263; Indian Creek Reservoir 1275
Athens: Home Place Acres Park 1273
Bastrop: Chemin-a-Haut State Park 1259
Baton Rouge: Camp Avondale 1250; Capitol Historical Trail 1253; Pearl River Management Area 1296
Benton: Cypress Black Bayou Recreation Area 1265
Blanchard: Jacobs Nature Park 1277
Bogalusa: Lake Vista Nature Preserve Trail 1289
Boyce: KOA-Alexandria West/Kincaid Lake 1282
Chalmette: Chalmette Historical Trail 1258
Clinton: Istrouma Trail 1276
Columbia: Riverton Lake Campground 1299
Crown Point: Bayou Barn 1245
Destrehan: Little Red Church Historic Trail 1290
Doyline: Lake Bistineau State Park 1286
Epps: Poverty Point State Commemorative Area 1298

Eunice: Cajun Campground 1249
Gardner: Kincaid Reservoir 1280; Valentine Lake 1305
Hackberry: Sabine National Wildlife Refuge 1300
Hammond: Hidden Oaks Campground 1272; Yogi Bear's Jellystone New Orleans-Hammond 1306
Henderson: Frenchman's Wilderness 1269
Homer: Kisatchie National Forest 1281; Lake Claiborne State Park 1287
Houma: Capri Court 1254
Independence: Indian Creek Campground 1274
Jeanerette: Lake Fausse Point 1288
Jena: Catahoula National Wildlife Refuge 1257
Lafayette: Acadiana City Park 1242; Camp Mt. Bayou 1251; Lafayette Natural History Museum 1285
Lake Arthur: Lacassine National Wildlife Refuge 1284
Lake Charles: Sam Houston Jones State Park 1302

LOUISIANA

Laplace: Harahan Historic Trail 1270; Harahan Levee Hike 1271
Loranger: Sweetwater Ranch & Campground 1304; Zemurray Gardens 1307
Madisonville: Fairview-Riverside State Park 1267
Mandeville: Fountainebleau State Park 1268
Mansfield: Mansfield Commemorative Trail 1294
Metarie: Spanish Fort Trail 1303
Minden: Caney Lakes Recreation Area 1252
Monroe: D'Arbonne National Wildlife Refuge 1266
Morgan City: Kemper Wilderness Park 1279
New Orleans: Bienville Trail 1247; Carrollton Historical Trail 1255; Jean Lafitte National Historical Park 1278; Louisiana Nature and Science Center 1292; St. Bernard State Park 1301
Pineville: Buhlow Lake 1248; Kisatchie National Forest 1281
Port Allen: Carruth Historic Trails 1256
Port Hudson: Port Hudson State Commemorative Area 1297
Robeline: Los Adaes State Commemorative Area 1291
St. Francisville: Audubon State Commemorative Area 1244
Sulphur: Creole Nature Trail 1264
Tickfaw: Cherokee Beach and Campgrounds 1260
Ville Platte: Chicot State Park 1261; Louisiana State Arboretum 1293
Vinton: KOA-Vinton/Lake Charles 1283
Westwego: Bayou Segnette State Park 1246
Whitehall: Christien Campground 1262
Woodworth: Alexander State Forest 1243
Zwolle: North Toledo Bend State Park 1295

MAINE

Acadia Mountain Trail *see* entry 1308.

1308 **Acadia National Park**, P.O. Box 177, Bar Harbor, ME 04609, (207) 288-3338. 200 miles. Named trails: Acadia Mountain 2.5, Bar Island, Beech Cliff, Beech Mountain 1.8, Beehive 1.2, The Bowl, Bubble Rock, Cadillac Mountain 1.8, Canada Cliffs, Dorr Mountain 1.5, Eagle Lake, Gorge Path, Gorham Mountain 6.0, Gorham Mountain Ridge 4.0, Great Head, Hadlock Brook Loop 3.9, Hadlock Valley Loop Carriage Road 4.2, Jordan Cliffs, Jordan Pond Loop 3.3(l), Jordan Pond Nature, Kebo Mountain 1.5, Long Pond 2.9, North Ridge, Norumbega Mountain 2.5, Ocean Path 1.8, Pemetic Mountain 2.0, Penobscot Mountain, Precipice 1.6, Sargent Mountain, Ship Harbor Nature 1.25, Shore Path, South Ridge 7.0, Summit, West Face, Western Mountains, Wild Gardens of Acadia Nature, Witch Hole Loop Carriage Road 3.5, Wonderland. (LGU; EAN; EGH; FNE; WCD; FMV; AYH; MNE; SNE; GFA; GNP; NPV; WTW; DGW; NPE; OTB; AGW; CGA; EMW; NET; FDN; WNE; GNA)

1309 **Acres of Wildlife**, SR 113/11, P.O. Box 2W, Steep Falls, ME 04085, (207) 675-3211. (WCD)

Agamenticus Trail *see* entry 1313.

1310 **Aldus Lakeside Camping**, SR 131, Belfast, ME 04915, (207) 342-5618. (WCD)

1311 **Allagash Wilderness Waterway**, Bureau of Parks and Recreation, State House, Station 22, Augusta, ME 04333, (207) 289-3821. (SNE; GNA)

1312 **Allen Pond Campground**, North Mountain Rd., Greene, ME 04236, (207) 946-7439. (WCD)

1313 **Appalachian Mountains**, Maine Appalachian Trail Club, P.O. Box 283, Augusta, ME 04330; or Appalachian Mountain Club, 5 Joy St., Boston, MA 02108. Named trails: Agamenticus 0.5(s), Arnold, Bald Mountain 3.5(s), Bear Mountain 1.0(s), Bigelow Range, Caribou Mountain 3.5(s), Champlain Mountain 1.0(s), Coburn Mountain 4.0(s), Doubletop Mountain 4.5(s), East Spur, Hunt Trail (Up Mt. Katahdin) 5.2(s), Mount Battie 1.0(s), Mount Kineo 0.3(s), Mount Zircon 0.7(s), Old Spec Mountain 1.5(s), Ossipee Mountain 0.3(s), Pleasant Mountain 1.8(s), Rumford Whitecap Mountain 2.0(s), Sabattus Mountain 1.5(s), Saddleback Mountain 3.5(s), Squaw Mountain 3.75(s), Stone Mountain 1.5(s), Streaked Mountain 1.0(s), Tumbledown 3.0(s), Tumbledown Dick Mountain 1.0(s). (BMG; MGV)

1314 **Appalachian Side Trails** (not listed elsewhere), Maine Appalachian Trail Club, P.O. Box 283, Augusta, ME 04330. Named trails: Beemis Valley, Gulf, Range, White Brook Side. (ATG #1)

1315 **Appalachian Trail** (see separate entry 4948 in interstate section).

Arnold Trail *see* entry 1313.

1316 **Aroostook State Park**, US 1, Presque Isle, ME 04769, (207) 768-8341. (MNE)

Bald Mountain Trail *see* entry 1313.

Bald Rock Mountain Trail *see* entry 1322.

Bar Island Trail *see* entry 1308.

1317 **Baxter State Park**, 64 Balsam Dr., Millinocket, ME 04462, (207) 723-5140. 178 miles. Named trails: Chimney Pond, Daicey Pond Nature, Freeze-Out, Hunt, Knife Edge, Roaring Brook Nature, Sandy Stream Pond, South Branch Nature,

MAINE

South Turner Mountain. (LGU; EGH; FNE; GOP; MNE; SNE; OTB; NET; GNA; GTB)
Bear Mountain Trail *see* entry 1313.
Beech Cliff Trail *see* entry 1308.
Beech Mountain Trail *see* entry 1308.
Beehive Trail *see* entry 1308.
Beemis Valley Trail *see* entry 1314.
1318 Big Skye Acres, Rt. 1, Box 590, Pownal, ME 04069, (207) 688-4147. (WCD)
Bigelow Mountain Trail *see* entry 1319.
1319 Bigelow Preserve, Bureau of Public Lands, Maine Department of Conservation, State House, Station 22, Augusta, ME 04333, (207) 289-3061. Named trails: Bigelow Mountain 4.5, Firewarden's. (EGH; SNE)
Bigelow Range Trail *see* entry 1313.
Birch Point Trail *see* entry 1379.
1320 Blueberry Pond Campground, Rt. 4, Box 4364, Freeport, ME 04032, (207) 688-4421. (WCD)
The Bowl Trail *see* entry 1308.
1321 Bradbury Mountain State Park, Pownal, ME 04069, (207) 688-4712. (SNE)
Bubble Rock Trail *see* entry 1308.
Cadillac Mountain Trail *see* entry 1308.
1322 Camden Hills State Park, Rt. 1, Belfast Rd., Camden, ME 04843, (207) 236-3109. 25.0 miles. Named trails: Bald Rock Mountain 3.0(s), Hemlock, Maiden Cliff, Mount Megunticook 3.5(s), Ragged Mountain, Scenic, Tablelands 3.5(s). (EGH; FNE; WCD; MNE; SNE; DGW; AFW; GNA)
Canada Cliffs Trail *see* entry 1308.
1323 Canal Bridge Camping Area, SR 5, Fryeburg, ME 04037, (207) 935-2286. (WCD)
Caribou Mountain Trail *see* entry 1313.
Carlo Col Trail *see* entry 1361.
Casco Bay Trail *see* entry 1416.
Champlain Mountain Trail *see* entry 1313.
1324 Chewonki Campgrounds, P.O. Box 261, Chewonki Rd., Wiscasset, ME 04578, (207) 882-7426. (WCD)

Chimney Pond Trail *see* entry 1317.
1325 Cobscook Bay State Park, Dennysville, ME 04628, (207) 726-4412. (WCD; MNE; SNE; GNA)
Coburn Mountain Trail *see* entry 1313.
1326 College of the Atlantic Nature Trail, College of the Atlantic, Bar Harbor, ME 04609, (207) 288-5015. (GOP)
1327 Colonial Ramblings, 71 York St., York, ME 03909. 1.6-5.0 miles loops. Awards available. (AA 1992)
Daicey Pond Nature Trail *see* entry 1317.
1328 Deboullie Management Unit, Bureau of Public Lands, Maine Department of Conservation, State House, Station 22, Augusta, ME 04333, (207) 289-3061. (SNE)
1329 Deer Farm Campground, Tufts Pond Rd., Kingfield, ME 04947, (207) 265-4599. (WCD)
1330 Desert of Maine, Desert Rd., Dept. W, Freeport, ME 04032, (207) 865-6962. (WCD)
1331 Donnell Pond/Tunk Lake, Bureau of Public Lands, Maine Department of Conservation, State House, Station 22, Augusta, ME 04333, (207) 289-3061. (SNE)
Dorr Mountain Trail *see* entry 1308.
Doubletop Mountain Trail *see* entry 1313.
1332 Down East Family Camping, SR 27, Wiscasset, ME 04578, (207) 882-5431. (WCD)
1333 Duck Lake Management Unit, Bureau of Public Lands, Maine Department of Conservation, State House, Station 22, Augusta, ME 04333, (207) 289-3061. (GFC; SNE)
1334 Eagle Lake Management Unit, Bureau of Public Lands, Maine Department of Conservation, State House, Station 22, Augusta, ME 04333, (207) 289-3061. (SNE)
Eagle Lake Trail *see* entry 1308.
East Point Sanctuary Trail *see* entry 1340.
East Spur Trail *see* entry 1313.
1335 Fernald's Neck Preserve, Maine

Chapter, The Nature Conservancy, 122 Main St., P.O. Box 338, Topsham, ME 04086, (207) 729-5181. (SNE)

1336 **Ferry Beach State Park**, SR 9, Saco, ME 04072, (207) 283-0067. (MNE)

Firewarden's Trail see entry 1319.

1337 **Four Ponds Management Unit**, Bureau of Public Lands, Maine Department of Conservation, State House, Station 22, Augusta, ME 04333, (207) 289-3061. (GFC; SNE)

Freeze-Out Trail see entry 1317.

1338 **Frye Mountain Game Management Area**, Department of Inland Fisheries and Wildlife, 284 State St., Augusta, ME 04333, (207) 289-3651. (SNE; GNA)

1339 **Georgia-Pacific Corporation Lands**, Woodland, ME 04694, (207) 427-3311. (SNE)

1340 **Gilsland Farm**, Maine Audubon Society, 118 US 1, Falmouth, ME 04105, (207) 781-2330. Named trails: East Point Sanctuary 2.0(l). (SNE)

Goose Eye Trail see entry 1361.

Gorge Path see entry 1308.

Gorham Mountain Ridge Trail see entry 1308.

Gorham Mountain Trail see entry 1308.

1341 **Grafton Notch State Park**, Newry, ME 04261, (207) 824-2912. Named trails: Skyline 3.5. (GOP; SNE)

Great Head Trail see entry 1308.

1342 **Great Wass Island Preserve**, Maine Chapter, The Nature Conservancy, P.O. Box 338, 122 Main St., Topsham, ME 04086, (207) 729-5181. 3.5 miles. (GOP; SNE)

1343 **Greenville Area**, The Greathouse at Moosehead Lake and Squaw Mountain, Pritham Avenue, SR 6/15, Greenville, ME 04442, (207) 695-2278. (AYH)

Gulf Trail see entry 1314.

Hadlock Brook Loop Trail see entry 1308.

Hadlock Valley Loop Carriage Road see entry 1308.

1344 **Halfway Brook Campground**, SR 102, Tremont, ME 04653, (207) 244-3464. (WCD)

1345 **Hebron Pines Campground**, SR 124, Hebron, ME 04238, (207) 966-2179. (WCD)

Hemlock Trail see entry 1322.

1346 **Hermit Island**, SR 216, Small Point, ME 04567, (207) 443-2101. (WCD)

1347 **Holbrook Island Sanctuary**, District Supervisor, Bureau of Parks and Recreation, P.O. Box 120, Liberty, ME 04949, (207) 589-4286. 2.0 miles. (GNA)

1348 **Holeb Management Unit**, Bureau of Public Lands, Maine Department of Conservation, State House, Station 22, Augusta, ME 04333, (207) 289-3061. Named trails: Sally Mountain. (SNE)

Hunt Trail see entry 1313.

Hunt Trail see entry 1317.

1349 **Indian Point/Blagden Preserve**, Maine Chapter, The Nature Conservancy, P.O. Box 338, 122 Main St., Topsham, ME 04086, (207) 729-5181. (SNE)

1350 **Jay-to-Farmington Trail**, Scott D. Ramsey, Supervisor, Off Road Vehicles, Bureau of Parks, Department of Conservation, Station 22, Augusta, ME 04333, (207) 289-4957. 14.0 miles straight. (GRT)

Jordan Cliffs Trail see entry 1308.

Jordan Pond Loop Trail see entry 1308.

Jordan Pond Nature Trail see entry 1308.

1351 **Josephine Newman Sanctuary**, Maine Audubon Society, Gilsland Farm, 118 US 1, Falmouth, ME 04105, (207) 781-2330. (SNE)

Kebo Mountain Trail see entry 1308.

1352 **Kezar Lake Camping Area**, Rt. 1, Box 246W, Lovell, ME 04051, (207) 925-1631. (WCD)

Knife Edge Trail see entry 1317.

1353 **KOA-Patten Pond**, US 1, Ellsworth, ME 04605, (207) 667-5645. (WCD)

1354 **KOA-Skowhegan-Canaan**, US 2, Canaan, ME 04924, (207) 474-2858. (WCD)

1355 **Lagrange Right-of-way Trail**, Scott D. Ramsey, Supervisor, Off Road Vehicles, Bureau of Parks, Department of Conservation, Station 22, Augusta, ME 04333, (207) 289-4957. 12.0 miles straight. (GRT)

1356 **Lamoine State Park**, SR 184, P.O. Box 1077, Ellsworth, ME 04605, (207) 667-4778. (WCD)

1357 **LaVerna and Rachel Carson Salt Pond Preserves**, Maine Chapter, The Nature Conservancy, P.O. Box 338, 122 Main St., Topsham, ME 04086, (207) 729-5181. (SNE)

1358 **Lily Bay State Park**, Greenville, ME 04441, (207) 695-2700. (WCD; SNE; GNA)

1359 **Little Squaw Management Unit**, Bureau of Public Lands, Maine Department of Conservation, State House, Station 22, Augusta, ME 04333, (207) 289-3061. (SNE)

Long Pond Trail *see* entry 1308.

1360 **Loring AFB FAMCAMP**, Loring Air Force Base, SR 89E, Caribou, ME 04736. (WCD)

1361 **Mahoosuc Mountains Management Unit**, Bureau of Public Lands, Maine Department of Conservation, State House, Station 22, Augusta, ME 04333, (207) 289-3061. Named trails: Carlo Col, Goose Eye, Mahoosuc Notch, Speck Pond. (GFC; SNE)

Mahoosuc Notch Trail *see* entry 1361.

Maiden Cliff Trail *see* entry 1322.

1362 **Maine High Adventure Trails**, Maine National High Adventure Area, P.O. Box 607, Howland, ME 04448, (207) 732-4845. (HUN)

1363 **Maine Wilderness Camps & Campground**, SR 6, Springfield, ME 04487, (207) 738-5052. (WCD)

1364 **Malabeam Lake FAMCAMP**, SR 89, Loring AFB, Caribou, ME 04736, (207) 999-2432. (WCD)

1365 **Mast Landing Sanctuary**, Maine Audubon Society, Gilsland Farm, 188 US 1, Falmouth, ME 04105, (207) 781-2330. (SNE)

1366 **Mattawamkeag Wilderness Park**, P.O. Box 5, Mattawamkeag, ME 04459, (207) 736-4881. 15.0 miles. (SNE)

1367 **Meadowbrook Camping Area**, HCR 32, Box 280W, Campbell's Pond Rd., Bath, ME 04530, (207) 443-4967 or (800) 370-CAMP. (WCD)

Moore's Pond Trail *see* entry 1378.

1368 **Moose Pond Campground**, Rt. 1, Box 1650, Harmony, ME 04942, (207) 683-2160 or (207) 683-2033 or fax (207) 683-6291. (WCD)

1369 **Moosehead Lake**, Moosehead Lake Region Chamber of Commerce, P.O. Box 581, Greenville, ME 04441, (207) 695-2702. (MNE)

1370 **Moosehorn National Wildlife Refuge**, P.O. Box 1077, Calais, ME 04619, (207) 454-3521. 60.0 miles. (SNE; WTW; GNW)

Mount Battie Trail *see* entry 1313.

1371 **Mount Blue State Park**, Shore Rd., Weld, ME 04285, (207) 585-2347. Named trails: Mount Blue 3.25(l). (WCD; MNE; SNE; GNA)

Mount Blue Trail *see* entry 1371.

Mount Kineo Trail *see* entry 1313.

Mount Megunticook Trail *see* entry 1322.

Mount Zircon Trail *see* entry 1313.

1372 **Mullen Woods Preserve**, Maine Chapter, The Nature Conservancy, P.O. Box 338, 122 Main St., Topsham, ME 04086, (207) 729-5181. (SNE)

1373 **North Maine Woods Forest**, P.O. Box 421, Ashland, ME 04732, (207) 764-6213. (GFC; SNE; GNA)

North Ridge Trail *see* entry 1308.

1374 **Northport Travel Park**, US 1, Belfast, ME 04915, (207) 338-2077. (WCD)

Norumbega Mountain Trail *see* entry 1308.

Ocean Path *see* entry 1308.

1375 **Old Massachusetts Homestead**, US 1, Lincolnville, ME 04849, (207) 789-5135. (WCD)

1376 **Old Narrow Gauge Volunteer Nature Trail**, Town Clerk, Town Office, 128 Water St., Randolph, ME 04346, (207) 582-5808. 2.4 miles straight. (GRT)

Old Spec Mountain Trail *see* entry 1313.

Ossipee Mountain Trail *see* entry 1313.

1377 **Packard's Moorings Camping Area**, SR 150, Sebec Lake, ME 04482, (207) 997-3300. (WCD)

1378 **Peaks-Kenny State Park**, Dover-

Foxcroft, ME 04426, (207) 564-2003. Named trails: Moore's Pond. (WCD; MNE; SNE; GNA)

Pemetic Mountain Trail *see* entry 1308.

Penobscot Mountain Trail *see* entry 1308.

1379 **Petit Manan National Wildlife Refuge**, P.O. Box 279, Milbridge, ME 04658, (207) 546-2124. Named trails: Birch Point 4.0(l), Petit Manan 4.5(s), Shore 5.0. (SNE; GNA)

Petit Manan Trail *see* entry 1379.

Pleasant Mountain Trail *see* entry 1313.

1380 **Pleasant River Campground**, US 2, Bethel, ME 04217, (207) 836-3575. (WCD)

1381 **Point Sebago**, Point Sebago Rd., Casco, ME 04015, (207) 655-3821. (WCD)

1382 **Potter's Place**, Baker's Grant Rd., Lebanon, ME 04027, (207) 457-1341. (WCD)

Precipice Trail *see* entry 1308.

1383 **Quoddy Head State Park**, Lubec, ME 04652. (SNE; GFA; OTB)

1384 **R. Waldo Tyler Wildlife Management Area**, Department of Inland Fisheries and Wildlife, 284 State St., Augusta, ME 04333, (207) 289-5253. (SNE)

1385 **Rachel Carson National Wildlife Refuge**, Rt. 2, Box 751, Wells, ME 04090, (207) 646-9226. (LGU; MNE; SNE)

Ragged Mountain Trail *see* entry 1322.

Range Trail *see* entry 1314.

1386 **Rangeley State Park**, Rangeley, ME 04970, (207) 864-3858. (SNE)

1387 **Recompence Shore Campsites**, Wolf's Neck Rd., Freeport, ME 04032, (207) 865-9307. (WCD)

1388 **Richardsontown Lake Management Unit**, Bureau of Public Lands, Department of Conservation, State House, Station 22, Augusta, ME 04333, (207) 289-3061. (GFC; SNE)

1389 **River Run Canoe & Camping**, P.O. Box 90, Brownfield, ME 04010, (207) 452-2500. (WCD)

Roaring Brook Nature Trail *see* entry 1317.

1390 **Rocky Lake Management Unit**, Bureau of Public Lands, Maine Department of Conservation, State House, Station 22, Augusta, ME 04333, (207) 289-3061. (GFC; SNE)

1391 **Roosevelt Campobello International Park**, P.O. Box 97, Lubec, ME 04652, (506) 752-2922. (NPE)

1392 **Round Pond Management Unit**, Bureau of Public Lands, Maine Department of Conservation, State House, Station 22, Augusta, ME 04333, (207) 289-3061. (GFC; SNE)

1393 **Ruffingham Wildlife Management Area**, Department of Inland Fisheries, 284 State St., Augusta, ME 04333, (207) 289-5253. (SNE)

1394 **Ruffit Campgrounds**, SR 127, Dresden, ME 04342, (207) 737-8893. (WCD)

Rumford Whitecap Mountain Trail *see* entry 1313.

Sabattus Mountain Trail *see* entry 1313.

Saddleback Mountain Trail *see* entry 1313.

Sally Mountain Trail *see* entry 1348.

1395 **Sandy Beach Campground**, SR 201, Madison, ME 04950, (207) 474-5975. (WCD)

Sandy Stream Pond Trail *see* entry 1317.

Sargent Mountain Trail *see* entry 1308.

1396 **Scarborough Marsh**, Maine Audubon Society, Gilsland Farm, 118 US 1, Falmouth, ME 04105, (207) 781-2330. (SNE)

Scenic Trail *see* entry 1322.

1397 **Schoodis Point Recreation Area**, SR 186, Winter Harbor, ME 04693, (207) 963-5537. (WCD)

1398 **Scraggly Lake Management Unit**, Bureau of Public Lands, Maine Department of Conservation, State House, Station 22, Augusta, ME 04333, (207) 289-3061. (SNE)

1399 **Sebago Lake Resort & Campground**, Rt. 1, Box 9360, SR 114, Sebago Lake, ME 04075, (207) 787-3671. (WCD)

1400 **Sebago Lake State Park**, Harrison Rd., Naples, ME 04055, (207) 693-6612. (SNE; GNA)

MAINE

1401 **Seboeis Lake Management Unit,** Bureau of Public Lands, Maine Department of Conservation, State House, Station 22, Augusta, ME 04333, (207) 289-3061. (SNE)
1402 **Sennebec Lake Campground,** SR 131, Appleton, ME 04862, (207) 785-4250. (WCD)
1403 **Shady Oaks Campground,** P.O. Box 549, Bucksport, ME 04416, (207) 469-6004. (WCD)
Ship Harbor Nature Trail see entry 1308.
Shore Path see entry 1308.
Shore Trail see entry 1379.
Skyline Trail see entry 1341.
1404 **The Somerset Motor Lodge,** US 201, Skowhegan, ME 04976, (207) 474-2227. (WCD)
1405 **South Arm Campground,** P.O. Box 310, Andover, ME 04216, (207) 784-3566. (WCD)
South Branch Nature Trail see entry 1317.
1406 **South Portland Greenbelt South,** Jerre Bryant, City Manager, City Hall, 25 Cottage Rd., South Portland, ME 04106, (207) 767-3201. 2.5 miles straight. (GRT)
South Ridge Trail see entry 1308.
South Turner Mountain Trail see entry 1317.
Speck Pond Trail see entry 1361.
1407 **Sprague Neck Campsites,** SR 191, East Machias, ME 04630, (207) 259-8285. (WCD)
Spruce Hill Trail see entry 1415.
1408 **Squa Pan Lake,** Bureau of Public Lands, Maine Department of Conservation, State House, Station 22, Augusta, ME 04333, (207) 289-3061. (SNE)
Squaw Mountain Trail see entry 1313.
1409 **Stanwood Sanctuary and Homestead Museum,** Bar Harbor Rd., Ellsworth, ME 04605, (207) 667-8460. (MNE; OTB)
1410 **Steep Falls Wildlife Management Area,** Department of Inland Fisheries and Wildlife, 284 State St., Augusta, ME 04333, (207) 289-5253. (SNE)
1411 **Steve Powell Wildlife Management Area,** Department of Inland Fisheries and Wildlife, 284 State St., Augusta, ME 04333, (207) 289-5253. (SNE)
Stone Mountain Trail see entry 1313.
Streaked Mountain Trail see entry 1313.
Summit Trail see entry 1308.
Tablelands Trail see entry 1322.
Tumbledown Dick Mountain Trail see entry 1313.
Tumbledown Trail see entry 1313.
1412 **Vaughn Woods Memorial,** SR 91, South Berwick, ME 03908. (SNE)
1413 **Vernon S. Walker Wildlife Management Area,** Department of Inland Fisheries and Wildlife, 284 State St., Augusta, ME 04333, (207) 289-5253. (SNE)
1414 **Walnut Grove Campground,** Rt. 1, Box 260, Alfred, ME 04002, (207) 324-1207. (WCD)
West Face Trail see entry 1308.
Western Mountains Trail see entry 1308.
White Brook Side Trail see entry 1314.
1415 **White Mountain National Forest,** Evans Notch Ranger District, Rt. 2, Box 2270, Bethel, ME 04217, (207) 824-2134; or Forest Supervisor, 719 Main St., P.O. Box 638, Laconia, NH 03247, (603) 524-6450. Named trails: Spruce Hill. (EGH; FNE; NNE; SNE; MEG)
Wild Gardens of Acadia Nature Trail see entry 1308.
Witch Hole Loop Carriage Road see entry 1308.
1416 **Wolfe's Neck Woods State Park,** Wolfe's Neck Rd., Portland, ME 04101, (207) 865-4465. Named trails: Casco Bay. (FMV; MNE; NET)
Wonderland Trail see entry 1308.

Generally:
Bureau of Public Lands, Department of Conservation, State House, Station 22, Augusta, ME 04333, (207) 289-3061. (SNE)
Maine Bureau of Parks and Recreation, State House, Station 22, Augusta, ME 04333, (207) 289-3821. (EGH)

Index (by city)

Alfred: Walnut Grove Campground 1414
Allagash: Deboullie Management Unit 1328; Round Pond Management Unit 1392
Andover: South Arm Campground 1405
Appleton: Sennebec Lake Campground 1402
Ashland: North Maine Woods Forest 1373
Augusta: Appalachian Mountains 1313; Jay-to-Farmington Trail 1350; Lagrange Right-of-Way Trail 1355; Little Squaw Management Unit 1359; R. Waldo Tyler Wildlife Management Area 1384; Ruffingham Wildlife Management Area 1393; Steve Powell Wildlife Management Area 1411; Vernon S. Walker Wildlife Management Area 1413
Bar Harbor: Acadia National Park 1308; College of the Atlantic Nature Trail 1326
Bath: Meadowbrook Camping Area 1367
Beals: Great Wass Island Preserve 1342
Belfast: Aldus Lakeside Camping 1310; Northport Travel Park 1374
Bethel: Mahoosuc Mountains Management Unit 1361; Pleasant River Campground 1380; White Mountain National Forest 1415
Bigelow: Bigelow Preserve 1319
Brownfield: River Run Canoe & Camping 1389
Bucksport: Holbrook Island Sanctuary 1347; Shady Oaks Campground 1403
Burlington: Duck Lake Management Unit 1333
Calais: Moosehorn National Wildlife Refuge 1370
Camden: Camden Hills State Park 1322
Canaan: KOA-Skowhegan-Canaan 1354
Caribou: Loring AFB FAMCAMP 1360; Malabeam Lake FAMCAMP 1364
Casco: Point Sebago 1381
Clayton Lake: Allagash Wilderness Waterway 1311
Dennysville: Cobscook Bay State Park 1325
Dover-Foxcroft: Peaks-Kenny State Park 1378
Dresden: Ruffit Campgrounds 1394
Eagle Lake: Eagle Lake Management Unit 1334

East Machias: Rocky Lake Management Unit 1390; Sprague Neck Campsites 1407
East Sullivan: Donnell Pond/Tunk Lake 1331
Ellsworth: KOA-Patten Pond 1353; Lamoine State Park 1356; Stanwood Sanctuary and Homestead Museum 1409
Falmouth: Gilsland Farm 1340; Josephine Newman Sanctuary 1351; Mast Landing Sanctuary 1365
Freeport: Blueberry Pond Campground 1320; Desert of Maine 1330; Recompence Shore Campsites 1387
Fryeburg: Canal Bridge Camping Area 1323
Greene: Allen Pond Campground 1312
Greenville: Greenville Area 1343; Lily Bay State Park 1358; Moosehead Lake 1369
Harmony: Moose Pond Campground 1368
Hebron: Hebron Pines Campground 1345
Howland: Maine High Adventure Trails 1362
Kingfield: Deer Farm Campground 1329
Lebanon: Potter's Place 1382
Liberty: Frye Mountain Game Management Area 1338
Lincolnville: Old Massachusetts Homestead 1375
Lovell: Kezar Lake Camping Area 1352
Lubec: Quoddy Head State Park 1383; Roosevelt Campobello International Park 1391
Madison: Sandy Beach Campground 1395
Madrid: Four Ponds Management Unit 1337
Mattawamkeag: Mattawamkeag Wilderness Park 1366
Milbridge: Petit Manan National Wildlife Refuge 1379
Millinocket: Baxter State Park 1317
Moose River: Holeb Management Unit 1348
Naples: Sebago Lake State Park 1400
Newburyport: LaVerna and Rachel Carson Salt Pond Preserves 1357
Newry: Grafton Notch State Park 1341
Portland: Wolfe's Neck Woods State Park 1416
Pownal: Big Skye Acres 1318; Bradbury Mountain State Park 1321

MAINE *Index* 93

Presque Isle: Aroostook State Park 1316
Randolph: Old Narrow Gauge Volunteer Nature Trail 1376
Rangeley: Rangeley State Park 1386
Richardsontown: Richardsontown Lake Management Unit 1388
Saco: Ferry Beach State Park 1336
Scarborough: Scarborough Marsh 1396
Sebago Lake: Sebago Lake Resort & Campground 1399
Sebec Lake: Packard's Moorings Camping Area 1377
Seboeis: Seboeis Lake Management Unit 1401
Shin Pond: Scraggly Lake Management Unit 1398
Skowhegan: The Somerset Motor Lodge 1404
Small Point: Hermit Island 1346
South Berwick: Vaughn Woods Memorial 1412

South Portland: South Portland Greenbelt South 1406
Springfield: Maine Wilderness Camps & Campground 1363
Squa Pan: Squa Pan Lake 1408
Steep Falls: Acres of Wildlife 1309; Steep Falls Wildlife Management Area 1410
Topsham: Fernald's Neck Preserve 1335; Mullen Woods Preserve 1372
Tremont: Halfway Brook Campground 1344
Weld: Mount Blue State Park 1371
Wells: Rachel Carson National Wildlife Refuge 1385
Winter Harbor: Schoodis Point Recreation Area 1397
Wiscasset: Chewonki Campgrounds 1324; Down East Family Camping 1332
Woodland: Georgia-Pacific Corporation Lands 1339
York: Colonial Ramblings 1327

Maryland

1417 **Annapolis Pathways**, Maryland Historical Trails, P.O. Box 419, Glen Burnie, MD 21061. 10.0 miles. Awards available. (HTA)

1418 **Antietam Battlefield Historical Trail**, Mason-Dixon Council, BSA, 1200 Crestwood, P.O. Box 2133, Hagerstown, MD 21742-2133, (301) 739-1211; or Antietam National Battlefield, P.O. Box 158, Sharpsburg, MD 21782. 10.5 miles loop. Awards available. (SAR 1993)

1419 **Appalachian Side Trails** (not listed elsewhere), Potomac Appalachian Trail Club, 1718 N St., N.W., Washington, DC 20036, (202) 638-5306. Named trails: Bear Spring Cabin 1.04(s), Devils Racecourse Shelter 0.42(s), Elk Ridge 5.78(s), White Rocks 0.28(s). (ATG #6)

1420 **Appalachian Trail** (see separate entry **4948** in interstate section).

1421 **Appalachian Trail**, Mason-Dixon Council, BSA, 1200 Crestwood, P.O. Box 2133, Hagerstown, MD 21742-2133, (301) 739-1211. 44.0 miles straight. Awards available. (AA 1990)

1422 **Assateague Island National Seashore**, Rt. 2, Box 294, Berlin, MD 21811, (301) 641-1441. Named trails: Backcountry 21.0, Candleberry 1.0. (LGU; EGH; ATM; GFC; MMA; DMA; NPV; NSS; CGA; GTB)

1423 **Assateague State Park**, Rt. 2, Box 293, Berlin, MD 28111, (410) 641-2120. (LGU; WCD; ATM; MMA; GNA)

Azalea Trail *see* entry 1467.

Backbone Mountain Trail *see* entry 1510.

Backcountry Trail *see* entry 1422.

1424 **Baltimore and Annapolis Trail**, Dave Dionne, Superintendent, Baltimore and Annapolis Trail Park, P.O. Box 1007, Severna Park, MD 21146, (410) 222-6244. 13.3 miles straight. (GRT)

1425 **Baltimore Historical Trails**, Baltimore Area Council, BSA, 701 Wyman Park Dr., Baltimore, MD 21211-2899, (410) 338-1700. Named trails: Cannon Segment 7.5(s), Railroad Segment 6.0(s), Shot Tower Segment 5.0(s), Thinker Segment 8.5(s). Awards available. (SAR 1993)

1426 **Battle of Bladensburg & The Star-Spangled Banner Trail**, National Capital Area Council, BSA, 9190 Wisconsin Ave., Bethesda, MD 20814, (301) 530-9360. 50.0 miles straight. Awards available. (AA 1990)

1427 **Battle Creek Cypress Swamp Sanctuary**, Gray's Rd., Prince Frederick, MD 20678, (301) 535-5327. (DMA)

Bear Spring Cabin Trail *see* entry 1419.

Bee Oak Trail *see* entry 1438.

1428 **Big Run State Park**, Savage River Rd., Luke, MD 21540. (ATM)

Big Savage Mountain Trail *see* entries 1497 and 1517.

Billy Goat Trail *see* entry 1465.

Bird Walk *see* entry 1441.

1429 **Black Trail**, Del-Mar-Va Council, BSA, 8th and Washington Sts., Wilmington, DE 19801. 2.25 miles. (DMV)

1430 **Blackwater National Wildlife Refuge**, P.O. Box 121, Cambridge, MD 21613, (410) 228-2677. (ATM; MMA; DBV; DMA; WTW; OTB; AMC; GNA; GNW)

Blueberry Trail *see* entry 1467.

1431 **C & O Canal Historic Trail**, Mason-Dixon Council, BSA, 1200 Crestwood Dr., Hagerstown, MD 21740, (301) 739-1211; or National Capital Area Council, BSA, 9190 Wisconsin Ave., Bethesda, MD

MARYLAND

20814-3897, (301) 530-9360; or Baltimore Area Council, BSA, 701 Wyman Park Dr., Baltimore, MD 21211; or Shenandoah Area Council, BSA, P.O. Box 892, 2300 Roosevelt Blvd., Winchester, VA 22601; or Potomac Council, BSA, P.O. Box 212, Cumberland, MD 21502; or Superintendent, C & O National Historical Park, P.O. Box 4, Sharpsburg, MD 21782. Section distances: 60.0, 64.5, 16.8, 15.0 and 28.7 miles straight. Awards available. (AA 1990)

1432 **C & O Canal Towpath Trail**, Maryland Historical Trails, P.O. Box 419, Glen Burnie, MD 21061; or Superintendent, C & O Canal National Historical Park, Sharpsburg, MD 21782; or C & O Monument Supt., P.O. Box 859, 120 Potomac St., Hagerstown, MD 21740. Named trails: General Braddock Section 50.0(s), George Washington Section 50.0(s), James Rumsley Section 50.0(s). Awards available. (HTA)

1433 **Cabin John Regional Park**, 7400 Tuckerman Ln., Rockville, MD 20852, (301) 299-4555 or (301) 495-2525. 3.0 miles. (MMA; GPW; NWA)

1434 **Calvert Cliffs State Park**, Rt. 2, Box 224B, Lusby, MD 20657, (301) 326-4728. 13.0 miles. (DMA; OTB; AMC; GNA; NWA)

Candleberry Trail see entry 1422.
Cannon Segment see entry 1425.
Canyon Trail see entry 1526.

1435 **Capitol KOA Nature Trail**, P.O. Box 149, 768 Cecil Ave., Millersville, MD 21108, (410) 923-2771. 1.0 mile. (WCD; NWA)

1436 **Carderock Recreation Area**, George Washington Memorial Pkwy., Carderock Springs, MD 20817, (301) 299-3613. (GPW)

1437 **Catoctin Mountain National Park**, National Park Services, Thurmont, MD 21788, (301) 663-9330. 50.0 miles. Named trails: Catoctin 26.0. (EGH; PGF; WCD; NAT; DMA; GFA; NPE; CGA; GPW; AMI; NWA; YNP; ANP)

Catoctin Trail see entry 1437.

1438 **Cedarville State Forest**, Cedarville National Resources Management Area, Rt. 4, Box 133, Brandywine, MD 20613, (301) 888-1622. 20.0 miles. Named trails: Bee Oak, Hidden Spring, Loop, Magnolia, Mistletoe, Panhandle, Plantation, South, Sunset, West, Wolf Dam. (WCD; ATM; MMA; NAT; OTB; GPW; AMC; GNA; NWA)

1439 **Chancellor's Point Natural History Area**, St. Mary's City, MD 20686. (NAT)

1440 **Chief Nemacolin's Trail**, Maryland Historical Trails, P.O. Box 419, Glen Burnie, MD 21061. 33.0 miles. Awards available. (HTA)

Circuit Hikes 1 & 2 see entry 1450.

1441 **Clinton Regional Park**, Thrift Rd., Clinton, MD 20735. Named trails: Bird Walk 1.5(l). (PTB)

1442 **Colonial Annapolis Historical Trail**, American Historical Trails, P.O. Box 769, Monroe, NC 28110, (704) 289-1604. 7.0-14.5 miles loop. Awards available. (SAR 1991)

1443 **Crow's Nest Campground**, P.O. Box 145, Thurmont, MD 21788, (301) 271-7632. (WCD)

1444 **Cunningham Falls State Park**, SR 77, Thurmont, MD 21788, (301) 271-7574. 25.0 miles. (EGH; PGF; WCD; ATM; MMA; DMA; GFA; NPE; CGA; GPW; AMI; GNA; NWA; YNP; ANP)

1445 **Cylburn Park and Arboretum**, 4915 Greenspring Ave., Baltimore, MD 21209, (410) 396-0180. (GFA; NWA)

1446 **Dan's Mountain Wildlife Management Area**, Warrior Mountain, Rt. 1, Box 97, Oldtown, MD 21555, (301) 395-5639. 6.0 miles. (GNA)

1447 **Deal Island Wildlife Management Area**, Wellington Work Center, Rt. 2, Box 95, Princess Anne, MD 21853, (410) 651-2320. 11.0 miles. (GNA)

1448 **Deep Creek Lake State Park**, Glendale Bridge Rd., Oakland, MD 21550, (410) 387-5563. 6.0 miles. (WCD; ATM; MMA; GNA)

Deer Run Nature Trail see entry 1501.

1449 **Defenders Trail**, Dundalk-Patapsco Neck Historical Society, P.O. Box 21781, Dundalk, MD 21222; or Gladys M. Echols, 3307 Yorkway, Dundalk, MD 21222, (410)

284-3315. 10.0 miles straight. Awards available. (AA 1992)

Devils Racecourse Shelter Trail *see* entry 1419.

Dogwood Nature Trail *see* entry 1467.

1450 **Doncaster State Forest**, SR 6, Doncaster, MD 20646, (301) 934-2282; or Project Forester, Maryland Forest Service, P.O. Box 535, Waldorf, MD 20601, (301) 645-5653. Named trails: Circuit Hike 1 2.0(l), Circuit Hike 2 2.0(l). (MMA; NWA; PTB)

Duck End Trail *see* entry 1451.

1451 **Eastern Neck National Wildlife Refuge**, Rt. 3, Box 225, Rock Hall, MD 21661, (410) 639-7056. 10.0 miles. Named trails: Duck End. (DBA; DMA; AMC; GNA; NWA; GNW)

1452 **Elk Neck State Forest**, c/o Regional Forester, Maryland Forest Service, 103 N. Main St., Bel Air, MD 21014, (410) 838-6920 or (410) 879-2492. 12.0 miles. (MMA; GNA)

1453 **Elk Neck State Park**, SR 272, North East, MD 21901, (410) 287-5333. Named trails: Red. (WCD; ATM; MMA; AMC; GNA)

Elk Ridge Trail *see* entry 1419.

Emma Strider Conservation Trail *see* entry 1518.

Field Trail *see* entry 1504.

1454 **Forbes Road Historic Trail**, Mason-Dixon Council, BSA, 1200 Crestwood, P.O. Box 2133, Hagerstown, MD 21742-2133, (301) 739-1211. 28.0 miles. Awards available. (AA 1990)

1455 **Fort Frederick State Park**, SR 56, Hagerstown, MD 21740, (301) 842-2155. (WCD; ATM; MMA)

1456 **Fort McHenry Trail**, Fort McHenry National Monument and Historic Shrine, Baltimore, MD 21230, (410) 962-4290. 1.0 mile. (CGA; ANP; YNP; NPG)

1457 **Fort Washington Park**, c/o National Capital Parks-East, 1900 Anacostia Dr., S.E., Washington, DC 20020, (301) 292-2110; or Fort Washington Park, Fort Washington Rd., Fort Washington, MD 20744, (301) 292-2112. (NPE; CGA; GPW)

1458 **Gambrill State Park**, Rt. 8, Box 260, Frederick, MD 21701, (301) 473-8360. 10.0 miles. Named trails: Lost Chestnut Nature. (ATM; MMA; GNA; NWA)

1459 **Garrett State Forest**, CR 20, Deer Park, MD 21550, (301) 334-2038. 6.0 miles. (MMA; GNA)

1460 **Gathland State Park**, Gapland, MD 21736, (301) 293-2420. (ATM)

1461 **General A.P. Hill's Forced March**, Maryland Historical Trails, P.O. Box 419, Glen Burnie, MD 21061. 14.0 miles. Awards available. (HTA)

General Braddock Section *see* entry 1432.

George Washington Section *see* entry 1432.

1462 **Goshen Scout Camp**, National Capital Council, BSA, 9190 Wisconsin Ave., Bethesda, MD 20814, (301) 530-9360; or Goshen Scout Camp, SR 601, P.O. Box 86, Goshen, VA 24439, (703) 987-5140. (SFC)

1463 **Governor Johnson Patriot Trail**, Maryland Historical Trails, P.O. Box 419, Glen Burnie, MD 21061. 10.0 miles. Awards available. (HTA)

1464 **Grant Conway Historic Trail**, Superintendent, Harpers Ferry National Historical Park, Harpers Ferry, WV 25425. 3.5 hours. (ATG #6; AMI; HTA)

1465 **Great Falls Park**, 9200 Old Dominion Dr., Great Falls, VA 22066, (301) 759-2915. 6.0 miles. Named trails: Billy Goat 5.0(l), Great Falls. (DMV; NAT; WCG; GPW)

Great Falls Trail *see* entry 1465.

1466 **Green Ridge State Forest**, Star Route, Flintstone, MD 21530, (301) 777-2345. Named trails: Green Ridge 26.0. (EGH; WCD; AMI; GNA)

Green Ridge Trail *see* entry 1466.

1467 **Greenbelt National Park**, Greenbelt Rd., Greenbelt, MD 20770, (301) 344-3948. 12.0 miles. Named trails: Azalea 1.2, Blueberry 1.2, Dogwood Nature 1.4. (PGF; WCD; MMA; NPE; NWA; PTB)

1468 **Greenbrier State Park**, US 40, Hagerstown, MD 21740, (301) 791-4767. (WCD; ATM; MMA; GNA)

Grist Mill Trail *see* entry 1501.

MARYLAND

1469 **Gunpowder Falls State Park**, P.O. Box 5032, 10815 Harford Rd., Glen Arm, MD 21057, (410) 592-2897. 70.0 miles. Named trails: Gunpowder South, Panther Branch. (ATM; MMA; AMI; GNA; NWA)
Gunpowder South Trail see entry 1469.
Gwynns Falls Trail see entry 1478.
1470 **Hampton National Historic Site Trail**, 535 Hampton Ln., Towson, MD 21204, (410) 823-7054. 1.0 mile. (DMA)
1471 **Herrington Manor**, CR 20, Oakland, MD 21550. (ATM)
Hidden Spring Trail see entry 1438.
1472 **Holiday Park Campground**, P.O. Box 277, Greensboro, MD 21639, (410) 482-6797 or (800) 992-6691. (WCD)
1473 **Idylwild Wildlife Management Area**, Department of Natural Resources, Federalsburg, MD 21632, (410) 754-8686. 25.0 miles. (GNA)
1474 **Indian Springs Wildlife Management Area**, Rt. 1, Box 118, Big Pool, MD 21711, (301) 842-3355 or (301) 842-2702. (GNA)
Inlet Trail see entry 1504.
James Rumsley Section see entry 1432.
1475 **Jefferson Patterson Park and Museum**, SR 265, Prince Frederick, MD 20678, (301) 586-0050. (DMA)
1476 **Jug Bay Natural Area**, Rt. 1, Box 3380, Upper Marlboro, MD 20772, (301) 627-6074. (NAT; AMC)
1477 **KOA-Snug Harbor**, Rt. 2, Box 369A, Williamsport, MD 21795, (301) 223-7571 or (800) 457-3096. (WCD)
Lake Trail see entry 1504.
1478 **Leakin and Gwynns Falls**, Department of Recreation and Parks, City of Baltimore, Druid Hill Park, Baltimore, MD 21217, (410) 523-4643. Named trails: Gwynns Falls 1.5. (NWA)
1479 **Lenhok'sin Trail Camp Programs**, National Capital Area Council, BSA, 9190 Wisconsin Ave., Bethesda, MD 20814, (301) 530-9360. (HUN)
1480 **Little Bennett Regional Park**, 23701 Frederick Rd., Clarksburg, MD 20871, (301) 972-9222. (WCD)

1481 **Little Orleans Campground**, Orleans Rd., Little Orleans, MD 21766, (301) 478-2325. (WCD)
Loop Trail see entry 1438.
Lost Chestnut Nature Trail see entry 1458.
1482 **Louise F. Cosca Regional Park**, 11000 Thrift Rd., Clinton, MD 20735, (301) 868-1397. 3.0 miles. (NWA)
Magnolia Trail see entry 1438.
1483 **Mansfield's Approach Trail**, Maryland Historical Trails, P.O. Box 419, Glen Burnie, MD 21061. 11.0 miles. Awards available. (HTA)
1484 **Martinak State Park Trail**, Deep Shore Rd., Denton, MD 21629, (410) 479-1619. 2.0 miles loop. (WCD; DMV)
1485 **Maryland Heights-Buggy Rock Trail**, Del-Mar-Va Council, BSA, 8th and Washington Sts., Wilmington, DE 19801. 4.6-9.8 miles. (DMV)
1486 **Maydale Nature Center**, Naturalist, Maydale Nature Center, 1726 Briggs Chaney Rd., Colesville, MD 20904, (301) 384-9447. 1.7 miles. (NWA)
1487 **McKee-Beshers Wildlife Management Area**, c/o District Manager, Strider Work Center, 12510 Clopper Rd., Germantown, MD 20767, (301) 428-0438. (GNA)
1488 **McLaw's Approach Trail**, Maryland Historical Trails, P.O. Box 419, Glen Burnie, MD 21061. 28.0 miles. Awards available. (HTA)
1489 **Merkle Wildlife Management Area**, c/o Cheltenham Work Center, 11000 Old Indian Head Rd., Upper Marlboro, MD 20870, (301) 372-8128. 7.0 miles. (NAT; GNA)
1490 **Milburn Landing Nature Trail**, Milburn Landing Recreation Area, Rt. 1, Pocomoke City, MD 21815. (CBP)
Mistletoe Trail see entry 1438.
1491 **Monocacy Battle Trail**, Maryland Historical Trails, P.O. Box 419, Glen Burnie, MD 21061; or Monocacy National Battlefield, c/o Antietam National Battlefield, P.O. Box 158, Sharpsburg, MD 21782, (301) 432-5124. 10.0 miles. Awards available. (NPE)
1492 **Monocacy Natural Resources**

Management Area, P.O. Box 141, Beallsville, MD 20704. 4.0 miles. (GNA)
1493 **Morris Meadow Recreation Farm,** Freeland Rd., Freeland, MD 21053, (410) 329-6636 or (800) 643-7036. (WCD)
1494 **Mt. Nebo Wildlife Management Area,** Star Route 1, Box 45, Oakland, MD 21550, (410) 334-4255. (GNA)
1495 **Myrtle Grove Work Center,** District Manager, Rt. 2, Box 2209, La Plata, MD 20646, (301) 743-5161. (NWA)
1496 **Needwood Lake Park,** Avery Rd., Rockville, MD 20855, (301) 948-5053. (GPW)
1497 **New Germany State Park,** Rt. 2, Grantsville, MD 21536, (301) 895-5453. Named trails: Big Savage Mountain 17.0. (ATM; MMA; OTB; GNA)
1498 **Northern Central Railroad Trail,** Dave Davis, Manager, Gunpowder Falls State Park, P.O. Box 5032, Glen Arm, MD 21057, (410) 592-2897. 20.0 miles straight. (GRT)
1499 **Number Nine Trolley Line Trail,** Charles Kines, Regional Superintendent, Baltimore County Department of Recreation and Parks, 301 Washington Ave., Towson, MD 21204, (410) 887-3829. 1.5 miles straight. (GRT)
1500 **Oxon Hill Farm Trail,** National Capital Parks-East, 1900 Anacostia Drive, S.E., Washington, DC 20020, (301) 839-1177. 0.5 mile. (CGA)
Panhandle Trail see entry 1438.
Panther Branch Trail see entry 1469.
1501 **Patapsco Valley State Park,** 1100 Hilton Ave., Baltimore, MD 21227, (410) 747-6602. 15.0 miles. Named trails: Deer Run Nature, Grist Mill, Saw Mill Branch, Switchback 5.0. (WCD; ATM; MMA; GPW; AMI; GNA; NWA)
1502 **Patuxent River Park,** Maryland-National Capital Park and Planning Commission, Rt. 1, Box 3380, Upper Marlboro, MD 20870, (301) 627-6074. 4.5 miles. (ATM; GNA; NWA)
1503 **Patuxent River State Park Trail,** 17400 Annapolis Rock Rd., Woodbine, MD 21797, (301) 489-4646. 0.5 mile. (NAT; NWA)
1504 **Piney Run Park,** 30 Martz Rd., Sykesville, MD 21784, (410) 795-3274. 4.0 miles. Named trails: Field, Inlet, Lake. (NWA)
1505 **Piscataway Park,** c/o National Capital Parks-East, 1900 Anacostia Dr., S.E., Washington, DC 20020, (301) 472-9227. (NPE)
Plantation Trail see entry 1438.
1506 **Pocomoke River State Park,** SR 364, Pocomoke City, MD 21851, (410) 632-2566. (WCD; ATM; MMA)
1507 **Pocomoke State Forest,** Rt. 2, Box 99, Pocomoke City, MD 21851, (410) 632-2566. 75.0 miles. (MMA; GNA)
1508 **Point Lookout State Park,** SR 5, Scotland, MD 20687, (301) 872-5688. (WCD; ATM; MMA; DBV; DMA; OTB)
1509 **Potomac Heritage Trail** (see separate entry **4957** in interstate section).
1510 **Potomac State Forest,** Deer Park, MD 21550, (301) 334-2038; or Potomac State Forest, SR 219N, Oakland, MD 21550, (301) 334-3296. 8.0 miles. Named trails: Backbone Mountain. (MMA; GNA)
Railroad Segment see entry 1425.
1511 **Ramblin' Pines Campground,** 801 Hoods Mill Rd., Woodbine, MD 21797, (301) 795-5161. (WCD)
Red Trail see entry 1453.
Red Trail see entry 1513.
1512 **Rock Creek Regional Park,** 6700 Needwood Rd., Derwood, MD 20855, (301) 762-9500. (NWA)
Rocks Nature Trail see entry 1513.
1513 **Rocks State Park,** 3318 Rocks Chrome Hill Rd., Jarretsville, MD 21084, (410) 557-7994. Named trails: Red, Rocks Nature 0.5. (ATM; OTB; AMI; GNA)
1514 **Rocky Gap State Park,** SR 40, Cumberland, MD 21502, (301) 777-2138; or Rocky Gap State Park, Rt. 1, Box 90, Flintstone, MD 21530, (301) 777-2138. 8.0 miles. (ATM; DMP; DBV; DMA; GNA)
1515 **Rodney Scout Reservation,** Del-Mar-Va Council, BSA, 8th and Washington Sts., Wilmington, DE 19801, (302) 652-3741; or Rodney Scout Reservation, Rt. 2, Box 398, North East, MD 21901, (410) 287-5888. (SFC)

MARYLAND

Sandy Point Nature Trail *see* entry 1516.

1516 **Sandy Point State Park**, Rt. 2, Box 137, Annapolis, MD 21401, (410) 974-1249 or (410) 757-1841. Named trails: Sandy Point Nature 2.7. (ATM; GNA)

1517 **Savage River State Forest**, US 40, Grantsville, MD 21536, (301) 895-5759. 180 miles. Named trails: Big Savage Mountain 17.0. (EGH; WCD; MMA; GNA)

Saw Mill Branch Trail *see* entry 1501.

1518 **Seneca Creek State Park**, P.O. Box 2235, Gaithersburg, MD 20760, (301) 924-2127. Named trails: Emma Strider Conservation. (ATM; MMA; GPW; GNA; NWA)

1519 **Sharpsburg Line Trail**, Maryland Historical Trails, P.O. Box 419, Glen Burnie, MD 21061. 11.0 miles. Awards available. (HTA)

Shot Tower Segment *see* entry 1425.

1520 **Sideling Hill Wildlife Management Area**, c/o District Wildlife Manager, Billmeyer Work Center, Star Route, Flintstone, MD 21530, (301) 478-2525. (GNA)

1521 **Smallwood Nature Trail**, Smallwood State Park, P.O. Box 25, Rison, MD 20681, (301) 743-7613. (NWA)

1522 **Snavely Ford Nature Trail**, Antietam National Battlefield, P.O. Box 158, Sharpsburg, MD 21782. 2.25 miles. (HTA)

1523 **Soldiers Delight Natural Environment Area**, 4830 Deer Park Rd., Owings Mills, MD 21117, (410) 922-3044. (AMI; NWA)

South Trail *see* entry 1438.

1524 **Sugarloaf Mountain**, Information Officer, Sugarloaf Regional Trails, P.O. Box 87, Stronghold, Dickerson, MD 20842, (301) 926-4510; or Stronghold, Inc., P.O. Box 55, Dickerson Station, MD 20753. (ATM; GFA; GPW; AMI; GNA; NWA; PTB)

Sunset Trail *see* entry 1438.

1525 **Susquehanna State Park**, 801 Stafford Rd., Havre de Grace, MD 21078, (410) 939-0643. 3.0 miles. (WCD; ATM; MMA; GNA)

1526 **Swallow Falls State Park**, c/o Herrington Manor State Park, Rt. 5, Box 122, Oakland, MD 21550, (410) 339-9180. 10.0 miles. Named trails: Canyon. (ATM; MMA; OTB; GNA)

Switchback Trail *see* entry 1501.

Thinker Segment *see* entry 1425.

1527 **Tuckahoe State Park**, Rt. 1, Box 23, Queen Anne, MD 21657, (410) 634-2810. (WCD; ATM)

1528 **Upper Rock Creek Regional Park**, 6700 Needwood Rd., Rockville, MD 20855, (301) 948-5053. (ATM; NAT)

1529 **Warrior Mountain Wildlife Management Area**, Rt. 1, Box 97, Oldtown, MD 21555, (301) 395-5639. (GNA)

1530 **Washington Monument State Park**, US 40A, Boonsboro, MD 21713, (301) 432-8065. (ATM; MMA; OTB)

1531 **Watersedge Trail**, Public Information Officer, Maryland-National Capital Park and Planning Commission, Montgomery County, 8787 Georgia Ave., Silver Spring, MD 20907, (301) 589-1480. 6.5 miles. (NWA)

1532 **Watkins Regional Park**, Rt. 2, Box 2328, Upper Marlboro, MD 20870, (301) 249-9220. 5.0 miles. (NWA)

West Trail *see* entry 1438.

1533 **Wheaton Regional Park**, 12012 Kemp Mill Rd., Wheaton, MD 20902, (301) 622-0056. 4.0 miles. (NWA; PTB)

White Rocks Trail *see* entry 1419.

Wolf Dam Trail *see* entry 1438.

1534 **Woodland Nature Trail**, Audubon Naturalist Society of the Central Atlantic States, 8940 Jones Mill Rd., Chevy Chase, MD 20815, (301) 652-9188. (NAT; WCG)

1535 **Woodlands Camping Resort**, 265 Starkey Ln., Elkton, MD 21921, (410) 398-4414. (WCD)

1536 **Wye Island Natural Resources Area**, c/o Department of Natural Resources, State of Maryland, Tawes State Office Bldg., Annapolis, MD 21401, (410) 269-2230. 6.0 miles. (AMC; CBP)

Generally:
Maryland Forest, Park and Wildlife Service, Tawes State Office Bldg., C-2, Annapolis, MD 21401, (410) 374-3771. (EGH)

Index (by city)

Annapolis: Colonial Annapolis Historical Trail 1442; Sandy Point State Park 1516; Wye Island Natural Resources Area 1536

Baltimore: Baltimore Historical Trails 1425; Cylburn Park and Arboretum 1445; Fort McHenry Trail 1456; Leakin and Gwynns Falls 1478; Patapsco Valley State Park 1501

Berlin: Assateague Island National Seashore 1422; Assateague State Park 1423

Bethesda: Lenhok'sin Trail Camp Programs 1479

Big Pool: Indian Springs Wildlife Management Area 1474

Bladensburg: Battle of Bladensburg & The Star-Spangled Banner Trail 1426

Boonsboro: Washington Monument State Park 1530

Brandywine: Cedarville State Forest 1438

Cambridge: Blackwater National Wildlife Refuge 1430

Carderock Springs: Carderock Recreation Area 1436

Chevy Chase: Woodland Nature Trail 1534

Clarksburg: Little Bennett Regional Park 1480

Clinton: Clinton Regional Park 1441; Louise F. Cosca Regional Park 1482

Colesville: Maydale Nature Center 1486

Cumberland: Rocky Gap State Park 1514

Deer Park: Garrett State Forest 1459; Potomac State Forest 1510

Denton: Martinak State Park Trail 1484

Derwood: Rock Creek Regional Park 1512

Dickerson: Sugarloaf Mountain 1524

Doncaster: Doncaster State Forest 1450

Dundalk: Defenders Trail 1449

Elkton: Woodlands Camping Resort 1535

Federalsburg: Idylwild Wildlife Management Area 1473

Flintstone: Green Ridge State Forest 1466; Rocky Gap State Park 1514; Sideling Hill Wildlife Management Area 1520

Fort Washington: Fort Washington Park 1457

Frederick: Gambrill State Park 1458

Freeland: Morris Meadow Recreation Farm 1493

Gaithersburg: Seneca Creek State Park 1518

Gapland: Gathland State Park 1460

Germantown: McKee-Beshers Wildlife Management Area 1487

Glen Arm: Gunpowder Falls State Park 1469; Northern Central Railroad Trail 1498

Glen Burnie: Annapolis Pathways 1417; C & O Canal Towpath Trail 1432; Chief Nemacolin's Trail 1440; General A.P. Hill's Forced March 1461; Governor Johnson Patriot Trail 1463; Mansfield's Approach Trail 1483; McLaw's Approach Trail 1488; Sharpsburg Line Trail 1519

Goshen, VA: Goshen Scout Camp 1462

Grantsville: New Germany State Park 1497; Savage River State Forest 1517

Great Falls: Great Falls Park 1465

Greenbelt: Greenbelt National Park 1467

Greensboro: Holiday Park Campground 1472

Hagerstown: Appalachian Trail 1421; C & O Canal Historic Trail 1431; Fort Frederick State Park 1455; Greenbrier State Park 1468

Harpers Ferry, WV: Grant Conway Historic Trail 1464; Maryland Heights-Buggy Rock Trail 1485

Havre de Grace: Susquehanna State Park 1525

Jarretsville: Rocks State Park 1513

La Plata: Myrtle Grove Work Center 1495

Little Orleans: Little Orleans Campground 1481

Luke: Big Run State Park 1428

Lusby: Calvert Cliffs State Park 1434

Millersville: Capitol KOA Nature Trail 1435

North East: Black Trail 1429; Elk Neck State Forest 1452; Elk Neck State Park 1453; Rodney Scout Reservation 1515

Oakland: Deep Creek Lake State Park 1448; Herrington Manor 1471; Mt. Nebo Wildlife Management Area 1494; Potomac State Forest 1510; Swallow Falls State Park 1526

Oldtown: Dan's Mountain Wildlife Management Area 1446; Warrior Mountain Wildlife Management Area 1529

Owings Mills: Soldiers Delight Natural Environment Area 1523
Pocomoke City: Milburn Landing Nature Trail 1490; Pocomoke State Forest 1507
Prince Frederick: Battle Creek Cypress Swamp Sanctuary 1427; Jefferson Patterson Park and Museum 1475
Princess Anne: Deal Island Wildlife Management Area 1447
Queen Anne: Tuckahoe State Park 1527
Rison: Smallwood Nature Trail 1521
Rock Hall: Eastern Neck National Wildlife Refuge 1451
Rockville: Cabin John Regional Park 1433; Needwood Lake Park 1496; Upper Rock Creek Regional Park 1528
St. Mary's City: Chancellor's Point Natural History Area 1439
Scotland: Point Lookout State Park 1508
Severna Park: Baltimore and Annapolis Trail 1424
Sharpsburg: Antietam Battlefield Historical Trail 1418; Monocacy Battle Trail 1491; Snavely Ford Nature Trail 1522
Silver Spring: Watersedge Trail 1531
Sykesville: Piney Run Park 1504
Thurmont: Catoctin Mountain National Park 1437; Crow's Nest Campground 1443; Cunningham Falls State Park 1444
Towson: Hampton National Historic Site Trail 1470; Number Nine Trolley Line Trail 1499
Upper Marlboro: Jug Bay Natural Area 1476; Merkle Wildlife Management Area 1489; Patuxent River Park 1502; Watkins Regional Park 1532
Washington, DC: Oxon Hill Farm Trail 1500; Piscataway Park 1505
Wheaton: Wheaton Regional Park 1533
Williamsport: KOA-Snug Harbor 1477
Woodbine: Patuxent River State Park Trail 1503; Ramblin' Pines Campground 1511

MASSACHUSETTS

Agawon Trail *see* entry 1538.
Alander Trail *see* entry 1721.
1537 **Ames Nowell State Park**, Linwood St., Abington, MA 02351. 5.0 miles. (GBP)
1538 **Appalachian Side Trails** (not listed elsewhere), Appalachian Trail Conference, P.O. Box 807, Harpers Ferry, WV 25425, (304) 535-6331; or Appalachian Mountain Club, Pinkham Notch Camp, Gorham, NH 03581, (604) 466-2727. Named trails: Agawon, Bellows Pipe, Bellows Pipe Ski, Broad Brook, Cheshire Harbor, Deer Hill, Gould Farm, Hopper, Money Brook, Mt. Prospect, Overlook, Pine Cobble, Race Brook, South Taconic, Undermountain. (ATG #3; BMG)
1539 **Appalachian Trail** (see separate entry **4948** in interstate section).
1540 **Appalachian Trail in Massachusetts**, Great Trails Council, BSA, 88 Old Windsor Rd., Dalton, MA 01226, (413) 684-3542. 85.0 miles (in segments of 5-20 miles each). Awards available. (AA 1992)
1541 **Arcadia Nature Center and Wildlife Sanctuary**, Easthampton, MA 01027, (413) 584-3009. 4.0 miles. (SNE)
1542 **Ashumet Holly Reservation**, 286 Ashumet Rd., East Falmouth, MA 02536, (508) 563-6390. 1.25 miles. Named trails: Crater Loop, English Holly, Holly, Pond. (FNE; NAT; SNE; SWC)
Atlantic White Cedar Swamp Trail *see* entry 1572.
1543 **Bartholomew's Cobble**, P.O. Box 233, Ashley Falls, MA 01222, (413) 298-8600; or Trustees of Reservations, 224 Adams St., Milton, MA 02186. 6.0 miles. Named trails: Ledges Interpretive. (FRN; SNE; NET; TBB; ANI; GNA)
Base Path *see* entry 1547.

1544 **Bash-Bish Falls State Forest**, c/o Mt. Washington State Forest, Copake, NY 12517, (413) 528-0330. 15.0 miles. (NET; ANI; GNA)
1545 **Beartown State Forest**, Blue Hill Rd., Monterey, MA 01245, (413) 528-0904. Named trails: Mt. Wilcox 4.4(l). (SNE; TBB; GNA)
Beau Bridge Trail *see* entry 1657.
Beech Forest Trail *see* entry 1572.
Bellows Pipe Ski Trail *see* entry 1538.
Bellows Pipe Trail *see* entry 1538.
1546 **Birch Hill Wildlife Management Area**, Division of Fisheries and Game, Temple St., West Boylston, MA 01583, (617) 835-3607. 31.0 miles. (SNE; GNA)
Black Duck Creek Trail *see* entry 1605.
Blue Dot Trail *see* entry 1547.
1547 **Blue Hills Reservation and Fowl Meadows**, 695 Hillside St., Milton, MA 02186, (617) 698-5840 or (617) 333-0690. 300 miles. Named trails: Base Path, Blue Dot, Border Path, Burma Road, Chestnut Run Path, Cliff Path, Coon Hollow Path, Dalton Path, 5 Corners Path, Half Way Path, Hancock Hill Path, Hemenway Hill Path, Houghton Path, North Sky Line, Ponkapog Pond, Puddle Path, Red Dot, South Sky Line, Wolcott Path, Yellow Dot. (MNE; NAT; GBP; GNA)
1548 **Blue Hills State Reservation**, 20 Somerset St., Boston, MA 02108, (617) 727-5114. (EGH; SNE)
1549 **Blue Hills Trails**, Witch Trail Committee, 157 Circuit Rd., Winthrop, MA 02152, (617) 836-2626. 2.0 and 8.0 miles loops. Awards available. (AA 1994)
Bog Nature Trail *see* entry 1576.
1550 **Bolton Flats Wildlife Management**

Area, Wildlife District Manager, Temple St., West Boylston, MA 01583, (506) 835-3607. (SNE)

Border Path see entry 1547.

1551 **Borderland State Park**, Massapoag Ave., North Easton, MA 02334, (617) 238-6566. 6.0 miles. (SNE; GBP)

1552 **Boston Bicentennial Trail of Freedom**, American Historical Trails, Inc., P.O. Box 769, Monroe, NC 28110, (704) 289-1604. 5.5-11.75 miles. Awards available. (AA 1992)

1553 **Boston Harbor Islands State Park**, 349 Lincoln St./SR 3A, Hingham, MA 02043, (617) 740-1605. (WCD; GFC)

1554 **Boston's Black Heritage Trail**, Boston African American National Historic Site, 46 Joy St., Boston, MA 02114, (617) 742-5415. 1.6 miles. (LGU; GNM; NPE; CGA; NET)

1555 **Boulder Brook Trail**, Kelly Park, Boulder Brook Reservation, Elmwood Rd., Wellesley, MA 02181. (GBP)

Brace Mountain to Riga Lake Trail see entry 1721.

1556 **Bradley W. Palmer State Park**, Asbury St., Topsfield, MA 01983, (617) 887-5931. 10.0 miles. (GBP)

1557 **Bread and Roses Strike Trail**, Bread and Roses Strike Trail Associates, 37 Linehan St., Lawrence, MA 01841. 3.5 miles loop. Awards available. (AA 1994)

Briar Patch Path see entry 1671.

1558 **Brimfield State Forest**, US 20, Brimfield, MA 01010, (413) 245-9966. 24.0 miles. (MNE; SNE; GNA)

Broad Brook Trail see entry 1538.

1559 **Broadmoor Wildlife Sanctuary**, 280 Eliot St., Natick, MA 01760, (617) 655-2296. 9.0 miles. (NAT; SNE)

1560 **Buffumville Reservoir**, Public Affairs Officer, U.S. Army Engineer Division, New England, 424 Trapelo Rd., Waltham, MA 02154. (LRA)

Burma Road see entry 1547.

Buttonbush Trail see entry 1572.

1561 **Callahan State Park**, Millwood St., Framingham, MA 01701, (617) 653-9641. 5.0 miles. (GBP)

1562 **Camp Cacholot**, Moby Dick Council, BSA, 39 Grove St., New Bedford, MA 92740, (617) 993-9978. (SFC)

1563 **Camp Child**, Moby Dick Council, BSA, 39 Grove St., New Bedford, MA 02740, (617) 993-9978. (SFC)

1564 **Camp Noquochoke**, Moby Dick Council, BSA, 39 Grove St., New Bedford, MA 02740, (617) 993-9978. (SFC)

1565 **Camp Squanto**, Old Colony Council, BSA, 2348 Washington St., Canton, MA 02021, (617) 828-8360; or Camp Squanto, P.O. Box 931, South Carver, MA 02368, (617) 224-2010. (SFC)

1566 **Campbell Falls State Park**, Massachusetts Division of Forests and Parks, 100 Cambridge St., Boston, MA 02202, (617) 727-3180. (SNE)

1567 **Canoe Meadows Wildlife Sanctuary**, Holmes Rd., Pittsfield, MA 01201, (413) 637-0320. 5.0 miles. Named trails: Sacred Way, Wolf Pine. (MNE; SNE)

1568 **Cape Cod-Barnstable County**, The Cape Cod Animal Hospital, West Barnstable, MA 02558; or Govone Grain and Feed, SR 130, Forestdale, MA 02644; or Maushop Farm, Cotuit, MA 02635; or Flying B Ranch, Pine Ln., Barnstable, MA 02630; or Circle B Ranch, SR 28, Hyannis, MA 02601. Named trails: Cotuit Highlands 59.0, Dopple Bottom 67.0, Hathaway Ponds 19.0, Mashapee Pond 40.1, Mill Pond 2.0, Mystic Lake 14.0, Race Lane 12.0, Town Line 16.0, Wequaquet Lake 52.8. (HTN)

1569 **Cape Cod Bikeway/Recreational Trail**, Division of Forests, Parks and Recreation, 100 Cambridge St., Boston, MA 02202, (617) 727-3180. 16.3 miles. (GNA)

1570 **Cape Cod Campresort**, Thomas Landers Rd., East Falmouth, MA 02536, (508) 548-1458 or (800) 777-2175. (WCD)

1571 **Cape Cod Museum of Natural History**, SR 6A, Brewster, MA 02631. Named trails: North 0.25(l), South 0.75(l). (SWC)

1572 **Cape Cod National Seashore**, National Parks Service, South Wellfleet, MA 02663, (617) 349-3785. 40.0 miles. Named trails: Atlantic White Cedar Swamp 1.25, Beech Forest 1.0, Buttonbush 0.25(l), Fort

Hill (Red Maple Swamp) 1.5, Great Island 8.0(l), Indian Hill 0.25, Nauset Marsh 1.5, Pilgrim Spring 0.5(l), Salt Pond 1.0(l), Small's Swamp 0.5(l). (LGU; MNE; SNE; GFA; NPV; WYW; DGW; NSS; NPE; CGA; AFW; FDN; HTA; GNA; HTN; SWC)

Cape Cod Rail Trail see entry 1697.

1573 **Cape Poge Wildlife Refuge**, Trustees of Reservations, 572 Essex St., Beverly, MA 01915, (508) 921-1944. (SNE)

1574 **Catamount State Forest**, Catamount State Forest, c/o Mohawk Trail State Forest, SR 2, Charlemont, MA 01339, (413) 339-5504. 14.0 miles. (SNE; GNA)

1575 **Charles River Pathway**, Newton Conservation Commission, 1000 Commonwealth Ave., Newton, MA 02159. 8.0 miles. (GBP)

1576 **Charles W. Ward Reservation**, 5 Ward Ln., Andover, MA 01845. Named trails: Bog Nature. (SNE)

Cheshire Harbor Trail see entry 1538.

1577 **Chester-Blandford State Forest**, Chester, MA 01050, (413) 354-6347. 10.0 miles. (SNE; GNA)

1578 **Chesterwood Nature Trail**, Chesterwood Estate, SR 183, Stockbridge, MA 01262. (NET)

Chestnut Run Path see entry 1547.

1579 **Circle CG Farm**, 131 N. Main St., Bellingham, MA 02019, (508) 966-1136. (WCD)

1580 **Clarksburg State Forest**, Middle Rd., Clarksburg, MA 01247, (413) 442-8928. (SNE; TBB; GNA)

1581 **Clarksburg State Park**, Middle Rd., North Adams, MA 01247, (413) 663-6312. (WCD)

Cliff Path see entry 1547.

1582 **Cookson State Forest**, West St., Sandisfield, MA 01255, (413) 258-4774. (TBB)

Coon Hollow Path see entry 1547.

Cotuit Highlands Trail see entry 1568.

1583 **Country Aire Campground**, P.O. Box 286, SR 2, Mohawk Trail, MA 01339, (413) 625-2996. (WCD)

1584 **Crane Pond Wildlife Management Area**, Wildlife District Manager, Harris St., P.O. Box 86, Acton, MA 01720, (508) 263-4647. (SNE)

1585 **Crane Wildlife Management Area**, Wildlife District Manager, Southeast Wildlife District, 195 Bourndak Rd., Buzzards Bay, MA 02532, (617) 759-3406. (SNE; GNA)

Crater Loop Trail see entry 1542.

Curtis Trail see entry 1602.

1586 **Cutler Park**, Needham and Dedham Banks of Charles River, Boston, MA 02135. Named trails: Kenrick Street 1.5(l), Riverdale 1.0. (GBP)

1587 **D.A.R. State Forest**, SR 112, Goshen, MA 01032, (413) 268-7098. 9.0 miles. (WCD; GNA)

Dalton Path see entry 1547.

1588 **Daniel Webster Wildlife Sanctuary**, South Shore Regional Center, 2000 Main St., Marshfield, MA 02050, (617) 837-9400. (SNE)

Deer Hill Trail see entry 1538.

1589 **Derby Wharf Historic Trail**, Salem Maritime National Historic Site, Custom House, Derby St., Salem, MA 01970, (617) 744-4323. 1.0 mile loop. (CGA)

Dike Trail see entry 1605.

Discovery Hill Path see entry 1671.

Dopple Bottom Trail see entry 1568.

1590 **Dorothy F. Rice Sanctuary for Wildlife**, Rice Rd., Peru, MA 01050, (413) 655-2681. 12.0 miles. (SNE; TBB; GNA)

1591 **Duvall Nature Trail**, Hoosac Valley High School, SR 116, Adams, MA 01220. 2.0 miles. (TBB)

1592 **East Mt. State Reservation**, SR 7, Great Barrington, MA 01230, (413) 528-2000. (TBB)

Elbow Trail see entry 1658.

English Holly Trail see entry 1542.

1593 **Erving State Forest**, Church St., Erving, MA 01344, (508) 544-3939. 14.0 miles. (WCD; SNE; GNA)

1594 **Eugene D. Moran Wildlife Management Area**, Division of Fisheries and Wildlife, Western Wildlife District Manager, 400 Hubbard Ave., Pittsfield, MA 01201, (413) 447-9789. (GNA)

1595 **Falmouth Shining Sea Trail**, Kevin

Lynch, P.O. Box 372, Peaticket, MA 02536, (508) 968-5859. 3.2 miles straight. (GRT)

1596 **Federated Women's Clubs State Forest**, c/o Otter River State Forest, Baldwinville, MA 01436, (617) 939-8962. (GNA)

1597 **Felix Neck Wildlife Sanctuary**, Edgartown-Vineyard Haven Rd., P.O. Box 494, Vineyard Haven, Martha's Vineyard, MA 02568, (508) 627-4850. 6.0 miles. Named trails: Orange, Shad, Yellow. (MNE; NAT; SNE; GFA; SWC)

1598 **Five Colleges Bikeway**, Daniel O'Brian, Bikeway and Rail Trail Planner, Department of Environmental Management, Division of Resource Conservation, 100 Cambridge St., Rm. 1404, Boston, MA 02202, (617) 727-3160 ext. 557. 9.0 miles straight. (GRT)

5 Corners Path see entry 1547.

1599 **Footsteps of Our Founders Trail**, Moby Dick Council, BSA, 39 Grove St., New Bedford, MA 02740-3498, (508) 993-9978 or (508) 678-2858. 6.5 miles loop. Awards available. (AA 1994)

1600 **Forest Park**, US 5, Springfield, MA 01101. (MNE)

Fort Hill Trail see entry 1572.

1601 **Freedom Trail**, Greater Boston Council, BSA, 891 Centre St., Boston, MA 02130-2796, (617) 522-4000. 5.0 miles. Awards available. (AA 1992)

1602 **Garden in the Woods**, Hemenway Rd., Framingham, MA 01701, (508) 877-6574. (SNE)

Goose Pond Nature Trail see entry 1737.

Gould Farm Trail see entry 1538.

1603 **Granville State Forest**, W. Hartland Rd., Granville, MA 01034, (413) 357-6611. 3.0 miles. (WCD; MNE; SNE; GNA)

Gray Birch Trail see entry 1721.

1604 **Great Brook Farm State Park**, North St., Carlisle, MA 01741, (617) 369-6312. 7.0 miles. (GBP)

Great Island Trail see entry 1572.

1605 **Great Meadows National Wildlife Refuge**, Weir Hill Rd., Sudbury, MA 01776, (508) 443-4661. Named trails: Black Duck Creek, Dike 1.5, Timber, Weir Hill, Wood Duck. (MNE; NAT; SNE; GFA; OTB; AFW; GBP; GNA; GNW)

1606 **H.O. Cook State Forest**, c/o Mohawk Trail State Forest, SR 2, Charlemont, MA 01339, (413) 339-5504. (SNE; GNA)

Half Way Path see entry 1547.

1607 **Hammond Pond Woods**, Hammond Pond Pkwy., Boston, MA 02120. 10.0 miles. (GBP)

Hancock Hill Path see entry 1547.

1608 **Hancock Shaker Trail**, Great Trails Council, BSA, 88 Old Windsor Rd., Dalton, MA 01226, (413) 684-3542. 6.0 miles. Awards available. (AA 1992)

Hank's Place Trail see entry 1690.

1609 **Harold Parker State Forest**, Middleton Rd., North Andover, MA 01845, (617) 686-3391. 11.0 miles. (WCD; SNE; GBP)

Hathaway Ponds Trail see entry 1568.

1610 **Hawley State Forest**, Hawley, MA 01070, (413) 634-8858. 8.0 miles. (GNA)

Hellcat Swamp Wildlife Trail see entry 1677.

Hemenway Hill Path see entry 1547.

1611 **Heritage Walking Tour**, Boston Chamber of Commerce, 69 Rogers St., Boston, MA 02127. (RTH)

1612 **High Ridge Wildlife Management Area**, Wildlife District Manager, Temple St., West Boylston, MA 01583, (508) 835-3607. (SNE)

1613 **Hinsdale Flats Wildlife Management Area**, Wildlife District Manager, 400 Hubbard Ave., Pittsfield, MA 01201, (413) 447-9789. (SNE)

1614 **Hiram H. Fox Wildlife Management Area**, Wildlife District Manager, 400 Hubbard Ave., Pittsfield, MA 01201, (413) 447-9789. (SNE)

1615 **Hockomock Swamp Wildlife Management Area**, Wildlife District Manager, Southeast Wildlife District, 195 Bourndale Rd., Buzzards Bay, MA 02352, (617) 759-3406. 15.0 miles. (SNE; GNA)

Holly Trail see entry 1542.

1616 **Hopkins Memorial Forest**, Bulkley St., Williamstown, MA 01267, (413) 458-3080. (TBB)

1617 **Hopkinton State Park**, Cedar St., Hopkinton, MA 01748, (508) 435-4303. (SNE)
  Hopper Trail see entry 1538.
  Houghton Path see entry 1547.
1618 **Hubbardton Wildlife Management Area**, Wildlife District Manager, Temple St., West Boylston, MA 01583, (508) 835-3607. (SNE)
1619 **Ice Glen Nature Preserve**, Ice Glen Rd., Stockbridge, MA 01262. (TBB)
  Indian Hill Trail see entry 1572.
  Indian Monument Trails see entry 1651.
  Indian Trail see entry 1648.
1620 **Indianhead Campground**, SR 3A, Plymouth, MA 02360, (508) 888-3688. (WCD)
1621 **Ipswich River Sanctuary**, Perkins Row, Topsfield, MA 01983, (617) 887-9264. 15.0 miles. (NAT; SNE; OTB; GBP; GNA)
1622 **Isaac Davis Trail**, Scouters of the Isaac Davis Trail, P.O. Box 763, Acton, MA 01720. 7.0 miles straight. Awards available. (AA 1992)
1623 **John C. Phillips Wildlife Sanctuary**, Division of Fisheries and Wildlife, 100 Cambridge St., Boston, MA 02202, (617) 727-3151. (SNE)
1624 **John Wing Trail**, Wing Island, SR 6A, Brewster, MA 02631. 1.3 miles loop. (SWC)
1625 **Kenneth Dubuque Memorial State Forest**, Hawley, MA 01070, (413) 339-6631. 43.0 miles. (SNE)
  Kenrick Street Trail see entry 1587.
  Kettle Hole Trail see entry 1677.
1626 **Knightville Dam**, Public Affairs Officer, U.S. Army Corps of Engineers, New England Division, Trapelo Rd., Waltham, MA 02154. (LRA)
1627 **KOA-Plymouth Rock**, P.O. Box 616, Dept. W, US 44, Middleboro, MA 02346, (508) 947-6435. (WCD)
1628 **KOA-Sturbridge Webster Family Kampground**, SR 16, Webster, MA 01570, (508) 943-1895. (WCD)
1629 **Lake Denison State Park**, Winchendon, MA 01475, (617) 297-1609. (GNA)
1630 **Laughing Brook Education Center and Wildlife Sanctuary**, 789 Main St., Hampden, MA 01036, (413) 566-8034. (MNE)
  Ledges Interpretive Trail see entry 1543.
1631 **Leominster State Forest**, P.O. Box 32, East Princeton, MA 01517, (617) 874-2303. 28.0 miles. (SNE; GNA)
1632 **Leslie's Retreat Trail**, Witch Trail Committee, 157 Circuit Rd., Winthrop, MA 02152, (617) 836-2626. 6.0-10.0 miles. Awards available. (AA 1994)
1633 **Long Hill Reservation**, Sedgewick Gardens, 572 Essex St., Beverly, MA 01915, (617) 922-1536. (NAT)
1634 **Long Point Wildlife Refuge**, Trustees of Reservations, 224 Adams St., Milton, MA 02186, (617) 698-2066. (SNE)
1635 **Lowell Holly Reservation**, S. Sandwich Rd., Sandwich, MA 02563. 2.0 miles. Named trails: Wheeler. (SWC)
1636 **Lynn Woods Reservation**, Penny Brook Rd., Lynn, MA 01905. 30.0 miles. (MNE; GBP)
1637 **Malachi Brook Wildlife Sanctuary**, South Shore Sanctuaries, SR 3A, Marshfield, MA 02050, (617) 837-9500. 3.0 miles. (GBP)
1638 **Martha's Vineyard State Forest Trail**, West Tisbury, MA 02575. 1.0 mile loop. (SWC)
1639 **Martin Burns Wildlife Management Area**, Wildlife District Manager, Harris St., P.O. Box 86, Acton, MA 01720, (508) 263-4347. (SNE)
  Mashapee Pond Trail see entry 1568.
  Massachusetts-Sunset Rock Trail see entry 1721.
1640 **Massasoit State Park**, Middleboro Ave., East Taunton, MA 02718, (617) 822-7405. 5.0 miles. (WCD; GBP)
1641 **Metacomet-Monadnock Trail** (see separate entry **4952** in interstate section).
1642 **Middlesex Fells Reservation**, Pond St., Stoneham, MA 02180, (617) 438-5690. 50.0 miles. Named trails: Skyline. (GBP)
1643 **Midstate Trail**, Trails Program, Massachusetts Department of Environmental Management, 225 Friend St.,

Boston, MA 02114; or Midstate Trail Committee, P.O. Box 155, Clinton, MA 01510. 89.0 miles. (EGH; SNE; GNA)

Mill Pond Trail *see* entry 1568.

1644 **Millers River Wildlife Management Area**, District Wildlife Manager, Temple St., West Boylston, MA 01583, (508) 835-3607. (SNE)

1645 **Minute Man Trail**, Minute Man National Historical Park, P.O. Box 160, Concord, MA 01742, (617) 369-6993. 1.0 mile. (PGF; CGA)

1646 **Minuteman Bikeway**, Alan McClennen, Jr., Director of Planning and Community Development, Town Hall, 730 Massachusetts Ave., Arlington, MA 02174, (617) 646-1000 ext. 4130. 11.0 miles straight. (GRT)

1647 **Mohawk Trail**, Orange, MA 01364. 65.0 miles. (GFA)

1648 **Mohawk Trail State Forest**, P.O. Box 7, SR 2, Charlemont, MA 01339, (413) 339-5504. Named trails: Indian. (EGH; WCD; SNE; OTB; GNA)

Money Brook Trail *see* entry 1538.

1649 **Monomoy National Wildlife Refuge**, Morris Island, MA 02633, (617) 945-0594 (June-Sept.). 8.0 miles. (MNE; SNE; GNA)

1650 **Monroe State Forest**, Monroe, MA 01350, (413) 424-7600. 9.0 miles. (SNE; GNA)

1651 **Monument Mountain**, US 7, Great Barrington, MA 01230; or Trustees of Reservations, 224 Adams St., Milton, MA 02186. Named trails: Indian Monument. (NET; TBB)

1652 **Moore State Park**, Worcester, MA 01602. (OTB)

1653 **Moose Hill Wildlife Sanctuary**, 300 Moose Hill St., Sharon, MA 02067, (617) 784-5691. 6.0 miles. (SNE; GBP)

1654 **Mt. Everett State Reservation**, East St., Mt. Washington, MA 01258, (413) 528-0330. (TBB)

1655 **Mount Grace State Forest**, Warwick, MA 01364, (617) 544-7474. 9.0 miles. (SNE; GNA)

1656 **Mt. Greylock State Reservation**, P.O. Box 138, Notch Rd., North Adams, MA 01247, (413) 499-4262. 35.0 miles. (EGH; WCD; SNE; TBB; GNA)

Mt. Prospect Trail *see* entry 1538.

1657 **Mount Tom Reservation**, P.O. Box 985, Northampton, MA 01064, (413) 527-4805. 20.0 miles. Named trails: Beau Bridge. (EGH; SNE; ANI; GNA)

1658 **Mount Washington State Forest**, Mount Washington, MA 01258, (413) 528-0330. 15.0 miles. Named trails: Elbow. (EGH; GFC; SNE; DGW)

Mt. Wilcox Trail *see* entry 1545.

1659 **Myles Standish State Forest**, P.O. Box 66, Cranberry Rd., South Carver, MA 02366, (617) 866-2526. (WCD; MNE; SNE; GBP; GNA)

Mystic Lake Trail *see* entry 1568.

Nauset Marsh Trail *see* entry 1572.

1660 **Nickerson State Park** *see* entry 1697. (GRT; SNE)

1661 **Norcross Wildlife Sanctuary**, Monson-Wales Rd., Wales, MA 01081, (413) 267-9654. (GFA)

1662 **Normandy Farm Family Campground**, 72 West St., Dept. W, Foxboro, MA 02035, (508) 543-7600. (WCD)

1663 **Norris Reservation**, West St., Norwell, MA 02061. 3.0 miles. (GBP)

1664 **North Hill Marsh Wildlife Sanctuary**, South Shore Regional Center, 2000 Main St., Marshfield, MA 02050, (617) 837-9400. (SNE)

North Sky Line Trail *see* entry 1547.

North Trail *see* entry 1571.

1665 **Northampton Bikeway**, George Andrikidis, Northampton Department of Public Works, 125 Locust St., Northampton, MA 01060, (413) 586-6950. 2.6 miles straight. (GRT)

Northfield Mountain Nature Trail *see* entry 1666.

1666 **Northfield Mountain Recreation and Environmental Center**, Rt. 2, Box 117, Northfield, MA 01360, (413) 659-3714; or Monroe & Isabel Smith AYH-Hostel, 51 Highland Ave., Northfield, MA 01360, (413) 498-5311 ext. 502. 29.0 miles. Named trails: Northfield Mountain Nature, Shadow Lake Nature. (FNE; AYH; MNE; SNE; GFA)

1667 **Northfield-Warwick State Forest**,

c/o Mount Grace State Forest, Warwick, MA 01364, (617) 544-7474. 27.0 miles. (GNA)
Northrop Trail see entry 1721.
1668 **Notchview Reservation**, Windsor, MA 01270, (413) 684-0148; or Trustees of Reservations, 224 Adams St., Milton, MA 02186. 25.0 miles. (EGH; TBB; GNA)
1669 **Oak Haven Campground**, SR 19, Wales, MA 01081, (413) 245-7148. (WCD)
1670 **October Mountain State Forest**, Washington Mt. Brook Rd., Lee, MA 01238, (413) 243-1778. 12.0 miles. (WCD; SNE; TBB; GNA)
1671 **The Old Briar Patch**, Gully Ln., Sandwich, MA 02563. 2.0 miles. Named trails: Briar Patch Path, Discovery Hill Path, Springside. (SWC)
1672 **The Old Saw Mill Campground**, Longhill Rd., P.O. Box 377, West Brookfield, MA 01585, (508) 867-2427. (WCD)
1673 **Old Town Hill Reservation**, Newman Rd., Newbury, MA 01951; or Trustees of Reservations, 572 Essex St., Beverly, MA 01915, (508) 921-1944. Named trails: Old Town Hill 1.5. (SNE; GBP)
Old Town Hill Trail see entry 1673.
Orange Trail see entry 1597.
1674 **Otis State Forest**, SR 23, Otis, MA 01253. (TBB)
1675 **Otter River State Forest**, US 202, Winchendon, MA 01475, (508) 939-8962. 15.0 miles. (WCD; GNA; LRA)
Overlook Trail see entry 1538.
1676 **Oxboro National Wildlife Refuge**, c/o Great Meadows National Wildlife Refuge, 191 Sudbury Rd., Concord, MA 01742, (617) 369-5518. (GNA)
1677 **Parker River National Wildlife Refuge**, Northern Blvd., Plum Island, Newburyport, MA 01950, (617) 465-5753. 10.0 miles. Named trails: Hellcat Swamp Wildlife, Kettle Hole. (FNE; MNE; NAT; SNE; OTB; NET; GBP; GNA; GNW)
1678 **Partridge Hollow Camping Area**, P.O. Box 41, Monson, MA 01057, (413) 267-5122. (WCD)
1679 **Pearl Hill State Park**, New Fitchburg Rd., West Townsend, MA 01469, (508) 597-8802. (WCD)

1680 **Peru State Forest**, c/o Chester-Blandford State Forest, Huntington, MA 01050, (413) 354-6347. 7.5 miles. (GNA)
1681 **Peru Wildlife Management Area**, Wildlife District Manager, 400 Hubbard Ave., Pittsfield, MA 01201, (413) 447-9789. (SNE)
1682 **Phillipston Wildlife Management Area**, Wildlife District Manager, Temple St., West Boylston, MA 01583, (508) 835-3607. (SNE)
Pilgrim Spring Trail see entry 1572.
1683 **Pine Acres Family Campground**, Bechan Rd., Oakham, MA 01068, (508) 882-9509. (WCD)
1684 **Pine Banks Park**, 1087 Main St., Melrose, MA 02176, (617) 324-0822. 4.0 miles. (GBP)
Pine Cobble Trail see entry 1538.
Pine Hollow Trail see entry 1694.
1685 **Pinewood Lodge Campground**, 190 Pinewood Rd., Plymouth, MA 02360, (508) 746-3548 or (508) 746-6495. (WCD)
1686 **Pirate Legend Trek & Trail**, Witch Trail Committee, 157 Circuit Rd., Winthrop, MA 02152, (617) 836-2626. 4.0 & 10.0 miles. Awards available. (AA 1994)
1687 **Pittsfield State Forest**, Cascade St., Pittsfield, MA 01201, (413) 442-8992. 30.0 miles. Named trails: Taconic Crest, Taconic Skyline 20.0. (EGH; WCD; SNE; TBB; GNA)
1688 **Pleasant Valley Wildlife Sanctuary**, 472 W. Mountain Rd., Lenox, MA 01240, (413) 637-0320. 14.0 miles. Named trails: Trail of the Ledges 3.0(l). (MNE; SNE; OTB; NET; TBB; GNA)
Pond Trail see entry 1542.
Ponkapog Pond Trail see entry 1547.
Powers Trail see entry 1690.
1689 **Privacy Campground**, SR 43, Hancock, MA 01237, (413) 458-3125. (WCD)
Puddle Path see entry 1547.
1690 **Quabbin Reservoir**, 485 Ware Rd., Belchertown, MA 01007, (413) 323-6306. 10.0 miles. Named trails: Hank's Place 1.75, Powers 2.0. (SNE; ANI; GNA)
1691 **Quabog Wildlife Management Area**, c/o Division of Fisheries and Wildlife, 100 Cambridge St., Boston, MA 02202, (617) 727-3151; or District Wildlife

MASSACHUSETTS

Manager, Temple St., West Boylston, MA 01583, (508) 835-3607. 3.0 miles. (SNE; GNA)

1692 **Quarries Footpath**, Peter Church or Steve Ovellette, Quincy Quarries Historic Site, Metropolitan District Commission, 695 Hillside St., Milton, MA 02186, (617) 698-1802. 1.0 mile straight. (GRT)

Race Brook Trail see entry 1538.
Race Lane Trail see entry 1568.

1693 **Ravenswood Park**, SR 127, Manchester, MA 01944. (GBP)

Red Dot Trail see entry 1547.
Red Maple Swamp Trail see entry 1572.

1694 **Richard T. Crane, Jr. Memorial Reservation**, Trustees of Reservations, Northeast Regional Supervisor, Argilla Rd., Ipswich, MA 01938, (617) 356-4354. Named trails: Pine Hollow. (SNE; GNA)

Riverdale Trail see entry 1587.

1695 **Rock Meadow**, Mill St., Belmont, MA 02178. (GBP)

1696 **Rocky Woods Reservation**, Hartford St., Medford, MA 02052, (617) 359-6333. 12.0 miles. (GBP)

1697 **Roland C. Nickerson State Park**, SR 6A, Brewster, MA 02631, (508) 896-3491. Named trails: Cape Cod Rail 19.6(s). (EGH; WCD)

Sacred Way Trail see entry 1567.

1698 **Salem Heritage Trail**, National Park Service Information Center, Museum Place Mall, Salem, MA 01970, (617) 741-3648. 1.3 miles. (LGU)

1699 **Salem Maritime National Historic Site**, Custom House, Derby St., Salem, MA 01970. (NPV)

1700 **Salisbury Beach State Reservation**, SR 1A, Salisbury, MA 01952, (508) 462-4481. (WCD)

Salt Pond Trail see entry 1572.

1701 **Sandisfield State Forest**, West St., Sandisfield, MA 01255, (617) 258-4774. 20.0 miles. (GFC; SNE; TBB; GNA)

1702 **Sandy Neck Beach**, SR 6A & 149, Barnstable, MA 02630. 5.0 miles. (SWC)

1703 **Sandy Pond Campground**, 834 Bourne Rd., South Plymouth, MA 02360, (508) 759-9336. (WCD)

1704 **Savoy Mountain State Forest**, SR 2, Florida, MA 01247, (413) 663-8469. 24.0 miles. (EGH; WCD; MNE; SNE; TBB; GNA)

1705 **Scusset Beach State Park**, Scusset Rd., Sagamore, MA 02561, (508) 888-0859. (WCD)

1706 **The Seaside Trail**, Harding's Beach, Harding's Beach Rd., Chatham, MA 02633. 1.2 miles loop. (SWC)

Shad Trail see entry 1597.
Shadow Lake Nature Trail see entry 1666.

1707 **Shady Pines Campground**, P.O. Box D, Loop Rd., Savoy, MA 01256, (413) 743-2694. (WCD)

1708 **Shawme Crowell State Forest**, SR 130, Sandwich, MA 02563, (508) 888-0351. (WCD)

1709 **Sheriff's Meadow Trail**, Sheriff's Meadow Wildlife Preserve, Edgarton, Martha's Vineyard, MA 02539. 0.6 mile loop. (SWC)

1710 **Sky Line Trail**, Witch Trail Committee, 157 Circuit Rd., Winthrop, MA 02152, (617) 836-2626. 7.0 miles loop. Awards available. (AA 1994)

Skyline Trail see entry 1642.
Small's Swamp Trail see entry 1572.

1711 **Sons of Liberty Trail**, Witch Trail Committee, 157 Circuit Rd., Winthrop, MA 02152, (617) 836-2626. 10.0 miles. Awards available. (AA 1994)

South Sky Line Trail see entry 1547.
South Taconic Trail see entry 1538.
South Trail see entry 1571.

1712 **Southwest Corridor Park Trail**, Alan Morris, Parkland Manager, Southwest Corridor Park, 38 New Heath St., Jamaica Plain, MA 02130, (617) 727-0057. 5.0 miles straight. (GRT)

1713 **Spirit of '76 Trail**, Witch Trail Committee, 157 Circuit Rd., Winthrop, MA 02152, (617) 836-2626. 2.0 miles. Awards available. (AA 1994)

Springside Trail see entry 1671.

1714 **Stanley Park**, 400 Western Ave., Westfield, MA 01085, (413) 568-9312. (MNE)

Stissing Mountain Circular Trail see entry 1721.

MASSACHUSETTS

1715 **Stony Brook Nature Center and Wildlife Sanctuary**, North St., Norfolk, MA 02056, (617) 528-3140. (GFA)

1716 **Stony Brook Reservation**, Turtle Pond Pkwy., West Roxbury and Hyde Park, MA 02136, (617) 364-9683. 12.0 miles. (GFA)

1717 **Summit Hill Campground**, SR 8, Washington, MA 01235, (413) 623-5761. (WCD)

Sunset Rock Trail *see* entry 1721.

1718 **Sunsetview Farm Camping Area**, 57 Town Farm Rd., Monson, MA 01057, (413) 267-9269. (WCD)

1719 **Sutton Falls Camping Area**, Manchaug Rd., West Sutton, MA 01590, (508) 865-3898. (WCD)

1720 **Sweetwater Forest**, P.O. Box 1797, Brewster, MA 02631, (508) 896-3773. (WCD)

Taconic Crest Trail *see* entry 1687.
Taconic Skyline Trail *see* entry 1687.

1721 **Taconics Mountains**, New York-New Jersey Trail Conference, 232 Madison Ave., Rm. 908, New York, NY 10116, (212) 685-9699. Named trails: Alander, Brace Mountain to Riga Lake 3.5(s), Gray Birch, Massachusetts-Sunset Rock, Northrop 1.3(s), Stissing Mountain Circular 1.7(l), Sunset Rock. (NYW)

1722 **Talbot's Point**, Old County Rd., East Sandwich, MA 02537. 1.5 miles. (SWC)

Timber Trail *see* entry 1605.

1723 **Tolland State Forest**, Reservoir Rd., Otis, MA 01008, (413) 269-6002. 10.0 miles. (WCD; SNE; TBB; GNA)

Town Line Trail *see* entry 1568.
Trail of the Ledges *see* entry 1688.

1724 **Travelers Woods of New England**, River St., Bernardston, MA 01337, (413) 648-9105. (WCD)

1725 **Tyringham Cobble**, Jerusalem Rd., Tyringham, MA 01264, (413) 243-1749; or Trustees of Reservations, 224 Adams St., Milton, MA 02186. (TBB)

Undermountain Trail *see* entry 1538.

1726 **Upton State Forest**, Massachusetts Division of Forests and Parks, 100 Cambridge St., Boston, MA 02202, (617) 727-3180. 6.0 miles. (SNE)

1727 **Village Green Campground**, US 20, Brimfield, MA 01010, (413) 245-3504. (WCD)

1728 **Wachusett Meadow Wildlife Sanctuary**, P.O. Box 268, Princeton, MA 01541, (617) 424-2712. 11.0 miles. (MNE; SNE; GFA; GNA)

1729 **Wachusett Mountain State Reservation**, Mountain Rd., Princeton, MA 01541, (617) 464-2987. 13.0 miles. (SNE; GNA)

1730 **Wagon Wheel Camping Area**, Wendell Depot Rd., Orange, MA 01355, (508) 544-3425. (WCD)

1731 **Wakely Holly Sanctuary and Recreation Area**, Cotuit Rd., Sandwich, MA 02563. 2.1 miles. (SWC)

1732 **Walden Pond Trail**, Walden Pond State Reservation, 915 Walden St., Concord, MA 01742, (617) 369-3254. 1.7 miles loop. (FRN; MNE; NAT; AFW; GBP)

1733 **Walker Island Family Campground**, Rt. 2, Box 131, Chester, MA 01011, (413) 354-2295. (WCD)

1734 **Walking Tours of Harvard**, 8 Garden St., Cambridge, MA 02138, (617) 495-1573. (GFA)

1735 **Ward Reservation**, c/o Stevens-Coolidge Place, 139 Andover St., North Andover, MA 01845. 9.0 miles. (GBP)

1736 **Weir Hill Reservation**, 6 Stevens-Coolidge Pl., 139 Andover St., North Andover, MA 01845. 7.0 miles. (GBP)

Weir Hill Trail *see* entry 1605.

1737 **Wellfleet Bay Wildlife Sanctuary**, P.O. Box 236, South Wellfleet, MA 02663, (617) 349-2615. 5.0 miles. Named trails: Goose Pond Nature, World of Water 1.5. (MNE; NAT; SNE; OTB; GNA; SWC)

1738 **Wendell State Forest**, Rt. 1, Wendell Rd., Wendell, MA 01379, (413) 659-3797. 32.0 miles. (SNE; GNA)

Wequaquet Lake Trail *see* entry 1568.
Wheeler Trail *see* entry 1635.

1739 **White Birch Campground**, North St., Whately, MA 01093, (413) 665-4941. (WCD)

1740 **Whitney and Thayer Woods**, Cohasset and Hingham, MA 02043. 12.0 miles. (GBP)

MASSACHUSETTS   *Index*   111

1741 Willard Brook State Forest, SR 119, West Townsend, MA 01469, (508) 597-8802. 18.0 miles. (WCD; SNE; GNA)
1742 **Willowdale State Forest**, Massachusetts Division of Forests and Parks, 100 Cambridge St., Boston, MA 02202, (617) 727-3180. (SNE)
1743 **Winding Brook Campground**, South St., Douglas, MA 01516, (508) 476-7549. (WCD)
1744 **Windsor State Forest**, River Rd., Windsor, MA 01270, (413) 684-8469. 3.0 miles. (WCD; SNE; TBB; GNA)
1745 **Winter Island City Park**, Winter Island Rd., Salem, MA 01970, (508) 745-9430. (WCD)
1746 **Witch Trail**, Witch Trail Committee, 157 Circuit Rd., Winthrop, MA 02152, (617) 836-2626. 10.0 miles straight. Awards available. (AA 1994)
  Wolcott Path *see* entry 1547.
  Wolf Pine Trail *see* entry 1567.
1747 **Wompatuck State Park**, Union St., Hingham, MA 02043, (617) 749-7160. 10.0 miles. Named trails: Wompatuck. (WCD; NAT; SNE; GBP; GNA)

Wompatuck Trail *see* entry 1747.
Wood Duck Trail *see* entry 1605.
1748 **The Wood Lot Campground**, Stafford St., P.O. Box 968, Charlton City, MA 01508, (800) 255-4153. (WCD)
  World of Water Trail *see* entry 1737.
1749 **World's End Reservation**, Martin's Ln., Hingham, MA 02043. 6.0 miles. (GBP)
1750 **Yarmouth Botanic Trails**, SR 6A, Yarmouth Port, MA 02675. 1.25 miles. (SWC)
  Yellow Dot Trail *see* entry 1547.
  Yellow Trail *see* entry 1597.
1751 **Yogi Bear's Sturbridge Jellystone Park Camp Resort**, P.O. Box 600, Sturbridge, MA 01566, (508) 347-2336 or (508) 347-9570. (WCD)

Generally:
Corps of Engineers, New England Division, 424 Trapelo Rd., Waltham, MA 02254. (GFC)
Massachusetts Division of Forests and Parks, 100 Cambridge St., Boston, MA 02202, (617) 727-3180. (EGH)

Index (by city)

Abington: Ames Nowell State Park 1537
Acton: Crane Pond Wildlife Management Area 1584; Isaac Davis Trail 1622; Martin Burns Wildlife Management Area 1639
Adams: Duvall Nature Trail 1591
Andover: Charles W. Ward Reservation 1576
Arlington: Minuteman Bikeway 1646
Ashley Falls: Bartholomew's Cobble 1543
Baldwinville: Birch Hill Wildlife Management Area 1546; Federated Women's Clubs State Forest 1596
Barnstable: Cape Cod-Barnstable County 1568; Sandy Neck Beach 1702
Belchertown: Quabbin Reservoir 1690
Bellingham: Circle CG Farm 1579
Bernardston: Travelers Woods of New England 1724
Beverly: Cape Poge Wildlife Refuge 1573; Long Hill Reservation 1633
Boston: Blue Hills State Reservation 1548; Boston Bicentennial Trail of Freedom 1552; Boston's Black Heritage Trail 1554; Cape Cod Bikeway/Recreational Trail 1569; Cutler Park 1586; Five Colleges Bikeway 1598; Freedom Trail 1601; Hammond Pond Woods 1607; Heritage Walking Tour 1611; John C. Phillips Wildlife Sanctuary 1623
Brewster: Cape Cod Museum of Natural History 1571; John Wing Trail 1624; Nickerson State Park 1660; Roland C. Nickerson State Park 1697; Sweetwater Forest 1720
Brimfield: Brimfield State Forest 1558; Village Green Campground 1727
Cambridge: Walking Tours of Harvard 1734
Carlisle: Great Brook Farm State Park 1604
Charlemont: Catamount State Forest 1574; H.O. Cook State Forest 1606; Mohawk Trail State Forest 1648

Charlton City: The Wood Lot Campground 1748
Chatham: The Seaside Trail 1706
Chester: Chester-Blandford State Forest 1577; Walker Island Family Campground 1733
Clarksburg: Clarksburg State Forest 1580
Clayton: Campbell Falls State Park 1566
Clinton: Midstate Trail 1643
Cohasset: Whitney and Thayer Woods 1740
Concord: Minute Man Trail 1645; Oxboro National Wildlife Refuge 1676; Walden Pond Trail 1732
Copake, NY: Bash-Bish Falls State Forest 1544
Dalton: Appalachian Trail in Massachusetts 1540
Douglas: Winding Brook Campground 1743
East Falmouth: Ashumet Holly Reservation 1542; Cape Cod Campresort 1570
East Princeton: Leominster State Forest 1631
East Sandwich: Talbot's Point 1722
East Taunton: Massasoit State Park 1640
Easthampton: Arcadia Nature Center and Wildlife Sanctuary 1541
Erving: Erving State Forest 1593
Fall River: Footsteps of Our Founders Trail 1599
Falmouth: Crane Wildlife Management Area 1585
Florida: Savoy Mountain State Forest 1704
Foxboro: Normandy Farm Family Campground 1662
Framingham: Callahan State Park 1561; Garden in the Woods 1602
Goshen: D.A.R. State Forest 1587
Granville: Granville State Forest 1603
Great Barrington: East Mt. State Reservation 1592; Monument Mountain 1651
Hampden: Laughing Brook Education Center and Wildlife Sanctuary 1630
Hancock: Hancock Shaker Trail 1608; Privacy Campground 1689
Hawley: Hawley State Forest 1610; Kenneth Dubuque Memorial State Forest 1625
Hingham: Boston Harbor Islands State Park 1553; Whitney and Thayer Woods 1740; Wompatuck State Park 1747; World's End Reservation 1749

Hopkinton: Hopkinton State Park 1617
Huntington: Peru State Forest 1680
Ipswich: Richard T. Crane, Jr. Memorial Reservation 1694; Willowdale State Forest 1742
Jamaica Plain: Southwest Corridor Park Trail 1712
Lawrence: Bread and Roses Strike Trail 1557
Lee: October Mountain State Forest 1670
Lenox: Pleasant Valley Wildlife Sanctuary 1688
Lexington: Sons of Liberty Trail 1711
Lynn: Lynn Woods Reservation 1636; Pirate Legend Trail and Trek 1686
Manchester: Ravenswood Park 1693
Marblehead: Leslie's Retreat Trail 1632; Spirit of '76 Trail 1713
Marshfield: Daniel Webster Wildlife Sanctuary 1588; Malachi Brook Wildlife Sanctuary 1637; North Hill Marsh Wildlife Sanctuary 1664
Martha's Vineyard: Felix Neck Wildlife Sanctuary 1597; Sheriff's Meadow Trail 1709
Medford: Rocky Woods Reservation 1696
Melrose: Pine Banks Park 1684
Middleboro: KOA-Plymouth Rock 1627
Milton: Blue Hills Reservation 1547; Blue Hills Trails 1549; Hockomock Swamp Wildlife Management Area 1615; Long Point Wildlife Refuge 1634; Notchview Reservation 1668; Quarries Footpath 1692
Mohawk Trail: Country Aire Campground 1583
Monroe: Monroe State Forest 1650
Monson: Partridge Hollow Camping Area 1678; Sunsetview Farm Camping Area 1718
Monterey: Beartown State Forest 1545
Morris Island: Monomoy National Wildlife Refuge 1649
Mount Washington: Mt. Everett State Reservation 1654; Mount Washington State Forest 1658
Natick: Broadmoor Wildlife Sanctuary 1559
New Bedford: Camp Cacholot 1562; Camp Child 1563; Camp Noquochoke 1564
New York, NY: Taconics Mountains 1721
Newbury: Old Town Hill Reservation 1673

MASSACHUSETTS   *Index*   113

Newburyport: Parker River National Wildlife Refuge 1677
Newton: Charles River Pathway 1575
Norfolk: Stony Brook Nature Center and Wildlife Sanctuary 1715
North Adams: Clarksburg State Park 1581; Mt. Graylock State Reservation 1656
North Andover: Harold Parker State Forest 1609; Ward Reservation 1735; Weir Hill Reservation 1736
North Easton: Borderland State Park 1551
Northampton: Mount Tom Reservation 1657; Northampton Bikeway 1665
Northfield: Northfield Mountain Recreation and Environmental Center 1666
Norwell: Norris Reservation 1663
Oakham: Pine Acres Family Campground 1683
Orange: Mohawk Trail 1647; Wagon Wheel Camping Area 1730
Otis: Otis State Forest 1674; Tolland State Forest 1723
Peaticket: Falmouth Shining Sea Trail 1595
Peru: Dorothy F. Rice Sanctuary for Wildlife 1590
Pittsfield: Canoe Meadows Wildlife Sanctuary 1567; Hinsdale Flats Wildlife Management Area 1613; Hiram H. Fox Wildlife Management Area 1614; Peru Wildlife Management Area 1681; Pittsfield State Forest 1687
Plymouth: Indianhead Campground 1620; Pinewood Lodge Campground 1685
Princeton: Wachusett Meadow Wildlife Sanctuary 1728; Wachusett Mountain State Reservation 1729
Sagamore: Scusset Beach State Park 1705
Salem: Derby Wharf Historic Trail 1589; Salem Heritage Trail 1698; Salem Maritime National Historic Site 1699; Winter Island City Park 1745; Witch Trail 1746
Salisbury: Salisbury Beach State Reservation 1700
Sandisfield: Cookson State Forest 1582; Sandisfield State Forest 1701
Sandwich: Lowell Holly Reservation 1635; The Old Briar Patch 1671; Shawme Crowell State Forest 1708; Wakely Holly Sanctuary 1731
Savoy: Shady Pines Campground 1707
Sharon: Moose Hill Wildlife Sanctuary 1653

South Carver: Camp Squanto 1565; Myles Standish State Forest 1659
South Plymouth: Sandy Pond Campground 1703
South Wellfleet: Cape Cod National Seashore 1572; Wellfleet Bay Wildlife Sanctuary 1737
Springfield: Forest Park 1600
Stockbridge: Chesterwood Nature Trail 1578; Ice Glen Nature Preserve 1619
Stoneham: Middlesex Fells Reservation 1642; Sky Line Trail 1710
Sturbridge: Yogi Bear's Sturbridge Jellystone Park Camp Resort 1751
Sudbury: Great Meadows National Wildlife Refuge 1605
Topsfield: Bradley W. Palmer State Park 1556; Ipswich River Sanctuary 1621
Tyringham: Tyringham Cobble 1725
Upton: Upton State Forest 1726
Wales: Norcross Wildlife Sanctuary 1661; Oak Haven Campground 1669
Waltham: Buffumville Reservoir 1560; Knightville Dam 1626
Warwick: Mount Grace State Forest 1655; Northfield-Warwick State Forest 1667
Washington: Summit Hill Campground 1717
Webster: KOA-Sturbridge Webster Family Kampground 1628
Wellesley: Boulder Brook Trail 1555
Wendell: Wendell State Forest 1738
West Boylston: Bolton Flats Wildlife Management Area 1550; High Ridge Wildlife Management Area 1612; Hubbardton Wildlife Management Area 1618; Millers River Wildlife Management Area 1644; Phillipston Wildlife Management Area 1682
West Brookfield: The Old Saw Mill Campground 1672; Quabog Wildlife Management Area 1691
West Sutton: Sutton Falls Camping Area 1719
West Tidbury: Martha's Vineyard State Forest Trail 1638
West Townsend: Pearl Hill State Park 1679; Willard Brook State Forest 1741
Westfield: Stanley Park 1714
Whately: White Birch Campground 1739
Williamstown: Hopkins Memorial Forest 1616

Winchendon: Lake Denison State Park 1629; Otter River State Forest 1675
Windsor: Eugene D. Moran Wildlife Management Area 1594
Worcester: Moore State Park 1652
Yarmouth Port: Yarmouth Botanic Trails 1750

MICHIGAN

1752 **Addison-Oaks County Park**, Romeo Rd., Rochester, MI 48307, (810) 693-2432. (WCD)
1753 **Albert E. Sleeper State Park**, US 25, Caseville, MI 48725, (517) 856-4411. (ATW; WCD; MGL)
Albert Stoll, Jr. Memorial Trail see entry 1868.
1754 **Alcona County Park**, Au Sable Rd., Glennie, MI 48737. (WCD)
1755 **Algonac State Park**, SR 29, Algonac, MI 48001, (313) 765-5605. (WCD)
1756 **Allegan State Game Area**, 4590 118th Ave., Allegan, MI 49010. 23.0 miles. (EGH)
1757 **Allegan State Recreation Area**, 116th Ave., Allegan, MI 49010. (WCD)
Alligator Hill Trail see entry 1992.
1758 **Alpena Waterfowl Sanctuary**, Sportsmen's Island and Alpena Waterfowl Sanctuary, US 23N, Alpena, MI 49707. (MGL)
1759 **Alpine Campground**, US 2, Bessemer, MI 49911, (800) 348-0805. (WCD)
1760 **Bald Mountain State Park**, SR 24, Pontiac, MI 48343. (ATW)
1761 **Baraga State Park**, US 41, Baraga, MI 49908, (906) 353-6558. (ATW; WCD)
1762 **Battle Creek Linear Park Trail**, Linn Kracht, Recreation Superintendent, City of Battle Creek, Parks and Recreation Department, 124 E. Michigan Ave., Battle Creek, MI 49017, (616) 966-3431. 17.0 miles straight. (GRT)
1763 **Baw Beese Trail**, Mark Reynolds, Recreation Director, 43 McCollum, Hillsdale, MI 49242, (517) 437-3579. 6.0 miles straight planned, current as to 2.0 miles. (GRT)
1764 **Bay City State Park**, 3582 State Park Dr., Bay City, MI 48706, (517) 684-3020. Named trails: Chickadee Nature, Frank N. Anderson 0.75. (ATW; GRT; WCD; MGL)
Bay de Noc-Grand Island Trail see entry 1846.
1765 **Bay Hampton Rail Trail**, Al McFayden, City of Bay City, 301 Washington St., Bay City, MI 48708, (517) 894-8154; or Dick Hart, Hampton Township, P.O. Box 187, Bay City, MI 48707, (517) 893-7541. 6.0 miles straight. (GRT)
Beaver Basin Loop Trail see entry 1952.
Beaver Lodge Trail see entry 1938.
1766 **Beaver Pete's Trail**, Allen Keto, Assistant Area Forest Ranger, Norway Forest Area, Copper Country State Forest, US 2, Norway, MI 49870, (906) 563-9247. 20.0 miles straight. (GRT)
1767 **Beech Grove Campground**, Breen Rd., Emmett, MI 48022, (810) 395-7042. (WCD)
Beechwood Trail see entry 1872.
1768 **Belle Isle**, E. Jefferson Ave. & E. Grand Blvd., Detroit, MI 48207, (313) 267-7157. (ATW)
1769 **Bergland to Sidnaw Trail**, Martin Nelson, Area Forest Manager, Copper Country State Forest, P.O. Box 400, Baraga, MI 49908, (906) 353-6651. 45.0 miles straight. (GRT)
1770 **Ber-Wa-Ga-Na Campground**, 3526 Sanilac Rd., Vassar, MI 48768, (517) 673-7125. (WCD)
1771 **Betsie River Campground**, Riverside Canoes & Betsie River Campground, Lindy Ave., Thompsonville, MI 49683, (616) 378-2386. (WCD)
1772 **Betsie River Campsite**, River Rd., Frankfort, MI 49635, (616) 352-9535. (WCD)

MICHIGAN

1773 **Bewabic State Park**, US 2, Crystal Falls, MI 49920. (ATW)

1774 **Big Bend Campground**, 513 Conrad Rd., Standish, MI 48658, (517) 653-2484. (WCD)

1775 **Bill Nicholls Trail**, Duane St. Ours, District Fire and Recreation Specialist, Copper Country State Forest, P.O. Box 440, Baraga, MI 49908, (906) 353-6651. 55.0 miles straight. (GRT)

1776 **Blackrick's Campgrounds**, Sidney St., Crystal, MI 48818, (517) 235-4222. (WCD)

1777 **Blandford Nature Center**, 1715 Hillburn Ave. NW, Grand Rapids, MI 49501, (616) 453-6192. (ATW; MGL; GFA)

1778 **Bob-a-Ron Lake & Park**, Warren Woods Rd., Three Oaks, MI 49128, (616) 469-3894. (WCD)

1779 **Brighton State Park**, Chilson Rd., Brighton, MI 48116, (313) 229-6566. (WCD)

1780 **Brimley State Park**, SR 221, Brimley, MI 49715. (ATW)

1781 **Brower County Park**, Polk Rd., Stanwood, MI 49346, (616) 823-2561. (WCD)

Bruno's Run Loop Trail *see* entry 1846.

1782 **Cadillac Travel Trailer Park**, E. Boon Rd., Cadillac, MI 49601, (616) 775-9724. (WCD)

1783 **Camp Agawam**, Clinton Valley Council, BSA, 4479 Pontiac Lake Rd., Pontiac, MI 48054, (810) 682-7407; or Camp Agawam, 1301 W. Clarkston Rd., Lake Orion, MI 48035, (810) 693-8821. (SFC)

1784 **Camp Gerber**, West Michigan Shores Council, BSA, 1935 Monroe Ave., Grand Rapids, MI 49505, (616) 363-3828; or Camp Gerber, 1733 Owassippi Rd., Twin Lake, MI 49457, (616) 894-4928. (SFC)

1785 **Camp Greilick**, Scenic Trails Council, BSA, 2308 US 31S, Traverse City, MI 49684, (616) 938-2200; or Camp Greilick, (616) 946-4263. (SFC)

1786 **Camp Hiawatha**, Hiawatha Land Council, BSA, 2210 US 41S, Marquette, MI 49855, (906) 249-1461; or Camp Hiawatha, Munising, MI 49862, (906) 387-2714. (SFC)

1787 **Camp Holoka**, Tall Pine Council, BSA, 202 E. Boulevard Dr., Flint, MI 48503-1894, (810) 235-2531 or fax (810) 235-5052. (AA 1992)

1788 **Camp Owassippi**, Chicago Area Council, BSA, 300 Adams St., Chicago, IL 60606, (312) 782-3990; or Camp Owassippi, Twin Lake, MI 49457, (616) 894-4061. (SFC)

1789 **Camp Rotary**, Lake Huron Area Council, BSA, 5001 S. Eleven Mile Rd., Auburn, MI 48611, (517) 695-5593; or Camp Rotary, Clare, MI 48617, (517) 386-7943. (SFC)

1790 **Camp Tapico**, Tall Pine Council, BSA, 202 E. Boulevard Dr., Flint, MI 48503-1894, (810) 235-2531 or fax (810) 235-5052; or Camp Tapico, (616) 258-9302. (AA 1992)

1791 **Camp Teetonkah**, Land O'Lakes Council, BSA, P.O. Box 1342, Jackson, MI 49204, (517) 782-0567; or Camp Teetonkah, 51 Highland Dr., Jackson, MI 49201, (517) 522-4634. (SFC)

1792 **Camper's Paradise Resort**, 8733 E. 25 Rd., Rapid River, MI 49878, (906) 474-6106. (WCD)

1793 **Carl G. Fenner Arboretum**, 2020 Mt. Hope Ave., Lansing, MI 48911, (517) 483-4224. (ATW; MGL)

1794 **Chain O'Lakes Campground**, SR 88, Bellaire, MI 49615, (616) 533-8432. (WCD)

Chapel Loop Trail *see* entry 1952.

1795 **Charles Mears State Park**, US 31 Bus., Pentwater, MI 49449, (616) 869-2051. (WCD)

1796 **Charlton Park Village and Museum**, SR 79, Hastings, MI 49058, (616) 945-3775. (ATW)

1797 **Cheboygan State Park**, US 23, Cheboygan, MI 49721, (616) 627-2811. (ATW; MGL)

1798 **Chelsea Hospital Fitness Trail**, Phillip Bonham, Vice President, Chelsea Community Hospital, 775 S. Main, Chelsea, MI 48118, (313) 475-3998. 1.0 mile. (GRT)

MICHIGAN

Chickadee Nature Trail *see* entry 1764.
1799 **Chief Pontiac Trail**, Clinton Valley Council, BSA, 1100 County Center Dr., W., Pontiac, MI 48053, (810) 338-0035 or fax (810) 338-0039. 16.7 miles straight. Awards available. (AA 1991)
1800 **Chippewa Nature Center**, 400 S. Badour Rd., Midland, MI 48640, (517) 631-0830. 12.0 miles. (ATW; WCD)
1801 **Chippewa River Campground**, Magruder Rd., Middleville, MI 49333, (800) 686-2447. (WCD)
1802 **Circle S Campground**, Trowbridge Rd., Wolverine, MI 49799, (616) 525-8300. (WCD)
1803 **Clear Lake State Park**, SR 33, Atlanta, MI 49709, (517) 785-4388. (ATW; WCD)
Coalwood Trail *see* entry 1846.
1804 **Coldbrook County Park**, MN Ave., Kalamazoo, MI 49001, (616) 383-8778. (WCD)
1805 **Crooked Lake County Park**, LaChance Rd., Lake City, MI 49651, (616) 839-4945. (WCD)
Cross Trail *see* entry 1957.
Crystal Falls to Iron River Trail *see* entry 1866.
Crystal Falls to Stager Trail *see* entry 1866.
1806 **Crystal Forest Campground**, Norconk Rd., Bear Lake, MI 49614, (616) 864-2323. (WCD)
1807 **Crystal Lake Best Holiday Trav-L-Park**, P.O. Box 142, 1884 Hansen Rd., Scottville, MI 49454, (616) 757-4510. (WCD)
1808 **Cuwe Wilderness Trail**, Tall Pine Council, BSA, 202 E. Boulevard Dr., Flint, MI 48503-1894, (810) 235-2531 or fax (810) 235-5052. 22.0 miles loop. Awards available. (AA 1992)
Daisy Farm Trail *see* entry 1868.
1809 **Double R Ranch**, 4424 Whites Bridge Rd., Smyrna, MI 48887, (616) 794-0520. (WCD)
Dune Climb Trail *see* entry 1992.
1810 **Dune Lake Campground**, CR 376, Coloma, MI 49038, (616) 764-8941. (WCD)

East Chickenbone Trail *see* entry 1868.
1811 **Ed Henning County Park**, Croton Dr., Newaygo, MI 49337, (616) 652-9191. (WCD)
1812 **El Rancho Alanson RV Resort**, 6732 M-68, Alanson, MI 49706, (616) 548-2600. (WCD)
1813 **Ella Sharp Memorial Park**, 4th St., Jackson, MI 49203, (517) 788-4066. (ATW)
Empire Bluff Trail *see* entry 1992.
1814 **Empire Campground**, Stormer Rd., Empire, MI 49630, (616) 326-5285. (WCD)
1815 **Enchanted Acres Campground**, Harvey Lake Rd., Highland, MI 48356, (810) 887-5135. (WCD)
Escarpment Trail *see* entry 1957.
1816 **Evergreen Acres Campground**, Ludington Dr., Farwell, MI 48622, (800) 842-4870. (WCD)
1817 **F.J. McLain State Park**, SR 203, Hancock, MI 49930, (906) 482-0278. (ATW; WCD)
1818 **Father Marquette National Memorial**, Straits State Park, 720 Church St., St. Ignace, MI 49781, (906) 643-8620. (CGA)
1819 **Fayette State Park**, SR 183, Garden, MI 49835, (906) 644-2603. (ATW; WCD)
1820 **Felch Grade Trail**, Allen Keto, Assistant Area Forest Ranger, Norway Forest Area, Copper Country State Forest, US 2, Norway, MI 49870, (906) 563-9247. 45.0 miles straight. (GRT)
Feldtmann Lake Trail *see* entry 1868.
Feldtmann Ridge Trail *see* entry 1868.
1821 **Fernwood Nature Center**, Botanic Gardens and Arts & Crafts Center, 13988 Range Line Rd., Niles, MI 49120, (616) 683-8653 or (616) 695-6491. (ATW; MGL)
1822 **Fisherman's Island State Park**, US 31, Champion, MI 49814, (616) 547-6641. (ATW; WCD)
1823 **Fitzgerald Park**, SR 43, Grand Ledge, MI 48837. (ATW)
1824 **Forester County Park**, SR 25, Port Sanilac, MI 48469. (WCD)

1825 **For-Mar Nature Preserve and Arboretum**, N. Genesee Rd., Flint, MI 48506, (810) 736-7100. (MGL)
1826 **Fort Custer Recreation Area**, 5163 W. Fort Custer Dr., Augusta, MI 59012, (616) 731-4200. (ATW; WCD)
1827 **Fort Trodd Family Campground**, 6350 Lapeer Rd., Goodells, MI 48027, (810) 987-4889. (WCD)
1828 **Fort Wilkins State Park**, US 41, Copper Harbor, MI 49918, (906) 289-4215. (ATW; WCD)
1829 **Four Seasons Family Campground**, Orban Rd., Grass Lake, MI 49240, (517) 522-8584. (WCD)

Fox River Pathway *see* entry 1889.
Frank N. Anderson Trail *see* entry 1764.

1830 **Freda Trail**, Duane St. Ours, District Fire and Recreation Specialist, Copper Country State Forest, P.O. Box 440, Baraga, MI 49908, (906) 353-6651. 11.2 miles straight. (GRT)
1831 **Gateway Park Campground**, Hallett Rd., Hillsdale, MI 49242, (517) 437-7005. (WCD)
1832 **Genesee Recreation Area**, I-475 exit 11, Flint, MI 48506, (810) 736-7100. (ATW)
1833 **Gerald E. Eddy Geology Center**, 16345 McClure Rd., Waterloo, MI 49240, (313) 475-3170. (ATW)
1834 **Gillaspie's Ponderosa Campground**, Ionia Rd., Vermontville, MI 49096, (517) 726-0016. (WCD)
1835 **Gillette Visitor Center**, US 31, Muskegon, MI 49440, (616) 798-3573. (ATW)
1836 **Gitchee Gumee Campground & RV Park**, SR 28, Marquette, MI 49855, (906) 249-9102. (WCD)

Government Peak Trail *see* entry 1957.

1837 **Grand Marais Trail**, Bruce Veneberg, Area Forest Manager, Shingleton Forest Area, Lake Superior State Forest, M-28, Shingleton, MI 49884, (906) 452-6227. 41.7 miles straight. (GRT)
1838 **Grand Rogue Campground & Canoe Livery**, 6400 W. River Dr., Belmont, MI 49306, (616) 361-1053. (WCD)

Greenstone Ridge Trail *see* entry 1868.
1839 **H & R Campground**, Foco Rd., Standish, MI 48658, (517) 846-6443. (WCD)
1840 **Haas Hidden Hill Campground**, SR 61, Harrison, MI 48625, (517) 539-9372. (WCD)
1841 **Hancock/Calumet Trail**, Duane St. Ours, District Fire and Recreation Specialist, Copper Country State Forest, P.O. Box 440, Baraga, MI 49908, (906) 353-6651. 12.5 miles straight. (GRT)
1842 **Harrisville State Park**, US 23, Harrisville, MI 48740. (ATW)
1843 **Hart-Montague Bicycle Trail State Park**, Peter Lundborg, Silver Lake State Park, Rt. 1, Box 254, Mears, MI 49436, (616) 873-3083. 22.5 miles straight. (GRT)
1844 **Hartwick Pines State Park**, SR 93, Grayling, MI 49738, (517) 348-7068. Named trails: Virgin Pines Foot. (ATW; WCD; OTB)

Hatchet Lake Trail *see* entry 1868.
Haywire Trail *see* entry 1846.
Hemlock Trail *see* entry 1952.

1845 **Henes Park**, Henes Park Dr., Menominee, MI 49858, (906) 863-2656. (ATW; WCD)
1846 **Hiawatha National Forest**, 2727 N. Lincoln Rd., Escanaba, MI 49829, (906) 786-4062; or Sault Ste. Marie Ranger District, 4000 I-75 Bus. Spur, Sault Ste. Marie, MI 49783, (906) 635-5311. 150 miles. Named trails: Bay de Noc-Grand Island 40.0, Bruno's Run Loop, Coalwood 24.0(s), Haywire 36.0(s), Juniper 0.5, Soo/Strongs 32.3(s). (ATW; GRT; EGH; WCD; GFC; MGL; FGU; HTM)
1847 **Hidden Lake Gardens**, SR 50, Tipton, MI 49287, (517) 431-2060. (ATW)
1848 **Hidden Valley Campground**, Plumb School Rd., Sturgis, MI 49091, (616) 651-9870. (WCD)
1849 **Higgins Lake Family Campground & Mobile Park**, CR 100, Roscommon, MI 48653, (517) 821-6891. (WCD)
1850 **High Country Pathway**, Michigan Department of Natural Resources, P.O. Box 30028, Lansing, MI 48909. 50.0 miles loop. (EGH)

1851 **Highland State Park**, SR 59, Highland, MI 48357. (ATW)
1852 **Hill and Hollow Campground**, Bus. SR 31, Pentwater, MI 49449, (616) 869-5811. (WCD)
1853 **Holiday Camping Resort**, Rt. 1, Box 97B, Stony Lake Rd., New Era, MI 49446, (616) 861-5290. (WCD)
1854 **Holiday Shores**, Goodall Rd., Durand, MI 48429, (517) 288-4444. (WCD)
1855 **Holly State Recreation Area**, 8100 Grange Hall Rd., Holly, MI 48442, (810) 634-8811. 30.0 miles. (ATW; EGH; WCD)
1856 **Horseshoe Lake Campground**, Horseshoe Lake Rd., Gwinn, MI 49841, (906) 346-9937. (WCD)
1857 **Hudson Mills Metropark**, N. Metropark Rd., Ann Arbor, MI 48103, (800) 24P-ARKS. (ATW; MGL)
Huginnin Cove Loop Trail see entry 1868.
1858 **Hungry Horse Wilderness Campground**, 142nd Ave., Dorr, MI 49323, (616) 681-9836. (WCD)
Huron Forest Snowmobile Trail see entry 1859.
1859 **Huron National Forest**, 421 S. Mitchell St., Cadillac, MI 49601, (616) 775-2421; or Harrisville Ranger District, P.O. Box 286, Harrisville, MI 48740, (517) 724-6471. Named trails: Huron Forest Snowmobile 95.0. (ATW; GRT; EGH; WCD; GFC; MGL; FGU; FNG)
1860 **Indian Lake State Park**, SR 149, Manistique, MI 49854, (906) 341-2355. (ATW; MGL)
Indian Portage Trail see entry 1868.
1861 **Indian River-KOA**, US 27, Indian River, MI 49749, (616) 238-0910. (WCD)
1862 **Indian Springs Park**, White Lake Rd., Clarkston, MI 48346. (ATW)
1863 **Interlochen State Park**, SR 137, Interlochen, MI 49643, (616) 276-9511. (ATW; WCD)
1864 **Ionia State Park**, SR 66, Ionia, MI 48846. (ATW)
1865 **Irish Hills Resort Kampground**, 16230 US 12, Cement City, MI 49233, (517) 592-6751. (WCD)

1866 **Iron Range**, Duane St. Ours, District Fire and Recreation Specialist, Copper Country State Forest, P.O. Box 440, Baraga, MI 49908, (906) 353-6651. Named trails: Crystal Falls to Iron River 25.0(s), Crystal Falls to Stager 11.0(s). (GRT)
Iron's Area Tourist Association Snowmobile Trail see entry 1909.
Ishpeming Trail see entry 1868.
1867 **Island Lake State Recreation Area**, US 23, Brighton, MI 48116, (313) 229-7067. (ATW; MGL)
Island Mine Trail see entry 1868.
1868 **Isle Royale National Park**, Michigan Trail Riders Association, Rt. 5, Box 312-A, Traverse City, MI 49684; or Isle Royale National Park, 87 N. Ripley St., Houghton, MI 49931, (906) 482-0984. 175 miles. Named trails: Albert Stoll, Jr. Memorial 2.3, Daisy Farm 2.0, East Chickenbone, Feldtmann Lake 2.5, Feldtmann Ridge 2.5, Greenstone Ridge 45.0, Hatchet Lake, Huginnin Cove Loop 7.0, Indian Portage 10.6, Ishpeming, Island Mine 5.0, Kneutson Historic, Lake Richie 2.3, Lane Cove 2.8, Lighthouse Loop, Lookout Louise 1.0, McCargoe Cove 2.2, Minont Ridge 26.0, Mott Island Circuit, Mount Franklin 2.2, Mount Ojibway 1.7, Raspberry Island, Rock Harbor 10.5, Siskiwit Falls, Stoll Loop, Tobin Harbor 3.0, Washington Creek, Windigo Nature 1.25, Windigo Nature Walk 1 hour. (ATW; LGU; EGH; PGF; GFC; MGL; GNP; NPV; WTW; NPE; CGA; IRN; BHT; HTM; IFT)
1869 **J.W. Wells State Park**, SR 35, Cedar River, MI 49813, (906) 863-9747. (WCD)
1870 **Ja Do Park Campground**, US 12, Clinton, MI 49236, (517) 431-2111. (WCD)
1871 **Juniper Hills**, 10500 US 12, P.O. Box 427, Brooklyn, MI 49230, (517) 592-6803. (WCD)
Juniper Trail see entry 1846.
1872 **Kalamazoo Nature Center**, 7000 N. Westnedge St., Kalamazoo, MI 49002, (616) 381-1574. Named trails: Beechwood, Marsh. (ATW; OTB)
1873 **Kal-Haven Trail Sesquicentennial State Park**, David Marsh, Van Buren State

Park, 23960 Ruggles Rd., South Haven, MI 49090, (616) 637-4984. 34.1 miles straight. (GRT)
1874 **Kalkaska Campground**, SR 72, Kalkaska, MI 49646, (616) 258-9863. (WCD)
1875 **Kensington Metropark**, Kent Lake, Detroit, MI 48231, (313) 685-1561. (ATW; MGL)
1876 **Kent Trail**, Roger Sabine, Kent County Road and Park Commission, 1500 Scribner, N.W., Grand Rapids, MI 49504, (616) 242-6948. 15.0 miles straight. (GRT)
1877 **Keweenaw Trail**, Duane St. Ours, District Fire and Recreation Specialist, Copper Country State Forest, P.O. Box 440, Baraga, MI 49908, (906) 353-6651. 21.0 miles straight. (GRT)
1878 **Kirby Creek Travel Park**, Deren Rd., Ludington, MI 49431, (616) 843-3995. (WCD)
1879 **Kiwanis Trail**, Ray Maxe, Adrian City Hall, 100 E. Church St., Adrian, MI 49221, (517) 263-2161. 8.5 miles straight. (GRT)

Kneutson Historic Trail see entry 1868.

1880 **KOA-Acres & Trails**, Forest Ave., Ortonville, MI 48462, (517) 739-5115. (WCD)
1881 **KOA-Benton Harbor/St. Joseph**, Coloma-Riverside Rd., Benton Harbor, MI 49002, (616) 849-3333. (WCD)
1882 **KOA-Cadillac**, SR M115, Cadillac, MI 49601, (616) 825-2012. (WCD)
1883 **KOA-Duke Creek**, White Creek Ave., Cedar Springs, MI 49319, (616) 696-9648. (WCD)
1884 **KOA-Newberry/Tahquamenon**, Rt. 1, Box 783, Newberry, MI 49868, (906) 293-5762. (WCD)
1885 **Lake Antoine County Park**, CR 396, Iron Mountain, MI 49801, (906) 774-8875. (WCD)
1886 **Lake George Campground**, Old State Rd., Lake George, MI 48633, (517) 588-6848. (WCD)
1887 **Lake Gogebic State Park**, SR 64, Marenisco, MI 49947. (ATW)
1888 **Lake Hudson State Park**, SR 156, Hudson, MI 49247. (ATW)

Lake Richie Trail see entry 1868.
1889 **Lake Superior State Forest**, 309 W. McMillan Ave., Newberry, MI 49868, (906) 293-5131; or Lake Superior State Forest, M-28, Shingleton, MI 49884, (906) 452-6227. Named trails: Fox River Pathway. (EGH; MGL)

Lake Superior Trail see entry 1957.
1890 **Lakelands Trail State Park**, Jon LaBossiere, Pinckney State Recreation Area, 8555 Silver Hill, Pinckney, MI 48169, (313) 426-4913. 36.0 miles straight. (GRT)
1891 **Lakeport State Park**, SR 25, Port Huron, MI 48060, (810) 327-6765. (ATW; WCD)

Lakeshore Trail see entry 1952.
1892 **Lakeside Campground**, Prang St., Jones, MI 49061, (616) 244-8490. (WCD)
1893 **Lakeside Trail**, Eric DeLong, Village Manager, Village of Spring Lake, 102 W. Savidge St., Spring Lake, MI 49456, (616) 842-1393. 1.75 miles straight. (GRT)

Lane Cove Trail see entry 1868.
1894 **Lansing Cottonwood Campground**, 5339 S. Aurelius Rd., Lansing, MI 48911, (517) 393-3200. (WCD)
1895 **Lansing River Trail**, Peter Stoughton, Parks and Recreation, 124 W. Michigan, Lansing, MI 48933, (517) 483-4277. 6.0 miles straight. (GRT)
1896 **Leelanau Pines Campground**, CR 643, Cedar, MI 49621, (616) 228-5742. (WCD)
1897 **Leelanau State Park**, SR 201, Northport, MI 49670. (WCD)
1898 **Leisure Valley Campground**, 40851 CR 669, Decatur, MI 49045, (616) 423-7122. (WCD)

Lighthouse Loop Trail see entry 1868.

Little Carp River Trail see entry 1957.
1899 **Living Waters**, Shurte St., Cassopolis, MI 49031, (616) 445-5110. (WCD)

Lookout Louise Trail see entry 1868.
1900 **Lost Lake Scout Reservation**, Clinton Valley Council, BSA, 4479 Pontiac Lake Rd., Pontiac, MI 48054, (810) 682-7407; or Lost Lake Scout Reservation,

MICHIGAN

9248 Poplar, Lake, MI 48632, (517) 544-2551. (SFC)
Lost Lake Trail *see* entry 1957.
1901 **Lost Valley Campground**, 3700 E. Sage Lake Rd., Lupton, MI 48635, (517) 473-2201. (WCD)
1902 **Lower Huron Park**, Waltz Rd., Belleville, MI 48111. (ATW)
1903 **Ludington State Park**, P.O. Box 709, SR 116, Ludington, MI 49431, (616) 843-8671. 18.0 miles. (ATW; EGH; WCD; LBE)
1904 **Mackinac Island State Park**, Mackinac Island, MI 49757. (OTB)
1905 **Mackinaw/Alanson Trail**, Duane Hoffman, District Fire and Recreation Specialist, Mackinaw State Forest, P.O. Box 660, Gaylord, MI 49735, (517) 732-3541. 24.0 miles straight. (GRT)
1906 **Mackinaw Mill Creek Camping**, P.O. Box 728, Mackinaw City, MI 49701, (616) 436-5584. (WCD)
1907 **Mackinaw State Forest**, P.O. Box 660, Gaylord, MI 49735, (517) 732-3541. (WCD)
1908 **Macon Campground**, Ford Hwy., Tecumseh, MI 49286, (517) 423-5659. (WCD)
1909 **Manistee National Forest**, 421 S. Mitchell St., Cadillac, MI 49601, (616) 775-2421; or Manistee National Forest, 1658 Manistee Hwy., Manistee, MI 49660, (616) 723-2211. Named trails: Iron's Area Tourist Association Snowmobile 22.0(s), Nordhouse Dunes 15.0(s). (ATW; GRT; EGH; GFC; MGL; FGU; NFG)
Marsh Trail *see* entry 1872.
Marsh Trail *see* entry 1952.
1910 **Matthaei Botanical Gardens**, University of Michigan, 1800 N. Dixboro Rd., Ann Arbor, MI 48105, (313) 998-7060. (ATW)
1911 **Maybury Urban State Park**, 8 Mile Rd., Detroit, MI 48203. (ATW)
McCargoe Cove Trail *see* entry 1868.
1912 **McClure Riverfront Park Trail**, Susan Rieske, Superintendent of Parks, City Hall, 112 W. Cass, Albion, MI 49224, (517) 629-5535. 0.2 mile straight. (GRT)
1913 **Merrill Lake County Park**, SR 66, Barryton, MI 49305, (517) 382-7158. (WCD)
1914 **Metamora-Hadley State Recreation Area**, Hero Rd., Lapeer, MI 48446, (810) 797-4439. (ATW; WCD)
1915 **Metro Beach**, 16 Mile Rd., Mount Clemens, MI 48044. (ATW)
1916 **Michaywe Travel Trailer Resort**, Brink Rd., Gaylord, MI 49735, (517) 939-8723. (WCD)
1917 **Michigan's Shore-to-Shore Riding-Hiking Trail**, Michigan Department of Natural Resources, P.O. Box 30028, Lansing, MI 48909; or State Forest Field Office, Tawas, MI 48730; or Department of Natural Resources, Betsie State Forest, (616) 325-4611; or Michigan Trail Riders Association, 2864 Beitner Rd., Traverse City, MI 49684; or Au Sable State Forest, (517) 348-6371. 308 miles. (ATW; EGH; FGU; HTA; LBE; BHT; HTM; IFT)
1918 **Mill Creek State Historic Park**, US 23, Mackinaw City, MI 49701, (616) 436-7301. (ATW)
1919 **Minnow Lake Campground**, 6 Mile Rd., Brimley, MI 49715, (906) 632-6980. (WCD)
Minot Ridge Trail *see* entry 1868.
Mott Island Circuit Trail *see* entry 1868.
1920 **Mott Lake AYH-Hostel**, G-6511 N. Genesee Rd., Flint, MI 48506, (810) 736-5760. (AYH)
Mount Franklin Trail *see* entry 1868.
Mount Ojibway Trail *see* entry 1868.
Munising Falls Trail *see* entry 1952.
1921 **Muskallonge Lake State Park**, SR 123, Newberry, MI 49868, (906) 658-3338. (ATW; WCD)
1922 **Muskegon River Camp & Canoe**, N. River Rd., Evart, MI 49631, (616) 734-3808. (WCD)
1923 **Muskegon State Park**, Giles Rd., North Muskegon, MI 49440, (616) 744-3480. (ATW; WCD; MGL)
1924 **Newaygo State Park**, 36th St., Newaygo, MI 49337, (517) 856-4452. (WCD)
Nordhouse Dunes Trail *see* entry 1909.
1925 **North Country Trail** (see separate entry **4955** in interstate section).

1926 **North Higgins Lake State Park**, Military Rd., Roscommon, MI 48653. (ATW; WCD)
    North Mirror Lakes Trail see entry 1957.
1927 **Northwoods Scout Reservation**, Chief Okemos Council, BSA, 4000 W. Michigan Ave., Lansing, MI 48917, (517) 321-7278; or Northwoods Scout Reservation, 3552 Lakeshore Dr., Lupton, MI 48635, (517) 473-2305. (SFC)
1928 **Nub Lake Campground**, Bus. SR 31N, Niles, MI 49120, (616) 683-0670. (WCD)
1929 **Oak Grove Resort Campground**, Ottawa Beach Rd., Holland, MI 49424, (616) 399-9230. (WCD)
1930 **Oak Knoll Campground**, CR B86, Montague, MI 49437, (616) 894-6063. (WCD)
1931 **Oak Shores Resort Campground**, 28th St., Vicksburg, MI 49097, (616) 649-4689. (WCD)
1932 **The Oaks**, Cutler Rd., Munith, MI 49259, (517) 596-2165. (WCD)
    Old Indian Trail see entry 1992.
1933 **Old Mill Creek State Park**, US 23, Mackinaw City, MI 49701, (616) 436-7301. (WCD)
1934 **Onaway State Park**, SR 211, Onaway, MI 49765, (517) 733-8279. (ATW; WCD)
1935 **Ontonagon County Park**, SR 64, Bergland, MI 49910, (906) 575-3420. (WCD)
1936 **Orchard Beach State Park**, SR 110, Manistee, MI 49660, (616) 723-7422. (ATW; WCD; MGL)
1937 **Ortonville State Park**, SR 15, Ortonville, MI 48462. (ATW)
1938 **Ottawa National Forest**, Forest Supervisor, US 2E, Ironwood, MI 49938, (906) 932-1330; or District Ranger, P.O. Box 276, Watersmeet, MI 49969, (906) 358-4551. 200 miles. Named trails: Beaver Lodge, Watersmeet/Land O'Lakes 8.0(s). (ATW; GRT; EGH; WCD; MGL; FGU)
1939 **Otter Lake Campground**, HC 50, Buckhorn Rd., Munising, MI 49862, (906) 387-4648 or (906) 387-3559. (WCD)
    Overlook Trail see entry 1957.

1940 **P.H. Hoeft State Park**, US 23, Rogers City, MI 49779, (517) 734-2543. (ATW; WCD)
1941 **P.J. Hoffmaster State Park**, US 31, Grand Haven, MI 49417. (ATW)
1942 **PJ's Family Campground**, Williamston Rd., Stockbridge, MI 49285, (517) 565-3044. (WCD)
1943 **Paddle Brave Canoe & Campground Resort**, Lancewood/Steckert Bridge Rd., Roscommon, MI 48653, (517) 275-5273. (WCD)
1944 **Paint Creek Trail**, Linda Gorecki, Trailways Coordinator, Paint Creek Trailways Commission, 4393 Collins Rd., Rochester, MI 48064, (810) 651-9260. 10.5 miles straight. (GRT)
1945 **Paul Bunyan Scout Reservation**, Lake Huron Area Council, BSA, 5001 S. Eleven Mile Rd., Auburn, MI 48611, (517) 695-5593; or Paul Bunyan Scout Reservation, Kalkaska, MI 49646, (616) 258-4644. (SFC)
1946 **Paw Paw River Campgrounds**, SR 140, Watervliet, MI 59098, (616) 463-5454. (WCD)
1947 **Pentoga County Park**, CR 424, Iron River, MI 49935, (906) 265-3979. (WCD)
1948 **Pere Marquette Rail-Trail of Mid-Michigan**, Bill Gibson, Director, Midland County Parks and Recreation Department, 220 W. Ellsworth St., Midland, MI 48640-5194, (517) 832-6870. 30.0 miles straight. (GRT)
1949 **Pere Marquette State Forest**, N. Arbutus Rd., Traverse City, MI 49684, (616) 775-9727. (WCD)
1950 **Peshekee to Clowry ORV Trail**, Dennis Nezich, Area Forest Manager, Ishpeming Forest Area, Escanaba River State Forest, 1985 US 41, Ishpeming, MI 49849, (906) 485-1031. 6.1 miles straight. (GRT)
1951 **Petosky State Park**, US 31, Petosky, MI 49770, (616) 347-2311. (ATW; WCD)
    Philip Hart Nature Trail see entry 1992.
1952 **Pictured Rocks National Lakeshore**, P.O. Box 40, Munising, MI 49862, (906) 387-2607. Named trails: Beaver Basin Loop, Chapel Loop 9.0, Hemlock

MICHIGAN

0.7(l), Lakeshore 42.8, Marsh 0.5, Munising Falls 0.25(l), Sand Point Marsh 0.5. (ATW; LGU; EGH; PGF; GFC; MGL; RTR; NPV; OTB; CGA; LBE)

1953 **Pinckney State Recreation Area**, 8555 Silver Hill Rd., Pinckney, MI 48169, (313) 426-4913. (ATW; EGH; WCD)

1954 **Pine Shores Campground**, Mackinac Trail Rd., St. Ignace, MI 49781, (906) 643-9160. (WCD)

Platte Pines Trail *see* entry 1992.

1955 **Pleasure Point RV Condominium Resort**, Musson Rd., Six Lakes, MI 48886, (517) 365-3133. (WCD)

1956 **Pontiac Lake State Park**, SR 59, Pontiac, MI 48343. (ATW)

1957 **Porcupine Mountain Wilderness State Park**, Star Route, Box 314, SR 107, Ontonagon, MI 49953, (906) 885-5275. 90.0 miles. Named trails: Cross, Escarpment, Government Peak, Lake Superior, Little Carp River, Lost Lake, North Mirror Lakes, Overlook, Union Spring. (ATW; LGU; EGH; MGL; IFT)

1958 **Port Crescent State Park**, SR 25, Port Austin, MI 48467. (ATW)

1959 **Potawatomi Trail**, Wolverine Council, BSA, 1979 Huron Pkwy., Ann Arbor, MI 48104-4199, (313) 971-7100; or Dee Slate, 20120 Bartell Rd., Gregory, MI 48137. 5.0 miles. Awards available. (AA 1991)

1960 **President Ford Trail**, West Michigan Shores Council, BSA, 1935 Monroe Ave., NW, Grand Rapids, MI 49505-6295, (616) 363-3828. 2.0 miles. Awards available. (AA 1992)

1961 **Presque Isle Park**, Marquette, MI 49855, (906) 228-0460. (ATW)

1962 **Proud Lake State Recreation Area**, Wixom Rd., Wixom, MI 48393. (ATW; WCD)

Pyramid Point Trail *see* entry 1992.

1963 **Ramada Inn Campground**, US 2, Manistique, MI 49854, (906) 341-6911. (WCD)

Raspberry Island Trail *see* entry 1868.

1964 **Ray-Wood Campgrounds**, Lance Lake Rd., Wolverine, MI 49799, (616) 525-8373. (WCD)

1965 **Red Pines Campground**, Condensery Rd., Carson City, MI 48811, (517) 584-3031. (WCD)

1966 **Republic/Champion Grade Trail**, Dennis Nezich, Area Forest Manager, Ishpeming Forest Area, Escanaba River State Forest, 1985 US 41, Ishpeming, MI 49849, (906) 485-1031. 8.0 miles straight. (GRT)

1967 **Rifle River Recreation Area**, Rose City Rd., Lupton, MI 48635, (517) 473-2258. (ATW; WCD)

1968 **River Park Campground**, P.O. Box 185, Grayling, MI 49738, (517) 348-9092. (WCD)

1969 **River Pines RV Park & Campground**, 600 River Rd., Ontonagon, MI 49953, (906) 884-4600 or (800) 424-1520. (WCD)

1970 **Riverbend Campground & Canoe Rental**, Main St., Omer, MI 48749, (517) 653-2576. (WCD)

1971 **Rivertail Park Trail**, Mary Scheurer, City of Portland Parks and Recreation Department, 259 Kent St., Portland, MI 48875, (517) 647-7985. 2.25 miles straight. (GRT)

1972 **Rochester-Utica Recreation Area**, Utica, MI 48318. (OTB)

Rock Harbor Trail *see* entry 1868.

1973 **Roscoe McHiggins Campground**, 3800 W. Federal Hwy., Roscommon, MI 48653, (517) 275-8151. (WCD)

1974 **Rustic Potawatomie Recreation Area**, Bell Rd., Girard, MI 49094, (517) 278-4284. (WCD)

1975 **Salmon Run Campground**, Felch Rd., Grant, MI 49327, (616) 834-5494. (WCD)

Sand Point Marsh Trail *see* entry 1952.

1976 **Sandy Beach County Park**, 30th St., White Cloud, MI 49349, (616) 689-1229. (WCD)

1977 **Sandy Oak Village**, Owens Dr., Houghton Lake, MI 48629, (800) 323-0220. (WCD)

1978 **Saugatuck State Park**, SR 31, Saugatuck, MI 49453. (ATW)

1979 **School Section Lake**, 9-Mile Rd., Mecosta, MI 49332, (616) 972-7450. (WCD)

MICHIGAN

1980 **Scottville Riverside City Park,** Main St., Scottville, MI 49454, (616) 757-4729. (WCD)

1981 **Seney National Wildlife Refuge,** Star Route, Seney, MI 49883, (906) 586-9851. Named trails: Seney 1.4. (LGU; MGL; GFA; WTW; GNW; IFT)
Seney Trail *see* entry 1981.

1982 **Seven Lakes State Park,** US 23, Holly, MI 48442. (ATW)

1983 **Shardi's Hide-Away,** 340 N. Loomis, Mount Pleasant, MI 48858, (517) 773-4268. (WCD)

1984 **Sharp Park,** Deep Lake Rd., Middleville, MI 49333, (616) 795-3856. (WCD)

1985 **Sherwood Forest Campground,** 5563 Sherwood Hwy., Olivet, MI 49076, (616) 749-9468. (WCD)

1986 **Shiawassee National Wildlife Refuge,** 6975 Mower Rd., Saginaw, MI 48601, (517) 777-5930. Named trails: Shiawassee 5.0. (GNW)
Shiawassee Trail *see* entry 1986.

1987 **Shrine of the Pines,** SR 37, Baldwin, MI 49304, (616) 745-7892. (ATW)

1988 **Sibley Park,** Park Ln., Sibley, MI 48183. (GFA)

1989 **Silver Lake State Park,** US 31, Mears, MI 49436. (ATW)

1990 **Singing Sands RV Park,** 74th St., South Haven, MI 49090, (616) 637-3919. (WCD)
Siskiwit Falls Trail *see* entry 1868.

1991 **Skegemog Lake Pathway,** Dennis Vitton, Area Forest Manager, 2089 Birch, Kalkaska, MI 49646, (616) 258-9471. 0.75 mile straight. (GRT)

1992 **Sleeping Bear Dunes National Lakeshore,** P.O. Box 277, Empire, MI 49630, (616) 326-5134. 50.0 miles. Named trails: Alligator Hill, Dune Climb 1.5(s), Empire Bluff, Old Indian, Philip Hart Nature, Platte Pines, Pyramid Point. (ATW; LGU; EGH; WCD; GFC; MGL; RTR; NPV; OTB; CGA; LBE)

1993 **Sleepy Bear Campground,** SR 72, Empire, MI 49630, (616) 326-5566. (WCD)

1994 **Sleepy Hollow State Park,** US 27, Lansing, MI 48906. (ATW)

1995 **Sno-Trac Camper Village,** CR F-97, Lovells, MI 49756, (517) 348-9494. (WCD)

1996 **Snow Lake Kampground,** Snows Lake Rd., Fenwick, MI 48834, (517) 248-3224. (WCD)

1997 **Somerset Beach Campground,** Fairway Blvd., Somerset Center, MI 49282, (517) 688-3783. (WCD)
Soo/Strongs Trail *see* entry 1846.

1998 **South Higgins Lake State Park,** SR 76, Roscommon, MI 48653, (517) 821-6374. (ATW; WCD)

1999 **Spaulding Lake Campground,** 2305 Bell Rd., Niles, MI 49120, (616) 684-1393. (WCD)

2000 **Spring Brook Pathway,** Jerry Lawrence, Area Forest Manager, Gaylord Field Office, P.O. Box 667, Gaylord, MI 49735, (517) 732-3541. 6.25 miles straight. (GRT)

2001 **Spring Valley Lake Recreation Area Campground,** 18th Ave., Bloomingdale, MI 49026, (616) 521-3136. (WCD)

2002 **State Line Trail,** Duane St. Ours, District Fire and Recreation Specialist, Copper Country State Forest, P.O. Box 440, Baraga, MI 49908, (906) 353-6651; or Joey M. Spano, West Bloomfield Parks and Recreation Commission, 3325 Middlebelt Rd., West Bloomfield, MI 48323, (313) 334-5660. 107.1 miles straight. (GRT)

2003 **Sterling State Park,** N. Dixie Hwy. and State Park Rd., Monroe, MI 48161, (313) 289-2715. (ATW; MGL; LBE)
Stoll Loop Trail *see* entry 1868.

2004 **Stony Creek Metropark,** 26-Mile Rd., Detroit, MI 48231, (313) 781-4242. (ATW; MGL)

2005 **Stony Haven Campground,** Rt. 1, New Era, MI 49446, (616) 861-5201. (WCD)

2006 **Summer Oaks Clothing-Optional Lake Resort,** Sunshine Ln., Battle Creek, MI 49017, (616) 962-1600. (WCD)

2007 **Sunken Lake Campground,** Leer Rd., Posen, MI 49776. (ATW)

2008 **Tahquemenon Falls State Park,** Star Route 48, Box 225, SR 123, Paradise, MI 49768, (906) 492-3415. 25.0 miles. (ATW; EGH; WCD; OTB; IFT)

MICHIGAN

2009 **Tawas Point State Park**, Tawas Point Lighthouse Rd., East Tawas, MI 48730. (ATW; WCD)

2010 **Three Braves Campground**, 400 Able Rd., Buchanan, MI 49107, (616) 695-9895. (WCD)

2011 **Timberland Game Ranch & Campground**, N. Territorial Rd., Dexter, MI 48130, (313) 475-8679. (WCD)

Tobin Harbor Trail see entry 1868.

2012 **Traverse Area Recreation Trail (TART)**, Mike Dillenbeck, Manager, Grand Traverse County Road Commission, 3949 Silver Lake Rd., Traverse City, MI 49684, (616) 922-4848. 7.75 miles straight. (GRT)

2013 **Traverse City State Park**, US 31, Traverse City, MI 49684. (ATW)

2014 **Tri Lakes Campground**, Perrett Rd., Marshall, MI 49068, (616) 781-2297. (WCD)

2015 **Tri Ponds Family Camp Resort**, Dumont Rd., Allegan, MI 49010, (616) 673-4740. (WCD)

2016 **Twin Bears Campground and Cabins**, SR 37, Baldwin, MI 49304, (616) 745-7648. (WCD)

2017 **Twin Lakes State Park**, SR 26, Mass City, MI 49948, (906) 288-3321. (WCD)

2018 **Twin Pines Campground & Canoe Livery**, Wheeler Rd., Concord, MI 49237, (517) 524-6298. (WCD)

2019 **Tyler Creek Recreation Area**, 13495 92nd St. SE, Alto, MI 49302, (616) 868-6751. (WCD)

Union Spring Trail see entry 1957.

2020 **Vagabond Campground-Resort**, CR 513, Rapid River, MI 49878, (906) 474-6122. (WCD)

2021 **Van Riper State Park**, US 41, Champion, MI 49814, (906) 339-4461. (ATW; WCD)

Virgin Pines Foot Trail see entry 1844.

2022 **Waffle Farm Camp**, Union City Rd., Coldwater, MI 49036, (517) 278-4315. (WCD)

2023 **Wagener County Park**, SR 25, Harbor Beach, MI 48441, (517) 479-9131. (WCD)

2024 **Walnut Hills Campground**, Lehring Rd., Durand, MI 48429, (517) 634-9782. (WCD)

2025 **Warren Dunes State Park**, Red Arrow Hwy., Sawyer, MI 49125, (616) 426-4013. (ATW; WCD; MGL)

Washington Creek Trail see entry 1868.

2026 **Water Tower Travel Trailer Park**, SR 24, Lapeer, MI 48446, (810) 664-8660. (WCD)

2027 **Waterloo State Recreation Area**, 16345 McClure Rd., Chelsea, MI 48118, (313) 475-8307. 20.0 miles. (ATW; EGH; WCD)

2028 **Waterloo-Pinckney Hiking Trail**, Wolverine Council, BSA, 1979 Huron Pkwy., Ann Arbor, MI 48104-4199, (313) 971-7100. 16.0 miles straight. (AA 1991)

Watersmeet/Land O'Lakes Trail see entry 1938.

2029 **West Bloomfield Trail Network**, Joey M. Spano, West Bloomfield Parks and Recreation Commission, 3325 Middlebelt Rd., West Bloomfield, MI 48323, (313) 334-5660. 5.3 miles. (GRT)

2030 **West Campus Bicycle Path**, Dan Klenczar, Physical Plant, Eastern Michigan University, Ypsilanti, MI 48197, (313) 487-4194. 1.0 mile straight. (GRT)

2031 **Wheel Inn Campground**, 240 Fogg Rd., P.O. Box 613, Leslie, MI 49251, (517) 589-8097. (WCD)

2032 **White Cloud City Campgrounds**, Wilcox St., White Cloud, MI 49349, (616) 689-1094. (WCD)

2033 **White River Campground**, 735-WT 1 Fruitvale Rd., Montague, MI 49437, (616) 894-4708. (WCD)

2034 **Whitehouse Nature Center**, I-94, Albion, MI 49224, (517) 629-2030. (ATW)

2035 **Wilderness State Park**, Wilderness Park Rd., Mackinaw City, MI 49701, (616) 436-5381. (ATW; WCD; OTB; LBE)

2036 **Wildwood Acres Campground**, Goose Lake Rd., Jonesville, MI 49250, (517) 524-7149. (WCD)

2037 **Willow Metropark**, Willow Rd., Flat Rock, MI 48134. (ATW)

Windigo Nature Trail see entry 1868.

MICHIGAN

Windigo Nature Walk *see* entry 1868.
2038 **Wood Lake Scout Reservation**, North Indiana Council, BSA, 1433 N. Side Blvd., South Bend, IN 46515, (219) 289-0337; or Wood Lake Scout Reservation, 10891 Withers St., Jones, MI 49061, (616) 435-7533. (SFC)
2039 **Woodland Waters**, 79720 Kidder Rd., Almont, MI 48003, (810) 798-3422. (WCD)
2040 **Yankee Springs State Park**, A-42, Bradley, MI 49311. (ATW)
2041 **Yogi Bear's Jellystone Camp Resort**, Rt. 1, Box 740, Grayling, MI 49738, (517) 348-2157. (WCD)
2042 **Yogi Bear's Jellystone Park**, 4050 Hammond Rd., Traverse City, MI 49684, (616) 947-2770 or (800) 558-2954. (WCD)
2043 **Yogi Bear's Jellystone Park Camp-Resort of Holly**, Grange Hall Rd., Holly, MI 48442, (810) 634-8621. (WCD)
2044 **Yogi Bear's Jellystone Park Indian River**, SR 68, Indian River, MI 49749, (616) 238-8259. (WCD)
2045 **Young State Park**, CR 73, Boyne City, MI 49712, (616) 582-7523. (ATW; WCD)

Generally:
Department of Natural Resources, Parks Division, 5th Floor, Mason Bldg., P.O. Box 30028, Lansing, MI 48909, (517) 373-1220. (EGH)
Michigan Trailfinders Club, 2680 Rockhill N.E., Grand Rapids, MI 49505. (EGH)

Index (by city)

Adrian: Kiwanis Trail 1879
Alanson: El Rancho Alanson RV Resort 1812; Mackinaw/Alanson Trail 1905
Albion: McClure Riverfront Park Trail 1912; Whitehouse Nature Center 2034
Algonac: Algonac State Park 1755
Allegan: Allegan State Game Area 1756; Allegan State Recreation Area 1757; Tri Ponds Family Camp Resort 2015
Almont: Woodland Waters 2039
Alpena: Alpena Waterfowl Sanctuary 1758
Alto: Tyler Creek Recreation Area 2019
Ann Arbor: Hudson Mills Metropark 1857; Matthaei Botanical Gardens 1910; Potawatomi Trail 1959; Waterloo-Pinckney Hiking Trail 2028
Atlanta: Clear Lake State Park 1803
Augusta: Fort Custer Recreation Area 1826
Baldwin: Shrine of the Pines 1987; Twin Bears Campground and Cabins 2016
Baraga: Baraga State Park 1761; Bergland to Sidnaw Trail 1769; Bill Nicholls Trail 1775; Freda Trail 1830; Hancock/Calumet Trail 1841; Iron Range 1866; Keweenaw Trail 1877; State Line Trail 2002
Barryton: Merrill Lake County Park 1913
Battle Creek: Battle Creek Linear Park Trail 1762; Summer Oaks Clothing-Optional Lake Resort 2006
Bay City: Bay City State Park 1764; Bay Hampton Rail Trail 1765
Bear Lake: Crystal Forest Campground 1806
Bellaire: Chain O'Lakes Campground 1794
Belleville: Lower Huron Park 1902
Belmont: Grand Rogue Campground & Canoe Livery 1838
Benton Harbor: KOA-Benton Harbor/St. Joseph 1881
Bergland: Ontonagon County Park 1935
Bessemer: Alpine Campground 1759
Bloomingdale: Spring Valley Lake Recreation Area 2001
Boyne City: Young State Park 2045
Bradley: Yankee Springs State Park 2040
Brighton: Brighton State Park 1779; Island Lake State Recreation Area 1867
Brimley: Brimley State Park 1780; Minnow Lake Campground 1919
Brooklyn: Juniper Hills 1871
Buchanan: Three Braves Campground 2010
Cadillac: Cadillac Travel Trailer Park 1782; Huron National Forest 1859; KOA-Cadillac 1882; Manistee National Forest 1909

Carson City: Red Pines Campground 1965
Caseville: Albert E. Sleeper State Park 1753
Cassopolis: Living Waters 1899
Cedar: Leelanau Pines Campground 1896
Cedar River: J.W. Wells State Park 1869
Cedar Springs: KOA-Duke Creek 1883
Cement City: Irish Hills Resort Kampground 1865
Champion: Fisherman's Island State Park 1822; Van Riper State Park 2021
Cheboygan: Cheboygan State Park 1797
Chelsea: Chelsea Hospital Fitness Trail 1798; Waterloo State Recreation Area 2027
Clare: Camp Rotary 1789
Clarkston: Indian Springs Park 1862
Clinton: Ja Do Park Campground 1870
Coldwater: Waffle Farm Camp 2022
Coloma: Dune Lake Campground 1810
Concord: Twin Pines Campground & Canoe Livery 2018
Copper Harbor: Fort Wilkins State Park 1828
Crystal: Blackrick's Campgrounds 1776
Crystal Falls: Bewabic State Park 1773
Decatur: Leisure Valley Campground 1898
Detroit: Belle Isle 1768; Kensington Metropark 1875; Maybury Urban State Park 1911; Stony Creek Metropark 2004
Dexter: Timberland Game Ranch 2011
Dorr: Hungry Horse Wilderness Campground 1858
Durand: Holiday Shores 1854; Walnut Hills Campground 2024
East Tawas: Tawas Point State Park 2009
Emmett: Beech Grove Campground 1767
Empire: Empire Campground 1814; Sleeping Bear Dunes National Lakeshore 1992; Sleepy Bear Campground 1993
Escanaba: Hiawatha National Forest 1846
Evart: Muskegon River Camp & Canoe 1922
Farwell: Evergreen Acres Campground 1816
Fenwick: Snow Lake Kampground 1996
Flat Rock: Willow Metropark 2037
Flint: Camp Holoka 1787; Camp Tapico 1790; Cuwe Wilderness Trail 1808; For-Mar Nature Preserve and Arboretum 1825; Genesee Recreation Area 1832; Mott Lake AYH-Hostel 1920
Frankfort: Betsie River Campsite 1772

Garden: Fayette State Park 1819
Gaylord: Mackinaw State Forest 1907; Michaywe Travel Trailer Resort 1916; Spring Brook Pathway 2000
Girard: Rustic Potawatomie Recreation Area 1974
Glennie: Alcona County Park 1754
Goodells: Fort Trodd Family Campground 1827
Grand Haven: P.J. Hoffmaster State Park 1941
Grand Ledge: Fitzgerald Park 1823
Grand Rapids: Blandford Nature Center 1777; Kent Trail 1876; President Ford Trail 1960
Grant: Salmon Run Campground 1975
Grass Lake: Four Seasons Family Campground 1829
Grayling: Hartwick Pines State Park 1844; River Park Campground 1968; Yogi Bear's Jellystone Camp Resort 2041
Gwinn: Horseshoe Lake Campground 1856
Hancock: F.J. McLain State Park 1817
Harbor Beach: Wagener County Park 2023
Harrison: Haas Hidden Hill Campground 1840
Harrisville: Harrisville State Park 1842; Huron National Forest 1859
Hastings: Charlton Park Village and Museum 1796
Highland: Enchanted Acres Campground 1815; Highland State Park 1851
Hillside: Baw Beese Trail 1763; Gateway Park Campground 1831
Holland: Oak Grove Resort Campground 1929
Holly: Holly State Recreation Area 1855; Seven Lakes State Park 1982; Yogi Bear's Jellystone Park-Camp Resort of Holly 2043
Houghton: Isle Royale National Park 1868
Houghton Lake: Sandy Oak Village 1977
Hudson: Lake Hudson State Park 1888
Indian River: Indian River-KOA 1861; Yogi Bear's Jellystone Park Indian River 2044
Interlochen: Interlochen State Park 1863
Ionia: Ionia State Park 1864
Iron Mountain: Lake Antoine County Park 1885
Iron River: Pentoga County Park 1947
Ironwood: Ottawa National Forest 1938

Ishpeming: Peshekee to Clowry ORV Trail 1950; Republic/Champion Grade Trail 1966
Jackson: Camp Teetonkah 1791; Ella Sharp Memorial Park 1813
Jones: Lakeside Campground 1892; Wood Lake Scout Reservation 2038
Jonesville: Wildwood Acres Campground 2036
Kalamazoo: Coldbrook County Park 1804; Kalamazoo Nature Center 1872
Kalkaska: Kalkaska Campground 1874; Paul Bunyan Scout Reservation 1945; Skegemog Lake Pathway 1991
Lake: Lost Lake Scout Reservation 1900
Lake City: Crooked Lake County Park 1805
Lake George: Lake George Campground 1886
Lake Orion: Camp Agawam 1783
Lansing: Carl G. Fenner Arboretum 1793; High Country Pathway 1850; Lansing Cottonwood Campground 1894; Lansing River Trail 1895; Sleepy Hollow State Park 1994
Lapeer: Metamora-Hadley State Recreation Area 1914; Water Tower Travel Trailer Park 2026
Leslie: Wheel Inn Campground 2031
Lovells: Sno-Trac Camper Village 1995
Ludington: Kirby Creek Travel Park 1878; Ludington State Park 1903
Lupton: Lost Valley Campground 1901; Northwoods Scout Reservation 1927; Rifle River Recreation Area 1967
Mackinac Island: Mackinac Island State Park 1904
Mackinaw City: Mackinaw Mill Creek Camping 1906; Mill Creek State Historic Park 1918; Old Mill Creek State Park 1933; Wilderness State Park 2035
Manistee: Manistee National Forest 1909; Orchard Beach State Park 1936
Manistique: Indian Lake State Park 1860; Ramada Inn Campground 1963
Marenisco: Lake Gogebic State Park 1887
Marquette: Gitchee Gumee Campground & RV Park 1836; Presque Isle Park 1961
Marshall: Tri Lakes Campground 2014
Mass City: Twin Lakes State Park 2017
Mears: Hart-Montague Bicycle Trail State Park 1843; Silver Lake State Park 1989

Mecosta: School Section Lake 1979
Menominee: Henes Park 1845
Middleville: Chippewa River Campground 1801; Sharp Park 1984
Midland: Chippewa Nature Center 1800; Pere Marquette Rail-Trail of Mid-Michigan 1948
Monroe: Sterling State Park 2003
Montague: Oak Knoll Campground 1930; White River Campground 2033
Mount Clemens: Metro Beach 1915
Mount Pleasant: Shardi's Hide-Away 1983
Munising: Camp Hiawatha 1786; Otter Lake Campground 1939; Pictured Rocks National Lakeshore 1952
Munith: The Oaks 1932
Muskegon: Gillette Visitor Center 1835
New Era: Holiday Camping Resort 1853; Stony Haven Campground 2005
Newaygo: Ed Henning County Park 1811; Newaygo State Park 1924
Newberry: KOA-Newberry/Tahquamenon 1884; Lake Superior State Forest 1889
Niles: Fernwood Nature Center 1821; Nub Lake Campground 1928; Spaulding Lake Campground 1999
North Muskegon: Muskegon State Park 1923
Northport: Leelanau State Park 1897
Norway: Beaver Pete's Trail 1766; Felch Grade Trail 1820
Olivet: Sherwood Forest Campground 1985
Omer: Riverbend Campground & Canoe Rental 1970
Onaway: Onaway State Park 1934
Ontonagon: Porcupine Mountain Wilderness State Park 1957; River Pines RV Park & Campground 1969
Ortonville: KOA-Acres & Trails 1880; Ortonville State Park 1937
Paradise: Tahquemenon Falls State Park 2008
Pentwater: Charles Mears State Park 1795; Hill and Hollow Campground 1852
Petosky: Petosky State Park 1951
Pinckney: Lakelands Trail State Park 1890; Pinckney State Recreation Area 1953
Pontiac: Bald Mountain State Park 1760; Chief Pontiac Trail 1799; Pontiac Lake State Park 1956
Port Austin: Port Crescent State Park 1958

Port Huron: Lakeport State Park 1891
Port Sanilac: Forester County Park 1824
Portland: Rivertail Park Trail 1971
Posen: Sunken Lake Campground 2007
Rapid River: Camper's Paradise Resort 1792; Vagabond Campground-Resort 2020
Rochester: Addison-Oaks County Park 1752; Paint Creek Trail 1944
Rogers City: P.H. Hoeft State Park 1940
Roscommon: Higgins Lake Family Campground & Mobile Park 1849; North Higgins Lake State Park 1926; Paddle Brave Canoe & Campground Resort 1943; Roscoe McHiggins Campground 1973; South Higgins Lake State Park 1998
Saginaw: Shiawassee National Wildlife Refuge 1986
St. Ignace: Father Marquette National Memorial 1818; Pines Shores Campground 1954
Saugatuck: Saugatuck State Park 1978
Sault Ste. Marie: Hiawatha National Forest 1846
Sawyer: Warren Dunes State Park 2025
Scottville: Crystal Lake Best Holiday Trav-L-Park 1807; Scottville Riverside City Park 1980
Seney: Seney National Wildlife Refuge 1981
Shingleton: Grand Marais Trail 1837; Lake Superior State Forest 1889
Sibley: Sibley Park 1988
Six Lakes: Pleasure Point RV Condominium Resort 1955
Smyrna: Double R Ranch 1809
Somerset Center: Somerset Beach Campground 1997
South Haven: Kal-Haven Trail Sesquicentennial State Park 1873; Singing Sands RV Park 1990
Spring Lake: Lakeside Trail 1893

Standish: Big Bend Campground 1774; H & R Campground 1839
Stanwood: Brower County Park 1781
Stockbridge: PJ's Family Campground 1942
Sturgis: Hidden Valley Campground 1848
Tawas: Michigan's Shore-to-Shore Riding-Hiking Trail 1917
Tecumseh: Macon Campground 1908
Thompsonville: Betsie River Campground 1771
Three Oaks: Bob-a-Ron Lake & Park 1778
Tipton: Hidden Lake Gardens 1847
Traverse City: Camp Greilick 1785; Pere Marquette State Forest 1949; Traverse Area Recreation Trail 2012; Traverse City State Park 2013; Yogi Bear's Jellystone Park 2042
Twin Lake: Camp Gerber 1784; Camp Owassippi 1788
Utica: Rochester-Utica Recreation Area 1972
Vassar: Ber-Wa-Ga-Na Campground 1770
Vermontville: Gillaspie's Ponderosa Campground 1834
Vicksburg: Oak Shores Resort Campground 1931
Waterloo: Gerald E. Eddy Geology Center 1833
Watersmeet: Ottawa National Forest 1938
Watervliet: Paw Paw River Campgrounds 1946
West Bloomfield: West Bloomfield Trail Network 2029
White Cloud: Sandy Beach County Park 1976; White Cloud City Campgrounds 2032
Wixom: Proud Lake State Recreation Area 1962
Wolverine: Circle S Campground 1802; Ray-Wood Campgrounds 1964
Ypsilanti: West Campus Bicycle Path 2030

MISSISSIPPI

2046 **Archusa Creek Water Park**, SR 18, Quitman, MS 39355. (ATA)

2047 **Arkabutla Reservoir**, Corps of Engineers, SR 304, Hernando, MS 38632. (ATA)

2048 **Askew's Landing Campground**, Rt. 2, Box 353, Edwards, MS 39066, (601) 852-2331. (WCD)

2049 **Atwood Water Park**, US 84, Monticello, MS 39654, (601) 587-2711. (WCD; ATA)

2050 **Beaver Dam Nature Trail**, Wilfred Dick, Rt. 4, Magnolia, MS 39652. 5.0-25.0 miles. Awards available. (HTA)

2051 **Bienville National Forest**, 100 W. Capitol St., Suite 1141, Jackson, MS 32969, (601) 961-4391. (WCD; ATA; GFC; MSE; FGU; NFG)

2052 **Big Creek Water Park**, US 84, Laurel, MS 39440. (ATA)

Black Creek National Recreation Trail see entry 2070.

2053 **Bogue Chitto Water Park**, US 98, McComb, MS 39648. (ATA; OTB)

2054 **Buccaneer State Park**, US 90, Waveland, MS 39576, (601) 467-3822. (WCD; MSE)

2055 **Bullen Creek Nature Trail**, Natchez Trace Parkway, Rt. 1, NT-143, Tupelo, MS 38801, (601) 842-1572. (NPE)

2056 **Burnside Lake Park**, SR 15, Philadelphia, MS 39350. (ATA)

2057 **Camp Tallaha**, Delta Area Council, BSA, Rt. 3, Box 1, 1010 Lee Dr., Clarksdale, MS 38614, (601) 624-9091; or Camp Tallaha, Rt. 1, Charleston, MS 38921, (601) 647-2887. (SFC)

2058 **Carver Point State Park**, SR 7, Rt. 2, Coffeeville, MS 38922, (601) 628-5199. (OMS)

2059 **Catherine "Kitty" Bryan Dill Memorial Bikeway**, Dewel G. Brasher, Jr., City Manager, P.O. Box 1117, West Point, MS 39773, (601) 494-2573. 1.2 miles straight. (GRT)

2060 **Chewalla Lake and Recreation Area**, c/o U.S. Forest Service, 100 W. Capitol St., Suite 1141, Jackson, MS 39269, (601) 960-4391. (NAT)

2061 **Chewalla Nature Trail**, Shiloh Military Trail, P.O. Box 17507, Memphis, TN 38117. 10.0 miles loop. Awards available. (AA 1992)

2062 **Chickasaw Hill Campground**, Corps of Engineers—Enid Lake, US 51, Courtland, MS 38620, (601) 563-4571. (WCD)

2063 **Choctaw Lake Park**, SR 15, Ackerman, MS 39735. (ATA)

2064 **Clarkco State Park**, US 45, Meridian, MS 39301, (601) 776-6651. (WCD; ATA; MSE)

2065 **Clear Springs Park**, FR 104, Meadville, MS 39653. (ATA)

2066 **Coal Bluff Park**, SR 483, Canton, MS 39046, (601) 654-7726. (WCD; ATA)

2067 **Columbus Lock East**, US 45N, Columbus, MS 39701. (ATA)

2068 **Crossroads Water Park**, SR 26, Crossroads, MS 38701. (ATA)

Deer Meadow Road Nature Trail see entry 2081.

2069 **Delta National Forest**, SR 16, Yazoo City, MS 39194; or Forest Supervisor, 100 W. Capitol St., Suite 1141, Jackson, MS 39269, (601) 965-4391. (MSE; FGU)

2070 **DeSoto National Forest**, 100 W. Capitol St., Suite 1141, Jackson, MS 39269, (601) 965-4391; or Biloxi Ranger District, 251 US 49S, P.O. Box 62, McHenry, MS 39561, (601) 928-5291. 76.0

MISSISSIPPI

miles. Named trails: Black Creek National Recreation 41.0, Tuxachanie National Recreation 22.0(s). (SAR 1990)

2071 **d'Iberville Trail**, Rt. 6, Box 134, Biloxi, MS 39532. 8.5 miles. Awards available. (HTA)

2072 **D'Lo Water Park**, Old US 49, Mendenhall, MS 39114, (601) 847-4310 or (601) 847-1725. (WCD; ATA; MSE)

2073 **Dry Creek Water Park**, US 49, Mount Olive, MS 39119. (ATA)

2074 **Dub Patten Campground**, Corps of Engineers—Arkabutla Lake, Tate Rd., Coldwater, MS 38618, (601) 562-6261. (WCD)

2075 **Flat Branch Campground & RV Park**, US 49, Gulfport, MS 39501, (601) 832-2267. (WCD)

2076 **Flint Creek Water Park**, SR 29, Wiggins, MS 39577. (ATA)

2077 **George Payne Cossar State Park**, SR 32, Oakland, MS 38948, (601) 623-7356. (WCD; ATA; MSE)

2078 **Golden Memorial State Park**, SR 35, Walnut Grove, MS 39189, (601) 253-2237. (ATA; MSE)

2079 **Goshen Springs Campground**, SR 43, Jackson, MS 39205, (601) 354-3448. (WCD)

2080 **Grand Gulf Park Trail**, Rt. 2, Box 389, Port Gibson, MS 39150. 10.0 miles. Awards available. (SAR 1992)

2081 **Great River Road State Park**, Great River Rd., Rosedale, MS 38769, (601) 759-6762. Named trails: Deer Meadow Road Nature. (WCD; ATA; MSE; NAT; OTB)

2082 **Grenada Lake**, Resource Manager, Grenada Lake, P.O. Box 903, Grenada, MS 38901, (601) 226-5911 or (601) 226-1679. Named trails: Lost Bluff Hiking 2.5. (ATA; MSE; LRA)

2083 **Gulf Islands National Seashore**, 3500 Park Rd., Ocean Springs, MS 39564, (601) 875-0821. (WCD; MSE)

2084 **Hillside National Wildlife Refuge**, P.O. Box 107, Yazoo City, MS 39194, (601) 235-4355. (GNW)

2085 **Holly Springs National Forest**, FR 611, Holly Springs, MS 38634; or Forest Supervisor, 100 W. Capitol St., Suite 1141, Jackson, MS 32969, (601) 965-4391. (WCD; ATA; GFC; MSE; FGU)

2086 **Holmes County State Park**, US 51, Kosciusko, MS 39090, (601) 653-3351. (WCD; ATA; MSE)

2087 **Holmes Water Park**, SR 27, Tylertown, MS 39667. (ATA)

2088 **Homochitto National Forest**, 350 Milner Bldg., P.O. Box 1292, Jackson, MS 39250, (601) 965-4391. (ATA; MSE; FGU; NFG)

2089 **Hugh White State Park**, SR 8, Grenada, MS 38901, (601) 266-4934. (ATA; MSE)

2090 **J.P. Coleman State Park**, Rt. 5, Box 503, Iuka, MS 38852, (601) 423-6515. (FTS; ATA)

2091 **Jacinto Nature Trails**, SR 356, Corinth, MS 38834, (601) 287-4296. (FTS)

Jeff Busby Nature Trail see entry 2092.

2092 **Jeff Busby State Park**, P.O. Box 20305, Jackson, MS 39209. Named trails: Jeff Busby Nature 20 minutes. (FTS)

2093 **John W. Kyle State Park**, SR 315, Sardis, MS 38666, (601) 487-1345. (WCD; ATA; MSE)

2094 **Lake Lowndes State Park**, SR 69, Columbus, MS 39702, (601) 328-2110. (WCD; ATA; MSE)

2095 **LeFleur's Bluff State Park**, SR 25N, Jackson, MS 39205, (601) 987-3985. (WCD; ATA)

2096 **Legion State Park**, Old SR 25, Louisville, MS 39339, (601) 773-8323. (MSE)

2097 **Leroy Percy State Park**, P.O. Box 176, Hollandale, MS 38748, (601) 827-5320. (ATA; MSE; OMS)

2098 **Lichterman Nature Center**, 5992 Quince Rd., Memphis, TN 38119, (901) 726-4775. (NAT)

2099 **Little Black Creek Water Park**, Old Purvis-Lumberton Hwy., Lumberton, MS 39455. (ATA)

Little Mountain Trail see entry 2110.
Little Swan Trail see entry 2110.
Lonesome Pine Horse Trail see entry 2110.
Lost Bluff Hiking Trail see entry 2082.

MISSISSIPPI

2100 **Luxapilla Creek Park**, SR 69, Columbus, MS 39701. (ATA)
2101 **Marathon Lake Park**, FR 506, Forest, MS 39074. (ATA)
2102 **Maynor Creek Water Park**, US 84W, Waynesboro, MS 39367. (ATA)
2103 **Mazalea Travel Park**, 8220 W. Oaklawn, Biloxi, MS 39532, (601) 392-8575 or (601) 392-5348. (WCD)
2104 **McLeod Water Park**, SR 603, Bay St. Louis, MS 39520, (601) 467-1894. (WCD; ATA)
2105 **Merit Water Park**, SR 43, Mendenhall, MS 39114. (ATA)
2106 **Mississippi Agriculture & Forestry Museum**, Lakeland Dr., Jackson, MS 39208. (MSE)
2107 **Mississippi Petrified Forest Campground**, SR 22, Flora, MS 39071, (601) 879-8189. (WCD; ATA; MSE; OTB)
2108 **Mount Locus Environmental Study Trail**, Natchez Trace Parkway, Rt. 5, NT-143, Tupelo, MS 38801. (OMS)
2109 **Natchez State Park**, US 61, Natchez, MS 39120, (601) 442-2658. (WCD; ATA; MSE)
2110 **Natchez Trace National Scenic Trail** (see separate entry **4954** in interstate section). Side trails not listed elsewhere: Little Mountain 1.0, Little Swan 2.3, Lonesome Pine Horse 15.0, Old Town Overlook 4.6, Old Trace 3.5, Owens Creek 5.0-10.0, Tupelo Horse 3.5. For addresses, see interstate section.
2111 **Nathan Bedford Forrest Trail**, P.O. Box 17507, Memphis, TN 38117. 16.0 miles loop. Awards available. (AA 1990)
2112 **Nita Lake Resort**, Nita Lake Rd., Fulton, MS 38843, (601) 652-3602. (WCD)
2113 **Noxubee National Wildlife Refuge**, Rt. 1, Box 84, Brooksville, MS 39739, (601) 323-5548. 50.0 miles. (GFA; OTB; GNW)
2114 **Okatibbee Lake**, Reservoir Manager, P.O. Box 98, Collinsville, MS 39325. (ATA; LRA)
2115 **Okatibbee Water Park**, SR 19, Meridian, MS 39307. (ATA)
2116 **Oktibbeha County Lake**, US 82, Starkville, MS 39759. (ATA)

Old Town Overlook Trail *see* entry 2110.
Old Trace *see* entry 2110.
2117 **Outlet Channel Campground**, Mississippi Park Commission—Grenada Lake, SR 333, Grenada, MS 38901. (WCD)
Owens Creek Trail *see* entry 2110.
2118 **Oxbow RV Park**, SR 7, Grenada, MS 38901, (601) 226-0751. (WCD)
2119 **Paul B. Johnson State Park**, US 49, Hattiesburg, MS 39401, (601) 582-7721. (WCD; ATA; MSE)
2120 **Percy Quin State Park**, Rt. 3, McComb, MS 39648, (601) 684-3931. 1.5-25.0 miles loops. (WCD; ATA; OMS)
2121 **River Bend RV Resort**, 10707 SR 613N, Escatawpa, MS 39552-1366, (601) 475-2429. (WCD)
2122 **Riverside Park**, SR 25, Jackson, MS 39205. (ATA)
2123 **Roosevelt State Park**, SR 13, Morton, MS 39117, (601) 732-6316. (WCD; ATA)
2124 **Salmen Scout Reservation**, New Orleans Area Council, BSA, P.O. Box 1146, Metairie, LA 70004, (504) 885-9800; or Salmen Scout Reservation, Rt. 2, Box 388, Perkinston, MS 39573, (601) 255-1336. (SFC)
2125 **Sandhill Crane National Wildlife Refuge**, Mississippi Crane National Wildlife Refuge, 7200 Crane Ln., Gautier, MS 39553, (601) 497-2380 or (601) 497-6322. (MSE; NAT; GNW)
2126 **Sardis Lake**, Resource Manager, Rt. 2, Box 500, Sardis, MS 38666. (ATA; LRA)
2127 **Shepard State Park**, US 90, Pascagoula, MS 39581. (ATA)
2128 **Sleepy Hollow Campground**, SR 389, Houston, MS 38851, (601) 456-4387. (WCD)
2129 **South Abutment Campground**, Corps of Engineers—Arkabutla Lake, Tate Rd., Coldwater, MS 38618, (601) 562-6261. (WCD)
2130 **Timber Lake Campground**, Spillway Dr., Jackson, MS 39205. (WCD)
2131 **Timberlanes Camp & Dude Ranch**

Resort, Rt. 2, Box 150, Wesson, MS 39191, (601) 643-5656. (WCD)
2132 **Tishomingo State Park**, SR 25, Tishomingo, MS 38873, (601) 438-6914. (WCD; ATA)
  Tombigbee Horse Trail *see* entry 2133.
2133 **Tombigbee National Forest**, Natchez Trace Pkwy., Tupelo, MS 38801; or Forest Supervisor, 100 W. Capitol St., Suite 1141, Jackson, MS 39269, (601) 965-4391; or District Ranger, Rt. 1, Box 98A, Ackerman, MS 39735, (601) 285-3264. Named trails: Tombigbee Horse 9.0-15.0. (ATA; MSE; FGU)
2134 **Tombigbee State Park**, SR 6, Tupelo, MS 38801, (601) 842-7669. (ATA; MSE)
2135 **Trace State Park**, Rt. 1, Box 254, Belden, MS 38826, (601) 489-2958. (ATA; MSE)
  Tupelo Horse Trail *see* entry 2110.
2136 **Turkey Creek Water Park**, Decatur, MS 39327. (ATA)
2137 **Turkey Fork Lake**, SR 63, Richton, MS 39476. (ATA)
  Tuxachanie National Recreation Trail *see* entry 2070.
2138 **Tuxachanie Trail**, Tuxachanie Trail, Inc., P.O. Box 14, Gulfport, MS 39501. 11.0 miles straight. Awards available. (SAR 1990)
2139 **Vicksburg National Military Park**

Trail & Trek, Eugene G. Buglewicz, 503 Lakeside Dr., Vicksburg, MS 39180. 7.0, 12.0 and 14.0 miles loops. Awards available. (AA 1991)
2140 **Wall Doxey State Park**, SR 7, Holly Springs, MS 38634, (601) 252-4231. (WCD; ATA; MSE)
2141 **Wallace Creek**, Corps of Engineers—Enid Lake, Enid, MS 38927, (601) 563-4571. (WCD)
2142 **Water Valley Landing Campground**, Corps of Engineers—Enid Lake, SR 32, Water Valley, MS 38965, (601) 563-4571. (WCD)
2143 **Waverly Ferry**, Corps of Engineers, SR 50, West Point, LA 39773. (ATA)
2144 **Whispering Pines AOK Campground**, US 49, Hattiesburg, MS 39402, (601) 268-2747. (WCD)
2145 **Yazoo National Wildlife Refuge**, Rt. 1, Box 286, Hollandale, MS 38748, (601) 839-2638. 26.0 miles. (GNW)

Generally:
Executive Director, Department of Natural Resources, 700 Robert E. Lee Bldg., Jackson, MS 39207-9998, (601) 354-6321. (SFC)
National Forests in Mississippi Hiking Trails, Supervisor's Office, U.S. Forest Service, 100 Capitol St., Suite 1141, Jackson, MS 39269, (601) 965-4391. (EGH)

Index (by city)

Ackerman: Choctaw Lake Park 2063; Tombigbee National Forest 2133
Baldwyn: Nathan Bedford Forrest Trail 2111
Bay St. Louis: McLeod Water Park 2104
Belden: Trace State Park 2135
Biloxi: d'Iberville Trail 2071; Mazalea Travel Park 2103
Brooksvile: Noxubee National Wildlife Refuge 2113
Canton: Coal Bluff Park 2066
Charleston: Camp Tallaha 2057
Coffeeville: Carver Point State Park 2058
Coldwater: Dub Patten Campground 2074; South Abutment Campground 2129

Collinsville: Columbus Lock East 2067; Lake Lowndes State Park 2094; Luxapilla Creek Park 2100
Corinth: Jacinto Nature Trails 2091
Courtland: Chickasaw Hill Campground 2062
Crossroads: Crossroads Water Park 2068
Decatur: Turkey Creek Water Park 2136
Edwards: Askew's Landing Campground 2048
Enid: Wallace Creek 2141
Escatawpa: River Bend RV Resort 2121
Flora: Mississippi Petrified Forest Campground 2107

Forest: Bienville National Forest 2051; Marathon Lake Park 2101
Fulton: Nita Lake Resort 2112
Gautier: Sandhill Crane National Wildlife Refuge 2125
Grenada: Grenada Lake 2082; Hugh White State Park 2089; Outlet Channel Campground 2117; Oxbow RV Park 2118
Gulfport: Flat Branch Campground & RV Park 2075
Hattiesburg: Paul B. Johnson State Park 2119; Whispering Pines AOK Campground 2144
Hernando: Arkabutla Reservoir 2047
Hollandale: Leroy Percy State Park 2097; Yazoo National Wildlife Refuge 2145
Holly Springs: Holly Springs National Forest 2085; Wall Doxey State Park 2140
Houston: Sleepy Hollow Campground 2128
Iuka: J.P. Coleman State Park 2090
Jackson: Chewalla Lake and Recreation Area 2060; Goshen Springs Campground 2079; Jeff Busby State Park 2092; LeFleur's Bluff State Park 2095; Mississippi Agriculture & Forestry Museum 2106; Riverside Park 2122; Timber Lake Campground 2130
Kosciusko: Holmes County State Park 2086
Laurel: Big Creek Water Park 2052
Louisville: Legion State Park 2096
Lumberton: Little Black Creek Water Park 2099
Magnolia: Beaver Dam Nature Trail 2050
McComb: Bogue Chitto Water Park 2053; Percy Quin State Park 2120
McHenry: DeSoto National Forest 2070
Meadville: Clear Springs Park 2065; Homochitto National Forest 2088
Memphis, TN: Chewalla Nature Trail 2061; Lichterman Nature Center 2098
Mendenhall: D'Lo Water Park 2072; Merit Water Park 2105

Meridian: Clarkco State Park 2064; Okatibbee Water Park 2115
Monticello: Atwood Water Park 2049
Morton: Roosevelt State Park 2123
Mount Olive: Dry Creek Water Park 2073
Natchez: Natchez State Park 2109
Oakland: George Payne Cossar State Park 2077
Ocean Springs: Gulf Islands National Seashore 2083
Pascagoula: Shepard State Park 2127
Perkinston: Salmen Scout Reservation 2124
Philadelphia: Burnside Lake Park 2056
Port Gibson: Grand Gulf Park Trail 2080
Quitman: Archusa Creek Water Park 2046
Richton: Turkey Fork Lake 2137
Rosedale: Great River Road State Park 2081
Sardis: John W. Kyle State Park 2093; Sardis Lake 2126
Starkville: Oktibbeha County Lake 2116
Tishomingo: Tishomingo State Park 2132
Tupelo: Bullen Creek Nature Trail 2055; Mount Locus Environmental Study Trail 2108; Tombigbee National Forest 2133; Tombigbee State Park 2134
Tylertown: Holmes Water Park 2087
Vicksburg: Vicksburg National Military Park Trail & Trek 2139
Walnut Grove: Golden Memorial State Park 2078
Water Valley: Water Valley Landing Campground 2142
Waveland: Buccaneer State Park 2054
Waynesboro: Maynor Creek Water Park 2102
Wesson: Timberlanes Camp & Dude Ranch Resort 2131
West Point: Catherine "Kitty" Bryan Dill Memorial Bikeway 2059; Waverly Ferry 2143
Wiggins: Flint Creek Water Park 2076
Yazoo City: Delta National Forest 2069; Hillside National Wildlife Refuge 2084

New Hampshire

Adams Slide Trail *see* entry 2254.
Ammonoosuc Ravine Trail *see* entry 2227.

2146 **Annett State Forest**, 105 Loudon Rd., Concord, NH 03301, (603) 271-2214. (SNE; GNA)

2147 **Appalachian Side Trails** (not listed elsewhere), Dartmouth Outing Club, Robinson Hall, P.O. Box 9, Hanover, NH 03755, (603) 646-2428; or Appalachian Mountain Club, 5 Joy St., Boston, MA 02108. Named trails: Arethusa-Ripley Falls, Around-Lonesome-Lake, Atwell Hill, Austin Brook, Beaver Brook, Black Angel, Camel, Caps Ridge, Carlo Col, Cascade Brook, Centennial, Clark Pond Loop, Cornice, Daniel Webster (Scout), Davis Path, Denduskeag, Dryad Falls, East Spur, Edmands Path, Eyebrow, Fishin' Jimmy, Gale River, Glencliff, Goose Eye, Gordon Pond, Great Gully, Hale Brook, Hurricane, Imp, Israel Ridge Path, Jefferson Loop, Jewell, Kedron Flume, Kinsman Pond, Kinsman Ridge, Lambert Ridge, Ledyard Spring, Lend-a-Hand, Link, Lost Pond, Lowe's Path, Monroe Loop, Mt. Clinton, Mt. Cube, Mt. Eisenhower, Mt. Eisenhower Loop, Nelson Crag, Nineteen Mile Brook, North Carter, North Twin Spur, Old Speck, Ore Hill, Parapet, Peabody Brook, Quinttown, Rattle River, Real Brook, Ridge, Shookumchuck, Stony Brook, Success, Velvet Rocks Shelter Loop, Velvet Rocks Shelter, Webster Cliff, Webster-Jackson, Wildcat Ridge, Willey Range. (BMG; ATG #2)

2148 **Appalachian Trail** (see separate entry **4948** in interstate section).

2149 **Apple Hill Campground**, SR 142, Bethlehem, NH 03574, (603) 869-2238. (WCD)

Arethusa-Ripley Falls Trail *see* entry 2147.
Around-Lonesome-Lake Trail *see* entry 2147.
Artist's Bluff Trail *see* entry 2254.
Atwell Hill Trail *see* entry 2147.
Base Area Loop Trail *see* entry 2254.
Basin-Cascades Trail *see* entry 2174.

2150 **Beach Hill Campground**, US 302, Twin Mountain, NH 03595, (603) 846-5521. (WCD)

2151 **Beachwood Shores Campground**, HC 66, Bonnyman Rd., East Wakefield, NH 03830, (603) 539-4272. (WCD)

2152 **Bear Brook State Park**, SR 28, Allenstown, NH 03275, (603) 485-9874. 30.0 miles. (NHG; NHH; WCD; EGH; GNA)

Beaver Brook Trail *see* entry 2147.

2153 **Belknap County Park**, SR 11A, Gilford, NH 03237, (603) 293-4344. (WCD)

Benton Trail *see* entry 2254.
Black Angel Trail *see* entry 2147.
Black Pond Trail *see* entry 2254.
Blow-Me-Down Natural Area Trail *see* entry 2232.
Blow-Me-Down Ravine Trail *see* entry 2232.
Bondcliff Trail *see* entry 2253.
Boot Spur Trail *see* entry 2253.
Boulder Loop Trail *see* entry 2253.

2154 **Branch Brook Campground**, P.O. Box 390, Campton, NH 03223, (603) 726-7001. (WCD)

Brook Trail *see* entry 2254.
Brooks Trail *see* entry 2248.
Camel Trail *see* entry 2147.

2155 **Camp Carpenter**, Daniel Webster Council, BSA, P.O. Box 128, 571 Holt Ave., Manchester, NH 03105, (603) 625-6431. (SFC)

2156 **Camp Wanockset**, Nashua Valley Council, BSA, Rt. 2, Box 128, Lancaster, MA 01523, (617) 534-3532. (SFC)
Caps Ridge Trail *see* entry 2147.
2157 **Cardigan Forest, Reservation and State Park**, SR 188, Orange, NH 03741. 50.0 miles. Named trails: West Ridge. (NHG; EGH; GNA)
Carlo Col Trail *see* entry 2147.
Carriage Road Trail *see* entry 2254.
Carrigan Notch Trail *see* entry 2254.
Carter-Moriah Trail *see* entry 2254.
Cascade Brook Trail *see* entry 2147.
Cascade Link-Old Ski Path-Red Spot Trail *see* entry 2207.
2158 **Cascades-Waterfalls Trail**, Balsams Hotel, SR 26, Dixville Notch, NH 03576. (NET)
Cedar Brook Trail *see* entry 2253.
Centennial Trail *see* entry 2147.
Champney Falls Trail *see* entry 2253.
2159 **Charles L. Pierce Wildlife and Forest Reservation**, Society for the Protection of New Hampshire Forests, 54 Portsmouth St., Concord, NH 03301, (603) 224-9945. (SNE)
2160 **Chocorua Camping Village**, P.O. Box 118, West Ossipee, NH 03890, (603) 323-8536 or (800) 462-2426. (WCD)
Clark Pond Loop Trail *see* entry 2147.
2161 **Cog Railway RV Park**, Base Rd., Twin Mountain, NH 03595, (603) 846-5404. (WCD)
2162 **Coleman State Park**, Rt. 1, Diamond Pond Rd., Colebrook, NH 03576, (603) 237-4520. (MNE; SNE; OTB; GNA)
2163 **Connecticut Lakes State Forest**, Pittsburg, NH 03592, (603) 538-6965. (SNE)
Cornice Trail *see* entry 2147.
2164 **Crawford Notch General Store & Campground**, Star Route, Box 302, Bartlett, NH 03812, (603) 374-2779. (WCD)
2165 **Crawford Notch State Park**, SR 302, Harts Location, NH 03812, (603) 374-2272. Named trails: Mount Willard. (NHG; NHH; WCD; MNE; SNE; GNA)
Crawford Path *see* entry 2227.
Daniel Webster (Scout) Trail *see* entry 2147.

Daniel Webster Trail *see* entry 2253.
Davis Path *see* entry 2147.
2166 **Deer Mountain State Campground**, Pittsburg, NH 03592, (603) 271-3456. (NHH)
2167 **Deering Wildlife Preserve**, Audubon Society of New Hampshire, P.O. Box 528B, Concord, NH 03301, (603) 224-9909. (SNE)
Denduskeag Trail *see* entry 2147.
Dilley Trail *see* entry 2198.
2168 **Dixville Notch State Park**, SR 26, Dixville Notch, NH 93576, (603) 788-3155. (NHG; NHH)
Dry River Trail *see* entry 2253.
Dryad Falls Trail *see* entry 2147.
East Branch Trail *see* entry 2253.
East Spur Trail *see* entry 2147.
2169 **Echo Lake State Park**, Bartlett, NH 03812, (603) 356-2627. (NHG; NHH; SNE)
2170 **Echo Valley Campground**, Rt. 1, Box 392, Lyndeborough, NH 03082, (603) 654-9246. (WCD)
2171 **Enfield Wildlife Management Area**, Fox State Forest, 34 Bridge St., Concord, NH 03301, (603) 271-3421. 20.0 miles. Named trails: Mushroom, Tree Identification Loop. (SNE; GNA)
Ethan Pond Trail *see* entry 2253.
Eyebrow Trail *see* entry 2147.
Falling Waters Trail *see* entry 2254.
2172 **Field 'N Forest Recreation Area**, 278 Bond's Corner Rd., Hancock, NH 03449, (603) 525-3568. (NHG; WCD)
Fishin' Jimmy Trail *see* entry 2147.
Flat Mountain Pond Trail *see* entry 2253.
The Flume *see* entry 2174.
Flume Slide Trail *see* entry 2254.
Forest Nature Trail *see* entry 2212.
2173 **Fox State Forest**, P.O. Box 1175, School St., Hillsboro, NH 03244, (603) 464-3453. 20.0 miles. (NHG; NHH; EGH; SNE)
Franconia Brook Trail *see* entry 2253.
2174 **Franconia Notch State Park**, Franconia, NH 03580, (603) 823-5563 or (603) 823-9513; or Flume Visitors Center, (603) 745-8391. Named trails: Basin-Cascades,

NEW HAMPSHIRE

The Flume 2.0(l), Greenleaf 2.5, Lake 1.5, Old Bridle 3.0. (NHG; LGU; NHH; WCD; MNE; SNE; GNA)
    Franconia Ridge Trail see entry 2254.
2175 **Franklin Falls Flood Control Area,** Fish and Game Department, P.O. Box 2003, 34 Bridge St., Concord, NH 03301, (603) 271-3421. (SNE; GNA)
2176 **Friendly Beaver Campground,** Old Coach Rd., New Boston, NH 03070, (603) 487-5570. (WCD)
    Frost Trail see entry 2253.
    Gale River Trail see entry 2147.
2177 **Gap Mountain,** Society for the Protection of New Hampshire Forests, 54 Portsmouth St., Concord, NH 03301, (603) 224-9945. (SNE)
    Garfield Ridge Trail see entry 2254.
    Garfield Trail see entry 2254.
2178 **Gile Memorial State Forest,** 105 Loudon Rd., Concord, NH 03301. (SNE)
    Glencliff Trail see entry 2147.
    Goose Eye Trail see entry 2147.
    Gorge Brook Trail see entry 2254.
2179 **Grafton Pond,** Society for the Protection of New Hampshire Forests, 54 Portsmouth St., Concord, NH 03301, (603) 224-9945. (SNE)
    Great Gulf Trail see entry 2253.
    Great Gully Trail see entry 2147.
2180 **Greeley Ponds Trail,** Greeley Ponds, North Woodstock, NH 03262. 3.0 miles straight. (OTB)
2181 **Greenfield State Park,** SR 136, Greenfield, NH 03047, (603) 547-3497. (NHG; WCD)
    Greenleaf Trail see entries 2174 and 2254.
    Guinea Pond Trail see entry 2253.
    Gulfside Trail see entry 2227.
2182 **Gunstock Recreation Area,** SR 11A, Gilford, NH 03246, (603) 293-4341. (MNE)
    Hale Brook Trail see entry 2147.
2183 **Harris Center for Conservation Education,** King's Hwy., Hancock, NH 03449, (603) 525-3394. (NHG)
    Hawker Ridge Trail see entry 2253.
2184 **Hay Reservation,** Society for the Protection of New Hampshire Forests, 54 Portsmouth St., Concord, NH 03301,
(603) 224-9945. (SNE)
2185 **Hemenway State Forest,** New Hampshire Division of Parks and Recreation, P.O. Box 856, Concord, NH 03301, (603) 271-3254. (SNE; GNA)
2186 **Hillcrest Campground,** Dover Rd., Rt. 2, Box 801, Chichester, NH 03263, (800) 338-9488. (WCD)
2187 **Hopkinton and Everett Lakes,** Fish and Game Department, P.O. Box 2003, 34 Bridge St., Concord, NH 03301, (603) 271-3421; or U.S. Army Corps of Engineers, Franklin Falls Dam, P.O. Box 351, Franklin, NH 03235. (SNE; GNA)
    Hurricane Trail see entry 2147.
    Imp Trail see entry 2147.
    Israel Ridge Path see entry 2147.
2188 **Jacobs Brook Campground,** Archertown Rd., Orford, NH 03777, (603) 353-9210. (WCD)
    Jefferson Loop Trail see entry 2147.
    Jewell Trail see entry 2147.
2189 **John Hay National Wildlife Refuge,** SR 103A, Newbury, NH 03255, (603) 763-5041 or (603) 763-2452. (NHG)
2190 **John Wingate Weeks Historic Site,** US 3, Lancaster, NH 03584, (603) 788-4004. (NHG)
2191 **Jones Brook Wildlife Management Area,** Fish and Game Department, P.O. Box 2003, 34 Bridge St., Concord, NH 03301, (603) 271-3421. (SNE)
    Kedron Flume Trail see entry 2147.
    Kinsman Pond Trail see entry 2147.
    Kinsman Ridge Trail see entry 2147.
2192 **Knights Hill Nature Park,** New London, NH 03257. (GFA)
2193 **KOA-Cherry Mountain,** P.O. Box 148, Twin Mountain, NH 03595, (800) 743-5819. (WCD)
2194 **Lake Francis State Park,** US 3, Pittsburg, NH 03592. (SNE; OTB)
    Lake Trail see entry 2174.
    Lambert Ridge Trail see entry 2147.
    Ledyard Spring Trail see entry 2147.
    Lend-a-Hand Trail see entry 2147.
    Liberty Spring Trail see entry 2254.
    Liberty Trail see entry 2254.
    Lincoln Brook Trail see entry 2253.
    Lincoln Woods Trail see entry 2253.
    Link Trail see entry 2147.

2195 **Little Nature Museum**, 59 Boyce Rd., Weare, NH 03281, (603) 529-7180. (NHG; GFA)
2196 **Living Water Campground**, P.O. Box 158W, Twin Mountain, NH 03595, (603) 846-5513. (WCD)
2197 **Lonesome Lake**, Lafayette Campground, Franconia Notch, NH 03580. Named trails: Ridge Path 0.5, Wildwood Path 0.5. (NET)
  Lonesome Lake Trail see entry 2254.
  Lost Pond Trail see entry 2147.
2198 **Lost River Reservation**, SR 112, Kinsman Notch, NH 03251, (603) 745-8031; or Society for the Protection of New Hampshire Forests, 54 Portsmouth St., Concord, NH 03301, (603) 224-9945. Named trails: Dilley. (MNE; SNE)
2199 **Lost River Valley Campground**, Rt. 1, Box 44W, North Woodstock, NH 03262, (603) 745-8321. (WCD)
  Lowe's Path see entry 2147.
  Madison Gulf Trail see entry 2253.
  Mahoosuc Notch Trail see entry 2254.
  Mahoosuc Trail see entry 2254.
2200 **Mason Railroad Trail**, Liz Fletcher, Mason Conservation Commission, Mann House, Darling Hill Rd., Mason, NH 03048, (603) 878-2070. 6.7 miles straight. (GRT)
2201 **Mead Wilderness Base**, Daniel Webster Council, BSA, P.O. Box 128, 571 Holt Ave., Manchester, NH 03105, (603) 625-6431. (HUN)
2202 **Meriden Bird Sanctuary**, Main St., Meriden, NH 03770, (603) 542-4883. (NHG)
2203 **Metacomet-Monadnock Trail** (see separate entry **4952** in interstate section).
2204 **Milan Hill State Park**, Milan, NH 03588, (603) 788-3155. (NHG)
2205 **Mile Away Campground**, 41 Old W. Hopkinton Rd., Henniker, NH 03242, (603) 428-7616. (WCD)
2206 **Miller State Park**, SR 101, Peterborough, NH 03458, (603) 547-3497. Named trails: Wapack 21.0. (NHG; NHH; SNE)
2207 **Monadnock State Park**, SR 124, Jaffrey Center, NH 03452, (603) 532-8862. 39.0 miles. Named trails: Cascade Link-Old Ski Path-Red Spot, Pumpelly, White Cross, White Dot. (NHG; NHH; WCD; EGH; MNE; SNE; NET)
2208 **Monadnock-Sunapee Greenway**, Appalachian Mountain Club, 5 Joy St., Boston, MA 02108; or Society for the Protection of New Hampshire Forests, 54 Portsmouth St., Concord, NH 03301, (603) 224-9945. 51.0 miles. (EGH)
  Monroe Loop Trail see entry 2147.
2209 **Moose Brook State Park**, Rt. 1, Berlin, NH 03570, (603) 466-3860. (MNE; SNE; GNA)
2210 **Moose Hillock Campground**, Rt. 1, Box 96W, Warren, NH 03279, (603) 764-5294 or (800) 539-2267. (WCD)
  Moriah Brook Trail see entry 2253.
  Mount Clay Loop Trail see entry 2227.
  Mt. Clinton Trail see entry 2147.
  Mt. Cube Trail see entry 2147.
  Mt. Eisenhower Loop Trail see entry 2147.
  Mt. Eisenhower Trail see entry 2147.
2211 **Mount Kearsarge**, New Hampshire Division of Parks and Recreation, P.O. Box 856, Concord, NH 03301, (603) 271-3254. (GNA)
2212 **Mount Monadnock**, Society for the Protection of New Hampshire Forests, 54 Portsmouth St., Concord, NH 03301, (603) 224-9945. Named trails: Forest Nature. (SNE; GNA)
2213 **Mount Sunapee State Park**, SR 103, Newbury, NH 03255, (603) 763-2356. (NHG; NHH; SNE; GNA)
  Mount Willard Trail see entry 2165.
  Mushroom Trail see entry 2171.
  Nelson Crag Trail see entry 2147.
  Nineteen Mile Brook Trail see entry 2147.
  North Carter Trail see entry 2147.
  North Province Ridge Trail see entry 2254.
  North Twin Spur Trail see entry 2147.
  North Twin Trail see entry 2253.
2214 **Northstar Campground**, SR 10, Newport, NH 03773, (603) 863-4001. (WCD)

2215 **Odiorne Point State Park**, SR 1A, Rye, NH 03870, (603) 436-8043 or (603) 436-7406. (NHG; FNE; SNE; GNA)
Old Bridle Path see entry 2174.
Old Speck Trail see entry 2147.
Oliverian Trail see entry 2253.
Ore Hill Trail see entry 2147.
Osgood Trail see entry 2253.
2216 **Ossipee Lake/Heath Pond Bog**, Division of Parks and Recreation, P.O. Box 856D, Concord, NH 03301, (603) 271-3254. (SNE)
2217 **Otter Lake Campground**, Otterville Rd., New London, NH 03257, (603) 763-5600. (WCD)
2218 **Oxbow Campground**, SR 149, Hillsborough, NH 03244, (603) 464-5952. (WCD)
2219 **Paradise Point Nature Center**, North Shore Rd., Hebron, NH 03241, (603) 744-3516 or (603) 224-9909. (NHG; SNE)
Parapet Trail see entry 2147.
Patte Brook Auto Tour see entry 2253.
2220 **Pawtuckaway State Park**, SR 107, Raymond, NH 03077, (603) 895-3031. (NHG; NHH; SNE; GNA)
Peabody Brook Trail see entry 2147.
2221 **Peabody Forest**, Society for the Protection of New Hampshire Forests, 54 Portsmouth St., Concord, NH 03301, (603) 224-9945. Named trails: Peabody. (SNE)
Peabody Trail see entry 2221.
2222 **Pillsbury State Park**, SR 31, Washington, NH 03280, (603) 863-2860. 2.0 miles. (NHG; NHH; SNE; GNA)
2223 **Pine River State Forest**, Division of Forests and Lands, P.O. Box 856, State House Annex, Concord, NH 03301, (603) 271-2214. (SNE; GNA)
Piper Trail see entry 2253.
2224 **Pisgah State Park**, Chesterfield, NH 03443, (603) 239-8153. 30.0 miles. (NHG; NHH; SNE; GNA)
2225 **Poetry-Nature Trail**, Robert Frost Farm Historic Site, SR 28, Derry, NH 03038, (603) 432-3091. 0.5 mile. (NHG; MNE; WON)
2226 **Pondicherry Wildlife Refuge Trail**, Audubon Society of New Hampshire, P.O. Box 528B, 3 Silk Farm Rd., Concord, NH 03301, (603) 224-9909. (SNE; GNA)
2227 **Presidential Range**, Forest Supervisor, White Mountain National Forest, P.O. Box 638, Laconia, NH 03246. Named trails: Ammonoosuc Ravine 2.26, Crawford Path, Gulfside 6.25(s), Mount Clay Loop, Valley Way 3.47(s). (HFI; HTN)
Pumpelly Trail see entry 2207.
Quinttown Trail see entry 2147.
Rail 'n River Nature Trail see entry 2253.
Rattle River Trail see entry 2147.
Real Brook Trail see entry 2147.
2228 **Rhododendron Natural Area**, SR 119, Fitzwilliam, NH 03447, (603) 632-8862. Named trails: Rhododendron. (NHG; NHH; OTB; GNA)
Rhododendron Trail see entry 2228.
Ridge Path see entry 2197.
Ridge Trail see entry 2147.
2229 **Road's End Farm Hiking Center**, Jackson Hill Rd., Chesterfield, NH 03443, (603) 363-4703. (FNE)
Rob Brook Trail see entry 2253.
2230 **Rockingham Recreational Trail**, Paul Gray, Chief, Department of Trails, New Hampshire Department of Resources and Economic Development, P.O. Box 856, Concord, NH 03302, (603) 271-3254. 22.5 miles straight. (GRT)
Rocky Branch Trail see entry 2253.
2231 **Rollins State Park**, SR 103, Warner, NH 03278, (603) 239-8153. (NHG; NHH)
2232 **Saint-Gaudens National Historic Site**, Rt. 3, Box 73, SR 12A, Cornish, NH 03745-9704, (603) 675-2175. Named trails: Blow-Me-Down Natural Area 2.5, Blow-Me-Down Ravine 0.25. (NPF; NPV; NPE; OTB; CGA)
2233 **Sanguinary Ridge**, New Hampshire Division of Parks and Recreation, P.O. Box 856, Concord, NH 03301, (603) 271-3254. (SNE)
Sanguinary Ridge Trail see entry 2254.
Sawyer River Trail see entry 2253.
2234 **Seven Maples Camping Area**, P.O. Box 587, Hancock, NH 03449, (603) 525-3321. (WCD)

Shelburne Trail *see* entry 2253.
2235 **Shieling State Forest**, Old Street Rd., Peterborough, NH 03458, (603) 271-3457. 8.0 miles. (NHG; NHH)
Shoal Pond Trail *see* entry 2253.
Shookumchuck Trail *see* entry 2147.
Six Husbands Trail *see* entry 2254.
Smartsbrook Trail *see* entry 2253.
Snapper Ski Trail *see* entry 2254.
South Province Ridge Trail *see* entry 2254.
Sphinx Trail *see* entry 2254.
2236 **SPNHF-Bretzfelder Memorial Park**, Prospect St., Bethlehem, NH 03574, (603) 444-6228. (NHG)
2237 **Squam Lakes**, Science Center of New Hampshire at Squam Lakes, P.O. Box 204, Holderness, NH 03245, (603) 968-7194 or (603) 968-7336; or Squam Lakes Association, Plymouth, NH 03264. 40.0 miles. (WCD)
2238 **Squam Lakeside Farm Campground**, SR 25, Ashland, NH 03217, (603) 968-7227. (WCD)
2239 **Stoneham Island Nature Center**, P.O. Box 1097, Meredith, NH 03253, (603) 279-7278. (NHG)
Stony Brook Trail *see* entry 2147.
2240 **Storrs Pond Recreation Area**, P.O. Box 106, Hanover, NH 03755, (603) 643-2134. (WCD)
Success Trail *see* entry 2147.
2241 **Sugar River Recreation Trail**, Paul Gray, Chief, Department of Trails, New Hampshire Department of Resources and Economic Development, P.O. Box 856, Concord, NH 03302, (603) 271-3254. 8.0 miles straight. (GRT)
2242 **Surry Mountain Camping Area**, P.O. Box 271, Keene, NH 03431, (603) 352-9770. (WCD)
2243 **Swain Brook Campground**, P.O. Box 157, Beech Hill Rd., Wentworth, NH 03282, (603) 764-5537. (NHG)
2244 **Taves Reservation**, Society for the Protection of New Hampshire Forests, 54 Portsmouth St., Concord, NH 03301, (603) 224-9945. (SNE)
2245 **Terrace Pines**, P.O. Box 98W, Center Ossipee, NH 03814, (603) 539-6210. (WCD)

Thoreau Falls Trail *see* entry 2253.
2246 **Thousand Acres Family Campground**, US 3, Franklin, NH 03235, (603) 934-4440. (WCD)
Tree Identification Loop Trail *see* entry 2171.
Tuckerman Ravine Trail *see* entry 2253.
Tunnel Brook Trail *see* entry 2254.
Twin Brook Trail *see* entry 2253.
2247 **Twin Mountain Fish & Wildlife Center**, SR 3, Whitefield, NH 03598, (603) 846-5108. (NHG)
Twinway Trail *see* entry 2253.
Upper Nanamocomuck Trail *see* entry 2253.
2248 **Urban Forestry Center**, 45 Elwyn Rd., Portsmouth, NH 03801, (603) 431-6774. Named trails: Brooks. (NHG; NHH)
Valley Way Trail *see* entry 2227.
Velvet Rocks Shelter Loop Trail *see* entry 2147.
Velvet Rocks Shelter Trail *see* entry 2147.
2249 **Wapack National Wildlife Refuge**, SR 101, Peterborough, NH 03458. Named trails: Wapack Nature 3.0, Wapack 21.0. (NHG; SNE; GNA)
Wapack Nature Trail *see* entry 2249.
Wapack Trail *see* entries 2206 and 2249.
Webster Cliff Trail *see* entry 2147.
Webster-Jackson Trail *see* entry 2147.
2250 **Wellington State Beach**, SR 3A, Bristol, NH 03222, (603) 744-2197. (NHG)
West Milan Trail *see* entry 2253.
West Ridge Trail *see* entry 2157.
Westside Trail *see* entry 2253.
2251 **White Birches Mountain Camping Park**, 218 SR 2, Shelburne, NH 03581, (603) 466-2022. (WCD)
White Cross Trail *see* entry 2207.
White Dot Trail *see* entry 2207.
2252 **White Lake State Park**, SR 16, West Ossipee, NH 03890, (603) 323-7350. (WCD; MNE; SNE; GNA)
2253 **White Mountain National Forest**, Federal Bldg., 719 Main St., P.O. Box 638, Laconia, NH 03246; or Ammonoosuc

NEW HAMPSHIRE 141

Ranger District, Trudeau Rd., P.O. Box 239, Bethlehem, NH 03574, (603) 869-2626; or Androscoggin Ranger District, 80 Glen Rd., Gorham, NH 03581, (603) 466-2713; or Saco Ranger District, Kancamagus Hwy., P.O. Box 274, Conway, NH 03818, (603) 447-5448; or Evans Notch Ranger District, Bridge St., Bethel, ME 04217, (207) 824-2134; or Pemigewasset Ranger District, Rt. 3, Box 15, 127 Highland St., Plymouth, NH 03264, (603) 536-1310. 1200 miles. Named trails: Bondcliff 6.0(s), Boot Spur, Boulder Loop, Cedar Brook 5.7(s), Champney Falls, Daniel Webster, Dry River 10.5(s), East Branch 8.0(s), Ethan Pond 5.6(s), Flat Mountain Pond 9.0(s), Franconia Brook 7.2(s), Frost, Great Gulf 7.76(s), Guinea Pond 4.0(s), Hawker Ridge, Lincoln Brook, Lincoln Woods 2.7(s), Madison Gulf, Moriah Brook 5.3(s), North Twin 4.3(s), Oliverian 3.5(s), Osgood, Patte Brook Auto Tour, Piper, Rail 'n River Nature, Rob Brook 2.0(s), Rocky Branch 9.0(s), Sawyer River 4.0(s), Shelburne 5.0(s), Shoal Pond, Smartsbrook, Thoreau Falls 5.1(s), Tuckerman Ravine 4.1, Twin Brook, Twinway, Upper Nanamocomuck 9.3(s), West Milan 12.0(s), Westside, Wild River 7.7(s), Wilderness 6.0(s), York Pond 6.5(s), Zeacliff 2.5(s). (NHG; BPM; GRT; NHH; WCD; EGH; FMV; GOP; MNE; SNE; NET; FGU; GNA; NFG; IFT)

2254 **White Mountains**, Reservations Secretary, AMC Pinkham Notch Camp, Gorham, NH 03581, (603) 466-3994; or White Mountains National Forest, P.O. Box 638, Laconia, NH 03247, (603) 524-6450. Named trails: Adams Slide 1.26(s), Artist's Bluff, Base Area Loop 1.25(s), Benton 3.5(s), Black Pond 0.83(s), Brook 4.2(s), Carriage Road 5.0(s), Carrigan Notch 0.5(s), Carter-Moriah 13.9(s), Falling Waters 2.8(s), Flume Slide 3.45(s), Franconia Ridge 5.0(s), Garfield 5.0(s), Garfield Ridge 6.53(s), Gorge Brook 2.7(s), Greenleaf 3.25(s), Liberty 4.5(s), Liberty Spring 3.45(s), Lonesome Lake, Mahoosuc 27.24, Mahoosuc Notch 2.75, North Province Ridge 1.12(s), Sanguinary Ridge, Six Husbands 4.42(s), Snapper Ski 1.1(s), South Province Ridge 1.0(s), Sphinx 1.0(s), Tunnel Brook 6.5(s). (LGU; FNE; PTD; BMG; AGW; NET; GTB; HTN)

Wild River Trail see entry 2253.
Wildcat Ridge Trail see entry 2147.
Wilderness Trail see entry 2253.

2255 **Wildwood Campground**, Old Coach Rd., New Boston, NH 03070, (603) 487-3300. (WCD)

Wildwood Path see entry 2197.

2256 **Willard Pond Preserve**, Audubon Society of New Hampshire, P.O. Box 528B, Concord, NH 03301, (603) 224-9909. (SNE)

Willey Range Trail see entry 2147.

2257 **Winslow State Park**, SR 11, Wilmot Flat, NH 03287, (603) 526-6168 or (603) 927-4724 or (603) 763-2452. (NHG; NHH)

2258 **Wolfeboro/Sanbornville Recreational Trail**, Town of Wolfeboro, P.O. Box 629, Wolfeboro, NH 03894, (603) 569-3900; or Paul Gray, Chief of Off-Highway Vehicles, New Hampshire Department of Resources and Economic Development, Trails Bureau, P.O. Box 856, Concord, NH 03302, (603) 271-3254. 12.0 miles straight. (GRT)

York Pond Trail see entry 2253.
Zeacliff Trail see entry 2253.

Generally:

New England Trail Conference, 33 Knollwood Dr., East Longmeadow, MA 01028, (203) 342-1425 or (413) 732-3719. (EGH)

New Hampshire Department of Resources and Economic Development, P.O. Box 856, Concord, NH 03302, (603) 271-3254. (GRT)

New Hampshire Division of Parks and Recreation, 105 Loudoun Rd., Concord, NH 03301, (603) 271-3254. (EGH)

Index (by city)

Allenstown: Bear Brook State Park 2152
Ashland: Squam Lakeside Farm Campground 2238
Bartlett: Crawford Notch General Store & Campground 2164; Echo Lake State Park 2169
Berlin: Moose Brook State Park 2209
Bethel: White Mountain National Forest 2253
Bethlehem: Apple Hill Campground 2149; SPNHF-Bretzfelder Memorial Park 2236; White Mountain National Forest 2253
Bristol: Wellington State Beach 2250
Campton: Branch Brook Campground 2154
Center Ossipee: Ossipee Lake/Heath Pond Bog 2216; Pine River State Forest 2223; Terrace Pines 2245
Chesterfield: Pisgah State Park 2224; Road's End Farm Hiking Center 2229
Chichester: Hillcrest Campground 2186
Chocorua: Hemenway State Forest 2185
Colebrook: Coleman State Park 2162
Concord: Annett State Forest 2146; Charles L. Pierce Wildlife and Forest Reservation 2159; Deering Wildlife Preserve 2167; Enfield Wildlife Management Area 2171; Gap Mountain 2177; Gile Memorial State Forest 2178; Grafton Pond 2179; Hay Reservation 2184; Jones Brook Wildlife Management Area 2191; Monadnock-Sunapee Greenway 2208; Peabody Forest 2221; Rockingham Recreational Trail 2230; Sanguinary Ridge 2233; Sugar River Recreation Trail 2241; Taves Reservation 2244
Conway: White Mountain National Forest 2253
Cornish: Saint-Gaudens National Historic Site 2232
Derry: Poetry-Nature Trail 2225
Dixville Notch: Dixville Notch State Park 2168
East Wakefield: Beachwood Shores Campground 2151
Fitzwilliam: Rhododendron Natural Area 2228
Franconia: Franconia Notch State Park 2174
Franconia Notch: Lonesome Lake 2197
Franklin: Franklin Falls Flood Control Area 2175; Hopkinton and Everett Lakes 2187; Thousand Acres Family Campground 2246
Gilford: Belknap County Park 2153; Gunstock Recreation Area 2182
Gorham: White Mountain National Forest 2253; White Mountains 2254
Greenfield: Greenfield State Park 2181
Hancock: Field 'N Forest Recreation Area 2172; Harris Center for Conservation Education 2183; Seven Maples Camping Area 2234; Willard Pond Preserve 2256
Hanover: Storrs Pond Recreation Area 2240
Harts Location: Crawford Notch State Park 2165
Hebron: Paradise Point Nature Center 2219
Henniker: Mile Away Campground 2205
Hillsboro: Fox State Forest 2173
Hillsborough: Oxbow Campground 2218
Holderness: Squam Lakes 2237
Jaffrey Center: Monadnock State Park 2207; Mount Monadnock 2212
Keene: Surry Mountain Camping Area 2242
Kinsman Notch: Lost River Reservation 2198
Laconia: Presidential Range 2227; White Mountain National Forest 2253
Lancaster: Camp Wanockset 2156; John Wingate Weeks Historic Site 2190
Lyndeborough: Echo Valley Campground 2170
Manchester: Camp Carpenter 2155; Mead Wilderness Base 2201
Mason: Mason Railroad Trail 2200
Meredith: Stoneham Island Nature Center 2239
Meriden: Meriden Bird Sanctuary 2202
Milan: Milan Hill State Park 2204
New Boston: Friendly Beaver Campground 2176; Wildwood Campground 2255
New London: Knights Hill Nature Park 2192; Otter Lake Campground 2217
Newbury: John Hay National Wildlife Refuge 2189; Mount Sunapee State Park 2213

Newport: Northstar Campground 2214
North Woodstock: Greeley Ponds Trail 2180; Lost River Valley Campground 2199
Orange: Cardigan State Park 2157
Orford: Jacobs Brook Campground 2188
Peterborough: Miller State Park 2206; Shieling State Forest 2235; Wapack National Wildlife Refuge 2249
Pittsburg: Connecticut Lakes State Forest 2163; Deer Mountain State Campground 2166; Lake Francis State Park 2194
Plymouth: White Mountain National Forest 2253
Portsmouth: Urban Forestry Center 2248
Raymond: Pawtuckaway State Park 2220
Rye: Odiorne Point State Park 2215
Shelburne: White Birches Mountain Camping Park 2251
Twin Mountain: Beach Hill Campground 2150; Cog Railway RV Park 2161; KOA-Cherry Mountain 2193; Living Water Campground 2196
Warner: Rollins State Park 2231
Warren: Moose Hillock Campground 2210
Washington: Pillsbury State Park 2222
Weare: Little Nature Museum 2195
Wentworth: Swain Brook Campground 2243
West Ossipee: Chocorua Camping Village 2160; White Lake State Park 2252
Whitefield: Pondicherry Wildlife Refuge Trail 2226; Twin Mountain Fish & Wildlife Center 2247
Wilmot Flat: Mount Kearsarge 2211; Winslow State Park 2257
Wolfeboro: Wolfeboro/Sanbornville Recreational Trail 2258

NEW JERSEY

2259 **Abram S. Hewitt State Forest**, c/o Wawayanda State Park, P.O. Box 198, Highland Lakes, NJ 97422, (201) 764-4120. Named trails: Bearfort Ridge 2.5. (NNY; GNA)

Absegami Nature Trail *see* entry 2266.

2260 **Allaire State Park**, P.O. Box 218, Farmingdale, NJ 07727, (201) 938-2371. (WCD; ATP; OTB; DNJ; NNY; GNA)

2261 **Allamuchy Mountain State Park**, Willow Grove-Waterloo Rd., Hackettstown, NJ 07840, (201) 852-3790. (ATP; MMA; DNJ)

Allis Trail *see* entry 2352.

Allison Trail *see* entry 2359.

2262 **Alpine Area**, Henry Hudson Dr., Alpine, NJ 07620, (201) 768-1360. (MMA)

2263 **Appalachian Side Trails** (not listed elsewhere), New York-New Jersey Trail Conference, 232 Madison Ave., Rm. 908, New York, NY 10116, (212) 685-9699. Named trails: Blue Dot, Buttermilk Falls, Iris, Jacob's Ladder, Mount Tammany, River Ridge, Stony Brook, Swenson, Tinsley. (ATG #4; NYW)

2264 **Appalachian Trail** (see separate entry **4948** in interstate section).

2265 **Assunpink Wildlife Management Area**, Nacote Creek Lab, Star Route 9, Absecon, NJ 08201, (609) 652-9519. (AMC; NNY; GNA)

2266 **Bass River State Forest**, Stage Rd., New Gretna, NJ 08224, (609) 296-2554 or (609) 296-1114. Named trails: Absegami Nature. (WCD; ATP; DNJ; AMC; GNA)

2267 **Batona Trail**, Batona Hiking Club, c/o Robert E. Raine, 514 Inman Terr., Willow Grove, PA 19090; or Batona Trail, 1233 Princess Ave., Camden, NJ 08103; or Laura Cramer, Batona Club, 6244-A Mulberry St., Philadelphia, PA 19135; or Whit Korshiak, 219 Moore St., Lenola, NJ 08057. 51.0 miles. Awards available. (EGH; GOP; NJD; OTB; AMI; HTA; NHY; BHT; GTB; CBP; NYW)

2268 **Battle of Monmouth Historic Trail**, Monmouth Council, BSA, P.O. Box 188, Oakhurst, NJ 07755-0188, (908) 531-3636. 11.0 miles straight. Awards available. (AA 1993)

Bearfort Ridge Trail *see* entry 2259.

2269 **Beaver Hill Campground**, P.O. Box 353, Sussex, NJ 07461, (201) 827-0670 or (800) 229-CAMP. (WCD)

2270 **Beaver Swamp Wildlife Management Area**, Division of Fish, Game and Shellfisheries, P.O. Box 1809, Trenton, NJ 08625, (609) 292-9450. (GNA)

2271 **Belleplain State Forest**, P.O. Box 450, CR 550, Woodbine, NJ 08270, (609) 861-2404. 6.5 miles. (ATP; GNA)

2272 **Bergen County Nature Trail**, Bergen County Wildlife Center, Crescent Ave. W., Wyckoff, NJ 07481, (201) 891-5571. 0.67 mile. (NNY)

2273 **Berkshire Valley Wildlife Management Area**, Jim Munson, Crew Supervisor, Black River Wildlife Management Area, P.O. Box 52, North Rd., Chester, NJ 07930, (908) 879-6252. 3.0 miles straight. (GRT; GNA)

2274 **Birch Grove City Park**, Burton Rd., Northfield, NJ 08225, (609) 641-3778. (WCD)

2275 **Black River Wildlife Management Area Trail**, Jim Munson, Crew Supervisor, Black River Wildlife Management Area, P.O. Box 52, North Rd., Chester, NJ 07930, (908) 879-6252. 5.0 miles straight. (GRT; GNA)

NEW JERSEY 145

Blue Dot Trail see entry 2263.
Blue Trail see entry 2390.

2276 **Bordentown Walking Tour**, Bordentown Historical Society Visitor's Center, 302 Farnsworth St., Bordentown, NJ 08505, (201) 286-1740. (NJO)

Braille Nature Trail see entry 2311.

2277 **Brigantine National Wildlife Refuge**, P.O. Box 72, Oceanville, NJ 08231, (609) 652-1665. Named trails: Leeds Eco-Trail. (AMC; GNA; GNW)

2278 **Brookdale Park**, Essex County Department of Parks, Recreation & Cultural Affairs, 115 Clifton Ave., Newark, NJ 07104, (201) 482-6400. 6.0 miles. Named trails: Brookline Interpretive. (NNY)

Brookline Interpretive Trail see entry 2278.

2279 **Bull's Island State Recreation Area**, Rt. 1, Box 4-Canal, Belle Mead, NJ 08502, (201) 873-3050. (AMI)

Burnt Meadow Trail see entry 2352.
Butler to Montville Trail see entry 2352.
Buttermilk Falls Trail see entry 2263.

2280 **Camp Carr**, c/o Hunterdon County YMCA, Allerton Rd., Clinton, NJ 08809, (908) 782-1030. (WCD)

2281 **Camp Lewis**, Bayonne Council, BSA, 41 E. 25th St., Bayonne, NJ 07002, (201) 436-0100. (SFC)

2282 **Camp Watchung**, Watchung Council, BSA, 1170 US 22W, Mountainside, NJ 07092, (201) 624-9191. (SFC)

2283 **Campgaw Mountain County Reservation**, Campgaw Rd., Mahwah, NJ 07436, (201) 646-2680. (DNJ; NNY)

2284 **Cannonball Trail**, Sacred Heart School, 622 Valley Brook Ave., Lyndhurst, NJ 07071. 17.0 miles. Awards available. (HTA)

Cannonball Trail see entry 2352.

2285 **Cape May County Park**, Crest Haven Rd., Cape May Court House, NJ 08210. (ATP)

2286 **Cape May Point State Park**, Cape May Point, NJ 08212, (609) 884-2159. (ATP; DBV; DMA; OTB; AMI; GNA)

2287 **Capoolong Creek Wildlife Management Area Trail**, Steve Smyser, Clinton Wildlife Management Area, Rt. 3, Box 409, Hampton, NJ 08827, (908) 735-8793. 3.0 miles straight. (GRT)

2288 **Captain Joshua Huddy Revolutionary Trail**, Ocean County Council, BSA, 1518 Ridgeway Rd., P.O. Box 1247, Toms River, NJ 08754, (201) 349-1037. 7.0 miles loop. Awards available. (AA 1992)

Carris Hill Trail see entry 2352.

2289 **Cattus Island County Park**, 1170 Cattus Island Blvd., Toms River, NJ 08753, (908) 270-6960. (ATP)

Cedar Ridge Interpretive Trail see entry 2291.
Cedar Swamp Trail see entry 2402.

2290 **Celery Farm Trail**, Mr. Stiles Thomas, P.O. Box 168, Allendale, NJ 07401, (201) 327-4600. 2.0 miles. (NNY)

2291 **Center for Environmental Studies**, 621 Eagle Rock Ave., Roseland, NJ 07068, (201) 228-2210. Named trails: Cedar Ridge Interpretive, Eagle Rock Reservation 3.5, Sensitivity, Swinefield Interpretive. (GFA; NJO; DNJ; NNY)

2292 **Cheesequake State Park**, Golden State Pkwy., Matawan, NJ 07747, (201) 566-2161. Named trails: Green, Red, Yellow. (WCD; ATP; MMA; NAT; DNJ; AMC; NNY; GNA)

2293 **Chips Folly Family Campground**, P.O. Box 56, New Gretna, NJ 08224, (609) 296-4434. (WCD)

2294 **Colliers Mills Wildlife Management Area**, c/o Nacote Creek Lab, Star Route 9, Absecon, NJ 08201, (609) 652-9519. (NNY; GNA)

2295 **Colonial Park Trail**, Public Information Officer, Somerset County Park Commission, P.O. Box 837, Somerville, NJ 08876, (201) 722-1200. (NNY)

2296 **Cooper Environmental Center**, 1170 Cattus Island Blvd., Toms River, NJ 08753, (201) 270-6960. (MMA)

2297 **Cora Hartshorn Arboretum and Bird Sanctuary**, 324 Forest Dr. S., Short Hills, NJ 07078, (201) 376-3587. 3.0 miles. (MMA; NNY)

2298 **Corson's Inlet State Park**, Ocean Dr., Strathmere, NJ 08248. (ATP; DMJ)

Crosswoods Interpretive Trail see entry 2346.

2299 **Delaware and Raritan Canal State**

Park, Rt. 1, Box 4, 643 Canal Rd., Somerset, NJ 08873, (908) 873-3050. Named trails: Delaware and Raritan Canal State Park Multi-Use 72.0(s). (GRT; ATP; NJO; GTB; DNJ)

Delaware and Raritan Canal State Park Multi-Use Trail *see* entry 2299.

Delaware Palisades and Ringing Rocks Trail *see* entry 2397.

2300 **Delaware Water Gap National Recreation Area**, River Rd., Bushkill, PA 18324, (717) 588-6637. (ATP; EGH; NJD; OTB; DNJ; AMI; GNA)

2301 **Dennis Creek Wildlife Management Area**, Jake's Landing Rd., Dennisville, NJ 08214. (GNA)

The Devil's Tea Table Trail *see* entry 2397.

Dinosaur Quarry Trail *see* entry 2373.

Dogwood Trail *see* entry 2377.

2302 **Double Trouble Nature Trail**, Double Trouble State Park, Double Trouble, NJ 08734. 1.25 miles. (OTB)

Eagle Rock Reservation Trail *see* entry 2291.

2303 **East Hill Preserve**, Dept. of Parks, Borough of Tenafly, 107 Grove St., Tenafly, NJ 07670, (201) 569-7275. 4.3 miles. (NNY)

Eastview Trail *see* entry 2346.

2304 **Edgar Felix Memorial Bikeway**, Thomas B. White, Director, Wall Township Parks and Recreation, 2700 Allaire Rd., Wall, NJ 07719, (908) 449-8444. ext. 250. 3.6 miles straight. (GRT)

2305 **Edward G. Bevan Wildlife Management Area**, Division of Fish, Game and Shellfisheries, P.O. Box 1809, Trenton, NJ 08625, (609) 292-9450. (GNA)

2306 **Edwin B. Forsyth National Wildlife Refuge**, P.O. Box 72, Great Creek Rd., Oceanville, NJ 08231, (609) 652-1665. Named trails: People's. (ATP; DBV; DMA; NJO; OTB)

2307 **Englewood-Bloomers Area**, Henry Hudson Dr., Englewood Cliffs, NJ 07632, (201) 768-1360. (MMA)

Ernest Walter Trail *see* entry 2352.

2308 **Estelle Manor County Park**, SR 50, Mays Landing, NJ 08330. (ATP)

Farm Woodlot Interpretive Trail *see* entry 2373.

Firehouse Trail *see* entry 2352.

2309 **Flat Rock Brook Center**, P.O. Box 571, Englewood, NJ 07631, (201) 567-1800. (NNY)

2310 **Flatbrook-Roy Wildlife Management Area**, Division of Fish, Game and Shellfisheries, P.O. Box 1809, Trenton, NJ 08625, (609) 292-9450. (GNA)

2311 **Frelinghuysen Arboretum**, 53 E. Hanover Ave., P.O. Box 1295R, Morristown, NJ 07960, (201) 285-6166 or (201) 326-7600. 4.0 miles. Named trails: Braille Nature. (ATP; MMA; GFA; NJO; NNY)

2312 **Garden States Arts Center Trail**, Garden States Arts Center, Telegraph Hill Park, Holmdel, NJ 07733, (908) 442-9200. (ATP)

2313 **Garret Mountain Reservation**, Mountain Ave., Paterson, NJ 07501, (201) 881-4832; or Passaic County Park Commission, Lambert Castle, 5 Valley Rd., Paterson, NJ 07503, (201) 742-6373. (MMA; NNY)

2314 **Gateway National Recreation Area**, Floyd Bennett Field, Brooklyn, NY 11234, (212) 252-9150; or Sandy Hook Unit, P.O. Box 437, Highlands, NJ 07732, (201) 872-0115. (ATP; OTB; AMC; GNA)

2315 **Glassboro Wildlife Management Area**, Division of Fish, Game and Shellfisheries, P.O. Box 1809, Trenton, NJ 08625, (609) 292-9450. (GNA)

2316 **Great Swamp National Wildlife Refuge**, RD 1, Box 148, Basking Ridge, NJ 07920, (201) 647-1222. 10.0 miles. Named trails: Ground Pine, Mountain Laurel. (MMA; GFA; NJO; OTB; AMI; NNY; GNA; GNW)

2317 **Great Swamp Outdoor Education Center Trail**, Morris County Park Commission, 247 Southern Blvd., Chatham, NJ 07928, (201) 635-6629. 1.0 mile. (NNY)

Green Trail *see* entry 2292.

Green Trail *see* entry 2326.

2318 **Greenbrook Sanctuary**, Palisades Nature Association, P.O. Box 155, Alpine, NJ 07620, (201) 768-1360 or (201) 569-5698. 6.5 miles. (NNY)

NEW JERSEY

2319 **Greenwood Forest Wildlife Management Area**, Division of Fish, Game and Shellfisheries, P.O. Box 1809, Trenton, NJ 08625, (609) 292-9450. (GNA)

Ground Pine Trail *see* entry 2316.

2320 **Hacklebarney State Park**, Rt. 2, Long Valley, NJ 07853, (201) 879-5677. (NNY)

2321 **Hamburg Mountain Wildlife Management Area**, Joseph M. Penkala, Regional Superintendent, New Jersey Fish, Game and Wildlife, Rt. 9, Box 9126, Newton, NJ 07860. 5.0 miles straight. (GRT)

2322 **Hedden County Park**, Reservoir Ave. & Concord Rd., Dover, NJ 07801. (DNJ)

2323 **Heislerville Wildlife Management Area**, Division of Fish, Game and Shellfisheries, P.O. Box 1809, Trenton, NJ 08625, (609) 292-9450. (GNA)

2324 **Helyar Woods Nature Trail**, Helyar Woods, Forestry & Wildlife Section, Cook College, P.O. Box 231, Rutgers University, New Brunswick, NJ 08903, (201) 932-8915. 0.67 mile loop. (NNY)

Hemlock Trail *see* entry 2391.

2325 **Henry Hudson Trail**, Faith Hahn, Supervising Planner, Monmouth County Park System, Newman Springs Rd., Lincroft, NJ 07738, (908) 842-4000. 9.0 miles straight planned, current as to 6.0 miles. (GRT)

2326 **Herrontown Woods Arboretum**, Naturalist, Mercer County Park Commission, P.O. Box 1777, 640 S. Broad St., Trenton, NJ 08607, (609) 989-6530. 3.0 miles. Named trails: Green, Red, Yellow. (AMI; NNY)

Hewitt Trail *see* entry 2352.

Hewitt-Butler Trail *see* entry 2354.

Hexenkopf Rock Trails *see* entry 2397.

High Mountain Brook Trail *see* entry 2352.

2327 **High Point State Park**, Rt. 4, Box 07461, SR 23, Sussex, NJ 07641, (201) 875-4800. Named trails: Monument, Old. (WCD; ATP; EGH; MMA; NJO; OTB; DNJ; NNY; GNA)

2328 **Holmdel Park**, Longstreet Rd., Holmdel, NJ 07733, (201) 946-2669; or Monmouth County Park System, P.O. Box 326, Newman Springs Rd., Lincroft, NJ 07738, (201) 842-4000. 7.0 miles. (DNJ; NNY)

Horse Pond Mountain Trail *see* entry 2352.

2329 **Indian Rock Resort & Campground**, Rt. 6, Box 292B, Jackson, NJ 08527, (908) 928-0034 or (800) 442-4954. (WCD)

Iris Trail *see* entry 2263.

2330 **Island Beach State Park**, Seaside Park, NJ 08752, (201) 793-0506. (ATP; OTB; AMC; NNY; GNA)

Jacob's Ladder Trail *see* entry 2263.

2331 **James A. McFaul Wildlife Center**, Crescent Ave., Wyckoff, NJ 07481, (201) 891-5571. (ATP; MMA)

Jennings Hollow Trail *see* entry 2352.

2332 **Jenny Jump State Forest**, P.O. Box 150, Hope, NJ 07844, (201) 459-4366. Named trails: Notch Vista Nature 0.5. (ATP; DNJ; NNY; GNA)

2333 **Jockey Hollow Trail**, Morris-Sussex Area Council, BSA, 12 Mt. Pleasant Tpk., Denville, NJ 07834, (201) 361-1800. 17.5 miles straight. Awards available. (AA 1992)

2334 **John D. Kuser Natural Area Trail**, Rt. 4, Box 287, Sussex, NJ 07461, (201) 875-4800. (AMI)

Kitchell Lake Trail *see* entry 2352.

2335 **Lake Lenape Park**, Old Harding Hwy., Mays Landing, NJ 08330. (ATP)

Laurel Pond Trail *see* entry 2402.

2336 **Lebanon State Forest**, SR 70, New Lisbon, NJ 08064, (609) 726-1191. (WCD; ATP; DNJ; AMI; GNA)

Leeds Eco-Trail *see* entry 2277.

2337 **Leonard J. Buck Garden**, Layton Rd., Far Hills, NJ 07931, (908) 234-2677. (ATP)

2338 **Lester G. MacNamara Wildlife Management Area**, Division of Fish, Game and Shellfisheries, P.O. Box 1809, Trenton, NJ 08625, (609) 292-9450. (GNA)

2339 **Lewis Morris Park**, Morris County Park Commission, 53 E. Hanover Ave., P.O. Box 1295R, Morristown, NJ 07960, (201) 285-6166. (NNY)

2340 **Linwood Bikepath**, Mary Boileau, City Clerk, Linwood City Hall, 400 Poplar Ave., Linwood, NJ 08221, (609) 927-4108. 1.3 miles straight. (GRT)
Little-Chism Trail see entry 2359.
2341 **Loantaka Brook Reservation**, Morris County Park Commission, 53 E. Hanover Ave., P.O. Box 1295R, Morristown, NJ 07960, (201) 285-6166. (NNY)
Long Path see entry 2358.
2342 **Lord Stirling Park**, Somerset County Environmental Education Center, 190 Lord Stirling Rd., Basking Ridge, NJ 07920, (201) 766-2489. 9.0 miles. (NNY)
2343 **Lorrimer Nature Center**, 790 Ewing Ave., Franklin Lakes, NJ 07417, (201) 891-1211. (NNY)
Lower Trail see entry 2352.
Macopin Trail see entry 2352.
2344 **Mahlon Dickerson Reservation**, Morris County Park Commission, 53 E. Hanover Ave., P.O. Box 1295R, Morristown, NJ 07960, (201) 285-6166. (NNY)
2345 **Manahawkin Wildlife Management Area**, Division of Fish, Game and Shellfisheries, P.O. Box 1809, Trenton, NJ 08625, (609) 292-9450. (GNA)
2346 **Mills Reservation**, Essex County Department of Parks, Recreation & Cultural Affairs, 115 Clinton Ave., Newark, NJ 07104, (201) 482-6400. Named trails: Crosswoods Interpretive, Eastview. (DNJ; NNY)
2347 **Millstone Valley Historic Trail**, Thomas A. Edison Council, BSA, 2757 Woodbridge Ave., P.O. Drawer L, Edison, NJ 08818, (201) 494-0305. 10.0 miles straight. Awards available. (SAR 1993)
Mine Trail see entry 2352.
2348 **Monmouth Battlefield State Park**, Freehold, NJ 07728, (201) 462-9616. (NJO)
2349 **Monroe Township Bikepath**, Allison J. Munch, Community Affairs Director, Department of Parks and Recreation, Monroe Township, 3rd Floor, Town Hall, 125 Virginia Ave., Williamstown, NJ 08094, (609) 728-9823. 1.5 miles straight. (GRT)
Monument Trail see entry 2327.
2350 **Morris County Outdoor Education Center**, Southern Blvd., Meyersville, NJ 07933, (201) 766-2489. (AMI)
2351 **Morristown National Historical Park**, Washington Pl., P.O. Box 1136R, Morristown, NJ 07960, (201) 539-2085 or (201) 539-2016 or (201) 539-2017. Named trails: Morristown, Primrose Brook 0.5(l). (NPE; CGA; NNY)
Morristown Trail see entry 2351.
Mount Tammany Trail see entry 2263.
Mountain Laurel Trail see entry 2316.
Mountain Spring Trail see entry 2352.
Museum Trail see entry 2377.
Nature Trail see entry 2377.
New Hope to Washington Crossing State Park and Side Trip to Bowman's Hill see entry 2397.
2352 **New Jersey Highlands**, New York-New Jersey Trail Conference, 232 Madison Ave., Rm. 908, New York, NY 10116, (212) 685-9699. Named trails: Allis, Burnt Meadow 0.8, Butler to Montville 7.8(s), Cannonball 4.5(s), Carris Hill 1.0(s), Ernest Walter 1.4(s), Firehouse 1.67(s), Hewitt, High Mountain Brook, Horse Pond Mountain 2.0(s), Jennings Hollow, Kitchell Lake, Lower 1.7(s), Macopin 2.5(s), Mine 5.4(l), Mountain Spring 0.75(s), Otter Hole 2.0(s), Post Brook 3.0(s), State Line 1.15(s), Stirling Ridge 8.4(s), Stone Hunting House 0.5(s), Stonetown Circular 9.5(l), Suffern-Midvale 12.0(s), Torne 1.0(s), Towaco-Pompton 8.0(s), West Brook 1.0(s), Wyanokie Circular 8.7(l). (NYW)
2353 **New Jersey Pine Barrens**, c/o Wharton State Forest, Batsto, Rt. 1, Hammonton, NJ 08037, (609) 561-3262. (NJD; NAT)
2354 **Norvin Green State Forest**, c/o Ringwood State Park, P.O. Box 1304, Ringwood, NJ 07456, (201) 962-7031. 36.0 miles. Named trails: Hewitt-Butler 11.0. (EGH; NNY; GNA)
Notch Vista Nature Trail see entry 2332.
2355 **Ocean County Park**, SR 88, Lakewood, NJ 08701. (ATP)

NEW JERSEY

Old Trail *see* entry 2327.

2356 **Old Troy Park**, Reynolds Ave., Township of Parsippany-Troy Hills, NJ 07054. (DNJ)

Orange Trail *see* entry 2390.

Otter Hole Trail *see* entry 2352.

2357 **Oyster Shell Road Historic Trail**, Burlington County Council, BSA, P.O. Box 246, Rancocas, NJ 08073, (609) 261-5850. Awards available. (NHT)

2358 **Palisades Historic Trails**, Bergen Council, BSA, 1060 Main St., P.O. Box 4237, River Edge, NJ 07661-0937, (201) 342-8600. Named trails: Long Path 11.3, Shore 12.5. Awards available. (NHT; HTA)

2359 **Palisades Interstate Park**, Palisades Nature Association, P.O. Box 155, Alpine, NJ 07620, (201) 768-1360; or Palisades Interstate Park Commission, Administration Bldg., Bear Mountain, NY 10911. Named trails: Allison 8.5, Little-Chism 1.5, Palisades Long Path National Recreation 11.0, Palisades Shore National Recreation 13.0. (EGH; NFG; NYW)

Palisades Long Path National Recreation Trail *see* entry 2359.

Palisades Shore National Recreation Trail *see* entry 2359.

2360 **Parvin State Park**, Rt. 1, CR 540, Elmer, NJ 08318, (609) 692-7039. 8.0 miles. (WCD; ATP; OTB; DNJ; AMI; GNA)

2361 **Pasadena Wildlife Management Area**, Division of Fish, Game and Shellfisheries, P.O. Box 1809, Trenton, NJ 08625, (609) 292-9450. (GNA)

2362 **Passaic River Park**, River Rd., Passaic, NJ 07055. (DNJ)

2363 **Patriots' Path**, Al Kent, Morris County Park Commission, P.O. Box 1295, Morristown, NJ 07962, (201) 326-7600. 12.0 miles straight. (GRT)

2364 **Peaslee Wildlife Management Area**, Division of Fish, Game and Shellfisheries, P.O. Box 1809, Trenton, NJ 08625, (609) 292-9450. (GNA)

2365 **Penn State Forest**, c/o Bass River Forest, New Gretna, NJ 08224, (609) 296-2554 or (609) 296-1114. 15.0 miles. (ATP; DNJ; GNA)

People's Trail *see* entry 2306.

2366 **Pequannock Watershed**, NWCDC, P.O. Box 319, Newfoundland, NJ 07435, (201) 697-2850. 30.0 miles. (EGH)

2367 **Pequest Wildlife Management Area**, Jim Munson, Crew Supervisor, Black River Wildlife Management Area, P.O. Box 52, North Rd., Chester, NJ 07930, (908) 879-6252. 4.0 miles straight. (GRT)

2368 **Pilgrim Lake Campground**, P.O. Box 129, New Gretna, NJ 08224, (609) 296-4723. (WCD)

Post Brook Trail *see* entry 2352.

Primrose Brook Trail *see* entry 2351.

Ralph Stover State Park Trail *see* entry 2397.

2369 **Ramapo Mountain State Forest**, P.O. Box 225, Oakland, NJ 07436, (201) 337-0960. 42.0 miles. (EGH; NNY)

2370 **Ramapo Valley County Reservation**, Bergen County Wildlife Center, Crescent Ave., Wyckoff, NJ 07481, (201) 891-5571. (DNJ; NNY)

Red Trail *see* entry 2292.

Red Trail *see* entry 2326.

Red Trail *see* entry 2390.

2371 **Reeves-Reed Arboretum**, 165 Hobart Ave., Summit, NJ 07901, (201) 273-8787. 2 trails 0.75 mile each. (NNY)

Riegelsville to Easton and Return on NJ Side *see* entry 2397.

2372 **Rifle Camp Park**, Rifle Camp Rd., West Paterson, NJ 07424. (MMA)

Riker Hill Interpretive Trail *see* entry 2373.

2373 **Riker Hill Park**, Essex County Department of Parks, Recreation & Cultural Affairs, 115 Clifton Ave., Newark, NJ 07104, (201) 482-6400. Named trails: Dinosaur Quarry, Farm Woodlot Interpretive, Riker Hill Interpretive. (NNY)

2374 **Ringwood State Park**, P.O. Box 1304, Sloatsburg Rd., Ringwood, NJ 07456, (201) 962-7031 or (201) 962-7047. 30.0 miles. (ATP; EGH; MMA; OTB; DNJ; NNY; GNA)

River Ridge Trail *see* entry 2263.

2375 **Ross Dock**, Henry Hudson Dr., Alpine, NJ 07620, (201) 768-1360. (MMA)

2376 **Round Valley State Recreation**

Area, Rt. 1, Round Valley Rd., Lebanon, NJ 08833, (201) 236-6355. Named trails: Round Valley 10.0(l). (WCD; ATP; MMA; DNJ; NNY; GNA)
Round Valley Trail *see* entry 2376.
2377 **Scherman-Hoffman Wildlife Sanctuaries**, Hardscrabble Rd., P.O. Box 693, Bernardsville, NJ 07924, (201) 766-5787. 5.0 miles. Named trails: Dogwood, Museum, Nature. (AMI; NNY; GNA)
2378 **Schooley's Mountain Park**, Camp Washington & Springtown Rds., Washington Twp., NJ 07882. (DNJ)
Sensitivity Trail *see* entry 2291.
2379 **Shark River Park**, Monmouth County Park System, Newman Springs Rd., Lincroft, NJ 07738, (201) 842-4000. (NNY)
Shore Trail *see* entry 2358.
2380 **Silas Condict Park**, Ricker Rd., Kinnelon Twp., NJ 07405. (DNJ)
2381 **Skylands Botanical Gardens**, Ringwood, NJ 07456. (GFA)
2382 **Somerset County Park**, Commission Environmental Education Center, 190 Lord Stirling Rd., Basking Ridge, NJ 07920, (906) 766-2489. (ATP)
2383 **South Mountain Reservation**, Essex County Department of Parks, Recreation & Cultural Affairs, 115 Clinton Ave., Newark, NJ 07104, (201) 482-6400. 20.0 miles. Named trails: Turtle Back Rock Interpretive. (ATP; MMA; DNJ; NNY)
2384 **Spruce Run State Park**, SR 31, Clinton, NJ 08809. (ATP)
2385 **Stafford Forge Wildlife Management Area**, Division of Fish, Game and Shellfisheries, P.O. Box 1809, Trenton, NJ 08625, (609) 292-9450. (GNA)
State Line Trail *see* entry 2352.
2386 **Stephens-Saxton Falls State Park**, c/o Stokes State Forest, Rt. 2, Box 260, Branchville, NJ 07826, (201) 948-3820. (NNY)
Stirling Ridge Trail *see* entry 2352.
Stockton Circular and Green Sergeant's Bridge *see* entry 2397.
2387 **Stokes State Forest**, Rt., Box 260, Branchville, NJ 07826, (201) 948-3820. 75.0 miles. Named trails: Tinsley Geological. (WCD; EGH; NJD; DNJ; AMI; GNA)
Stone Hunting House Trail *see* entry 2352.
Stonetown Circular Trail *see* entry 2352.
Stony Brook Trail *see* entry 2263.
Suffern-Midvale Trail *see* entry 2352.
2388 **Sussex Branch Railroad Trail**, Steve Ellis, Superintendent, Swartswood State Park, P.O. Box 123, Swartswood, NJ 07877-0123, (201) 383-5230. 13.0 miles straight planned, current as to 2.6 miles. (GRT)
2389 **Swartswood State Park**, Newton Swartswood Rd., Newton, NJ 07860, (201) 383-5230. (WCD; ATP)
Swenson Trail *see* entry 2263.
Swinefield Interpretive Trail *see* entry 2291.
2390 **Terrace Pond**, Sussex Woodlands, P.O. Box 338, Hewitt, NJ 07421. Named trails: Blue 1.5(s), Orange 3.0(s), Red 3.6(s), White 1.2(l), Yellow 2.5(s). (NYW)
Tinsley Geological Trail *see* entry 2387.
Tinsley Trail *see* entry 2263.
Torne Trail *see* entry 2352.
2391 **Tourne Park**, Poweville & Old Denville Rds., Boonton Twp., NJ 07005; or Morris County Park Commission, 53 E. Hanover Ave., P.O. Box 1259R, Morristown, NJ 07960, (201) 285-6166. Named trails: Hemlock. (DNJ; NNY)
Towaco-Pompton Trail *see* entry 2352.
2392 **Traction Line Recreation Trail**, Albert Kent, Patriots' Path Coordinator, Morris County Park Commission, 53 E. Hanover Ave., P.O. Box 1295, Morristown, NJ 07962-1295, (201) 326-7600. 2.0 miles straight. (GRT)
2393 **Troy Meadows Trail**, Chief Ranger, Troy Meadows Wildlife Preserves, Inc., P.O. Box 194, Hopacong, NJ 07843, (201) 398-5318. 2.5 miles. (NNY)
2394 **Turkey Swamp County Park**, P.O. Box 866, Nomoco Rd., Freehold, NJ 07728, (201) 462-7286. (ATP; MMA; OTB; NNY)
Turtle Back Rock Interpretive Trail *see* entry 2383.

NEW JERSEY

2395 **Turtle Run Campground**, Turtle Creek Rd., Wading River, NJ 08224, (609) 965-5343. (WCD)

Uhlerstown Circular Trail *see* entry 2397.

Uhlerstown to Upper Black Eddy *see* entry 2397.

2396 **U.S. Army ARDEC-Picatinny Arsenal**, Lake Denmark Rd., Dover, NJ 07801, (201) 724-4484. (WCD)

2397 **Upper Delaware Valley**, New York-New Jersey Trail Conference, 232 Madison Ave., Rm. 908, New York, NY 10116, (212) 685-9699. Named trails: Delaware Palisades and Ringing Rocks 8.0-9.0, The Devil's Tea Table 11.0, Hexenkopf Rock 11.0-12.0, New Hope to Washington Crossing State Park and Side Trip to Bowman's Hill 8.0-9.0, Ralph Stover State Park 10.0-11.0, Riegelsville to Easton and Return on NJ Side 18.0, Stockton Circular and Green Sergeant's Bridge 12.0-14.0, Uhlerstown Circular 12.0, Uhlerstown to Upper Black Eddy 10.0, Washington Crossing to Trenton and Return on NJ Side 15.0. (NYW)

2398 **Victory Trail**, Watchung Area Council, BSA, 905 Watchung Ave., Plainfield, NJ 07060. 13.0 miles. Awards available. (HTA)

2399 **Voorhees State Park**, Rt. 2, Box 80, SR 513, Glen Gardner, NJ 08826, (201) 638-6969. (NNY)

2400 **Washington Crossing State Park**, Rt. 1, Box 337, Titusville, NJ 08560, (609) 737-0623. Named trails: Nature Center. (GNA)

Washington Crossing to Trenton and Return on NJ Side *see* entry 2397.

2401 **Watchung Reservation**, Director, Trailside Nature & Science Center, Coles Ave. & New Providence Rd., Mountainside, NJ 07092, (201) 232-5930. (MMA; DNJ; NNY)

2402 **Wawayanda State Park**, P.O. Box 198, Highland Lakes, NJ 07422, (201) 764-4120. 20.0 miles. Named trails: Cedar Swamp, Laurel Pond. (ATP; EGH; OTB; DNJ; AMI; NNY; GNA)

2403 **Weis Ecology Center**, 150 Snake Den Rd., Ringwood, NJ 07456, (201) 835-2160. 40.0 miles. (DNJ; NNY)

West Brook Trail *see* entry 2352.

2404 **Wetlands Salt Marsh Trail**, Wetlands Institute and Museum, Stone Harbor Blvd., Stone Harbor, NJ 08247, (609) 368-1211. (MMA; DBV)

2405 **Wharton State Forest**, Batsto, Rt. 4, Hammonton, NJ 08037, (609) 561-0024; or Wharton State Forest, c/o Regional Office, National Park Service, 143 S. Third St., Philadelphia, PA 19106; or Pinelands Commission, P.O. Box 7, New Lisbon, NJ 08064. 400 miles. (ATP; PGF; NAT; OTB; GNA)

White Trail *see* entry 2390.

2406 **Whittingham Wildlife Management Area**, c/o Clinton Wildlife Management Area, P.O. Box 409, Hampton, NJ 08827, (201) 735-8793. (NNY; GNA)

2407 **Worthington State Forest**, Old Mine Rd., Columbia, NJ 07832, (201) 841-9575. 20.0 miles. (WCD; ATP; EGH; DNJ; GNA)

Wyanokie Circular Trail *see* entry 2352.

Yellow Trail *see* entry 2292.
Yellow Trail *see* entry 2326.
Yellow Trail *see* entry 2390.

2408 **Yogi Bear's Jellystone Park Camp Resort**, P.O. Box 48, Jackson, NJ 08527, (908) 928-0500 or (609) 758-2235. (WCD)

Generally:
Commissioner, Department of Environmental Protection, P.O. Box 1390, Trenton, NJ 08625, (609) 292-2885. (SFC)

Division of Fish, Game and Shellfisheries, P.O. Box 1809, Trenton, NJ 08625, (609) 292-9450. (GNA)

New Jersey Division of Parks and Forestry, CN 404, Trenton, NJ 08625. (EGH)

Index (by city)

Absecon: Assunpink Wildlife Management Area 2265; Colliers Mills Wildlife Management Area 2294
Allendale: Celery Farm Trail 2290
Alpine: Alpine Area 2262; Greenbrook Sanctuary 2318; Palisades Interstate Park 2359; Ross Dock 2375
Basking Ridge: Great Swamp National Wildlife Refuge 2316; Lord Stirling Park 2342; Somerset County Park 2382
Bayonne: Camp Lewis 2281
Belle Meade: Bull's Island State Recreation Area 2279
Bernardsville: Scherman-Hoffman Wildlife Sanctuaries 2377
Boonton Twp.: Tourne Park 2391
Bordentown: Bordentown Walking Tour 2276
Branchville: Stephens-Saxton Falls State Park 2386; Stokes State Forest 2387
Bushkill: Delaware Water Gap National Recreation Area 2300
Butler: New Jersey Highlands 2352
Camden: Batona Trail 2267
Cape May Court House: Beaver Swamp Wildlife Management Area 2270; Cape May County Park 2285
Cape May Point: Cape May Point State Park 2286
Chatham: Great Swamp Outdoor Education Center 2317
Chester: Berkshire Valley Wildlife Management Area 2273; Black River Wildlife Management Area 2275; Pequest Wildlife Management Area 2367
Clinton: Spruce Run State Park 2384
Columbia: Worthington State Forest 2407
Dennisville: Dennis Creek Wildlife Management Area 2301
Double Trouble: Double Trouble Nature Trail 2302
Dover: Hedden County Park 2322; U.S. Army ARDEC-Picatinny Arsenal 2396
Elmer: Parvin State Park 2360
Englewood: Flat Rock Brook Center 2309
Englewood Cliffs: Englewood-Bloomers Area 2307
Far Hills: Leonard J. Buck Garden 2337
Farmingdale: Allaire State Park 2260

Franklin Lakes: Lorrimer Nature Center 2343
Freehold: Battle of Monmouth Historic Trail 2268; Monmouth Battlefield State Park 2348; Turkey Swamp County Park 2394
Glassboro: Glassboro Wildlife Management Area 2315
Glen Gardner: Voorhees State Park 2399
Hackettstown: Allamuchy Mountain State Park 2261
Hammonton: New Jersey Pine Barrens 2353; Wharton State Forest 2405
Hampton: Capoolong Creek Wildlife Management Area Trail 2287; Whittingham Wildlife Management Area 2406
Heislerville: Heislerville Wildlife Management Area 2323
Hewitt: Terrace Pond 2390
Highland Lakes: Abram S. Hewitt State Forest 2259; Wawayanda State Park 2402
Holmdel: Garden States Arts Center 2312; Holmdel Park 2328
Hopacong: Troy Meadows Trail 2393
Hope: Jenny Jump State Forest 2332
Jackson: Indian Rock Resort & Campground 2329; Yogi Bear's Jellystone Park Camp Resort 2408
Kingston: Millstone Valley Historic Trail 2347
Kinnelon Twp.: Silas Condict Park 2380
Lakehurst: Pasadena Wildlife Management Area 2361
Lakewood: Ocean County Park 2355
Lebanon: Round Valley State Recreation Area 2376
Lincroft: Henry Hudson Trail 2325; Shark River Park 2379
Linwood: Linwood Bikepath 2340
Long Valley: Hacklebarney State Park 2320
Lyndhurst: Cannonball Trail 2284
Mahwah: Campgaw Mountain County Reservation 2283
Manahawkin: Greenwood Forest Wildlife Management Area 2319; Manahawkin Wildlife Management Area 2345
Matawan: Cheesequake State Park 2292
Mays Landing: Estelle Manor County Park 2308; Lake Lenape Park 2335

NEW JERSEY Index 153

Meyersville: Morris County Outdoor Education Center 2350
Millville: Edward G. Bevan Wildlife Management Area 2305; Peaslee Wildlife Management Area 2364
Morristown: Frelinghuysen Arboretum 2311; Jockey Hollow Trail 2333; Lewis Morris Park 2339; Loantaka Brook Reservation 2341; Mahlon Dickerson Reservation 2344; Morristown National Historical Park 2351; Patriots' Path 2363
Mountainside: Camp Watchung 2282; Watchung Reservation 2401
New Brunswick: Helyar Woods Nature Trail 2324
New Gretna: Bass River State Forest 2266; Chips Folly Family Campground 2293; Penn State Forest 2365; Pilgrim Lake Campground 2368
New Lisbon: Lebanon State Forest 2336
New York, NY: Gateway National Recreation Area 2314
Newark: Brookdale Park 2278; Mills Reservation 2346; Riker Hill Park 2373; South Mountain Reservation 2383
Newfoundland: Pequannock Watershed 2366
Newton: Hamburg Mountain Wildlife Management Area 2321
Northfield: Birch Grove City Park 2274
Oakland: Ramapo Mountain State Forest 2369
Oceanville: Brigantine National Wildlife Refuge 2277; Edwin B. Forsyth National Wildlife Refuge 2306
Parsippany-Troy Hills: Old Troy Park 2356
Passaic: Passaic River Park 2362
Paterson: Garret Mountain Reservation 2313
Plainfield: Victory Trail 2398
Rancocas: Oyster Shell Road Historic Trail 2357
Riegelsville: Upper Delaware Valley 2397
Ringwood: Norvin Green State Forest 2354; Ringwood State Park 2374; Skylands Botanical Gardens 2381; Weis Ecology Center 2403

River Edge: Palisades Historic Trails 2358
Roseland: Center for Environmental Studies 2291
Seaside Park: Island Beach State Park 2330
Short Hills: Cora Hartshorn Arboretum and Bird Sanctuary 2297
Somerset: Delaware and Raritan Canal State Park 2299
Somerville: Colonial Park Trail 2295
Stone Harbor: Wetlands Salt Marsh Trail 2404
Strathmere: Corson's Inlet State Park 2298
Summit: Reeves-Reed Arboretum 2371
Sussex: Beaver Hill Campground 2269; High Point State Park 2327; John D. Kuser Natural Area 2334
Swartswood: Sussex Branch Railroad Trail 2388; Swartswood State Park 2389
Tenafly: East Hill Preserve 2303
Titusville: Washington Crossing State Park 2400
Toms River: Captain Joshua Huddy Revolutionary Trail 2288; Cattus Island County Park 2289; Cooper Environmental Center 2296
Trenton: Herrontown Woods Arboretum 2326
Tuckahoe: Lester G. MacNamara Wildlife Management Area 2338
Tuckerton: Stafford Forge Wildlife Management Area 2385
Tuttles Corner: Flatbrook-Roy Wildlife Management Area 2310
Wading River: Turtle Run Campground 2395
Wall: Edgar Felix Memorial Bikeway 2304
Washington Twp.: Schooley's Mountain Park 2378
West Paterson: Rifle Camp Park 2372
Williamstown: Monroe Township Bikepath 2349
Woodbine: Belleplain State Forest 2271
Wyckoff: Bergen County Nature Trail 2272; James A. McFaul Wildlife Center 2331; Ramapo Valley County Reservation 2370

NEW YORK

2409 **Adirondack Adventure Treks,** Adirondack Adventure Area, Northeast Region, BSA, P.O. Box 350, Dayton, NJ 08810, (201) 821-6500. (AA 1990)
2410 **Adirondack Camping Village,** P.O. Box 406, Lake George, NY 12845, (518) 668-5226. (WCD)
2411 **Adirondack Center Museum and Colonial Garden,** Court St., Elizabethtown, NY 12932, (518) 873-6466. (ANY)
2412 **Adirondack State Forest,** Adirondack Mountain Club, 714 Glen St., Glens Falls, NY 12801, (518) 793-7737; or Department of Environmental Conservation, Ray Brook, NY 12977, (518) 891-1370; or Department of Environmental Conservation, P.O. Box 220, Warrenburg, NY 12855, (518) 623-3671; or Department of Environmental Conservation, Northville, NY 12134, (518) 863-4545; or Adirondack Park Visitors Information Center, P.O. Box 3000, Paul Smith, NY 12970, (518) 327-3000. 2000 miles. Named trails: Independence River Section: Basket Factory Rd.-East Loop Rd.-Stillwater 3.5, Beach Mill Pond 7.1, Bills Pond 0.8, Emmet Hill Road Snowmobile 1.5, Fish 2.0, Francis Lake 0.5, Halfmoon Lake 1.0, McCarthy Road and Snowmobile 5.0, North Crossover Snowmobile 2.0, Panther Pond-Independence River 5.0, Panther Pond Loop 10.1, Stillwater Mountain 0.8, Sunday Lake 0.4. Big Moose Section: Bald (Rondaxe) Mountain 1.0, Billy's Bald Spot-Squash Pond 1.0, Black Mtn. Ski 5.3, Bubb Lake 2.3, Cascade Lake 5.4, Cascade Lake Link 1.1, Cathedral Pines 0.1, Chain Ponds 2.7, Constable Pond-West Mountain 8.1, Eagle Cliff 0.25, Foot Pond 1.0, Fourth Lake-Black Bear Mountain 3.0, Gull Lakes 1.2, Hermitage 1.3, Mays Pond 1.3, Moss Lake Circuit 2.5, Norridgewock 4.4, Queer Lake 5.9, Razorback Pond 2.0, Rocky Mountain 0.5, Russian Lake 0.7, Safford Pond 5.2, Scenic Mountain 4.5, Seventh Lake 2.2, Seventh Lake-Black Bear Mountain 2.5, Sister Lake 3.3, Snake Pond 0.5, Uncas 3.5, Uncas Road-Black Bear Mountain 2.2, Vista 4.4. Raquette Lake Section: Death Falls 0.3, Mohegan Lake Road 3.1, Raquette Lake-West Mountain 4.8, Sagamore Cascades 3.1, Sagamore North 3.2, Shallow Lake 1.4, Sucker Brook Bay 3.1, Tioga Point 5.2, Uncas Road-Mohegan Lake 3.5. Blue Mountain Lake Section: Blue Mountain 2.0, Cascade Pond 3.5, Castle Rock 1.2, Owls Head Mountain 7.2, Sargent Pond East 4.7, Tirrell Pond 3.1, Wilson Pond 2.9. Brantingham Section: Big Otter Lake West 5.7, Blueberry Snowmobile 1.5, Centennial Ski 3.7, Glenfield RR Snowmobile 2.4, Little Otter Lake Rd. & Confusion Flats, Otter Creek-Pine Lake 3.1, Pine Creek Loop 7.5, Pine Lake 6.2, Pine Mountain 2.5, Shingle Mill Falls 0.5, Silvermine and East Bridge 9.2, Steam Mill-Spring Hill 5.8. Old Forge-Thendara Section: Big Otter Lake East 7.8, Brown's Tract 5.9, Cedar Pond Lean-to 2.2, East Pond-Lost Creek 5.9, Middle Branch Lake 1.6, Middle Settlement Lake 3.7, Middle Settlement Lake Access 1.2, Nicks Lake Circuit 4.4, Remsen Falls-Nelson Lake Loop 18.5, Scusa Access 0.6. Moose River Recreation Area: Bear Pond 2.5, Beaver Lake 2.3, Helldiver Pond 0.2, Ice House Pond 0.4, Indian Lake 0.1, Indian River 5.4, Limekiln Creek-Third Lake 5.6, Limekiln Ski Routes 3.3, Lost Ponds 1.0, Mitchell Ponds 2.8, Moose River Plains 5.4, Muskrat Pond

0.1, Rock Dam 1.4, Sly Pond 5.4, Squaw Lake 0.4, White's Pond 3.1. McKeever-Woodgate Section: Bear Lake 6.2, Bear Lake-Woodhull Lake 2.2, Brandy Lake 1.7, Chub Pond 4.0, Gull Lake Loop 7.8, Otter Lake Outlet 1.1, Round Pond-Long Lake 5.1, Sand Lake Falls 7.6, Wolf Lake Landing Road 5.5, Woodhull Mountain 7.6, Woodhull Road 7.6. NY8 and North Lake Road Section: Baby Lake Falls 7.7, Honnedaga Brook 2.7, Little Salmon Lake 2.3, Little Woodhull Lake 4.0, Mad Tom 7.3, Middle Branch Marsh 5.2, Mill Creek Lake 3.8, South Lake 5.5, Stone Dam 3.5, Stone Dam Lake and Chub Pond 13.4, T Lake Falls 5.4, Twin Lakes Dam 3.1. Cedar River Section: Cedar Lakes 8.4, Cellar Pond 2.6, West Canada Lake 7.7. Beaver River Section: Pepperbox Access 0.5, Red Horse 5.3, Sunday Creek 0.3, Wilderness Lakes Tract Access 0.8. High Peaks Wilderness Area: Algonquin Peak Loop 8.0, Ampersand Mountain 5.6, Dix 6.7, Elk Lake-Dix 6.12, Indian Pass 10.6, Roaring Brook 3.57, Santanoni Preserve 10.2, Trail to Marcy from Elk Lake 10.96, Upper Works 10.11, Van Hoevenberg. Cranberry Lake Area: The Loop 16.0(l)(consisting of High Falls Truck 1.5, Leary 2.7, Cat Mountain 2.05, Dead Creek Flow Truck, Buck Pond, Six Mile Creek 4.2, Five Ponds-Wolf Pond-Sand Lake, Plains, and Big Deer Pond), Bear Mountain 2.4, Clear Pond 0.5, Curtins Pond 1.2, Darning Needle Pond 2.4, Moore's 2.0. Schroon Lake Area: Arnold Pond 1.5, Bear Pond 2.5, Berrymill Pond 4.9, Goose Pond 0.75, Gull Pond 0.75, Long Swing 11.0, Lost Pond 1.7, Peaked Hill 2.25, Pharaoh Lake 2.3, Pharaoh Mountain Firetower 2.75, Rock Pond-Clear Pond 3.25, Severance Hill 2.0, Short Swing 9.7, Spectacle Pond 1.6, Treadway Mountain 2.0. Lake George Region: Black Mountain 8.5, Black Mountain Firetower 2.75, Buck Mountain 6.6, Prospect Mountain 1.13, Tongue Mountain Range 18.0. Pharaoh Lake Wilderness Area: Pharaoh Mountain 6.0, Pharaoh Ponds Loop 15.0. Siamese Ponds Wilderness Area: Chimney Mountain 2.5, Siamese Ponds 13.2. West Canada Lakes Wilderness Area: Snowy Mountain 7.5, Wakely Mountain 6.4. Blue Ridge Wilderness Area: Rock, Cascade and Stephens Ponds 7.5. McKenzie Wilderness Area: McKenzie Mountain 10.6. Sentinel Range Wilderness Area: Pitchoff Mountain 5.2. Hoffman Notch Wilderness Area: Hoffman Notch 7.5. Giant Mountain Wilderness Area: Giant Mountain 6.6. Stony Creek, Hadley and the Eastern Section: Baldhead Mountain and Moose Mountain 3.6, Crane Mountain 1.4, Crane Mountain Pond and NW Range 2.7, Hadley Mountain 1.8, Huckleberry Mountain 2.5, Paint Mine Ruins 2.3, Prospect Mountain 1.4, Roundtop Mountain 2.6. Wilcox Lake Wild Forest and Baldwin Springs Section: Baldwin Springs via W. Stony Creek Road 6.5, Garnet Lake Canoe/Hike to Lizard Pond and Baldwin Springs 4.4, Harrisburg Lake to Baldwin Springs via Arrow Trail 7.4, Indian Pond, Mount Blue 2.0, Round Pond from Garnet Lake 2.3, Round Pond via Mud Pond 1.7, Tenant Creek Falls 2.1, Wilcox Lake from Brownell Camp via E. Stony Creek 5.2, Wilcox Lake from Willis Lake 6.3. Benson, Wells and Silver Lake Wilderness Section: Bartman 6.3, Cathead Mountain 1.6, Chase Lake 2.5, Cod Pond from Shanty Brook Trailhead 1.7, Dunning Pond from Gilmantown Road 1.0, Dunning Pond from NY 30 4.2, Kibby Pond 1.9, Murphy Lake from Creek Road 3.8, Murphy Lake from Pumpkin Hollow Road 4.5, Oregon Trail to Stewart Creek Flow 2.7, Pine Orchard and Jimmy Creek 4.8, Pine Orchard from Pumpkin Hollow Road 6.6, Piseco to Upper Benson-NP 23.1. Canada Lake, Caroga Lake, and Powley-Piseco Road Section: Bearpath Inn Trail to Sheriff Lake 2.5, Big Alderbed 3.1, Black Cat Lake 3.0, Clockmill Corners 4.0, Dry and Dexter Lakes 2.9, Glasgow Mills and Hillabrandt Valley 3.3, Good Luck Lake 1.8, Good Luck Mountain Cliffs 2.5, Irving Pond, Bellows Lake, Holmes Lake Loop to Peters Corners 8.3, Kane Mountain -E. 0.9, Kane Mountain-S. 0.7, Kane Mountain from Pine Lake

Campground 2.0, Meco Lake 2.0, Sand Lake 0.5, Sheriff Lake 1.1, Spectacle Lake from NY10 2.6, Third Lake from NY10 2.7. Northville-Placid Trail 146(s). Other Trails: Blue Ledge on the Hudson 5.0, Boreas Mountain 7.6, Catamount Mountain 3.8, Debar Mountain 7.0, Echo Cliffs on Panther Mountain 1.4, Falls on the West Branch of the Sacanda 6.0, Goodnow Mountain 3.0, High Lake Falls 11.0, John Brown's Tract 9.6, Murphy, Middle and Bernet Lakes 7.2, Nehasane Preserve 9.4, Peaked Mountain 8.2, Pillsbury Mountain 5.6, Pine Orchard 4.8, Pokamoonshine Mountain 2.0, Saint Regis Mountain 6.0, Vanderwhacker Mountain 5.8. (WCD; EGH; HAC; GOP; MNE; DBV; DMA; FHA; GAT-VII; GAT-V; GNA; GTB; HTN; IFT)

Algonquin Peak Loop Trail see entry 2412.

2413 **Allegany State Park**, Rt. 1, Salamanca, NY 14779, (716) 354-2535. 80.0 miles. (ANY; WCD; EGH; MNE; DMA; GNA)

2414 **Alley Park**, Alley Pond Environmental Center, 228-06 Northern Blvd., Douglastown, NY 11363, (212) 229-4000. Named trails: Pitobik 2.0, Turtle Pond. (NNY)

Allis Trail see entry 2418.

2415 **Alpine Lake Camping Resort**, 78 Heath Rd., Corinth, NY 12822, (518) 654-6260. (WCD)

2416 **Alps Family Campground**, SR 43, Averill Park, NY 12018, (518) 674-5565. (WCD)

2417 **American 1779 March of Anthony Wayne Trail**, Rockland County Council, BSA, 15 Frank Rd., P.O. Box 686, Stony Point, NY 10980, (914) 786-2771. 12.0 miles. Awards available. (AA 1992)

Ampersand Mountain Trail see entry 2412.

Anthony Wayne Trail see entry 2425.

2418 **Appalachian Side Trails** (not listed elsewhere), New York-New Jersey Trail Conference, 232 Madison Ave., Rm. 908, New York, NY 10116, (212) 685-9699. Named trails: Allis, Mountain Spring, Three Lakes. (ATG #4)

2419 **Appalachian Trail** (see separate entry **4948** in interstate section).

Arden-Surebridge Trail see entry 2425.

Arnold Pond Trail see entry 2412.

Arthur Trail see entry 2774.

2420 **Arthur W. Butler Memorial Sanctuary** (see Butler Memorial Sanctuary **2449**). (NAT)

2421 **Ausable Pines Campground**, Rt. 2, Box 156, Peru, NY 12972, (518) 561-1188 or (800) 545-0116. (WCD)

Baby Lake Falls Trail see entry 2412.

2422 **Bailey Arboretum Nature Trail**, Bayville Rd. & Feeks Ln., Lattingtown, NY 11560, (516) 292-4116. 1.0 mile loop. (NNY)

Bald (Rondaxe) Mountain Trail see entry 2412.

Baldhead Mountain and Moose Mountain Trail see entry 2412.

Baldwin Springs via W. Stony Creek Road see entry 2412.

Balsam Lake Mountain Trail see entry 2474.

Bank of the River Trail see entry 2667.

Bartman Trail see entry 2412.

Barton Swamp Trail see entry 2754.

2423 **Bashakill Wildlife Management Area**, Wildlife Manager, Region 3, Department of Environmental Conservation, New York State, 21 S. Putt Corners Rd., New Paltz, NY 12561, (914) 255-5453. (AMI; NNY; NNY)

Basin Ravine Trail see entry 2449.

Basin Trail see entry 2449.

Basket Factory Rd.-East Loop Rd.-Stillwater Spur Trail see entry 2412.

2424 **Bayard Cutting Arboretum**, P.O. Box 66, Montauk Hwy., Oakdale, NY 11769, (516) 581-1002. Named trails: Bird Watchers' Walk, Pinetum, Rhododendron, Swamp Cypress, Wildflower Walk. (MNE; OTB; NNY)

Beach Mill Pond Trail see entry 2412.

Bear Lake Trail see entry 2412.

Bear Lake-Woodhull Lake Trail see entry 2412.

Bear Mountain Trail see entry 2412.

NEW YORK

2425 **Bear Mountain-Harriman State Park**, SR 9W, Stony Point, NY 10980, (914) 786-2701; or Palisades Interstate Park Commission, New York Section, Bear Mountain, NY 10911, (914) 786-2701. 200 miles. Named trails: Anthony Wayne 2.7, Arden-Surebridge 5.0, Blue Disc 3.8, Breakneck Mountain 1.6, Conklin's Crossing 0.65, Crown Ridge 5.0, Deep Hollow Shelter 0.7, Diamond Mountain 0.4, Dunning 3.4, Hillburne-Sebago-Torne 4.7, Horn, Hurst 0.5, Kakiat 7.2, Lichen 0.5, Long Mountain-Torne 3.2, Major Welch 3.3, Nurian 3.3, Pine Meadow 6.2, Pittsboro Hollow, Popolopen Gorge 4.3, Quartz Brook, Raccoon Brook Hills 2.3, Ramapo-Dunderberg 20.8, Red Arrow, Red Cross 7.6, Reeves Brook, Seven Hills 6.8, Sherwood 1.9, Six Chins, Skannatai 4.8, Suffern-Bear Mountain 24.3, Timp-Torne 9.9, Tower 0.8, Triangle 4.9, Tuxedo-Mount Ivy 10.3, White Cross 1.9. (ANY; EGH; MNE; BMG; DBV; DMA; AMI; GNA; NYW)

Bear Pond Trail see entry 2412.

2426 **Bear Spring Mountain Wildlife Management Area**, Regional Wildlife Manager, Region 4 Wildlife Office, NYS Department of Environmental Conservation, Stamford, NY 12167, (607) 652-7364. 12.0 miles. (GNA)

2427 **Bear Swamp and Summer Hill State Forests**, Regional Forester, Region 7, P.O. Box 1169, Cortland, NY 13045, (607) 753-3095. (GNA)

Bearpath Inn Trail to Sheriff Lake see entry 2412.

2428 **Beaver Island State Park**, West River Pkwy., Buffalo, NY 14240, (716) 773-3271. (ANY; MNE)

2429 **Beaver Lake Nature Center**, 8477 E. Mud Lake Rd., Baldwinsville, NY 13027, (315) 638-2519. 10.0 miles. (ANY; MNE; GFA; NYP)

Beaver Lake Trail see entry 2412.
Beaver Pond Trail see entry 2506.
Becker Hollow Trail see entry 2474.
Becker Trail see entry 2474.

2430 **Belmont Lake State Park**, Southern State Pkwy., Babylon, NY 11702, (516) 667-5055. (ANY; NNY)

2431 **Belvedere Lake Campground**, SR 165, Rosebloom, NY 13450, (607) 264-8182. (WCD)

2432 **Benjamin Tallmadge National Historic Trail**, John Aleksak, 56 Hewes St., Port Jefferson Station, NY 11776, (516) 928-2867. 27.0 miles straight. Awards available. (AA 1992)

Berrymill Pond Trail see entry 2412.

2433 **Bethpage State Park**, Bethpage Pkwy., Bethpage, NY 11714, (516) 249-0701. (ANY; MNE)

Big Alderbead Trail see entry 2412.
Big Deer Pond Trail see entry 2412.
Big Otter Lake East Trail see entry 2412.
Big Otter Lake West Trail see entry 2412.
Bills Pond Trail see entry 2412.
Billy's Bald Spot-Squash Pond Trail see entry 2412.

2434 **Birchwood Acres Camping Resort**, P.O. Box 482-WD, Woodridge, NY 12789, (914) 434-4743. (WCD)

Bird Watchers' Walk see entry 2424.

2435 **Black Bear Mountain Trail**, Eighth Lake Public Campsite, SR 28, Inlet, NY 13360. 3.0 miles. (OTB)

Black Cat Lake Trail see entry 2412.
Black Mountain Firetower Trail see entry 2412.
Black Mtn. Ski Trail see entry 2412.
Black Mountain Trail see entry 2412.

2436 **Black Rock Forest**, Harvard Black Rock Forest, P.O. Box 483, Continental Rd., Cornwall, NY 12518, (914) 534-4517. 15.0 miles. (EGH; NNY)

Black Rock Hollow Trail see entry 2774.

Blackhead Range Trail see entry 2474.

Blue Disc Trail see entry 2425.

2437 **Blue Heron Park**, High Rock Park Conservation Center, 200 Nevada Ave., Staten Island, NY 10306, (212) 987-6233. (NNY)

Blue Ledge on the Hudson Trail see entry 2412.

Blue Mountain and Spinzenberg Circular see entry 2816.

2438 **Blue Mountain Lake**, Blue Mountain

Lake Association, Blue Mountain Lake, NY 12812. 3.0 miles. (MNE)

2439 **Blue Mountain Reservation**, Welcher Ave., Peekskill, NY 10566, (914) 737-2194; or County Naturalist, Westchester County, Department of Parks, Recreation & Conservation, 148 Martine Ave., White Plains, NY 10601, (914) 682-2637. 16.0 miles. (MNE; NNY)

Blue Mountain Trail see entry 2412.
Blue Trail see entry 2806.
Blueberry Snowmobile Trail see entry 2412.
Boreas Mountain Trail see entry 2412.

2440 **Bowman Lake State Park**, SR 220, Oxford, NY 13830, (607) 334-2718. (ANY; WCD)

2441 **Braddock Bay Park**, Braddock St., Rochester, NY 14612. (ANY)

2442 **Bradford State Forest**, Regional Forester, Region 8, 115 Liberty St., Bath, NY 14810, (607) 776-2165. (GNA)

Brandy Lake Trail see entry 2412.

2443 **Brasher Falls State Forest**, Regional Forester, Region 6, 30 Court St., Canton, NY 13617, (315) 386-4546. (GNA)

Breakneck Mountain Trail see entry 2425.
Breakneck Ridge Trail see entry 2686.
Brink of the Gorge Trail see entry 2667.

2444 **Brinton Brook Sanctuary**, Naturalist & Sanctuary Coordinator, Saw Mill River Audubon Society, Inc., 2660 Quaker Church Rd., Yorktown Heights, NY 10598, (914) 962-9330. (NNY)

2445 **British 1777 General Clinton Trail**, Rockland County Council, BSA, 15 Frank Rd., Rt. 2, Box 686, Stony Point, NY 10980, (914) 786-2771. 8.0 miles. Awards available. (AA 1992)

Brown's Tract Trail see entry 2412.

2446 **Bryant Preserve**, William Cullen Bryant Preserve, Northern Blvd., P.O. Box D, Roslyn, NY 11576, (516) 484-9337. (NNY)

Bubb Lake Trail see entry 2412.
Buck Mountain Trail see entry 2412.

Buck Pond Trail see entry 2412.

2447 **Buckhorn Island State Park**, Robert Moses Pkwy., Buffalo, NY 14240. (MNE)

2448 **Burnt-Rossman Hills State Forest**, Regional Forester, Region 4, Jefferson Rd., Stamford, NY 12167, (607) 652-7364. (GNA)

2449 **Butler Memorial Sanctuary**, Executive Director, Lower Hudson Chapter, The Nature Conservancy, Rt. 2, Chestnut Ridge Rd., Mount Kisco, NY 10549, (914) 666-5365. 10.0 miles. Named trails: Basin Ravine, Basin. (ANI; NNY; GNA)

2450 **Buttermilk Falls State Park**, SR 13, Ithaca, NY 14850, (607) 273-5761. Named trails: Gorge 5.0, Rim, Treman Lake 2.0(l). (ANY; WCD; MNE; DMA; GNA)

2451 **Buttermilk Falls Trail**, Buttermilk Falls County Park, Rockland County Park Commission, 380 Phillips Hill Rd., New City, NY 10956, (914) 425-5100. (NNY)

2452 **Camp at Camp Bell Campground**, SR 415, Campbell, NY 14821, (607) 527-3301. (WCD)

2453 **Camp at Ferenbaugh**, Rt. 3, Corning, NY 14830, (607) 962-6193 or (800) 582-6558. (WCD)

2454 **Camp Babcock-Hovey**, Finger Lakes Council, BSA, 55 E. Castle St., Geneva, NY 14456, (315) 789-1166; or Camp Babcock-Hovey, Rt. 2, Box 28, Quid, NY 14521, (607) 869-3841. (SFC)

2455 **Camp Barton**, Baden-Powell Council, BSA, P.O. Box 4, Dryden, NY 13053, (607) 844-8125; or Camp Barton, Frontenac Rd., Trumansburg, NY 14886, (607) 387-9250. (SFC)

2456 **Camp Boyhaven**, Schenectady County Council, BSA, 2 Union St., Schenectady, NY 12305, (518) 374-7733. (SFC)

2457 **Camp Crumhorn Mountain**, Otschodela Council, BSA, SR 23, Southside P.O. Box 1356, Oneonta, NY 13820, (607) 432-6491; or Camp Crumhorn Mountain, Rt. 1, Maryland, NY 12116, (607) 638-9050. (SFC)

2458 **Camp Hitchens Park**, Suffolk County Council, BSA, 7 Scouting Blvd., Medford, NY 11763, (516) 924-7000. (SFC)

2459 **Camp Massawepie**, Otetiana Council, BSA, 474 East Ave., Rochester, NY 14607, (716) 244-4210; or Camp Massawepie, Piercefield, NY 12973, (518) 359-3900. (SFC)

2460 **Camp Merz**, Allegheny Highlands Council, BSA, 50 Hough Hill Rd., Falconer, NY 14733, (716) 665-2697; or Camp Merz, Rt. 2, Box 41, Mayville, NY 14757, (716) 753-7194. (SFC)

2461 **Camp Portaferry**, Jefferson-Lewis Council, BSA, 6842 Leray St., Watertown, NY 13601, (315) 782-4751. (SFC)

2462 **Camp Russell**, General Herkimer Council, BSA, 427 N. Main St., Herkimer, NY 13350, (315) 866-1540. (SFC)

2463 **Camp Sabattis**, Watchung Council, BSA, 1170 US 22W, Mountainside, NJ 07092, (201) 624-9191; or Camp Sabattis, Long Lake, NY 12847, (518) 624-3767. (SFC)

2464 **Camp Sabattis**, Hiawatha Council, BSA, 900 W. Genesee St., Syracuse, NY 13204, (315) 474-8574. (SFC)

2465 **Camp Vigor**, Street Lawrence Council, BSA, P.O. Box 425, Canton, NY 13617, (315) 386-4571. (SFC)

2466 **Camp Wakpominee**, Mohican Council, BSA, 15 Pearl St., Glens Falls, NY 12801, (518) 792-5433; or Camp Wakpominee, Rt. 1, Sly Pond Rd., West Fort Ann, NY 12827, (518) 792-8849. (SFC)

2467 **Camp Woodworth Lake**, Sir Wm. Johnson Council, BSA, 38 Grand St., Gloversville, NY 12079, (518) 773-7313. (SFC)

2468 **Canada Hill, White Rock and Sugar Loaf**, New York-New Jersey Trail Conference, 232 Madison Ave., Rm. 908, New York, NY 10116, (212) 685-9699. Named trails: Canada Hill-White Rock 5.0-7.0(l), Sugar Loaf 2.3(l). (NYW)

Canada Hill-White Rock Trail see entry 2468.

2469 **Canal Education Center**, Cedar Bay Rd. and DeWitt, Syracuse, NY 13214. (GNA)

2470 **Capital District Wildlife Management Area**, Bureau of Wildlife, Department of Environmental Conservation, SR 10, Stamford, NY 12167, (607) 652-7364. 10.0 miles. (GNA)

2471 **Carlton Hill State Forest**, Regional Forester, Region 9, Rt. 1, Box 4, Jamestown, NY 14701, (716) 484-7161. (GNA)

Cascade Lake Link Trail see entry 2412.

Cascade Lake Trail see entry 2412.

2472 **Cascade Mountain Trail**, Cascade Lakes Day Use Area, SR 73, Keene, NY 12942. 2.5 miles. (OTB)

Cascade Pond Trail see entry 2412.

Casino Trail see entry 2686.

Castle Rock Trail see entry 2412.

Cat Mountain Trail see entry 2412.

Catamount Mountain Trail see entry 2412.

Cathead Mountain Trail see entry 2412.

Cathedral Pines Trail see entry 2412.

2473 **Catskill Aqueduct**, New York-New Jersey Trail Conference, 232 Madison Ave., Rm. 908, New York, NY 10116, (212) 685-9699. Named trails: Croton Reservoir to Hardscrabble Road 4.5(s), Mt. Taurus to Phillips Brook 3.0(s), Oregon Road to Croton Reservoir 7.0(s). (NYW)

2474 **Catskills Forest Preserve**, Catskill 3500 Club, 20 Cedar Ln., Cornwall, NY 12518; or New York-New Jersey Trail Conference, 232 Madison Ave., Rm. 908, New York, NY 10116, (212) 685-9699. Named trails: Balsam Lake Mountain 3.0(s), Becker, Blackhead Range 6.85(s), Becker Hollow 12.0(s), Curtis, Delaware Ridge-Line 18.8(s), Denning/Slide 6.35(s), The Devil's Path 19.65(s), Diamond Notch, Dry Brook Ridge 14.8(s), Escarpment 24.0(s), Giant Ledge-Panther Mountain 2.85(s), Hanley Corners 3.0(s), Hollow Tree Brook-Diamond Notch 4.8(s), Jimmy Dolan Notch 2.7(s), Long Path, Lost Clove 2.6(s), McKinley Hollow 2.65(s), Mink Hollow 12.0(s), Neversink-Hardenburg 12.9(s), North Lake Campground to NY 23A 4.5(s), North Lake to Notch Point 4.3(s), Pecoy Notch 1.9(s), Phoenicia-East Branch, Pine Hill/Eagle Mountain/West Branch 14.25(s), Seager-Dry Brook, Seager-Shandaken Brook 4.1(s), Shanty Hollow-Colonel's Chair 2.5(s), Steps, Tremper Mountain 6.75(s), Winnisook Lodge/Slide 2.85(s), Wittenberg/Cornell/Slide/Winnisook/Woodland Valley Trail 15.5(s). (ANY; EGH; MNE; DMA; AMI; GNA; GTB; WIC; IFT; NYW)

2475 **Catskills State Forest**, SR 23A, Haines Falls, NY 12436, (518) 589-5058. (WCD)

2476 **Caumsett State Park**, Rt. 3, Lloyd Harbor Rd., Huntington, NY (516) 423-1770. 10.0 miles. (NAT; NNY; GNA)

2477 **Cayuga County Trail**, Tom Higgins, Cayuga County Planning Board, 160 Genesee St., Auburn, NY 13021, (315) 253-1276. 15.0 miles straight. (GRT)

2478 **Cayuga Lake State Park**, SR 89, Seneca Falls, NY 13148, (315) 568-5163. (WCD)

2479 **Cedar Grove Campgrounds**, Schoharie Tpk., Catskill, NY 12414, (518) 945-1451. (WCD)

Cedar Lakes Trail see entry 2412.

Cedar Pond Lean-to Trail see entry 2412.

2480 **Cedar Valley Campsites**, S. Butler Rd., Morrisville, NY 13408, (315) 684-3033. (WCD)

Cellar Pond Trail see entry 2412.

Centennial Ski Trail see entry 2412.

2481 **Centers for Nature Education/Baltimore Woods**, Bishop Hill Rd., Marcellus, NY 13108, (315) 673-1350. (ANY)

2482 **Central Park**, Urban Park Rangers—Manhattan, NYC Department of Parks & Recreation, 16 W. 61st St., New York, NY 10023, (212) 397-3091. 50.0 miles. Named trails: Central Park Heritage National Recreation, Great Lawn Path 0.55, Reservoir Path 1.58. (NAT; NNY; CPH)

Central Park Heritage National Recreation Trail see entry 2482.

Chain Ponds Trail see entry 2412.

Chase Lake Trail see entry 2412.

Chatauqua West Trail see entry 2815.

2483 **Chateaugay-Winona State Forest**, Regional Forester, Region 6, Rt. 3, SR 26A, Lowville, NY 13617, (315) 376-3521. (GNA)

Chatfield Trail see entry 2774.

2484 **Chenango Valley State Park**, Chenango Forks, NY 13746, (607) 648-5251. (ANY; WCD; MNE; GNA)

2485 **Cherry Plain State Park**, Miller Rd., Stephentown, NY 12168. (ANY)

2486 **Cherry Valley State Forest**, Regional Forester, Region 4, Jefferson Rd., Stamford, NY 12167, (607) 652-7364. (GNA)

Chimney Mountain Trail see entry 2412.

2487 **Chittanango Falls State Park**, SR 13, Cazenovia, NY 13035, (315) 655-9620. (ANY; MNE; GNA)

2488 **Choate Sanctuary Trail**, Naturalist & Sanctuary Coordinator, Saw Mill River Audubon Society, Inc., 2660 Quaker Church Rd., Yorktown Heights, NY 10598. 0.75 mile loop. (NNY)

Chub Pond Trail see entry 2412.

2489 **Clarence Fahnestock Memorial State Park**, SR 301, Carmel, NY 10512, (914) 225-7207. 25.0 miles. (ANY; WCD; EGH; NNY; GNA; NYW)

2490 **Clark Reservation State Park**, Jamesville, NY 13078, (315) 492-1590. 3.0 miles. (ANY; GNA)

2491 **Clay Pit Ponds State Park Preserve**, 83 Neilson Ave., Staten Island, NY 10309, (212) 967-1976. (NNY)

Clear Pond Trail see entry 2412.

2492 **Clermont State Park**, US 9, Germantown, NY 12526, (518) 537-4240. (DMA)

Cliff Trail see entry 2666.

Clockmill Corners Trail see entry 2412.

2493 **Clove Lakes Park**, Urban Park Rangers—Staten Island, Clove Lakes/Silver Lake Parks, 1150 Clove Rd., Staten Island, NY 10301, (212) 442-1304 or (212) 442-7640. (NNY)

Clove Path see entry 2679.

Cod Pond from Shanty Brook Trailhead see entry 2412.

Compartment Trail see entry 2774.

2494 **Conesus Lake Campground**, 2202 E. Lake Rd., Conesus Lake, NY 14435, (716) 346-5472 or (716) 663-3840. (WCD)

Conklin's Crossing Trail see entry 2425.

2495 **Connetquot River State Park**, Sunrise Hwy., P.O. Box 505, Oakdale, NY

NEW YORK

11769, (516) 581-1005. 50.0 miles. (ANY; NAT; NNY; GNA)

Constable Pond-West Mountain Trail see entry 2412.

2496 **Constitution Island Marsh Sanctuary**, Rt. 2, Carmel, NY 10512, (914) 225-7207. (ANI)

2497 **Cooperstown Beaver Valley Campground**, Rt. 2, Box 646, Cooperstown, NY 13326, (607) 264-8431. (WCD)

2498 **Cooperstown Ringwood Farms Campground**, SR 80, Cooperstown, NY 13326, (800) 231-9114. (WCD)

2499 **Corning, Colonists, Cowboys and Crystal Historic Trail**, Five Rivers Council, BSA, 49 Liberty St., P.O. Box 807, Bath, NY 14810-0807, (607) 776-3861 or (800) 724-6099. 3.5 miles. Awards available. (AA 1993)

2500 **Country Hills Campground**, Rt. 2, Box 295, Marathon, NY 13803, (607) 849-3300. (WCD)

2501 **Covered Bridge Campsite**, Conklin Rd., Livingston Manor, NY 12758, (914) 439-5093. (WCD)

2502 **Cranberry Lake Park**, County Naturalist, Westchester County, Department of Parks, Recreation & Conservation, 148 Martine Ave., White Plains, NY 10601, (914) 682-2637. Named trails: Kensico Dam 0.5, Lake 1.5(l). (GFC; NNY)

2503 **Cranberry Lake Region**, New York Department of Environmental Conservation, 30 Court St., P.O. Box 109, Canton, NY 13617. (GFC)

Crane Mountain Pond and NW Range Trail see entry 2412.

Crane Mountain Trail see entry 2412.

Croton Reservoir to Hardscrabble Road see entry 2473.

2504 **Crown Point Reservation State Campground**, SR 9N/22, Crown Point, NY 12928, (518) 597-3603. (MNE)

Crown Ridge Trail see entry 2425.

2505 **Crystal Lake Park**, CR 17, Garrattsville, NY 13342, (607) 965-8265. (WCD)

2506 **Cumming Nature Center**, Gulick Rd., Naples, NY 14512, (716) 374-6160. Named trails: Beaver Pond 1.5, Iroquois 0.5(l), Pioneer 1.0. (ANY; MNE; DBV)

Curtins Pond Trail see entry 2412.

Curtis Trail see entry 2474.

2507 **Cuyler Hill State Forest**, Regional Forester, Region 7, P.O. Box 1169, Cortland, NY 13045, (607) 753-3095. (GNA)

2508 **D&H Canal Heritage Corridor Trail**, Rich White-Smith, New York Parks and Conservation Association, 35 Maiden Ln., Albany, NY 12207, (518) 434-1583; or JoEllen Donnelly, D&H Heritage Corridor Alliance, P.O. Box 176, Rosendale, NY 12472, (914) 338-5181. 90.0 miles straight planned, current as to 24.0 miles. (GRT)

2509 **Daggett Lake Campsites**, Glen-Athol Rd., Warrensburg, NY 12885, (518) 623-2198. (WCD)

2510 **Danby State Forest**, Regional Forester, Region 7, P.O. Box 1169, Cortland, NY 13045, (607) 753-3095. (GNA)

2511 **Darien Lake Nature Trail**, Darien Lake Theme Park, SR 90, Darien Center, NY 14040, (716) 599-4501. (DMA)

2512 **Darien Lakes State Park**, 9993 Allegheny Rd., Corfu, NY 14036, (716) 547-4727. (ANY; WCD; MNE)

Dark Hollow Trail see entry 2754.

Darning Needle Pond Trail see entry 2412.

2513 **Davis Wildlife Refuge Nature Trail**, Staten Island Institute of Arts and Sciences, 75 Stuyvesant Pl., Staten Island, NY 10301, (212) 727-1135. 1.5 miles. (NNY)

Dead Creek Flow Truck Trail see entry 2412.

Death Falls Trail see entry 2412.

Debar Mountain Trail see entry 2412.

2514 **Debar Wildlife Management Area**, Bureau of Wildlife, Ray Brook, NY 12977, (518) 891-1370. (GNA)

Deep Hollow Shelter Trail see entry 2425.

2515 **Deer River Campsite**, Red Tavern Rd., Duane, NY 12953, (518) 483-0060. (WCD)

2516 **Deer River State Forest**, Regional Forester, Ray Brook, NY 12977, (518) 891-1370. 22.0 miles. (GNA)

2517 **Deer Run Campgrounds**, Deer Run

Dr., Mechanicville, NY 12118, (518) 664-2804. (WCD)

Delaware Ridge-Line Trail *see* entry 2474.

2518 **Delta Lake State Park**, SR 46, Rome, NY 13440, (315) 337-4670. (ANY; WCD; MNE)

Denning/Slide Trail *see* entry 2474.

2519 **Devil's Hole State Park**, Robert Moses Pkwy., Niagara Falls, NY 14302. (ANY)

The Devil's Path *see* entry 2474.

Diamond Mountain Trail *see* entry 2425.

Diamond Notch Trail *see* entry 2474.

Dix Trail *see* entry 2412.

2520 **Dorchester Park**, SR 26, Whitney Point, NY 13862. (ANY)

2521 **Dream Lake Campground**, Buffalo Rd., Warsaw, NY 14569, (716) 786-5172. (WCD)

Dry and Dexter Lakes Trail *see* entry 2412.

Dry Brook Ridge Trail *see* entry 2474.

Dunning Pond from Gilmantown Road *see* entry 2412.

Dunning Pond from NY 30 *see* entry 2412.

Dunning Trail *see* entry 2425.

Eagle Cliff Trail *see* entry 2412.

2522 **East Ithaca Recreation Way**, Richard H. Schoch, Manager, Ithaca Parks and Open Space, 106 Seven Mile Dr., Ithaca, NY 14850, (607) 273-8035. 2.0 miles straight. (GRT)

East Pond Trail *see* entry 2599.

East Pond-Lost Creek Trail *see* entry 2412.

East Trail *see* entry 2646.

Echo Cliffs on Panther Mountain Trail *see* entry 2412.

2523 **Eleanor Roosevelt Trails**, Roosevelt-Vanderbilt National Historical Sites, 249 Albany Post Rd., Hyde Park, NY 12538, (914) 229-9115. (CGA)

Elk Lake-Dix Trail *see* entry 2412.

2524 **Elks-Brox City Park**, SR 97, Port Jervis, NY 12771, (914) 856-6034. (WCD)

2525 **Elmira Historic Trail**, Five Rivers Council, BSA, 49 Liberty St., P.O. Box 807, Bath, NY 14810, (607) 776-3861 or (800) 724-6099. 5.0-10.0 miles loop. Awards available. (AA 1993)

Emmet Hill Road Snowmobile Trail *see* entry 2412.

2526 **Empire Haven Nudist Park**, Rt. 3, Box 297, Moravia, NY 13118, (315) 497-0135. (WCD)

2527 **Erie Canal Towpath**, New York State Parks, Empire State Plaza, Albany, NY 12238. (DMA)

2528 **Erie Canal Trail**, Janice Fontanella, Site Manager, Schoharie Crossing State Historic Site, P.O. Box 140, Fort Hunter, NY 12069, (518) 829-7516. 90.0 miles straight. (GRT)

2529 **Erwin Wildlife Management Area**, Regional Wildlife Manager, New York State Department of Environmental Conservation, P.O. Box 57, Avon, NY 14414, (716) 226-2466. 5.0 miles. (GNA)

Escarpment Trail *see* entry 2474.

Esker Brook Walking Trail *see* entry 2681.

2530 **Eugene and Agnes Meyer Nature Preserve** *see* entry 2666.

2531 **Evangola State Park**, SR 5, Dunkirk, NY 14048, (716) 549-1802. (ANY; WCD; MNE)

2532 **Evergreen Camping Resort**, P.O. Box 431, Lake George, NY 12845, (518) 623-3207. (WCD)

2533 **Fair Haven Beach State Park**, SR 104A, Oswego, NY 13126, (315) 947-5205. (ANY; WCD; MNE)

Falls of the West Branch of the Sacanda Trail *see* entry 2412.

2534 **Fillmore Glen State Park**, SR 38, Moravia, NY 13118, (315) 497-0130. 5.0 miles. (ANY; MNE; GNA)

2535 **Finger Lakes National Forest**, P.O. Box W, Montour Falls, NY 14865, (607) 594-2750. 25.0 miles. (ANY)

2536 **Finger Lakes Trail**, Finger Lakes Trail Conference, P.O. Box 18048, Rochester, NY 14618, (716) 288-7191; or State Department of Environmental Conservation, Albany, NY 12201; or Finger Lakes Association, Dept. 6-B, 309 Lake St., Penn Yan, NY 14527-1831, (800)

548-4386. 775 miles. (LGU; EGH; HTN)
2537 **Fire Island National Seashore**, 120 Laurel St., Patchogue, NY 11772, (516) 289-4810. (LGU; WCD; PGF; GFC; NAT; DMA; NPV; CGA; NNY; GNA; YNP)
Fire Tower Trail see entry 2810.
2538 **Fish Creek Pond State Public Campground**, SR 30, Tupper Lake, NY 12986, (518) 891-4560. (MNE)
2539 **Fish Creek Wildlife Management Area**, Bureau of Wildlife, 317 Washington St., Watertown, NY 13601, (315) 782-0100. (GNA)
Fish Trail see entry 2412.
Five Ponds-Wolf Pond-Sand Lake Trail see entry 2412.
2540 **Flint Creek Campgrounds**, 1455 Phelps Rd., Middlesex, NY 14507, (716) 554-3567. (WCD)
2541 **Flushing Meadows-Corona Park**, Urban Park Rangers—Queens, Flushing Meadows-Corona Park, Administration Bldg., Corona, NY 11368, (212) 699-6722. 2.5 miles. Named trails: Turtle Pond Interpretive. (NNY)
Foot Pond Trail see entry 2412.
2542 **Forest Haven Campground**, Page Rd., Kennedy, NY 14747, (716) 267-5902. (WCD)
2543 **Forest Park**, Urban Park Rangers—Queens, Flushing Meadows-Corona Park, Administration Bldg., Corona, NY 11368, (212) 699-6722. (NNY)
Former Croton Lake Station to Lake Mahopac see entry 2693.
Forrest Trail see entry 2754.
2544 **Fort Niagara State Park**, P.O. Box 169, Robert Moses Pkwy., Youngstown, NY 14174, (716) 745-3802 or (716) 745-7611. (SAR 1994)
2545 **Fort Tryon Park**, Urban Park Rangers—Manhattan, NYC Department of Parks & Recreation, 16 W. 61st St., New York, NY 10023, (212) 397-3100. 8.0 miles. (NNY)
2546 **Four Mile Creek State Park**, SR 18, Youngstown, NY 14174. (ANY)
2547 **Four Winds Campground**, 7350 Tenefly Rd., Portageville, NY 14536, (716) 493-2794. (WCD)

Fourth Lake-Black Bear Mountain Trail see entry 2412.
Francis Lake Trail see entry 2412.
2548 **Frank E. Jadwin State Forest**, Regional Forester, Region 6, Rt. 3, SR 26A, Lowville, NY 13367, (315) 376-3521. (GNA)
2549 **Franklin Delano Roosevelt State Park**, 2957 Crompond Rd., Yorktown Heights, NY 10598, (914) 245-4434. (ANY; MNE)
2550 **Franklin Roosevelt Home**, Roosevelt-Vanderbilt National Historical Sites, 249 Albany Post Rd., Hyde Park, NY 12538, (914) 229-9115. (CTA)
2551 **French Creek Wildlife Management Area**, Bureau of Wildlife, 317 Washington St., Watertown, NY 13601, (315) 782-0100. (GNA)
Fringe of the Forest Trail see entry 2667.
2552 **Frost Ridge Campground**, Conlon Rd., LeRoy, NY 14482, (716) 768-4883 or (716) 768-9730. (WCD)
2553 **Ganondagan State Historic Site**, 1488 Victor-Holcomb Rd., Victor, NY 14564, (716) 924-5848. (SSI)
2554 **Gardiner Hill Campground**, P.O. Box 219-1A, Norway Rd., Lowman, NY 14861, (607) 732-9827. (WCD)
Garnet Lake Canoe/Hike to Lizard Pond and Baldwin Springs see entry 2412.
2555 **Garvies Point Museum & Preserve**, Barry Dr., Glen Cove, NY 11542, (516) 671-0300. 5.0 miles. (ANY; MNE; DMA; NNY)
2556 **Gateway National Recreation Area**, Floyd Bennett Field, Brooklyn, NY 11234, (718) 338-3575. (ANY; CGA)
2557 **Gedney Brook Sanctuary**, Naturalist & Sanctuary Coordinator, Saw Mill River Audubon Society, Inc., 2660 Quaker Church Rd., Yorktown Heights, NY 10598, (914) 962-9330. 1.5 miles. (NNY)
2558 **Genesee Country Campground**, P.O. Box 100, Caledonia, NY 14423, (716) 538-4200. (WCD)
2559 **Genesee Valley Greenway**, Robin Dropkin, Conservation Director, New York Parks and Conservation Association,

35 Maiden Ln., Albany, NY 12207, (518) 434-1583; or Fran Gotchik, Local Greenway Coordinator, New York Parks and Conservation Association, 46 Prince St., Rochester, NY 14607, (716) 271-3550. 50.0 miles straight planned, current as to 2.0 miles. (GRT)

Giant Ledge-Panther Mountain Trail see entry 2474.

Giant Mountain Trail see entry 2412.

2560 **Gilbert Lake State Park**, SR 215, Oneonta, NY 13820, (607) 432-2114. (ANY; WCD)

Glasgow Mills and Hillabrandt Valley see entry 2412.

Glenfield RR Snowmobile Trail see entry 2412.

2561 **Glimmerglass State Park**, E. Lake Rd., Cooperstown, NY 13326, (607) 547-8662. (ANY; MNE; DMA)

2562 **Golden Hill State Park**, Lower Lake Rd., Barker, NY 14012, (716) 795-3885. (ANY; WCD)

Goldens Bridge to Lake Mahopac see entry 2693.

Good Luck Lake Trail see entry 2412.

Good Luck Mountain Cliffs Trail see entry 2412.

Goodnow Mountain Trail see entry 2412.

Goose Pond Trail see entry 2412.

2563 **Gorge Trail**, Thomas F. Vogt, Stewardship Chair, Cazenovia Preservation Foundation, P.O. Box 432, Cazenovia, NY 13035, (315) 655-2397. 2.2 miles straight. (GRT)

Gorge Trail see entry 2450.

2564 **Grafton Lakes State Park**, SR 2, Grafton, NY 12082. (ANY)

Great Lawn Path see entry 2482.

2565 **Green Lakes State Park**, SR 5, Fayetteville, NY 13066, (315) 637-6111. (ANY; WCD; MNE; GNA)

2566 **Greenburgh Nature Center**, Dromore Rd., Scarsdale, NY 10583, (914) 723-3470. (NNY)

2567 **Greenwood Park**, SR 26, Endicott, NY 13760. (ANY)

2568 **Griffis AFB FAMCAMP**, Griffis Air Force Base, SR 365, Rome, NY 13440, (315) 330-2848. (WCD)

2569 **Griffis Sculpture Park**, Ahrens Rd., Ashford Hollow, NY 14171. (GFA; OTB)

Gull Lake Loop Trail see entry 2412.

Gull Lakes Trail see entry 2412.

Gull Pond Trail see entry 2412.

Hadley Mountain Trail see entry 2412.

Haiku Trail see entry 2580.

2570 **Hale Ravine Trail**, Nature Conservancy, Rt. 2, Chestnut Ridge Rd., Mount Kisco, NY 10549, (914) 666-5365. (ANI)

Halfmoon Lake Trail see entry 2412.

Hall of Pines Trail see entry 2774.

2571 **Hamlin Beach State Park**, Lake Ontario State Pkwy., Hamlin, NY 14464, (716) 964-2462. Named trails: Yanty Creek Nature. (ANY; WCD; MNE; OTB)

2572 **Hammond Hill and Yellow Barn State Forest**, Regional Forester, Region 7, P.O. Box 1169, Cortland, NY 13045, (607) 753-3095. (GNA)

Hanley Corners Trail see entry 2474.

2573 **Harriman Long Path National Recreation Trail**, Palisades Interstate Park Commission, Bear Mountain State Park, Bear Mountain, NY 10911, (914) 786-2701. 16.0 miles. (NFG)

Harrisburg Lake to Baldwin Springs via Arrow Trail see entry 2412.

2574 **Heckscher State Park**, Heckscher State Pkwy., East Islip, NY 11730, (516) 581-2100. (ANY; NNY)

Helldiver Pond Trail see entry 2412.

2575 **Hempstead Lake State Park**, Southern State Pkwy., Rockville Centre, NY 11572, (516) 766-1029. Named trails: Hempstead Lake 5.0(l). (ANY; NNY)

Hempstead Lake Trail see entry 2575.

2576 **Heritage Trail**, Otetiana Council, BSA, 474 East Ave., Rochester, NY 14607, (716) 244-4210. 15.0 miles. Awards available. (NHT; HTA)

Hermitage Trail see entry 2412.

2577 **Hickory Hill Family Campground**, 7531 Mitchellsville Rd., Bath, NY 14810, (607) 776-4345. (WCD)

2578 **Hickory Lake Campground**, Centerville Rd., Houghton, NY 14744, (716) 567-4211. (WCD)

2579 **High Falls Park Campground**, CR 23, Chateaugay, NY 12920, (518) 497-3156. (ANY; WCD)

High Falls Truck Trail *see* entry 2412.

High Lake Falls Trail *see* entry 2412.

2580 **High Rock Park**, High Rock Park Conservation Center, 200 Nevada Ave., Staten Island, NY 10306, (212) 987-6233. Named trails: Haiku. (MNE; NNY)

2581 **High Tor Wildlife Management Area**, Bureau of Wildlife, New York Department of Environmental Conservation, P.O Box 57, Avon, NY 14414, (716) 226-2466. 14.0 miles. (GNA)

2582 **Highbanks Campground**, Onoville Rd., Steamburg, NY 14783, (716) 354-4855. (WCD)

2583 **Higley Flow State Park**, Coldbrook Rd., South Colton, NY 13687, (315) 262-2880. 6.0 miles. (ANY; WCD; GNA)

2584 **Hill 'N Hollow Campsites**, P.O. Box 19, Hammondsport, NY 14840-0019, (607) 569-2711. (WCD)

Hillburne-Sebago-Torne Trail *see* entry 2425.

2585 **Hilltop Farm Campsites**, P.O. Box 138, Mountaindale, NY 12763, (914) 434-1017. (WCD)

2586 **Hither Hills State Park**, SR 27, Montauk, NY 11954, (516) 668-2554. 6.0 miles. (ANY; DBV; DMA; GNA)

Hoffman Notch Trail *see* entry 2412.

2587 **Holiday Hill Campground**, 7818 Marvin Hill Rd., Springwater, NY 14560, (716) 669-2600. (WCD)

Hollow Tree Brook-Diamond Notch Trail *see* entry 2474.

2588 **Hommocks Conservation Area**, Conservation Advisory Committee, Town of Mamaroneck, 740 W. Boston Post Rd., Mamaroneck, NY 10543, (914) 698-4929. (NNY)

Honnedaga Brook Trail *see* entry 2412.

2589 **Hook Mountain**, Palisades Interstate Park Commission, Bear Mountain State Park, Bear Mountain, NY 10911, (914) 786-2701. (NNY)

Horn Trail *see* entry 2425.

Huber Trail *see* entry 2774.

2590 **Huckleberry Lake**, New York Department of Environmental Conservation, 30 Court St., P.O. Box 109, Canton, NY 13617. (GFC)

Huckleberry Mountain Trail *see* entry 2412.

2591 **Hudson Highlands State Park**, Superintendent, Taconic State Park Commission, Staatsburg, NY 12580, (914) 889-4100. (NNY)

2592 **Hudson River Museum Trail**, 511 Warburton Ave., Yonkers, NY 10701, (914) 963-4550. 0.5 mile. (NNY)

2593 **Hudson Valley KOA Trail**, P.O. Box B134, Plattekill, NY 12568, (914) 564-2836. 0.5 mile. (NNY)

Hurst Trail *see* entry 2425.

2594 **Ice Caves National Landmark**, Ellenville, NY 12428. (OTB)

Ice House Pond Trail *see* entry 2412.

Indian Lake Trail *see* entry 2412.

Indian Pass Trail *see* entry 2412.

Indian Pond Trail *see* entry 2412.

2595 **Indian Ridge Campsite**, HC 2, Box 23, Leeds, NY 12451, (518) 943-3516. (WCD)

Indian River Trail *see* entry 2412.

Indian Trail *see* entry 2812.

2596 **Inwood Hill Park**, Urban Park Rangers—Manhattan, NYC Department of Parks & Recreation, 16 W. 61st St., New York, NY 10023, (212) 397-3100. (NNY)

2597 **Iroquois National Wildlife Refuge**, Rt. 1, Casey Rd., Bason, NY 14013, (716) 958-5445. Named trails: Swallow Hollow 1.0. (MNE; OTB; GNA; GNW)

Iroquois Trail *see* entry 2506.

Irving Pond, Bellows Lake, Holmes Lake Loop to Peters Corners *see* entry 2412.

2598 **Italy Hill State Forest**, Regional Forester, Region 8, 115 Liberty St., Bath, NY 14810, (607) 776-2165. 4.0 miles. (GNA)

2599 **Jamaica Bay**, Jamaica Bay Unit, Gateway National Recreation Area, Floyd Bennett Field, Brooklyn, NY 11234, (212) 252-9286. Named trails: East Pond, West Pond 2.0(l). (OTB; NNY)

2600 **Jamaica Bay Wildlife Refuge**, Crossbay Blvd., Jamaica, NY 11417, (718) 474-0613. (ANY)
2601 **James Baird State Park**, Taconic State Pkwy., Poughkeepsie, NY 12601. (ANY)
2602 **James D. Kennedy Memorial State Forest**, Regional Forester, Region 7, P.O. Box 1169, Cortland, NY 13045, (607) 753-3095. (GNA)
2603 **Jamestown Audubon Nature Center**, 1600 Riverside Rd., Jamestown, NY 14701. (ANY)
Jessup Trail see entry 2754.
Jimmy Dolan Notch Trail see entry 2474.
2604 **JJ's Pope Haven Campground**, SR 241, Randolph, NY 14772, (716) 358-4900. (WCD)
2605 **John Boyd Thacher State Park**, Rt. 1, Voorheesville, NY 12186, (518) 872-1237. 4.0 miles. (GNA)
John Brown's Tract Trail see entry 2412.
2606 **John C. Thompson Park**, State St., Watertown, NY 13601, (315) 785-7775. (TIT)
2607 **John F. Kennedy Memorial Wildlife Sanctuary**, Superintendent, Department of Beaches, Town Hall, Oyster Bay, NY 11771, (516) 922-5800 ext. 578. 4.5 miles. (NNY)
2608 **The John Kieran Nature Trail**, Marianne Anderson, Van Cortlandt and Pelham Bay Parks Administration, Bronx River Pkwy., Bronx, NY 10462, (212) 430-1890. 1.0 mile straight. (GRT)
2609 **Joseph Davis State Park**, Robert Moses Pkwy., Youngstown, NY 14174. (ANY)
2610 **Junction Campsite**, P.O. Box 316, Lake Clear Junction, NY 12945, (518) 891-9858. (WCD)
Kakiat Trail see entry 2425.
Kane Mountain-E. Trail see entry 2412.
Kane Mountain from Pine Lake Campground see entry 2412.
Kane Mountain-S. Trail see entry 2412.
2611 **Kayuta Lake Campground**, SR 28, Forestport, NY 13338, (315) 831-5077. (WCD)
2612 **Keewaydin State Park**, SR 12, Alexandria Bay, NY 13607. (ANY)
2613 **Kellystone Park**, Rt. 1, Nineveh, NY 13813, (607) 639-1090. (WCD)
Kensico Dam Trail see entry 2502.
2614 **Keuka Lake State Park**, SR 54A, Penn Yan, NY 14527, (315) 536-3666. (ANY; WCD; MNE)
Kibby Pond Trail see entry 2412.
2615 **Kinderhook Trail**, Town Recreation Commission, P.O. Box P, Niverville, NY 12130, (518) 758-9754; or Jim Tansey, Chairman of Kinderhook Rails-to-Trails, Rt. 1, Valatie, NY 12184. 8.0 miles straight planned, current as to 1.0 mile. (GRT)
2616 **King Phillip's Campsite**, US 9, Lake George, NY 12845, (518) 668-5763. (WCD)
2617 **Kitchawan Research Station**, Brooklyn Botanic Garden, 1000 Washington Ave., Brooklyn, NY 11225, (212) 622-4433. 5.0 miles. (NNY)
2618 **Kittatinny Campgrounds**, SR 97, Barryville, NY 12719, (914) 557-8611. (WCD)
2619 **KOA-Ausable Chasm**, SR 373, Ausable Chasm, NY 12911, (518) 834-9990. (WCD)
2620 **KOA-Cooperstown North**, Rt. 2, Box 88, Richfield Springs, NY 13439, (315) 858-0236. (WCD)
2621 **KOA-Herkimer Diamond Campground**, P.O. Box 510, Herkimer, NY 13350, (315) 891-7355. (WCD)
2622 **KOA-Hudson Valley** (see Hudson Valley KOA Trail **2593**). (WCD)
2623 **KOA-Lake Placid-Whiteface Mountain Kampground**, Fox Farm Rd., Wilmington, NY 12997, (518) 946-7878. (WCD)
2624 **KOA-Natural Bridge/Watertown**, P.O. Box 71A, Natural Bridge, NY 13665, (315) 644-4880. (WCD)
2625 **KOA-Old Forge**, P.O. Box 51, Old Forge, NY 13420, (315) 369-6011. (WCD)
2626 **KOA-Rome/Verona**, Blackman's Corner Rd., Verona, NY 13478, (315) 336-7318. (WCD)
2627 **KOA-Syracuse**, Plainville-Jack's Reef

Rd., Baldwinsville, NY 13027, (315) 635-6405. (WCD)

2628 **KOA-Unadilla/I-88/Oneonta**, Rt. 1, Box 186, Franklin, NY 13775, (607) 369-9030. (WCD)

2629 **KOA-Watkins Glen/Corning**, P.O. Box 228, Watkins Glen, NY 14891, (607) 535-7404. (WCD)

2630 **Kring Point State Park**, SR 12, Alexandria Bay, NY 13607, (315) 482-2444. (WCD)

2631 **Lake Chautaqua State Park**, Mayville, NY 14757. (OTB)

2632 **Lake Erie State Park**, SR 5, Dunkirk, NY 14048, (716) 792-9214. (ANY; WCD; MNE)

2633 **Lake George Area**, Lake George AYH-Hostel, P.O. Box 176, Lake George, NY 12845, (518) 668-2634. (AYH)

2634 **Lake George RV Park**, Rt. 3, Box 3223, Lake George, NY 12845-9765, (518) 792-3775. (WCD)

2635 **Lake Lauderdale Campground**, Rt. 1, Cambridge, NY 12816, (518) 677-8855. (WCD)

2636 **Lake Taghkanic State Park**, SR 23, Ancram, NY 12502, (518) 851-3631. 4.0 miles. (ANY; WCD; MNE; GNA)

Lake Trail see entry 2502.

2637 **Lakeside Beaches State Park**, Lake Ontario Pkwy., Albion, NY 14411, (716) 682-5246. (WCD)

2638 **Lakeview Wildlife Management Area**, New York Bureau of Wildlife, Department of Environmental Conservation, 217 Washington St., Watertown, NY 13601, (315) 782-0100. (GNA)

2639 **Larchmont Reservoir Conservation Area**, Conservation Advisory Committee, Town of Mamaroneck, 740 W. Boston Post Rd., Mamaroneck, NY 10543, (914) 698-4929. (NNY)

2640 **LaTourette Park**, Urban Park Rangers—Staten Island, Clove Lakes/Silver Lake Parks, 1150 Clove Rd., Staten Island, NY 10301, (212) 442-1304 or (212) 442-7640. 5.0 miles. (NNY)

2641 **Lazy River Campground**, 50 Bevier Rd., Gardiner, NY 12525, (914) 255-5193. (WCD)

Leary Trail see entry 2412.

2642 **Lebanon Reservoir Campground**, Reservoir Rd., Hamilton, NY 13346, (315) 824-2278. (WCD)

Ledge Trail see entry 2774.

2643 **Lehigh Memory Trail**, Williamsville Village Hall, 5565 Main St., Williamsville, NY 14221, (716) 632-4120. 0.71 mile straight. (GRT)

2644 **Lei-Ti Campground**, 9979 Francis Rd., Batavia, NY 14020, (716) 343-8600 or (800) HI LEI-TI. (WCD)

2645 **Lesser Wilderness State Forest**, Regional Forester, Region 6, Rt. 3, SR 26A, Lowville, NY 13367, (315) 376-3521. (GNA)

2646 **Letchworth State Park**, SR 19A, Portageville, NY 14536, (716) 493-2611. Named trails: East 18.0. (ANY; WCD; MNE; OTB; GNA)

Lichen Trail see entry 2425.

Limekiln Creek-Third Lake Trail see entry 2412.

Limekiln Ski Routes see entry 2412.

Little Otter Lake Rd. & Confusion Flats Trail see entry 2412.

Little Salmon Lake Trail see entry 2412.

2647 **Little Valley State Forest**, Regional Forester, Region 9, Rt. 1, Box 4, Jamestown, NY 14701, (716) 484-7161. (GNA)

Little Woodhull Lake Trail see entry 2412.

2648 **Livingston State Forest**, Regional Forester, Region 8, 115 Liberty St., Bath, NY 14810, (607) 776-2165. (GNA)

2649 **Long Island Greenbelt Trail**, Director, Greenbelt Trail Conference, Inc., 23 Deer Path Rd., Central Islip, NY 11722, (516) 234-3112. 34.0 miles straight. (NNY)

Long Mountain-Torne Trail see entry 2425.

2650 **Long Path**, New York-New Jersey Trail Conference, 232 Madison Ave., Rm. 908, New York, NY 10116, (212) 685-9699; or Catskill 3500 Club, 20 Cedar Ln., Cornwall, NY 12518; or Palisades Interstate Park Commission, Bear Mountain State Park, Bear Mountain, NY 10911, (914) 786-2701. 226 miles. (EGH)

2651 **Long Point on Lake Chautaqua**, SR 1, Maple Springs, NY 14756. (ANY)

Long Swing Trail *see* entry 2412.
The Loop *see* entry 2412.
2652 **Lost City of Tryon Trail**, Troop 55, Covenant United Methodist Church, 1124 Culver Rd., Rochester, NY 14609. 1.5 miles. Awards available. (AA 1994)
Lost Clove Trail *see* entry 2474.
Lost Lake Trail *see* entry 2412.
Lost Pond Trail *see* entry 2412.
Lost Ponds Trail *see* entry 2412.
2653 **Macomb Reservation State Park**, SR 22B, Schuyler Falls, NY 12985, (518) 643-9952. (WCD; MNE; GNA)
Mad Tom Trail *see* entry 2412.
2654 **Magic Pines RV Resort**, US 9, Lewis, NY 12950, (518) 873-2288. (WCD)
Major Welch Trail *see* entry 2425.
2655 **Manitoga Preserve**, Executive Director, Lower Hudson Chapter, The Nature Conservancy, Rt. 2, Chestnut Ridge Rd., Mount Kisco, NY 10549, (914) 666-5365. 4.0 miles. (ANY; NNY)
2656 **Margaret Lewis Norrie State Park**, US 9, Poughkeepsie, NY 12601, (914) 889-4646. (ANY; WCD)
2657 **Marine Nature Study Area**, Town of Hempstead, Slice Dr., Oceanside, NY 11572, (516) 766-1580. (NNY)
2658 **Marshlands Conservancy**, US 1, Boston Post Rd., Rye, NY 10580, (914) 835-4466. (NNY)
2659 **Mary Flagler Cary Arboretum**, The New York Botanical Garden, Bronx, NY 10458-5126, (212) 220-8700. (GGB)
2660 **Masonville State Forest**, Regional Forester, Region 4, Jefferson Rd., Stamford, NY 12167, (607) 652-7364. (GNA)
2661 **Massapequa State Park Trail**, Long Island State Park & Recreation Commission, Belmont Lake State Park, Babylon, NY 11702, (516) 669-1000. 3.0 miles loop. (NNY)
2662 **Max V. Shaul State Park**, SR 30, Middleburgh, NY 12122, (518) 827-4711. (ANY; WCD)
Mays Pond Trail *see* entry 2412.
McCarthy Road and Snowmobile Trail *see* entry 2412.
2663 **McConchie's Heritage Acres**, 2501 Northline Rd., Galway, NY 12074, (518) 882-6605. (WCD)

McKenzie Mountain Trail *see* entry 2412.
McKinley Hollow Trail *see* entry 2474.
2664 **Meadow-Vale Campsite**, Gilbert Lake Rd., Mt. Vision, NY 13810, (607) 293-8802. (WCD)
Meco Lake Trail *see* entry 2412.
2665 **Mendon Ponds Park**, SR 65, Rochester, NY 14615. (ANY)
2666 **Meyer Nature Preserve**, Executive Director, Lower Hudson Chapter, The Nature Conservancy, Rt. 2, Chestnut Ridge Rd., Mount Kisco, NY 10549, (914) 666-5365 or (914) 666-4221. 6.5 miles. Named trails: Cliff, Oregon, Ravine. (ANI; NNY)
2667 **Mianus River Gorge**, Mianus River Gorge Conservation Committee, Bartlett Arboretum, 157 Brookdale Rd., Stamford, CT 06903, (203) 322-9148. 5.0 miles. Named trails: Bank of the River, Brink of the Gorge, Fringe of the Forest. (EGH; NNY; GNA)
Middle Branch Lake Trail *see* entry 2412.
Middle Branch Marsh Trail *see* entry 2412.
Middle Settlement Lake Access Trail *see* entry 2412.
Middle Settlement Lake Trail *see* entry 2412.
Mill Creek Lake Trail *see* entry 2412.
2668 **Millard Fillmore Historic Trail**, Cayuga County Historian, Historic Old Post Office, 157 Genesee St., Auburn, NY 13021-3423, (315) 253-1300; or Cayuga County Council, BSA, Memorial City Hall, Auburn, NY 13021, (315) 252-9579. 10.0 miles loop. Awards available. (AA 1993)
2669 **Mills-Norris State Park**, US 9, Staatsburg, NY 12580, (914) 889-4100. (MNE)
Millwood to Croton Reservoir *see* entry 2693.
2670 **Mine Kill State Park**, Stamford, NY 12167, (518) 827-6111. (MNE)
2671 **Mineral Spring Falls Trail**, Executive Director, Lower Hudson Chapter,

The Nature Conservancy, Rt. 2, Chestnut Ridge Rd., Mount Kisco, NY 10549, (914) 666-5365. (NNY)

Mink Hollow Trail see entry 2474.

2672 **Minna Anthony Common Nature Center**, I-81 exit 51, Alexandria Bay, NY 13607, (315) 482-2479. (ANY; TIT)

2673 **Minnewaska State Park**, P.O. Box 893, New Paltz, NY 12561, (914) 255-0752; or Palisades Interstate Park Commission, Administration Bldg., Bear Mountain State Park, Bear Mountain, NY 10911, (914) 786-2701. (EGH; GNA)

Minnewaska Trail see entry 2679.

Mitchell Ponds Trail see entry 2412.

2674 **Mohawk Campground**, Rt. 2, Box 62, Cherry Valley, NY 13320, (607) 264-3241. (WCD)

2675 **Mohawk-Caughnawaga Museum Nature Trail**, SR 5, Fonda, NY 12068, (518) 853-3646. (GFA)

2676 **Mohawk-Hudson Bikeway**, Albany County Planning Department, 1 Lodge St., Albany, NY 12207, (518) 447-5660; or James G. Zambardino, Superintendent, Colonie Recreation and Parks Department, Rt. 1, Box 442, Cohoes, NY 12047, (518) 783-2760; or Elizabeth Orzel-Kaspar, Chairperson, Recreation Committee, Town of Niskayuna, 1335 Balltown Rd., Schenectady, NY 12309, (518) 374-7871; or Edwin D. Reilly, Supervisor, Town of Niskayuna, 1335 Balltown Rd., Schenectady, NY 12309, (518) 374-7710; or William Seber, Director, Department of Parks and Recreation, City Hall, Jay St., Schenectady, NY 12305, (518) 382-5152; or Denise Cahsmere, Senior Planner, Schenectady County Planning Department, 1 Broadway Center, Suite 800, Schenectady, NY 12305-2583, (518) 386-2225. 41.0 miles straight. (GRT)

2677 **Mohawk-Hudson Greenway**, Schenectady Chamber of Commerce, 240 Canal Sq., Schenectady, NY 12305, (518) 372-5656. 23.0 miles. (DMA)

Mohegan Lake Road see entry 2412.

2678 **Mohonk Preserve**, New Paltz, NY 12561, (914) 255-0919. (EGH)

2679 **Mohonk Trust Lands**, The Mohonk Trust, New Paltz, NY 12561, (914) 255-1000. Named trails: Clove Path, Minnewaska. (DMA; GNA; NYW)

2680 **Montauk Point State Park**, Montauk Hwy., Montauk, Long Island, NY 11954, (516) 668-2554. 4.0 miles. (ANY; MNE; GNA)

2681 **Montezuma National Wildlife Refuge**, Rt. 1, Box 1412, SR 5, Seneca Falls, NY 13148, (315) 568-5987. Named trails: Esker Brook Walking 1.4, Storage Pool Dyke 7.0. (ANY; DMA; GNA; GNW)

2682 **Montgomery Place**, SR 9G, Annandale-on-Hudson, NY 12504, (914) 758-5461. (MNE)

Moore's Trail see entry 2412.

Moose River Plains Trail see entry 2412.

2683 **Moreau Lake State Park**, US 9, Glens Falls, NY 12801, (518) 793-0511. (ANY; WCD)

2684 **Morgan Hill State Forest**, Regional Forester, Region 7, P.O. Box 1169, Cortland, NY 13045, (607) 753-3095. (GNA)

2685 **Morton National Wildlife Refuge**, Noyack Rd., Southampton, NY 11968, (516) 286-0485. 1.0 mile. (ANY; MNE; OTB)

Moss Lake Circuit Trail see entry 2412.

2686 **Mt. Beacon-Breakneck Ridge-Mt. Taurus Region**, New York-New Jersey Trail Conference, 232 Madison Ave., Rm. 908, New York, NY 10116, (212) 685-9699. Named trails: Breakneck Ridge, Casino 2.3(s), Three Notch 8.0(s), Washburn 2.0(s). (NYW)

Mount Blue Trail see entry 2412.

2687 **Mt. Kenyon Family Campground**, SR 9N, Lake Luzerne, NY 12846, (518) 696-2905. (WCD)

Mt. Taurus to Phillips Brook see entry 2473.

2688 **Mount Tom State Forest**, Regional Forester, Region 5, P.O. Box 220, Hudson St. Ext., Warrensburg, NY 12885, (518) 623-3671. (GNA)

Mountain Spring Trail see entry 2418.

Murphy Lake from Creek Road see entry 2412.

Murphy Lake from Pumpkin Hollow Road *see* entry 2412.

Murphy, Middle and Bernet Lakes Trail *see* entry 2412.

2689 **Museum of the Hudson Highlands**, The Boulevard, Cornwall-on-Hudson, NY 12520, (914) 534-7781. (NNY)

Muskrat Pond Trail *see* entry 2412.

2690 **Muttontown Nature Preserve**, Muttontown Ln., East Norwich, NY 11732, (516) 922-3123. (NNY)

2691 **Nathan Hale Historic Trail**, Howard Gray, 31 Turtle Cove Ln., Huntington, NY 11743-3867. 18.5 miles straight. Awards available. (AA 1992)

2692 **Nathaniel Cole Park**, Colesville Rd., Kirkwood, NY 13795. (ANY)

Nehasane Preserve Trail *see* entry 2412.

Neversink-Hardenburg Trail *see* entry 2474.

2693 **New York Central RR Former Rights of Way**, New York-New Jersey Trail Conference, 232 Madison Ave., Rm. 908, New York, NY 10116, (212) 685-9699. Named trails: Former Croton Lake Station to Lake Mahopac 10.5(s), Goldens Bridge to Lake Mahopac 7.2(s), Millwood to Croton Reservoir 30.0(s). (NYW)

2694 **Newton Battlefield Reservation**, SR 7, Elmira, NY 14901. (ANY)

2695 **Niagara Frontier Trail**, Greater Niagara Frontier Council, BSA, 401 Maryvale Dr., Cheektowaga, NY 14225. 30.0 miles auto tour. Awards available. (SAR 1994)

2696 **Niagara Reservation State Park**, Robert Moses Pkwy., Niagara Falls, NY 14302, (716) 278-1770. (SAR 1994)

Nicks Lake Circuit Trail *see* entry 2412.

2697 **Nissequogue River State Park**, Jericho Tpk., Smithtown, NY 11787, (516) 265-1054. 5.0 miles. (NNY; GNA)

Norridgewock Trail *see* entry 2412.

2698 **North Bay Park**, SR 3, Fulton, NY 13069, (315) 593-3408. (MNE)

2699 **North Country Trail** (see separate entry **4955** in interstate section).

2700 **North County Trailway**, Director of Park Facilities, Westchester County Department of Parks, Recreation and Conservation, 19 Bradhurst Ave., Hawthorne, NY 10532, (914) 285-7275. 10.0 miles straight. (GRT)

North Crossover Snowmobile Trail *see* entry 2412.

North Lake Campground to NY 23A *see* entry 2474.

North Lake to Notch Point *see* entry 2474.

Northville-Placid Trail *see* entry 2412.

Nurian Trail *see* entry 2425.

Nyack Circular Trail *see* entry 2712.

2701 **Oak Orchard Wildlife Management Area**, 12465 Podunk Rd., Medina, NY 14103. 10.0 miles. (MNE; NYP; GNA)

2702 **Oakland Valley Campground**, CR 7, Cuddebackville, NY 12729, (914) 754-8732. (WCD)

2703 **Ogden and Ruth Livingston Mills Memorial**, Old Post Rd., Hyde Park, NY 12538. (ANY)

Old Croton Aqueduct Hiking Trail *see* entry 2804.

2704 **Old Erie Canal State Park**, 122 Canal St., Canastota, NY 13032, (315) 687-7821. (MNE)

2705 **The Old New York Historical Trail**, Pat Golland c/o Bain, Historical Trail Committee, Man-A-Hattin Lodge 82, W.W.W., 10 Park Ave. #4J, New York, NY 10016, (212) 242-1100 ext. 240. 5.3 miles. Awards available. (AA 1992)

Ongiara Trail *see* entry 2821.

2706 **Oquaga Creek Park**, SR 206, Sidney, NY 13838. (ANY)

Oregon Road to Croton Reservoir *see* entry 2473.

Oregon Trail *see* entry 2666.

Oregon Trail to Stewart Creek Flow *see* entry 2412.

2707 **Orient Beach**, SR 25, Orient, NY 11957. (ANY)

2708 **Oswego Recreational Trail**, Darrell Kehoe, Crew Leader, Oswego County Highway Department, 46 E. Bridge St., Oswego, NY 13126, (315) 349-8331. 26.0 miles straight. (GRT)

2709 **Otsinigo Park**, US 11, Binghamton, NY 13902. (ANY)

NEW YORK 171

Otter Creek-Pine Lake Trail *see* entry 2412.

Otter Lake Outlet Trail *see* entry 2412.

2710 **Outlet Trail**, Virginia H. Gibbs, County Historian, 110 Court St., Penn Yan, NY 14527, (315) 536-5147. 7.5 miles straight. (GRT; MNE)

Owls Head Mountain Trail *see* entry 2412.

Paint Mine Ruins Trail *see* entry 2412.

2711 **Palisades Interstate Park**, Palisades Interstate Park Commission, Bear Mountain State Park, Bear Mountain, NY 10911, (914) 786-2701. Named trails: Long Path 27.25(s), Shore 11.0(s). (MNE; NNY)

2712 **Palisades Ridge**, New York-New Jersey Trail Conference, 232 Madison Ave., Rm. 908, New York, NY 10116, (212) 685-9699. Named trails: Nyack Circular 6.5(l), Piermont. (HFI; NYW)

2713 **Panama Rocks Park**, SR 474, Panama, NY 14767, (716) 728-2845. (MNE)

Panther Pond-Independence River Trail *see* entry 2412.

Panther Pond Loop Trail *see* entry 2412.

2714 **Paradise Park Campground**, P.O. Box 99, Reading Center, NY 14876, (607) 535-6600. (WCD)

2715 **Partridge Run Wildlife Management Area**, New York Department of Environmental Conservation, SR 10, Stamford, NY 12167, (607) 652-7364. 19.0 miles. (GNA)

Peaked Hill Trail *see* entry 2412.

Peaked Mountain Trail *see* entry 2412.

Pecoy Notch Trail *see* entry 2474.

2716 **Pelham Bay Park**, Supervisor, Urban Park Rangers—Bronx, Van Cortlandt Stadium, Van Cortlandt Park South, Broadway & 242nd St., Bronx, NY 10471, (212) 822-4336. (NNY)

2717 **Pelham Bay Park Historic Trail**, Greater New York Councils, BSA, 345 Hudson St., New York, NY 10014, (212) 242-1100. Awards available. (NHT)

Pepperbox Access Trail *see* entry 2412.

2718 **Perch River Wildlife Management Area**, Bureau of Wildlife, New York Department of Environmental Conservation, 317 Washington St., Watertown, NY 13601, (315) 782-0100. (GNA)

Pharaoh Lake Trail *see* entry 2412.

Pharaoh Mountain Firetower Trail *see* entry 2412.

Pharaoh Mountain Trail *see* entry 2412.

Pharaoh Ponds Loop Trail *see* entry 2412.

2719 **Phillips Creek State Forest**, Regional Forester, Region 9, Rt. 1, Box 4, Jamestown, NY 14701, (716) 484-7161. (GNA)

Phoenicia-East Branch Trail *see* entry 2474.

Piermont Trail *see* entry 2712.

Pillsbury Mountain Trail *see* entry 2412.

Pine Creek Loop Trail *see* entry 2412.

Pine Hill/Eagle Mountain/West Branch Trail *see* entry 2474.

Pine Lake Trail *see* entry 2412.

Pine Meadow Trail *see* entry 2425.

Pine Mountain Trail *see* entry 2412.

Pine Orchard and Jimmy Creek Trail *see* entry 2412.

Pine Orchard from Pumpkin Hollow Road *see* entry 2412.

Pine Orchard Trail *see* entry 2412.

2720 **Pine Valley Campground**, Boswell Hill Rd., Endicott, NY 13760, (607) 785-6868. (WCD)

Pinetum Trail *see* entry 2424.

2721 **Pinnacle Park**, Ackerson Rd., Addison, NY 14801. (ANY)

Pioneer Trail *see* entry 2506.

Piseco to Upper Benson-NP Trail *see* entry 2412.

Pitchoff Mountain Trail *see* entry 2412.

Pitobik Trail *see* entry 2414.

Pittsboro Hollow Trail *see* entry 2425.

2722 **Pixley Falls Park**, SR 46, Boonville, NY 13309. (ANY)

Plains Trail *see* entry 2412.
2723 **Planting Fields Arboretum**, Planting Fields Rd., Oyster Bay, NY 11771, (516) 922-9206. (MNE)
2724 **Point Au Roche Park**, SR 9, Plattsburgh, NY 12901. (ANY)
Pokamoonshine Mountain Trail *see* entry 2412.
Popolopen Gorge Trail *see* entry 2425.
2725 **Pop's Lake Campground**, Centerline Rd., Galway, NY 12074, (518) 883-8678. (WCD)
2726 **Portage Trail**, Allegheny Highlands Council, BSA, 50 Hough Hill Rd., P.O. Box 0261, Falconer, NY 14733-0261, (716) 665-2697. 11.5-13.5 miles straight. Awards available. (SAR 1991)
Prospect Mountain Trail *see* entry 2412.
2727 **Prospect Park**, NYC Department of Parks and Recreation, 64th St. & Fifth Ave., New York, NY 10021, (212) 360-1350; or Supervisor, Urban Park Rangers—Brooklyn, NYC Department of Parks & Recreation, 95 Prospect Park W., Brooklyn, NY 11215, (212) 856-4210. (NAT; NNY)
2728 **Putnam Pond State Public Campground**, SR 74, Ticonderoga, NY 12883, (518) 585-7280. (MNE)
Quartz Brook Trail *see* entry 2425.
Queer Lake Trail *see* entry 2412.
Raccoon Brook Hills Trail *see* entry 2425.
2729 **Rainbow Valley Campground**, High St., Bloomingburg, NY 12721, (914) 733-4767. (WCD)
Ramapo-Dunderberg Trail *see* entry 2425.
Raquette Lake-West Mountain Trail *see* entry 2412.
2730 **Rattlesnake Hill Wildlife Management Area**, P.O. Box 57, Avon, NY 14414, (716) 226-2466. 15.0 miles. (GNA)
Ravine Trail *see* entry 2666.
2731 **Raymond Esposito Trail**, Mary Martini, Village Clerk, Village Hall, 282 S. Broadway, Village of South Nyack, NY 10960, (914) 358-0287. 1.0 mile straight. (GRT)

Razorback Pond Trail *see* entry 2412.
Red Arrow Trail *see* entry 2425.
Red Cross Trail *see* entry 2425.
Red Horse Trail *see* entry 2412.
Red Trail *see* entry 2806.
Reeves Brook Trail *see* entry 2425.
Remsen Falls-Nelson Lake Loop Trail *see* entry 2412.
2732 **Rensselaerville State Forest**, Regional Forester, Region 4, Jefferson Rd., Stamford, NY 12167, (607) 652-7364. (GNA)
2733 **Reservoir Park**, SR 265 & 31, Niagara Falls, NY 14302. (ANY)
Reservoir Path *see* entry 2482.
Rhododendron Trail *see* entry 2424.
2734 **Richard "Bull" Smith Historical Trail**, Frank Klem, 15 Tanglewood Dr., Smithtown, NY 11787; or Explorer Post 1776, P.O. Box 3, Smithtown, NY 11787. 21.0 miles. Awards available. (HTA)
Richmontown Circular *see* entry 2768.
Rim Trail *see* entry 2450.
2735 **Rip Van Winkle Campground**, 14 Robinson St., Saugerties, NY 12477, (914) 246-8334. (WCD)
River Trail *see* entry 2810.
River Trail *see* entry 2816.
2736 **Riverforest Park**, 2526 River Forest Rd., Weedsport, NY 13166, (315) 834-9458 or (800) 772-2644. (WCD)
Roaring Brook Trail *see* entry 2412.
2737 **Robert H. Treman State Park**, SR 327, Newfield, NY 14867, (607) 273-3440. 8.0 miles. (WCD; DMA; GNA)
2738 **Robert Moses State Park**, SR 37, Massena, NY 13662, (315) 769-8663. (ANY; WCD; GNA)
2739 **Rochester, Syracuse and Eastern Trail**, David R. Morgan, Director of Parks, 1350 Turk Hill Rd., Fairport, NY 14450, (716) 223-5050. 8.0 miles straight planned, current as to 5.0 miles. (GRT)
Rock, Cascade and Stephens Ponds Trail *see* entry 2412.
2740 **Rock City Park Nature Trail**, SR 16, Olean, NY 14760, (716) 372-7790. 45 minutes. (DBV; OTB)
Rock Dam Trail *see* entry 2412.

NEW YORK

Rock Pond-Clear Pond Trail *see* entry 2412.
2741 **Rockland Lake Park**, US 9W, Nyack, NY 10960. (ANY)
Rocky Mountain Trail *see* entry 2412.
2742 **Rogers Environmental Education Center**, SR 80, Sherburne, NY 13460, (607) 674-4017. (ANY; MNE)
2743 **Rolling Acres Campground**, Pike Rd., Phoenicia, NY 12464, (716) 587-8557. (WCD)
2744 **Rosemond Campground & Motel**, P.O. Box 11, Woodridge, NY 12789, (914) 434-7433. (WCD)
2745 **Rotary Scout Training Center**, Governor Clinton Council, BSA, 257 Osborne Rd., Loudenville, NY 12211, (518) 459-5170. (SFC)
Round Pond-Long Lake Trail *see* entry 2412.
Round Pond via Mud Pond *see* entry 2412.
Roundtop Mountain Trail *see* entry 2412.
2746 **Royal Mountain Campsite**, Rt. 2, Box 177, Johnstown, NY 12095, (518) 762-1946. (WCD)
2747 **Russell Brook Campsite**, Russell Brook Rd., Cooks Falls/Roscoe, NY 12776, (607) 498-5416. (WCD)
Russian Lake Trail *see* entry 2412.
Safford Pond Trail *see* entry 2412.
Sagamore Cascades Trail *see* entry 2412.
Sagamore Ponds North Trail *see* entry 2412.
Saint Regis Mountain Trail *see* entry 2412.
2748 **Sampson State Park**, SR 96A, Geneva, NY 14456, (315) 585-6392. (ANY; WCD; MNE)
Sand Lake Falls Trail *see* entry 2412.
Sand Lake Trail *see* entry 2412.
2749 **Sands Point Park & Preserve**, 95 Middleneck Rd., Port Washington, NY 11050, (516) 883-1612. (ANY; NNY)
Santanoni Preserve Trail *see* entry 2412.
2750 **Saranac Lakes Park**, SR 3W, Saranac Lake, NY 12982. (ANY)

2751 **Saratoga Battlefield Historical Trail**, Saratoga County Council, BSA, 204 Malta Ave., Ballston Spa, NY 12020; or Saratoga National Historical Park, Rt. 1, Box 113-C, Stillwater, NY 12170, (518) 664-9821. 10.0 miles. Awards available. (ANY; PGF; DMA; NPE; CGA; HTA; NPG)
2752 **Saratoga Spa State Park**, I-87 exit 13N, Saratoga Springs, NY 12866, (518) 584-2535 or (518) 587-3330. (ANY)
Sargent Pond East Trail *see* entry 2412.
Scenic Mountain Trail *see* entry 2412.
2753 **Schroon River Campsite**, Horion Ave., Warrensburg, NY 12885, (518) 623-2171. (WCD)
2754 **Schunemunk Mountain**, New York-New Jersey Trail Conference, 232 Madison Ave., Rm. 908, New York, NY 10116, (212) 685-9699; or Mountainville Conservancy, Mountainville, NY 10953. 20.0 miles. Named trails: Barton Swamp, Dark Hollow, Forrest 2.3, Jessup 8.1, Sweet Clover 2.8, Western Ridge 2.3. (NYW)
2755 **Schuyler State Forest**, Regional Forester, Region 8, 115 Liberty St., Bath, NY 14810, (607) 776-2165. (GNA)
Scusa Access Trail *see* entry 2412.
Seager-Dry Brook Trail *see* entry 2474.
Seager-Shandaken Brook Trail *see* entry 2474.
2756 **Selkirk Shores State Park**, SR 3, Oswego, NY 13126, (315) 298-5737. (ANY; WCD; MNE)
2757 **Seton Falls Park**, New York City Department of Parks and Recreation, 64th St. & Fifth Ave., New York, NY 10021, (212) 360-1350. (NAT)
Seven Hills Trail *see* entry 2425.
Seventh Lake-Black Bear Mountain Trail *see* entry 2412.
Severance Hill Trail *see* entry 2412.
Shallow Lake Trail *see* entry 2412.
2758 **Shangri-La Camping Sites**, 3852 SR 98, Franklinville, NY 14737, (716) 676-2413 or (800) 866-2267. (WCD)
Shanty Hollow-Colonel's Chair Trail *see* entry 2474.

2759 **Sheldrake River,** Conservation Advisory Committee, Town of Mamaroneck, 740 W. Boston Post Rd., Mamaroneck, NY 10543, (914) 698-4929. (NNY)
  Sheriff Lake Trail *see* entry 2412.
  Sherwood Path *see* entry 2425.
2760 **Shindagin Hollow State Forest,** Regional Forester, Region 7, P.O. Box 1169, Cortland, NY 13045, (607) 753-3093. (GNA)
  Shingle Mill Falls Trail *see* entry 2412.
2761 **Shirley Path,** Lake Minnewaska Mountain Houses, Inc., Lake Minnewaska, New Paltz, NY 12561. (NYW)
  Shore Trail *see* entry 2711.
  Short Swing Trail *see* entry 2412.
  Siamese Ponds Trail *see* entry 2412.
  Silvermine and East Bridge Trails *see* entry 2412.
  Sister Lake Trail *see* entry 2412.
  Six Chins Trail *see* entry 2425.
  Six Mile Creek Trail *see* entry 2412.
2762 **Skaneateles Nature Trail,** Matthew Major, Recreation Supervisor, 24 Jordan St., Skaneateles, NY 13152, (315) 685-6726. 2.0 miles straight. (GRT)
  Skannatai Trail *see* entry 2425.
2763 **Skybrook Campground,** McCurdy Rd., Dansville, NY 14437, (716) 335-6880. (WCD)
2764 **Skyway Camping Resort,** P.O. Box 194, Greenfield Park, NY 12435, (914) 647-5747. (WCD)
  Sly Pond Trail *see* entry 2412.
  Snake Pond Trail *see* entry 2412.
  Snowy Mountain Trail *see* entry 2412.
  South Lake Trail *see* entry 2412.
2765 **South Shore Nature Center,** Department of Parks, Recreation & Cultural Affairs, Islip, NY 11751, (516) 224-5436. (NNY)
  South Taconic Trail *see* entry 2780.
2766 **Southwick Beach State Park,** SR 3, Woodville, NY 13698, (315) 846-5338. (ANY; WCD; GNA)
  Spectacle Lake from NY 10 *see* entry 2412.
  Spectacle Pond Trail *see* entry 2412.
2767 **Spruce Row Campsite,** 164 Kraft Rd., Ithaca, NY 14850, (607) 387-9225. (WCD)
  Spy Rock Trail *see* entry 2810.
  Squaw Lake Trail *see* entry 2412.
2768 **Staten Island Greenbelt,** Director, Conservation & The Outdoors, P.O. Box 284, New York, NY 10031, (212) 721-8156. 35.0 miles. Named trails: Richmontown Circular 13.0. (NNY)
2769 **Staten Island Recreation Trails,** Staten Island Unit, Gateway National Recreation Area, P.O. Box 37, Staten Island, NY 10306, (212) 351-8700. (NNY)
  Steam Mill-Spring Hill Trail *see* entry 2412.
  Steps Trail *see* entry 2474.
2770 **Stewart's Pond Campsite,** Antone Rd., Hadley, NY 12835, (518) 696-2779. (WCD)
  Stillwater Mountain Trail *see* entry 2412.
  Stone Dam Lake and Chub Pond Trail *see* entry 2412.
  Stone Dam Trail *see* entry 2412.
2771 **Stony Brook State Park,** SR 36, Dansville, NY 14437, (716) 335-8111. (ANY; WCD; MNE)
2772 **Stony Brook Walking Tour,** Stony Brook Village Center, P.O. Box 572, Stony Brook, NY 11790, (516) 751-2244. (ANY; WCD; MNE)
2773 **Stony Point Battlefield,** US 9W, Stony Point, NY 10980. (GNA)
  Storage Pool Dyke Trail *see* entry 2681.
2774 **Storm King-Black Rock Forest,** New York-New Jersey Trail Conference, 232 Madison Ave., Rm. 908, New York, NY 10116, (212) 685-9699; or Palisades Interstate Park Commission, Bear Mountain State Park, Bear Mountain, NY 10911, (914) 786-2701. Named trails: Arthur, Black Rock Hollow, Chatfield, Compartment, Hall of Pines, Huber, Ledge, Reservoir, Ryerson, Sachett Mountain 1.5, Scenic 7.2, Secor, Stillman 10.5, Stropel, Sutherland, Swamp, White Oak. (GOP; NYW)
  Sucker Brook Bay Trail *see* entry 2412.
  Suffern-Bear Mountain Trail *see* entry 2425.

NEW YORK

2775 **Sugar Creek Glen Campground**, P.O. Box 143W, Dansville, NY 14437, (716) 335-6294. (WCD)

Sugar Loaf Trail see entry 2468.

2776 **Sullivan County Rail-Trail**, Peter Rhulen, Sullivan County Rails-to-Trails Conservancy, Inc., 217 Broadway, Monticello, NY 12701, (914) 794-8000 ext. 222. 14.0 miles straight. (GRT)

Sunday Creek Trail see entry 2412.
Sunday Lake Trail see entry 2412.

2777 **Sunken Meadow State Park**, Sunken Meadow State Pkwy., Kings Park, NY 11754, (516) 269-4333. (ANY; MNE; DBV; DMA; NNY)

Swallow Hollow Trail see entry 2597.
Swamp Cypress Trail see entry 2424.
Sweet Clover Trail see entry 2754.

2778 **Swiss Trail Campsites**, SR 9N, Lake Luzerne, NY 12846, (518) 696-3591. (WCD)

T Lake Falls Trail see entry 2412.

2779 **Tackapausha Museum and Preserve**, Washington Ave., Seaford, NY 11783, (516) 785-2802 or 292-4266. (ANY; NYO; NNY)

2780 **Taconic State Park**, SR 344, Copake Falls, NY 12517, (518) 329-3993. 25.0 miles. Named trails: South Taconic. (ANY; WCD; EGH; MNE; GNA)

2781 **Target Rock National Wildlife Refuge**, Lloyd Neck, Huntington, Long Island, NY 11743, (516) 271-2409. (MNE; GNW)

2782 **Taughannock Falls State Park**, SR 89, Ithaca, NY 14850, (607) 387-3639. 8.0 miles. (ANY; WCD; MNE; DBV; DMA; OTB)

2783 **Teatown Lake Reservation**, Spring Valley Rd., Ossining, NY 10562, (914) 762-2912. 12.0 miles. (ANY; NNY)

2784 **Ten Mile River Historic Trail**, Ten Mile River Scout Camps, 1481 CR 26, Narrowsburg, NY 12764, (914) 252-3911 ext. 160. 36.0 miles straight. Awards available. (AA 1994)

Tenant Creek Falls Trail see entry 2412.

2785 **Terry Mountain State Forest**, Regional Forester, Region 5, Ray Brook, NY 12977, (518) 891-1370. (GNA)

2786 **Theodore Roosevelt Memorial Sanctuary & Trailside Museum**, Cove Rd., Oyster Bay, NY 11771, (516) 922-3200. (MNE)

Third Lake from NY 10 see entry 2412.

2787 **Thompson's Lake State Park**, SR 157A, East Berne, NY 12059, (518) 872-1674. (ANY; WCD)

Three Lakes Trail see entry 2418.
Three Notch Trail see entry 2686.

2788 **Tifft Farm Nature Preserve**, 1200 Furhmann Blvd., Buffalo, NY 14240. (GFA)

Timp-Torne Trail see entry 2425.
Tioga Point Trail see entry 2412.
Tirrell Pond Trail see entry 2412.

2789 **Titusville Mountain State Forest**, Regional Forester, Region 5, Ray Brook, NY 12977, (518) 891-1370. (GNA)

2790 **Tonawanda Wildlife Management Area**, Bureau of Wildlife, New York Department of Conservation, P.O. Box 57, Avon, NY 14414, (716) 226-2466. 30.0 miles. (GNA)

Tongue Mountain Range Trail see entry 2412.

2791 **Top-A-Rise Camping Area**, Dean School Rd., Falconer, NY 14733, (716) 287-3222. (WCD)

Tower Trail see entry 2425.
Trail to Marcy from Elk Lake see entry 2412.

2792 **Trail's End Campsite**, Hinckley Rd., Hinckley, NY 13438, (315) 826-7220. (WCD)

Treadway Mountain Trail see entry 2412.
Treman Lake Trail see entry 2425.
Tremper Mountain Trail see entry 2474.
Triangle Trail see entry 2425.

2793 **Triple-R Campground**, 3487 Bryant Hill Rd., Franklinville, NY 14737, (716) 676-3856. (WCD)

2794 **Trumansburg Area**, Podunk Home Hostel, Podunk Rd., Trumansburg, NY 14886, (607) 387-9277. (AYH)

2795 **Tug Hill State Forest**, Regional Forester, Region 6, Rt. 3, Lowville, NY 13367, (315) 376-3521. (GNA)

2796 **Tug Hill Wildlife Management Area**, Bureau of Wildlife, 317 Washington St., Watertown, NY 13601, (315) 782-0100 ext. 311. 4.8 miles. (GNA)

2797 **Tumble Hill Campground**, 10551 Atlanta Back Rd., Cohocton, NY 14826, (716) 384-5248. (WCD)

Turtle Pond Interpretive Trail see entry 2541.

Turtle Pond Trail see entry 2414.

Tuxedo-Mount Ivy Trail see entry 2425.

Twin Lakes Dam Trail see entry 2412.

2798 **Udalls Cove Wildlife Preserve**, Aurora Gareiss, President, Udalls Cove Preservation Committee, Inc., 3107 Douglas Rd., Douglastown, NY 11363, (212) 229-4809. (NAT; NNY)

Uncas Road-Black Bear Mountain Trail see entry 2412.

Uncas Road-Mohegan Lake Trail see entry 2412.

Uncas Trail see entry 2412.

2799 **Uncle Sam Bikeway**, Robert J. Weaver, Commissioner, Troy Parks and Recreation Department, 1 Monument Sq., Troy, NY 12180, (518) 270-4600. 3.8 miles straight. (GRT)

2800 **Up the Creek Campground**, SR 3, Woodville, NY 13698, (315) 846-5809. (WCD)

2801 **Upper and Lower Lakes Wildlife Management Area**, Bureau of Wildlife, 317 Washington St., Watertown, NY 13601, (315) 782-0100 ext. 311. (GNA)

Upper Works Trail see entry 2412.

2802 **Valeria Home Trail**, Manager, Valeria Home, Oscawana, NY 10561. 4.0 miles loop. (NYW)

2803 **Valley Stream State Park**, Southern State Pkwy., Valley Stream, NY 11580, (516) 825-4128. (NNY)

2804 **Van Cortlandt Park**, Supervisor, Urban Park Rangers—Bronx, Van Cortlandt Stadium, Van Cortlandt Park South, Broadway & 242nd St., Bronx, NY 10471, (212) 822-4336. Named trails: Old Croton Aqueduct Hiking. (NNY)

Van Hoevenberg Trail see entry 2412.

Vanderwhacker Mountain Trail see entry 2412.

2805 **Verona Beach State Park**, SR 13, Oneida, NY 13421, (315) 762-4463. (ANY; MNE)

Vista Trail see entry 2412.

2806 **Vroman's Nose Historic Trail**, Otschodela Council, BSA, P.O. Box 1356, Oneonta, NY 13820-1356, (607) 432-6491. 1.8 miles loop (includes Blue, Red and Yellow Trails). Awards available. (AA 1994)

2807 **Wagon Wheel Campground**, CR 74, Prattsburg, NY 14873, (607) 522-3270. (WCD)

Wakely Mountain Trail see entry 2412.

2808 **Wakonda Family Campground**, HCR 1, Box 40, River Rd., Pottersville, NY 12860, (518) 494-2610. (WCD)

2809 **Wallkill Valley Rail Trail**, Roland Bahret, Wallkill Valley Rail-Trail Association, Inc., P.O. Box 1048, New Paltz, NY 12561, (914) 255-1436. 8.7 miles straight. (GRT)

2810 **Ward Pound Ridge Reservation**, P.O. Box 461, Cross River, NY 10518, (914) 763-3993 or (914) 763-3493. 35.0 miles. Named trails: Fire Tower, River, Spy Rock. (ANY; EGH; MNE; ANI; NNY)

2811 **Warren County Bikeway**, Patrick Beland, Director, Warren County Parks and Recreation Department, 261 Main St., Warrensburg, NY 12855, (518) 623-2877. 10.0 miles straight. (GRT)

Washburn Trail see entry 2686.

2812 **Watkins Glen State Park**, SR 414, Watkins Glen, NY 14891, (607) 535-4511. 10.0 miles. Named trails: Indian. (ANY; WCD; DMA; GNA)

2813 **Wellesley Island State Park**, SR 12, Alexandria Bay, NY 13607, (315) 482-2722. 20.0 miles. (ANY; WCD; MNE; GNA)

2814 **Wertheim National Wildlife Refuge**, Smith St. S., Shirley, NY 11967, (516) 286-0485. (ANY; MNE)

West Canada Lake Trail see entry 2412.

West Pond Trail see entry 2599.

NEW YORK

2815 **West Side Trail State Forest**, Regional Forester, Region 9, Rt. 1, Box 4, Jamestown, NY 14701, (716) 484-7161. Named trails: Chatauqua West 15.0. (GNA)

2816 **Westchester County**, New York-New Jersey Trail Conference, 232 Madison Ave., Rm. 908, New York, NY 10116, (212) 685-9699. Named trails: Blue Mountain and Spinzenberg Circular 5.0(l), River. (NYW)

2817 **Westchester County Historic Trail**, Westchester-Putnam Council, BSA, 1000 North St., White Plains, NY 10605-5198, (914) 949-6180. Varying mileage auto tour. Awards available. (AA 1994)

2818 **Westcott Beach State Park**, SR 3, Sackets Harbor, NY 13685, (315) 938-5083. (ANY; MNE)

Western Ridge Trail see entry 2754.

2819 **Westmoreland Sanctuary**, Director/Naturalist, Westmoreland Sanctuary, Chestnut Ridge Rd., Mt. Kisco, NY 10549, (914) 666-8448. 10.0 miles. (NNY)

2820 **Whetstone Gulf State Park**, Bureau of Wildlife, SR 12D, Lowville, NY 13367, (315) 376-6630. 5.0 miles. (WCD; GNA)

2821 **Whirlpool State Park**, Robert Moses Pkwy., Niagara Falls, NY 14301, (716) 278-1770. Named trails: Ongiara. (SAR 1994)

2822 **Whispering Woods Campground**, Walker Rd., Long Lake, NY 12847, (518) 624-5121. (WCD)

2823 **White Birches Campsites**, Nauvoo Rd., Windham, NY 12496, (518) 734-3266. (WCD)

White Cross Trail see entry 2425.

White's Pond Trail see entry 2412.

Wilcox Lake from Brownell Camp via E. Stony Creek Trail see entry 2412.

Wilcox Lake from Willis Lake see entry 2412.

Wilderness Lakes Tract Access Trail see entry 2412.

Wildflower Walk see entry 2424.

2824 **Wildwood State Park**, SR 25A, Wading River, NY 11792, (516) 929-4314. (ANY; WCD)

2825 **Wilkinson Trail-Saratoga Battlefield**, Saratoga County Council, BSA, 204 Malta Ave., Ballston Spa, NY 12020, (518) 885-5352. Awards available. (NHT)

2826 **Wilmington Recreation Area**, SR 86, Wilmington, NY 12997, (518) 946-7172. (MNE)

2827 **Wilson Hill Wildlife Management Area**, Bureau of Wildlife, 317 Washington St., Watertown, NY 13601, (315) 782-0100 ext. 311. 0.5 mile. (GNA)

2828 **Wilson M. Powell Wildlife Sanctuary**, Alan Devoe Bird Club, Old Chatham, NY 12136, (518) 794-7434. (ANI)

Wilson Pond Trail see entry 2412.

2829 **Wilson-Tuscarora State Park**, SR 18, Wilson, NY 14172. (ANY)

2830 **Winding Hills County Park**, 500 SR 416, Montgomery, NY 12549, (914) 457-5950. (WCD)

Winnisook Lodge/Slide Trail see entry 2474.

2831 **Wintergreen Park**, Canajoharie, NY 13317, (518) 673-5508. (GFA)

Wittenberg/Cornell/Slide/Winnisook/Woodland Valley Trail see entry 2474.

Wolf Lake Landing Road see entry 2412.

2832 **Wolfe's Pond Park**, Urban Park Rangers–Staten Island, Clove Lakes/Silver Lake Parks, 1150 Clove Rd., Staten Island, NY 10301, (212) 442-1304 or (212) 442-7640. (NNY)

2833 **Wood Ridge Camping Area**, Wood Ridge Ln., Little Valley, NY 14755, (716) 938-6767. (WCD)

Woodhull Mountain Trail see entry 2412.

Woodhull Road Trail see entry 2412.

2834 **Woodland Hills Campground**, 86 Fog Hill Rd., Austerlitz, NY 12017, (518) 392-3557. (WCD)

2835 **Woodstock on the Lake Campground**, Darling Rd., Bethel, NY 12720, (914) 583-6210. (WCD)

2836 **Woodstream Campsite**, 5440 School Rd., Gainesville, NY 14066, (716) 493-5643. (WCD)

Yanty Creek Nature Trail see entry 2571.

2837 **Yawger Brook Family Campsites**, Rt. 3, Auburn, NY 13021, (315) 252-8969. (WCD)

Yellow Trail *see* entry 2806.
2838 **Yogi Bear's Jellystone Park**, SR 373, Port Kent, NY 12975, (518) 834-9011. (WCD)

Generally:
New York Department of Environmental Conservation, 30 Court St., P.O. Box 109, Canton, NY 13617. (GFC)
New York - New Jersey Trail Conference, 232 Madison Ave., Rm. 908, New York, NY 10116, (212) 685-9699. (EGH)

Index (by city)

Addison: Pinnacle Park 2721
Albany: Erie Canal Towpath 2527; Mohawk-Hudson Bikeway 2676
Albion: Lakeside Beaches State Park 2637
Alexandria Bay: Keewaydin State Park 2612; Kring Point State Park 2630; Minna Anthony Common Nature Center 2672; Wellesley Island State Park 2813
Ancram: Lake Taghkanic State Park 2636
Annandale-on-Hudson: Montgomery Place 2682
Ashford Hollow: Griffis Sculpture Park 2569
Attica: Carlton Hill State Forest 2471
Auburn: Cayuga County Trail 2477; Yawger Brook Family Campsites 2837
Ausable Chasm: KOA-Ausable Chasm 2619
Austerlitz: Woodland Hills Campground 2834
Averill Park: Alps Family Campground 2416
Avon: Rattlesnake Hill Wildlife Management Area 2730
Babylon: Belmont Lake State Park 2430; Massapequa State Park Trail 2661
Baldwinsville: Beaver Lake Nature Center 2429; KOA-Syracuse 2627
Ballston Spa: Saratoga Battlefield Historical Trail 2751; Wilkinson Trail-Saratoga Battlefield 2825
Barcelona: Portage Trail 2726
Barker: Golden Hill State Park 2562
Barnes Corners: Tug Hill State Forest 2795
Barryville: Kittatinny Campgrounds 2618
Bason: Iroquois National Wildlife Refuge 2597
Batavia: Lei-Ti Campground 2644
Bath: Hickory Hill Family Campground 2577

Bear Mountain: Harriman Long Path National Recreation Trail 2573; Hook Mountain 2589; Palisades Interstate Park 2711; Storm King-Black Rock Forest 2774
Berne: Partridge Run Wildlife Management Area 2715
Bethel: Woodstock on the Lake Campground 2835
Bethpage: Bethpage State Park 2433
Binghamton: Otsinigo Park 2709
Bloomingburg: Rainbow Valley Campground 2729
Blue Mountain Lake: Blue Mountain Lake 2438
Boonville: Pixley Falls Park 2722
Brasher Falls: Brasher Falls State Forest 2443
Brooktondale: Shindagin Hollow State Forest 2760
Buffalo: Beaver Island State Park 2428; Buckhorn Island State Park 2447; Tifft Farm Nature Preserve 2788
Caledonia: Genesee Country Campground 2558
Cambridge: Lake Lauderdale Campground 2635
Campbell: Camp at Camp Bell Campground 2452
Canajoharie: Wintergreen Park 2831
Canandaigua: High Tor Wildlife Management Area 2581
Canastota: Old Erie Canal State Park 2704
Canton: Cranberry Lake Region 2503
Carmel: Clarence Fahnestock Memorial State Park 2489; Constitution Island Marsh Sanctuary 2496
Catskill: Cedar Grove Campgrounds 2479

NEW YORK Index 179

Cazenovia: Chittanango Falls State Park 2487; Gorge Trail 2563
Central Islip: Long Island Greenbelt Trail 2649
Chateaugay: Chateaugay-Winona State Forest 2483; High Falls Park Campground 2579
Chenango Forks: Chenango Valley State Park 2484
Cherry Valley: Cherry Valley State Forest 2486; Mohawk Campground 2674
Cobleskill: Burnt-Rossman Hills State Forest 2448
Cohocton: Tumble Hill Campground 2797
Conesus Lake: Conesus Lake Campground 2494
Cooks Falls/Roscoe: Russell Brook Campsite 2747
Cooperstown: Cooperstown Beaver Valley Campground 2497; Cooperstown Ringwood Farms Campground 2498; Glimmerglass State Park 2561
Copake Falls: Taconic State Park 2780
Corfu: Darien Lakes State Park 2512
Corinth: Alpine Lake Camping Resort 2415
Corning: Bradford State Forest 2442; Camp at Ferenbaugh 2453; Corning, Colonists, Cowboys and Crystal Historic Trail 2499
Cornwall: Black Rock Forest 2436; Catskills Forest Preserve 2474
Cornwall-on-Hudson: Museum of the Hudson Highlands 2689
Cortland: Bear Swamp and Summer Hill State Forests 2427; Cuyler Hill State Forest 2507
Cross River: Ward Pound Ridge Reservation 2810
Crown Point: Crown Point Reservation State Campground 2504
Cuddebackville: Oakland Valley Campground 2702
Danby: Danby State Forest 2510
Dansville: Skybrook Campground 2763; Stony Brook State Park 2771; Sugar Creek Glen Campground 2775
Darien Center: Darien Lake Nature Trail 2511
Dayton: Adirondack Adventure Treks 2409

Deer River: Deer River State Forest 2516
Douglastown: Alley Park 2414; Udalls Cove Wildlife Preserve Trail 2798
Dryden: Hammond Hill and Yellow Barn State Forest 2572
Duane: Debar Wildlife Management Area 2514; Deer River Campsite 2515
Dunkirk: Evangola State Park 2531; Lake Erie State Park 2632
East Berne: Thompson's Lake State Park 2787
East Islip: Heckscher State Park 2574
East Norwich: Muttontown Nature Preserve 2690
Edwards: Huckleberry Lake 2590
Elizabethtown: Adirondack Center Museum and Colonial Garden 2411
Ellenville: Ice Caves National Landmark 2594
Elmira: Elmira Historic Trail 2525; Newton Battlefield Reservation 2694
Endicott: Greenwood Park 2567; Pine Valley Campground 2720
Erwin: Erwin Wildlife Management Area 2529
Fairport: Rochester, Syracuse and Eastern Trail 2739
Falconer: Top-A-Rise Camping Area 2791
Fayetteville: Green Lakes State Park 2565
Five Corners: Phillips Creek State Forest 2719
Fonda: Mohawk-Caughnawaga Museum Nature Trail 2675
Forestport: Kayuta Lake Campground 2611
Fort Hunter: Erie Canal Trail 2528
Franklin: KOA-Unadilla/I-88/Oneonta 2628
Franklinville: Shangri-La Camping Sites 2758; Triple-R Campground 2793
French Creek: French Creek Wildlife Management Area 2551
Fulton: North Bay Park 2698
Gainesville: Woodstream Campsite 2836
Galway: McConchie's Heritage Acres 2663; Pop's Lake Campground 2725
Gardiner: Lazy River Campground 2641
Garrattsville: Crystal Lake Park 2505
Geneva: Sampson State Park 2748
Germantown: Clermont State Park 2492
Glen Cove: Garvies Point Museum & Preserve 2555

Glens Falls: Adirondack State Forest 2412; Moreau Lake State Park 2683
Gloversville: Camp Woodworth Lake 2467
Grafton: Grafton Lakes State Park 2564
Greenfield Park: Skyway Camping Resort 2764
Hadley: Stewart's Pond Campsite 2770
Haines Falls: Catskills State Forest 2475
Hamilton: Lebanon Reservoir Campground 2642
Hamlin: Hamlin Beach State Park 2571
Hammondsport: Hill 'N Hollow Campsites 2584
Hawthorne: North Country Trailway 2700
Herkimer: Camp Russell 2462; KOA-Herkimer Diamond Campground 2621
Hinckley: Trail's End Campsite 2792
Houghton: Hickory Lake Campground 2578
Huntington: Caumsett State Park 2476; Nathan Hale Historic Trail 2691; Target Rock National Wildlife Refuge 2781
Hyde Park: Eleanor Roosevelt Trails 2523; Franklin Roosevelt Home 2550; Ogden and Ruth Livingston Mills Memorial 2703
Inlet: Black Bear Mountain Trail 2435
Islip: South Shore Nature Center 2765
Italy Hill: Italy Hill State Forest 2598
Ithaca: Buttermilk Falls State Park 2450; East Ithaca Recreation Way 2522; Spruce Row Campsite 2767; Taughannock Falls State Park 2782
Jamaica: Jamaica Bay Wildlife Refuge 2600
Jamestown: Jamestown Audubon Nature Center 2603
Jamesville: Clark Reservation State Park 2490
Johnstown: Royal Mountain Campsite 2746
Keene: Cascade Mountain Trail 2472
Kennedy: Forest Haven Campground 2542
Kings Park: Sunken Meadow State Park 2777
Kirkwood: Nathaniel Cole Park 2692
Lake Clear Junction: Junction Campsite 2610
Lake George: Adirondack Camping Village 2410; Evergreen Camping Resort 2532; King Phillip's Campsite 2616; Lake George Area 2633; Lake George RV Park 2634

Lake Luzerne: Mt. Kenyon Family Campground 2687; Swiss Trail Campsites 2778
Lattingtown: Bailey Arboretum Nature Trail 2422
Leeds: Indian Ridge Campsite 2595
LeRoy: Frost Ridge Campground 2552
Lewis: Magic Pines RV Resort 2654
Little Valley: Little Valley State Forest 2647; Wood Ridge Camping Area 2833
Livingston: Livingston State Forest 2648
Livingston Manor: Covered Bridge Campsite 2501
Long Lake: Camp Sabattis 2463; Whispering Woods Campground 2822
Loudenville: Rotary Scout Training Center 2745
Lowman: Gardiner Hill Campground 2554
Malone: Titusville Mountain State Forest 2789
Mamaroneck: Hommocks Conservation Area 2588; Larchmont Reservoir Conservation Area 2639; Sheldrake River 2759
Maple Springs: Long Point on Lake Chautaqua 2651
Marathon: Country Hills Campground 2500
Marcellus: Centers for Nature Education/ Baltimore Woods 2481
Martinsburg: Lesser Wilderness State Forest 2645; Whetstone Gulf State Park 2820
Maryland: Camp Crumhorn Mountain 2457
Masonville: Masonville State Forest 2660
Massena: Robert Moses State Park 2738; Wilson Hill Wildlife Management Area 2827
Mayville: Camp Merz 2460; Lake Chautaqua State Park 2631
Mechanicville: Deer Run Campgrounds 2517
Medford: Camp Hitchens Park 2458
Medina: Oak Orchard Wildlife Management Area 2701
Middleburgh: Max V. Shaul State Park 2662
Middlesex: Flint Creek Campgrounds 2540
Millwood: New York Central RR Former Rights of Way 2693

Montauk: Hither Hills State Park 2586; Montauk Point State Park 2680
Montgomery: Winding Hills County Park 2830
Monticello: Sullivan County Rail-Trail 2776
Montour Falls: Finger Lakes National Forest 2535
Moravia: Empire Haven Nudist Park 2526; Fillmore Glen State Park 2534; Millard Fillmore Historic Trail 2668
Morrisville: Cedar Valley Campsites 2480
Mount Kisco: Arthur W. Butler Memorial Sanctuary 2420; Butler Memorial Sanctuary 2449; Eugene and Agnes Meyer Nature Preserve 2530; Hale Ravine Trail 2570; Manitoga Preserve 2655; Meyer Nature Preserve 2666; Mineral Spring Falls Trail 2671; Westmoreland Sanctuary 2819
Mt. Vision: Meadow-Vale Campsite 2664
Mountaindale: Hilltop Farm Campsites 2585
Mountainville: Schunemunk Mountain 2754
Naples: Cumming Nature Center 2506
Narrowsburg: Ten Mile River Historic Trail 2784
Natural Bridge: KOA-Natural Bridge/Watertown 2624
New City: Buttermilk Falls Trail 2451
New Paltz: Minnewaska State Park 2673; Mohonk Preserve 2678; Mohonk Trust Lands 2679; Shirley Path 2761; Wallkill Valley Rail Trail 2809
New York City: Canada Hill et al. 2468; Catskill Aqueduct 2473; Long Path 2650; Mt. Beacon et al. 2686; Seton Falls Park 2757
  Bronx: The John Kieran Nature Trail 2608; Mary Flagler Cary Arboretum 2659; Pelham Bay Park 2716; Pelham Bay Park Historic Trail 2717; Van Cortlandt Park 2804
  Brooklyn: Gateway National Recreation Area 2556; Jamaica Bay 2599; Kitchawan Research Station 2617; Prospect Park 2727
  Manhattan: Central Park 2482; Fort Tryon Park 2545; Inwood Hill Park 2596; The Old New York Historical Trail 2705

  Queens: Flushing Meadows-Corona Park 2541; Forest Park 2543
  Staten Island: Blue Heron Park 2437; Clay Pit Ponds State Park Preserve 2491; Clove Lakes Park 2493; Davis Wildlife Refuge Nature Trail 2513; High Rock Park 2580; LaTourette Park 2640; Staten Island Greenbelt 2768; Staten Island Recreation Trails 2769; Wolfe's Pond Park 2832
Newfield: Robert H. Treman State Park 2737
Niagara Falls: Devil's Hole State Park 2519; Niagara Frontier Trail 2695; Niagara Reservation State Park 2696; Reservoir Park 2733; Whirlpool State Park 2821
Nineveh: Kellystone Park 2613
Niverville: Kinderhook Trail 2615
Nyack: Palisades Ridge 2712; Rockland Lake Park 2741
Oakdale: Bayard Cutting Arboretum 2424; Connetquot River State Park 2495
Oceanside: Marine Nature Study Area 2657
Old Chatham: Wilson M. Powell Wildlife Sanctuary 2828
Old Forge: KOA-Old Forge 2625
Olean: Rock City Park Nature Trail 2740
Oneida: Verona Beach State Park 2805
Oneonta: Gilbert Lake State Park 2560
Orient: Orient Beach 2707
Oscawana: Valeria Home Trail 2802
Ossining: Teatown Lake Reservation 2783
Oswego: Fair Haven Beach State Park 2533; Oswego Recreational Trail 2708; Selkirk Shores State Park 2756
Oxford: Bowman Lake State Park 2440
Oyster Bay: John F. Kennedy Memorial Wildlife Sanctuary 2607; Planting Fields Arboretum 2723; Theodore Roosevelt Memorial Sanctuary & Trailside Museum 2786
Panama: Panama Rocks Park 2713
Parkers Corners: Tug Hill Wildlife Management Area 2796
Patchogue: Fire Island National Seashore 2537
Paul Smith: Adirondack State Forest 2412
Peekskill: Blue Mountain Reservation 2439
Penn Yan: Keuka Lake State Park 2614; Outlet Trail 2710

Peru: Ausable Pines Campground 2421; Terry Mountain State Forest 2785
Phoenicia: Rolling Acres Campground 2743
Piercefield: Camp Massawepie 2459
Plattekill: Hudson Valley KOA Trail 2593; KOA-Hudson Valley 2622
Plattsburgh: Point Au Roche Park 2724
Pope Mills: Fish Creek Wildlife Management Area 2539
Port Jefferson Station: Benjamin Tallmadge National Historic Trail 2432
Port Jervis: Elks-Brox City Park 2524
Port Kent: Yogi Bear's Jellystone Park 2838
Port Washington: Sands Point Park & Preserve 2749
Portageville: Four Winds Campground 2547; Letchworth State Park 2646
Pottersville: Wakonda Family Campground 2808
Poughkeepsie: James Baird State Park 2601; Margaret Lewis Norrie State Park 2656
Prattsburg: Wagon Wheel Campground 2807
Quid: Camp Babcock-Hovey 2454
Randolph: JJ's Pope Haven Campground 2604
Reading Center: Paradise Park Campground 2714
Rensselaerville: Rensselaerville State Forest 2732
Richfield Springs: KOA-Cooperstown North 2620
Rochester: Braddock Bay Park 2441; Finger Lakes Trail 2536; Genesee Valley Greenway 2559; Heritage Trail 2576; Lost City of Tryon Trail 2652; Mendon Ponds Park 2665
Rockville Centre: Hempstead Lake State Park 2575
Rome: Delta Lake State Park 2518; Griffis AFB FAMCAMP 2568
Rosebloom: Belvedere Lake Campground 2431
Rosendale: D&H Canal Heritage Corridor Trail 2508
Roslyn: Bryant Preserve 2446
Rye: Marshlands Conservancy 2658
Sacketts Harbor: Westcott Beach State Park 2818
Salamanca: Allegany State Park 2413

Saranac Lake: Saranac Lakes Park 2750
Saratoga Springs: Saratoga Spa State Park 2752
Saugerties: Rip Van Winkle Campground 2735
Scarsdale: Greenburgh Nature Center 2566
Schenectady: Camp Boyhaven 2456; Mohawk-Hudson Greenway 2677
Schuyler Falls: Macomb Reservation State Park 2653
Seaford: Tackapausha Museum and Preserve 2779
Seneca Falls: Cayuga Lake State Park 2478; Montezuma National Wildlife Refuge 2681
Sherburne: Rogers Environmental Education Center 2742
Sherman: West Side Trail State Forest 2815
Shinhopple: Bear Spring Mountain Wildlife Management Area 2426
Shirley: Wertheim National Wildlife Refuge 2814
Sidney: Oquaga Creek Park 2706
Skaneateles: Skaneateles Nature Trail 2762
Smithtown: Nissequogue River State Park 2697; Richard "Bull" Smith Historical Trail 2734
South Colton: Higley Flow State Park 2583
South Nyack: Raymond Esposito Trail 2731
Southampton: Morton National Wildlife Refuge 2685
Springwater: Holiday Hill Campground 2587
Staatsburg: Hudson Highlands State Park 2591; Mills-Norris State Park 2669
Stamford: Mine Kill State Park 2670
Stamford, CT: Mianus River Gorge 2667
Steamburg: Highbanks Campground 2582
Stephentown: Capital District Wildlife Management Area 2470; Cherry Plain State Park 2485
Stony Brook: Stony Brook Walking Tour 2772
Stony Point: American 1779 March of Anthony Wayne Trail 2417; Bear Mountain-Harriman State Park 2425; British 1777 General Clinton Trail 2445; Stony Point Battlefield 2773
Syracuse: Camp Sabattis 2464; Canal Education Center 2469
Ticonderoga: Putnam Pond State Public Campground 2728

Tonawanda: Tonawanda Wildlife Management Area 2790
Troy: Mount Tom State Forest 2688; Uncle Sam Bikeway 2799
Trumansburg: Camp Barton 2455; Trumansburg Area 2794
Truxton: Morgan Hill State Forest 2684
Tupper Lake: Fish Creek Pond State Public Campground 2538
Valley Stream: Valley Stream State Park 2803
Verona: KOA-Rome/Verona 2626
Victor: Ganondagan State Historic Site 2553
Virgil: James D. Kennedy Memorial State Forest 2602
Voorheesville: John Boyd Thacher State Park 2605
Wading River: Wildwood State Park 2824
Warrensburg: Daggett Lake Campsites 2509; Schroon River Campsite 2753; Warren County Bikeway 2811
Warsaw: Dream Lake Campground 2521
Watertown: Camp Portaferry 2461; Frank E. Jadwin State Forest 2548; John C. Thompson Park 2606; Lakeview Wildlife Management Area 2638; Perch River Wildlife Management Area 2718; Upper and Lower Lakes Wildlife Management Area 2801
Watkins Glen: KOA-Watkins Glen/Corning 2629; Schuyler State Forest 2755; Watkins Glen State Park 2812
Weedsport: Riverforest Park 2736
West Fort Ann: Camp Wakpominee 2466
West Middleburgh: Vroman's Nose Historic Trail 2806
White Plains: Cranberry Lake Park 2502; Westchester County 2816; Westchester County Historic Trail 2817
Whitney Point: Dorchester Park 2520
Williamsville: Lehigh Memory Trail 2643
Wilmington: KOA-Lake Placid-Whiteface Mountain Kampground 2623; Wilmington Recreation Area 2826
Wilson: Wilson-Tuscarora State Park 2829
Windham: White Birches Campsites 2823
Woodridge: Birchwood Acres Camping Resort 2434; Rosemond Campground & Motel 2744
Woodville: Southwick Beach State Park 2766; Up the Creek Campground 2800
Wurtsboro: Bashakill Wildlife Management Area 2423
Yonkers: Hudson River Museum Trail 2592
Yorktown Heights: Brinton Brook Sanctuary 2444; Franklin Delano Roosevelt State Park 2549; Gedney Brook Sanctuary 2557
Youngstown: Fort Niagara State Park 2544; Joseph Davis State Park 2609

NORTH CAROLINA

2839 **Adventure Trail Campground,** P.O. Box 1673, Cherokee, NC 28719, (704) 497-3651. (WCD)
   Alder Trail see entry 2886.
   American Beech Nature Trail see entry 2967.
2840 **Appalachian Side Trails** (not listed elsewhere), Appalachian Trail Conference, Inc., P.O. Box 807, Harpers Ferry, WV 25425-0807. Named trails: Bear Pen Creek, Board Camp 2.2, Breakneck Ridge 2.0, Chasteen 5.5, Chunky Gal 20.0, Crain Branch 5.0, Dixon, Mount Sterling 0.5, Mount Sterling Gap 7.5, Pounding Mill, Round Bottom 2.8, Shuckstack 5.2, Squibb Creek, Tow String 6.5, Upper Creek 7.5, Upper Sassafras Gap 3.1, Walnut Bottoms 59.5, Wesser Creek 12.0, Whiteoak Flats, Wilderness 1.0. (ATG #9)
2841 **Appalachian Trail** (see separate entry **4948** in interstate section).
2842 **Appalachian Village Campground,** Old Marshall Hwy., Asheville, NC 28804, (704) 645-5847. (WCD)
   Apple Barn Connector Road see entry 2856.
2843 **Apple Tree Group Camp,** District Ranger, U.S. Forest Service, P.O. Box 469, Franklin, NC 28734. Named trails: Appletree 2.0, Choga 6.0, Diamond Valley 1.0, Junaluska 4.0, Laurel Creek 2.0, London Bald 9.0, Nantahala 6.0, Tusquitee Loop 8.5. (BHT)
   Apple Tree Trail see entry 2953.
   Appletree Trail see entry 2843.
   Arch Rock Trail see entry 2897.
2844 **Arrowood Glade,** Franklin, NC 28734. (ATN)
   Art Loeb Trail see entries 2856 and 2964.

2845 **Asbury Trail,** SEJ Commission on Archives & History, The United Methodist Church, P.O. Box 804, Lake Junaluska, NC 28745, (704) 456-6650 or (704) 456-9226. 27.0 miles straight. Awards available. (AA 1991)
2846 **B. Everett Jordan Reservoir,** US 64, Apex, NC 27502. (ATN)
   Babel Tower Trail see entry 2964.
   Backside Trail see entry 2882.
   Badin Lake Trail see entry 2997.
   Bald Knob Ridge Trail see entry 2856.
   Balsam Mountain Nature Trail see entry 2856.
   Balsam Mountain Trail see entry 2898.
   Balsam Trail see entry 2948.
2847 **Bandit's Roost Park,** Corps of Engineers—W. Kerr Scott Reservoir, RPR 1141, Wilkesboro, NC 28697, (910) 921-2177. (WCD)
   Basin Creek Trail see entry 2856.
   Bass Lake Carriage Trail see entry 2856.
   Baxter Creek Trail see entry 2898.
   Beacon Heights Trail see entry 2856.
2848 **Bear Den Campground,** Rt. 3, Box 284, Spruce Pine, NC 28777, (704) 765-2888. (WCD)
   Bear Pen Creek Trail see entry 2840.
   Bear Pen Gap Trail see entry 2856.
   Bearpen Gap Trail see entry 2953.
   Beaugard Ridge Trail see entry 2898.
   Becks Branch Trail see entry 2898.
   Bee Gum Branch Trail see entry 2898.
   Beech Gap Trail see entry 2898.
   Beech Gap Trail see entry 2953.
2849 **Beech Mountain,** Banner Elk, NC 28604. (ATN)

Beech Trail *see* entry 3005.
2850 **Benton MacKaye Trail** (see separate entry 4950 in interstate section).
2851 **Bentonville Battlefield Trail**, Tuscarora Council, BSA, P.O. Box 1436, Goldsboro, NC 27533, (910) 734-1714; or T.L. Walden, P.O. Box 18832, Raleigh, NC 27619. 14.0 miles loop. Awards available. (SAR 1992)
Big Branch Trail *see* entry 2898.
Big Butt Trail *see* entry 2856.
2852 **Big Cove Campground**, Morgan Branch Rd., Asheville, NC 28801, (704) 667-9376. (WCD)
Big Creek Trail *see* entry 2898.
Big East Fork of Pigeon River Trail *see* entry 2964.
Big Fat Branch Trail *see* entry 2925.
Big Fork Ridge Trail *see* entry 2898.
Big Glassy Mountain Trail *see* entry 2870.
Big Indian Trail *see* entry 2953.
2853 **Big Laurel Creek Trail**, Carolina Wilderness, P.O. Box 488, Hot Springs, NC 28743, (800) 872-7437. 8.0 miles. (WRE)
Big Laurel Falls Trail *see* entry 2953.
Big Poplar Trail *see* entry 2898.
Big Rocks Trail *see* entry 2945.
Big Snowbird Trail *see* entry 2953.
Big Stack Gap Branch Trail *see* entry 2925.
Bird Trail *see* entry 2876.
Black Bottom Carriage Road *see* entry 2856.
Black Rock Cliffs Trail *see* entry 2897.
2854 **Bladen Lakes State Forest**, Division of Forest Resources, P.O. Box 27687, Raleigh, NC 27611, (919) 733-4141. (GNA)
2855 **Blue Ridge Foothills Family Campground**, Snowhill Church Circle Rd., Dobson, NC 27017, (800) 554-1477. (WCD)
2856 **Blue Ridge Parkway**, 400 BB&T Bld., One Pack Square, Asheville, NC 28801, (704) 271-4779. Named trails: Apple Barn Connector Road 0.2, Art Loeb 30.0, Bald Knob Ridge 2.8, Balsam Mountain Nature 0.6, Basin Creek 3.3, Bass Lake Carriage 1.7, Beacon Heights 0.35, Bear Pen Gap 2.8, Big Butt 6.0, Black Bottom Carriage Road 0.5, Bluff Mountain 7.5, Bluff Ridge 2.8, Boone Fork 4.9, Brinegar Cabin Walk 0.1, Buck Springs 6.2, Camp Creek 0.06, Cascades, Case Camp Ridge 1.5, Cedar Ridge 4.5, Chestoa View Loop 0.8, Chestoa View Overlook, Cold Prong Loop 0.3, Crabtree Falls Loop 2.5, Craggy Gardens, Craggy Pinnacle 1.2, Cumberland Knob 0.6, Deep Gap 2.0, Deer Park Carriage Road 0.7, Deerlick Gap Overlook 2.0, Devils Courthouse, Devils Courthouse Overlook 0.75, Douglas Falls 4.0, Duggers Creek Loop, Duncan Carriage 2.5, East Fork Access 0.2, Elk Run, Figure Eight 0.5, Flat Rock, Flat Rock Craggy Gardens, Flat Rock Ridge 5.0, Flat Top Mountain, Flat Top Mountain Carriage Road 2.8, Fodderstock 1.0, Fox Hunters' Paradise Overlook 0.2, Frying Pan Mountain 1.9, Glassmine Falls 0.5, Glassmine Falls Overlook, Gorge, Grassy Gap Fire Road 6.5, Grassy Knob, Graveyard Fields Loop 2.2, Green Knob, Gully Creek 2.5, Halwood Jackson Overlook 6,000', Harkening Hill, Haywood Gap, Humpback Rocks, John Rock, Jumpinoff Rocks 1.0, Lake Shore, Laurel Mountain, Linville Falls 2.1, Linville Gorge 0.7, Linville River Bridge 0.1, Little Glad Mill Pond 0.2, Lost Cove Ridge 3.1, The Maze 2.3, Mount Pisgah 1.25, Mountains to Sea Access 0.4, Picnic Area Connector 0.5, Picnic Area Loop 0.3, Pilot Rock, Plunge Basin Overlook 0.2, Polls Gap, Price Lake Loop 2.5, Rich Mountain Carriage Road 5.1, Richland Balsam 1.4, Rock Creek Bridge Carriage Road 1.7, Rocky Knob, Shulls Mill Road Extension 0.5, Shut-In 16.8, Sims Creek 0.1, Sleepy Gap 1.0, Snooks Nose 3.8, Thompson Creek, Three Knobs Overlook, Tompkins Knob 0.6, Trout Lake 1.0, Upper Boone Fork 0.55, Waterrock Knob 0.55, Watkins Carriage Road 3.8, Wildcat Rocks 0.1, Woods Mountain, Woods Mountain Access 2.1. (WCD; EGH; ATN; WBR; GFC; NPV; CGA; BRM; GNA; YNP; ANP)
2857 **Blueberry Hill Campground**, SR

53, Burgaw, NC 28425, (910) 259-5669. (WCD)
   Bluff Loop Trail *see* entry 2938.
   Bluff Mountain Trail *see* entry 2856.
   Bluff Ridge Trail *see* entry 2856.
   Board Camp Trail *see* entry 2840.
   Bob Bald Trail *see* entry 2925.
   Bobbit Hole Trail *see* entry 2889.
2858 **Bob's Creek Pocket Wilderness Trail,** Public Relations Department, Bowater Southern Paper Co., Calhoun, TN 37309. 3.5-8.0 miles loops. Awards available. (AA 1990)
   Bone Valley Trail *see* entry 2898.
   Booger Man Trail *see* entry 2898.
2859 **Boone Fork Trail,** Julian Price Memorial Park, Blowing Rock, NC 26805, (704) 963-5911. (FTS; GFC; GMG)
2860 **Boone's Cave State Park,** SR 150, Salisbury, NC 28146; or c/o North Carolina State Parks, West District Office, Rt. 2, Box 224M, Troutman, NC 28166. Named trails: Daniel Boone 0.5(s). (ATN; PNC; GNC)
   Bote Mountain Trail *see* entry 2898.
   Bower's Bog Trail *see* entry 3004.
2861 **Brackett's Cedar Park Campgrounds,** SR 10, Polkville, NC 28090, (704) 538-7124. (WCD)
   Bradley Fork Trail *see* entry 2898.
   Breakneck Ridge Trail *see* entry 2840.
   Brinegar Cabin Walk *see* entry 2856.
2862 **Buck Creek Campground,** Tom Creek Rd., Marion, NC 28752, (704) 724-4888. (WCD)
2863 **Buck Hill Campground,** US 19E, Spruce Pine, NC 28777, (704) 765-4641. (WCD)
   Buck Springs Trail *see* entry 2856.
   Buckquarter Creek Trail *see* entry 2889.
2864 **Bunker Hill Covered Bridge Nature Trail,** Hickory, NC 28601, (704) 465-0363. (MMA)
2865 **Buxton Woods Nature Trail,** SR 12, Buxton, NC 27920. 0.75 mile loop. (OTB)
   Bynum Bluff Trail *see* entry 2964.
   Cabe's Land Trail *see* entry 2889.
   Caldwell Fork Trail *see* entry 2898.
   Calloway Trail *see* entry 2896.

Camp Alice Trail *see* entry 2948.
Camp Creek Trail *see* entry 2856.
Campbell's Creek Loop Trail *see* entry 2967.
Campground Trail *see* entry 2871.
Canal Trail *see* entry 2961.
2866 **Cane Creek County Park,** 5213 Harkey Rd., Waxhaw, NC 28173, (704) 843-3919. (WCD; ATN)
2867 **Cape Fear Historic Trail,** Cape Fear Council, BSA, 110 Longstreet Dr., P.O. Box 7156, Wilmington, NC 28406, (910) 395-1100. 6.0 miles loop. Awards available. (SAR 1991)
   Cape Hatteras Beach Trail *see* entry 2868.
2868 **Cape Hatteras National Seashore,** Rt. 1, Box 675, Manteo, NC 27954, (919) 473-2111; or Pea Island National Wildlife Refuge, P.O. Box 150, Rodanthe, NC 27968, (919) 987-2394. Named trails: Cape Hatteras Beach 75.8, Hammock Hills Nature, Nature 0.75, Thomas Harriot Nature 0.2. (AA 1991)
2869 **Cape Lookout National Seashore,** P.O. Box 690, 415 Front St., Beaufort, NC 28516, (919) 728-2121. (RTR; NPV; GNA; ANP)
2870 **Carl Sandburg Home National Historic Site,** P.O. Box 395, Flat Rock, NC 28731, (704) 693-4178. Named trails: Big Glassy Mountain 1.3, Little Glassy Mountain Trail 0.2. (GMG; NPV; NPE; CGA)
2871 **Carolina Beach State Park,** P.O. Box 475, Carolina Beach, NC 28428, (910) 458-8206. 5.0 miles. Named trails: Campground, Fly Trap Loop 0.5(l), Sandhills, Snow's Cut, Sugarloaf, Swamp. (ATN; MMA; PNC; GNC; GNA)
   Carriage Drive Trail *see* entry 2960.
   Cascades Trail *see* entry 2856.
   Case Camp Ridge Trail *see* entry 2856.
   Cataloochee Divide Trail *see* entry 2898.
   Cedar Point Tideland Trail *see* entry 2880.
   Cedar Ridge Trail *see* entry 2856.
   Cedar Rock Trail *see* entry 2988.
   Cedar Top Trail *see* entry 2953.

NORTH CAROLINA

Chasteen Fork Trail *see* entry 2898.
Chasteen Trail *see* entry 2840.
2872 **Chatuge Lake**, US 64, Hayesville, NC 28904. (ATN)
2873 **Cherokee Campground**, Bus. US 19N, Cherokee, NC 28719, (704) 497-6901. (WCD)
Chestnut Branch Trail *see* entry 2898.
Chestnut Oak Self-guided Nature Trail *see* entry 2906.
Chestoa View Loop Trail *see* entry 2856.
Chestoa View Overlook Trail *see* entry 2856.
2874 **Chimney Rock Park**, P.O. Box 38, US 64/74, Chimney Rock, NC 28720, (704) 625-9611. (ATN; GMG; MMA; BRM)
Choga Trail *see* entry 2843.
Chunky Gal Trail *see* entry 2840.
2875 **Clemons State Forest**, Clayton, NC 27520. (ATN)
2876 **Cliffs of the Neuse State Park**, Rt. 2, Box 50, Seven Springs, NC 28578, (919) 778-6234. Named trails: Bird 0.75(l), Galax 0.5(l), River, Spanish Moss 0.5(l). (WCD; ATN; MMA; PNC; GNC; GNA)
2877 **Cliffside Lake**, Highlands, NC 28741. (ATN)
Cold Prong Loop Trail *see* entry 2856.
Cold Spring Branch Trail *see* entry 2898.
Cold Spring Knob Trail *see* entry 2925.
Cole Mill Trail *see* entry 2889.
Collins Creek Trail *see* entry 2898.
Company Mill Trail *see* entry 3005.
Conley Cove Trail *see* entry 2964.
Cook's Wall Trail *see* entry 2906.
Cooper Creek Trail *see* entry 2898.
Corridor Trail *see* entry 2961.
Cox's Mountain Trail *see* entry 2889.
2878 **Cozy Cove Campground**, US 176, Saluda, NC 28773, (704) 749-4366. (WCD)
Crabtree Creek Self-guided Trail *see* entry 3005.
Crabtree Falls Loop Trail *see* entry 2856.

Crag Way Trail *see* entry 2896.
Craggy Gardens Trail *see* entry 2856.
Craggy Pinnacle Trail *see* entry 2856.
Crain Branch Trail *see* entry 2840.
2879 **Creekside Mountain Camping**, P.O. Box 251, Bat Cave, NC 28710, (800) 248-8118. (WCD)
2880 **Croatan National Forest**, Forest Supervisor, 50 S. French Broad Ave., Asheville, NC 28802; or District Ranger, US Forest Service, 435 Thurman Rd., New Bern, NC 28560, (919) 638-5628. 28.0 miles. Named trails: Cedar Point Tideland, Neusiok 22.0. (WCD; EGH; ATN; GNC; MMA; FGU; GNA)
2881 **Cross Country Campground**, 1851 SR 150E, Denver, NC 28037, (704) 483-5897. (WCD)
2882 **Crowders Mountain State Park**, Rt. 1, Box 159, Kings Mountain, NC 28086, (704) 867-1181. Named trails: Backside 1.0(s), Crowders 3.2(s), Fern Nature 0.9(s), Lake 1.0(l), Pinnacle 1.7(s), Rocktop 2.25(s), Tower 2.0(s), Turn-Back 1.2(s). (ATN; PNC; GNC; GNA)
Crowders Trail *see* entry 2882.
Cumberland Knob Trail *see* entry 2856.
Dam Site Trail *see* entry 2938.
2883 **Dan Nicholas Park**, Bringle Ferry Rd., Salisbury, NC 28146, (704) 636-2089 or (704) 636-0154. (WCD; ATN; MMA)
Daniel Boone Scout Trail *see* entry 2897.
Daniel Boone Trail *see* entry 2860.
2884 **Davis' River Campground**, SR 251, Asheville, NC 28801, (704) 658-0772. (WCD)
Deep Creek Trail *see* entry 2898.
Deep Gap Trail *see* entry 2856.
Deep Gap Trail *see* entry 2948.
2885 **Deep River Park**, Trogdon Pond Rd., Asheboro, NC 27203, (910) 629-4069. (WCD)
Deeplow Gap Trail *see* entry 2898.
Deer Park Carriage Road *see* entry 2856.
Deerlick Gap Overlook Trail *see* entry 2856.

Demonstration Trail *see* entry 2917.
Densons Creek Nature Trail *see* entry 2997.
Devils Courthouse Trail *see* entry 2856.
Devil's Hole Trail *see* entry 2964.
Diamond Valley Trail *see* entry 2843.
Dixon Trail *see* entry 2840.
Dogwood Trail *see* entry 2983.
Dogwood Trail *see* entry 3005.
Double Gap Trail *see* entry 2898.
Douglas Access Trail *see* entry 2856.
Duggers Creek Loop Trail *see* entry 2856.

2886 **Duke Power State Park**, North Carolina State Parks, West District Office, Rt. 2, Box 224M, Troutman, NC 28166, (704) 528-6350. Named trails: Alder 0.8(l), Lakeshore 5.4(l). (WCD; ATN; MMA; PNC)

Duncan Carriage Trail *see* entry 2856.
Dunnagan Trail *see* entry 2889.

2887 **Durham Trail**, Durham Trails and Greenways Commission, 101 City Hall Plaza, Durham, NC 27701, (919) 683-4137. 170 miles. Includes Pearl Mill Trail and Quarry Trail. (IGT)

Dutchman's Creek Trail *see* entry 2997.
Eagle Creek Trail *see* entry 2898.
East Fork Access Trail *see* entry 2856.

2888 **Elk River Campground**, Elk River Rd., Elk Park, NC 28622, (704) 733-0455. (WCD)

Elk Run Trail *see* entry 2856.
Elliott Coues Nature Trail *see* entry 2894.
Enloe Creek Trail *see* entry 2898.

2889 **Eno River State Park**, Rt. 2, Box 436-C, Durham, NC 27705, (919) 383-1686. Named trails: Bobbit Hole 2.5(l), Buckquarter Creek 1.5, Cabe's Land 1.5(l), Cole Mill 1.25(s), Cox's Mountain 2.5(l), Dunnagan 1.7(l), Eno Trace Self-guided Nature 1.0, Fanny's Ford 1.0(l), Holden's Mill 2.6(l), Pea Creek 1.25, Pump Station 2.25(l). (ATN; PNC; GNC; GNA)

Eno Trace Self-guided Nature Trail *see* entry 2889.

Fall Mountain Trail *see* entry 2945.

2890 **Falls Lake State Recreation Area**, 12700 Bay Leaf Rd., Raleigh, NC 27614, (919) 846-9991. (WCD; ATN; MMA)

Fanny's Ford Trail *see* entry 2889.
Fern Nature Trail *see* entry 2882.
Figure Eight Trail *see* entry 2856.
First Flat Rock Trail *see* entry 2988.
Fish Traps Trail *see* entry 2967.
Flat Creek Trail *see* entry 2898.
Flat Rock Craggy Gardens Trail *see* entry 2856.
Flat Rock Ridge Trail *see* entry 2856.
Flat Rock Trail *see* entry 2856.
Flat Top Mountain Carriage Road *see* entry 2856.
Flatty Creek Trail *see* entry 2896.
Fly Trap Loop Trail *see* entry 2871.
Fodderstock Trail *see* entry 2856.

2891 **Fontana Lake Park**, SR 28, Fontana Village, NC 28733. (ATN)

Forest Walk *see* entry 2917.
Fork Mountain Trail *see* entry 2964.
Fork Ridge Trail *see* entry 2898.
Forney Creek Trail *see* entry 2898.
Forney Ridge Trail *see* entry 2898.

2892 **Fort Fisher Air Force Recreation Area**, US 421, Kure Beach, NC 28449, (910) 458-6546. (WCD)

2893 **Fort Fisher State Historical Site**, P.O. Box 68, US 421, Kure Beach, NC 28449. (WCD)

2894 **Fort Macon State Park**, P.O. Box 127, Atlantic Beach, NC 28557, (919) 726-3775. Named trails: Elliott Coues Nature 0.4(l). (ATN; MMA; PNC)

Fox Hunters' Paradise Trail *see* entry 2856.
Fox Trail *see* entry 2983.
Frying Pan Mountain Trail *see* entry 2856.
Galax Trail *see* entry 2876.
Garden Creek Trail *see* entry 2988.
Gingercake Trail *see* entry 2964.
Glassmine Falls Overlook Trail *see* entry 2856.
Glassmine Falls Trail *see* entry 2856.

2895 **Goose Creek Recreation & RV Park**, Goose Creek Rd., Cherokee, NC 28719, (704) 497-3052. (WCD)

2896 **Goose Creek State Park**, Rt. 2, Box 372, Washington, NC 27889, (919) 923-2191. Named trails: Calloway 0.4(s), Crag Way 1.0(s), Flatty Creek 0.7(l), Goose Creek 2.9(s), Grandfather Trail Extension 1.2(s), Ivey Gut 2.1(s), Live Oak 1.2(s), Profile 2.6(s), Ragged Point 0.25(s). (ATN; PNC; GNC; GNA)

Goose Creek Trail *see* entry 2896.

Gorge Trail *see* entry 2856.

2897 **Grandfather Mountain**, P.O. Box 995, Linville, NC 28646, (704) 733-2013 or (800) 468-7325. 25.0 miles. Named trails: Arch Rock 1.0(s), Black Rock Cliffs 1.3(s), Daniel Boone Scout 3.0(s), Grandfather 3.9(s), Shanty Spring 1.8(s), Tanawha 14.15, Underwood 0.5(s). (LGU; ATN; WBR; GMG; MMA)

Grandfather Trail *see* entry 2897.

Grandfather Trail Extension *see* entry 2896.

Grassy Branch Trail *see* entry 2898.

Grassy Gap Fire Road *see* entry 2856.

Grassy Knob Trail *see* entry 2856.

Grassy Ridge Trail *see* entry 2961.

Graveyard Fields Loop Trail *see* entry 2856.

2898 **Great Smoky Mountains National Park**, Gatlinburg, TN 37738, (615) 436-1200. 850 miles. Named trails: Big Creek Section: Baxter Creek 6.0(s), Big Branch, Big Creek 5.8(s), Chestnut Branch 2.1(s), Gunter Fork 4.5(s), Low Gap 2.3(s), Swallow Fork 3.8(s), Yellow Creek 5.2(s); Cataloochee Section: Big Fork Ridge 2.8(s), Big Poplar, Booger Man 3.8(s), Caldwell Fork 5.8(s), Cataloochee Divide 11.5(s), Double Gap 2.2(s), Little Cataloochee 5.0(s), McKee Branch 2.5(s), Mount Sterling Ridge 7.7(s), Palmer Creek 4.6(s), Pig Pen (a/k/a Long Branch) 3.6(s), Pretty Hollow Gap 4.0(s), Rough Fork 8.0(s); Raven Fork Section: Balsam Mountain 9.9(s), Beech Gap 3.0(s), Enloe Creek 3.6(s), Flat Creek 2.6(s), Hyatt Bald 2.9(s), Hyatt Ridge 9.5(s), Raven Fork 6.4(s), Spruce Mountain 4.8(s); Oconaluftee Section: Becks Branch, Bradley Fork 5.3(s), Chasteen Fork 4.0(s), Collins Creek 4.2(s), Grassy Branch 2.3(s), Hughes Ridge 11.8(s), Kanati Fork 3.0(s), Kephart Prong 2.1(s), Mingus Creek 5.6(s), Newton Bald 4.8(s), Porters Creek, Richland Mountain 4.3(s), Smokemont Loop 5.9(l), Sweat Heifer 3.6(s), Taywa Creek 3.6(s); Deep Creek Section: Beaugard Ridge 5.0(l), Cooper Creek 2.3(s), Deep Creek 12.0(s), Deeplow Gap 3.8(s), Fork Ridge 4.9(s), Indian Creek 6.8(s), Noland Divide 11.5(s), Pole Road Creek 3.2(s), Spruce Fir Nature, Stone Pile Gap, Sunkota Ridge 4.8(s), Thomas Divide 14.1(s); Noland and Forney Creeks Section: Bee Gum Branch 2.9(s), Forney Creek 11.4(s), Forney Ridge 6.8(s), Jonas Creek 4.0(s), Jumpup Ridge 5.8(s), Noland Creek 9.5(s), Springhouse Branch 2.8(s), Welch Ridge 6.8(s); Hazel Creek Section: Bone Valley 1.7(s), Cold Spring Branch 3.9(s), Hazel Creek 15.0(s), Jenkins Ridge 5.9(s), Sugar Fork 2.4(s); Twentymile and Eagle Creeks Section: Bote Mountain, Eagle Creek 9.1(s), Long Hungry Ridge 4.4(s), Lost Cove 3.1(s), Pinnacle Creek 3.5(s), Shuckstack Tower 9.0(l), Twentymile Creek 5.3(s). (WCD; EGH; ATN; MMA; GNP; WGS; GNA; HGS; IFT)

2899 **Green Acres Family Camping Resort**, Rt. 2, Box 200, Williamston, NC 27892, (919) 792-3939. (WCD)

Green Knob Trail *see* entry 2856.

2900 **Greenfield Gardens**, US 421, Wilmington, NC 28401, (910) 341-7855. (MMA)

Grindstone Trail *see* entry 2961.

2901 **Guilford Courthouse Historic Trail**, Old North State Council, BSA, 1405 Westover Terr., P.O. Box 29046, Greensboro, NC 27429-9046, (910) 378-9166 or (800) 367-9166 or fax (910) 378-9169; or Guilford Courthouse National Military Park, P.O. Box 9806, Greensboro, NC 27408, (910) 288-1776. 6.5 miles loop. Awards available. (SAR 1993)

Gully Creek Trail *see* entry 2856.

Gum Swamp Trail *see* entry 3004.

2902 **GUMPAC Trail**, Greater Uwharrie Mountains Preservation and Appreciation Committee, c/o Yadkin-Pee Dee River Basin Committee, 232 Richmond Rd., Salisbury, NC 28444. (PGE)

NORTH CAROLINA

Gunter Fork Trail *see* entry 2898.
2903 **Hagan-Stone Park**, Hagan-Stone Park Rd., Greensboro, NC 27406, (910) 674-0472. (ATN; MMA)
Halwood Jackson Overlook Trail *see* entry 2856.
Hammock Hills Nature Trail *see* entry 2868.
2904 **Hammocks Beach State Park**, Rt. 2, Box 136-B, Swansboro, NC 28584, (910) 326-4881. 3.5 miles. (ATN; GNA)
2905 **Hanging Dog Recreation Area**, U.S. Forest Service, Tusquitee Ranger District, US 19/64/129, Murphy, NC 28906, (704) 837-5152. (GMG)
2906 **Hanging Rock State Park**, P.O. Box 186, SR 1011, Danbury, NC 27016, (910) 593-8480. Named trails: Chestnut Oak Self-guided Nature 0.75(l), Cook's Wall, Hanging Rock 0.7, Indian Creek, Lower Cascades, Moore's Knob 4.2(l), Tory's Den, Upper Cascades 0.2(s), Window Falls 0.6(s), Wolf Rock. (WCD; ATN; MMA; PNC; GNC; GNA)
Hanging Rock Trail *see* entry 2906.
Hangover Lead Trail *see* entry 2925.
Haoe Trail *see* entry 2925.
Harkening Hill Trail *see* entry 2856.
Hattaway Mountain Trail *see* entry 2945.
Hawksbill Trail *see* entry 2964.
Haywood Gap Trail *see* entry 2856.
Hazel Creek Trail *see* entry 2898.
Hemlock Nature Trail *see* entry 2983.
2907 **Hemphill Mountain Campground**, Rt. 2, Box 282-A, Waynesville, NC 28786, (704) 926-0331. (WCD)
2908 **The Heritage**, Heritage Farm Rd., Southern Pines, NC 28387, (910) 949-3433. (WCD)
Hickory Branch Trail *see* entry 2953.
2909 **Hidden Valley Campground**, SR 1303, Taylorsville, NC 28681, (704) 632-4483. (WCD)
2910 **Hidden Valley Family Campground**, Deacon Dr., Marion, NC 28752, (704) 652-7208. (WCD)
2911 **Highlands Nature Center**, US 64, Highlands, NC 28741. (MMA)
2912 **Historic Bethabara Park**, 2147 Bethabara Rd., Winston-Salem, NC 27106, (910) 924-8191. (MMA)
History Trail *see* entry 2943.
2913 **Hitching Post RV Park**, Wildcat Rd., Deep Gap, NC 28618, (704) 264-5367. (WCD)
2914 **Hiwassee Lake**, SR 294, Murphy, NC 29806. (ATN)
Hoffman Nature Trail *see* entry 2992.
Holden's Mill Trail *see* entry 2889.
2915 **Holly Bluff Family Campground**, Rt. 3, Box 247, Asheboro, NC 27203, (910) 857-2761. (WCD)
2916 **Holly Ridge Family Campground**, Rt. 1, Box 39, Boonville, NC 27011, (910) 367-7756. (WCD)
Holly Road Trail *see* entry 3004.
2917 **Holmes State Forest**, Rt. 4, Box 308, Hendersonville, NC 28739, (704) 692-0100. Named trails: Demonstration 2.0, Forest Walk 0.5. (ATN; BRM)
2918 **Honey Bear Campground**, Rt. 3, Box 110, Boone, NC 28607, (704) 963-4004. (WCD)
Hughes Ridge Trail *see* entry 2898.
2919 **Hump Mountain Trail**, Tocane Ranger District, U.S. Forest Service, P.O. Box 128, Burnsville, NC 28714, (704) 682-6146. 20.0 miles loop. (HAC)
Humpback Rocks Trail *see* entry 2856.
Hurricane Creek Trail *see* entry 2953.
Hyatt Bald Trail *see* entry 2898.
Hyatt Ridge Trail *see* entry 2898.
Ike Branch Trail *see* entry 2925.
2920 **Indian Creek Campground**, Big Cove Rd., Cherokee, NC 28719, (704) 497-4361. (WCD)
Indian Creek Trail *see* entry 2898.
Indian Creek Trail *see* entry 2906.
Ivy Gut Trail *see* entry 2896.
Jenkins Ridge Trail *see* entry 2898.
2921 **Jockey's Ridge Trail**, Jockey's Ridge State Park, P.O. Box 592, Nags Head, NC 27959, (919) 441-7132. 22.0 miles loop. (AA 1991)
2922 **John H. Kerr Reservoir**, Reservoir Manager, Rt. 1, Box 76, Boydton, VA 23917, (804) 738-6662. (ATN; GNA)

NORTH CAROLINA

John Rock Trail see entry 2856.
John Wasilik Memorial Poplar Trail see entry 2953.
Jomeokee Trail see entry 2961.
Jonas Creek Trail see entry 2898.
2923 Jones Lake State Park, Rt. 2, Box 945, Elizabethtown, NC 28337, (910) 588-4550. Named trails: Lake 3.0(l), Lower, Nature 1.0(l). (WCD; ATN; MMA; PNC)
2924 Jordan Lake State Recreation Area, US 64, Apex, NC 27502, (919) 362-0586. (WCD)
2925 Joyce Kilmer/Slick Rock Wilderness, c/o Nantahala National Forest, P.O. Box 2750, Asheville, NC 28802. 60.0 miles. Named trails: Big Fat Branch 1.6, Big Stack Gap Branch 1.8, Bob Bald 1.6, Cold Spring Knob 2.4, Hangover Lead, Haoe 5.5(s), Ike Branch 3.0(s), Little Santeetlah Creek 4.6, Little Slickrock Creek 3.4, Naked Ground 4.5(s), Nichols Cove, Plaque Loop 1.0, Slickrock Creek, Stratton Bald 8.5(s), Unicoi Mountain 8.8, Yellowhammer Gap. (GMG; MMA; BRM; FGU; WPS; HGS; IFT)
Jumpinoff Rocks Trail see entry 2856.
Jumpup Ridge Trail see entry 2898.
Junaluska Trail see entry 2843.
Kanati Fork Trail see entry 2898.
Kephart Prong Trail see entry 2898.
2926 Kerr Lake State Recreation Area, Rt. 3, Box 800, Henderson, NC 27536, (919) 438-7791. (ATN; PNC; LRA)
Kimsey Creek Trail see entry 2953.
2927 KOA-Cherokee Great Smokies, Star Route, Box 39, Cherokee, NC 28719, (704) 497-9711 or fax (704) 497-6776. (WCD)
2928 Kountry Kampground, US 441, Franklin, NC 28734, (704) 524-4339. (WCD)
2929 Lake James State Park, SR 126, Marion, NC 28752, (704) 652-5047. (WCD; ATN)
2930 Lake Myers RV Resort, Rt. 1, Box 90, Mocksville, NC 27028, (704) 492-7736 or fax (704) 492-2351. (WCD)
Lake Shore Trail see entry 2856.
Lake Trail see entry 2882.

Lake Trail see entry 2923.
Lakeshore Trail see entry 2886.
Lanier's Falls Trail see entry 2967.
2931 Latta Plantation Park, Sample Rd., Charlotte, NC 28204, (704) 875-1391. (MMA)
Laurel Creek Trail see entry 2843.
Laurel Mountain Trail see entry 2856.
Laurel Self-guided Trail see entry 2945.
Ledges Springs Trail see entry 2961.
2932 Libba Cotton Trail, Roy Willford, Planning and Economic Development Coordinator, P.O. Box 829, Carrboro, NC 27510, (919) 968-7714. 0.5 mile straight. (GRT)
Linville Falls Trail see entry 2856.
Linville Gorge Trail see entries 2856 and 2964.
Linville River Bridge Trail see entry 2856.
Little Cataloochee Trail see entry 2898.
Little Creek Loop Trail see entry 2967.
Little East Fork Trail see entry 2964.
Little Glad Mill Pond Trail see entry 2856.
Little Glassy Mountain Trail see entry 2870.
Little Pinnacle Trail see entry 2961.
2933 Little River Camping Resort, SR 64, Brevard, NC 28712, (704) 877-4475. (WCD)
Little Santeetlah Creek Trail see entry 2925.
Little Slickrock Creek Trail see entry 2925.
Live Oak Trail see entry 2896.
London Bald Trail see entry 2843.
Long Branch Trail see entry 2898.
Long Branch Trail see entry 2953.
Long Hungry Ridge Trail see entry 2898.
Loop Trail see entry 3005.
2934 Lost Cove Campground, US 19, Cherokee, NC 28719, (704) 497-6168. (WCD)
Lost Cove Ridge Trail see entry 2856.

Lost Cove Trail *see* entry 2898.
Low Gap Trail *see* entry 2898.
Lower Cascades Trail *see* entry 2906.
Lower Falls Trail *see* entry 2983.
Lower Ridge Trail *see* entry 2953.
Lower Trail *see* entry 2923.

2935 **Mattamuskeet National Wildlife Refuge**, Rt. 1, Box N-2, Swanquarter, NC 27885, (919) 926-4021. 20.0 miles. (GNA; GNW)

The Maze *see* entry 2856.

2936 **McDowell County Park**, York Rd., Charlotte, NC 28278, (704) 588-5225. (WCD)

McKee Branch Trail *see* entry 2898.

2937 **Meadowbrook Resort**, 9 Indian Creek Rd., Maggie Valley, NC 28751, (704) 926-1821. (WCD)

2938 **Medoc Mountain State Park**, Rt. 3, Box 219G, Enfield, NC 27823, (919) 445-2280. Named trails: Bluff Loop 2.8(l), Dam Site 0.7, Stream and Discovery Loop 2.1(l), Summit 3.0(l). (ATN; PNC; GNC; GNA)

2939 **Merchants Millpond State Park**, Rt. 1, Box 141-A, Gatesville, NC 27938, (919) 357-1191. Named trails: Millpond Loop 6.7(l). (WCD; ATN; MMA; PNC; AMC; GNC)

Middle Falls Trail *see* entry 2953.

2940 **Midway Campground & RV Resort**, Rt. 4, Box 199B, Statesville, NC 28677, (704) 546-7615. (WCD)

Millpond Loop Trail *see* entry 2939.

2941 **Mine Branch Family Campground**, Rt. 1, Box 398, Blowing Rock, NC 28605, (704) 264-2170. (WCD)

Mingus Trail *see* entry 2898.

Mooney Falls Trail *see* entry 2953.

2942 **Moonshine Creek Campground**, P.O. Box 10, Balsam, NC 28707, (704) 586-6666. (WCD)

2943 **Moore's Creek Battlefield Trail**, Moore's Creek National Battlefield, P.O. Box 69, Currie, NC 28435, (910) 283-5591 (for trail brochure); or Cape Fear Council, BSA, P.O. Box 7156, Wilmington, NC 28406 (for patches). 1.3 miles loop (includes History Trail 1.0 and Tarheel Trail 0.3). Awards available. (SAR 1993)

Moore's Knob Trail *see* entry 2906.

2944 **Moravian Falls Campground**, CR 1372, Moravian Falls, NC 28654, (910) 667-6150. (WCD)

Morrow Mountain Loop Trail *see* entry 2945.

2945 **Morrow Mountain State Park**, Rt. 5, Box 430, SR 1719, Albemarle, NC 28001, (704) 982-4402. Named trails: Big Rocks 2.5(s), Fall Mountain 3.75, Hattaway Mountain 2.0(l), Laurel Self-guided 0.6(l), Morrow Mountain Loop 0.8(l), Morrow Mountain 3.0(s), Quarry 0.6(l), Sugarloaf Mountain 2.75(l), Three Rivers Self-guided 0.6(l). (WCD; ATN; MMA; PNC; GNC; GNA)

2946 **Moses H. Cone Memorial Park**, Blue Ridge Pkwy., Boone, NC 28607, (704) 295-7938. (LGU; MMA)

2947 **Mount Jefferson State Park**, 1481 Mount Jefferson State Park Rd., West Jefferson, NC 28694, (910) 246-9653. Named trails: Rhododendron 1.1(s), Summit 0.3(s). (ATN; MMA; PNC)

2948 **Mount Mitchell State Park**, Rt. 5, Box 700, Burnsville, NC 28714, (704) 675-4611. 33.0 miles. Named trails: Balsam 0.75(s), Camp Alice, Deep Gap 3.0(s), Mount Mitchell 6.0(s), Old Mitchell 1 hour. (EGH; ATN; MMA; PNC; BRM; GNC; GNA)

Mount Mitchell Trail *see* entry 2948.

Mount Pisgah Trail *see* entry 2856.

Mount Sterling Gap Trail *see* entry 2840.

Mount Sterling Ridge Trail *see* entry 2898.

2949 **Mountain Cove Campground & Trout Pond**, Still Fork Creek Rd., Busick, NC 28711, (704) 675-5362. (WCD)

2950 **Mountain Paradise Campground**, US 221, Marion, NC 28752, (704) 756-4085. (WCD)

Mountain Trail *see* entry 2961.

Mountains to Sea Access Trail *see* entry 2856.

2951 **Mountains to Sea Trail**, North Carolina State Trails Coordinator, Division of Parks and Recreation, 512 N. Salisbury St., Raleigh, NC 27611. 700

miles straight planned, current as to about 250 miles. (EGH; WBR)

2952 **Nags Head Woods Preserve**, Rt. 1, Box 631, Manteo, NC 27954, (919) 473-5282. (AMC)
   Naked Ground Trail *see* entry 2925.
2953 **Nantahala National Forest**, 100 Otis St., P.O. Box 2750, Asheville, NC 28802, (704) 257-4200; or Cheoah Ranger District, USFS, Rt. 1, Box 16A, Robbinsville, NC 28771, (704) 479-6431; or Highland Ranger District, USFS, P.O. Box 749, Highlands, NC 28741, (704) 526-2562; or Tusquitee Ranger District, 201 Woodland Dr., Murphy, NC 28906, (704) 837-5152; or Wayah Ranger District, P.O. Box 469, Franklin, NC 28734, (704) 524-6441. 450 miles. Named trails: Apple Tree 2.0, Bearpen Gap 2.0, Beech Gap 2.0, Big Indian 2.0, Big Laurel Falls 0.5, Big Snowbird 12.7, Cedar Top 8.0, Hickory Branch 1.5, Hooper Bald 11.5, Hurricane Creek 2.0, John Wasilik Memorial Poplar 0.7, Kimsey Creek 3.7, Long Branch 2.3, Lower Ridge 3.5, Middle Falls 1.0, Mooney Falls 0.1, Park Creek 6.0, Sassafras Lick 1.5, Snowbird Mountain 12.0, Timber Ridge 2.5. (WCD; EGH; ATN; GFC; MMA; FGU; GNC; GNA)
   Nantahala Trail *see* entry 2843.
2954 **Natural Science Center of Greensboro**, 4301 Lawndale Dr., Greensboro, NC 27408, (910) 288-3769. (MMA)
   Nature Trail *see* entry 2868.
   Nature Trail *see* entry 2923.
   Neusiok Trail *see* entry 2880.
2955 **New River State Park**, SR 88, Jefferson, NC 28640. (ATN)
   Newton Bald Trail *see* entry 2898.
   Nichols Cave Trail *see* entry 2925.
   Noland Creek Trail *see* entry 2898.
   Noland Divide Trail *see* entry 2898.
2956 **North Carolina Botanical Gardens**, Laurel Hill Rd., Chapel Hill, NC 27514, (919) 967-2246. (ATN; MMA; GNA)
2957 **North Carolina Museum of Life and Science**, 433 Murray Ave., Durham, NC 27704, (919) 477-0431. Named trails: Prehistory. (ATN; FTS)
   North Pond Trail *see* entry 2959.
   North Slope Trail *see* entry 2964.

Northington's Ferry Trail *see* entry 2967.
   Old Butt Knob Trail *see* entry 2964.
   Old Mitchell Trail *see* entry 2948.
2958 **Orchard Lake Campground & RV Park**, Mountain Page Rd., Saluda, NC 28773, (704) 749-3901. (WCD)
   Palmer Creek Trail *see* entry 2898.
   Park Creek Trail *see* entry 2953.
   Pea Creek Trail *see* entry 2889.
2959 **Pea Island National Wildlife Refuge**, P.O. Box 1026, Manteo, NC 27954, (919) 987-2394. Named trails: North Pond 4.0(l). (OTB; GNA; GNW)
   Pearl Mill Trail *see* entry 2887.
2960 **Pettigrew State Park**, Rt. 1, Box 336, Creswell, NC 27928, (919) 797-4475. Named trails: Carriage Drive 4.1(s). (ATN; PNC; GNC)
   Picnic Area Connector Trail *see* entry 2856.
   Picnic Area Loop Trail *see* entry 2856.
   Pig Pen Trail *see* entry 2898.
2961 **Pilot Mountain State Park**, Rt. 1, Box 21, Pinnacle, NC 27043, (910) 325-2355. Named trails: Canal 0.5, Corridor, Grassy Ridge 1.0, Grindstone 2.1(s), Jomeokee 0.75(l), Ledges Springs 1.6(l), Little Pinnacle 100 yards, Mountain 2.5(s), Sassafras Nature 0.5(l). (WCD; ATN; MMA; PNC; GNC; GNA)
   Pilot Rock Trail *see* entry 2856.
   Pinch In Trail *see* entry 2964.
   Pine Barrens Trail *see* entry 3004.
   Pine Gap Trail *see* entry 2964.
   Pine Island Trail *see* entry 3004.
2962 **The Pines RV Park**, US 64, Franklin, NC 28734, (704) 524-4490. (WCD)
   Pinnacle Creek Trail *see* entry 2898.
   Pinnacle Trail *see* entry 2882.
2963 **Pioneer Village Family Campground**, Rt. 2, Box 155A, Pinnacle, NC 27043, (910) 325-2582. (WCD)
2964 **Pisgah National Forest**, District Ranger, U.S. Forest Service, P.O. Box 8, Pisgah National Forest, NC 28768; or District Ranger, P.O. Box 519, Marion, NC 28752, (704) 652-4841. 550 miles. Named trails: Art Loeb 32.0, Babel Tower 2.4, Big East Fork of Pigeon River 4.0,

Bynum Bluff, Conley Cove 2.8, Devil's Hole, Fork Mountain 6.0, Gingercake, Hawksbill 0.8, Linville Gorge 13.2, Little East Fork 5.8, North Slope, Old Butt Knob 3.0, Pinch In, Pine Gap 2.6, Sandy Flats, Shining Creek 4.5(s), Shortoff 9.4, Spence Ridge 2.4, Table Rock 1.6. (EGH; ATN; GFC; GMG; MMA; FGU; GNC; GNA; WPS; BHT; IFT)

Plaque Loop Trail *see* entry 2925.
Plunge Basin Overlook Trail *see* entry 2856.
Pole Road Creek Trail *see* entry 2898.
Polls Gap Trail *see* entry 2856.
Porters Creek Trail *see* entry 2898.
Possum Trail *see* entry 2983.
Pounding Mill Trail *see* entry 2840.
Prehistory Trail *see* entry 2957.
Pretty Hollow Gap Trail *see* entry 2898.
Price Lake Loop Trail *see* entry 2856.
Profile Trail *see* entry 2896.
Pump Station Trail *see* entry 2889.

2965 **Pungo National Wildlife Refuge**, P.O. Box 267, Plymouth, NC 27962, (919) 793-2143. (GNA)

Quarry Trail *see* entry 2887.
Quarry Trail *see* entry 2945.
Ragged Point Trail *see* entry 2896.

2966 **Rainbow Springs Campground**, 1626 Old Murphy Rd., Franklin, NC 28734, (704) 524-6376 or (800) 524-8293. (WCD)

Raven Fork Trail *see* entry 2898.
Raven Rock Loop Trail *see* entry 2967.

2967 **Raven Rock State Park**, Rt. 3, Box 1005, Lillington, NC 27546, (919) 893-4888. Named trails: American Beech Nature 1.0(l), Campbell's Creek Loop 5.3(l), Fish Traps 1.1(s), Lanier's Falls 0.4(l), Little Creek Loop 1.4(l), Northington's Ferry 4.4(l), Raven Rock Loop 2.1(l). (ATN; MMA; PNC; GNC; GNA)

2968 **Reed Gold Mine State Historic Site**, SR 200, Stanfield, NC 28163, (704) 786-8337. (ATN; OTB)

Reedy Creek Self-guided Trail *see* entry 3005.

Rhododendron Trail *see* entry 2947.
Rich Mountain Carriage Road *see* entry 2856.
Richland Balsam Trail *see* entry 2856.
Richland Mountain Trail *see* entry 2898.

2969 **River to Sea Bikeway**, Joseph Huegy, Transportation Planner, City of Wilmington, P.O. Box 1810, Wilmington, NC 28402, (910) 341-7888. 8.0 miles straight. (GRT)

River Trail *see* entry 2876.

2970 **River Valley Campground**, P.O. Box 462, Cherokee, NC 28719, (704) 497-3540. (WCD)

2971 **Rivercamp USA**, CR 1308, Piney Creek, NC 28663, (910) 359-8231. (WCD)

2972 **Riverside Campground**, SR 45, Belhaven, NC 27810, (919) 943-2849. (WCD)

Rock Creek Bridge Carriage Road *see* entry 2856.
Rocktop Trail *see* entry 2882.

2973 **Rocky Bluff Park**, SR 209, Hot Springs, NC 28743. (ATN)

Rocky Knob Trail *see* entry 2856.

2974 **Rose Creek Mine & Campground**, CR 1372, Franklin, NC 28734, (704) 524-3225. (WCD)

Rough Fork Trail *see* entry 2898.
Round Bottom Trail *see* entry 2840.

2975 **Salisbury-Spencer Trail**, American Historical Trails, Inc., P.O. Box 769, Monroe, NC 28110, (704) 289-1604. 4.2-8.5 miles straight. Awards available. (SAR 1993)

Sal's Branch Trail *see* entry 3005.

2976 **Sand Ridge Nature Trail**, Lake Waccamaw State Park, c/o Singletary Lake State Park, Rt. 1, Box 63, Kelly, NC 28448, (910) 669-2928. 1.5 miles straight. (PNC)

Sandhills Trail *see* entry 2871.
Sandy Flats Trail *see* entry 2964.
Sassafras Lick Trail *see* entry 2953.
Sassafras Nature Trail *see* entry 2961.

2977 **Sauratown Trail**, Sauratown Trail Committee, 280 S. Liberty St., Winston-Salem, NC 27101. (PNC)

NORTH CAROLINA

Sawtooth Trail *see* entry 2983.
2978 **Schiele Museum of Natural History and Planetarium**, 1500 E. Garrison Blvd., Gastonia, NC 28054, (704) 864-3962. (WCD)
    Shanty Spring Trail *see* entry 2897.
    Shining Creek Trail *see* entry 2964.
    Shortoff Trail *see* entry 2964.
    Shuckstack Tower Trail *see* entry 2898.
    Shuckstack Trail *see* entry 2840.
    Shulls Mill Road Extension Trail *see* entry 2856.
    Shut-In Trail *see* entry 2856.
    Sims Creek Trail *see* entry 2856.
2979 **Singing Waters Camping Resort**, Trout Creek Rd., Tuckasegee, NC 28783, (704) 293-5872. (WCD)
2980 **Singletary Lake State Park**, Rt. 1, Box 63, Kelly, NC 28448, (910) 669-2928. Named trails: Singletary Lake 1.0. (ATN; PNC; GNC)
    Singletary Lake Trail *see* entry 2980.
    Sleepy Gap Trail *see* entry 2856.
    Slickrock Creek Trail *see* entry 2925.
2981 **Smithfield Best Holiday Trav-L-Park**, Rt. 4, Box 189, Four Oaks, NC 27524, (919) 934-3181. (WCD)
    Smokemont Loop Trail *see* entry 2898.
2982 **Smokemont Park**, Newfound Gap Rd., Cherokee, NC 28719. (ATN)
    Snooks Nose Trail *see* entry 2856.
    Snowbird Mountain Trail *see* entry 2953.
    Snow's Cut Trail *see* entry 2871.
2983 **South Mountains State Park**, Rt. 1, Box 206-C, Connelly Springs, NC 28612, (704) 433-4772. Named trails: Dogwood, Fox, Hemlock Nature 0.25(s), Lower Falls 0.5(s), Possum, Sawtooth, Upper Falls 0.9(s). (ATN; PNC; GNC)
2984 **South Tow River**, District Ranger, U.S. Forest Service, P.O. Box 128, Burnsville, NC 28714. (HTA)
    Spanish Moss Trail *see* entry 2876.
    Spence Ridge Trail *see* entry 2964.
2985 **Spring Valley Park**, SR 59, Fayetteville, NC 28302, (910) 425-1505. (WCD)
    Springhouse Branch Trail *see* entry 2898.

2986 **Springmaid Mountain Campground**, Rt. 3, Box 376, Spruce Pine, NC 28777, (704) 765-2353. (WCD)
    Spruce Fir Nature Trail *see* entry 2898.
    Spruce Mountain Trail *see* entry 2898.
    Squibb Creek Trail *see* entry 2840.
2987 **Steel Creek Park**, Rt. 7, Box 412L, Morganton, NC 28655, (704) 433-5660. (WCD)
    Stone Mountain Loop Trail *see* entry 2988.
2988 **Stone Mountain State Park**, Star Route 1, Box 17, Roaring Gap, NC 28668, (910) 957-8185. 14.0 miles. Named trails: Cedar Rock 0.7(s), First Flat Rock, Garden Creek 7.0(s), Stone Mountain Loop, Wolf Rock Loop 2.7(l). (WCD; ATN; MMA; PNC; OTB; GNA)
    Stone Pile Gap Trail *see* entry 2898.
    Stratton Bald Trail *see* entry 2925.
    Stream and Discovery Loop Trail *see* entry 2938.
2989 **Strollway**, Jack Steelman, Winston-Salem Development Office, P.O. Box 2511, Winston-Salem, NC 27102, (910) 727-2741. 1.2 miles straight. (GRT)
    Sugar Fork Trail *see* entry 2898.
    Sugarloaf Mountain Trail *see* entry 2945.
    Sugarloaf Trail *see* entry 2871.
    Summit Trail *see* entry 2947.
2990 **Sundowner Campground**, SR 69, Hayesville, NC 28904, (704) 389-3241. (WCD)
    Sunkota Ridge Trail *see* entry 2898.
    Swallow Fork Trail *see* entry 2898.
    Swamp Trail *see* entry 2871.
    Sweat Heifer Trail *see* entry 2898.
    Sycamore Trail *see* entry 3005.
    Table Rock Trail *see* entry 2964.
    Tanawha Trail *see* entry 2897.
2991 **Tanglewood County Park**, P.O. Box 1040, SR 158, Clemmons, NC 27012, (910) 766-0591. (WCD; MMA)
    Tarheel Trail *see* entry 2943.
    Taywa Creek Trail *see* entry 2898.
2992 **Theodore Roosevelt State Natural Area**, P.O. Box 127, Atlantic Beach, NC 28512, (919) 726-3775. Named trails: Hoffman Nature 0.4. (PNC; GNC)

Thomas Divide Trail *see* entry 2898.
Thomas Harriot Nature Trail *see* entry 2868.
Thompson Creek Trail *see* entry 2856.
Three Knobs Overlook Trail *see* entry 2856.
Three Rivers Self-guided Trail *see* entry 2945.
Timber Ridge Trail *see* entry 2953.
Tompkins Knob Trail *see* entry 2856.
Tory's Den Trail *see* entry 2906.
Tow String Trail *see* entry 2840.
Tower Trail *see* entry 2882.
Trout Lake Trail *see* entry 2856.
2993 Turkey Creek Campground, SR 28, Almond, NC 28702, (704) 488-9866. (WCD)
Turn-Back Trail *see* entry 2882.
Tusquitee Loop Trail *see* entry 2843.
2994 Tuttle State Forest, SR 18, Morganton, NC 28655. (ATN)
Twentymile Creek Trail *see* entry 2898.
2995 Twin Lakes Campground & Yacht Basin, Rt. 2, Box 605, Chocowinity, NC 27817, (919) 946-5700. (WCD)
2996 Twin Rivers Campground, CR 1549, Piney Creek, NC 28663, (910) 982-3456. (WCD)
Underwood Trail *see* entry 2897.
Unicoi Mountain Trail *see* entry 2925.
Upper Boone Fork Trail *see* entry 2856.
Upper Cascades Trail *see* entry 2906.
Upper Creek Trail *see* entry 2840.
Upper Falls Trail *see* entry 2983.
Upper Sassafras Gap Trail *see* entry 2840.
2997 Uwharrie National Forest, 100 Otis St., P.O. Box 2750, Asheville, NC 28802, (704) 257-4200; or Uwharrie Trail Club, P.O. Box 2073, Asheboro, NC 27206. 50.0 miles. Named trails: Badin Lake 5.6, Densons Creek Nature 2.0, Dutchman's Creek 9.5, Uwharrie National Recreation 33.6. (EGH; ATN; GFC; PNC; FGU; GNC; GNA)

Uwharrie National Recreation Trail *see* entry 2997.
2998 Valle Crucis Campground, CR 1112, Valle Crucis, NC 28691, (704) 963-4423. (WCD)
2999 Van Hoy Farms Family Campground, Jericho Rd., Union Grove, NC 28689, (704) 539-5493. (WCD)
3000 W. Kerr Scott Lake, Corps of Engineers, Wilmington District, P.O. Box 1890, Wilmington, NC 28401; or Reservoir Manager, W. Kerr Scott Reservoir, P.O. Box 182, Wilkesboro, NC 28697. (ATN; GFC; LRA)
Walnut Bottoms Trail *see* entry 2840.
Waterrock Knob Trail *see* entry 2856.
Watkins Carriage Road *see* entry 2856.
3001 Waynesborough State Park, US 117, Goldsboro, NC 27530. (ATN)
Welch Ridge Trail *see* entry 2898.
Wesser Creek Trail *see* entry 2840.
3002 West Point on the Eno, Durham, NC 27701. (ATN)
3003 Western North Carolina Nature Center, Gashes Creek Rd., Asheville, NC 28803, (704) 298-5600. (ATN; MMA)
3004 Weymouth Woods/Sandhills Nature Preserve, 400 N. Fort Bragg Rd., Southern Pines, NC 28387, (910) 692-2167. Named trails: Bower's Bog, Gum Swamp 0.4(l), Holly Road 1.9(s), Pine Barrens 1.0(l), Pine Island 0.4(s). (ATN; MMA; PNC; GNA)
Whiteoak Flats Trail *see* entry 2840.
Wildcat Rocks Trail *see* entry 2856.
Wilderness Trail *see* entry 2840.
3005 William B. Umstead State Park, Rt. 8, Box 130, Raleigh, NC 27612, (919) 787-3033. Named trails: Beech 0.5(s), Company Mill 3.5(l), Crabtree Creek Self-guided 1.0(l), Dogwood 1.1(s), Loop 0.5(l), Reedy Creek Self-guided 1.2(l), Sal's Branch 2.4(l), Sycamore 5.1(l). (WCD; ATN; MMA; PNC; GNC)
Window Falls Trail *see* entry 2906.
Wolf Rock Loop Trail *see* entry 2988.
Wolf Rock Trail *see* entry 2906.

NORTH CAROLINA   **Index**   197

Woods Mountain Access Trail *see* entry 2856.
Woods Mountain Trail *see* entry 2856.
Yellow Creek Trail *see* entry 2898.
Yellowhammer Gap Trail *see* entry 2925.
3006 **Yogi Bear's Jellystone Park**, Rt. 6, Box 1004, Lumberton, NC 28358, (910) 739-4372. (WCD)
3007 **Yogi in the Smokies**, Star Route, Box 54, Cherokee, NC 28719, (704) 497-9151. (WCD)
3008 **Zooland Family Campground**, Rt. 5, Box 353, Asheboro, NC 27203, (910) 381-3422. (WCD)

Generally:
Secretary, Department of Natural Resources and Community Development, 512 N. Salisbury St., Raleigh, NC 27611, (919) 733-4181. (EGH)
North Carolina State Trails Coordinator, Division of Parks and Recreation, Yorkshire Center, 12700 Bayleaf Rd., Raleigh, NC 27614. (WBR)
U.S. Army Corps of Engineers, Wilmington District, P.O. Box 1890, Wilmington, NC 28401. (GFC)

Index (by city)

Albemarle: Morrow Mountain State Park 2945
Almond: Turkey Creek Campground 2993
Apex: B. Everett Jordan Reservoir 2846; Jordan Lake State Recreation Area 2924
Asheboro: Deep River Park 2885; Holly Bluff Family Campground 2915; Uwharrie National Forest 2997; Zooland Family Campground 3008
Asheville: Appalachian Village Campground 2842; Big Cove Campground 2852; Blue Ridge Parkway 2856; Croatan National Forest 2880; Davis' River Campground 2884; Joyce Kilmer/Slick Rock Wilderness 2925; Nantahala National Forest 2953; Uwharrie National Forest 2997; Western North Carolina Nature Center 3003
Atlantic Beach: Fort Macon State Park 2894; Theodore Roosevelt State Natural Area 2992
Balsam: Moonshine Creek Campground 2942
Banner Elk: Beech Mountain 2849
Bat Cave: Creekside Mountain Camping 2879
Beaufort: Cape Lookout National Seashore 2869
Belhaven: Riverside Campground 2972
Bentonville: Bentonville Battlefield Trail 2851

Blowing Rock: Boone Fork Trail 2859; Mine Branch Family Campground 2941
Boone: Honey Bear Campground 2918; Moses H. Cone Memorial Park 2946
Boonville: Holly Ridge Family Campground 2916
Boydton: John H. Kerr Reservoir 2922
Brevard: Little River Camping Resort 2933
Burgaw: Blueberry Hill Campground 2857
Burnsville: Hump Mountain Trail 2919; Mount Mitchell State Park 2948; South Tow River 2984
Busick: Mountain Cove Campground & Trout Pond 2949
Carolina Beach: Carolina Beach State Park 2871
Carrboro: Libba Cotton Trail 2932
Chapel Hill: North Carolina Botanical Gardens 2956
Charlotte: Latta Plantation Park 2931; McDowell County Park 2936
Cherokee: Adventure Trail Campground 2839; Cherokee Campground 2873; Goose Creek Recreation & RV Park 2895; Indian Creek Campground 2920; KOA-Cherokee Great Smokies 2927; Lost Cove Campground 2934; River Valley Campground 2970; Smokemont Park 2982; Yogi in the Smokies 3007
Chimney Rock: Chimney Rock Park 2874

NORTH CAROLINA

Chocowinity: Twin Lakes Campground & Yacht Basin 2995
Clayton: Clemons State Forest 2875
Clemmons: Tanglewood County Park 2991
Connelly Springs: South Mountains State Park 2983
Creswell: Pettigrew State Park 2960
Currie: Moore's Creek Battlefield Trail 2943
Danbury: Hanging Rock State Park 2906
Deep Gap: Hitching Post RV Park 2913
Denver: Cross County Campground 2881
Dobson: Blue Ridge Foothills Family Campground 2855
Durham: Durham Trail 2887; Eno River State Park 2889; North Carolina Museum of Life and Science 2957; West Point on the Eno 3002
Elizabethtown: Jones Lake State Park 2923
Elk Park: Elk River Campground 2888
Enfield: Medoc Mountain State Park 2938
Fayetteville: Spring Valley Park 2985
Flat Rock: Carl Sandburg Home National Historic Site 2870
Fontana Village: Fontana Lake Park 2891
Four Oaks: Smithfield Best Holiday Trav-L-Park 2981
Franklin: Apple Tree Group Camp 2843; Arrowood Glade 2844; Kountry Kampground 2928; Nantahala National Forest 2953; The Pines RV Park 2962; Rainbow Springs Campground 2966; Rose Creek Mine & Campground 2974
Gastonia: Schiele Museum of Natural History and Planetarium 2978
Gatesville: Merchants Millpond State Park 2939
Gatlinburg: Great Smoky Mountains National Park 2898
Goldsboro: Waynesborough State Park 3001
Greensboro: Guilford Courthouse Historic Trail 2901; Hagan-Stone Park 2903; Natural Science Center of Greensboro 2954
Hayesville: Chatuge Lake 2872; Sundowner Campground 2990
Henderson: Kerr Lake State Recreation Area 2926
Hendersonville: Holmes State Forest 2917
Highlands: Cliffside Lake 2877; Highlands Nature Center 2911; Nantahala National Forest 2953

Hot Springs: Big Laurel Creek Trail 2853; Rocky Bluff Park 2973
Jefferson: New River State Park 2955
Kelly: Sand Ridge Nature Trail 2976; Singletary Lake State Park 2980
Kings Mountain: Crowders Mountain State Park 2882
Kure Beach: Fort Fisher Air Force Recreation Area 2892; Fort Fisher State Historical Site 2893
Lake Junaluska: Asbury Trail 2845
Lillington: Raven Rock State Park 2967
Linville: Grandfather Mountain 2897
Lumberton: Yogi Bear's Jellystone Park 3006
Maggie Valley: Meadowbrook Resort 2937
Manteo: Cape Hatteras National Seashore 2868; Nags Head Woods Preserve 2952; Pea Island National Wildlife Refuge 2959
Marion: Bob's Creek Pocket Wilderness Trail 2858; Buck Creek Campground 2862; Hidden Valley Family Campground 2910; Lake James State Park 2929; Mountain Paradise Campground 2950; Pisgah National Forest 2964
Mocksville: Lake Myers RV Resort 2930
Moravian Falls: Moravian Falls Campground 2944
Morganton: Steel Creek Park 2987; Tuttle State Forest 2994
Murphy: Hanging Dog Recreation Area 2905; Hiawassee Lake 2914; Nantahala National Forest 2953
Nags Head: Jockey's Ridge Trail 2921
New Bern: Croatan National Forest 2880
Piney Creek: Rivercamp USA 2971; Twin Rivers Campground 2996
Pinnacle: Pilot Mountain State Park 2961; Pioneer Village Family Campground 2963
Plymouth: Pungo National Wildlife Refuge 2965
Polkville: Brackett's Cedar Park Campgrounds 2861
Raleigh: Bladen Lakes State Forest 2854; Falls Lake State Recreation Area 2890; Mountains to Sea Trail 2951; William B. Umstead State Park 3005
Roaring Gap: Stone Mountain State Park 2988

NORTH CAROLINA Index

Robbinsville: Nantahala National Forest 2953
Rodanthe: Cape Hatteras National Seashore 2868
Salisbury: Dan Nicholas Park 2883; GUM-PAC Trail 2902; Salisbury-Spencer Trail 2975
Saluda: Cozy Cove Campground 2878; Orchard Lake Campground & RV Park 2958
Seven Springs: Cliffs of the Neuse State Park 2876
Southern Pines: The Heritage 2908; Weymouth Woods/Sandhills Nature Preserve 3004
Spruce Pine: Bear Den Campground 2848; Buck Hill Campground 2863; Springmaid Mountain Campground 2986
Stanfield: Reed Gold Mine State Historic Site 2968
Statesville: Midway Campground & RV Resort 2940
Swanquarter: Mattamuskeet National Wildlife Refuge 2935
Swansboro: Hammocks Beach State Park 2904

Taylorsville: Hidden Valley Campground 2909
Troutman: Boone's Cave State Park 2860; Duke Power State Park 2886
Tuckasegee: Singing Waters Camping Resort 2979
Union Grove: Van Hoy Farms Family Campground 2999
Valle Crucis: Valle Crucis Campground 2998
Washington: Goose Creek State Park 2896
Waxhaw: Cane Creek County Park 2866
Waynesville: Hemphill Mountain Campground 2907
West Jefferson: Mount Jefferson State Park 2947
Wilkesboro: Bandit's Roost Park 2847; W. Kerr Scott Lake 3000
Williamston: Green Acres Family Camping Resort 2899
Wilmington: Cape Fear Historic Trail 2867; Greenfield Gardens 2900; River to Sea Bikeway 2969
Winston-Salem: Historic Bethabara Park 2912; Sauratown Trail 2977; Strollway 2989

OHIO

3009 **A.W. Marion State Park**, Warner Huffer Rd., Circleville, OH 43113, (614) 474-3386. (WCD; ATI; MGL)

3010 **Adams Lake State Park**, SR 41, West Union, OH 45693. (ATI)

Adamsville Trail see entry 3032.

3011 **Akron/Bike and Hike Trail**, John R. Daily, Director, Akron Metropolitan Park District, 975 Treaty Line Rd., Akron, OH 44313, (216) 867-5511; or Steve Coles, Chief of Planning, Cleveland Metroparks, 4101 Fulton Pkwy., Cleveland, OH 44144, (216) 351-6300 ext. 238. 29.0 miles straight. (GRT)

3012 **Alum Creek State Park**, US 36/SR 37, Delaware, OH 43015, (614) 548-4631 or (800) BUCKEYE. (WCD; ATI; MGL)

3013 **Anthony Wayne Trail** (Fallen Timbers Segment), Toledo Area Council, BSA, One Stranahan Sq., P.O. Box 337, Toledo, OH 43691-1492, (419) 241-7293. 15.0 miles straight. Awards available. (AA 1989; SAR 1966)

3014 **Anthony Wayne Trail** (Fort Finney Segment), Dan Beard Council, BSA, 2331 Victory Pkwy., Cincinnati, OH 45206, (513) 961-2336 or (800) 772-6887, fax (513) 961-2688; or O.A. Lodge #462, BSA, 3007 Vernon Pl., Cincinnati, OH 45219. 35.5 miles straight. Awards available. (AA 1991)

3015 **Anthony Wayne Trail** (Fort Hamilton Segment), Dan Beard Council, BSA, 2331 Victory Pkwy., Cincinnati, OH 45206, (513) 961-2336 or (800) 772-6887, fax (513) 961-2688; or O.A. Lodge 462, BSA, 3007 Vernon Pl., Cincinnati, OH 45219. 32.8 miles straight. Awards available. (AA 1991)

3016 **Anthony Wayne Trail** (Fort St. Clair Segment), Mound Builders Area Council, BSA, 29 City Centre Plaza, Middletown, OH 45042; or O.A. Lodge 495, c/o Miami Valley Council, BSA, 4999 Northcutt Pl., Dayton, OH 45414. 39.7 miles straight. Awards available. (COC; HTA)

Arboretum Trail see entry 3114.

3017 **Atwood Lake Park**, CR 93, Mineral City, OH 44656, (216) 343-6780. (WCD; ATI)

3018 **Auburn Lake Park**, SR 103, New Washington, OH 44854, (419) 492-2110. (WCD)

3019 **Aullwood Audubon Center and Farm**, 1000 Aullwood Rd., Dayton, OH 45414, (513) 890-7360. (MGL)

3020 **Austin Lake Park and Campground**, Austin Lake Rd., Toronto, OH 43964, (614) 544-5253. (WCD)

3021 **Barkcamp State Park**, SR 149, Belmont, OH 43718, (614) 484-4064. (WCD; ATI)

3022 **Beaumont Scout Reservation**, Greater Cleveland Council, BSA, Woodland Ave. & E. 22nd St., Cleveland, OH 44115, (216) 861-6060. 4.0 & 6.5 miles loops. Awards available. (AA 1989; SAR 1967)

3023 **Beaver Creek State Park**, SR 7, East Liverpool, OH 43920, (216) 385-3091. 15.0 miles. Named trails: Dogwood, Fisherman's, Gretchen's Lock, Pine Ridge, Vondergreen. (AA 1994)

3024 **Belden Camp Trail**, Greater Cleveland Council, BSA, Woodland Ave. & E. 22nd St., Cleveland, OH 44115, (216) 861-6060. 5.0 miles loop. Awards available. (SAR 1989)

3025 **Berlin Lake**, Reservoir Manager, Deerfield, OH 44411. (LRA)

3026 **Bicentennial Trail**, Ohio Power

Company, Att. Bill Homeister, P.O. Box 328, McConnelsville, OH 43756. 13.0 miles. (COC)

Bike and Hike Trail *see* entry 3064.

3027 **Blackhand Gorge Bikeway**, William Daehler, Administrator, Comprehensive Planning Section, Division of Natural Areas and Preserves, Ohio Department of Natural Resources, Fountain Sq., Columbus, OH 43224, (614) 265-6395. 4.0 miles straight. (GRT)

3028 **Blackhand Gorge State Nature Preserve**, SR 146, Newark, OH 43055. Named trails: Chestnut, Owl Hollow. (OTB)

3029 **Blue Heron Trail**, BSA Troop 184, c/o Larry Young, 585 SR 571, Union City, OH 45390, (513) 968-5577. 15.0 miles straight. Awards available. (AA 1992)

3030 **Blue Rock State Park**, CR 45, Duncan Falls, OH 43734, (614) 674-4794. (WCD; ATI; MGL)

Bluewater Trail *see* entry 3154.

3031 **Bob Board Park**, Rochester Rd., East Rochester, OH 44625, (216) 894-2360. (WCD)

3032 **Bob Evans Farms**, P.O. Box 330, Rio Grande, OH 45674, (614) 245-5305. 12.0 miles. Adamsville 1.0, Gatewood-Adamsville Cutoff, Grandma Gatewood 2.0, Nehemiah Wood 2.0. (AA 1992)

3033 **Bruckner Nature Center**, 5995 Horseshoe Bend Rd., Troy, OH 45373, (513) 698-6493. 6.0 miles. (ATI; OOB)

3034 **Buccaneer Campsite**, 1408 SR 307W, Jefferson, OH 44047, (216) 576-2881. (WCD)

3035 **Buck Creek State Park**, SR 4, Springfield, OH 44501, (513) 322-5284. (WCD; ATN; MGL)

3036 **Buckeye Lake-KOA**, SR 79, Buckeye Lake, OH 43008, (614) 928-0706. (WCD)

3037 **Buckeye Trail**, Buckeye Trail Association, P.O. Box 254, Worthington, OH 43085. 1158 miles loop. Section distances: Akron 40.0(s), Belle Valley 55.0(s), Bowerston 58.0(s), Burton 54.0(s), Caesar Creek 51.0(s), Chapin Forest 31.0(s), Defiance 53.0(s), Delphos 38.0(s), Fremont 48.0(s), Loveland 41.0(s), Massillon 48.0(s), Medina 53.0(s), Mogadore 52.0(s), New Straitsville/Norwalk 50.0(s), Old Man's Cave 61.0(s), Scioto Trail 52.0(s), Sinking Spring 36.0(s), St. Marys 41.0(s), Stockport 63.0(s), Tinkers Creek 29.0(s), Troy 54.0(s), Waterville 44.0(s), West Union 59.0(s), Williamsburg 47.0(s). Awards available. (SAR 1990)

3038 **Burr Oak State Park**, Rt. 2, Box 286, Glouster, OH 45732, (614) 466-0652. Named trails: Burr Oak 29.0. (WCD; EGH; ATI; MGL)

Burr Oak Trail *see* entry 3038.

3039 **Caesar Creek State Park**, 8570 Center Rd., Waynesville, OH 45068, (513) 897-3055. 30.0 miles. (WCD; EGH; ATI; MGL)

Calico Bush Trail *see* entry 3131.

California Junction Trail *see* entry 3040.

3040 **California Woods Nature Preserve**, Jim Farsing, California Woods Recreation Center, 5400 Kellogg Ave., Cincinnati, OH 45228, (513) 231-8678. Named trails: California Junction 1.0(s). (GRT)

3041 **Camelot Camping Grounds**, 17837 Warwick Rd., Marshallville, OH 44645, (216) 855-5225. (WCD)

3042 **Camp Toodik Family Campground & Canoe Livery**, 7700 TR 462, Loudonville, OH 44842, (419) 994-3835 or (800) 322-2663. (WCD)

Camp Trail *see* entry 3114.

3043 **Captain Martin Bates Trail**, Scoutmaster, BSA Troop 456, Seville, OH 44273. 15.0 miles. Awards available. (COC)

3044 **Carriage Hill Reserve**, Shull Rd., Dayton, OH 45424, (513) 879-0461. (ATI)

3045 **Cascade & Elywood Parks**, City Hall, 7303 Avon Belden Rd., Elyria, OH 44035, (216) 322-0926. (ATI; MGL; NAT)

3046 **Cave Lake Park**, Bell Hollow Rd., Sinking Spring, OH 45172, (513) 588-3252. (WCD)

3047 **Cedarlane Campgrounds**, 2926 N.E. Catawba Rd., Port Clinton, OH 43452, (419) 797-9907. (WCD)

3048 **Celina-Coldwater Bikeway**, Mike Sovinski, Celina Engineering Department,

426 W. Market, Celina, OH 45822, (419) 586-1144. 4.6 miles straight. (GRT)

3049 **Chaparral Family Campground**, 10136 Middletown Rd., Salem, OH 44460, (216) 337-9381. (WCD)

3050 **Charles Mill Lake Park**, SR 430, Mansfield, OH 44903, (419) 368-6885. (WCD; ATI)

Chestnut Trail see entry 3028.

3051 **Chief Blackhoof Trail**, Bill Collins, Fort Amanda Trading Post, RR 4, Fort Amanda Rd., Cridersville, OH 45806. 8.5 miles straight. Awards available. (AA 1994)

3052 **Chief Logan's Gap Camping Resort & Marina**, P.O. Box 38, Ripley, OH 45167, (513) 392-4722. (WCD)

3053 **Chief Wapa Tecumseh Trail**, Paul Nuss, Rt. 1, New Knoxville, OH 45871. 24.5 miles straight. Awards available. (AA 1991)

Chuck Wagon Trail see entry 3154.

3054 **Cincinnati Nature Center**, 4949 Tealtown Rd., Cincinnati, OH 45234. (TOV)

3055 **Clear Water Trail**, Bill Collins, Fort Amanda Trading Post, RR 4, Fort Amanda Rd., Cridersville, OH 45806. 18.0 miles straight. Awards available. (AA 1994)

3056 **Clinton Lake Camping**, TR 122, Republic, OH 44867, (419) 585-3331. (WCD)

3057 **Country Acres Campground**, Minyoung Rd., Ravenna, OH 44266, (216) 358-2774. (WCD)

3058 **The Covered Bridge Trail**, Boy Scout Troop 101, c/o John Eufinger, 110 S. Court St., Marysville, OH 43040. 14.0 miles. Awards available. (COC)

3059 **Cowan Lake State Park**, Dalton Rd., Wilmington, OH 45177, (513) 289-2105. (WCD; ATI; MGL)

3060 **Cox Arboretum**, 6733 Springboro Pike, Dayton, OH 45449, (513) 434-9005. 1.5 miles. (ATI; GFA)

3061 **Cozy-Dale Campground**, 10623 Cozaddale-Murdock Rd., Goshen, OH 45122, (513) 722-1692. (WCD)

3062 **Crane Creek State Park**, 19000 W. SR 1, Oak Harbor, OH 43449, (419) 898-2495. (ATI; MGL; NAT)

3063 **Cross's Campground**, US 127, Camden, OH 45311, (513) 452-1535. (WCD)

3064 **Cuyahoga Valley National Recreation Area**, Akron, OH 44309, (216) 650-4636. Named trails: Bike and Hike, Daffodil, Wetmore Bridle. (SAR 1994)

3065 **Cuyahoga Valley Trail**, Marnoc Lodge, O.A., Great Trail Council, BSA, P.O. Box 68, 1601 S. Main St., Akron, OH 44309-0068. 13.0 miles loop. Awards available. (SAR 1990)

Daffodil Trail see entry 3064.

3066 **Dan Beard Riverwalk Trail**, Dan Beard Council, BSA, 2331 Victory Pkwy., Cincinnati, OH 45206, (513) 961-2336. 5.0 miles loop. Awards available. (AA 1992)

3067 **Dawes Arboretum**, 7770 Jacksontown Rd., SE, Newark, OH 43055, (614) 323-2355. (MGL)

3068 **Deer Creek State Park**, 20635 Waterloo Rd., Mt. Sterling, OH 43143, (614) 869-3124 or (614) 869-3508. (WCD; ATI; MGL)

Deer Loop Trail see entry 3187.

3069 **Delaware State Park**, US 23, Delaware, OH 43015, (614) 369-2761. (WCD; ATI; MGL)

3070 **Delphos Historical Trail**, Charles A. Rohrbacher, 187 Michelle Dr., Delphos, OH 45833. 7.5 miles loop. Awards available. (AA 1990)

3071 **Dillon State Park**, SR 146, Zanesville, OH 43701, (614) 453-4377. (WCD; MGL)

Dogwood Trail see entry 3023.

3072 **Dogwood Valley Resort Family Campground**, TR 99, Mount Gilead, OH 43338, (419) 946-5230. (WCD)

3073 **East Fork State Park**, P.O. Box 119, Bethel, OH 45106, (513) 734-4323. 60.0 miles. (WCD; EGH; ATI; MGL)

3074 **East Harbor State Park**, 1169 N. Buck Rd., Lakeside-Marblehead, OH 43440, (419) 734-4424. (WCD; ATI; MGL; NAT)

3075 **Edge of Appalachia Preserve**, Cincinnati Museum of Natural History, 1720 Gilbert Ave., Cincinnati, OH 45202, (513) 621-3889. (GOP 1991)

3076 **Edwin H. Davis State Memorial**,

TR 129, Peebles, OH 45660, (614) 297-2300. (ATI)

3077 **Emerald Necklace Trails**, Greater Cleveland Council, BSA, Woodland Ave. & E. 22nd St., Cleveland, OH 44115, (216) 861-6060. 4 sections 10.0-16.0 miles straight each. Awards available. (SAR 1989)

3078 **Enon Beach Campground**, 2401 Enon Rd., Springfield, OH 45502, (513) 882-6431. (WCD)

3079 **Faraway Trail**, Frank M. Fauver, 123 W. Leggett St., Wauseon, OH 43567, (419) 335-9363. 15.1 miles loop. Awards available. (AA 1994)

3080 **Fernwood State Forest**, Ohio Department of Natural Resources, Division of Forestry, Fountain Sq., Columbus, OH 43224, (614) 265-7000. (GFC)

3081 **Findley State Park**, SR 58, Wellington, OH 44090, (216) 647-4490. (WCD; ATI)

Fisherman's Trail see entry 3023.

3082 **Flint Ridge State Memorial and Museum**, CR 668, Brownsville, OH 43721, (614) 787-2476. (ATI; OOB)

3083 **Forked Run State Park**, SR 124, Reedsville, OH 45772, (614) 378-6206. (WCD; ATI)

3084 **Ft. Amanda-Ft. Barbee Trail**, Bob Suchland, c/o Goodyear Tire & Rubber Co., P.O. Box 288, St. Marys, OH 45885; or Trail Committee, P.O. Box 181, St. Marys, OH 45885; or Four Rivers Trail Committee, c/o Troop 235 BSA, 825 Creighton Ave., Dayton, OH 45410. 20.0 miles. Awards available. (HTA; COC)

3085 **Fort Ancient**, Middleboro Rd., Lebanon, OH 45036, (513) 932-4421. (ATI)

3086 **Fort Hill Nature Preserve**, SR 41, Sinking Spring, OH 45172. (ATI)

3087 **Fort Hill Trail**, Fort Hill State Memorial, TR 256, Chillicothe, OH 45601. 2000' straight. (MGL)

3088 **Four Rivers Trail**, Four Rivers Trail Committee, c/o Troop 235 BSA, 825 Creighton Ave., Dayton, OH 45410. 11.5 miles. Awards available. (AA 1992)

Gatewood-Adamsville Cutoff Trail see entry 3032.

3089 **Geneva State Park**, SR 534, Geneva-on-the-Lake, OH 44041, (216) 466-8600. (WCD; ATI; MGL)

3090 **Glen Helen Scout Trail**, Milton Lord, 1360 Rice Rd., Yellow Springs, OH 45387. 10.0 miles loop. Awards available. (AA 1990)

3091 **Grand Lake St. Marys State Park**, SR 703, St. Marys, OH 45885, (419) 394-3611. (WCD; ATI)

Grandma Gatewood Trail see entry 3032.

3092 **Great Seal State Park**, 825 Rocky Rd., Chillicothe, OH 45601, (614) 773-2726. 20.0 miles. (EGH; ATI)

Gretchen's Lock Trail see entry 3023.

3093 **Happy Hills Family Campground**, SR 278, Nelsonville, OH 45764, (614) 385-6720. (WCD)

3094 **Happy Hunting Ground Trail**, Miami Valley Council, BSA, 4999 Northcutt Pl., Dayton, OH 45414. 12.78 miles loop. Awards available. (AA 1992)

3095 **Harrison Lake State Park**, US 20, Fayette, OH 43521, (419) 237-2593. (WCD; ATI)

3096 **Headlands Beach State Park**, SR 44, Painesville, OH 44077. (ATI)

3097 **Heritage Trail**, Hancock Park District, 819 Park St., Findlay, OH 45840. 20.0 miles straight. Awards available. (AA 1991)

3098 **Hidden Hills Campground**, Loper Rd., Newark, OH 43055, (614) 763-2750. (WCD)

3099 **Hidden Hollow Campground**, Fresno Rd., Carrollton, OH 44615, (216) 735-2553. (WCD)

3100 **Hide Away Hollow**, Pancake-Clarkson Rd., Rogers, OH 44455, (216) 227-3626. (WCD)

3101 **Hocking Hills State Park**, 20160 SR 664, Logan, OH 43138, (614) 385-6841. 20.0 miles. (WCD; EGH; ATI; MGL; OOB)

3102 **Holden Arboretum**, 9500 Sperry Rd., Mentor, OH 44060, (216) 946-4400. (ATI; NAT; OOB; SAR 1965)

3103 **Honeycreek Valley Campground**, 1219 Honeycreek Rd. W., Bellville, OH 44813, (419) 896-2777. (WCD)

3104 **Hoover Reservoir**, Sunbury Rd., Columbus, OH 43230, (614) 882-4145. (MGL)
  Horace Mann Trail *see* entry 3114.
3105 **Hueston Woods State Park**, SR 732, Oxford, OH 45056, (513) 523-6347. (WCD; ATI; MGL)
3106 **Huffman Prairie Overlook Trail**, Elwood J. Ensor, Miami Valley Regional Bicycle Committee, 1304 Horizon Dr., Fairborn, OH 45324-5816, (513) 879-2068 or (513) 255-4097. 5.5 miles straight planned, current as to 3.0 miles. (GRT)
3107 **Independence Dam State Park**, SR 24, Defiance, OH 43512, (419) 784-3263. (WCD; ATI; MGL)
3108 **Indian Creek Camping Resort**, 4710 Lake Rd. E., Geneva-on-the-Lake, OH 44041-9449, (216) 466-8191 or fax (216) 466-6900. (WCD)
3109 **Indian Lake State Park**, US 33, Bellefontaine, OH 43311, (513) 843-2098. (WCD; ATI; MGL)
3110 **Indian Mound Campground**, TR 24, Athens, OH 45701, (614) 664-8700. (WCD)
3111 **Indian Trail Campground**, US 250, Fitchville, OH 44851, (419) 929-1135. (WCD)
  Inner Trail *see* entry 3248.
3112 **Jeffco Lakes Campground**, Hayes Rd., Andover, OH 44003, (216) 293-7485. (WCD)
3113 **Jefferson Lake State Park**, SR 43, Richmond, OH 43444, (614) 765-4459. (WCD; ATI)
3114 **John Bryan State Park and Clifton Gorge State Nature Preserve**, 3790 SR 370, Yellow Springs, OH 45387, (513) 767-1274. Named trails: Arboretum 1.2(l), Camp 1.0(s), Horace Mann, John L. Rich 1.3(s), Narrows, North Gorge, North Rim 2.0(s), Orton Memorial 1.0(s), Pittsburgh-Cincinnati Stage Coach 1.3(s), Poplar 0.3(s), Swimming Pool Road 0.2(s). (WCD; ATI; MGL)
  John L. Rich Trail *see* entry 3114.
3115 **Johnny Appleseed Trail**, Johnny Appleseed Council, BSA, 445 W. Longview Ave., Mansfield, OH 44905, (419) 522-5091. 20.9 miles straight. Awards available. (AA 1991)
3116 **Kelleys Island Trail**, Kelleys Island Chamber of Commerce, P.O. Box 783M, Kelleys Island, OH 43438-0783, (419) 746-2360. 9.0 miles loop. (LGU; WCD; ATI; FHO; MGL)
3117 **Kiser Lake State Park**, SR 235, St. Paris, OH 43072, (513) 362-3822. (WCD; ATI)
  Kit Cricket Training Trail *see* entry 3154.
3118 **KOA-Bear Creek Resort Ranch**, Haut Rd., Canton, OH 44706, (216) 484-3901. (WCD)
3119 **KOA-Big Sandy-Toledo/Maumee**, 4035 SR 295, Swanton, OH 43558, (419) 826-8784. (WCD)
3120 **KOA-Butler/Mohican**, Bunkerhill Rd., Butler, OH 44822, (419) 883-3314. (WCD)
3121 **KOA-Dayton Tall Timbers Resort**, 7796 Wellbaum Rd., Brookville, OH 45309, (513) 833-3888 or (800) 432-CAMP. (WCD)
3122 **KOA-Hocking Hills**, SR 664, Logan, OH 43138, (614) 385-4295. (WCD)
3123 **Kokosing Gap Trail**, Phil Samuell, President of the Board of Directors, Kokosing Gap Trail, P.O. Box 129, Gambier, OH 43022, (614) 427-4509 or (614) 587-6267. 9.0 miles straight planned, current as to 4.2 miles. (GRT)
3124 **Kokosing Valley Camp & Canoe**, US 36, Howard, OH 43028, (614) 599-7056. (WCD)
3125 **Kool Lakes Family Campground & Recreation Resort**, SR 282, Parkman, OH 44080, (216) 548-8436. (WCD)
3126 **La Trainee de L'Explorateur Trail**, Trailmaster, Troop 83 BSA, 4416 Colerain Ave., Cincinnati, OH 45223. 10.0 miles. Awards available. (COC)
3127 **Lake Alma State Park**, SR 349, Wellston, OH 45692, (614) 384-4474. (WCD; ATI; MGL)
3128 **Lake Erie Nature & Science Center**, 28728 Wolf Rd., Bay Village, OH 44140, (216) 871-2900. (ATI)
3129 **Lake Hill Campground**, Musselman Rd., Chillicothe, OH 45601, (614) 998-5648. (WCD)

OHIO

3130 **Lake Hope State Park**, SR 278, Zaleski, OH 45698, (614) 596-5253. (WCD)

3131 **Lake Katherine State Nature Preserve**, CR 59, Jackson, OH 45640, (614) 286-2487. Named trails: Calico Bush, Pine Ridge 2.0, Salt Creek 2.0. (OOB)

3132 **Lake Logan State Park**, SR 664, Logan, OH 43138, (614) 385-3444. (ATI; MGL)

3133 **Lake Loramie State Park**, SR 362, Fort Loramie, OH 45845, (513) 295-2011. (WCD; ATI)

3134 **Lake Park Recreation Area**, 23253 SR 83, Coshocton, OH 43812, (614) 622-7528. (WCD)

3135 **Lake Snowden Recreation Area**, US 50, Albany, OH 45710, (614) 698-6373. (WCD)

3136 **Lake Vesuvius Park**, SR 93, Ironton, OH 45638. (ATI)

3137 **Lazy R Campground**, Dry Creek Rd., Newark, OH 43055, (614) 366-4385. (WCD)

3138 **Lazy River Resort Campground**, Rt. 1, Pioneer, OH 43554, (419) 485-4411. (WCD)

3139 **Leesville Southfork Marina**, Deer Rd., Sherrodsville, OH 44675, (614) 269-5371. (WCD; ATI)

3140 **Leo Petroglyph State Memorial**, CR 28, Coalton, OH 45621, (216) 297-2300. (ATI)

3141 **Lil Beaver Park**, Trinity Church Rd., Lisbon, OH 44432, (216) 223-1167. (WCD)

3142 **Little Miami Bike Route**, Tim Smith, Director, Springfield Parks and Recreation, City Hall, 76 E. High St., Springfield, OH 45502, (513) 324-7348. 3.0 miles straight. (GRT)

3143 **Little Miami Scenic Park Trail**, Little Miami Scenic Park, 8570 E. SR 73, Waynesville, OH 45068, (513) 897-3055. 45.0 miles straight. (GRT; EGH; ATI)

3144 **Logan Trail**, 643 Weyant Ave., Columbus, OH 43213, (614) 235-7026. 10.0 & 21.0 miles loops. Awards available. (AA 1991)

3145 **Magee Marsh Wildlife Area**, Port Clinton, OH 43452. (OTB)

3146 **Malabar Farm State Park**, Pleasant Valley Rd., Mansfield, OH 44903, (419) 892-2784; or Malabar Farm AYH-Hostel, Rt. 1, Box 465-A, Lucas, OH 44843, (419) 892-2055. (ATI; AYH; MGL; OTB)

3147 **Mar-Lynn Lake Park**, 187 SR 303, Streetsboro, OH 44241, (216) 650-2552. (WCD)

3148 **Mary Jane Thurston State Park**, SR 65, Bowling Green, OH 43402, (419) 832-7662. (ATI; MGL)

3149 **Maumee Bay State Park**, 6505 Cedar Point Rd., Oregon, OH 43618, (419) 836-7758. (WCD; ATI; MGL; NAT)

3150 **Meadow Lake Resort**, Woodville Pk., Urbana, OH 43078, (513) 652-3400. (WCD)

3151 **Meadowbrook Park**, SR 18, Bascom, OH 44809, (419) 937-2242. (WCD)

3152 **Miami Conservancy Trail**, O.A. Lodge 495, c/o Miami Valley Council, BSA, 4999 Northcutt Pl., Dayton, OH 45414. 21.3 miles. Awards available. (MVC; HTA)

3153 **Miami-Erie Trail**, John Lunz, Jr., 302 Columbia St., St. Marys, OH 45885. 8.0 miles straight. Awards available. (AA 1994)

3154 **Miami Valley Training Trails**, Miami Valley Council, BSA, 4999 Northcutt Pl., Dayton, OH 45414. Named trails: Bluewater Training 6.12(l), Chuck Wagon 5.0, Kit Cricket Training 4.62(l), Old Two-Path 5.0, Red Stallion Training 5.20(l), Triangle Training 6.21(l). Awards available. (AA 1992)

3155 **Miami Whitewater Forest**, I-74, Cincinnati, OH 45214. (ATI)

3156 **Middletown Historic Trail**, Mound Builders Area Council, BSA, 29 City Centre Plaza, Middletown, OH 45042. 6.8 miles. Awards available. (COC)

3157 **Mill Creek Park**, Mahoning Ave., Youngstown, OH 44509, (216) 740-7108; or Youngstown Department of Parks and Recreation, 26 S. Phelps St., Youngstown, OH 44503, (216) 744-4171. (NAT)

3158 **Mill Creek Park Trail**, Mahoning Valley Council, BSA, 3712 Leffingwell Rd., Canfield, OH 44406, (216) 477-7248.

10.0 miles loop. Awards available. (AA 1993)

3159 **Mineral Springs Lake Resort,** Mineral Springs Rd., Peebles, OH 45660, (513) 587-3132. (WCD)

3160 **Mohican State Park,** P.O. Box 22, SR 97, Loudonville, OH 44842, (419) 994-4290. (WCD; ATI; NAT)

3161 **Mohican Wilderness,** Wally Rd., Loudonville, OH 44842, (614) 599-6741. (WCD)

3162 **Mosquito Creek State Park,** SR 5, Bazetta, OH 44481, (216) 637-2856. (WCD; ATI; MGL)

3163 **Mound City Group National Monument,** 16062 SR 104, Chillicothe, OH 45601, (614) 774-1125. (GNM; NPS; NPV; SSI; NPE; CGA; ANP)

3164 **Mount Airy Forest and Arboretum,** 5083 Colerain Ave., Cincinnati, OH 45223, (513) 352-4080. (WCD; ATI; MGL)

3165 **Mt. Gilead State Park,** SR 95, Mt. Gilead, OH 43338, (419) 946-1961. (ATI; MGL)

3166 **Mount Pleasant,** Rising Park, N. High St., Lancaster, OH 43130. (MGL)

Narrows Trail *see* entry 3114.

Nehemiah Wood Trail *see* entry 3032.

North Gorge Trail *see* entry 3114.

North Rim Trail *see* entry 3114.

3167 **Oak Openings Trail,** Oak Openings Park Manager, 4139 Girdham Rd., Swanton, OH 43558, (419) 862-6463; or Toledo Area Council, BSA, One Stranahan Sq., Toledo, OH 43604-1492, (419) 241-7293. 17.0 miles loop. Awards available. (AA 1991)

3168 **Ohio Canal Greenway,** Russ Edgington, Licking Park District, 4309 Lancaster Rd., Granville, OH 43023, (614) 587-2535. 2.8 miles straight. (GRT)

3169 **Ohio City Trail,** Greater Cleveland Council, BSA, Woodland Ave. & E. 22nd St., Cleveland, OH 44115, (216) 861-6060. 4.5 miles loop. Awards available. (SAR 1990)

Old Two-Path Trail *see* entry 3154.

3170 **Olive Branch Campground,** 6985 Wilmington Rd., Orgonia, OH 45054, (513) 932-4399. (WCD)

Orton Memorial Trail *see* entry 3114.

3171 **Ottawa National Wildlife Refuge,** 14000 W. SR 2, Oak Harbor, OH 43449, (419) 897-0211. 7.0 miles. (GNW)

3172 **Ottawa Park,** Parkside Blvd., Toledo, OH 43607. (GNW)

Owl Hollow Trail *see* entry 3028.

3173 **Paint Creek State Park,** US 50, Bainbridge, OH 45612, (614) 365-1401. (WCD; ATI; MGL)

3174 **Panther Trails Campground,** Peck-Wadsworth Rd., Wellington, OH 44090, (216) 647-5453. (WCD)

3175 **Paradise Lake Park,** Rochester Rd., East Rochester, OH 44625, (216) 525-7726. (WCD)

Paw Paw Trail *see* entry 3187.

3176 **Pier-Lon Park,** Vandemark Rd., Medina, OH 44256, (216) 667-2311. (WCD)

3177 **Pike Lake State Park,** Potts Hill Rd., Bainbridge, OH 45612, (614) 493-2212. (WCD; ATI)

Pine Ridge Trail *see* entry 3023.

Pine Ridge Trail *see* entry 3131.

Pittsburgh-Cincinnati Stage Coach Trail *see* entry 3114.

3178 **Platt Park,** SR 78, Woodsfield, OH 43793. (ATI)

3179 **Pleasant Hill Lake Park,** SR 95, Perrysville, OH 44864. (ATI)

3180 **Poor Farmer's Campsite,** 7211 N. Lostcreek-Shelby Rd., Fletcher, OH 45326, (513) 368-2449. (WCD)

Poplar Trail *see* entry 3114.

3181 **Portage Lakes State Park,** SR 93, Akron, OH 44309, (216) 644-2220. (WCD; ATI; MGL)

3182 **Possum Creek Reserve,** Gettysburg Ave., Dayton, OH 45406. (ATI)

3183 **Punderson State Park,** P.O. Box 338, 10755 Kinsman Rd., Newberry, OH 44065, (216) 564-2279. (WCD; ATI; MGL; NAT)

3184 **Pymatuning State Park,** Lake Rd., Andover, OH 44003, (216) 293-6329. (WCD; ATI)

3185 **Quail Hollow State Park,** Congress Lake Rd., Hartville, OH 44632. (ATI)

Red Stallion Trail *see* entry 3154.

Redbud Trail *see* entry 3187.

3186 **Rippling Stream Campground**, SR 156, Baltimore, OH 43105, (614) 862-6065. (WCD)

3187 **Rocky Fork State Park**, N. Shore Dr., Hillsboro, OH 45133, (513) 393-4284. Named trails: Deer Loop, Paw Paw, Redbud. (WCD; ATI; OTB)

3188 **Sally Buffalo Park**, SR 9, Cadiz, OH 43907, (614) 942-3213. (WCD)

  Salt Creek Trail *see* entry 3131.

3189 **Salt Fork State Park**, US 22, Cambridge, OH 43725, (614) 439-3521. (WCD; ATI; MGL)

3190 **Sandy Beaver Trail**, Columbiana Council, BSA, 37748 Furnace Rd., Lisbon, OH 44432. 19.0 miles. Awards available. (COC; HTA)

3191 **Scioto Bike Path**, Mollie O'Donnell, Landscape Architect, City of Columbus Recreation and Parks Department, 420 W. Whittier St., Columbus, OH 43215, (614) 645-3300. 4.75 miles straight. (GRT)

3192 **Scioto Trail State Park**, SR 372, Waverly, OH 45690, (614) 663-2125. (WCD; ATI)

3193 **Sea Lake Resort**, 250 Treat Rd., Aurora, OH 44402, (216) 562-4423. (WCD)

3194 **Senecaville Lake Park**, SR 574, Senecaville, OH 43780, (614) 685-6013. (WCD; ATI)

3195 **Seven Caves**, US 50, Bainbridge, OH 45612, (513) 365-1283. (ATI)

3196 **Shadow Lake Campground**, Miltonsburg/Calais Rd., Woodsfield, OH 43793, (614) 472-5468. (WCD)

3197 **Shaker Lakes Regional Nature Center**, 2600 S. Park Blvd., Shaker Heights, OH 44120, (216) 321-5935. (MGL; NAT)

3198 **Sharon Woods Park**, Reading Rd., Cincinnati, OH 45241. (ATI)

3199 **Shawnee Backpack Trail**, Ohio Deparment of Natural Resources, Division of Forestry, Fountain Sq., Columbus, OH 43224. 22.8-49.7 miles. (COC; HTM)

3200 **Shawnee Lookout**, US 50, Cincinnati, OH 45243. (ATI)

3201 **Shawnee State Forest**, Rt. 5, Box 151C, Portsmouth, OH 45662, (614) 858-6685. 60.0 miles. (EGH)

3202 **Shawnee State Park**, SR 125, Portsmouth, OH 45662, (614) 858-6621. (WCD; ATI; OOB)

3203 **Shawnee Trail**, Scioto Area Council, BSA, P.O. Box 1305, Portsmouth, OH 45662; or Ron Miller, Star Route, Box 60, Portsmouth, OH 45662. 14.0 miles. Awards available. (HTA)

3204 **Sherwood Forrest**, SR 83, Lodi, OH 44254, (216) 667-2156. (WCD)

3205 **Silver Moccasin Trail** (includes Golden Lamb Trail and Little Miami Trail), Mound Builders Area Council, BSA, 29 City Centre Plaza, Middletown, OH 45042. Awards available. (MVC; HTA)

3206 **Sloan's Hickory Lake Campground**, 26 TR 1300, West Salem, OH 44287, (419) 869-7587. (WCD)

3207 **Spring Valley Campground**, 8000 Dozer Rd., Cambridge, OH 43725, (614) 439-9291. (WCD)

3208 **Stavich Bicycle Trail**, Gary Slaven, Falcon Foundry, 6th & Water Sts., P.O. Box 301, Lowellville, OH 44436-0301, (216) 536-6221. 12.0 miles. (GRT)

3209 **Stonelick State Park**, SR 727, Blanchester, OH 45107, (513) 625-7544. (WCD; ATI)

3210 **Strouds Run State Park**, US 50, Athens, OH 45701, (614) 592-2302. (WCD; ATI; MGL)

3211 **Sugarcreek Reserve**, Wilmington Pk., Cincinnati, OH 45214. (ATI)

  Swimming Pool Road Trail *see* entry 3114.

3212 **Sycamore State Park**, SR 49, Trotwood, OH 45426. (ATI)

3213 **Tamsin Park Camping Resort**, Akron/Cleveland Rd., Peninsula, OH 44264, (216) 650-0579. (WCD)

3214 **Tappan Lake Park**, CR 55, Cadiz, OH 43907, (614) 922-3649. (WCD; ATI)

3215 **Tar Hollow State Park**, SR 327, Laurelville, OH 43135, (614) 887-4818. (WCD; ATI)

3216 **Terrace Lakes Campground**, TR 462, Sullivan, OH 44880, (419) 736-3463. (WCD)

3217 **Thomas J. Evans Bike Trail**, The Thomas J. Evans Foundation, P.O. Box

4212, Newark, OH 43055, (614) 345-9711. 14.5 miles straight. (GRT)

3218 **Thunderbird Trail**, Dan Beard Council, BSA, 2331 Victory Pkwy., Cincinnati, OH 45206. 5.0 miles. Awards available. (AA 1994)

3219 **Tinkers Creek State Park**, Aurora-Hudson Rd., Portage, OH 43451. (ATI)

3220 **Tomorrow's Stars Music Park**, US 40, Springfield, OH 45501, (513) 324-2267. (WCD)

3221 **Top 'o the Caves Campground**, Chapel Ridge Rd., Logan, OH 43138, (800) 967-2434. (WCD)

3222 **Town and Country Camp Resort**, 7555 Shilling Rd., West Salem, OH 44287, (419) 853-4550. (WCD)

3223 **Towpath Trail**, Buckeye Council, BSA, 5136 Tuscarawas St. W., Canton, OH 44708. 15.0 miles loop. Awards available. (AA 1991)

3224 **Tree Haven Campground**, Miller-Paul Rd., Westerville, OH 43081, (614) 965-3469. (WCD)

Triangle Training Trail see entry 3154.

3225 **Turtle Creek Campground**, Hardin-Wapak Rd., Sidney, OH 45365, (513) 492-3104. (WCD)

3226 **Twin Hill Park**, SR 799, Freeport, OH 43973, (614) 658-3275. (WCD)

3227 **Valley Lake Park**, SR 305, Southington, OH 44470, (216) 898-1819. (WCD)

3228 **Van Buren Lake State Park**, SR 613, Van Buren, OH 45889, (419) 299-3461. (WCD; ATI)

3229 **Vesuvius Furnace Historical Trail**, Delbert E. Tennant, 749 High St., Coal Grove, OH 45638; or Scioto Area Council, BSA, 1239 Second St., P.O. Box 1305, Portsmouth, OH 45662; or District Ranger, Wayne National Forest, Ironton, OH 45638. 16.0 miles. Awards available. (HTA; COC)

Vondergreen Trail see entry 3023.

3230 **Wahkeena Nature Preserve**, CR 86, Lancaster, OH 43130, (614) 297-2606. (ATI)

3231 **Warren Western Reserve Historical Trail**, Ron Kay, 8442 E. Market St., Warren, OH 44483, (216) 372-1049. 7.0 miles loop. Awards available. (SAR 1990)

3232 **Wayne National Forest**, Forest Supervisor, 3527 10th St., Bedford, IN 47421, (812) 275-5987; or Ironton Ranger District, 710 Park Ave., Ironton, OH 45638, (614) 532-3223; or Athens Ranger District, 219 Columbus Rd., Athens, OH 45701, (614) 592-6644, or Marietta Ranger District, Rt. 1, Box 132, Marietta, OH 45750, (614) 373-9055. 50.0 miles. Named trails: Wildcat Hollow 13.0(l). (WCD; EGH; ATI; MGL; FGU; TOV)

3233 **West Branch State Park**, 5708 Ellsworthy Rd., Ravenna, OH 44266, (216) 296-3239. (WCD; ATI; MGL; NAT)

Wetmore Bridle Trails see entry 3064.

3234 **Whispering Hills Family Campground**, P.O. Box 607, Shreve, OH 44676, (216) 567-2137 or (800) 992-2435. (WCD)

Wildcat Hollow Trail see entry 3232.

3235 **Wildcat Woods Campground**, 1355 Wildcat Rd., Greenville, OH 45331, (513) 548-7921. (WCD)

3236 **The Wilderness Center**, US 250, Wilmot, OH 44689, (216) 359-5235. (ATI; GFA; MGL; NAT)

3237 **Wilderness Trace**, Wilderness Trace Committee, 339 Binns Blvd., Columbus, OH 43204. 10.0 miles. Awards available. (COC)

3238 **Wildwood Preserve Metropark**, 5120 W. Central Ave., Toledo, OH 43615, (419) 535-3058. (NAT; OOB)

3239 **Wilmot Wilderness Center** (see The Wilderness Center **3236**).

3240 **Winter Bushwack**, BSA Troop 184, c/o Larry Young, 585 SR 571, Union City, OH 45390, (513) 968-5577. 10.0 miles. Awards available. (AA 1994)

3241 **Winter's Recreational Area**, SR 347, Raymond, OH 43067, (513) 246-4011. (WCD)

3242 **Winton Woods Park**, Winton Rd., Cincinnati, OH 45224. (ATI)

3243 **Withrow Nature Preserve**, Five Mile Rd., Cincinnati, OH 45230, (513) 385-4653. (IGC)

3244 **Wolf Run State Park**, SR 177, Cald-

well, OH 43724, (614) 732-5035. (WCD; ATI)
3245 **Wooded Acres Campground**, 2232 CR 106, Lindsey, OH 43442, (419) 665-2414. (WCD)
3246 **Woodland Mound Park Trail**, Woodland Mound Park, US 52, Cincinnati, OH 45255, (513) 521-7275. 1.0 mile. (IGC)
3247 **Woodside Lake Park**, 2256 Frost Rd., Streetsboro, OH 44241, (216) 626-4251. (WCD)
Wright Brothers Historical Walking Trail see entry 3248.
3248 **Wright Memorial Trail** (includes Inner Trail 12.0, Wright Brothers Historical Walking Trail), P.O. Box 905, Fairborn, OH 45324. (SAR 1991)
3249 **Wyandot Trail**, Harding Area Council, BSA, 2365 Marion-Mount Gilead Rd., Marion, OH 43302, (614) 389-4615; or Wyandot Trail, c/o BSA Troop 24, Green Camp, OH 43322. 17.0 miles. Awards available. (COC)
3250 **Xenia to Yellow Springs Bikeway**, Charles E. Dressler, Greene County Park District, 651 Dayton-Xenia Rd., Xenia, OH 45385, (513) 376-7440. 9.7 miles straight. (GRT)

3251 **Yogi Bear's Jellystone Park Mansfield**, Black Rd., Mansfield, OH 44901, (419) 886-2267. (WCD)
3252 **Zaleski Backpacking Trail**, Ohio Department of Natural Resources, Division of Forestry, Fountain Sq., Columbus, OH 43224. 21.7 miles. (COC; GTB)
3253 **Zaleski State Forest Trail**, Zaleski, OH 45698, (614) 596-5781. (EGH)
3254 **Zane Caverns**, 7092 SR 540, Bellefontaine, OH 43311, (513) 592-0891. (WCD; MGL)
3255 **Zanesville Riverfront Bikepath**, Ernie Bynum, Recreation Director, City of Zanesville, 401 Market St., Zanesville, OH 43701, (614) 455-0609. 2.9 miles straight. (GRT)
3256 **Zoar Valley Trail**, Buckeye Council, BSA, 5136 Tuscarawas St. W., Canton, OH 44708. 12.0 miles straight. Awards available. (AA 1991)

Generally:
Ohio Department of Natural Resources, Division of Parks and Recreation, Fountain Sq. C-1, Columbus, OH 43224, (614) 265-7000. (EGH)

Index (by city)

Adelphi: Logan Trail 3144
Akron: Akron/Bike and Hike Trail 3011; Cuyahoga Valley National Recreation Area 3064; Portage Lakes State Park 3181
Albany: Lake Snowden Recreation Area 3135
Andover: Jeffco Lakes Campground 3112; Pymatuning State Park 3184
Athens: Indian Mound Campground 3110; Strouds Run State Park 3210; Wayne National Forest 3232
Aurora: Sea Lake Resort 3193
Bainbridge: Paint Creek State Park 3173; Pike Lake State Park 3177; Seven Caves 3195
Baltimore: Rippling Stream Campground 3186

Bascom: Meadowbrook Park 3151
Bay Village: Lake Erie Nature & Science Center 3128
Bazetta: Mosquito Creek State Park 3162
Bellefontaine: Indian Lake State Park 3109; Zane Caverns 3254
Belleville: Honeycreek Valley Campground 3103
Belmont: Barkcamp State Park 3021
Bethel: East Fork State Park 3073
Blanchester: Stonelick State Park 3209
Bloomingdale: Fernwood State Forest 3080
Bolivar: Zoar Valley Trail 3256
Bowling Green: Mary Jane Thurston State Park 3148
Brookville: KOA-Dayton Tall Timbers Resort 3121

Brownsville: Flint Ridge State Memorial and Museum 3082
Buckeye Lake: Buckeye Lake-KOA 3036
Butler: KOA-Butler/Mohican 3120
Cadiz: Sally Buffalo Park 3188; Tappan Lake Park 3214
Caldwell: Wolf Run State Park 3244
Cambridge: Salt Fork State Park 3189; Spring Valley Campground 3207
Camden: Cross's Campground 3063
Canal Fulton: Towpath Trail 3223
Canton: KOA-Bear Creek Resort Ranch 3118
Carrollton: Hidden Hollow Campground 3099
Celina: Celina-Coldwater Bikeway 3048
Chillicothe: Fort Hill Trail 3087; Great Seal State Park 3092; Lake Hill Campground 3129; Mound City Group National Monument 3163
Cincinnati: California Woods Nature Preserve 3040; Cincinnati Nature Center 3054; Dan Beard Riverwalk Trail 3066; Edge of Appalachia Preserve 3075; La Trainee de L'Explorateur Trail 3126; Miami Whitewater Forest 3155; Mount Airy Forest and Arboretum 3164; Sharon Woods Park 3198; Shawnee Lookout 3200; Sugarcreek Reserve 3211; Winton Woods Park 3242; Withrow Nature Preserve 3243; Woodland Mound Park Trail 3246
Circleville: A.W. Marion State Park 3009
Cleveland: Emerald Necklace Trails 3077; Ohio City Trail 3169
Clifton: Winter Bushwack 3240
Coalton: Leo Petroglyph State Memorial 3140
Columbus: Hoover Reservoir 3104; Scioto Bike Path 3191; Shawnee Backpack Trail 3199; Wilderness Trace 3237
Coshocton: Lake Park Recreation Area 3134
Dayton: Aullwood Audubon Center and Farm 3019; Blue Heron Trail 3029; Carriage Hill Reserve 3044; Cox Arboretum 3060; Four Rivers Trail 3088; Happy Hunting Ground Trail 3094; Miami Conservancy Trail 3152; Miami Valley Training Trails 3154; Possum Creek Reserve 3182; Wright Memorial Trail 3248

Deerfield: Berlin Lake 3025
Defiance: Independence Dam State Park 3107
Delaware: Alum Creek State Park 3012; Delaware State Park 3069
Delphos: Delphos Historical Trail 3070
Duncan Falls: Blue Rock State Park 3030
East Liverpool: Beaver Creek State Park 3023
East Rochester: Bob Board Park 3031; Paradise Lake Park 3175
Elyria: Cascade & Elywood Parks 3045
Fairborn: Huffman Prairie Overlook Trail 3106
Fayette: Harrison Lake State Park 3095
Findlay: Heritage Trail 3097
Fitchville: Indian Trail Campground 3111
Fletcher: Poor Farmer's Campsite 3180
Fort Loramie: Lake Loramie State Park 3133
Franklin: Thunderbird Trail 3218
Freeport: Twin Hill Park 3226
Gambier: Kokosing Gap Trail 3123
Geneva-on-the-Lake: Geneva State Park 3089; Indian Creek Camping Resort 3108
Glouster: Burr Oak State Park 3038
Goshen: Cozy-Dale Campground 3061
Grafton: Belden Camp Trail 3024
Granville: Ohio Canal Greenway 3168
Green Camp: Wyandot Trail 3249
Greenville: Wildcat Woods Campground 3235
Hamilton: Anthony Wayne Trail (Fort Finney Segment) 3014; Anthony Wayne Trail (Fort Hamilton Segment) 3015
Hartville: Quail Hollow State Park 3185
Hillsboro: Rocky Fork State Park 3187
Howard: Kokosing Valley Camp & Canoe 3124
Ironton: Lake Vesuvius Park 3136; Vesuvius Furnace Historical Trail 3229; Wayne National Forest 3232
Jackson: Lake Katherine State Nature Preserve 3131
Jefferson: Buccaneer Campsite 3034
Kelleys Island: Kelleys Island Trail 3116
Lakeside-Marblehead: East Harbor State Park 3074
Lancaster: Mount Pleasant 3166; Wahkeena Nature Preserve 3230

OHIO

Laurelville: Tar Hollow State Park 3215
Lebanon: Fort Ancient 3085
Lindsey: Wooded Acres Campground 3245
Lisbon: Lil Beaver Park 3141; Sandy Beaver Trail 3190
Lodi: Sherwood Forrest 3204
Logan: Hocking Hills State Park 3101; KOA-Hocking Hills 3122; Lake Logan State Park 3132; Top 'o the Caves Campground 3221
Loudonville: Camp Toodik Family Campground & Canoe Livery 3042; Mohican State Park 3160; Mohican Wilderness 3161
Lowellville: Stavich Bicycle Trail 3208
Mansfield: Charles Mill Lake Park 3050; Johnny Appleseed Trail 3115; Malabar Farm State Park 3146; Yogi Bear's Jellystone Park Mansfield 3251
Marietta: Wayne National Forest 3232
Marshallville: Camelot Camping Grounds 3041
Marysville: The Covered Bridge Trail 3058
Maumee: Anthony Wayne Trail (Fallen Timbers Segment) 3013
McConnelsville: Bicentennial Trail 3026
Medina: Pier-Lon Park 3176
Mentor: Holden Arboretum 3102
Middletown: Anthony Wayne Trail (Fort St. Clair Segment) 3016; Middletown Historic Trail 3156; Silver Moccasin Trail 3205
Mineral City: Atwood Lake Park 3017
Minster: Chief Wapa Tecumseh Trail 3053
Mount Gilead: Dogwood Valley Resort Family Campground 3072; Mt. Gilead State Park 3165
Mt. Sterling: Deer Creek State Park 3068
Nelsonville: Happy Hills Family Campground 3093
New Washington: Auburn Lake Park 3018
Newark: Blackhand Gorge Bikeway 3027; Blackhand Gorge State Nature Preserve 3028; Dawes Arboretum 3067; Hidden Hills Campground 3098; Lazy R Campground 3137; Thomas J. Evans Bike Trail 3217
Newberry: Punderson State Park 3183
Oak Harbor: Crane Creek State Park 3062; Ottawa National Wildlife Refuge 3171
Oregon: Maumee Bay State Park 3149
Orgonia: Olive Branch Campground 3170
Oxford: Hueston Woods State Park 3105
Painesville: Headlands Beach State Park 3096
Parkman: Kool Lakes Family Campground & Recreation Resort 3125
Peebles: Edwin H. Davis State Memorial 3076; Mineral Springs Lake Resort 3159
Peninsula: Cuyahoga Valley Trail 3065; Tamsin Park Camping Resort 3213
Perrysville: Pleasant Hill Lake Park 3179
Pioneer: Lazy River Resort Campground 3138
Port Clinton: Cedarlane Campgrounds 3047; Magee Marsh Wildlife Area 3145
Portage: Tinkers Creek State Park 3219
Portsmouth: Shawnee State Forest 3201; Shawnee State Park 3202; Shawnee Trail 3203
Ravenna: Country Acres Campground 3057; West Branch State Park 3233
Raymond: Winter's Recreational Area 3241
Reedsville: Forked Run State Park 3083
Republic: Clinton Lake Camping 3056
Richmond: Jefferson Lake State Park 3113
Rio Grande: Bob Evans Farms 3032
Ripley: Chief Logan's Gap Camping Resort & Marina 3052
Rock Creek: Beaumont Scout Reservation 3022
Rogers: Hide Away Hollow 3100
St. Johns: Chief Blackhoof Trail 3051
St. Marys: Ft. Amanda-Ft. Barbee Trail 3084; Grand Lake St. Marys State Park 3091; Miami-Erie Trail 3153
St. Paris: Kiser Lake State Park 3117
Salem: Chaparral Family Campground 3049
Senecaville: Senecaville Lake Park 3194
Seville: Captain Martin Bates Trail 3043
Shaker Heights: Shaker Lakes Regional Nature Center 3197
Sherrodsville: Leesville Southfork Marina 3139
Shreve: Whispering Hills Family Campground 3234
Sidney: Turtle Creek Campground 3225
Sinking Spring: Cave Lake Park 3046; Fort Hill Nature Preserve 3086
Southington: Valley Lake Park 3227
Springfield: Buck Creek State Park 3035;

Enon Beach Campground 3078; Little Miami Bike Route 3142; Tomorrow's Stars Music Park 3220
Streetsboro: Mar-Lynn Lake Park 3147; Woodside Lake Park 3247
Sullivan: Terrace Lakes Campground 3216
Swanton: KOA-Big Sandy-Toledo/Maumee 3119; Oak Openings Trail 3167
Toledo: Ottawa Park 3172; Wildwood Preserve Metropark 3238
Toronto: Austin Lake Park and Campground 3020
Trotwood: Sycamore State Park 3212
Troy: Bruckner Nature Center 3033
Urbana: Meadow Lake Resort 3150
Van Buren: Van Buren Lake State Park 3228
Wapakoneta: Clear Water Trail 3055
Warren: Warren Western Reserve Historical Trail 3231
Wauseon: Faraway Trail 3079
Waverly: Scioto Trail State Park 3192
Waynesville: Caesar Creek State Park 3039; Little Miami Scenic Park Trail 3143

Wellington: Findley State Park 3081; Panther Trails Campground 3174
Wellston: Lake Alma State Park 3127
West Salem: Sloan's Hickory Lake Campground 3206; Town and Country Camp Resort 3222
West Union: Adams Lake State Park 3010
Westerville: Tree Haven Campground 3224
Wilmington: Cowan Lake State Park 3059
Wilmot: The Wilderness Center 3236; Wilmot Wilderness Center 3239
Woodsfield: Platt Park 3178; Shadow Lake Campground 3196
Worthington: Buckeye Trail 3037
Xenia: Xenia to Yellow Springs Bikeway 3250
Yellow Springs: Glen Helen Scout Trail 3090; John Bryan State Park 3114
Youngstown: Mill Creek Park 3157; Mill Creek Park Trail 3158
Zaleski: Lake Hope State Park 3130; Zaleski Backpacking Trail 3252; Zaleski State Forest 3253
Zanesville: Dillon State Park 3071; Zanesville Riverfront Bikepath 3255

Pennsylvania

Abbott Run Trail *see* entry 3662.

3257 **Alan Seeger Natural Area**, Office of Public Information, Department of Environmental Resources, P.O. Box 1467, Harrisburg, PA 17120, (717) 787-2657. Named trails: Greenwood Spur-Johnson, Mill Race. (OJP; AMI)

3258 **Allegheny National Forest**, P.O. Box 847, 222 Liberty St., Warren, PA 16365, (814) 723-5150; or Marienville Ranger District, Marienville, PA 16347, (814) 927-6628; or Ridgway Ranger District, Rt. 1, Box 28A, Ridgway, PA 15853, (814) 776-6172; or Sheffield Ranger District, Rt. 6, Sheffield, PA 16347, (814) 968-3232. 150 miles. Named trails: Deerlick Cross-Country Ski 9.0(s), Heart's Content Cross-Country Ski 7.7(s), Marienville ATV/Bike 36.0(s), Mill Creek Loop 16.7(l), Tidioute Riverside RecTrek 2.5(s), Twin Lakes 14.7(s). (GRT; LGU; WCD; ATP; EGH; GFC; MMA; OJP; OTB; FGU; GNA; GTB)

3259 **Allegheny Portage Railroad National Historic Site**, P.O. Box 189, Cressona, PA 16630, (814) 886-8176. 7.5 miles. (GRT; ATP; GNM; NPS; NPV; NPE; GNA)

3260 **Allegheny River Trail**, Franklin Area Chamber of Commerce, 1256 Liberty St., Suite 2, Franklin, PA 16323, (814) 432-5823. 14.0 miles straight. (GRT)

3261 **Almost Heaven Campground**, SR 154, Forksville, PA 18616, (717) 924-3458. (WCD)

Amos Branch Trail *see* entry 3627.

3262 **Andorra Natural Area**, Northwestern Ave., Philadelphia, PA 19118, (215) 242-5610. Named trails: Azalea Loop, Beech Row, Bell's Mill, Big Tree, Central Loop, Ginger, Harper, Nursery, Wood Thrush. (OJP)

Ant Mound Trail *see* entry 3448.

3263 **Appalachian Campsites**, P.O. Box 72W, Shartlesville, PA 19554, (610) 488-6319. (WCD)

3264 **Appalachian Side Trails** (not listed elsewhere), Keystone Trails Association, P.O. Box 251, Cogan Station, PA 17728. Named trails: Arndt 1.1(s), Eagles Nest, North 1.6(s), Old Mine, Sand Spring, Shikellamy, South, Sunset Rocks 2.4(s), Tom Lowe, Victoria, Wildcat Rocks. (BMG; ATG #5)

3265 **Appalachian Trail** (see separate entry 4948 in interstate section).

3266 **Archbold Pothole State Park**, c/o Lackawanna State Park, Rt. 1, Box 230, Dalton, PA 18414, (717) 945-3239. (PSP; OJP)

3267 **The Armstrong Trail**, Susan Torrence, Armstrong County Tourist Bureau, 402 E. Market St., Kittanning, PA 16201, (412) 548-3226. 48.0 miles straight. (GRT)

Arndt Trail *see* entry 3264.

3268 **Arrowhead Trail**, Joanne F. Nelson, Director, Peters Township Department of Parks and Recreation, 610 E. McMurray Rd., McMurray, PA 15317, (412) 942-5000. 6.0 miles straight planned, current as to 3.5 miles. (GRT)

3269 **Artillery Ridge Campground**, 610 Taneytown Rd., Gettysburg, PA 17325, (717) 334-1288. (WCD)

Ash Hollow Trail *see* entry 3627.

Audubon Trail *see* entry 3580.

3270 **Audubon Wildlife Sanctuary**, Audubon Pawlings Rd., Audubon, PA 19407, (215) 666-5593. Named trails: Green 1.0(l), Mill Grove 6.0. (VFM; ATP; NAT; GFA; OJP; GNA)

Azalea Loop Trail *see* entry 3262.

3271 **Bake Oven Campground**, P.O. Box

D, Ashfield, PA 18212, (717) 386-2911. (WCD)
3272 **Baker Park YMCA Campground,** 400 E. Pothouse Rd., Phoenixville, PA 19460, (215) 933-5861. (WCD)
3273 **Baker Trail,** American Youth Hostels, Inc., 6300 Fifth Ave., Pittsburgh, PA 15232, (412) 362-8181. 141 miles. Awards available. (AA 1992)
  Bakers Run Trail see entry 3627.
3274 **Bald Eagle Campsite,** SR 350, Tyrone, PA 16686, (814) 684-3485. (WCD)
3275 **Bald Eagle State Forest,** P.O. Box 147, Laurelton, PA 17835, (717) 922-3344. (WCD)
3276 **Bald Eagle State Park,** Rt. 1, Box 56, Howard, PA 16841, (814) 625-2447. 8.0 miles. (MMA; PSP)
  Bald Hill Trail see entry 3305.
  Barbour Rock Nature Way Trail see entry 3560.
  Bear Hollow Trail see entry 3627.
3277 **Bear Meadows Natural Area,** Office of Public Information, Department of Environmental Resources, P.O. Box 1467, Harrisburg, PA 17120, (717) 787-2657. (OJP)
  Bear Pen Hollow Trail see entry 3627.
3278 **Bear Run Campground,** Rt. 1, Portersville, PA 16051, (412) 368-3564. (EGH)
3279 **Bear Run Nature Reserve,** SR 381, Ohiopyle, PA 15470, (412) 329-8501; or c/o Western Pennsylvania Conservancy, 316 4th Ave., Pittsburgh, PA 15222. 20.0 miles. (EGH)
  Beartown Rocks Trail see entry 3451.
  Beaver Run Trail see entry 3377.
  Bechtel Trail see entry 3627.
  Beech Row Trail see entry 3262.
3280 **Beechwood Farms Nature Preserve,** 614 Dorseyville Rd., Pittsburgh, PA 15238, (412) 963-6100. Named trails: Goldenrod 5.0, Meadow View, Pine Hollow, Spring Hollow, Violet. (ATP; POB; OJP)
  Beechwood Trail see entry 3627.
  Bell's Mill Trail see entry 3262.
3281 **Beltzville State Park,** Rt. 3, Box 242, Lehighton, PA 18235, (610) 377-0045. 16.0 miles. (ATP; PSP; GNA; LRA)

3282 **Benjamin Franklin Historical Trail,** American Historical Trails, Inc., P.O. Box 769, Monroe, NC 28110, (704) 289-1604. 4.5-8.3 miles loop. Awards available. (SAR 1993)
  Benson Trail see entry 3627.
3283 **Berks County Heritage Center,** Red Bridge Rd., Reading, PA 19612, (610) 374-8839. Named trails: Union Canal Biking and Hiking 5.0. (ATP)
3284 **The Berry Patch Campground,** P.O. Box 370, Honey Brook, PA 19344, (610) 273-3720. (WCD)
3285 **Bethany Christian Campground,** Charleroi, PA 15022, (412) 483-6235. (WCD)
3286 **Betzwood Rail Trail,** Scott Kalbach, Chief Park Ranger, Valley Forge National Historic Park, P.O. Box 953, Valley Forge, PA 19481, (610) 783-1045. 2.0 miles straight. (GRT)
  Big Boyer Trail see entry 3627.
3287 **Big Pocono State Park,** P.O. Box 173, Henryville, PA 18332, (717) 629-0320 or (717) 433-9991. 10.0 miles. Named trails: Old Railroad 8.4(s). (GRT; ATP; DBV; DMA; PSP; AMI; GNA)
  Big Ridge Trail see entry 3627.
  Big Round Top Loop Trail see entry 3399.
  Big Sandy Trail see entry 3627.
3288 **Big Spring State Park,** SR 272, New Germantown, PA 17071. (ATP)
  Big Tree Trail see entry 3262.
  Billy Yank Trail see entry 3398.
  Birch Trail see entry 3344.
3289 **Birchview Farm Campground,** Rt. 9, Coatesville, PA 19320, (610) 384-0500. (WCD)
3290 **Black Bear Campground,** Rt. 1, Lewis Run, PA 16738, (814) 362-1394. (WCD)
  Black Forest Trail see entry 3446.
  Black Forest Trail see entry 3650.
3291 **Black Moshannon State Park,** Rt. 1, Box 183, Philipsburg, PA 16866, (814) 342-1101. 16.0 miles. Named trails: Moss-Hanne. (WCD; ATP; MMA; PSP; GNA)
  Black Willow Water Trail see entry 3494.
  Blazing Star Trail see entry 3439.

Blue Blaze Trail *see* entry 3627.
3292 **Blue Knob State Park**, Rt. 1, Box 449, Imler, PA 16655, (814) 276-3576. 16.0 miles. (WCD; ATP; MMA; PSP; GNA)
3293 **Blue Marsh Lake**, SR 183, Reading, PA 19612. (ATP)
3294 **Blue Rocks Family Campground**, Rt. 2, SR 143, Lenhartsville, PA 19534, (610) 756-6366. (WCD; MMA)
Blue Trail *see* entry 3691.
Boardwalk Loop Trail *see* entry 3652.
Bobcat Trail *see* entry 3474.
Bobsled Hollow Trail *see* entry 3627.
Boiler Run Trail *see* entry 3627.
Boone Road Trail *see* entry 3627.
3295 **Boulder Woods Campground**, Camp Sky Mount Rd., Quakertown, PA 18951, (215) 257-7178. (WCD)
Boulevard Trail *see* entry 3537.
Boundary Line Trail *see* entry 3627.
Boundary Trail *see* entry 3448.
3296 **Bowman's Hill State Wildflower Preserve**, Office of Public Information, Department of Environmental Resources, P.O. Box 1467, Harrisburg, PA 17120, (717) 787-2657. Named trails: Bucks County, Fern, Marshmarigold, Wherry Fern, Woods' Edge. (OJP)
3297 **Box Huckleberry Natural Area Trail**, Office of Public Information, Department of Environmental Resources, P.O. Box 1467, Harrisburg, PA 17120, (717) 787-2657. 0.25 mile. (OJP)
Boyer Trail *see* entry 3627.
3298 **Braddock's Crossing Trail**, John P. English, 1031 East End Ave., Pittsburgh, PA 15221, (412) 731-6651; or Greater Pittsburgh Council, BSA, Flag Plaza—1275 Bedford Ave., Pittsburgh, PA 15219-3699, (412) 471-2927. 10.0 miles. Awards available. (AA 1993)
3299 **Brady Run County Park**, SR 51, New Brighton, PA 15066, (412) 846-5600. (WCD)
3300 **Brandywine River Museum**, US 1, Chadds Ford, PA 19317, (610) 388-7601. (ATP; MMA)
3301 **Brenner's Meadow Run Camping & Cabins**, Nelson Rd., Farmington, PA 15437, (412) 329-4097. (WCD)

Bridal Veil Falls Trail *see* entry 3309.
Brink Hollow Trail *see* entry 3627.
3302 **Bristol Spurline Park Trail**, Fidel Esposito, Manager, or Maria Fields, Administrative Assistant, Borough of Bristol, 250 Pound St., Bristol, PA 19007, (610) 788-3828. 2.0 miles straight. (GRT)
Brown Trail *see* entry 3301.
3303 **Bruce Lake Natural Area**, Office of Public Information, Department of Environmental Resources, P.O. Box 1467, Harrisburg, PA 17120, (717) 787-2657. Named trails: Brown, Panther Swamp, Rock Oak Ridge, West Branch Bruce Lake. (OJP; AMI)
Bruce Lake Trail *see* entry 3574.
3304 **Brush Creek Campground**, Star Route 2, Breezewood, PA 15533, (814) 735-4035. (WCD)
Brush Hollow Trail *see* entry 3586.
3305 **Buchanan State Forest**, Rt. 2, Box 3, McConnellsburg, PA 17233, (717) 485-3148. Named trails: Bald Hill 5.8(l), Little Mountain 12.1(l), Tuscarora. (EGH; GNA)
Buck Trail *see* entry 3539.
3306 **Buckaloons Access Area**, US 62, Warren, PA 16365. (ATP)
Buckhorn Trail *see* entry 3627.
3307 **Bucktail Camping Resort**, 1029 Mann Creek Rd., Mansfield, PA 16933, (717) 662-2923. (WCD)
3308 **Bucktail State Park**, Rt. 1, Box 1-A, Emporium, PA 15834, (814) 486-3365; or Bucktail State Park Association, P.O. Box 506, Lock Haven, PA 17745, (717) 748-9214. Named trails: East Branch. (PSP; OJP; GNA)
Bull Run Trail *see* entry 3627.
3309 **Bushkill Falls**, US 209, Bushkill, PA 18324, (717) 588-6682. Named trails: Bridal Veil Falls 1.0(s), Bushkill Falls 1.5. (ATP; DBV; PSP)
Bushkill Falls Trail *see* entry 3309.
3310 **Bushy Run Battlefield**, SR 993, Greensburg, PA 15601, (412) 527-5584. (MMA)
3311 **Butler-Freeport Community Trail**, Ron Bennett, President, Butler-Freeport Community Trail Council, P.O. Box 533,

Saxonburg, PA 16056, (412) 352-4783. 20.0 miles straight planned, current as to 3.0 miles. (GRT)

3312 **Caesar's Paradise Stream**, SR 940, Mount Pocono, PA 18344, (717) 839-8881 or (800) 233-4141. (MMA)

Caldwell Run Trail see entry 3627.

3313 **Caledonia State Park**, 40 Rocky Mt. Rd., Fayetteville, PA 17222, (717) 352-2161. 10.0 miles. (WCD; ATP; MMA; PSP; GNA)

3314 **Camp Anawanna**, Greater Pittsburgh Council, BSA, Flag Plaza–1275 Bedford Ave., Pittsburgh, PA 15129-3699, (412) 471-2927. (SFC)

3315 **Camp Baker**, Greater Pittsburgh Council, BSA, Flag Plaza–1275 Bedford Ave., Pittsburgh, PA 15129-3699, (412) 471-2927. (SFC)

3316 **Camp Charles Campgrounds**, Blue Mountain Dr., Bangor, PA 18013, (610) 588-0553. (WCD)

3317 **Camp Custaloga**, French Creek Council, BSA, 1815 Robison Rd. W., Erie, PA 16509, (814) 868-5571. (SFC)

3318 **Camp Elk Lick**, Allegheny Highlands Council, BSA, 50 Hough Hill Rd., Falconer, NY 14753, (716) 665-4753; or Camp Elk Lick, Rt. 3, Border Rd., Smethport, PA 16749, (814) 465-9991. (SFC)

3319 **Camp Guyasuta**, Allegheny Trails Council, BSA, Flag Plaza–1275 Bedford Ave., Pittsburgh, PA 15219-3699, (412) 471-2927. (SFC)

3320 **Camp Minsi**, Minsi Trails Council, BSA, P.O. Box 2424, Lehigh Valley, PA 18001, (610) 264-8551. (SFC)

3321 **Camp Olmstead**, Chief Cornplanter Council, BSA, 316 4th Ave., Warren, PA 16365, (814) 723-6700; or Camp Olmstead, Rt. 1, Russell, PA 16345, (814) 757-8719. (SFC)

3322 **Camp Roaring Run**, Penns Woods Council, BSA, 501 15th St., Windber, PA 15963, (814) 467-5557; or Camp Roaring Run, Rt. 1, Boswell, PA 15531, (814) 629-5294. (SFC)

3323 **Camp Twin Echo**, East Valley Area Council, BSA, 510 10th Ave., Munhall, PA 15120, (412) 462-9100; or Camp Twin Echo, Rt. 1, New Florence, PA 15944, (412) 238-6939. (SFC)

3324 **Camp Wopononock**, Penns Woods Council, BSA, 501 15th St., Windber, PA 15963, (814) 467-5557; or Camp Wopononock, Rt. 1, Fallentimber, PA 16639, (814) 687-3265. (SFC)

3325 **Camp-A-While**, Rt. 1, Box 334, Hegins, PA 17938, (717) 682-8696. (WCD)

Cannon Hole Trail see entry 3627.

3326 **Canoe Creek State Park**, Rt. 2, Box 560, Hollidaysburg, PA 16648, (814) 695-6807. 8.0 miles. (ATP; MNE; PSP)

Canyon Vista Trail see entry 3691.

3327 **Cape Lookout State Park**, Bowmansville AYH-Hostel, P.O. Box 157, Bowmansville, PA 17507, (610) 445-4131. (AYH)

3328 **Carlisle Historical Trail**, American Historical Trails, Inc., P.O. Box 769, Monroe, NC 28110, (704) 289-1604. 4.0-8.0 miles loop. Awards available. (SAR 1993)

3329 **Carpenter's Woods**, c/o Andorra Natural Area, Northwestern Ave., Philadelphia, PA 19118, (215) 242-5610. (NAT)

Central Loop Trail see entry 3262.

3330 **Chapman State Park**, Rt. 1, Box 1610, Clarendon, PA 16313, (814) 723-5030. Named trails: Tanbark 25.0. (WCD; ATP; MMA; PSP; GNA; IFT)

Charcoal Hearth Trail see entry 3448.

3331 **Charles F. Lewis Natural Area**, Office of Public Information, Department of Environmental Resources, P.O. Box 1467, Harrisburg, PA 17120, (717) 787-2657. Named trails: Clark Run. (OJP)

3332 **Cherry Springs State Forest Picnic Area**, c/o Denton Hill State Park, P.O. Box 407, Coudersport, PA 16915, (814) 435-6372. (GNA)

3333 **Cherry Springs State Park**, c/o Lyman Run State Park, P.O. Box 204, Galeton, PA 16922, (814) 435-6444. 1.0 mile. (ATP; PSP)

Chicken Farm Trail see entry 3627.

Chillisuagi Trail see entry 3516.

3334 **Christmas Pines Campground**, P.O. Box 375, Auburn, PA 17922, (717) 366-8866. (WCD)

Chrome Trail *see* entry 3539.
Chuck Keiper Trail *see* entry 3627.
Clark Run Trail *see* entry 3331.
3335 **Clear Creek State Forest**, P.O. Box 705, Clarion, PA 16214, (814) 226-1901. 45.0 miles. (EGH)
3336 **Clear Creek State Park**, Rt. 1, Box 82, Sigel, PA 15860, (814) 752-2368. 16.0 miles. (WCD; MMA; PSP; GNA)
3337 **Cliff Park**, Cliff Park Inn, Rt. 2, Box 8562, Milford, PA 18337, (717) 296-6491 or (800) 225-6535. (MMA)
3338 **Codorus State Park**, Rt. 3, Box 118, Hanover, PA 17331, (717) 637-2816. 15.0 miles. (WCD; ATP; MMA; PSP)
Cold Fork Trail *see* entry 3627.
3339 **Colonel Crawford Park**, Rt. 2, Box 134-I, Sagertown, PA 16433, (814) 724-6879. (MMA)
3340 **Colonel Denning State Park**, Rt. 3, Box 2250, Newville, PA 17241, (717) 776-5272. Named trails: Flat Rock 2.5. (WCD; ATP; PSP; AMI; GNA)
Colonial Trail *see* entry 3513.
3341 **Colton Point State Park**, US 6, Wellsboro, PA 16901, (717) 724-3061. 4.0 miles. (WCD; ATP; PSP; OTB; GNA)
Commissioner Run Trail *see* entry 3627.
3342 **Conemaugh River Lake**, Conemaugh Dam, Rt. 1, Box 702, SR 981, Saltsburg, PA 15681, (412) 459-7240. (ATP; GNA)
3343 **Conewago Trail**, John Gerencser, Recreation Coordinator, Lancaster County Parks and Recreation, 1050 Rockford Rd., Lancaster, PA 17602, (717) 299-8215. 5.0 miles straight. (GRT)
Conservation Trail *see* entry 3509.
3344 **Cook Forest State Park**, P.O. Box 120, Cooksburg, PA 16217, (814) 744-8407. 30.0 miles. Named trails: Birch, Deer Park, Hemlock, Indian, Longfellow, Nature 1.5, Rhododendron, Seneca. (WCD; ATP; MMA; PSP; OJP; GNA)
Coon Run Trail *see* entry 3627.
3345 **Cooper's Lake Campground**, Currie Dr., Portersville, PA 16051, (412) 368-8710. (WCD)
3346 **Council Cup Campground**, Rt. 3, Box 3500, Wapwallopen, PA 18660, (717) 379-2566. (WCD)
3347 **Cowanesque Lake**, Corps of Engineers, Lawrenceville, PA 16929. (ATP)
3348 **Cowans Gap State Park**, HC 17266, Fort Loudon, PA 17224, (717) 485-3948. 10.0 miles. (WCD; ATP; PSP; GNA)
Cowlick Trail *see* entry 3627.
3349 **Cranberry Run Campground**, 489 Hallett Rd., East Stroudsburg, PA 18301, (717) 421-1462. (WCD)
3350 **Crooked Creek State Park**, Rt. 3, Ford City, PA 16226, (412) 763-3161. (GNA)
Crowley Trail *see* entry 3627.
3351 **Crystal Cave Park**, US 222, Kutztown, PA 19530, (610) 683-6765. (ATP; MMA)
Cumberland County Biker/Hiker Trail *see* entry 3561.
3352 **Curwensville Lake**, SR 453, Curwensville, PA 16833. (ATP)
Cut Off Trail *see* entry 3627.
3353 **Daniel Boone Homestead**, 400 Boone Rd., Birdsboro, PA 19508, (610) 582-4900. (VFM; MMA; OJP)
Dark Hollow Trail *see* entry 3627.
Dead Horse Trail *see* entry 3627.
3354 **Deer Meadow Campground**, HC 1, Box 27, Cooksburg, PA 16217, (814) 927-8125. (WCD)
Deer Park Trail *see* entry 3344.
Deer Path Nature Trail *see* entry 3509.
Deerlick Cross-Country Ski Trail *see* entry 3258.
3355 **Deihl's Camping Resort**, Rt. 4, Bloomsburg, PA 17815, (717) 683-5212. (WCD)
3356 **Delaware Canal State Park**, Rt. 1, Box 615-A, Upper Black Eddy, PA 18972, (610) 982-5560. 60.0 miles. (ATP; PSP)
3357 **Delaware Canal Trail**, Bucks County Council, BSA, 225 Green St., Doylestown, PA 18901, (215) 348-9436. 10.0-48.0 miles. Awards available. (AA 1992)
3358 **Delaware & Lehigh Canal Trail**, Hugh Moore Historical Park and Museums, 200 S. Delaware Dr., P.O. Box 877, Easton, PA 18044, (610) 250-6700. 12.5 miles. Awards available. (HTA)

3359 **Delaware State Forest**, P.O. Box 150, 474 Clearview Ln., Stroudsburg, PA 18360, (717) 424-3001. Named trails: Thunder Swamp 28.0. (EGH; GNA)

3360 **Delaware Water Gap National Recreation Area**, Bushkill, PA 18324, (717) 588-6637. 26.0 miles. (MMA; NPV; POB; NPE; OJP; CGA)

3361 **Denton Hill State Park**, c/o Lyman Run State Park, P.O. Box 204, Galeton, PA 16922, (814) 635-6444. 2.0 miles. (PSP)

3362 **Dingmans Campground**, Rt. 2, Box 20, Dingmans Ferry, PA 18328, (717) 828-2266. (WCD)

3363 **Dingmans Falls Trail**, Dingmans Falls Visitors Center, SR 739, Dingmans Ferry, PA 18328, (717) 828-2319. 0.5 mile. (DMA; AMI)

Dismal Run Trail see entry 3441.
Doe Trail see entry 3539.

3364 **Dogwood Acres Campground**, SR 944, Newville, PA 17241, (717) 776-5203. (WCD)

3365 **Dogwood Haven Family Camp Grounds**, 16 Lodi Hill Rd., Upper Black Eddy, PA 18972, (610) 982-5402. (WCD)

3366 **Donegal Mills Plantation**, Musser Rd., Mount Joy, PA 17552, (717) 653-2168. (ATP)

Donut Hole Trail see entry 3627.

3367 **Dorflinger-Suydam Wildlife Sanctuary**, Long Ridge Rd., White Mills, PA 18973, (717) 253-2564. (ATP)

Double Run Nature Trail see entry 3496.
Dougherty Hollow Trail see entry 3627.
Dougherty Trail see entry 3627.

3368 **Downtown Gettysburg Walking Tour**, Gettysburg Travel Council, Inc., 35 Carlisle St., Gettysburg, PA 17325, (717) 334-6274. (CBP)

Drake Hollow Trail see entry 3627.

3369 **Drummer Boy Campground**, 1300 Hanover Rd., Gettysburg, PA 17325, (800) 336-DBOY. (WCD)

Drury Ridge Trail see entry 3627.
Durham Trail see entry 3513.
Dutchmans Trail see entry 3627.
Eagles Nest Trail see entry 3264.

3370 **Eagles Peak Campground**, Rt. 1, Box 397WR, Robesonia, PA 19551, (610) 589-4800. (WCD)

3371 **East Branch Lake**, Corps of Engineers, Pittsburgh District, Federal Bldg., 1000 Liberty Ave., Pittsburgh, PA 15222. (GFC)

East Branch Trail see entry 3308.
East End Trail see entry 3382.

3372 **Echo Valley Park**, 52 Camp Rd., Tremont, PA 17981, (717) 695-3659. (WCD)

Eddy Lick Trail see entry 3627.
Elder Run Trail see entry 3509.
Elk Hollow Trail see entry 3627.

3373 **Elk State Forest**, Rt. 1, Box 327, Emporium, PA 15834, (814) 483-3354. 111 miles. Named trails: Pine Tree, Quehanna 50.0(l). (GNA)

3374 **Elk State Park**, c/o Bendigo State Park, P.O. Box A, Johnsonburg, PA 15845, (814) 965-2646. 2.0 miles. (ATP; PSP; GNA)

3375 **Endless Mountain Riding Trail**, Niki Mack, President, Bridgewater Riding Club, P.O. Box 21, Montrose, PA 18843, (717) 278-1318. 14.0 miles straight. (GRT)

3376 **Erie Historical Trail**, Langundowi Lodge #46, French Creek Council, BSA, 1815 Robison Rd. W., Erie, PA 16509-4905, (814) 868-5571. 7.0 miles. Awards available. (AA 1994)

3377 **Erie National Wildlife Refuge**, Rt. 2, Box 191, Guys Mills, PA 16327, (814) 789-3585. Named trails: Beaver Run, Tsunga Nature 1.6. (MMA; OJP; GNA; GNW)

3378 **Evansburg State Park**, May Hall Rd., P.O. Box 258, Collegeville, PA 19426, (610) 489-3729. 6.0 miles. (VFM; ATP; PSP)

3379 **Evergreen Lake**, 2375 Benders Dr., Bath, PA 18014, (610) 837-6401. (WCD)

Evergreen Trail see entry 3591.

3380 **Fairmount Park Bikeway National Recreation Trail**, Fairmount Park Commission, Memorial Hall, West Park, Philadelphia, PA 17131, (215) 879-4062. 8.5 miles. (ATP; NFG)

Fallen Timber Trail see entry 3586.
Ferncliff Trail see entry 3542.

3381 **Ferryboat Campsites,** US 11/15, Liverpool, PA 17045, (717) 444-3200 or (800) 759-8707. (WCD)
  Fields Run Trail *see* entry 3627.
  Fish Run Trail *see* entry 3382.
  Flat Ridge Trail *see* entry 3627.
  Flat Rock Trail *see* entry 3340.
3382 **Forbes State Forest,** 132 W. Main St., Ligonier, PA 15658, (412) 238-9533. Named trails: East End, Fish Run, Mile, Spruce Run, White Deer, Wolf Rocks. (AA 1992)
3383 **Forbes Trail,** John P. English, 1031 East End Ave., Pittsburgh, PA 15221, (412) 731-6651; or Greater Pittsburgh Council, BSA, Flag Plaza—1275 Bedford Ave., Pittsburgh, PA 15219-3699, (412) 471-2927. 20.0 miles. Awards available. (AA 1993)
3384 **Forest H. Dutlinger Natural Area,** Office of Public Information, Department of Environmental Resources, P.O. Box 1467, Harrisburg, PA 17120, (717) 787-2657. Named trails: Beech Bottom. (OJP)
  Fork Hill Trail *see* entry 3627.
3385 **Fort Hunter Mansion,** Front St., Harrisburg, PA 17101, (717) 599-5751. (ATP)
3386 **Fort Necessity National Battlefield,** Rt. 2, Box 528, The National Pike, Farmingham, PA 15437, (412) 329-5512. (NPS; NPE; OTB; CGA)
3387 **Fort Roberdeau,** Kettle St., Altoona, PA 16602, (814) 695-5541. (ATP)
3388 **Fort Washington State Park,** 500 Bethlehem Pike, Fort Washington, PA 19034, (215) 645-2942. 5.0 miles. (VFM; ATP; MMA; PSP)
  Four Ridge Trail *see* entry 3627.
3389 **Fowlers Hollow State Park,** c/o Colonel Denning State Park, Rt. 3, Box 2250, Newville, PA 17241, (717) 776-5272. 2.0 miles. (ATP; PSP)
3390 **Frances Slocum State Park,** 565 Mt. Olivet Rd., Wyoming, PA 18644, (717) 696-3525. 5.0 miles. (WCD; ATP; PSP)
3391 **Freedom Shrine Historic Trail,** Bucks County Council, BSA, 225 Green St., Doylestown, PA 18901, (215) 348-9436. 2 hours. Awards available. (NHT; DMV)

3392 **French Creek State Park,** Rt. 1, Box 448, Elverson, PA 19520, (610) 582-1514. 32.0 miles. (WCD; ATP; EGH; MMA; NAT; PSP)
  Frenchman Trail *see* entry 3627.
3393 **Frick Park,** 2005 Beechwood Blvd., Pittsburgh, PA 15217. (MMA)
3394 **Friendship Hill National Historic Site,** Rt. 2, Box 528, Farmington, PA 15437, (912) 329-5512. 5.0 miles. (NPF)
3395 **Gallitzin State Forest,** 131 Hillcrest Dr., Ebensburg, PA 15931, (814) 472-8320. Named trails: Old "56," Wolf Rocks. (GNA)
  Ganoga Glen Trail *see* entry 3591.
3396 **Gaslight Campground,** SR 208, Emlenton, PA 16373, (412) 867-6981. (WCD)
3397 **General Forbes Trail,** East Boroughs Council, BSA, 519 Penn Ave., Wilkinsburg, PA 15221. (MVC)
3398 **Gettysburg Heritage Trails,** York-Adams Area Council, BSA, 800 E. King St., York, PA 17403-1797, (717) 843-0901. Named trails: Billy Yank 9.0(l), Johnny Reb 3.5(l). Awards available. (SAR 1993)
3399 **Gettysburg National Military Park,** Gettysburg, PA 17325, (717) 334-1124. Named trails: Big Round Top Loop 1.0(l), High Water Mark 0.75. (SAR 1993)
3400 **Ghost Town Trail,** Ed Patterson, Indiana County Parks, Rt. 2, Box 157-J, Indiana, PA 15701, (412) 463-8636. 19.5 miles straight planned, current as to 12.0 miles. (GRT)
3401 **Gifford Pinchot State Park,** 2200 Rosstown Rd., Lewisberry, PA 17339, (717) 432-5011. 8.0 miles. (WCD; ATP; MMA; PSP; GNA)
  Ginger Trail *see* entry 3262.
  Ginseng Hollow Trail *see* entry 3627.
  Glacier Ridge Trail *see* entry 3518.
  Glen Leigh Trail *see* entry 3591.
3402 **Goddard Park Vacationland Campgrounds,** Goddard State Park Rd., Sandy Lake, PA 16145, (412) 253-4645. (WCD)
  Golden Eagle Trail *see* entry 3650.
  Goldenrod Trail *see* entry 3280.
  Goldenrod Trail *see* entry 3627.

PENNSYLVANIA

Goose Woods Nature Trail *see* entry 3516.

3403 **Gouldsboro State Park**, SR 611, Mount Pocono, PA 18344, (717) 894-8336. 22.0 miles. (ATP; MMA; DBV; DMA; PSP; GNA)

3404 **Granite Hill Campground & Waterpark**, 3340-W Fairfield Rd., Gettysburg, PA 17325, (717) 642-8742 or (800) 642-TENT. (WCD)

Gravel Lick Trail *see* entry 3627.

3405 **Gray Squirrel Campsites**, Walker Lake Rd., Beaver Springs, PA 17812, (717) 837-0333. (WCD)

Great Gorge Trail *see* entry 3542.

3406 **Great Shamokin Path**, Pam Meade, President, Cowanshannock Creek Watershed Association, P.O. Box 307, Rural Valley, PA 16249, (412) 783-6692. 4.0 miles straight. (GRT)

3407 **Green Lane Reservoir Park**, Hill Rd., Green Lane, PA 18054, (610) 234-4863. (VFM)

Green Trail *see* entry 3270.

3408 **Greene County Historical Museum**, Old SR 21, Waynesburg, PA 15370, (412) 627-3204. (ATP)

3409 **Greenwood Furnace State Park**, Rt. 2, Box 118, Huntingdon, PA 16652, (717) 667-3808. 2.0 miles. (WCD; ATP; MMA; PSP; GNA)

Greenwood Spur-Johnson Trail *see* entry 3257.

Gruger Hollow Trail *see* entry 3627.

3410 **Haleeka Campsites**, US 15, Williamsport, PA 17701, (717) 998-2489. (WCD)

3411 **Happy Acres Campground**, Little Pine Creek Rd., Waterville, PA 17776, (717) 753-8221. (WCD)

Harbrac Trail *see* entry 3627.

3412 **Harecreek Campground**, Rt. 2, Scotia-Corry, PA 16407, (814) 664-9684. (WCD)

Harper Trail *see* entry 3262.

3413 **Harrisburg Historical Trail**, American Historical Trails, Inc., P.O. Box 769, Monroe, NC 28110, (704) 289-1604. 6.0 miles straight. Awards available. (SAR 1993)

3414 **Hawk Mountain Sanctuary**, Rt. 2, Kempton, PA 19529, (610) 756-6961. Named trails: Hawk Mountain 0.75. (ATP; BMG; OTB; AMI; GNA)

Heart's Content Cross-Country Ski Trail *see* entry 3258.

3415 **Hemlock Lake County Park**, SR 286, Rossiter, PA 15772, (412) 463-8636. (MMA)

Hemlock Trail *see* entry 3344.

Hemlock Trail *see* entry 3474.

Hendricks Trail *see* entry 3627.

3416 **Heritage Reservation**, Greater Pittsburgh Council, BSA, Flag Plaza—1275 Bedford Ave., Pittsburgh, PA 15129, (412) 471-2927. (SFC)

3417 **Heritage Walking Tour**, Colonial York County Visitors and Tourist Bureau, 1455 Mount Zion Rd., York, PA 17402, (717) 755-9638. (SFC)

3418 **Hershey's Fur Center**, SR 94, York Springs, PA 17372, (717) 528-4412. (WCD)

3419 **Hibernia Park**, Cedar Knoll Rd., Downingtown, PA 19335, (610) 384-0290. (ATP; MMA)

3420 **Hickory Run Family Camping Resort**, 285 Greenville Rd., Denver, PA 17517, (800) 458-0612. (WCD)

3421 **Hickory Run State Park**, Rt. 1, Box 81, White Haven, PA 18661, (717) 443-9991. 36.0 miles. Named trails: Stone 1.0. (WCD; ATP; EGH; MMA; DBV; DMA; PSP; AMI; GNA)

3422 **Hidden Valley Camping Resort**, Rt. 2, Mifflinburg, PA 17844, (717) 966-1330. (WCD)

3423 **Hidden Valley Resort**, 1 Craighead Dr., Somerset, PA 15501, (814) 443-6454 or (800) 458-0175. (MMA)

High Rock Trail *see* entry 3496.

High Water Mark Trail *see* entry 3399.

3424 **Highland Campground**, Rt. 2, Box 283, Dalton, PA 18414, (717) 586-9972 or (717) 586-8836. (WCD)

Highland Trail *see* entry 3591.

3425 **Hills Creek State Park**, Rt. 2, Box 328, Wellsboro, PA 16901, (717) 724-4246. 5.0 miles. (WCD; ATP; MMA; PSP; GNA)

Hilltop Nature Trail *see* entry 3518.

Hirlinger Trail *see* entry 3591.
3426 **Historic Lancaster Walking Tour**, Headquarters, 100 S. Queen St., Lancaster, PA 17603, (717) 392-1776; or Downtown Visitors Center, Brunswick Mall, Chestnut St., Lancaster, PA 17602. (ATP; DBV; DMA; RTH)
3427 **Holiday Pines Campgrounds**, Rt. 1, Box 324, Loganton, PA 17747, (717) 725-CAMP. (WCD)
3428 **Hopewell Furnace Nature Trail**, Hopewell Furnace National Historic Site, Rt. 1, Box 345, Elverson, PA 19520, (610) 582-8773. 0.5 mile. (NPS; NPE; CGA; YNP; ANP; NPG)
3429 **Horse-Shoe Trail**, Horse-Shoe Trail Club, Attn: Treasurer, 509 Cheltena Ave., Jenkintown, PA 19046, (215) 887-1549. 130 miles. Awards available. (AA 1992)
Horseshoe Trail *see* entry 3509.
Horseshoe Trail *see* entry 3633.
Huling Ridge Trail *see* entry 3627.
3430 **Huntsdale Fish Cultural Station**, SR 233, Carlisle, PA 17013. 15.0 miles. (OTB)
3431 **Hyner Run State Park**, P.O. Box 46, Hyner, PA 17738, (717) 923-0257. 1.0 mile. Named trails: Hyner View. (WCD; ATP; PSP; GNA)
Hyner View Trail *see* entry 3431.
3432 **Idlewood Campground**, Big Shanty Rd., Lafayette, PA 16740, (814) 362-1719. (WCD)
Impoundment Trail *see* entry 3652.
3433 **Indian Creek Valley Hiking and Biking Trail**, Evelyn Dix, Secretary, Salt Lick Township, P.O. Box 403, Melcroft, PA 15462, (412) 455-2866. (GRT)
3434 **Indian Head Recreational Campgrounds**, 340 Reading St., Rupert, PA 17815, (717) 784-6150 or (717) 356-2144. (WCD)
Indian Pipe Trail *see* entry 3657.
3435 **Indian Steps Museum**, Indian Steps Rd., Airville, PA 17302, (717) 862-3948. (ATP)
Indian Trail *see* entry 3344.
Industrial Heritage Trail *see* entry 3513.
3436 **Iron Horse Trail**, Ernie Geanette, Bureau of Forestry, Rt. 1, Box 42A, Blain, PA 17006, (717) 536-3191. 10.0 miles straight. (GRT)
3437 **Ives Run Recreation Area**, Corps of Engineers—Tioga Lake, SR 287, Tioga, PA 16946, (717) 835-5281. (WCD)
J.U. Hollow Trail *see* entry 3627.
3438 **Jacobsburg State Park**, 835 Jacobsburg Rd., Wind Gap, PA 18091, (610) 759-7616. 7.5 miles. (ATP; PSP)
3439 **Jennings State Park**, Jennings Environmental Education Center, Rt. 1, Slippery Rock, PA 16057, (412) 794-6011. 7.0 miles. Named trails: Blazing Star, Massasauga, Prairie Loop, Ridge. (PSP; OJP)
Jennings Trail *see* entry 3580.
3440 **Jim Thorpe Camping Resort**, P.O. Box 328, Jim Thorpe, PA 18229, (717) 325-2644. (WCD)
3441 **John J. Tyler Arboretum**, Tyler Arboretum Educational Center, 515 Painter Rd., Lima, PA 19060, (215) 566-9133 or (215) 566-5431. 20.0 miles. Named trails: Dismal Run, Painter Brothers, Pinetum, Pink Hill, Rocky Run, Wilderness. (ATP; MMA; NAT; OJP; AMI; CBP)
Johnny Reb Trail *see* entry 3398.
Johnson-Ferney Trail *see* entry 3627.
3442 **Johnstown Flood National Memorial**, P.O. Box 247, Lake Rd., Cressona, PA 16630, (814) 886-8176 or (814) 495-4643. (ATP; NPS; CGA; YNP; ANP)
Jordan Hollow Trail *see* entry 3627.
3443 **Junction 19-80 Campground**, Rt. 6, Mercer, PA 16137, (412) 748-4174. (WCD)
Juneberry Trail *see* entry 3627.
3444 **Keen Lake Camping & Cottage Resort**, Rt. 1, Box 1976, Waymart, PA 18472, (717) 488-5522 or (717) 488-6161. (WCD)
Kelly Field Trail *see* entry 3627.
3445 **Ken's Woods Campground**, Mink Pond Rd., Bushkill, PA 18324, (717) 588-6381. (WCD)
3446 **Kettle Creek State Park**, HCR 62, Box 96, Renovo, PA 17764, (717) 923-0206. 2.0 miles. Named trails: Black Forest. (WCD; ATP; MMA; PSP; GNA)
3447 **Keystone State Park**, Rt. 2, Box 101, Derry, PA 15627, (412) 668-2939. 5.0 miles. (WCD; ATP; PSP; GNA)

Kildoo Nature Trail *see* entry 3504.
King Hollow Trail *see* entry 3627.

3448 **Kings Gap State Park**, Kings Gap Environmental Education and Training Center, 500 Kings Gap Rd., Carlisle, PA 17013, (717) 486-5031. 15.0 miles. Named trails: Ant Mound, Boundary, Charcoal Hearth, Watershed. (PSP; OJP)

3449 **Kinzua Bridge Historic Trail**, Allegheny Highlands Council, BSA, 50 Hough Hill Rd., P.O. Box 0261, Falconer, NY 14733-0261. Mileage varies. Awards available. (AA 1991)

3450 **Kinzua Bridge State Park**, US 6, Mount Jewett, PA 16740, (814) 965-2646. (ATP)

3451 **Kittanning State Forest**, Rt. 1, Box 471, Clarion, PA 16214, (814) 764-3251. Named trails: Beartown Rocks. (GNA)

3452 **Kline High Adventure Base**, Susquehanna Council, BSA, 815 Northway Rd., Williamsport, PA 17701, (717) 326-5121; or Kline High Adventure Base, SR 44, Waterville, PA 17776. (SFC)

3453 **KOA-Allentown-Lehigh Valley Kampground**, Rt. 2, Box 2301, New Tripoli, PA 18066, (610) 298-2160. (WCD)

3454 **KOA-Bellefonte/State College**, 2381 Jacksonville Rd., Bellefonte, PA 16823, (814) 355-7912. (WCD)

3455 **KOA-Delaware Water Gap**, Rt. 6, Box 6196, East Stroudsburg, PA 18301, (717) 223-8000. (WCD)

3456 **KOA-Gettysburg**, 20 Knox Rd., Gettysburg, PA 17325, (717) 642-5713. (WCD)

3457 **KOA-Kinzua East**, Kinzua Heights, Bradford, PA 16701, (814) 368-3662. (WCD)

3458 **KOA-Mercer/Grove**, Rt. 6, Box 6794, Mercer, PA 16137, (412) 748-3160. (WCD)

3459 **KOA-Tunkhannock**, P.O. Box 768, Tunkhannock, PA 18657, (717) 836-4122. (WCD)

3460 **KOA-Washington**, Vance Station Rd., Washington, PA 15301, (412) 225-7590. (WCD)

3461 **Kooser State Park**, Rt. 4, Box 256, Somerset, PA 15501, (814) 445-8673. 1.0 mile. (WCD; ATP; MMA; PSP; GNA)

Kyler Fork Trail *see* entry 3627.
Kyler Trail *see* entry 3627.

3462 **L & M Campgrounds**, Rt. 1, Penn Run, PA 15765, (412) 479-3264. (WCD)

3463 **Lacawac Sanctuary**, Rt. 1, Lake Ariel, PA 18463, (717) 689-9494. (AMI)

3464 **Lackawanna State Park**, Rt. 1, Box 230, Dalton, PA 18414, (717) 945-3239. 6.0 miles. (WCD; ATP; PSP)

3465 **Lake Aldred Park**, SR 425, York, PA 17405. (ATP)

3466 **Lake Erie Park**, SR 5, Erie, PA 16501. (ATP)

3467 **Lake In Wood Camp Travel Park**, 576 Yellow Hill Rd., Narvon, PA 17555, (610) 445-5525. (WCD)

3468 **Lake Raystown Resort**, SR 994, Emporium, PA 15834, (800) 628-4262. (WCD)

Lake Trail *see* entry 3474.

3469 **Lake Wallenpaupack**, SR 590, Hamlin, PA 18427. (ATP; DMA)

3470 **Lambs Creek Hike and Bike Trail**, Richard J. Koeppel, Park Manager, U.S. Army Corps of Engineers, Rt. 1, Box 65, Tioga, PA 16946, (717) 835-5281. 3.2 miles straight. (GRT)

3471 **Lancaster Junction Trail**, John Gerencser, Recreation Coordinator, Lancaster County Parks and Recreation, 1050 Rockford Rd., Lancaster, PA 17602, (717) 299-8215. 2.5 miles straight. (GRT)

Laura Smith Trail of History *see* entry 3516.

3472 **Laurel Highlands Camping**, P.O. Box 188, Donegal, PA 15628, (412) 593-6325 or (412) 593-6326. (WCD)

3473 **Laurel Highlands Hiking Trail**, Laurel Ridge State Park, Rt. 3, Box 246, Rockwood, PA 15557. 70.0 miles. Awards available. (AA 1992)

3474 **Laurel Hill State Park**, Rt. 4, Box 130, Somerset, PA 15501, (814) 445-7725. Named trails: Bobcat, Hemlock, Lake, Martz, Ridge, Tramroad. (AA 1992)

3475 **Laurel Ridge State Park**, Rt. 3, Box 246, Rockwood, PA 15557, (412) 455-3744. 94.0 miles. (PSP; GNA)

Laurelly Fork Trail *see* entry 3627.

3476 **Leaser Lake Park**, SR 143, Jacksonville, PA 18014. (ATP)

3477 **Ledgedale Recreation Area**, Pennsylvania Power & Light Co., Ledgedale Rd., Hawley, PA 18428, (717) 689-2181. (WCD)
  Lee Hollow Trail see entry 3627.
  Left Branch Trail see entry 3627.
  Left Fork Trail see entry 3627.
3478 **Lehigh Gorge Campground**, SR 940, White Haven, PA 18661, (717) 443-9191. (WCD)
3479 **Lehigh Gorge State Park**, Rt. 2, Box 56, Weatherly, PA 18255, (717) 427-8161. 30.0 miles. Named trails: Lehigh Gorge State Park 25.0(s). (GRT; PSP)
  Lehigh Gorge State Park Trail see entry 3479.
3480 **Leonard Harrison State Park**, SR 660, Wellsboro, PA 16901, (717) 724-3061. (WCD; ATP)
3481 **LeTort Spring Run Nature Trail**, Kenwood Giffhorn, Executive Director, LeTort Regional Authority, 415 Franklin St., Carlisle, PA 17013, (717) 249-6139. 1.4 miles straight. (GRT)
  Lick Mountain Run Trail see entry 3627.
3482 **Lincoln Caverns**, US 22, Huntingdon, PA 16652, (814) 643-0268. (ATP)
3483 **Linn Run State Park**, P.O. Box 527, Ligonier, PA 15658, (412) 238-6623. 5.0 miles. (ATP; PSP)
  Little Boyer Trail see entry 3627.
  Little Buckhorn Trail see entry 3627.
3484 **Little Buffalo State Park**, Rt. 2, Box 256, Newport, PA 17074, (717) 567-9255. 7.0 miles. (ATP; PSP)
3485 **Little Juniata Water Gap Natural Area**, Office of Public Information, Department of Environmental Resources, P.O. Box 467, Harrisburg, PA 17120, (717) 787-2657. (OJP)
3486 **Little Mexico Campground**, Rt. 1, Box 179, Winfield, PA 17889, (717) 374-9742. (WCD)
  Little Mountain Trail see entry 3305.
3487 **Little Pine State Park**, HC 63, Waterville, PA 17776-9705, (717) 753-8209. 13.0 miles. Named trails: Tiadaghton. (WCD; ATP; PSP; GNA)
3488 **Little Red Barn Campground**, Old Bethlehem Rd., Quakertown, PA 18951, (215) 536-1984. (WCD)
3489 **The Locust**, US 22/522, Lewistown, PA 17044, (717) 248-3974. (WCD)
3490 **Locust Lake State Park**, SR 1006, Mahanoy City, PA 17948, (717) 467-2404. 5.0 miles. (WCD; ATP; PSP)
  Log Hollow Trail see entry 3627.
  Lonely Trail see entry 3627.
  Lonesome Pine Trail see entry 3539.
  Long Fork Trail see entry 3627.
  Long Hollow Trail see entry 3627.
  Long Trail see entry 3627.
  Longfellow Trail see entry 3344.
  Lookout Trail see entry 3560.
  Loop Trail see entry 3657.
3491 **Lorimer Park**, Moredon Rd., Abington, PA 19001, (215) 947-3477. (VFM)
3492 **Lower Perkiomen Park**, Mill Rd., Oaks, PA 19456, (610) 666-5371. (VFM)
3493 **Lower Trail**, Palmer Brown, President, or Jennifer Barefoot, Rails-to-Trails of Blair County, Inc., 221 High St., Williamsburg, PA 16693, (814) 832-2400. 11.0 miles straight. (GRT)
3494 **Loyalhanna Lake**, Rt. 2, Saltsburg, PA 15681, (412) 639-9013. Named trails: Black Willow Water 1.0, Steeplebush. (GNA)
3495 **Loyalsock Creek**, Office of Public Information, Department of Environmental Resources, P.O. Box 1467, Harrisburg, PA 17120, (717) 787-2657. Named trails: Double Run Nature 0.5, High Rock 0.5. (OJP)
3496 **Loyalsock Trail**, Williamsport Alpine Club, 50 Huffman St., P.O. Box 501, Williamsport, PA 17703, (717) 322-7757. 59.28 miles straight. Awards available. (AA 1992)
3497 **Lyman Run State Park**, Twp. Rd., Galeton, PA 16922, (814) 435-6444. (WCD)
  M.U. Hollow Trail see entry 3627.
  Marienville ATV/Bike Trail see entry 3258.
3498 **Marsh Creek State Park**, 675 Park Rd., Downington, PA 19335, (610) 458-8515. 6.0 miles. (ATP; PSP)
  Marsh Creek Trail see entry 3627.
3499 **Martins Creek Park**, LR 48025, Martins Creek, PA 18063. (ATP)

Martz Trail *see* entry 3474.
3500 **Mason-Dixon Trail**, Mason-Dixon Trail System, c/o John and Marie Pittenger, 143 Devonshire, Wilmington, DE 19803. 204 miles. (EGH)
Massasauga Trail *see* entry 3439.
3501 **Mauch Chunk Lake Park**, Jim Thorpe, PA 18229. (ATP)
3502 **Maurice Brown Self-Guided Nature Trail**, Lacawac Sanctuary, Rt. 1, Box 518, Lake Ariel, PA 18436, (717) 689-9494. (OJP)
3503 **Maurice K. Goddard State Park**, Rt. 3, Box 91, Sandy Lake, PA 16145, (412) 253-4833. 14.0 miles. (ATP; PSP)
McCloskey Trail *see* entry 3627.
McClure Ridge Trail *see* entry 3627.
3504 **McConnell's Mill State Park**, Rt. 2, Box 16, Portersville, PA 16051, (412) 368-8091. 7.0 miles. Named trails: Kildoo Nature. (ATP; MMA; PSP; GNA)
3505 **McDade Park**, Keyser Ave., Scranton, PA 18504, (717) 961-6764. (MMA)
McElhenny Trail *see* entry 3627.
Meadow Trail *see* entry 3657.
Meadow View Trail *see* entry 3280.
3506 **Memorial Lake State Park**, Rt. 1, Box 7045, Grantville, PA 17028, (717) 865-6470. 2.0 miles. (ATP; PSP)
3507 **Merli-Sarnoski Park**, SR 106, Carbondale, PA 18407, (717) 876-1714. (MMA)
3508 **Michaux State Forest**, 10099 Lincoln Way E., Fayetteville, PA 17222, (717) 352-2211. (EGH; GNA)
Middle Creek Trail *see* entry 3509.
3509 **Middlecreek Wildlife Management Area**, SR 897, Kleinfeltersville, PA 17039, (717) 733-1512 or (717) 949-3582. 9.0 miles. Named trails: Conservation 1.4, Deer Path Nature, Elder Run, Horseshoe, Middle Creek, Millstone. (MMA; NAT; OJP; GNA)
3510 **Mid-State Trail**, PSOC Hiking Division, 4 Intramural Bldg., University Park, PA 16802; or Mid-State Trail Association, P.O. Box 167, 227 Kimport Ave., Boalsburg, PA 16827, (814) 237-7703. 206 miles. Awards available. (AA 1993)
Mile Trail *see* entry 3382.
Mill Creek Loop Trail *see* entry 3258.

Mill Grove Trail *see* entry 3270.
Mill Hollow Trail *see* entry 3627.
Mill Race Trail *see* entry 3257.
Millstone Trail *see* entry 3509.
3511 **Milton Loop County Park**, SR 389, Dayton, PA 16222, (412) 548-3223. (WCD)
3512 **Milton State Park**, c/o Shikellamy State Park, Bridge Ave., Sunbury, PA 17801, (717) 286-7880. 1.0 mile. (ATP; PSP)
Mineral Springs Trail *see* entry 3580.
3513 **Minsi Trails Council Historical Trails**, Minsi Trails Council, BSA, P.O. Box 20624, Lehigh Valley, PA 18002-0624, (610) 264-8551. Named trails: Colonial 12.0, Durham 12.0, Industrial Heritage 13.0, Moravian 14.0, Nazareth 13.0, Sullivan-Wilderness 12.0, Uncas 13.5. (AA 1992)
3514 **Mirror Lake Camping**, Rt. 1, New Florence, PA 15944, (412) 235-9983. (WCD)
Mix Hollow Trail *see* entry 3627.
3515 **Monongahela National Forest**, American Youth Hostels, 6300 Fifth Ave., Pittsburgh, PA 15232; or Monongahela National Forest, USDA Bldg., 200 Sycamore St., Elkins, WV 26241-3962, (304) 636-1800. 780 miles. (AA 1992)
3516 **Montour Preserve**, Rt. 1, Box 292, SR 54, Turbotville, PA 17772, (717) 437-3131; or Pennsylvania Power & Light Co., Washingtonville, PA 17884. Named trails: Chillisuagi 4.25, Goose Woods Nature 0.75, Laura Smith Trail of History 25 minutes. (ATP; OJP; MMA)
3517 **Montour Trail**, Tom Tix, The Montour Trail Council, P.O. Box 11866, Pittsburgh, PA 15228-0866, (412) 831-2030. 55.0 miles straight. (GRT)
3518 **Moraine State Park**, Rt. 1, Box 212, Portersville, PA 16051, (412) 368-8811. 10.0 miles. Named trails: Glacier Ridge 7.0, Hilltop Nature. (ATP; MMA; PSP; OTB; GNA)
Moravian Trail *see* entry 3513.
3519 **Morris Arboretum**, 9414 Meadowbrook Ave., Philadelphia, PA 19118, (215) 247-5777. (NAT)
3520 **Moshannon State Forest**, 1229 S.

Second St., Box 341, Clearfield, PA 16830, (814) 765-5361. Named trails: Quehanna 50.0(l). (GNA)

3521 **Mt. Davis Natural Area**, Office of Public Information, Department of Environmental Resources, P.O. Box 1467, Harrisburg, PA 17120, (717) 787-2657. Named trails: High Point, Mt. Davis 0.25, Shelter Rock, Tub Mill Run. (OJP)

3522 **Mt. Pisgah State Park**, Rt. 3, Box 362, Troy, PA 16947, (717) 297-2734. 10.0 miles. (ATP; PSP; OTB)

3523 **Mount Pocono Campground**, P.O. Box 65, Mt. Pocono, PA 18344, (717) 839-7573. (WCD)

3524 **Mountain Creek Campground**, 349 Pine Grove Rd., Gardners, PA 17324, (717) 486-7681. (WCD)

3525 **Mountain Pines Resort**, Rt. 1, Box 715, Champion, PA 15622, (412) 455-3300. (WCD)

3526 **Mountain Springs Camping Resort**, Mountain Rd., Shartlesville, PA 19554, (610) 488-6854. (WCD)

3527 **Mountain Vista Campground**, Rt. 2, Box 2190, East Stroudsburg, PA 18301, (717) 223-0111. (WCD)

3528 **Moyer's Mountain Retreat**, P.O. Box 3843, Gettysburg, PA 17325, (800) 955-0208. (WCD)

3529 **Muddy Run Park**, SR 372, Buck Run, PA 17901. (ATP)

3530 **Muddy Run Recreation Park**, Philadelphia Electric Co., Bethesda Church Rd., Holtwood, PA 17532, (717) 284-4325. (WCD)

Mudlick Trail *see* entry 3627.

3531 **National Trails Towpath Bike Trail of Palmer and Bethlehem Townships**, H. Robert Daws, Chairman, Palmer Township Board of Supervisors, P.O. Box 3039, Palmer, PA 18043, (610) 253-7191. 7.8 miles straight. (GRT)

Nature Trail *see* entry 3344.

Nature Trail *see* entry 3547.

3532 **Nay Aug Park**, Arthur Ave. & Mulberry St., East Scranton, PA 18510, (717) 348-4186 or (717) 348-4189. (MMA)

Nazareth Trail *see* entry 3513.

Nelson Trail *see* entry 3627.

3533 **Neshaminy State Park**, 263 Dunks Ferry Rd., Bensalem, PA 19020, (215) 639-4538. 3.0 miles. (PSP)

3534 **Newlin Mill Park**, US 1, Glen Mills, PA 19342, (610) 459-2359. 3.0 miles. (ATP; MMA)

3535 **Nittany Mountain Campground**, Rt. 1, Box 1383, New Columbia, PA 17856, (717) 568-5541. (WCD)

3536 **Nockamixon State Park**, 1542 Mountain View Dr., Quakertown, PA 18951, (215) 538-2151 or (215) 257-3646. 3.0 miles. (ATP; DMP; NAT; PSP; GNA)

3537 **Nolde Forest State Park**, Rt. 1, Box 392, Reading, PA 19607, (610) 775-1411. 33.0 miles. Named trails: Boulevard, Watershed. (PSP; OJP)

3538 **North Country Trail** (see separate entry **4955** in interstate section).

North Fork Trail *see* entry 3627.

North Trail *see* entry 3264.

3539 **Nottingham Serpentine Barrens**, US 1, Nottingham, PA 19362, (610) 932-9195. Named trails: Buck, Chrome, Doe, Lonesome Pine. (ATP; OJP; AMI)

Nursery Trail *see* entry 3262.

3540 **O & W Road Trail**, Phil Pass, Rail Trail Council of Northeast Pennsylvania, P.O. Box 100, Clifford, PA 18413, (717) 222-3333. 32.0 miles straight planned, current as to 6.0 miles. (GRT)

3541 **Oak Creek Campgrounds**, P.O. Box 128W, Bowmansville, PA 17507, (610) 445-6161. (WCD)

Oak Ridge Trail *see* entry 3627.

3542 **Ohiopyle State Park**, P.O. Box 105, Ohiopyle, PA 15470, (412) 329-8591; or Larry Ridenour, President, Regional Trail Corporation, Rt. 12, Box 203, Greensburg, PA 15601, (412) 355-5872. 67.0 miles. Named trails: Ferncliff, Great Gorge, Youghiogheny River. (GRT; LGU; WCD; ATP; EGH; AYH; MMA; DMA; PSP; GNA; OJP; LRA)

3543 **Oil Creek Camp-Resort**, Rt. 3, Box 217, Titusville, PA 16354, (814) 827-1023. (WCD)

Oil Creek Hiking Trail *see* entry 3544.

3544 **Oil Creek State Park**, Rt. 1, Box 207, Oil City, PA 16301, (814) 676-5915. Named trails: Oil Creek Hiking 36.0, Oil

Creek State Park 9.7(s). (GRT; ATP; EGH)

Oil Creek State Park Trail *see* entry 3544.

Old "56" Trail *see* entry 3395.

Old Mine Trail *see* entry 3264.

Old Railroad Trail *see* entry 3287.

3545 Old Trader's Path Trail, Moraine Trails Council, BSA, 830 Morton Ave., Butler, PA 16001, (412) 287-6791. Awards available. (MVC)

Old Wagon Trail *see* entry 3580.

3546 Ole Bull State Park, HCR 62, Box 9, Cross Fork, PA 17729, (814) 435-2169. 2.0 miles. (WCD; ATP; MMA; PSP; GNA)

3547 Otter Creek, Superintendent, Pennsylvania Power & Light Co., Rt. 3, Box 345, Holtwood, PA 17532, (717) 284-2278 or (717) 862-3628. Named trails: Nature 0.5, Otter Creek, Urey. (OJP; AMI)

Otter Creek Trail *see* entry 3547.

3548 Otter Lake Camp Resort, P.O. Box 850, Marshalls Creek, PA 18335, (717) 223-0123. (WCD)

3549 Outflow Camping Area, Corps of Engineers—Tionesta Lake, SR 36, Tionesta, PA 16353, (814) 755-3512. (WCD)

Oxbow Hollow Trail *see* entry 3627.

Painter Brothers Trail *see* entry 3441.

Panther Swamp Trail *see* entry 3301.

Park Line Trail *see* entry 3627.

3550 Parker Dam State Park, Rt. 1, Box 165, Penfield, PA 15849, (813) 765-5082. (WCD; ATP; MMA; PSP; GNA)

Parker Hollow Trail *see* entry 3627.

Patchel Trail *see* entry 3627.

Pats Ridge Trail *see* entry 3627.

3551 Patterson State Park, c/o Lyman Run State Park, P.O. Box 204, Galeton, PA 16922, (814) 435-6444. 1.0 mile. (ATP; PSP)

3552 Penn Highlands Campground, Rhine Run Rd., Russell, PA 16345, (814) 757-8406. (WCD)

3553 Penn Roosevelt State Forest, US 322, Milroy, PA 17063. (ATP; OTB)

Penns Creek Trail *see* entry 3568.

3554 Pennsylvania Dutch Campsite, P.O. Box 337, Shartlesville, PA 19554, (610) 488-6268. (WCD)

3555 Pequea Creek Campground, Pennsylvania Power & Light Co., SR 324, Pequea, PA 17565, (717) 284-4587. (WCD)

Perry Trail *see* entry 3627.

3556 Pettecote Junction Camping Park, P.O. Box 14, Cedar Run, PA 17727, (717) 353-7183. (WCD)

3557 Philadelphia Bicentennial Trail of Freedom, American Historical Trails, Inc., P.O. Box 769, Monroe, NC 28221, (704) 289-1604. 5.25-7.75 miles loop. Awards available. (AA 1992)

3558 Philadelphia to Valley Forge Bikeway, John H. Wood, Chief of Open Space Planning, Montgomery County Planning Commission, Court House, Norristown, PA 19404, (610) 278-3736. 21.0 miles straight. (GRT)

3559 Pine Cradle Lake Family Campground, Rome, PA 18837, (717) 247-2424. (WCD)

3560 Pine Creek Gorge, Office of Public Information, Department of Environmental Resources, P.O. Box 1467, Harrisburg, PA 17120, (717) 787-2657. Named trails: Barbour Rock Nature Way 1.0(l), Lookout, Turkey Path 1.5, West Rim. (OJP)

3561 Pine Grove Furnace State Park, Rt. 2, Box 399B, Gardners, PA 17324, (717) 486-7174. Named trails: Cumberland County Biker/Hiker 5.5(s). (GRT; WCD; ATP; AYH; MMA; PSP; GNA)

Pine Hollow Trail *see* entry 3280.

3562 Pine Lane Campground, SR 5, Lake City, PA 16423, (814) 774-4808. (WCD)

3563 Pine Ridge County Park, US 22, Blairsville, PA 15717, (412) 463-8636. (MMA)

Pine Tree Trail *see* entry 3373.

Pinetum Trail *see* entry 3441.

Pink Hill Trail *see* entry 3441.

3564 Pioneer Campground, SR 220, Laporte, PA 18626, (717) 946-9971. (WCD)

3565 Pioneer Park Campground, Dept. W, Rt. 4, SR 31W, Somerset, PA 15501, (814) 445-6348. (WCD)

Pitch Pine Trail *see* entry 3627.

3566 Plainfield Township Trail, Anita Bray, Supervisor/Secretary, Plainfield

Board of Supervisors, 517 Getz Rd., Nazareth, PA 18064, (610) 759-6944. 6.7 miles straight. (GRT)

Plantation Trail *see* entry 3627.

3567 **Pocono Vacation Park**, Rt. 5, Box 5214-A, Stroudsburg, PA 18360, (717) 424-2587. (WCD)

3568 **Poe Paddy State Park**, SR 45, Millheim, PA 16854, (814) 349-8778. Named trails: Penns Creek 25.0. (WCD; ATP; PSP; GNA)

3569 **Poe Valley State Park**, c/o Reeds Gap State Park, Rt. 1, Milroy, PA 17063, (814) 349-8778. 6.0 miles. (PSP; GNA)

Polypody Trail *see* entry 3657.

3570 **Poor Richard's Trail**, Tourist Center, 1525 John F. Kennedy Blvd., Philadelphia, PA 19103. 2.5-4.5 miles. (HTA)

3571 **Potomac Heritage Trail** (see separate entry 4957 in interstate section).

Prairie Loop Trail *see* entry 3439.

3572 **Presque Isle State Park**, Presque Isle Blvd., Erie, PA 16505, (814) 871-4251. 20.0 miles. (ATP; MMA; DBV; PSP; OJP; OTB; AGW; GNA)

3573 **Prince Gallitzin State Park**, Rt. 2, Box 79, Patton, PA 16668, (814) 674-3691. 9.0 miles. (WCD; ATP; MMA; PSP; GNA)

3574 **Promised Land State Park**, Rt. 1, Box 96, Greentown, PA 18426, (717) 676-3428. 29.0 miles. Named trails: Bruce Lake 2.5. (WCD; ATP; MMA; DBV; DMA; PSP; GNA; CBP)

3575 **Prouty Places State Park**, c/o Lyman Run State Park, P.O. Box 204, Galeton, PA 16922, (814) 435-6444. 1.0 mile. (ATP; PSP)

3576 **PW&S Railroad Hiking-Biking Trail**, Lysle S. Sherwin, Executive Director, Loyalhanna Watershed Association, P.O. Box 561, Ligonier, PA 15658, (412) 238-7560. 29.0 miles straight. (GRT)

3577 **Pymatuning State Park**, P.O. Box 425, Jamestown, PA 16134, (814) 932-3141; or Pymatuning State Park, Rt. 1, Andover, OH 44003, (216) 293-6030. 3.5 miles. Named trails: Pymatuning State Park 1.7(s). (GRT; ATP; MMA; PSP; GNA)

Pymatuning State Park Trail *see* entry 3577.

3578 **Pymatuning Waterfowl Area**, Mercer St., Linesville, PA 16424, (814) 683-5545; or Pennsylvania Game Commission, P.O. Box 1567, Harrisburg, PA 17120, (717) 787-6286. (ATP; GNA)

3579 **Quakertown Area**, Weisel AYH-Hostel, Rt. 3, Box 307, Quakertown, PA 18951, (215) 536-8749. (AYH)

Quehanna Trail *see* entries 3373 and 3520.

3580 **Raccoon Creek State Park**, Rt. 1, Box 79, Patton, PA 16668, (814) 647-3691. 13.0 miles. Named trails: Audubon, Jennings, Mineral Springs, Old Wagon, Valley 1.5. (WCD; ATP; MMA; PSP; OTB)

3581 **Rachel Carson Trail**, American Youth Hostels, 6300 Fifth Ave., Pittsburgh, PA 15232, (412) 362-8181. 32.3 miles. Awards available. (AA 1992)

3582 **Railroad Grade Trail**, R.J. Koeppel, Park Manager, U.S. Army Corps of Engineers, Rt. 1, Box 65, Tioga, PA 16946-9733, (717) 835-5281. 2.6 miles straight. (GRT)

3583 **Rainbow Mountain Family Campground**, SR 670, Honesdale, PA 18431, (717) 253-0424. (WCD)

3584 **Ralph Stover State Park**, 6011 State Park Rd., Pipersville, PA 18947, (610) 982-5560. 1.0 mile. (ATP; DBV; DMA; PSP)

Rands Hole Trail *see* entry 3627.

3585 **Ravensburg State Park**, SR 880, Jersey Shore, PA 17723, (717) 966-1455. 1.0 mile. (WCD; PSP)

Ravine Trail *see* entry 3657.

3586 **Raymond B. Winter State Park**, Rt. 2, Mifflinburg, PA 17844, (717) 966-1455. 6.0 miles. Named trails: Brush Hollow, Fallen Timber. (WCD; ATP; PSP; GNA)

3587 **Raystown Dam and Lake**, Corps of Engineers, Rt. 1, Heston, PA 16647, (814) 659-3405. Named trails: Terrace Mountain 13.5. (ATP; MMA; GNA)

3588 **Red Oak Campground**, Reservoir Rd., Scandia, PA 16365, (814) 757-8507. (WCD)

3589 **Red Ridge Lake Campground**, Rt. 1, Box 98, Zion Grove, PA 17985, (717) 384-4760 or (215) 543-7733. (WCD)

Red X Trail *see* entry 3691.
Reeder Trail *see* entry 3627.
3590 **Reeds Gap State Park**, Rt. 1, Box 276A, Milroy, PA 17063-9735, (717) 667-3622. 5.0 miles. (ATP; MMA; PSP)
Reynolds Spring Trail *see* entry 3650.
Rhododendron Trail *see* entry 3344.
3591 **Ricketts Glen State Park**, Rt. 2, Box 130, Benton, PA 17814-8905, (717) 477-5675. 20.0 miles. Named trails: Evergreen, Ganoga Glen, Glen Leigh, Highland, Hirlinger. (WCD; ATP; EGH; PSP; OJP; AMI; GNA)
Ridge Trail *see* entry 3439.
Ridge Trail *see* entry 3474.
Ridge Trail *see* entry 3627.
3592 **Ridley Creek State Park**, Sycamore Mills Rd., Media, PA 19063, (215) 566-4800. 12.0 miles. (ATP; MMA; NAT; PSP; GNA)
3593 **Ringing Rocks Park**, SR 663, Pottstown, PA 19464, (610) 323-3472. (MMA)
Ritchie Trail *see* entry 3627.
River Hollow Trail *see* entry 3627.
3594 **Riverfront Campground**, P.O. Box 64, Duncannon, PA 17020, (717) 834-5252. (WCD)
3595 **River's Edge Family Campground**, Rt. 1, Box 518C, Connellsville, PA 15425, (412) 628-4880. (WCD)
3596 **Riverview Park**, Riverview Ave., Pittsburgh, PA 15202, (412) 321-2400. (MMA)
3597 **Roaring Run Trail**, Andy Schreffler, Director, Roaring Run Watershed Association, 215 Rovel St., Apollo, PA 15613, (412) 568-1483. 1.5 miles straight. (GRT)
Robbins Ridge Trail *see* entry 3627.
Robbins Run Trail *see* entry 3627.
3598 **Robinson's Hideaway Campground**, SR 994E, Entriken, PA 16638, (814) 658-3663. (WCD)
Rock Hollow Trail *see* entry 3627.
Rock Oak Ridge Trail *see* entry 3301.
Rock Run Trail *see* entry 3627.
Rocky Run Trail *see* entry 3441.
3599 **Rocky Springs Campground**, Butler St., Mercer, PA 16137, (412) 662-4415. (WCD)

3600 **Rose Point Campground**, Rt. 4, Box 410W, New Castle, PA 16101, (412) 924-2415. (WCD)
Ross Camp Trail *see* entry 3627.
3601 **Rothrock State Forest**, P.O. Box 403, 401 Penn St., Huntingdon, PA 16652, (814) 643-2340. (EGH; GNA)
Round Island Run Trail *see* entry 3627.
3602 **Rustic Meadows Camping & Golf Resort**, 1980 Turnpike Rd., Elizabethtown, PA 17022, (717) 367-7718. (WCD)
3603 **Ryerson Station State Park**, Rt. 1, Box 77, Wind Ridge, PA 15380, (412) 428-4254. 10.0 miles. (WCD; ATP; PSP)
3604 **S.B. Elliott State Park**, SR 153, Clearfield, PA 16830, (814) 765-5082. 3.0 miles. (WCD; ATP; MMA; PSP; OTB; GNA)
Salt Lick Trail *see* entry 3627.
3605 **Salt Spring State Park**, c/o Lackawanna State Park, Rt. 1, Box 230, Dalton, PA 18414, (717) 945-3239. 2.0 miles. (PSP)
3606 **Samuel Justus Recreational Trail**, Richard A. Castonguay, Secretary, Cranberry Township, P.O. Box 378, Seneca, PA 16346, (814) 676-8812. 5.8 miles straight. (GRT)
3607 **Samuel S. Lewis State Park**, c/o Gifford Pinchot State Park, 2200 Rosstown Rd., Lewisberry, PA 17339, (717) 432-5011. 1.0 mile. (PSP)
Sand Rock Trail *see* entry 3627.
Sand Spring Trail *see* entry 3264.
Sandy Ridge Trail *see* entry 3627.
Sandy Trail *see* entry 3627.
3608 **Sandy Valley Campground**, Rt. 1, Box 110, White Haven, PA 18661, (717) 636-0770. (WCD)
3609 **Saunderosa Park**, SR 456, Mercersburg, PA 17236, (717) 328-2216. (WCD)
Savage Trail *see* entry 3627.
3610 **Schenley Park**, Forbes Ave. & Schenley Dr., Pittsburgh, PA 15235. (ATP; MMA)
3611 **Schuylkill Center for Environmental Education**, 8480 Hagy's Mill Rd., Roxborough, PA 19129, (610) 482-7300. 7.0 miles. (MMA; NAT; CBP)
3612 **Scottyland Camping Resort**, Rt. 2,

Box 208, Rockwood, PA 15557, (814) 926-3200. (WCD)
Seneca Trail see entry 3344.
Seth L. Myers Nature Trail see entry 3616.

3613 **Shady Rest Campground**, Eyers Grove Rd., Bloomsburg, PA 17815, (717) 458-6327. (WCD)
Shaney Brook Trail see entry 3627.

3614 **Shawnee State Park**, P.O. Box 67, Schellsburg, PA 15559, (814) 733-4218. 12.0 miles. (WCD; ATP; MMA; PSP; GNA)
Shear Trap Trail see entry 3627.

3615 **Shenango Public Use Area**, Corps of Engineers—Shenango Lake, SR 18, Sharon, PA 16148, (412) 962-7746. (WCD)

3616 **Shenango River Lake**, 2442 Kelly Rd., Sharpsville, PA 16150, (412) 962-2315. 15.0 miles. Named trails: Seth L. Myers Nature 0.5. (GNA; LRA)

3617 **Shenango Trail**, French Creek Council, BSA, 1815 Robison Rd. W., Erie, PA 16509, (814) 868-5571; or Custaloga Council, BSA, 300 W. State St., Sharon, PA 16146. 18.0 miles. Awards available. (AA 1994)

3618 **Shikellamy State Park**, Bridge Ave., Sunbury, PA 17801, (717) 286-7880. 2.0 miles. (ATP; PSP)
Shikellamy Trail see entry 3264.
Shingle Mill Hollow Trail see entry 3627.
Shintown Run Trail see entry 3627.
Shoemaker Trail see entry 3627.

3619 **Shohola Waterfowl Management Area**, Pennsylvania Game Commission, P.O. Box 1567, Harrisburg, PA 17120, (717) 787-6286. (GNA)
Short Bend Trail see entry 3627.

3620 **Silver Canoe Campground**, SR 210, Sagamore, PA 16250, (412) 783-6000. (WCD)
Sinking Spring Trail see entry 3627.

3621 **Sinnemahoning State Park**, Rt. 1, Box 172, Austin, PA 16720, (814) 647-8901. 5.0 miles. (WCD; ATP; PSP; GNA)

3622 **Sizerville State Park**, Rt. 1, Box 238-A, Emporium, PA 15834, (814) 486-5605. 5.0 miles. (WCD; ATP; PSP; GNA)

Slaughtering Ground Trail see entry 3627.
Slide Hollow Trail see entry 3627.

3623 **Slumber Valley Campground**, US 6, Meshoppen, PA 18630, (717) 833-5208. (WCD)
Smiths Run Trail see entry 3627.

3624 **Snyder-Middleswarth State Park**, c/o Reeds Gap State Park, Rt. 1, Box 276A, Milroy, PA 17063, (717) 667-3622. Named trails: Swift Run. (GNA)
South Link Trail see entry 3650.
South Trail see entry 3264.

3625 **Spring Gulch Resort Campground**, 475 Lynch Rd., New Holland, PA 17557, (717) 354-3100 or (800) 255-5744. (WCD)
Spring Hollow Trail see entry 3280.

3626 **Springton Manor Farm**, Springton Rd., Downingtown, PA 19335, (610) 942-2450. (WCD)

3627 **Sproul State Forest**, Star Route, Shintown, Renovo, PA 17764, (717) 923-1450. 468 miles. Named trails: Amos Branch, Ash Hollow, Bakers Run, Bear Hollow, Bear Pen Hollow, Bechtel, Beechwood, Benson, Big Boyer, Big Ridge, Big Sandy, Blue Blaze, Bobsled Hollow, Boiler Run, Boone Road, Boundary Line, Boyer, Brink Hollow, Buckhorn, Bull Run, Caldwell Run, Cannon Hole, Chicken Farm, Chuck Keiper 50.0(l), Cold Fork, Commissioner Run, Coon Run, Cowlick, Crowley, Cut Off, Dark Hollow, Dead Horse, Donut Hole 52.0(s), Dougherty, Dougherty Hollow, Drake Hollow, Drury Ridge, Dutchmans, Eddy Lick, Elk Hollow, Fields Run, Flat Ridge, Fork Hill, Four Ridge, Frenchman, Ginseng Hollow, Goldenrod, Gravel Lick, Gruger Hollow, Harbrac, Hendricks, Huling Ridge, J.U. Hollow, Johnson-Ferney, Jordan Hollow, Juneberry, Kelly Field, King Hollow, Kyler, Kyler Fork, Laurelly Fork, Lee Hollow, Left Branch, Left Fork, Lick Mountain Run, Little Boyer, Little Buckhorn, Log Hollow, Lonely, Long, Long Fork, Long Hollow, M.U. Hollow, Marsh Creek, McCloskey, McClure Ridge, McElhenny, Mill Hollow, Mix Hollow, Mudlick, Nelson, North Fork, Oak Ridge, Oxbow Hollow, Park Line,

Parker Hollow, Patchel, Pats Ridge, Perry, Pitch Pine, Plantation, Rands Hole, Reeder, Ridge, Ritchie, River Hollow, Robbins Ridge, Robbins Run, Rock Hollow, Rock Run, Ross Camp, Round Island Run, Salt Lick, Sand Rock, Sandy, Sandy Ridge, Savage, Shaney Brook, Shear Trap, Shingle Mill Hollow, Shintown Run, Shoemaker, Short Bend, Sinking Spring, Slaughtering Ground, Slide Hollow, Smiths Run, Stible Hole, Stone, Stone Bridge, Stout Hollow, Summerson Run, 3 Point Hollow, Three Ridge, Tub, Turkey, Twin Springs, Upper Doctor Greene, Van Ripper, Walker, Water Trough, Waterfall, Weaver, West Branch Lick Run, Whetham Tower, Wideview, Wildcat, Wolf Run, Wolf Run Supply. (AA 1994)

Spruce Run Trail *see* entry 3382.

3628 **Starlite Camping Resort**, 1500 Furnace Hill Rd., Stevens, PA 17578, (717) 733-9655 or (800) 521-3599. (WCD)

3629 **State Game Lands No. 35 & 159**, Game Commission, P.O. Box 1567, Harrisburg, PA 17120, (717) 787-3633; or Northeast Division Headquarters, Rt. 4, Box 220, Dallas, PA 18612, (717) 675-1143. (GNA)

3630 **State Game Lands No. 39 & 86**, Game Commission, P.O. Box 1567, Harrisburg, PA 17120, (717) 787-3633; or Northwest Division Headquarters, P.O. Box 31, 1509 Pittsburgh Rd., Franklin, PA 16323, (814) 412-3187. (GNA)

3631 **Stavich Bicycle Trail**, Gary Slaven, Falcon Foundry, 6th & Water Sts., P.O. Box 301, Lowellville, OH 44436-0301, (216) 536-6221. 12.0 miles straight. (GRT)

Steeplebush Trail *see* entry 3494.
Stible Hole Trail *see* entry 3627.

3632 **Stoevers Dam Recreational Area**, SR 343, Lebanon, PA 17042, (717) 273-6711 ext. 419. (MMA)

Stone Bridge Trail *see* entry 3627.
Stone Trail *see* entry 3421.
Stone Trail *see* entry 3627.

3633 **Stony Creek Valley**, Office of Public Information, Department of Environmental Resources, P.O. Box 1467, Harrisburg, PA 17120, (717) 787-2657. Named trails: Horseshoe, Water Tank, Yellow Springs. (OJP)

3634 **Stony Valley Railroad Grade Trail**, Roger L. Lehman, Chief, Federal-State Coordination Division, Pennsylvania Game Commission, 2001 Elmerton Ave., Harrisburg, PA 17100-9797, (717) 787-9612. 22.0 miles. (GRT)

Stout Hollow Trail *see* entry 3627.

3635 **Struble Trail**, Robert Folwell, Chester County Parks and Recreation Department, 235 W. Market St., West Chester, PA 19382, (215) 344-6415. 16.0 miles straight. (GRT)

Sullivan-Wilderness Trail *see* entry 3513.

Summerson Run Trail *see* entry 3627.

3636 **Sun Valley Campground**, P.O. Box 238, Bowmansville, PA 17507, (610) 445-6262. (WCD)

3637 **Sunrise Lake Family Campground**, P.O. Box 275W, Nicholson, PA 18446, (717) 942-6421 or (800) 326-9783. (WCD)

Sunset Rocks Trail *see* entry 3264.

3638 **Susquehanna Access Area**, Selinsgrove, PA 17870. (ATP)

3639 **Susquehanna Energy Information Center and Riverlands**, US 11, Berwick, PA 18603, (717) 542-2131 or (717) 759-4905. (ATP)

3640 **Susquehanna Park**, Williamsport, PA 17701. (ATP)

3641 **Susquehannock State Forest**, 8 E. Seventh St., Coudersport, PA 16915, (814) 274-8474. 500 miles. (EGH; GNA)

3642 **Susquehannock State Park**, c/o Gifford Pinchot State Park, 2200 Rosstown Rd., Lewisberry, PA 17339, (717) 432-5011. 8.0 miles. (PSP)

3643 **Susquehannock Trail**, Susquehannock Trail Club, P.O. Box 643, Coudersport, PA 16915; or Susquehannock Trail System, Secretary Elizabeth K. Ahn, Rt. 6, Ulysses, PA 16948. 85.0 miles loop. Awards available. (AA 1993)

3644 **Swatara State Park**, c/o Memorial Lake State Park, Rt. 1, Box 7045, Grantville, PA 17028, (717) 865-6470. (PSP)

Swift Run Trail *see* entry 3624.

3645 **Swiss Pines Japanese Garden**, Charlestown Rd., Malvern, PA 19355. (ATP)

3646 **Switchback Railroad Trail**, Dennis J. DeMara, Park Director, Carbon County Park and Recreation Department, 625 Lentz Trail Rd., Jim Thorpe, PA 18229, (717) 325-3669. 15.0 miles straight. (GRT)

3647 **Tall Oaks Campground**, SR 381, Farmington, PA 15437, (412) 329-4777. (WCD)

Tanbark Trail see entry 3330.

3648 **Tanglewood Camping**, P.O. Box 35, Covington, PA 16917, (717) 549-8299. (WCD)

3649 **Ten Mile Creek Access Area**, Prosperity, PA 15329. (ATP)

Terrace Mountain Trail see entry 3587.

3 Point Hollow Trail see entry 3627.

Three Ridge Trail see entry 3627.

Thunder Swamp Trail see entry 3359.

3650 **Tiadaghton State Forest**, Department of Environmental Resources, 423 E. Central Ave., South Williamsport, PA 17701, (717) 327-3450. 200 miles. Named trails: Black Forest 45.0(l), Golden Eagle 8.6(l), Reynolds Spring, South Link 6.0(s). (EGH; GNA; IFT)

Tiadaghton Trail see entry 3487.

Tidioute Riverside RecTrek Trail see entry 3258.

3651 **Tidioute Scout Reservation**, Northeast Ohio Council, BSA, 125 E. Erie St., Painesville, OH 44077, (216) 352-0631; or Tidioute Scout Reservation, Rt. 1, Box 236, Tidioute, PA 16351. (SFC)

3652 **Tinicum National Environmental Center**, Suite 104, Scott Plaza 2, Philadelphia, PA 19113, (215) 521-0662 or (215) 365-3118. Named trails: Boardwalk Loop, Impoundment. (DMP; MMA; NAT; OJP; AMC; GNA; GNW; CBP)

3653 **Tioga State Forest**, P.O. Box 94, 96 West Ave., Wellsboro, PA 16901, (717) 724-2868. Named trails: West Rim 30.0. (EGH; GNA)

3654 **Tioga-Hammond Lakes**, SR 287, Mansfield, PA 16933, (717) 835-5239. (ATP; MMA)

Tionesta Lake Nature Trail see entry 3655.

3655 **Tionesta Recreation Area**, Corps of Engineers—Tionesta Lake, SR 36, Tionesta, PA 16353, (814) 755-3512. Named trails: Tionesta Lake Nature. (WCD; GNA)

3656 **Tobyhanna State Park**, P.O. Box 387, Tobyhanna, PA 18466, (717) 894-8336. (WCD; ATP; AYH; MMA; DBV; DMA; PSP; GNA)

3657 **Todd Sanctuary**, Audubon Society of Western Pennsylvania, Beechwood Farms Nature Reserve, 614 Dorseyville Rd., Pittsburgh, PA 15238. Named trails: Indian Pipe, Loop, Meadow, Polypody, Ravine, Warbler. (LRA)

3658 **Tohickon Family Campground**, 8308 Covered Bridge Rd., Quakertown, PA 18951, (215) 536-7951. (WCD)

Tom Lowe Trail see entry 3264.

3659 **Tompkins Recreation Area**, Corps of Engineers—Tioga Lake, Bliss Rd., Lawrenceville, PA 16929, (717) 835-5281. (WCD)

Tramroad Trail see entry 3474.

3660 **Trexler Scout Reservation**, Minsi Trails Council, BSA, P.O. Box 2424, Lehigh Valley, PA 18001, (610) 264-8551; or Trexler Scout Reservation, SR 524, Kresgeville, PA 18333, (717) 629-0621. (SFC)

3661 **Triangle Acres Family Campground**, P.O. Box 413, Everett, PA 15537, (814) 784-3363. (WCD)

Trillium Trail see entry 3672.

3662 **Trough Creek State Park**, Rt. 1, Box 211, James Creek, PA 16657, (814) 658-3847. Named trails: Abbott Run. (WCD; ATP; PSP; OJP; AMI; GNA)

Tsunga Nature Trail see entry 3377.

Tub Trail see entry 3627.

3663 **Tucquan Park Family Campground**, River Rd., Holtwood, PA 17532, (717) 284-2156. (WCD)

Turkey Path Trail see entry 3560.

3664 **Turkey Trail**, Wellsboro Chamber of Commerce, P.O. Box 733, Wellsboro, PA 16901. (CBP)

Turkey Trail see entry 3627.

3665 **Tuscarora Hiking Trail**, Cowans Gap State Park, Fort Loudon, PA 17224; or Keystone Trails Association, P.O. Box 251, Cogan Station, PA 17728. 105 miles. (EGH; CBP)

3666 **Tuscarora State Forest**, Blain, PA 17006, (717) 536-3191. 131 miles. (EGH; GNA)
3667 **Tuscarora State Park**, Rt. 1, Box 1051, Barnesville, PA 18214, (717) 467-2404. 3.0 miles. (PSP)
Tuscarora Trail see entry 3305.
Twin Lakes Trail see entry 3258.
Twin Springs Trail see entry 3627.
3668 **Twin Streams Campground**, Rt. 1, Box 236, Morris, PA 16938, (717) 353-7251. (WCD)
3669 **Two Log Campground**, Rt. 2, Honey Brook, PA 19344, (610) 273-3068. (WCD)
3670 **Two Mile Run County Park**, Baker Rd., Franklin, PA 16323, (814) 676-6116. (WCD)
3671 **Tyler State Park**, SR 413 Bypass & Swamp Rd., Newtown, PA 18940, (610) 968-2021. 4.0 miles. (ATP; DMP; PSP)
3672 **Tytoona Natural Area**, Office of Public Information, Department of Environmental Resources, P.O. Box 1467, Harrisburg, PA 17120, (717) 787-2657. Named trails: Trillium. (OJP)
Uncas Trail see entry 3513.
Union Canal Biking and Hiking Trail see entry 3283.
Upper Doctor Greene Trail see entry 3627.
3673 **Upper Perkiomen Park**, SR 29, Green Lane, PA 18054, (610) 234-4528. (VFM)
Urey Trail see entry 3547.
3674 **Valley Forge Historical Trail**, Valley Forge Council, BSA, P.O. Box 806, Valley Forge, PA 19482, (610) 688-6900. 9.0 miles. Awards available. (AA 1992)
3675 **Valley Forge National Historical Park**, SR 23 & N. Guelph Rd., Valley Forge, PA 19482, (610) 783-1077. 5.0 miles. (VFM)
Valley Trail see entry 3580.
Van Ripper Trail see entry 3627.
Victoria Trail see entry 3264.
Violet Trail see entry 3280.
3676 **Virginia's Beach Campground**, SR 215, North Springfield, PA 16430, (814) 922-3261. (WCD)
3677 **W T Family Camping**, SR 115, Blakeslee, PA 18610, (717) 646-9255. (WCD)
Walker Trail see entry 3627.
Warbler Trail see entry 3657.
3678 **Warrior Trail**, Warrior Trail Association, Inc., Rt. 1, Box 35, Spraggs, PA 15362. 67.0 miles straight. Awards available. (AA 1992)
3679 **Warriors Path State Park**, c/o Canoe Creek State Park, Rt. 2, Box 560, Hollidaysburg, PA 16648, (814) 695-6807. 3.0 miles. (ATP; PSP)
3680 **Warwick Woods Family Camping Resort**, P.O. Box 280, St. Peters, PA 19470, (610) 286-9655. (WCD)
3681 **Washington Crossing Historic Trail**, Bucks County Council, BSA, 225 Green St., Doylestown, PA 18901, (610) 348-9436. 8.3 miles. Awards available. (AA 1992)
3682 **Washington Crossing Historical Park**, SR 32, New Hope, PA 18977, (610) 862-2924. (MMA)
3683 **Washington Trail**, Langundowi Lodge #46, French Creek Council, BSA, 1815 Robison Rd. W., Erie, PA 16509-4905, (814) 868-5571. 17.0 miles straight. Awards available. (AA 1991)
Water Tank Trail see entry 3633.
Water Trough Trail see entry 3627.
Waterfall Trail see entry 3627.
Watershed Trail see entry 3448.
Watershed Trail see entry 3537.
Weaver Trail see entry 3627.
3684 **Weiser State Forest**, P.O. Box 98, Cressona, PA 17929, (717) 385-2545. (GNA)
West Branch Bruce Lake Trail see entry 3301.
West Branch Lick Run Trail see entry 3627.
West Rim Trail see entry 3560.
West Rim Trail see entry 3653.
Whetham Tower Trail see entry 3627.
3685 **Whipple Dam State Park**, SR 26, State College, PA 16804, (814) 667-3808. 3.0 miles. (ATP; MMA; PSP)
3686 **Whispering Pines Camping Estates**, CR 19069, Benton, PA 17814, (717) 925-6810. (WCD)

3687 **White Clay Creek State Park**, P.O. Box 172, Landenburg, PA 19350, (215) 255-5415. 3.0 miles. (PSP)
  White Deer Trail see entry 3382.
  Wideview Trail see entry 3627.
  Wildcat Rocks Trail see entry 3264.
  Wildcat Trail see entry 3627.
  Wilderness Trail see entry 3441.
3688 **William Penn Trail**, Bucks County Council, BSA, 225 Green St., Doylestown, PA 18901, (610) 348-9436. 0.5-2.0 miles. Awards available. (AA 1992)
  Wolf Rocks Trail see entry 3382.
  Wolf Rocks Trail see entry 3395.
  Wolf Run Supply Trail see entry 3627.
  Wolf Run Trail see entry 3627.
  Wood Thrush Trail see entry 3262.
3689 **Woodburne Nature Trail**, Woodburne Forest and Wildlife Sanctuary, Rt. 1, Box 307, Montrose, PA 18801, (717) 278-3384. 1.0 mile. (OJP; AMI; GNA)
3690 **Woodland Park**, Rt. 4, Box 121, Ebensburg, PA 15931, (814) 472-9857 or (814) 472-7962. (WCD)
3691 **Worlds End State Park**, P.O. Box 62, Forksville, PA 18616-0062, (717) 924-3287. 12.0 miles. Named trails: Blue, Canyon Vista, Red X. (WCD; ATP; PSP; AMI; GNA)
3692 **Wyoming State Forest**, P.O. Box 439, Old Berwick Hwy., Bloomsburg, PA 17815, (717) 389-3606. (EGH; GNA)
3693 **Yellow Creek State Park**, US 422, Indiana, PA 15701, (412) 463-3850. 4.0 miles. (ATP; MMA; PSP)
  Yellow Springs Trail see entry 3633.
3694 **Yogi Bear's Jellystone Park Camp-Resort—Lancaster South/Quarryville**, 340 Blackburn Rd., Quarryville, PA 17566, (717) 786-3458. (WCD)
3695 **Yogi Bear's Jellystone Park Camp-Resort—Pocono Mountains**, Silver Valley Dr., Brodheadsville, PA 18322, (717) 992-4824. (WCD)
3696 **Yogi Bear's Jellystone Park Camp-Resort—Yogi-on-the-River**, Rt. 1, Box 116, Northumberland, PA 17857, (717) 473-8021. (WCD)
3697 **York City Historical Trail**, York-Adams Area Council, BSA, 800 E. King St., York, PA 17403, (717) 843-0901. 4.0 miles loop. Awards available. (SAR 1993)
3698 **York County Heritage Rail-Trail**, Tammy Klunk, Resource Coordinator, York County Parks, 400 Mundis Race Rd., York, PA 17402, (717) 771-9440. 22.0 miles straight planned, current as to 1.5 miles. (GRT)
3699 **Youghiogheny Reservoir**, US 40, Uniontown, PA 15401. (ATP)
  Youghiogheny River Trail see entry 3542.

Generally:
Bureau of State Parks, P.O. Box 1467, Harrisburg, PA 17105-1467, (717) 787-8800. (PSP)
Department of Environmental Resources, Bureau of Forestry, HCR 62, Box 90, Renovo, PA 17764. (HTA)
Office of Resources Management, Department of Environmental Resources, Rm. 202, Evangelical Press Bldg., Third & Reilly Sts., P.O. Box 1467, Harrisburg, PA 17120, (717) 787-2657. (OJP)
Pittsburgh Council, American Youth Hostels, Inc., 6300 Fifth Ave., Pittsburgh, PA 15232. (AYH)
U.S. Army Corps of Engineers, Pittsburgh District, Federal Bldg., 1000 Liberty Ave., Pittsburgh, PA 15222. (GFC)

Index (by city)

Abington: Lorimer Park 3491
Airville: Indian Steps Museum 3435
Altoona: Fort Roberdeau 3387
Apollo: Roaring Run Trail 3597
Ashfield: Bake Oven Campground 3271
Auburn: Christmas Pines Campground 3334
Audubon: Audubon Wildlife Sanctuary 3270
Austin: Sinnemahoning State Park 3621

234 Index PENNSYLVANIA

Bangor: Camp Charles Campgrounds 3316
Barnesville: Tuscarora State Park 3667
Bath: Evergreen Lake 3379
Beaver Springs: Gray Squirrel Campsites 3405
Bellefonte: KOA-Bellefonte/State College 3454
Bensalem: Neshaminy State Park 3533
Benton: Ricketts Glen State Park 3591; Whispering Pines Camping Estates 3686
Berwick: Susquehanna Energy Information Center and Riverlands 3639
Birdsboro: Daniel Boone Homestead 3353
Blain: Iron Horse Trail 3436; Tuscarora State Forest 3666
Blairsville: Pine Ridge County Park 3563
Blakeslee: W T Family Camping 3677
Bloomsburg: Deihl's Camping Resort 3355; Shady Rest Campground 3613; Wyoming State Forest 3692
Boalsburg: Mid-State Trail 3510
Boswell: Camp Roaring Run 3322
Bowmansville: Cape Lookout State Park 3327; Oak Creek Campgrounds 3541; Sun Valley Campground 3636
Bradford: KOA-Kinzua East 3457
Breezewood: Brush Creek Campground 3304
Bristol: Bristol Spurline Park Trail 3302
Brodheadsville: Yogi Bear's Jellystone Park Camp-Resort—Pocono Mountains 3695
Buck Run: Muddy Run Park 3529
Bushkill: Bushkill Falls 3309; Delaware Water Gap National Recreation Area 3360; Ken's Woods Campground 3445
Butler: Old Trader's Path Trail 3545
Cambridge Springs: Washington Trail 3683
Carbondale: Merli-Sarnoski Park 3507
Carlisle: Carlisle Historical Trail 3328; Huntsdale Fish Cultural Station 3430; Kings Gap State Park 3448; LeTort Spring Run Nature Trail 3481
Cedar Run: Pettecote Junction Camping Park 3556
Chadds Ford: Brandywine River Museum 3300
Champion: Mountain Pines Resort 3525
Charleroi: Bethany Christian Campground 3285
Clarendon: Chapman State Park 3330
Clarion: Clear Creek State Forest 3335; Kittanning State Forest 3451
Clearfield: Moshannon State Forest 3520; S.B. Elliott State Park 3604
Clifford: O & W Road Trail 3540
Coatesville: Birchville Farm Campground 3289
Collegeville: Evansburg State Park 3378
Connellsville: River's Edge Family Campground 3595
Cooksburg: Cook Forest State Park 3344; Deer Meadow Campground 3354
Coudersport: Cherry Springs State Forest Picnic Area 3332; Susquehannock State Forest 3641; Susquehannock Trail 3643
Covington: Tanglewood Camping 3648
Cressona: Allegheny Portage Railroad National Historic Site 3259; Johnstown Flood National Memorial 3442; Weiser State Forest 3684
Cross Fork: Ole Bull State Park 3546
Curwensville: Curwensville Lake 3352
Dalton: Archbold Pothole State Park 3266; Highland Campground 3424; Lackawanna State Park 3464; Salt Spring State Park 3605
Dayton: Milton Loop County Park 3511
Denver: Hickory Run Family Camping Resort 3420
Derry: Keystone State Park 3447
Dingmans Ferry: Dingmans Campground 3362; Dingmans Falls Trail 3363
Donegal: Laurel Highlands Camping 3472
Downington: Hibernia Park 3419; Marsh Creek State Park 3498; Springton Manor Farm 3626
Doylestown: Delaware Canal Trail 3357; Freedom Shrine Historic Trail 3391
Duncannon: Riverfront Campground 3594
East Scranton: Nay Aug Park 3532
East Stroudsburg: Cranberry Run Campground 3349; KOA-Delaware Water Gap 3455; Mountain Vista Campground 3527
Easton: Delaware & Lehigh Canal Trail 3358
Ebensburg: Gallitzin State Forest 3395
Elizabethtown: Rustic Meadows Camping & Golf Resort 3602
Elverson: French Creek State Park 3392; Hopewell Furnace Nature Trail 3428
Emlenton: Gaslight Campground 3396

PENNSYLVANIA Index 235

Emporium: Bucktail State Park 3308; Elk State Forest 3373; Lake Raystown Resort 3468; Sizerville State Park 3622
Entriken: Robinson's Hideaway Campground 3598
Erie: Camp Custaloga 3317; Erie Historical Trail 3376; Lake Erie Park 3466; Presque Isle State Park 3572; Shenango Trail 3617
Everett: Triangle Acres Family Campground 3661
Fallentimber: Camp Wopononock 3324
Farmingham: Fort Necessity National Battlefield 3386
Farmington: Brenner's Meadow Run Camping & Cabins 3301; Friendship Hill National Historic Site 3394; Tall Oaks Campground 3647
Fayetteville: Caledonia State Park 3313; Michaux State Forest 3508
Ford City: Crooked Creek State Park 3350
Forksville: Almost Heaven Campground 3261; Worlds End State Park 3691
Fort Loudon: Cowans Gap State Park 3348; Tuscarora Hiking Trail 3665
Fort Washington: Fort Washington State Park 3388
Franklin: Allegheny River Trail 3260; State Game Lands No. 39 & 86 3630; Two Mile Run County Park 3670
Freeport: Rachel Carson Trail 3581
Galeton: Cherry Springs State Park 3333; Denton Hill State Park 3361; Lyman Run State Park 3497; Patterson State Park 3551; Prouty Places State Park 3575
Gardners: Mountain Creek Campground 3524; Pine Grove Furnace State Park 3561
Gettysburg: Artillery Ridge Campground 3269; Downtown Gettysburg Walking Tour 3368; Drummer Boy Campground 3369; Gettysburg Heritage Trails 3398; Gettysburg National Military Park 3399; Granite Hill Campground & Westpark 3404; KOA-Gettysburg 3456; Moyer's Mountain Retreat 3528
Glen Mills: Newlin Mill Park 3534
Grantville: Memorial Lake State Park 3506; Swatara State Park 3644
Green Lane: Green Lane Reservoir Park 3407; Upper Perkiomen Park 3673

Greensburg: Bushy Run Battlefield 3310
Greentown: Promised Land State Park 3574
Guys Mills: Erie National Wildlife Refuge 3377
Hamlin: Lake Wallenpaupack 3469
Hanover: Codorus State Park 3338
Harrisburg: Alan Seeger Natural Area 3257; Andorra Natural Area 3262; Bear Meadows Natural Area 3277; Bowman's Hill State Wildflower Preserve 3296; Box Huckleberry Natural Area Trail 3297; Bruce Lake Natural Area 3303; Charles F. Lewis Natural Area 3331; Forest H. Dutlinger Natural Area 3384; Fort Hunter Mansion 3385; Harrisburg Historical Trail 3413; Little Juniata Water Gap Natural Area 3485; Loyalsock Creek 3495; Mt. Davis Natural Area 3521; Pine Creek Gorge 3560; Stony Creek Valley 3633; Stony Valley Railroad Grade Trail 3634; Tytoona Natural Area 3672
Hawley: Ledgedale Recreation Area 3477
Hegins: Camp-A-While 3325
Henryville: Big Pocono State Park 3287
Heston: Raystown Dam and Lake 3587
Hollidaysburg: Canoe Creek State Park 3326; Warriors Path State Park 3679
Holtwood: Muddy Run Recreation Park 3530; Otter Creek 3547; Tucquan Park Family Campground 3663
Honesdale: Rainbow Mountain Family Campground 3583
Honey Brook: The Berry Patch Campground 3284; Two Log Campground 3669
Howard: Bald Eagle State Park 3276
Huntingdon: Greenwood Furnace State Park 3409; Lincoln Caverns 3482; Rothrock State Forest 3601
Hyner: Hyner Run State Park 3431
Imler: Blue Knob State Park 3292
Indiana: Ghost Town Trail 3400; Yellow Creek State Park 3693
Jacksonville: Leaser Lake Park 3476
James Creek: Trough Creek State Park 3662
Jamestown: Pymatuning State Park 3577
Jenkintown: Horse-Shoe Trail 3429
Jersey Shore: Ravensburg State Park 3585
Jim Thorpe: Jim Thorpe Camping Resort 3440; Mauch Chunk Lake Park 3501; Switchback Railroad Trail 3646

Johnsonburg: Elk State Park 3374
Kempton: Hawk Mountain Sanctuary 3414
Kittanning: The Armstrong Trail 3267
Kleinfeltersville: Middlecreek Wildlife Management Area 3509
Kresgeville: Trexler Scout Reservation 3660
Kutztown: Crystal Cave Park 3351
Lafayette: Idlewood Campground 3432
Lake Ariel: Lacawac Sanctuary 3463; Maurice Brown Self-Guided Nature Trail 3502
Lake City: Pine Lane Campground 3562
Lancaster: Conewago Trail 3343; Historic Lancaster Walking Tour 3426; Lancaster Junction Trail 3471
Landenburg: White Clay Creek State Park 3687
Laporte: Pioneer Campground 3564
Laurelton: Bald Eagle State Forest 3275
Lawrenceville: Cowanesque Lake 3347; Tompkins Recreation Area 3659
Lebanon: Stoevers Dam Recreational Area 3632
Lehigh Valley: Camp Minsi 3320; Minsi Trails Council Historical Trails 3513
Lehighton: Beltzville State Park 3281
Lenhartsville: Blue Rocks Family Campground 3294
Lewis Run: Black Bear Campground 3290
Lewisberry: Gifford Pinchot State Park 3401; Samuel S. Lewis State Park 3607; Susquehannock State Park 3642
Lewistown: The Locust 3489
Ligonier: Linn Run State Park 3483; PW&S Railroad Hiking-Biking Trail 3576
Lima: John J. Tyler Arboretum 3441
Linesville: Pymatuning Waterfowl Area 3578
Liverpool: Ferryboat Campsites 3381
Loganton: Holiday Pines Campgrounds 3427
Lowellville, OH: Stavich Bicycle Trail 3631
Mahanoy City: Locust Lake State Park 3490
Malvern: Swiss Pines Japanese Garden 3645
Mansfield: Bucktail Camping Resort 3307; Tioga-Hammond Lakes 3654
Marienville: Allegheny National Forest 3258
Marshalls Creek: Otter Lake Camp Resort 3548
Martins Creek: Martins Creek Park 3499
McConnellsburg: Buchanan State Forest 3305
McMurray: Arrowhead Trail 3268
Media: Ridley Creek State Park 3592
Melcroft: Indian Creek Valley Hiking and Biking Trail 3433
Mercer: Junction 19-80 Campground 3443; KOA-Mercer/Grove 3458; Rocky Springs Campground 3599
Mercersburg: Saunderosa Park 3609
Meshoppen: Slumber Valley Campground 3623
Mifflinburg: Hidden Valley Camping Resort 3422; Raymond B. Winter State Park 3586
Milford: Cliff Park 3337
Millheim: Poe Paddy State Park 3568
Milroy: Penn Roosevelt State Forest 3553; Poe Valley State Park 3569; Reeds Gap State Park 3590; Snyder-Middleswarth State Park 3624
Montrose: Endless Mountain Riding Trail 3375; Woodburne Nature Trail 3689
Morris: Twin Streams Campground 3668
Morrisville: William Penn Trail 3688
Mount Jewett: Kinzua Bridge Historic Trail 3449; Kinzua Bridge State Park 3450
Mount Joy: Donegal Mills Plantation 3366
Mount Pocono: Caesar's Paradise Stream 3312; Gouldsboro State Park 3403; Mount Pocono Campground 3523
Narvon: Lake In Wood Camp Travel Park 3467
Nazareth: Plainfield Township Trail 3566
New Brighton: Brady Run County Park 3299
New Castle: Rose Point Campground 3600
New Columbia: Nittany Mountain Campground 3535
New Florence: Camp Twin Echo 3323; Mirror Lake Camping 3514
New Germantown: Big Spring State Park 3288
New Holland: Spring Gulch Resort Campground 3625
New Hope: Washington Crossing Historic Trail 3681; Washington Crossing Historical Park 3682

New Milford: State Game Lands No. 35 & 159 3629
New Tripoli: KOA-Allentown-Lehigh Valley Kampground 3453
Newport: Little Buffalo State Park 3484
Newtown: Tyler State Park 3671
Newville: Colonel Denning State Park 3340; Dogwood Acres Campground 3364; Fowlers Hollow State Park 3389
Nicholson: Sunrise Lake Family Campground 3637
Norristown: Philadelphia to Valley Forge Bikeway 3558
North Springfield: Virginia's Beach Campground 3676
Northumberland: Yogi Bear's Jellystone Park Camp-Resort 3696
Nottingham: Nottingham Serpentine Barrens 3539
Oaks: Lower Perkiomen Park 3492
Ohiopyle: Bear Run Nature Reserve 3279; Ohiopyle State Park 3542
Oil City: National Trails Towpath Bike Trail of Palmer and Bethlehem Townships 3531; Oil Creek State Park 3544
Patton: Prince Gallitzin State Park 3573; Raccoon Creek State Park 3580
Penfield: Parker Dam State Park 3550
Penn Run: L & M Campgrounds 3462
Pequea: Pequea Creek Campground 3555
Philadelphia: Benjamin Franklin Historical Trail 3282; Carpenter's Woods 3329; Fairmount Park Bikeway National Recreation Trail 3380; Morris Arboretum 3519; Philadelphia Bicentennial Trail of Freedom 3557; Poor Richard's Trail 3570; Tinicum National Environmental Center 3652
Philipsburg: Black Moshannon State Park 3291
Phoenixville: Baker Park YMCA Campground 3272
Pipersville: Ralph Stover State Park 3584
Pittsburgh: Baker Trail 3273; Beechwood Farms Nature Preserve 3280; Camp Anawanna 3314; Camp Baker 3315; Camp Guyasuta 3319; Forbes Trail 3383; Frick Park 3393; Heritage Reservation 3416; Monongahela National Forest 3515; Montour Trail 3517; Riverview Park 3596; Schenley Park 3610; Todd Sanctuary 3657
Portersville: Bear Run Campground 3278; Cooper's Lake Campground 3345; McConnell's Mill State Park 3504; Moraine State Park 3518
Pottstown: Ringing Rocks Park 3593
Prosperity: Ten Mile Creek Access Area 3649
Quakertown: Boulder Woods Campground 3295; Little Red Barn Campground 3488; Nockamixon State Park 3536; Quakertown Area 3579; Tohickon Family Campground 3658
Quarryville: Yogi Bear's Jellystone Park Camp-Resort 3694
Reading: Berks County Heritage Center 3283; Blue Marsh Lake 3293; Nolde Forest State Park 3537
Renovo: Kettle Creek State Park 3446; Sproul State Forest 3627
Ridgway: Allegheny National Forest 3258
Robesonia: Eagles Peak Campground 3370
Rockwood: Forbes State Forest 3382; Laurel Highlands Hiking Trail 3473; Laurel Ridge State Park 3475; Scottyland Camping Resort 3612
Rome: Pine Cradle Lake Family Campground 3559
Rossiter: Hemlock Lake County Park 3415
Roxborough: Schuylkill Center for Environmental Education 3611
Rupert: Indian Head Recreational Campgrounds 3434
Rural Valley: Great Shamokin Path 3406
Russell: Camp Olmstead 3321; Penn Highlands Campground 3552
Sagamore: Silver Canoe Campground 3620
Sagertown: Colonel Crawford Park 3339
St. Peters: Warwick Woods Family Camping Resort 3680
Saltsburg: Conemaugh River Lake 3342; Loyalhanna Lake 3494
Sandy Lake: Goddard Park Vacationland Campgrounds 3402; Maurice K. Goddard State Park 3503
Saxonburg: Butler-Freeport Community Trail 3311
Scandia: Red Oak Campground 3588
Schellsburg: Shawnee State Park 3614
Scotia-Corry: Harecreek Campground 3412

Scranton: McDade Park 3505
Selinsgrove: Susquehanna Access Area 3638
Seneca: Samuel Justus Recreational Trail 3606
Sharon: Shenango Public Use Area 3615
Sharpsville: Shenango River Lake 3616
Shartlesville: Appalachian Campsites 3263; Mountain Springs Camping Resort 3526; Pennsylvania Dutch Campsite 3554
Sheffield: Allegheny National Forest 3258
Shohola: Shohola Waterfowl Management Area 3619
Sigel: Clear Creek State Park 3336
Slippery Rock: Jennings State Park 3439
Smethport: Camp Elk Lick 3318
Somerset: Hidden Valley Resort 3423; Kooser State Park 3461; Laurel Hill State Park 3474; Pioneer Park Campground 3565
Spraggs: Warrior Trail 3678
State College: Whipple Dam State Park 3685
Stevens: Starlite Camping Resort 3628
Stroudsburg: Delaware State Forest 3359; Pocono Vacation Park 3567
Sunbury: Milton State Park 3512; Shikellamy State Park 3618
Tiadaghton: Tiadaghton State Forest 3650
Tidioute: Tidioute Scout Reservation 3651
Tioga: Ives Run Recreation Area 3437; Lambs Creek Hike and Bike Trail 3470; Railroad Grade Trail 3582
Tionesta: Outflow Camping Area 3549; Tionesta Recreation Area 3655
Titusville: Oil Creek Camp-Resort 3543
Tobyhanna: Tobyhanna State Park 3656
Tremont: Echo Valley Park 3372
Troy: Mt. Pisgah State Park 3522
Tunkhannock: KOA-Tunkhannock 3459
Turbotville: Montour Preserve 3516
Tyrone: Bald Eagle Campsite 3274
Uniontown: Youghiogheny Reservoir 3699
Upper Black Eddy: Delaware Canal State Park 3356; Dogwood Haven Family Camp Grounds 3365

Valley Forge: Betzwood Rail Trail 3286; Valley Forge Historical Trail 3674; Valley Forge National Historical Park 3675
Wapwallopen: Council Cup Campground 3346
Warren: Allegheny National Forest 3258; Buckaloons Access Area 3306
Washington: KOA-Washington 3460
Waterville: Happy Acres Campground 3411; Little Pine State Park 3487
Waymart: Keen Lake Camping & Cottage Resort 3444
Waynesburg: Greene County Historical Museum 3408
Weatherly: Lehigh Gorge State Park 3479
Wellsboro: Colton Point State Park 3341; Hills Creek State Park 3425; Leonard Harrison State Park 3480; Tioga State Forest 3653; Turkey Trail 3664
West Chester: Struble Trail 3635
White Haven: Hickory Run State Park 3421; Lehigh Gorge Campground 3478; Sandy Valley Campground 3608
White Mills: Dorflinger-Suydam Wildlife Sanctuary 3367
White Oak: Braddock's Crossing Trail 3298
Wilcox: East Branch Lake 3371
Wilkinsburg: General Forbes Trail 3397
Williamsburg: Lower Trail 3493
Williamsport: Haleeka Campsites 3410; Kline High Adventure Base 3452; Loyalsock Trail 3496; Susquehanna Park 3640
Wilmington: Mason-Dixon Trail 3500
Wind Gap: Jacobsburg State Park 3438
Wind Ridge: Ryerson Station State Park 3603
Winfield: Little Mexico Campground 3486
Wyoming: Frances Slocum State Park 3390
York: Heritage Walking Tour 3417; Lake Alfred Park 3465; York City Historical Trail 3697; York County Heritage Rail-Trail 3698
York Springs: Hershey's Fur Center 3418
Zion Grove: Red Ridge Lake Campground 3589

Rhode Island

3700 **Arcadia Management Area,** Arcadia Management Area, Rt. 1, Box 55, Hope Valley, RI 02832. 65.0 miles. (EGH; SNE; OTB; GNA)

3701 **Arcadia State Park,** Old Nooseneck Hill Rd., Hope Valley, RI 02832, (401) 539-7643 or (401) 539-2356. (SRI; WCD)

3702 **Bay Islands Park System,** Division of Parks and Recreation, 22 Hayes St., Providence, RI 02908, (401) 277-2635. (SNE)

3703 **Big River Management Area,** Division of Fish and Wildlife, Washington County Government Center, Tower Hill Rd., Wakefield, RI 02879, (401) 789-3094. (GNA)

3704 **Black Hut Management Area,** Division of Fish and Wildlife, Washington County Government Center, Tower Hill Rd., Wakefield, RI 02879, (401) 789-3094. 5.0 miles. (SNE; GNA)

3705 **Block Island,** Block Island Chamber of Commerce, P.O. Drawer D, Block Island, RI 02807, (401) 466-2982; or Block Island National Wildlife Refuge, Block Island, RI 02807. Named trails: Clayhead Nature. (LGU; FNE; FRN; GNA)

3706 **Bowdish Lake Camping Area,** US 44, Chepachet, RI 02814, (401) 568-8890. (WCD)

3707 **Buck Hill Family Campground,** Narragansett Council, BSA, 175 Broad St., Providence, RI 02903-4081, (401) 351-8700; or Buck Hill Family Campground, Rt. 1, Box 367, Wakefield Pond Rd., Pascoag, RI 02859, (401) 568-0456. (WCD; SFC)

3708 **Buck Hill Wildlife Management Area,** Division of Fish and Wildlife, Washington County Government Center, Tower Hill Rd., Wakefield, RI 02879, (401) 789-3094. (SNE)

3709 **Burlingame Complex,** Department of Environmental Management, 83 Park St., Providence, RI 02903, (401) 277-6800. 10.0 miles. (GNA)

3710 **Caratunk Wildlife Refuge,** 301 Brown Ave., Seekonk, MA 02771, (401) 761-8230. 7.0 miles. (SNE; GNA)

3711 **Carolina Game Management Area,** Division of Fish and Wildlife, Washington County Government Center, Tower Hill Rd., Wakefield, RI 02879, (401) 789-3094. 5.0 miles. (GNA)

3712 **Charles B. Parker Woodland,** Maple Valley Rd., Coventry, RI 02816; or Audubon Society of Rhode Island, 40 Bowen St., Providence, RI 02903, (401) 521-1670. 3.0 miles. Named trails: Yellow. (SNE; GFA; GNA)

Clayhead Nature Trail *see* entry 3705.

3713 **Cliff Walk,** Newport Chamber of Commerce, 10 America's Cup Ave., Newport, RI 02840, (401) 847-1600. 3.0 miles straight. (FNE; FRN; GFA; AGW; NET; FDN; WTN)

3714 **Colt State Park,** SR 114, Bristol, RI 02809, (401) 253-9062. (MNE)

3715 **Davis Memorial Wildlife Refuge Nature Trail,** Audubon Society of Rhode Island, 12 Sanderson Rd., Smithfield, RI 02917, (401) 231-6449. (SNE; GNA)

3716 **Diamond Hill State Park,** Diamond Hill Rd., Woonsocket, RI 02895. (WCD)

3717 **East Bay Bicycle Path,** Kevin O'Malley, Regional Manager, Colt State Park, Bristol, RI 02809, (401) 253-7482. 14.0 miles straight. (GRT)

3718 **Ell Pond and Long Pond,** Audubon Society of Rhode Island, 12 Sanderson

Rd., Smithfield, RI 02917, (401) 231-6449; or The Nature Conservancy, 294 Washington St., Rm. 850, Boston, MA 02108, (617) 542-1908. 3.0 miles. Named trails: Narragansett. (SNE; GNA)

3719 **Emilie Ruecker Wildlife Refuge**, Audubon Society of Rhode Island, 12 Sanderson Rd., Smithfield, RI 02917, (401) 231-6449. 1.5 miles. (GNA)

3720 **Fisherville Brook Wildlife Refuge**, Exeter, RI 02822, (401) 231-6444. (SRI)

3721 **George Washington Complex**, Department of Environmental Management, 83 Park St., Providence, RI 02903, (401) 277-6800. Named trails: Walkabout 8.0(l). (OTB; GNA)

3722 **George Washington Management Area**, Rt. 2, Box 2185, Chepachet, RI 02814, (401) 568-6700. (WCD; SNE)

3723 **Great Swamp Management Area**, Division of Fish and Wildlife, Washington County Government Center, Tower Hill Rd., Wakefield, RI 02879, (401) 789-3094. 5.0 miles. (GNA)

3724 **Greenwood Hill Family Campground**, SR 138, Hope Valley, RI 02832, (800) 232-7154. (WCD)

3725 **Kimball Wildlife Refuge**, US 1, Charlestown, RI 02813, (401) 521-1670 or (401) 231-6444. (MNE; OTB)

3726 **Lincoln Woods State Park**, Breakneck Hill Rd., Providence, RI 02904, (401) 723-7892. (MNE)

3727 **Melville Ponds City Park**, Sullivan Rd., Portsmouth, RI 02871, (401) 849-8212. (WCD)

3728 **Napatree Point Beach and Conservation Area**, Westerly, RI 02891. (SRI)

Narragansett Trail see entry 3718.

3729 **Newport Freedom Trail**, Narragansett Council, BSA, 175 Broad St., Providence, RI 02903-4081, (401) 351-8700. 20.0 miles loop. Awards available. (AA 1992)

3730 **Ninigret Conservation Area**, Frosty Drew Memorial Nature Center, c/o Department of Environmental Management, 22 Hayes St., Providence, RI 02908, (401) 277-2632. (SRI; SNE; GNA)

3731 **Norman Bird Sanctuary**, Third Beach Rd., Middletown, RI 02840, (401) 846-2577. 15.0 miles. (SNE; OTB; NEO; GNA)

3732 **Powder Mill Ledges Wildlife Refuge**, Audubon Society of Rhode Island, 12 Sanderson St., Smithfield, RI 02917, (401) 231-6449. (SNE)

3733 **Seapowet Marsh Management Area**, Division of Fish and Wildlife, Washington County Government Center, Tower Hill Rd., Wakefield, RI 02879, (401) 789-3094. (SNE)

3734 **Snake Den State Park**, Department of Environmental Management, 22 Hayes St., Providence, RI 02908, (401) 277-2632. (SNE)

3735 **Trestle Trail**, Department of Environmental Management, 83 Park St., Providence, RI 02903, (401) 277-6800; or Ginny Leslie, Senior Planner, Rhode Island Department of Environmental Management, Division of Planning and Development, 83 Park St., Providence, RI 02903, (401) 277-2776. 8.0 miles straight. (GRT; SNE; GNA)

3736 **Trustom Pond National Wildlife Refuge**, c/o Ninigret National Wildlife Refuge, P.O. Box 307, Charlestown, RI 02813, (401) 364-3106; or Audubon Society of Rhode Island, 12 Sanderson Rd., Smithfield, RI 02917, (401) 231-6449. (GNW)

Walkabout Trail see entry 3721.

3737 **Warwick City Park**, Asylum Rd., Warwick, RI 02886, (401) 738-2000 ext. 354. (MNE)

3738 **Wickaboxet Management Area**, Division of Fish and Wildlife, Washington County Government Center, Tower Hill Rd., Wakefield, RI 02879, (401) 789-3094. 5.0 miles. (SRI; GNA)

3739 **Winding Creek Trail**, Peace Dale, US 1, South Kingstown, RI 02881, (401) 789-9331 ext. 245. (FNE)

Yellow Trail see entry 3712.

Generally:
Rhode Island Department of Environmental Management, 22 Hayes St., Providence, RI 02908, (401) 277-6800. (EGH)

Index (by city)

Block Island: Block Island 3705
Bristol: Colt State Park 3714; East Bay Bicycle Path 3717
Carolina: Carolina Game Management Area 3711
Charlestown: Kimball Wildlife Refuge 3725; Ninigret Conservation Area 3730; Trustom Pond National Wildlife Refuge 3736
Chepachet: Bowdish Lake Camping Area 3706; George Washington Management Area 3722
Coventry: Charles B. Parker Woodland 3712
Coventry Center: Trestle Trail 3735
Exeter: Fisherville Brook Wildlife Refuge 3720
Frenchtown: Davis Memorial Wildlife Refuge Nature Trail 3715
Glendale: Black Hut Management Area 3704
Hope Valley: Arcadia Management Area 3700; Arcadia State Park 3701; Greenwood Hill Family Campground 3724
Middletown: Norman Bird Sanctuary 3731
Newport: Cliff Walk 3713; Newport Freedom Trail 3729
Nooseneck: Big River Management Area 3703
Pascoag: Buck Hill Family Campground 3707; Buck Hill Wildlife Management Area 3708
Portsmouth: Melville Ponds City Park 3727
Providence: Bay Islands Park System 3702; Lincoln Woods State Park 3726; Snake Den State Park 3734
Seekonk: Caratunk Wildlife Refuge 3710
Smithfield: Ell Pond and Long Pond 3718; Powder Mill Ledges Wildlife Refuge 3732
South Kingstown: Winding Creek Trail 3739
Tiverton: Emilie Ruecker Wildlife Refuge 3719; Seapowet Marsh Management Area 3733
Warwick: Warwick City Park 3737
West Glocester: George Washington Complex 3721
West Greenwich Center: Wickaboxet Management Area 3738
West Kingston: Great Swamp Management Area 3723
Westerly: Burlingame Complex 3709; Napatree Point Beach and Conservation Area 3728
Woonsocket: Diamond Hill State Park 3716

SOUTH CAROLINA

3740 **Aiken State Park**, 1145 State Park Rd., Windsor, SC 29856, (803) 649-2857. Named trails: Jungle Nature 2.4(l). (WCD; MMA; SCP; OTB; SCT; GNA)

Andrew Jackson Nature Trail *see* entry 3741.

3741 **Andrew Jackson State Park**, Rt. 1, Lancaster, SC 29720, (803) 285-3344. Named trails: Andrew Jackson Nature 1.1(l). (WCD; ATN; SCP; SCT)

Animal Forest Trail *see* entry 3763.

Artesian Nature Trail *see* entry 3832.

3742 **Asbury Hills United Methodist Camp**, Star Route, Box 65, Cleveland, SC 29635, (803) 836-3711. Named trails: Asbury 5.4(l), Blue 0.8(l), Yellow 1.0(l). (SCT)

Asbury Trail *see* entry 3742.

3743 **Baker Creek State Park**, Rt. 1, Box 219, McCormick, SC 29835, (803) 443-2457. (WCD; ATN; MMA; SCP)

Barnwell Lake Trail *see* entry 3744.

3744 **Barnwell State Park**, P.O. Box 147, Blackville, SC 29817, (803) 284-2212. Named trails: Barnwell Lake 1.5(l), Discovery 0.2(l). (WCD; MMA; SCT)

Bartram Trail (see entry **4949** in interstate section).

3745 **Bass Lake RV Campground**, Rt. 1, Box 750, Dillon, SC 29536, (803) 774-6153. (WCD)

3746 **Bear Island Game Management Area**, c/o Division of Wildlife and Freshwater Fisheries, P.O. Box 167, Columbia, SC 29202, (803) 758-6524. (GNA)

3747 **Beauty Trail**, Greater Florence Chamber of Commerce, 610 W. Palmetto St., P.O. Box 948, Florence, SC 29503, (803) 665-0515. 12.0 miles. (MMA)

Beaver Dam Trail *see* entry 3769.

3748 **Bethelwoods**, Rt. 4, Box 75-A, York, SC 29745, (803) 366-3722. Named trails: Bethelwoods Nature 0.8(l), Wagon Camp 0.8(l). (SCT)

Bethelwoods Nature Trail *see* entry 3748.

Big Ben Trail *see* entry 3882.

Billy Dreher Nature Trail *see* entry 3780.

3749 **Blue Ridge Historical Railroad Trail**, Blue Ridge Council, BSA, 2 Ridgeway Ave., P.O. Box 6628, Greenville, SC 29606-6628, (803) 233-8363. 15.0 miles straight. Awards available. (AA 1990)

3750 **Blue Ridge Railroad Historical Trail**, Hurley E. Badders, Executive Director, Pendleton District, Historical and Recreational Commission, P.O. Box 565, Pendleton, SC 29670, (803) 646-3782. 5.0 miles straight. (GRT)

Blue Trail *see* entry 3742.

Boardwalk Nature Trail *see* entry 3810.

Boardwalk Nature Trail *see* entry 3811.

Boosho Creek Nature Trail *see* entry 3849.

3751 **Boyd Hill Trail**, Rock Hill Recreation and Park Department, 211 S. Cherry Rd., Rock Hill, SC 29730, (803) 327-1136. 0.4 mile loop. (SCT)

Broad River Trail *see* entry 3882.

3752 **Brookgreen Gardens**, US 17, Murrells Inlet, SC 29576, (803) 237-4218. (ATN)

Bull Sluice Trail *see* entry 3882.

Bull's Island Wildlife Trail *see* entry 3760.

Buncombe Trail *see* entry 3882.

3753 **Caesars Head State Park**, P.O. Box 278, Cedar Mountain, NC 28718, (803) 836-6115. Named trails: Jones Creek 5.3(l),

242

SOUTH CAROLINA 243

Raven Cliffs Falls 4.6(l). (ATN; SCP; AGW; BRM; SCT)

3754 **Calhoun Falls State Park,** SR 81, Calhoun Falls, SC 29628, (803) 447-8097. (WCD)

3755 **Camp Gravatt Lake Trail,** Gravatt Camp Conference Center, Rt. 6, Box 200, Aiken, SC 29801, (803) 648-1817. 1.4 miles loop. (SCT)

3756 **Camp Thunderbird Nature Trail,** Camp Thunderbird, Rt. 7, Box 50, Clover, SC 29710, (803) 831-2121. 0.6 mile loop. (SCT)

3757 **Campers Paradise,** Rt. 5, Box 870, Manning, SC 29102, (803) 473-3550. (WCD)

3758 **Campobello-Gramling Trail,** Principal, Campobello-Gramling Elementary School, Campobello, SC 29322, (803) 472-6495. 0.8 mile loop. (SCT)

Canal Nature Trail see entry 3797.

Caney Fork Falls Trail see entry 3767.

3759 **Canoe Lake Nature Trail,** Camp Superintendent, Rt. 4, Box 232, Bennettsville, SC 29512, (803) 479-3051. 1.6 miles loop. (SCT)

3760 **Cape Romain National Wildlife Refuge,** Rt. 1, Box 191, Awendaw, SC 29429, (803) 928-3368. Named trails: Bull's Island Wildlife 2.0(l), Old Fort Loop 6.6(l), Sheephead Ridge Loop 3.7(l). (SCT; GNA; GNW)

3761 **Capers Island Park,** (803) 886-6680; or Wildlife and Marine Resources Department, P.O. Box 12559, Charleston, SC 29412, (803) 795-6350. (GNA)

3762 **Carolina Sandhills National Wildlife Refuge,** Rt. 2, Box 130, McBee, SC 29101, (803) 335-8401. Named trails: Whitetail 4.0(s), Woodland Pond 0.9(l). (ATN; OTB; GNA; GNW)

Charles Towne Garden Trail see entry 3763.

3763 **Charles Towne Landing State Park,** 1500 Old Town Rd., Charleston, SC 29407, (803) 556-4450. Named trails: Animal Forest 0.8(l), Charles Towne Garden 2.4(l). (ATN; SCP; SCT)

3764 **Charleston Bicentennial Trail of Freedom,** American Historical Trails, Inc., P.O. Box 769, Monroe, NC 28110, (704) 289-1604. 8.0-12.0 miles loop. Awards available. (SAR 1992)

Chattoga Trail see entry 3882.

3765 **Chauga Nature Trail,** Oconee County Parks and Recreation Commission, P.O. Box 188, Walhalla, SC 29691, (803) 638-9585. 0.5 mile loop. (SCT)

3766 **Cheraw State Park,** Rt. 2, Box 888, Cheraw, SC 29520, (803) 537-2215. Named trails: Dogwood Lake Nature 0.9(l), Lake Eureka, Wilderness 0.6(l). (WCD; ATN; MMA; SCP; GNA)

Cherokee Interpretive Trail see entry 3819.

Cherry Hill Nature Trail see entry 3882.

3767 **Chester State Park,** Rt. 2, Box 348, Chester, SC 29706, (803) 385-2680. Named trails: Caney Fork Falls 1.3(l). (WCD; ATN; SCP; SCT)

Cistern Boardwalk Trail see entry 3871.

3768 **Clark Hill Lake,** Resource Manager, Clarks Hill, SC 29821, (803) 333-2476. Named trails: Clark Hill 1.0(l), Modoc Nature 2.2(l). (SCT; GNA; LRA)

Clark Hill Trail see entry 3768.

Clarks Fork Trail see entry 3822.

3769 **Clemson University,** College of Forest and Recreational Resources, Clemson, SC 29631, (803) 656-3400 or (803) 656-4789. Named trails: Beaver Dam 0.8(s), Firetower 1.0(s), Horticultural Gardens 1.6(l), Indian Creek Forest 0.9(l), Issaqueena 4.0(l), Lawrence 2.2(l), Treaty Oak 0.4(l). (ATN; SCT)

3770 **Cleveland Park Trail,** Greenville Park and Recreational Services, P.O. Box 2207, Greenville, SC 29602, (803) 242-1250. 3.3 miles loop. (SCT)

3771 **Colleton State Park Nature Trail,** US 15, Canadys, SC 29433, (803) 538-8206. 0.4 mile loop. (WCD; ATN; MMA; SCP; SCT)

3772 **Colleton Trail,** Walterboro-Colleton County Recreation Commission, P.O. Box 173, Walterboro, SC 29488, (803) 549-2729. 2.6 miles loop. (SCT)

3773 **Congaree River Trail,** Parks and Recreation Department, 1932 Calhoun

St., Columbia, SC 29201, (803) 733-8331. 0.5 mile loop. (SCT)

3774 **Congaree Swamp National Monument**, P.O. Box 11938, Columbia, SC 29211, (803) 765-5571. 22.0 miles. (PGF; GNM; MMA; NPS; NPV; NPE; CGA; SCT)

Coquina Nature Trail see entry 3861.

3775 **Cowpens Battlefield Historical Trail**, Palmetto Council, BSA, 420 S. Church St., P.O. Box 6249, Spartanburg, SC 29304, (803) 585-4391. Awards available. (AA 1993)

3776 **Cowpens National Battlefield**, P.O. Box 308, Chesnee, SC 29323, (803) 461-2828/7077. (ATN; GNM; MMA; GFA; NPS; NPE; CGA; SCT)

3777 **Creek Trail**, Director, Whitten Center Camping and Nature Programs, P.O. Box 239, Clinton, SC 29325, (803) 833-2733. 1.3 miles straight. (SCT)

Croft Jogging Trail see entry 3778.

3778 **Croft State Park**, Rt. 4, Box 28-A, Spartanburg, SC 29302, (803) 585-0419. Named trails: Croft Jogging 0.5(l), Lake Johnson 5.5(l), Little Sycamore Nature 1.5(l). (WCD; ATN; MMA; SCP; SCT)

3779 **Devils Fork State Park**, SR 25, Walhalla, SC 29691, (803) 944-2639. (WCD)

Discovery Trail see entry 3744.

Dogwood Lake Nature Trail see entry 3766.

3780 **Dreher Island State Park**, Rt. 1, Box 356, Prosperity, SC 29127, (803) 364-4152. Named trails: Billy Dreher Nature 0.2(l). (WCD; ATN; MMA; SCP; SCT)

Duke Foothills Hiking Trail see entry 3789.

3781 **Duncan Park Trail**, Spartanburg City/County Parks and Recreation Dept., 168 W. Main St., Spartanburg, SC 29304, (803) 596-3733. 0.8 mile loop. (SCT)

3782 **Earlwood Park Trail**, Parks and Recreation Department, 1932 Calhoun St., Columbia, SC 29201, (803) 733-8331. 0.5 mile loop. (SCT)

East Fork Trail see entry 3882.

3783 **Edisto Beach State Park**, 8377 State Cabin Rd., Edisto Island, SC 29438, (803) 869-2156 or (803) 869-2756. Named trails: Indian Mound 3.6(l). (WCD; ATN; MMA; SCP; SCT; GNA)

3784 **Edisto Gardens**, Orangeburg Recreation Dept., 620 Middleton St., Orangeburg, SC 29115, (803) 534-6211. 1.5 miles loop. (SCT)

3785 **Edisto Nature Trail**, Westvaco Timberland Division, Southern Woodlands, P.O. Box WV, Summerville, SC 29483, (803) 871-5000. 1.0 mile loop. (SAR 1992)

Ellicott Rock Trail see entry 3882.

3786 **Explorer Trail**, Whitten Center Camping and Nature Programs, P.O. Box 239, Clinton, SC 29325, (803) 833-2733. 3.0 miles straight. (SCT)

3787 **Fewell Park Trail**, Rock Hill Recreation and Park Department, 211 S. Cherry Rd., Rock Hill, SC 29730, (803) 327-1136. 0.8 mile loop. (SCT)

Firetower Trail see entry 3769.

3788 **Foothills KOA of Spartanburg**, Campground Rd., Spartanburg, SC 29303, (803) 576-0970. (WCD)

3789 **Foothills Trail**, Project Recreation Supervisor, Duke Power Company, 422 South Church St., P.O. Box 33189, Charlotte, NC 28242, (704) 373-4011; or Foothills Trail Conference, P.O. Box 3041, Greenville, SC 29602. 74.8 miles straight, including Duke Foothills Hiking Trail 43.3(s). (AA 1992)

Fork Mountain Trail see entry 3882.

3790 **Fort Moultrie Trail**, Fort Moultrie National Monument, 1214 Middle St., Sullivans Island, SC 29482. 0.5 mile loop. (SAR 1992)

3791 **Fort Sumter National Monument**, 1214 Middle St., Sullivans Island, SC 29482, (803) 883-3123. (SAR 1992)

3792 **Fortune Springs Trail**, Fairfield County Recreation Commission, P.O. Box 73, Winnsboro, SC 29180, (803) 635-4725. 0.3 mile loop. (SCT)

3793 **Foster Park Trail**, Union County Recreation Department, South St., Union, SC 29379, (803) 427-1208. 0.6 mile loop. (SCT)

Four Holes Swamp Trail see entry 3794.

3794 **Francis Biedler Forest**, Sanctuary

Director, Rt. 1, Box 600, Harleyville, SC 29448, (803) 462-2150. Named trails: Four Holes Swamp 1.6(l). (ATN; MMA; OTB; SCT; GNA)

3795 **Francis Marion National Forest**, Francis Marion-Sumter National Forests, 1801 Assembly St., P.O. Box 2227, Columbia, SC 29202, (803) 765-5222; or Witherbee District, P.O. Box 196, McClellanville, SC 29458, (803) 887-3311. Named trails: Guilliard Lake 0.6(l), Jericho 20.0, Swamp Fox 21.0(s). (EGH; ATN; GFC; FGU; SCT; GNA)

3796 **Gateway Campground**, SR 17, Hardeeville, SC 29927, (803) 784-2267. (WCD)

3797 **Givhans Ferry State Park**, Rt. 3, Box 327, Ridgeville, SC 29472, (803) 873-0692. Named trails: Canal Nature 1.3(l). (WCD; ATN; SCP; SCT)

Gold Nugget Trail see entry 3822.

3798 **Granby Gardens Nature Trail**, Lexington County Recreation Commission, 1500 Dunbar Rd., Cayce, SC 29033, (803) 791-1361. 0.8 mile loop. (SCT)

Greenwood Lake Nature Trail see entry 3799.

3799 **Greenwood State Park**, Rt. 3, Box 108, Ninety Six, SC 29666, (803) 543-3535. Named trails: Greenwood Lake Nature 0.8(l). (SCT)

3800 **Guignard Park Trail**, Lexington County Recreation Commission, 1500 Dunbar Rd., Cayce, SC 29033, (803) 791-1361. 0.3 mile loop. (SCT)

Guilliard Lake Trail see entry 3795.

3801 **Hamilton Branch State Park**, US 221, McCormick, SC 29835, (803) 333-2223. (WCD)

3802 **Hampton Park**, Cleveland St., Charleston, SC 29403, (803) 724-7321. (MMA)

3803 **Hanging Rock Battle Trail**, Parks Recreation and Tourism, Suite 110, Edgar A. Brown Bldg., 1205 Pendleton St., Columbia, SC 29201, (803) 758-3622. 0.5 mile loop. (SCT)

3804 **Harbison Trail**, Harbison Recreation Center, 106 Hillpine Rd., Columbia, SC 29210, (803) 781-2281. 6.0 miles loop. (SCT)

3805 **Hartwell Lake Beaver Trail**, Resource Manager, Lake Hartwell, P.O. Box 278, Hartwell, GA 30643, (404) 376-4788. 0.7 mile loop. (SCT; LRA)

3806 **Hickory Knob State Resort Park**, Rt. 1, Box 199-B, McCormick, SC 29835, (803) 443-2151 or (803) 391-2450. Named trails: Turkey Ridge 0.3(l). (WCD; SCP; SCT)

Hilltop Trail see entry 3861.

3807 **Historic Camden Trail**, Camden District Heritage Foundation, P.O. Box 710, Camden, SC 29020, (803) 432-9841 or (803) 836-6115. 0.7 mile loop. (SAR 1992)

3808 **Hitchcock Woods**, Greater Aiken Chamber of Commerce, 400 Laurens St. NW, Aiken, SC 29801, (803) 648-0485. 20.0 miles. (SCT; GNA)

3809 **Hopeland Gardens Trail**, Aiken Recreation Department, P.O. Box 1177, Aiken, SC 29801, (803) 648-0151. 0.3 mile loop. (SCT)

Horn Creek Trail see entry 3882.

Horticultural Gardens Trail see entry 3769.

3810 **Hunting Island State Park**, Rt. 1, Box 668, Frogmore, SC 29920, (803) 838-2011; or Hunting Island State Park, 1175 Sea Island Pkwy., St. Helena Island, SC 29920. Named trails: Boardwalk Nature, Lighthouse. (WCD; ATN; FTS; MMA)

3811 **Huntington Beach State Park**, US 17, Murrells Inlet, SC 29576, (803) 237-4440. Named trails: Boardwalk Nature, Sea Oats. (WCD; ATN; MMA; SCP; GNA)

3812 **Indian Camp Forest Trail**, International Paper Co., Rt. 6, Box 123, Conway, SC 29526, (803) 347-3791. 0.3 mile loop. (SCT)

Indian Creek Forest Trail see entry 3769.

Indian Mound Trail see entry 3783.

3813 **Indian Shell Ring Loop Trail**, Sea Pines Plantation, Hilton Head Island, SC 29928, (803) 785-3333. 0.4 mile loop. (SCT)

3814 **Issaqueena Falls Trail**, Pendleton District Historical and Recreational Commission, 125 East Queen St., P.O. Box

234, Pendleton, SC 29670, (803) 646-3782. 0.2 mile loop. (SCT)
Issaqueena Trail *see* entry 3769.
3815 **James Island County Park,** 871 Riverland Dr., Charleston, SC 29412, (803) 795-9884. (WCD)
3816 **Jeffries Creek Trail,** City of Florence Recreation Department, P.O. Box 1476, Florence, SC 29503, (803) 665-3153. 0.8 mile loop. (SCT)
Jericho Trail *see* entry 3795.
Jones Creek Trail *see* entry 3753.
3817 **Jones Gap State Park,** 303 Jones Gap Rd., Marietta, SC 29661, (803) 836-3647. 5.0 miles. (SCP; GNA)
Jungle Nature Trail *see* entry 3740.
3818 **Kalmia Gardens Trail,** Kalmia Gardens of Coker College, Coker College, Hartsville, SC 29550, (803) 332-1381. 1.0 mile loop. (MMA; SCT)
Keowee-Toxaway Nature Trail *see* entry 3819.
3819 **Keowee-Toxaway State Park,** 108 Residence Dr., Sunset, SC 29685, (803) 868-2605. Named trails: Cherokee Interpretive 0.3(l), Keowee-Toxaway Nature 0.3(l), Raven Rock Hiking 4.2(l). (WCD; ATN; SCP; SCT; GNA)
Kings Creek Falls Trail *see* entry 3882.
3820 **Kings Mountain Battlefield Trail,** Palmetto Council, BSA, 420 S. Church St., P.O. Box 6249, Spartanburg, SC 29304, (803) 585-4391. 3.8 miles straight. Awards available. (AA 1992)
Kings Mountain Hiking Trail *see* entry 3822.
3821 **Kings Mountain National Military Park,** P.O. Box 40, Kings Mountain, NC 28086, (803) 936-7921. (NPS)
3822 **Kings Mountain State Park,** Rt. 2, Box 230, Blacksburg, SC 29702, (803) 222-3209. Named trails: Clarks Fork 14.0(l), Gold Nugget 2.3(l), Kings Mountain Hiking 15.0(l). (WCD; ATN; ANB; MMA; SCP; SCT; GNA; ANP)
3823 **KOA-Charleston,** US 78, Charleston, SC 29801, (803) 797-1045. (WCD)
3824 **KOA-Joanna/Clinton,** SR 66, Joanna, SC 29351, (803) 697-5105. (WCD)
3825 **KOA-Lake Hartwell Nature Trail,**

Lake Hartwell KOA, Rt. 11, Box 551, Anderson, SC 29621, (803) 287-3161. 1.2 miles loop. (WCD; SCT)
3826 **KOA-Point South,** US 17, Yemassee, SC 29945, (803) 726-5733. (WCD)
Lake Eureka Trail *see* entry 3766.
3827 **Lake Greenwood State Park** *see* entry 3799. (WCD; ATN; MMA; SCP)
3828 **Lake Hartwell State Park,** 19138-A S. SR 11, Fair Play, SC 29643, (803) 972-3352 or (803) 972-3561. (WCD; ATN; MMA; SCP)
Lake Johnson Trail *see* entry 3778.
Lake Placid Trail *see* entry 3854.
3829 **Lake Wateree State Park,** Rt. 4, Box 282E-5, Winnsboro, SC 29180, (803) 482-6126. (WCD; ATN; MMA; SCP)
Lakeshore Nature Trail *see* entry 3870.
Landsford Canal Nature Trail *see* entry 3830.
3830 **Landsford Canal State Park,** Rt. 1, Box 423, Catawba, SC 29704, (803) 789-5800. Named trails: Landsford Canal Nature 3.0(l). (ATN; MMA; SCP; OTB; SCT)
Laurel Hill Trail *see* entry 3871.
3831 **Laurens County Park Nature Trail,** Recreation Coordinator, Laurens YMCA Recreation Service, P.O. Box 519, Laurens, SC 29360, (803) 984-0144. 0.8 mile loop. (SCT)
Lawrence Trail *see* entry 3769.
3832 **Lee State Park,** Rt. 2, Box 202, Bishopville, SC 29010, (803) 428-3833. Named trails: Artesian Nature 1.0(l), Sandhill Nature 0.6(l). (WCD; ATN; MMA; SCP; SCT; GNA)
Lick Fork Lake Trail *see* entry 3882.
3833 **Lighthouse Nature Trail,** Rt. 1, Box 668, Frogmore, SC 29920, (803) 838-2011. 0.9 mile loop. (SCT)
Lighthouse Trail *see* entry 3810.
Little Pee Dee Nature Trail *see* entry 3834.
3834 **Little Pee Dee State Park,** Rt. 2, Box 250, Dillon, SC 29530, (803) 774-8872. Named trails: Little Pee Dee Nature 0.7(l). (WCD; ATN; SCP; SCT)
Little Sycamore Nature Trail *see* entry 3778.

SOUTH CAROLINA 247

Living on the Land Trail *see* entry 3882.
Long Cane Trail *see* entry 3882.
3835 **Lucas Park Trail**, City of Florence Recreation Department, P.O. Box 1476, Florence, SC 29503, (803) 665-3153. 0.6 mile loop. (SCT)
Lupine Nature Trail *see* entry 3864.
3836 **Lynches River State Park**, Rt. 1, Box 223, Coward, SC 29530, (803) 389-2785. Named trails: Stagecoach 1.1(l), Swamp Fox 0.6(l). (ATN; MMA; SCP; SCT)
Magnolia Gardens Trail *see* entry 3837.
3837 **Magnolia Plantation and Gardens**, Rt. 4, Charleston, SC 29407, (803) 571-1266. Named trails: Magnolia Gardens 1.7(l), Magnolia Wildlife 3.4(l). (LGU; SCT)
Magnolia Wildlife Trail *see* entry 3837.
3838 **Marsh Boardwalk Trail**, Rt. 1, Box 668, Frogmore, SC 29920, (803) 838-2011. 0.5 mile loop. (SCT)
3839 **Marsh Boardwalk Trail**, Murrells Inlet, SC 29576, (803) 237-4440. 0.3 mile loop. (SCT)
Marsh Trail *see* entry 3853.
3840 **Mauldin Park Trail**, Parks and Recreation Department, P.O. Box 675, Mauldin, SC 29662, (803) 288-3354. 0.5 mile loop. (SCT)
3841 **Maxcy Gregg Park Trail**, Parks and Recreation Department, 1932 Calhoun St., Columbia, SC 29201, (803) 733-8331. 0.3 mile loop. (SCT)
3842 **Middleton Place**, Rt. 4, Charleston, SC 29407, (803) 556-6020. 1.8 miles loop. (SCT)
3843 **Mile Creek Park**, SR 133, Clemson, SC 29631. (ATN)
Mill Pond Nature Trail *see* entry 3901.
Modoc Nature Trail *see* entry 3768.
Molly's Rock Trail *see* entry 3882.
3844 **Myrtle Beach State Park**, US 17S, Myrtle Beach, SC 19577, (803) 238-5325. Named trails: Sculptured Oak Nature 1.0(l). (WCD; ATN; MMA; SCP; SCT)
3845 **Newhall Audubon Preserve**, Palmetto Bay Rd., Hilton Head Island, SC 29928, (803) 671-2008. (FTS)
3846 **Ninety Six History Trail**, Ninety Six National Historic Site, P.O. Box 496, Ninety Six, SC 29666, (803) 543-4068. 1.0 mile loop. (ATN; ANB; GNM; NPS; NPE; CGA; SCT; YNP; ANP)
3847 **North Augusta Trail**, J. Robert Brooks, Director of Parks and Recreation, P.O. Box 6400, North Augusta, SC 29841, (803) 278-2358. 5.2 miles straight planned, current as to 1.0 mile. (GRT)
Oakpinolly Nature Trail *see* entry 3870.
3848 **Oconee State Park**, Star Route, Walhalla, SC 29691, (803) 638-5353; or Oconee State Park, 624 State Park Rd., Mountain Rest, SC 29664. Named trails: Oconee 3.2(l), Wormy Chestnut Nature 2.2(l). (WCD; ATN; MMA; SCP; BRM; SCT; GNA)
Oconee Trail *see* entry 3848.
3849 **Old Dorchester State Park**, 300 State Park Rd., Summerville, SC 29483, (803) 873-1740. Named trails: Boosho Creek Nature 0.7(l). (ATN; SCP; SCT)
Old Fort Loop Trail *see* entry 3760.
3850 **Old Santee Canal State Park**, 900 Stoney Landing Rd., Moncks Corner, SC 29461, (803) 899-5200. (ATN; SCP)
3851 **Old Walled City Trail**, Visitor Information Center, 85 Calhoun St., P.O. Box 975, Charleston Trident Chamber of Commerce, Charleston, SC 29402, (803) 722-8338. 2.3 miles loop. (SCT)
Osprey Trail *see* entry 3853.
3852 **Overmountain Victory National Historic Trail** (see separate entry 4956 in interstate section).
3853 **Palmetto Islands County Park**, 444 Neddlerush Pkwy., Mt. Pleasant, SC 29464, (803) 884-0832. Named trails: Marsh 0.6(l), Osprey 0.2(l), Palmetto Islands Nature 1.5(l). (ATN; MMA; SCT)
Palmetto Islands Nature Trail *see* entry 3853.
3854 **Paris Mountain State Park**, Rt. 12, Box 221, Greenville, SC 29609, (803) 244-5565 or (803) 292-3047. Named trails: Lake Placid 0.7(l), Paris Mountain 6.6(l). (WCD; ATN; MMA; SCP; SCT; GNA)

Paris Mountain Trail *see* entry 3854.
Parsons Mountain Trail *see* entry 3882.
3855 **Peachtree Rock Trail**, The South Carolina Nature Conservancy, P.O. Box 5475, Columbia, SC 29250, (803) 254-9049. 3.6 miles loop. (SCT)
3856 **Pinckney Island National Wildlife Refuge**, The Savannah Coastal Refuges Office, P.O. Box 8487, Savannah, GA 31412, (912) 652-4415. (AA 1993)
Pine Grove Trail *see* entry 3867.
3857 **Pine Ridge Family Campground**, Pine Ridge Campground Rd., Roebuck, SC 29376, (803) 576-0302. (WCD)
3858 **Pine Tree Hill Trail**, Indian Waters Council, BSA, 1825 Gadsden St., P.O. Box 144, Columbia, SC 29202-0144, (803) 765-9070. 10.5 miles straight. Awards available. (SAR 1992)
Pinnacle Trail *see* entry 3886.
Pleasant Ridge Nature Trail *see* entry 3859.
3859 **Pleasant Ridge State Park**, Rt. 2, Cleveland, SC 29635, (803) 836-6589. Named trails: Pleasant Ridge Nature 0.7(l). (OTB; SCT)
3860 **Pocotaligo Swamp Trail**, Clarendon County Recreation Dept., P.O. Box 831, Manning, SC 29102, (803) 473-3543. 0.5 mile loop. (SCT)
3861 **Poinsett State Park**, Rt. 1, Box 38, Wedgefield, SC 29168, (803) 494-8177. Named trails: Coquina Nature 1.8(l), Hilltop 0.6(s). (WCD; ATN; MMA; SCP; SCT; GNA)
Raven Cliffs Falls *see* entry 3753.
Raven Rock Hiking Trail *see* entry 3819.
3862 **Redcliffe State Park**, Rt. 2, Box 98, North Augusta, SC 29841, (803) 827-1473. Named trails: Redcliffe 1.7(l). (SCP; SCT)
Redcliffe Trail *see* entry 3862.
3863 **Reedy River Falls Trail**, Greenville Park and Recreational Services, P.O. Box 2207, Greenville, SC 29602, (803) 242-1250. 0.5 mile loop. (SCT)
3864 **Rivers Bridge State Park**, Rt. 1, Ehrhardt, SC 29081, (803) 267-3675. Named trails: Lupine Nature 0.4(l). (WCD; ATN; MMA; SCP; OTB; SCT)

3865 **Rocks Pond Campground**, Rt. 1, Box 432, Eutawville, SC 29048, (803) 492-7711. (WCD)
Rose Hill Nature Trail *see* entry 3866.
3866 **Rose Hill State Park**, Sardis Rd., Rt. 2, Union, SC 29379, (803) 427-5966. Named trails: Rose Hill Nature 0.6(l). (SCP; OTB; SCT)
3867 **Sadlers Creek State Park**, 940 Sadlers Creek Park Rd., Anderson, SC 29624, (803) 226-8950 or (803) 226-7156. Named trails: Pine Grove 0.6(l). (WCD; ATN; MMA; SCP; SCT)
Sandhill Nature Trail *see* entry 3832.
Sandhill Nature Trail *see* entry 3875.
3868 **Santee Coastal Reserve**, South Carolina Wildlife and Marine Resources Department, P.O. Box 37, McClellanville, SC 29458, (803) 546-8665. 6.2 miles. (SCT)
3869 **Santee National Wildlife Refuge**, Rt. 2, Box 66, Summerton, SC 29148, (803) 478-2217. Named trails: Santee Wildlife 1.1(l). (SCT)
3870 **Santee State Resort Park**, Rt. 1, Box 79, Santee, SC 29142, (803) 854-2408. Named trails: Lakeshore Nature 1.5(s), Oakpinolly Nature 0.9(l). (WCD; ATN; MMA; SCP; SCT)
Santee Wildlife Trail *see* entry 3869.
3871 **Savannah National Wildlife Refuge**, The Savannah National Coastal Refuges Office, P.O. Box 8487, Savannah, GA 31412, (912) 944-4415 or (912) 232-4321 ext. 415. 25.0 miles. Named trails: Cistern Boardwalk 0.5(l), Laurel Hill 6.3(l), Tupelo-Swamp Walk. (AA 1993)
3872 **Savannah River Swamp Trail**, Webb Wildlife Center, Garnett, SC 29922, (803) 625-3637. 3.6 miles loop. (SCT)
Sculptured Oak Nature Trail *see* entry 3844.
3873 **Sea Oats Nature Trail**, Superintendent, Murrells Inlet, SC 29576, (803) 237-4440. 1.0 mile loop. (SCT)
Sea Oats Trail *see* entry 3811.
3874 **Sea Pines Forest Preserve**, Sea Pines Resort, Hilton Head Island, SC 29928, (803) 671-7170. 7.0 miles. (FTS)

SOUTH CAROLINA

Sesqui Physical Fitness Trail *see* entry 3875.
3875 **Sesquicentennial State Park**, Rt. 3, Box 254, Columbia, SC 29206, (803) 788-2706. Named trails: Sandhill Nature 2.0(l), Sesqui Physical Fitness 3.5(l). (WCD; ATN; MMA; SCP; SCT)
3876 **Shady Oaks Family Campground**, Arthur Dr., Charleston, SC 29404, (803) 566-5271. (WCD)
Sheephead Ridge Loop Trail *see* entry 3760.
3877 **Siege of Charleston, S.C., Historical Trail**, American Historical Trails, Inc., P.O. Box 769, Monroe, NC 28110, (704) 289-1604. 7.0-11.5 miles loop. Awards available. (SAR 1992)
3878 **Simpsonville Nature Trail**, Simpsonville Parks and Recreation, P.O. Box 668, Simpsonville, SC 29681, (803) 963-5958. 0.5 mile loop. (SCT)
3879 **South Pine Street Trail**, Walterboro-Colleton County Recreation Commission, P.O. Box 173, Walterboro, SC 29488, (803) 549-2729. 0.3 mile loop. (SCT)
Spoon Auger Trail *see* entry 3882.
Stagecoach Trail *see* entry 3836.
3880 **Stoney Crest Plantation Campground**, Rt. 1, Box 36, Bluffton, SC 29910, (803) 757-3249. (WCD)
3881 **Sugar Loaf Mountain Trail**, Sand Hills State Forest, P.O. Box 128, Patrick, SC 29584, (803) 498-6478. 0.6 mile loop. (SCT; GNA)
3882 **Sumter National Forest**, Francis Marion-Sumter National Forests, 1801 Assembly St., P.O. Box 2227, Columbia, SC 29202; or Andrew Pickens District, Star Route, Walhalla, SC 29691, (803) 638-9568; or Tyger District, Duncan By-Pass, SR 176 (Drawer 10), Union, SC 29379, (803) 427-9858; or Enoree District, Rt. 1, Box 179, Whitmire, SC 29178, (803) 276-4810; or Edgefield District, 21 Bacon St., P.O. Box 30, Edgefield, SC 29824, (803) 637-5396; or Long Cane District, Rm. 201, Federal Bldg., Box 3168, Greenwood, SC 29646, (803) 229-2406. 200 miles. Named trails: Big Ben 2.7(s), Broad River 0.6(l), Bull Sluice 0.4(l), Buncombe 27.8(l), Chattoga 16.7(s), Cherry Hill Nature 0.5(l), East Fork 4.8(s), Ellicott Rock, Fork Mountain 6.3(s), Horn Creek 5.4(l), Kings Creek Falls 1.2(l), Lick Fork Lake 1.7(l), Living on the Land 0.5(l), Long Cane 22.2(s), Molly's Rock 0.7(l), Parsons Mountain 2.9(l), Spoon Auger 1.2(l), Tamasee Knob 4.2(l), Turkey Creek 22.9(s), Winding Stairs 3.4(l), Woods Ferry 1.0(l), Yellow Branch Nature 0.5(l). (WCD; EGH; ATN; GFC; MMA; OTB; FGU; SCT; GNA; NFG)
3883 **Swamp Fox National Recreation Trail**, Bill Craig, Recreation Staff Officer, U.S. Forest Service, 1835 Assembly St., Room 333, Columbia, SC 29201, (803) 253-3184. 21.0 miles straight. (GRT)
3884 **Swamp Fox Trail**, E.F. Holcombe, P.O. Box 30156, Charleston, SC 29417, (803) 884-9993; or Swamp Fox Trail Committee, UNALI'YI Lodge 236 O.A., Box 30150, Charleston, SC 29417. 12.5 and 14.5 miles straight. Awards available. (AA 1992)
3885 **Swan Lake Iris Gardens**, Sumter Park and Recreation Dept., 36 Artillery Dr., Sumter, SC 29150, (803) 773-9363. (MMA; SCT)
3886 **Table Rock State Park**, 246 Table Rock State Park Rd., Pickens, SC 29671, (803) 878-9813. Named trails: Pinnacle 7.2(l), Table Rock 6.8(l). (WCD; ATN; SCP; SCT; GNA)
Table Rock Trail *see* entry 3886.
Tamasee Knob Trail *see* entry 3882.
3887 **Timrod Park Trail**, City of Florence Recreation Department, P.O. Box 1476, Florence, SC 29503, (803) 665-3153. 1.0 mile loop. (MMA; SCT)
Treaty Oak Trail *see* entry 3769.
3888 **Tryon Park Trail**, Parks and Recreation, 226 Oakland Ave., Greer, SC 29651, (803) 877-9289. 0.2 mile loop. (SCT)
Tupelo-Swamp Walk *see* entry 3871.
Turkey Creek Trail *see* entry 3882.
Turkey Ridge Trail *see* entry 3806.
3889 **Turtle Island**, Wildlife and Marine Resources Department, P.O. Box 167, Columbia, SC 29202, (803) 758-8442. (GNA)
3890 **Virginia Acres Trail**, Aiken Recreation Department, P.O. Box 1177, Aiken,

SC 29801, (803) 648-0151. 1.0 mile loop. (SCT)
Wagon Camp Trail *see* entry 3748.
3891 **Waterfowl Pond Loop Trail**, Sea Pines Plantation, Hilton Head Island, SC 29928, (803) 785-3333. 0.9 mile loop. (SCT)
3892 **Webster Woods Trail**, Orangeburg Recreation Dept., 620 Middleton St., Orangeburg, SC 29115, (803) 534-6211. 0.5 mile loop. (SCT)
3893 **West Ashley Bikeway**, Kirk West, Department of Parks, 30 Mary Murray Dr., Charleston, SC 29403, (803) 724-7321. 2.0 miles straight. (GRT)
3894 **West Ashley Greenway**, Kirk West, Department of Parks, 30 Mary Murray Dr., Charleston, SC 29403, (803) 724-7321. 7.5 miles straight. (GRT)
3895 **Weston Lake Recreation Area**, Leesburg Rd., Columbia, SC 29209, (803) 751-5253. (WCD)
Whitetail Trail *see* entry 3762.
3896 **Whitten Exercise Trail**, Whitten Camping and Nature Programs, P.O. Box 239, Clinton, SC 29325, (803) 833-2733. 1.5 miles loop. (SCT)
3897 **Whooping Crane Conservancy**, Hilton Head Plantation, Hilton Head Island, SC 29928, (803) 681-5291. (FTS)
3898 **Wild Mint Trail**, Superintendent, Rt. 1, Box 219, McCormick, SC 29835, (803) 443-2457. 0.8 mile loop. (SCT)
3899 **Wildcat Nature Trail**, Program Section, Director of State Parks, Dept. of PRT, 1205 Pendleton St., Columbia, SC 29201, (803) 758-3622. 0.8 mile loop. (SCT)
Wilderness Trail *see* entry 3766.

3900 **Williams Park Trail**, Recreation Department, P.O. Box 94, Darlington, SC 29532, (803) 393-3626. 1.8 miles loop. (SCT)
Winding Stairs Trail *see* entry 3882.
Woodland Pond Trail *see* entry 3762.
3901 **Woods Bay State Park**, Rt. 1, Box 208, Olanta, SC 29114, (803) 659-4445. Named trails: Mill Pond Nature 0.9(l). (ATN; MMA; SCP; SCT)
Woods Ferry Trail *see* entry 3882.
Wormy Chestnut Nature Trail *see* entry 3848.
3902 **Wren's Camping Ground**, New DeLaughter Dr., Myrtle Beach, SC 29577, (803) 279-2488. (WCD)
3903 **Wylie Park Trail**, Chester County/City Park and Recreation Department, P.O. Box 771, Chester, SC 29706, (803) 385-2530. 0.3 mile loop. (SCT)
Yellow Branch Nature Trail *see* entry 3882.
Yellow Trail *see* entry 3742.
3904 **York County Nature Trail**, Museum of York County, Mt. Gallant Rd., Rock Hill, SC 29730, (803) 366-4116. 0.5 mile loop. (SCT)

Generally:
South Carolina Division of State Parks, Edgar Brown Bldg., 1205 Pendleton St., Columbia, SC 29201, (803) 253-6318. (EGH)
South Carolina Wildlife and Marine Resources Department, 1000 Assembly St., Rembert C. Dennis Bldg., P.O. Box 167, Columbia, SC 29201, (803) 758-0059. (GNA)

Index (by city)

Aiken: Camp Gravatt Lake Trail 3755; Hitchcock Woods 3808; Hopeland Gardens Trail 3809; Virginia Acres Trail 3890
Anderson: KOA-Lake Hartwell Nature Trail 3825; Sadlers Creek State Park 3867
Awendaw: Cape Romain National Wildlife Refuge 3760
Bennett's Point: Bear Island Game Management Area 3746
Bennettsville: Canoe Lake Nature Trail 3759
Bishopville: Lee State Park 3832

SOUTH CAROLINA **Index** 251

Blacksburg: Kings Mountain State Park 3822
Blackville: Barnwell State Park 3744
Bluffton: Stoney Crest Plantation Campground 3880
Calhoun Falls: Calhoun Falls State Park 3754
Camden: Historic Camden Trail 3807; Pine Tree Hill Trail 3858
Campobello: Campobello-Gramling Trail 3758
Canadys: Colleton State Park Nature Trail 3771
Catawba: Landsford Canal State Park 3830
Cayce: Granby Gardens Nature Trail 3798; Guignard Park Trail 3800
Cedar Mountain: Caesars Head State Park 3753
Charleston: Charles Towne Landing State Park 3763; Charleston Bicentennial Trail of Freedom 3764; Hampton Park 3802; James Island County Park 3815; KOA-Charleston 3823; Magnolia Plantation and Gardens 3837; Middleton Place 3842; Old Walled City Trail 3851; Shady Oaks Family Campground 3876; Siege of Charleston, S.C., Historical Trail 3877; Swamp Fox Trail 3884; West Ashley Bikeway 3893; West Ashley Greenway 3894
Cheraw: Cheraw State Park 3766
Chesnee: Cowpens Battlefield Historical Trail 3775; Cowpens National Battlefield 3776
Chester: Chester State Park 3767; Wylie Park Trail 3903
Clarks Hill: Clark Hill Lake 3768
Clemson: Clemson University 3769; Mile Creek Park 3843
Cleveland: Asbury Hills United Methodist Camp 3742; Pleasant Ridge State Park 3859
Clinton: Creek Trail 3777; Explorer Trail 3786; Whitten Exercise Trail 3896
Clover: Camp Thunderbird Nature Trail 3756
Columbia: Congaree River Trail 3773; Congaree Swamp National Monument 3774; Earlwood Park Trail 3782; Francis Marion National Forest 3795; Hanging Rock Battle Trail 3803; Harbison Trail 3804; Maxcy Gregg Park Trail 3841; Peachtree Rock Trail 3855; Sesquicentennial State Park 3875; Sumter National Forest 3882; Swamp Fox National Recreation Trail 3883; Turtle Island 3889; Weston Lake Recreation Area 3895; Wildcat Nature Trail 3899
Conway: Indian Camp Forest Trail 3812
Coward: Lynches River State Park 3836
Darlington: Williams Park Trail 3900
Dillon: Bass Lake RV Campground 3745; Little Pee Dee State Park 3834
Edgefield: Sumter National Forest 3882
Edisto Island: Edisto Beach State Park 3783
Ehrhardt: Rivers Bridge State Park 3864
Eutawville: Rocks Pond Campground 3865
Fair Play: Lake Hartwell State Park 3828
Florence: Beauty Trail 3747; Jeffries Creek Trail 3816; Lucas Park Trail 3835; Timrod Park Trail 3887
Frogmore: Hunting Island State Park 3810; Lighthouse Nature Trail 3833; Marsh Boardwalk Trail 3838
Garnett: Savannah River Swamp Trail 3872
Greenville: Cleveland Park Trail 3770; Foothills Trail 3789; Paris Mountain State Park 3854; Reedy River Falls Trail 3863
Greenwood: Sumter National Forest 3882
Greer: Tryon Park Trail 3888
Hardeeville: Gateway Campground 3796
Harleyville: Francis Biedler Forest 3794
Hartsville: Kalmia Gardens Trail 3818
Hartwell: Hartwell Lake Beaver Trail 3805
Hilton Head Island: Indian Shell Ring Loop Trail 3813; Newhall Audubon Preserve 3845; Sea Pines Forest Preserve 3874; Waterfowl Pond Loop Trail 3891; Whooping Crane Conservancy 3897
Joanna: KOA-Joanna/Clinton 3824
Kings Mountain, NC: Kings Mountain Battlefield Trail 3820; Kings Mountain National Military Park 3821
Lancaster: Andrew Jackson State Park 3741
Laurens: Laurens County Park Nature Trail 3831
Manning: Campers Paradise 3757; Pocotaligo Swamp Trail 3860
Marietta: Jones Gap State Park 3817
Mauldin: Mauldin Park Trail 3840

McBee: Carolina Sandhills National Wildlife Refuge 3762
McClellanville: Francis Marion National Forest 3795
McCormick: Baker Creek State Park 3743; Hamilton Branch State Park 3801; Hickory Knob State Resort Park 3806; Wild Mint Trail 3898
Moncks Corner: Old Santee Canal State Park 3850
Mt. Pleasant: Palmetto Islands County Park 3853
Murrells Inlet: Brookgreen Gardens 3752; Huntington Beach State Park 3811; Marsh Boardwalk Trail 3839; Sea Oats Nature Trail 3873
Myrtle Beach: Myrtle Beach State Park 3844; Wren's Camping Ground 3902
Ninety Six: Greenwood State Park 3799; Lake Greenwood State Park 3827; Ninety Six History Trail 3846
North Augusta: North Augusta Trail 3847; Redcliffe State Park 3862
Olanta: Woods Bay State Park 3901
Orangeburg: Edisto Gardens 3784; Webster Woods Trail 3892
Patrick: Sugar Loaf Mountain Trail 3881
Pendleton: Blue Ridge Railroad Historical Trail 3750; Issaqueena Falls Trail 3814
Pickens: Table Rock State Park 3886
Prosperity: Dreher Island State Park 3780
Ridgeville: Givhans Ferry State Park 3797
Rock Hill: Boyd Hill Trail 3751; Fewell Park Trail 3787; York County Nature Trail 3904
Roebuck: Pine Ridge Family Campground 3857

Santee: Santee State Resort Park 3870
Savannah, GA: Pinckney Island National Wildlife Refuge 3856; Savannah National Wildlife Refuge 3871
Simpsonville: Simpsonville Nature Trail 3878
Spartanburg: Croft State Park 3778; Duncan Park Trail 3781; Foothills KOA of Spartanburg 3788
Sullivans Island: Fort Moultrie Trail 3790; Fort Sumter National Monument 3791
Summerton: Santee National Wildlife Refuge 3869
Summerville: Edisto Nature Trail 3785; Old Dorchester State Park 3849
Sumter: Swan Lake Iris Gardens 3885
Sunset: Keowee-Toxaway State Park 3819
Union: Foster Park Trail 3793; Rose Hill State Park 3866; Sumter National Forest 3882
Walhalla: Chauga Nature Trail 3765; Devils Fork State Park 3779; Oconee State Park 3848; Sumter National Forest 3882
Walterboro: Colleton Trail 3772; South Pine Street Trail 3879
Wedgefield: Poinsett State Park 3861
West Union: Blue Ridge Railroad Historical Trail 3749
Whitehall Terrace: Capers Island Park 3761
Whitmire: Sumter National Forest 3882
Windsor: Aiken State Park 3440
Winnsboro: Fortune Springs Trail 3792; Lake Wateree State Park 3829
Yemassee: KOA-Point South 3826
York: Bethelwoods 3748

TENNESSEE

Abrams Falls Trail *see* entry 3977.
Ace Gap Trail *see* entry 3977.
Albright Grove Nature Trail *see* entry 3977.
Alum Cave Bluff Trail *see* entry 3905.
Alum Cave Trail *see* entry 3977.
Angel Falls Overlook Trail *see* entry 3917.
Anthony Creek Trail *see* entry 3977.
3905 **Appalachian Side Trails** (not listed elsewhere), Appalachian Trail Conference, Inc., P.O. Box 807, Harpers Ferry, WV 25425-0807; or Tennessee Eastman Hiking Club, P.O. Box 511, Kingsport, TN 37662. Named trails: Alum Cave Bluff 5.2, Big Pond 1.1, Bright's Trace, Chimneys 1.2, Clingman's Dome 0.5, Cosby 2.6, Fodderstock Mountain 2.8, Hazlewood Hollow 1.2, Holston Mountain, Horsely, Hungry Ridge 8.0, Huskey Gap I 2.5, Huskey Gap II 2.5, Jenkins Ridge 7.5, Morton Gap, Mount Cammerer 0.6, Old Flint Mill, Parson Bald 0.8, Trillium Branch 4.2, Vandeventer, Yellow Creek 10.5. (BMG; ATG #9).
3906 **Appalachian Trail** (see separate entry 4948 in interstate section).
3907 **Appalachian Trail**, Great Smoky Mountain Council, BSA, P.O. Box 51885, 6440 Papermill Rd., N.W., Knoxville, TN 37950-1885. 49.0 miles straight. Awards available. (AA 1989)
Artillery Trail *see* entry 3997.
Artillery Trail *see* entry 4056.
3908 **Audubon Acres**, 900 N. Sanctuary Rd., Chattanooga, TN 37421, (615) 892-1499. 8.0 miles. (TTN)
Bald River Trail *see* entry 3934.
Barkley Trail *see* entry 3997.
3909 **Battle of Nashville Trail**, Nashville Historical Trails, Inc., P.O. Box 299, Madison, TN 37116-0299. 13.7 miles loop. Awards available. (AA 1992)
3910 **Bays Mountain Park & Planetarium**, 853 Bays Mountain Park Rd. W., Kingsport, TN 37660, (615) 229-9447. 25.0 miles. (TTN; ATK; MSE)
Beard Cane Creek Trail *see* entry 3977.
3911 **Bearwaller Gap Hiking Trail**, Nashville Historical Trails, Inc., P.O. Box 299, Madison, TN 37116-0299. 6.0 miles straight. Awards available. (AA 1992)
3912 **Beech Bend**, SR 100, Parsons, TN 38363. (WCD)
3913 **Benton MacKaye Trail** (see separate entry 4950 in interstate section).
Big Creek Gulf Trail *see* entry 4053.
3914 **Big Cypress Tree State Natural Area**, US 45E & Kinney Rd., Greenfield, TN 38230, (901) 235-2700. (TTN)
Big Fiery Grizzard Trail *see* entry 4059.
Big Fodderstock Trail *see* entry 3934.
3915 **Big Hill Pond**, Jim Waldron (T341, BSA), 1626 Yorkshire Dr., Memphis, TN 38119; or Big Hill Pond, SR 57, Pocahontas, TN 38061, (901) 645-7967. 3.5-11.0 miles loop. Awards available. (TTN; ATK; HTA)
Big Pond Trail *see* entry 3905.
Big Poplar Trail *see* entry 3977.
3916 **Big Ridge State Rustic Park**, 1015 Big Ridge Rd., Maynardsville, TN 37807, (615) 992-5523. Named trails: Big Valley 6.0(l), The Cannonball 2.0(s), Lake 5.0(l). (TTN; MSE; TTR)
3917 **Big South Fork National River and Recreation Area**, P.O. Drawer 630, Oneida, TN 37841, (615) 879-4890; or

Great Smoky Mountain Council, BSA, 6440 Papermill Rd., NW, P.O. Box 51885, Knoxville, TN 37950-1885. 100 miles. Named trails: Angel Falls Overlook 6.0(l), Grand Gap Loop, Litton/Slaven Farm Loop 6.3(l), Oscar Blevins Loop 3.6(l). Awards available. (AA 1993)

Big Valley Trail *see* entry 3916.
Blanket Mountain Trail *see* entry 3977.

3918 **Bledsoe Creek State Camping Park**, 400 Zieglers Fort Rd., Gallatin, TN 37006, (615) 452-3706. (TTN; WCD; ATK; MSE)

3919 **Blue Beaver Trail**, P.O. Box 274, Signal Mountain, TN 37377-0274. 10.5 miles straight. Awards available. (SAR 1992)

Blue Hole Nature Trail *see* entry 4044.
Blue Trail *see* entry 4088.

3920 **Blue-Gray Trail**, Tennessee Division of Parks and Recreation, 701 Broadway, Nashville, TN 37243. 1.3 miles. (TTR)

Bluff Trail *see* entry 4005.

3921 **Booker T. Washington State Park**, 5801 Champion Rd., Chattanooga, TN 37416, (615) 894-4955. (TTN; ATK; GFC)

Boswell Trail *see* entry 3997.
Bote Mountain Ridge Trail *see* entry 3977.
Bote Mountain Road *see* entry 3977.
Boulevard Trail *see* entry 3977.
Boundary Trail *see* entry 3974.

3922 **Boxwell Reservation**, Middle Tennessee Council, BSA, P.O. Box 15565, Nashville, TN 37215, (615) 383-9724; or Boxwell Reservation, Rt. 4, Lebanon, TN 37987. (SFC)

Bright's Trace *see* entry 3905.

3923 **Britton Lane Trail**, Robert Hamlett, 63 Grove Ave., Jackson, TN 38301. 15.0 miles. Awards available. (HTA)

Brushy Mountain Trail *see* entry 3977.
Bryan's Fork Trail *see* entry 4061.
Buckhorn Gap Trail *see* entry 3977.

3924 **Buffalo Mountain Park**, Johnson City, TN 37605, (615) 283-5815. (TTN)

Bullhead Trail *see* entry 3977.

3925 **Burgess Falls State Natural Area Trail**, Rt. 6, Box 380, Sparta, TN 38583-8420, (615) 761-3338 or (615) 432-5312. 0.75 mile. (TTN; TTR)

Cades Cove Loop Trail *see* entry 3977.
Canal Loop Trail *see* entry 3997.
Cane Creek Overnight Trail *see* entry 3962.

3926 **Cane Creek Park**, I-40 exit 286, Cookeville, TN 38503, (615) 526-9591. (TTN)

The Cannonball Trail *see* entry 3916.

3927 **The Carter House Trail**, 1140 Columbia Ave., Franklin, TN 37064. 5.6 miles loop. Awards available. (AA 1993)

3928 **Cedars of Lebanon State Park**, US 231/SR 10, Lebanon, TN 37087, (615) 443-2769. Named trails: Hidden Springs 4.5(l). (WCD; ATK; MSE; TTR)

Center Furnace Trail *see* entry 3997.

3929 **Center Hill Lake**, Reservoir Manager, Center Hill Dam, Lancaster, TN 38569. (ATK; LRA)

3930 **Chattanooga Historic Trail**, Blue Beaver Trail, P.O. Box 274, Signal Mountain, TN 37377-0274. 10.0 miles loop. Awards available. (SAR 1992)

3931 **Chattanooga Nature Center at Reflection Riding**, Garden Rd., Chattanooga, TN 37419, (615) 821-1160. (SAR 1992)

3932 **Chattanooga West/Lookout Mt.-KOA**, Slyo Rd./Old Hales Gap Rd., Chattanooga, TN 37401, (706) 657-6815. (WCD)

3933 **Cherokee Lake Park**, SR 92, Jefferson City, TN 37760. (ATK)

3934 **Cherokee National Forest**, P.O. Box 2010, Cleveland, TN 37311; or Forest Supervisor, 2800 N. Ocoee St. N.W., Cleveland, TN 37311; or Larry Fleming, District Ranger, P.O. Box 339, Tellico Plains, TN 37385, (615) 253-2520. 640 miles. Named trails: Bald River 5.6(s), Big Fodderstock 8.6(s), Chestnut Mountain 1.3(s), Conasauga River 4.5(s), Crowder Branch 2.6(s), Grassy Branch 3.2(s), Greene Mountain 3.6(s), Gum Springs

1.3(s), Hemlock 3.0(s), Holston 7.0(s), Iron Mountain 20.0(s), Laurel Branch 3.0(s), Limestone Cove 9.0(s), Long Branch 2.7(s), McNabb Creek 3.9(s), Meadow Creek Mountain 15.0(s), North Fork Citico 5.0(s), Patty Ride 4.0(s), Pinnacle Tower 5.0(s), Rattlesnake Ridge, South Fork Citico 8.1(s), Unicoi 4.5(s), Wolf Ridge 8.3(l). (TTN; GRT; WCD; EGH; ATK; FGU; TTR).

3935 **Chester Frost Park**, Gold Point Cir., Hixson, TN 37415, (615) 842-0177. (MSE)

Chestnut Mountain Trail see entry 3934.

Chestnut Top Lead Trail see entry 3977.

3936 **Chickasaw Bluffs Trail**, Historical Hiking Trails, Inc., P.O. Box 17507, Memphis, TN 38117. 6.0 miles. Awards available. (AA 1990)

Chickasaw Bluffs Trail see entry 4007.

Chickasaw Bluffs-Meeman Trail see entry 4054.

3937 **Chickasaw State Rustic Park**, SR 100, Henderson, TN 38340, (901) 989-5141. (WCD; ATK)

3938 **Chilhowee Park**, FR 77, Cleveland, TN 37312. (ATK)

Chimney Top Trail see entry 3974.

Chimney Tops Trail see entry 3977.

Chimneys Trail see entry 3905.

3939 **Chucalissa Discovery Trail**, 2367 Strathmore Cir., Memphis, TN 38112. 6.0 miles. Awards available. (MVC; HTA)

3940 **City Lake Natural Area**, Bridgeway Rd., Cookeville, TN 38501, (615) 526-9591. (TTN)

Clear Creek Trail see entry 4018.

3941 **Cleveland Downtown Historic Greenway**, 2145 Keith St., Cleveland, TN 37311, (615) 472-6587. (TTN)

Cliff Trail see entry 4018.

Clingman's Dome Trail see entry 3905.

3942 **Collins River-Shellsford Trail**, Tennessee Division of Parks and Recreation, 701 Broadway, Nashville, TN 37243. (SAR 1992)

Compass Cross-County Trail see entry 4056.

Conasauga River Trail see entry 3934.

Confederate Advance Trail see entry 4056.

Cooper Road Trail see entry 3977.

3943 **Cordell Hull Lake**, Corps of Engineers, SR 85, Nashville, TN 37202. (ATK)

Cosby Creek Trail see entry 3977.

Cosby Trail see entry 3905.

Council of Trees Trail see entry 4044.

3944 **Cove Lake State Recreational Park**, US 25W, Caryville, TN 37714, (615) 562-8355. (TTN; WCD; ATK)

Cove Mountain Trail see entry 3977.

Cravens House Trail see entry 4005.

3945 **Crazy Horse Campground**, 4609 East Pkwy., Gatlinburg, TN 37738, (615) 436-4434. (WCD)

3946 **Cross Creeks National Wildlife Refuge**, Rt. 1, Box 229, Dover, TN 37058, (615) 232-7477. 12.0 miles. (GNW)

Crowder Branch Trail see entry 3934.

Cucumber Gap Trail see entry 3977.

3947 **Cumberland Gap National Historical Park**, P.O. Box 1848, Middlesboro, KY 40965, (606) 248-2817. (TTN)

3948 **Cumberland Mountain State Rustic Park**, Rt. 8, Box 322, Crossville, TN 38555, (615) 484-6138. (TTN; WCD; ATK; MSE)

3949 **Cumberland Trail**, Cumberland State Scenic Trail Headquarters, Cove Lake State Park, Rt. 2, Attn: Bobby Harbin, Caryville, TN 37714. 200-255 miles. Named sections: Cumberland Mountain 41.0(s), Walden Ridge 30.0(s), Catoosa 45.0(s), Grassy Cove. (AA 1992)

Curry Gap Trail see entry 3977.

3950 **Cypress Grove Nature Park**, US 70W, Jackson, TN 38301, (901) 424-1472. (MSE)

3951 **Dale Hollow Dam**, P.O. Box 276, Celina, TN 38551, (615) 243-3554; or Corps of Engineers, Nashville District, P.O. Box 1070, Nashville, TN 37202. (WCD; ATK; GFC; LRA)

3952 **Daniel Boone National Forest**, P.O. Box 727, Winchester, KY 40391.

Named trails: Sheltowee Trace National Preservation. (ATK; TTR)
3953 **David Crockett State Park**, P.O. Box 398, US 64, Laurenceburg, TN 38464, (615) 762-9408. (TTN; WCD; ATK; MSE)
Davis Ridge Trail see entry 3977.
3954 **Davy Crockett Birthplace Historical Park**, Limestone Rd., Greeneville, TN 37743, (615) 257-2167. (WCD)
3955 **Davy Crockett Lake**, SR 66, Sevierville, TN 37862. (ATK)
Devil's Backbone Trail see entry 3997.
3956 **Dogwood Trail** (f/k/a Fisherville Nature Trail), Eugene E. McKenzie, 1345 Hickory Ridge Cove, Memphis, TN 38116. 7.0 miles. Awards available. (AA 1992)
Door Connector Trail see entry 4053.
3957 **Downtown Loudon Walking Tour**, 318 Angel Row, Loudon, TN 37774, (615) 458-9020. (TTN)
3958 **Dudley Creek Travel Trailer Park**, US 441, Gatlinburg, TN 37738, (800) 462-4826. (WCD)
3959 **Dunbar Cave State Natural Area**, 401 Old Dunbar Cave Rd., Clarksville, TN 37043, (615) 648-5526. (TTN; ATK)
3960 **Eagle Roost Trail**, Skymont Scout Reservation, c/o Cherokee Area Council, BSA, 6031 Lee Hwy., Chattanooga, TN 37421, (615) 892-8323. (AA 1992)
3961 **Edgar Evins State Rustic Park**, SR 141, Silver Point, TN 38582, (615) 858-2114. (TTN; WCD; ATK)
Environmental Trail see entry 4056.
3962 **Fall Creek Falls State Resort Park**, SR 30, Pikeville, TN 37367, (615) 881-3241 or (615) 881-3297. 33.0 miles. Named trails: Cane Creek Overnight 25.0(l), Paw 4.0(s). (TTN; ATK; MSE; GFA; TTR)
Fiery Grizzard Trail see entry 4059.
Finley Cove Trail see entry 3977.
3963 **First Chickasaw Bluff Trail**, Ken Humphreys, P.O. Box 17507, Memphis, TN 38187, (901) 323-2739. 5.0-8.0 miles. Awards available. (AA 1992)
3964 **Floating Mill**, Corps of Engineers— Center Hill Reservoir, SR 56, Silver Point, TN 38582, (615) 858-4845. (WCD)

Fodderstock Mountain Trail see entry 3905.
3965 **Fort Donelson History-Nature Trail**, Fort Donelson National Military Park, P.O. Box F, Dover, TN 37058. 4.0 miles straight. Awards available. (AA 1990)
Fort Henry Trail System see entry 3997.
3966 **Fort Johnsonville Redoubts Trail**, Historical Hiking Trails, Inc., P.O. Box 17507, Memphis, TN 38187-0507, (901) 323-2739. 5.0 miles. Awards available. (AA 1990)
3967 **Fort Loudon State Historical Area**, Rt. 2, Box 565, Vonore, TN 37885, (615) 884-6217. Named trails: Island Loop, Nature. (AA 1992)
3968 **Fort Patrick Henry Lake**, SR 36, Kingsport, TN 37663. (ATK)
3969 **Fort Pillow Historical Trail & Trek**, Historical Hiking Trails, Inc., P.O. Box 17507, Memphis, TN 38187-0507, (901) 323-2739. Trail 10.0, Trek 5.0. Awards available. (AA 1992)
3970 **Fort Pillow State Historical Area**, Rt. 2, Box 108B-1, Henning, TN 38041, (901) 738-5581. 21.0 miles. (WCD; EGH; ATK)
3971 **Fort Sanders Neighborhood Walking Tour**, P.O. Box 1242, Knoxville, TN 37901. 2.0 miles. (HTA)
3972 **Foster Falls Small Wild Area**, US 41, Tracy City, TN 37387, (615) 924-2980. (WCD; MSE)
3973 **Franklin State Forest**, SR 41/64, St. Andrews, TN 37372. (ATK)
3974 **Frozen Head State Natural Area**, Rt. 2, Box 1302, Wartburg, TN 37887, (615) 346-3318; or Frozen Head State Park, Flat Fork Rd., Oak Ridge, TN 37830, (615) 346-3318. 50.0 miles. Named trails: Boundary 21.5(l), Chimney Top 3.4(s), North Old Mac Mountain 4.6(s), Panther Branch 3.5(s), South Old Mac Mountain 3.6(s), Spicewood Branch 4.5(s). (TTN; ATK; MSE; OTB; TTR)
Gabes Mountain Trail see entry 3977.
Garrison Creek Horse Trail see entry 4014.

Glen Falls Trail *see* entry 4005.
3975 **Golden Mountain Park**, SR 111, Sparta, TN 38583, (615) 526-5253. (TTN)
Goshen Prong Trail *see* entry 3977.
Grand Gap Loop Trail *see* entry 3917.
Grassy Branch Trail *see* entry 3934.
3976 **Great Smoky Jellystone Park Camp Resort**, SR 321, Gatlinburg, TN 37738, (615) 487-5534. (WCD)
3977 **Great Smoky Mountains National Park**, Gatlinburg, TN 37738, (615) 436-1200. 800 miles. Named trails: Cosby Section: Albright Grove Nature 7.0(l), Cosby Creek 2.5(s), Gabes Mountain 7.0(s), Henwallow Falls 3.5(l), Indian Camp Creek 2.3(s), Lower Mount Cammerer 7.6(s), Maddron Bald 5.0(s), Snake Den Mountain 5.0(s), Sutton Ridge 3.0(l); LeConte and Greenbrier Section: Alum Cave 5.5(s), Boulevard 5.1(s), Brushy Mountain 5.6(s), Bullhead 7.1(s), Greenbrier Pinnacle 3.5(s), Junglebrook Nature, Porters Creek 3.7(s), Rainbow Falls 6.6(s), Ramsey Cascade 2.5(s), Trillium Gap 6.5(s); Elkmont Section: Blanket Mountain 4.0(s), Chimney Tops 2.0(s), Cove Mountain 3.8(s), Cucumber Gap 2.4(s), Goshen Prong 7.3(s), Grotto Falls 3.0(s), Indian Gap 5.5(s), The Jumpoff 6.5(l), Little Brier, Little Buckhorn Gap, Meigs Mountain 8.7(s), Metcalf Bottoms 2.0(s), Miry Ridge 5.0(s), Road Prong 3.3(s), Rough Creek 3.4(s), Sugarland Mountain 11.5(s); Tremont Section: Bote Mountain Road 6.6(s), Buckhorn Gap 3.3(s), Curry Gap 3.0(s), Finley Cove 2.8(s), Greenbrier Ridge 8.4(s), Lead Cove, Lynn Camp Prong 3.3(s), Panther Creek 2.3(s), Spruce Flats, Spruce Flats Branch, West Prong 2.8(s); Cades Cove Section: Abrams Falls 6.9, Anthony Creek 3.4, Cades Cove Loop 11.0(l), Gregory Bald 6.9, Gregory Ridge 5.0, Hannah Mountain 7.5, Rabbit Creek 7.0, Russell Field 3.5; Boundary Trail Section: Ace Gap 5.8, Beard Cane Creek 4.3, Chestnut Top Lead 4.5, Cooper Road 4.7, Rich Mountain 4.2, Scott Mountain 3.8, Turkey Pen Ridge; Other Trails: Big Poplar 3.0(l), Bote Mountain Ridge 1.7(s), Davis Ridge 10.0(l), Laurel Falls 2.5(l), Leadbetter Ridge 6.0(l), Little Bottoms 5.0(l), Ogle Place 0.75, Roaring Fork Motor Nature 5.0, Spence Field 11.0(l). (SAR 1986)
Greenbrier Pinnacle Trail *see* entry 3977.
Greenbrier Ridge Trail *see* entry 3977.
Greene Mountain Trail *see* entry 3934.
Gregory Bald Trail *see* entry 3977.
Gregory Ridge Trail *see* entry 3977.
Grotto Falls Trail *see* entry 3977.
Guild Trail *see* entry 4005.
Gum Springs Trail *see* entry 3934.
Gum Springs Trail *see* entry 4005.
Hannah Mountain Trail *see* entry 3977.
Hardy Trail *see* entry 4005.
3978 **Harrison Bay State Recreational Park**, 8411 Harrison Bay Rd., Chattanooga, TN 37416, (615) 344-6214. (TTN; WCD; ATK; MSE)
Hazlewood Hollow Trail *see* entry 3905.
Hematite Trail *see* entry 3997.
Hemlock Trail *see* entry 3934.
3979 **Henry Horton State Resort Park**, P.O. Box 128, US 31A, Chapel Hill, TN 37034, (615) 364-2222. (TTN; WCD)
Henwallow Falls Trail *see* entry 3977.
3980 **Hidden Hollow Park**, 1901 Mt. Pleasant Rd., Cookeville, TN 38501, (615) 526-4038. (TTN)
Hidden Passage Trail *see* entry 4035.
Hidden Springs Trail *see* entry 3928.
3981 **Historic Trail of Tears Trail**, Jim Ruth, Justice Center, Bradley County, Cleveland, TN 37311; or Red Clay State Historic Park, 1140 Red Clay Park Rd., S.W., Rt. 6, Box 306, Cleveland, TN 37311, (615) 478-0339 or (615) 472-2627. 6.5 miles straight. Awards available. (AA 1992)
Historical Trails #1 & #3 *see* entry 4056.
Hogskin Branch Loop Trail *see* entry 4020.
Holston Mountain Trail *see* entry 3905.

Holston Trail *see* entry 3934.

3982 **Honey Creek Pocket Wilderness Trail**, Public Relations Department, Bowater Southern Paper Co., 5020 US 11S, Calhoun, TN 37309. 5.0 miles loop. Awards available. (AA 1994)

3983 **Honeysuckle Nature Trail**, Chucalissa Village, 1987 Indian Village Rd., Memphis, TN 38109, (901) 785-3160. (OTB)

Honker Trail *see* entry 3997.
Hoot Owl Trail *see* entry 4054.
Horsely Trail *see* entry 3905.
Hungry Ridge Trail *see* entry 3905.
Huskey Gap I & II Trails *see* entry 3905.

3984 **Ijams Nature Center**, 2915 Island Home Rd., Knoxville, TN 37920, (615) 577-4717. (TTN)

3985 **Indian Boundary Park**, Tellico Plains, TN 37385. (ATK)

3986 **Indian Camp Creek Campground**, SR 321, Gatlinburg, TN 37738, (615) 487-2493. (WCD)

Indian Camp Creek Trail *see* entry 3977.
Indian Gap Trail *see* entry 3977.

3987 **Indian Mountain State Camping Park**, Indian Mountain Rd., Jellico, TN 37762, (615) 784-7958. (TTN; WCD; ATK)

Iron Mountain Trail *see* entry 3934.
Island Loop Trail *see* entry 3967.

3988 **J. Percy Priest Reservoir**, Reservoir Manager, J. Percy Priest Resident Office, P.O. Box 2347, Nashville, TN 37214. (ATK; LRA)

Jackson Gap Trail *see* entry 4005.
Jenkins Ridge Trail *see* entry 3905.

3989 **Jim Oliver's Smoke House Campground**, SR 64, Monteagle, TN 37387, (615) 924-2268. (WCD)

3990 **John Muir Trail**, Hiwassee Ranger District, P.O. Box 255, Delano, TN 37325, (615) 263-5486. 17.0 miles. (GMG)

The Jumpoff Trail *see* entry 3977.
Junglebrook Nature Trail *see* entry 3977.
Kiddie Trail *see* entry 4005.

3991 **Kinser Park**, SR 70S, Greeneville, TN 37743, (615) 639-5912. (ATK; MSE)

3992 **Knoxville Heritage Walking Tour**, P.O. Box 1242, Knoxville, TN 37901. 2 hours. (HTA)

3993 **Knoxville Historic Trail**, Great Smoky Mountain Council, BSA, 6440 Papermill Rd., N.W., P.O. Box 51885, Knoxville, TN 37950-1885. 5.7-9.4 miles straight. Awards available. (SAR 1992)

3994 **KOA-Watt's Bar Dam Lake**, DeArmond Rd., Kingston, TN 37763, (615) 376-5880. (WCD)

3995 **Lady Finger Bluff Trail**, Tennessee Division of Parks and Recreation, 701 Broadway, Nashville, TN 37243. 2.5 miles loop. (TTR)

3996 **Lake Barkley**, SR 49, Dover, TN 37058. (ATK)

3997 **Land Between the Lakes**, Tennessee Valley Authority, Outdoor Recreation, 100 Van Morgan Dr., Golden Pond, KY 42211-9091, (502) 924-1225. 300 miles. Named trails: Artillery 4.9, Barkley, Boswell 0.4, Canal Loop 14.2(l), Center Furnace 0.3, Devil's Backbone 1.5, Fort Henry Trail System 26.0, Hematite 2.2, Honker 5.0, Long Creek 0.2, North-South Connector 1.7, North-South 65.0, Peytona 3.9, Picket Loop 2.9, Piney 2.3, Shortleaf Pine 1.6, Telegraph 7.5, Tennessee Ridge 1.8, Trail of These Hills 1.5, Waterfowl Loop 0.4(l), Woodland Walk 0.7, Wrangler. (AA 1992)

Laurel Branch Trail *see* entry 3934.

3998 **Laurel Creeks Campground**, US 154, Jamestown, TN 38556, (615) 879-7696. (WCD)

Laurel Falls Trail *see* entry 3977.
Laurel Falls Trail *see* entry 4053.

3999 **Laurel-Snow Pocket Wilderness National Recreation Trails**, Public Relations Department, Bowater Southern Paper Co., 5020 US 11S, Calhoun, TN 37309. 5.0-6.0 miles. Awards available. (AA 1994)

Lead Cove Trail *see* entry 3977.
Leadbetter Ridge Trail *see* entry 3977.
Lew Wallace Approach Trail *see* entry 4056.

4000 **Lichterman Nature Center**, 5992 Quince, Memphis, TN 38119, (901) 767-7322. (TTN)

TENNESSEE

4001 **Lillydale Campground**, SR 294, Livingston, TN 38570, (615) 823-4155. (WCD)
    Limestone Cove Trail see entry 3934.
    Little Bottoms Trail see entry 3977.
    Little Brier Trail see entry 3977.
    Little Buckhorn Gap Trail see entry 3977.

4002 **Little River Village Campground**, 8533 SR 73, Townsend, TN 37882, (615) 448-2241. (WCD)
    Litton/Slaven Farm Loop Trail see entry 3917.

4003 **Lone Mountain State Forest Nature Trail**, U.S. Department of the Interior, National Park Service, Obed Wild and Scenic River, P.O. Box 429, Wartburg, TN 37887, (615) 346-6294. 0.75 mile. (AA 1991)
    Long Branch Trail see entry 3934.
    Long Creek Trail see entry 3997.

4004 **Long Hunter State Recreational Park**, Hobson Pike, Hermitage, TN 37076, (615) 885-2422. (TTN)
    Long Trail see entry 4054.

4005 **Lookout Mountain**, Chickamauga and Chattanooga National Military Park, U.S. Department of the Interior, National Park Service, P.O. Box 2128, Fort Oglethorpe, GA 30742, (404) 866-9241. Named trails: Bluff 4.5(s), Cravens House, Glen Falls 0.9, Guild 1.0, Gum Springs 4.0, Hardy 1.2, Jackson Gap 0.6, Kiddie, Lower Truck, Mountain Beautiful 1.5, Rifle Pits, Shingle 0.7, Skyuka Spring 7.7(s), Upper Truck, Whiteside 0.6. (SAR 1992)

4006 **Loretta Lynn's Ranch**, Rt. 1, Hurricane Mills, TN 37078, (615) 296-7700. (WCD; MSE)
    Lower Mount Cammerer Trail see entry 3977.
    Lower Truck Trail see entry 4005.
    Lynn Camp Prong Trail see entry 3977.
    Maddron Bald Trail see entry 3977.
    McNabb Creek Trail see entry 3934.
    Meadow Creek Mountain Trail see entry 3934.
    Meeman-Shelby Compass Trail see entry 4054.

4007 **Meeman-Shelby Forest State Recreation Park**, P.O. Box 10, Bluff Rd., Millington, TN 38053, (901) 876-5215 or (901) 876-5201. 20.0 miles. Named trails: Chickasaw Bluffs 6.0(s), Shelby Forest 6.0(s). (TTN; WCD; EGH; ATK; MSE; NAT; TTR)
    Meigs Mountain Trail see entry 3977.

4008 **Memphis Historical Trail**, P.O. Box 17507, Memphis, TN 38117. 10.0 miles loop. Awards available. (AA 1991)

4009 **Meriwether Lewis Park**, SR 20 & Natchez Trace Pkwy., Hohenwald, TN 38462, (601) 680-4025. (TTN)
    Metcalf Bottoms Trail see entry 3977.
    Miry Ridge Trail see entry 3977.
    Montgomery Bell Overnight Trail see entry 4010.

4010 **Montgomery Bell State Resort Park**, P.O. Box 39, US 70, Burns, TN 37029, (615) 797-3101. Named trails: Montgomery Bell Overnight 11.7(l). (TTN; ATK; MSE; TTR)
    Morton Gap Trail see entry 3905.
    Mount Cammerer Trail see entry 3905.
    Mountain Beautiful Trail see entry 4005.

4011 **Mousetail Landing State Rustic Park**, P.O. Box 280B, Linden, TN 37096, (901) 847-0841. (TTN; WCD)

4012 **Narrows of the Harpeth State Historic Area**, P.O. Box 39, Burns, TN 37029, (615) 879-4026. (TTN)

4013 **Nashville Historical Trail**, Nashville Historical Trails, Inc., P.O. Box 299, Madison, TN 37116-0299. 11.0 miles. Awards available. (AA 1992)

4014 **Natchez Trace National Scenic Trail** (see separate entry **4954** in interstate section). Side trails not listed elsewhere: Garrison Creek Horse 24.5, Old Trace 1.7. (AA 1994)

4015 **Natchez Trace State Resort Park**, State Park Rd., Clarksburg, TN 38324, (901) 968-3742 or (901) 968-8176; or Natchez Trace State Resort Park, I-40 exit 116, Wildersville, TN 38388. Named trails: Red Leaves Backpacking 4.0-35.0. (TTN; WCD; ATK; MSE; HTA)

4016 **Nathan Bedford Forrest State Park**, SR 191, Eva, TN 38333, (901) 584-6356. 30.0 miles. (TTN; WCD; EGH; ATK; MSE)
  Natural Bridge Trail see entry 4035.
  Nature Trail see entry 3967.
4017 **Nolichucky Jack Trail**, Blue Beaver Trail, P.O. Box 274, Signal Mountain, TN 37377-0274. 20.0 miles loop. Awards available. (AA 1993)
4018 **Norris City Watershed**, Tennessee Division of Parks and Recreation, 701 Broadway, Nashville, TN 37243. 20.0 miles. Named trails: Clear Creek 3.0(s), Cliff 2.0(l), White Pine 4.4(l). (TTR)
4019 **Norris Dam State Park**, Rt. 1, Box 400, US 441, Lake City, TN 37769, (615) 494-0488 or (615) 426-7461. (TTN; MSE)
4020 **North Chickamauga Pocket Wilderness**, Public Relations Department, Bowater Southern Paper Co., 5020 US 11S, Calhoun, TN 37309. Named trails: Hogskin Branch Loop 1.5(l), Stevenson 7.8(s). (AA 1994)
  North Fork Citico Trail see entry 3934.
  North Old Mac Mountain Trail see entry 3974.
  North Plateau Trail see entry 4053.
4021 **North Ridge Trail**, Environmental Quality Advisory Board, Oak Ridge, TN 37830. 7.5 miles straight. (HTA)
  North-South Connector Trail see entry 3997.
  North-South Trail see entry 3997.
4022 **Obey River Campground**, SR 42, Livingston, TN 38570, (615) 864-6388. (WCD)
  Ogle Place Trail see entry 3977.
  Old Flint Mill Trail see entry 3905.
4023 **Old Hickory Reservoir**, Reservoir Manager, Old Hickory Resident Office, P.O. Box 511, Old Hickory, TN 37138. (ATK; LRA)
4024 **Old Stone Fort State Archaeological Area**, Rt. 7, Box 7400, Manchester, TN 37355, (615) 728-0751 or (615) 722-5073. (TTN; WCD; ATK; MSE)
  Old Trace see entry 4014.
  Oscar Blevins Loop Trail see entry 3917.

4025 **Oswald Dome Trail**, Hiwassee Ranger District, P.O. Box 255, Delano, TN 37325, (615) 263-5486. 5.0 miles. (GMG)
4026 **Outdoor Resort at Gatlinburg**, SR 321, Gatlinburg, TN 37738, (800) 677-5861. (WCD)
4027 **Overmountain Victory National Historic Trail** (see separate entry **4956** in interstate section).
4028 **Overton Park**, 2000 Gallaway Ave., Memphis, TN 38112, (901) 726-4725. (NAT)
4029 **Overton Zoological Trail**, 2367 Strathmore Cir., Memphis, TN 38112. 8.0-10.0 miles. Awards available. (MVC; HTA)
  Panther Branch Trail see entry 3974.
4030 **Panther Creek State Recreational Park**, 2010 Panther Creek Rd., Morristown, TN 37814, (615) 581-2623 or (615) 587-7046. (TTN; WCD; ATK; MSE)
  Panther Creek Trail see entry 3977.
4031 **Paris Landing State Resort Park**, US 79/SR 1, Buchanan, TN 38222, (901) 644-7359. (TTN)
4032 **Parksville Lake**, US 64, Cleveland, TN 37311. (ATK)
  Parson Bald Trail see entry 3905.
  Patty Ride Trail see entry 3934.
  Paw Trail see entry 3962.
4033 **Percy and Edwin Warner Parks**, SR 100, Nashville, TN 37202. (ATK)
4034 **Perimeter Trail**, Cherokee Area Council, BSA, 6031 Lee Hwy., Chattanooga, TN 37421, (615) 892-8323. 12.0 miles loop. Awards available. (AA 1994)
  Peytona Trail see entry 3997.
  Picket Loop Trail see entry 3997.
4035 **Pickett State Rustic Park**, Rock Creek Route, Box 174, Jamestown, TN 38556, (615) 879-5821. 50.0 miles. Named trails: Hidden Passage 8.0(l), Natural Bridge, Rock Creek 5.0(s). (TTN; WCD; EGH; ATK; GMG; MSE; OTB; TTR)
4036 **Pickwick Landing State Resort Park**, P.O. Box 15, SR 57, Pickwick Dam, TN 38365, (901) 689-3135. (TTN; WCD; ATK)
4037 **Piney River Trail**, Public Relations Department, Bowater Southern Paper

Co., 5020 US 11S, Calhoun, TN 37309. 10.0 miles. Awards available. (AA 1994)
Piney Trail see entry 3997.
Pink Trail see entry 4088.
Pinnacle Tower Trail see entry 3934.
4038 **Pinson Mounds State Archaeological Park**, 460 Ozier Rd., Jackson, TN 38301, (901) 988-5614. (ATK; MSE; GFA)
4039 **Port Royal State Historical Area**, 3300 Old Clarksville Hwy., Adams, TN 37010, (615) 358-9696. (TTN)
Porters Creek Trail see entry 3977.
4040 **Prentice Cooper State Forest**, SR 27, Kimball, TN 37347, (615) 658-5551. (TTN)
Rabbit Creek Trail see entry 3977.
4041 **Radnor Lake State Natural Area**, 1160 Otter Creek Rd., Nashville, TN 37215, (615) 373-3467. (TTN; MSE)
4042 **Ragland Bottom**, Corps of Engineers—Center Hill Reservoir, US 70, Smithville, TN 37166, (615) 597-7876. (WCD)
Rainbow Falls Trail see entry 3977.
4043 **Raleigh Historical Trail**, 3317 Crain Cove, Memphis, TN 38128. 4.0 miles loop. Awards available. (AA 1991)
Ramsey Cascade Trail see entry 3977.
Rattlesnake Ridge Trail see entry 3934.
4044 **Red Clay State Historic Area**, 1140 Red Clay Park Rd., S.W., Cleveland, TN 37311, (615) 478-0339. Named trails: Blue Hole Nature 0.3, Council of Trees 1.7. (TTN; HTA; LRA)
Red Leaves Backpacking Trail see entry 4015.
4045 **Reelfoot Lake State Resort Park**, SRs 21 & 78, Tiptonville, TN 38079, (901) 253-7756. (TTN; ATK)
4046 **Reelfoot National Wildlife Refuge**, P.O. Box 98, Samburg, TN 38254, (901) 538-2481. 12.0 miles. (WTW; GNW)
4047 **Return of the Eternal Flame Trail**, Jim Ruth, Justice Center, Bradley County, Cleveland, TN 37311; or Red Clay State Historic Park, 1140 Red Clay Park Rd., S.W., Cleveland, TN 37311, (615) 478-0339. 4.3 miles straight. (AA 1992)
4048 **Rich Mountain Loop Trail**, Great Smoky Mountain Council, BSA, 6440 Papermill Rd., NW, P.O. Box 51885, Knoxville, TN 37950-1885. 7.4 miles loop. Awards available. (AA 1990)
Rich Mountain Trail see entry 3977.
Rifle Pits Trail see entry 4005.
Road Prong Trail see entry 3977.
4049 **Roan Mountain State Resort Park**, Rt. 1, Box 236, SR 143, Roan Mountain, TN 37687, (615) 772-3303 or (615) 772-3303. 15.2 miles. (TTN; ATK; MSE; TTR)
Roaring Fork Motor Nature Trail see entry 3977.
4050 **Rock Creek Park**, US 23, Erwin, TN 37650. (ATK)
Rock Creek Trail see entry 4035.
4051 **Rock Island State Park**, SR 287, McMinnville, TN 37110, (615) 686-2471. (WCD)
4052 **Rocky Top Campground**, 496 Pearl Ln., Kingsport, TN 37617, (615) 323-2535 or (800) 542-6456. (WCD)
Rough Creek Trail see entry 3977.
Russell Field Trail see entry 3977.
4053 **Savage Gulf**, South Cumberland State Recreation Area, Rt. 1, Box 144H, Tracy City, TN 37387, (615) 924-2980; or Savage Gulf Preservation League, P.O. Box 102, McMinnville, TN 37110-0102; or Savage Gulf State Natural Area, Rt. 1, Box 127-H, Palmer, TN 37365; or Tennessee Trails Association, Inc., P.O. Box 4913, Chattanooga, TN 37405. Named trails: Big Creek Gulf 8.0, Door Connector 10.0(s), Laurel Falls 7.0, North Plateau 18.0(l). (MSE; TTR; WPS)
Scott Mountain Trail see entry 3977.
4054 **Shelby Forest**, 3547 Johnwood Dr., Memphis, TN 38122. Named trails: Chickasaw Bluffs-Meeman 5.0, Hoot Owl, Long, Meeman-Shelby Compass 5.0, Short. Awards available. (TTR)
Shelby Forest Trail see entry 4007.
4055 **Shellmound-Nickajack Dam Reservation**, Jasper, TN 37347, (615) 744-5300. (TTN; WCD)
Sheltowee Trace National Preservation Trail see entry 3952.
Shiloh Battlefield Trek see entry 4056.

Shiloh Cannon Trail *see* entry 4056.
Shiloh Indian Mounds Trek *see* entry 4056.
4056 **Shiloh Military Trails**, P.O. Box 17507, Memphis, TN 38117; or Trail Headquarters, Troop 343 Scout Hut, Kingsway Christian Church, 6319 Poplar Ave., Memphis, TN 38119, (901) 683-3505; or Shiloh National Military Park, Shiloh, TN 38376, (901) 689-5275. Named trails: Artillery 14.0, Compass Cross-Country 10.0, Confederate Advance 20.0, Environmental 12.0, Historical (#1) 14.0, Historical (#3) 14.0, Lew Wallace Approach 16.0, Shiloh Battlefield Trek 2.0, Shiloh Cannon 12.0, Shiloh Indian Mounds Trek 3.0. Awards available. (AA 1992)
Shingle Trail *see* entry 4005.
4057 **Shipp's Yogi Bear Jellystone Park**, 6728 Ringgold Rd., Chattanooga, TN 37412, (615) 892-8275. (WCD)
Short Trail *see* entry 4054.
Shortleaf Pine Trail *see* entry 3977.
Skyuka Spring Trail *see* entry 4005.
4058 **Smith's Camp on the Lake Campground**, Star Route, Box 42, Guild, TN 37340, (615) 942-4078. (WCD)
Snake Den Mountain Trail *see* entry 3977.
4059 **South Cumberland State Recreation Area**, Rt. 1, Box 2196, Monteagle, TN 37356, (615) 924-2980. 85.0 miles. Named trails: Big Fiery Grizzard 14.0(s), Fiery Grizzard 13.0(s). (TTN; BPM; EGH; HTA; ATK; MSE; GFA; TTR)
South Fork Citico Trail *see* entry 3934.
4060 **South Holston Lake**, US 421, Bristol, TN 37620. (ATK)
South Old Mac Mountain Trail *see* entry 3974.
Spence Field Trail *see* entry 3977.
Spicewood Branch Trail *see* entry 3974.
Spruce Flats Branch Trail *see* entry 3977.
Spruce Flats Trail *see* entry 3977.
4061 **Standing Stone State Rustic Park**, SR 52, Livingston, TN 38570, (615) 823-6347. Named trails: Bryan's Fork 5.0. (TTN; WCD; ATK; MSE; TTR)

4062 **Steele Creek Park**, P.O. Box 1189, Broad St., Bristol, TN 37620, (615) 764-4023. (TTN; ATK)
Stevenson Trail *see* entry 4020.
4063 **Stinging Fork Trail**, Public Relations Department, Bowater Southern Paper Co., 5020 US 11S, Calhoun, TN 37309. 3.0 miles. Awards available. (AA 1994)
4064 **Stones River National Battlefield**, Nashville Historical Trails, Inc., P.O. Box 299, Madison, TN 37116-299; also U.S. Department of the Interior, National Park Service, Stones River National Battlefield, 3501 Old Nashville Hwy., Murfreesboro, TN 37129, (615) 893-9501. 2.0-5.0 miles loop. Awards available. (AA 1992)
4065 **Sugar Hollow Park**, Lee Hwy., Bristol, VA 24201, (703) 645-7275. (TTN)
Sugarland Mountain Trail *see* entry 3975.
Sutton Ridge Trail *see* entry 3977.
4066 **Sweetwater Historical Trail**, Andrew McCampbell, 407 Mayes Ave., Sweetwater, TN 37874. 5.3 miles. Awards available. (AA 1993)
4067 **Sycamore Shoals State Historical Area**, 1651 W. Elk Ave., Elizabethton, TN 37643, (615) 543-5808. (TTN)
4068 **T.O. Fuller State Recreational Park**, 3269 Boxtown Rd., Memphis, TN 38109, (901) 529-7581 or (901) 785-3950. (TTN; ATK; MSE; NAT)
Telegraph Trail *see* entry 3997.
4069 **Tennessee Forrest Trail**, P.O. Box 17507, Memphis, TN 38187-0507, (901) 323-2739. 12.0 miles loop. Awards available. (AA 1991)
4070 **Tennessee National Wildlife Refuge**, P.O. Box 849, Paris, TN 38242, (901) 642-2091. 150 miles. (NAT; GNW)
Tennessee Ridge Trail *see* entry 3997.
4071 **Tims Ford State Rustic Park**, 570 Tims Ford Dr., Winchester, TN 37398, (615) 967-4457. (TTN; WCD; ATK)
4072 **Trail of Tears National Historic Trail** (see separate entry **4958** in interstate section).
4073 **Trail of the Lonesome Pine**, Tennessee Division of Parks and Recreation,

701 Broadway, Nashville, TN 37243. 75.0 miles. (TTR)
Trail of These Hills *see* entry 3997.
4074 **Tremont Hills Campground**, P.O. Box 5, Townsend, TN 37882, (615) 448-6363. (WCD)
Trillium Branch Trail *see* entry 3905.
Trillium Gap Trail *see* entry 3977.
Turkey Pen Ridge Trail *see* entry 3977.
4075 **Twin Creek RV Resort**, P.O. Box 1395, Gatlinburg, TN 37738, (615) 436-7081 or (800) 252-8077. (WCD)
4076 **Twin Forks Trail**, Tennessee Division of Parks and Recreation, 701 Broadway, Nashville, TN 37243. 22.0 miles straight. (TTR)
4077 **Twin Rocks Nature Trail**, Public Relations Department, Bowater Southern Paper Co., 5020 US 11S, Calhoun, TN 37309. 2.5 miles. Awards available. (AA 1994)
4078 **Unicoi Mountain Trail**, Hiwassee Ranger District, P.O. Box 255, Delano, TN 37325, (615) 263-1341. 5.0 miles. (GMG)
Unicoi Trail *see* entry 3934.
4079 **University of Tennessee Arboretum**, SR 62, Oak Ridge, TN 37830, (615) 438-3571. (TTN; ATK)
Upper Truck Trail *see* entry 4005.
4080 **Valley-KOA**, 5701 Fayetteville Rd., Pulaski, TN 38478, (615) 363-4600 or (800) 552-0307. (WCD)
Vandeventer Trail *see* entry 3905.
4081 **Virgin Falls Trail**, Public Relations Department, Bowater Southern Paper Co., 5020 US 11S, Calhoun, TN 37309. 8.0 miles. Awards available. (AA 1994)
4082 **Warriors Passage Trail**, 7816 Cedar Crest Rd., Knoxville, TN 37918. 15.0 miles straight. Awards available. (AA 1991)

4083 **Warrior's Path State Recreational Park**, Hemlock Park Rd., P.O. Box 5026, Kingsport, TN 37662, (615) 239-8531. (TTN; WCD; ATK; GMG; MSE)
4084 **Watauga Lake**, Elizabethton, TN 37643. (ATK)
Waterfowl Loop Trail *see* entry 3997.
4085 **Watts Bar Lake**, SR 68, Spring City, TN 37381. (ATK)
West Prong Trail *see* entry 3977.
4086 **Whispering Oaks Campground**, US 41, Manchester, TN 37355, (615) 728-0225. (WCD)
White Pine Trail *see* entry 4018.
Whiteside Trail *see* entry 4005.
4087 **Willow Grove**, SR 294, Livingston, TN 38570, (615) 823-4285. (WCD)
Wolf Ridge Trail *see* entry 3934.
4088 **Wolf River Trails**, Eugene E. McKenzie, 1345 Hickory Ridge Cove, Memphis, TN 38116; or Art Wolff, (901) 685-9706. Named trails: Blue 5.0(s), Pink, Yellow 5.0(s). Awards available. (AA 1992)
Woodland Walk *see* entry 3997.
Wrangler Trail *see* entry 3997.
Yellow Creek Trail *see* entry 3905.
Yellow Trail *see* entry 4088.

Generally:
Commissioner, Department of Conservation, 2611 West End Ave., Nashville, TN 32703, (615) 741-2301. (SFC)
Tennessee Division of Parks and Recreation, 701 Broadway, Nashville, TN 37243. (EGH)
Tennessee Tourist Development, P.O. Box 23170, Nashville, TN 37202, (615) 741-2158. (EGH)
Tennessee Trails Association, P.O. Box 41446, Nashville, TN 37204. (EGH)

Index (by city)

Adams: Port Royal State Historical Area 4039
Altamont: Eagle Roost Trail 3960; Perimeter Trail 4034
Bristol: South Holston Lake 4060; Steele Creek Park 4062; Sugar Hollow Park 4065
Buchanan: Paris Landing State Resort Park 4031

Burns: Montgomery Bell State Resort Park 4010; Narrows of the Harpeth State Historic Area 4012
Cades Cove: Rich Mountain Loop Trail 4048
Carthage: Bearwaller Gap Hiking Trail 3911
Caryville: Cove Lake State Recreational Park 3944; Cumberland Trail 3949
Celina: Dale Hollow Dam 3951
Chapel Hill: Henry Horton State Resort Park 3979
Chattanooga: Audubon Acres 3908; Booker T. Washington State Park 3921; Chattanooga Historic Trail 3930; Chattanooga Nature Center at Reflection Riding 3931; Chattanooga West/Lookout Mt.-KOA 3932; Harrison Bay State Recreational Park 3978; Shipp's Yogi Bear Jellystone Park 4057
Clarksburg: Natchez Trace State Resort Park 4015
Clarksville: Dunbar Cave State Natural Area 3959
Cleveland: Cherokee National Forest 3934; Chilhowee Park 3938; Cleveland Downtown Historic Greenway 3941; Historic Trail of Tears Trail 3981; Parksville Lake 4032; Red Clay State Historic Area 4044; Return of the Eternal Flame Trail 4047
Cookeville: Cane Creek Park 3926; City Lake Natural Area 3940; Hidden Hollow Park 3980
Crossville: Cumberland Mountain State Rustic Park 3948
Dayton: Laurel-Snow Pocket Wilderness National Recreation Trails 3999
Delano: John Muir Trail 3990; Oswald Dome Trail 4025; Unicoi Mountain Trail 4078
Derossett: Virgin Falls Trail 4081
Dover: Cross Creeks National Wildlife Refuge 3946; Fort Donelson History-Nature Trail 3965; Lake Barkley 3996
Elgin: Honey Creek Pocket Wilderness Trail 3982
Elizabethton: Sycamore Shoals State Historical Area 4067; Watauga Lake 4084
Erwin: Rock Creek Park 4050
Eva: Nathan Bedford Forrest State Park 4016

Fort Oglethorpe, GA: Lookout Mountain 4005
Franklin: The Carter House Trail 3927
Gallatin: Bledsoe Creek State Camping Park 3918
Gatlinburg: Crazy Horse Campground 3945; Dudley Creek Travel Trailer Park 3958; Great Smoky Jellystone Park Camp Resort 3976; Great Smoky Mountains National Park 3977; Indian Camp Creek Campground 3986; Outdoor Resort at Gatlinburg 4026; Twin Creek RV Resort 4075
Golden Pond, KY: Blue-Gray Trail 3920; Land Between the Lakes 3997
Greeneville: Davy Crockett Birthplace Historical Park 3954; Kinser Park 3991
Greenfield: Big Cypress Tree State Natural Area 3914
Guild: Smith's Camp on the Lake Campground 4058
Henderson: Chickasaw State Rustic Park 3937
Henning: Fort Pillow Historical Trail & Trek 3969; Fort Pillow State Historical Area 3970
Hermitage: Long Hunter State Recreational Park 4004
Hixson: Chester Frost Park 3935
Hohenwald: Meriwether Lewis Park 4009
Hurricane Mills: Loretta Lynn's Ranch 4006
Jackson: Britton Lane Trail 3923; Cypress Grove Nature Park 3950; Pinson Mounds State Archaeological Park 4038
Jamestown: Laurel Creeks Campground 3998; Pickett State Rustic Park 4035
Jasper: Shellmound-Nickajack Dam Reservation 4055
Jefferson City: Cherokee Lake Park 3933
Jellico: Indian Mountain State Camping Park 3987
Johnson City: Buffalo Mountain Park 3924
Kimball: Prentice Cooper State Forest 4040
Kingsport: Bays Mountain Park & Planetarium 3910; Fort Patrick Henry Lake 3968; Rocky Top Campground 4052; Warrior's Path State Recreational Park 4083
Kingston: KOA-Watt's Bar Dam Lake 3994

TENNESSEE   Index   265

Knoxville: Appalachian Trail 3907; Fort Sanders Neighborhood Walking Tour 3971; Ijams Nature Center 3984; Knoxville Heritage Walking Tour 3992; Knoxville Historic Trail 3993
Lake City: Norris Dam State Park 4019
Lancaster: Center Hill Lake 3929
Laurenceburg: David Crockett State Park 3953
Lebanon: Boxwell Reservation 3922; Cedars of Lebanon State Park 3928
Linden: Lady Finger Bluff Trail 3995; Mousetail Landing State Rustic Park 4011
Livingston: Lillydale Campground 4001; Obey River Campground 4022; Standing Stone State Rustic Park 4061; Willow Grove 4087
Lookout Mountain: Blue Beaver Trail 3919; Nolichucky Jack Trail 4017
Loudon: Downtown Loudon Walking Tour 3957
Manchester: Old Stone Fort State Archaeological Area 4024; Whispering Oaks Campground 4086
Maynardsville: Big Ridge State Rustic Park 3916
McMinnville: Collins River-Shellsford Trail 3942; Rock Island State Park 4051
Memphis: Chickasaw Bluffs Trail 3936; Chucalissa Discovery Trail 3939; Dogwood Trail 3956; First Chickasaw Bluff Trail 3963; Honeysuckle Nature Trail 3983; Lichterman Nature Trail 4000; Memphis Historical Trail 4008; Overton Park 4028; Overton Zoological Trail 4029; Shelby Forest 4054; T.O. Fuller State Recreational Park 4068; Wolf River Trails 4088
Middlesboro: Cumberland Gap National Historical Park 3947
Millington: Meeman-Shelby Forest State Recreation Park 4007
Monteagle: Jim Oliver's Smoke House Campground 3989; South Cumberland State Recreation Area 4059
Morristown: Panther Creek State Recreational Park 4030
Murphreesboro: Stones River National Battlefield 4064
Nashville: Battle of Nashville Trail 3909; Cordell Hull Lake 3943; J. Percy Priest Reservoir 3988; Nashville Historical Trail 4013; Percy and Edwin Warner Parks 4033; Radnor Lake State Natural Area 4041
New Johnsonville: Fort Johnsonville Redoubts Trail 3966
Norris: Norris City Watershed 4018
Oak Ridge: North Ridge Trail 4021; University of Tennessee Arboretum 4079
Old Hickory: Old Hickory Reservoir 4023
Oneida: Big South Fork National River and Recreation Area 3917
Paris: Tennessee National Wildlife Refuge 4070
Parsons: Beech Bend 3912
Pickwick Dam: Pickwick Landing State Resort Park 4036
Pikeville: Fall Creek Falls State Resort Park 3962
Pilot Knob: Tennessee Forrest Trail 4069
Pocahontas: Big Hill Pond 3915
Pulaski: Valley-KOA 4080
Raleigh: Raleigh Historical Trail 4043
Roan Mountain: Roan Mountain State Resort Park 4049
St. Andrews: Franklin State Forest 3973
Samburg: Reelfoot National Wildlife Refuge 4046
Sevierville: Davy Crockett Lake 3955
Shiloh: Shiloh Military Trails 4056
Silver Point: Edgar Evins State Rustic Park 3961; Floating Mill 3964
Smithville: Ragland Bottom 4042
Soddy-Daisy: North Chickamauga Pocket Wilderness 4020
Sparta: Burgess Falls State Natural Area Trail 3925; Golden Mountain Park 3975
Spring City: Piney River Trail 4037; Stinging Fork Trail 4063; Twin Rocks Nature Trail 4077; Watts Bar Lake 4085
Sweetwater: Sweetwater Historical Trail 4066
Tellico Plains: Cherokee National Forest 3934; Indian Boundary Park 3985; Warriors Passage Trail 4082
Tiptonville: Reelfoot Lake State Resort Park 4045
Townsend: Little River Village Campground 4002; Tremont Hills Campground 4074

Tracy City: Foster Falls Small Wild Area 3972; Savage Gulf 4053
Treadway: Trail of the Lonesome Pine 4073
Vonore: Fort Loudon State Historical Area 3967
Wartburg: Frozen Head State Natural Area 3974; Lone Mountain State Forest Nature Trail 4003
Winchester: Daniel Boone National Forest 3952; Tims Ford State Rustic Park 4071

Vermont

Adam Pond Trail *see* entry 4132.

4089 **Alburg Rail-Trail**, Trails Coordinator, Department of Forests, Parks and Recreation, 111 West St., Essex Junction, VT 05452, (802) 879-6565. 5.1 miles straight. (GRT)

4090 **Allis State Park**, Brookfield, VT 05036, (802) 276-3175. 2.5 miles. (VEG)

4091 **Amity Pond Natural Area**, Vermont Department of Forests and Parks, 103 S. Main, Waterbury, VT 05676, (802) 244-8711. (IGS)

4092 **Appalachian Side Trails** (not listed elsewhere), Appalachian Trail Conference Field Office, P.O. Box 122, 3rd Floor, Aldrich House, Mechanic St., Norwich, VT 05055, (802) 649-2816; or Green Mountain Club, P.O. Box 889, Montpelier, VT 05602. Named trails: Baker Peak, Bald Mountain, Branch Pond, Broad Brook, Bucklin, Dunville Hollow, Green Mountain, Homer Stone Brook, Keewaydin, Lake, Lye Brook, North Shore, Old Job, Pico Link, Pine Cobble, Shrewsbury Peak, Stratton Mountain, West Ridge, William Tucker. (BMG; ATG #2)

4093 **Appalachian Trail** (see separate entry **4948** in interstate section).

4094 **Ascutney State Park**, Back Mountain and Brownsville Rds., Windsor, VT 05089, (802) 674-2060 or (802) 886-2215. Named trails: Brownsville, Weathersfield, Windsor. (WCD; IGS; SNE; TVT; GNA)

4095 **Atherton Meadow Wildlife Area**, Wildlife Forester, Agricultural Center, Morrisville, VT 95661, (802) 888-4607; or District Wildlife Biologist, Rt. 1, Box 33, North Springfield, VT 05150, (802) 886-2215. (SNE)

Baker Peak Trail *see* entry 4092.

4096 **Bald Mountain Campground**, State Park Rd., Townshend, VT 05353, (802) 365-7510. (WCD)

Bald Mountain Trail *see* entry 4092.

4097 **Ball Mountain Lake**, Corps of Engineers, New England Division, 424 Trapelo Rd., Waltham, MA 92254. (GFC; TVT)

4098 **Bill Sladyk Wildlife Management Area**, District Wildlife Biologist, 180 Portland St., St. Johnsbury, VT 05819, (802) 748-8787. (SNE)

Black Creek Trail *see* entry 4148.

4099 **Bomoseen State Park**, West Shore Rd., Hubbardton, VT 05732, (802) 265-4242. 10.0 miles. (WCD; FNE; FMV; IGS; MNE; SNE; TVT; ANI; GNA)

4100 **Branbury State Park**, SR 53, Brandon, VT 05733, (802) 247-5925. Named trails: Falls of Llana 1.1, Silver Lake 3.0. (WCD; MNE; SNE; NET; GNA)

Branch Pond Trail *see* entry 4092.

4101 **Brighton State Park**, Island Pond, VT 05846, (802) 723-4360. 1.5 miles. (WCD; MNE; TVT; GNA)

Broad Brook Trail *see* entry 4092.

4102 **Bromley Mountain**, SR 11, Manchester Center, VT 05255. (NET)

Brownsville Trail *see* entry 4094.

Bucklin Trail *see* entry 4092.

4103 **Burlington Waterfront Bikeway**, Robert Whalen, Superintendent of Parks, Department of Parks and Recreation, 216 Leddy Park Rd., Burlington, VT 05401, (802) 864-0123. 8.5 miles straight. (GRT)

4104 **Burton Island State Park**, P.O. Box 123, St. Albans Bay, VT 05181, (802) 524-6353. (WCD; MNE; SNE; TVT; GNA)

4105 **Button Bay State Park**, Rt. 3, Vergennes, VT 05491, (802) 475-2377 or (802) 483-2314. Named trails: Cavity,

Champlain 0.25, South. (WCD; MNE; NFT; ANI; GNA)

4106 **Calvin Coolidge State Forest**, HCR 105, Plymouth, VT 05056, (802) 672-3612. Named trails: Reading Pond 5.0, Slack Hill 3.1. (IGS; MNE; SNE; TVT; VEG; GNA; GTB)

4107 **Camel's Hump Forest Reserve**, District Forester, Department of Forests, Parks, and Recreation, 103 S. Main St., Waterbury, VT 05676, (802) 828-3375. Named trails: Dean, Forestry. (EGH; SNE; ANI; GNA)

4108 **Camp Plymouth State Park**, SR 100, Plymouth, VT 05056, (802) 228-2025. Named trails: Echo Lake Vista 1.5. (IGS)

Canty Trail *see* entry 4124.

Cavity Trail *see* entry 4105.

4109 **Central Vermont Trail**, Trails Coordinator, Department of Forests, Parks and Recreation, 111 West St., Essex Junction, VT 05452, (802) 879-6565. 22.0 miles straight planned, current as to 8.0 miles. (GRT)

Champlain Trail *see* entry 4105.

4110 **Cornwall Swamp Wildlife Management Area**, Department of Fish and Wildlife, Waterbury Complex, 10 South, Waterbury, VT 05676, (802) 244-7331. (SNE)

4111 **Crown Point Camping Area**, Stoughton Pond Rd., Perkinsville, VT 05151, (802) 263-5555. (WCD)

4112 **Darling State Park**, East Burke, VT 05832. (GNA)

4113 **Dead Creek Waterfowl Area**, Department of Fish and Wildlife, Waterbury Complex, 10 South, Waterbury, VT 05676, (802) 244-7331. (SNE)

Dean Trail *see* entry 4107.

4114 **Deer Leap Trail**, Inn at Long Trail, Killington, VT 05751, (802) 775-7181. 2 hours. (TVT; VEG)

4115 **Delaware and Hudson Recreation Trail**, Gary Salmon, Trails Coordinator, Department of Forests, Parks and Recreation, Vermont Agency of Natural Resources, Rt. 2, Box 261, Pittsford, VT 05763, (802) 483-2314. 34.3 miles straight planned, current as to 20.0 miles. (GRT)

Dunville Hollow Trail *see* entry 4092.

East Branch Trail *see* entry 4124.

Echo Lake Vista Trail *see* entry 4108.

4116 **Elephant Mountain Camping Area**, SR 116, Bristol, VT 05443, (802) 453-3123. (WCD)

4117 **Elmore State Park**, P.O. Box 93, Lake Elmore, VT 05657, (802) 888-2982 or (802) 828-2454. (WCD; MNE; SNE; GNA)

4118 **Emerald Lake State Park**, P.O. Box 485, East Dorset, VT 05253, (802) 362-1655. (WCD; FNE; IGS; MNE; SNE; VEG; GNA)

Falls of Llana Trail *see* entry 4100.

Forestry Trail *see* entry 4107.

4119 **Fort Drummer State Park**, S. Main St., Brattleboro, VT 05301, (802) 254-2610. 1.0 mile. (WCD; FNE; TVT)

4120 **Gifford Woods State Park**, SR 100, Sherburne Center, VT 05482, (802) 775-5354. (WCD; IGS; MNE; SNE; ANI; GNA)

4121 **Grand Isle State Park**, US 2, South Hero, VT 05486, (802) 372-4300. (MNE)

4122 **Granville Gulf State Reservation**, Department of Forests, Parks and Recreation, Montpelier, VT 05602, (802) 828-3375. (GNA)

4123 **Green Mountain Audubon Nature Center**, Burlington, VT 05401, (802) 434-3068. (MNE)

4124 **Green Mountain National Forest**, Federal Bldg., 151 West St., Rutland, VT 05701, (802) 775-2579; or Manchester Ranger District, Manchester Center, VT 05255, (802) 362-2307; or Middlebury Ranger District, Middlebury, VT 05753, (802) 388-4362; or Rochester Ranger District, Rochester, VT 05767, (802) 767-4777. 130 miles. Named trails: Canty, East Branch 5.1(s), Robert Frost Wayside 0.75. (GRT; WCD; EGH; FNE; FMV; GFC; MNE; SNE; TVT; FGU; WNE; GNA; GTB; NFG)

Green Mountain Trail *see* entry 4092.

4125 **Greenwood Lodge and Campsites**, SR 9, Bennington, VT 05201, (802) 442-2547. (WCD)

4126 **Groton State Forest**, Marshfield,

VT 05658, (802) 584-3820; or George Plumb, Director of Recreation, Department of Forests, Parks and Recreation, Vermont Agency of Natural Resources, 103 S. Main St., Waterbury, VT 05676, (802) 244-8713. 40.0 miles. Named trails: Montpelier and Wells River 17.0. (GRT; WCD; EGH; MNE; SNE; OTB; GNA; GTB)

4127 **Half Moon State Park**, Town Rd., Hubbardton, VT 05732, (802) 775-5354. (WCD; FNE; FMV; IGS; TVT)

Hamilton Falls Trail see entry 4132.

4128 **Hawk Inn and Mountain Resort**, SR 100, Plymouth, VT 05056, (802) 672-3811. 11.0 miles. (IGS)

Hell Brook Trail see entry 4152.

History Hike see entry 4142.

Homer Stone Brook Trail see entry 4092.

4129 **Horseshoe Acres**, Andover-Weston Rd., Andover, VT 05143, (802) 875-2960. (WCD)

4130 **Hurricane Brook Wildlife Management Area**, Department of Fish and Game, Agency of Environmental Conservation, Montpelier, VT 04502, (802) 828-3371. (GNA)

4131 **Hurricane Hill Trail**, Hurricane Hill Refuge Area, North Hartland Rd., Hartford, VT 05047, (802) 295-9353. (IGS)

4132 **Jamaica State Park**, Town Rd., Jamaica, VT 05343, (802) 874-4600 or (802) 886-2215. Named trails: Adam Pond 2.0(l), Hamilton Falls 1.0(l), Overlook 0.9(s), Railroad Bed 3.0(s). (WCD; IGS; MNE)

Jay Peak Trail see entry 4133.

4133 **Jay State Forest**, District Forester, Department of Forests, Parks, and Recreation, 180 Portland St., St. Johnsbury, VT 05819, (802) 748-4890. Named trails: Jay Peak 1.7. (GNA)

Keewaydin Trail see entry 4092.

4134 **Kenolie Camping Village**, Brookline Rd., Newfane, VT 05345, (802) 365-7671. (WCD)

4135 **Lake Carmi State Park**, SR 236, North Sheldon, VT 05478, (802) 933-8383 or (802) 879-6565. (MNE)

4136 **Lake Dunmore Kampersville**, P.O. Box 214, Middlebury, VT 05753, (802) 352-4501. (WCD)

4137 **Lake St. Catherine State Park**, SR 30, Poultney, VT 05764. (MNE; TVT; NET)

4138 **Lake Shaftsbury State Park**, Historic SR 7A, Shaftsbury, VT 05262, (802) 375-9978. (IGS)

Lake Trail see entry 4092.

4139 **Lake Willoughby**, SR 5A, Lyndonville, VT 05851. (MNE)

4140 **Lewis Creek Wildlife Management Area**, District Wildlife Biologist, 111 West St., Essex Junction, VT 05452, (802) 878-1564. (SNE; GNA)

4141 **Linehurst Lake Campground**, SR 14, Barre, VT 05641, (802) 433-6662. (WCD)

4142 **Little River State Park**, Rt. 1, Little River Rd., Waterbury, VT 05676, (802) 244-7103. Named trails: History Hike. (WCD; FNE; MNE; SNE; TVT)

4143 **Long Trail**, Green Mountain Club, Inc., Rt. 1, Box 650, Waterbury Center, VT 05677, (802) 244-7037. 270 miles. Awards available. (AA 1992)

Lye Brook Trail see entry 4092.

4144 **Lye Brook Wilderness Trail**, Robert M. Pramuk, Recreation Forester, P.O. Box 519, Rutland, VT 05702, (802) 773-0300. 9.7 miles straight. (GRT; MNE; TVT; HTN)

4145 **Maidstone State Forest**, Forest Rd., Island Pond, VT 05846, (802) 676-3930 or (802) 828-2454. (WCD; MNE)

4146 **Maidstone State Park**, Rt. 1, Box 185, Guildhall, VT 05905, (802) 676-3930. (SNE)

Maquam Creek Trail see entry 4148.

4147 **Merck Forest**, P.O. Box 86, Rupert, VT 05768, (802) 394-7836. (TVT)

4148 **Missisquoi National Wildlife Refuge**, P.O. Box 163, Swanton, VT 05488, (802) 868-4781. Named trails: Black Creek, Maquam Creek. (MNE; SNE; TVT; OTB; ANI; GNA)

4149 **Molly Stark State Park**, SR 9, Wilmington, VT 05363, (802) 464-5460. 1.5 miles. (WCD; FNE; IGS; MNE; TVT; OTB; FDN)

VERMONT

Montpelier and Wells River Trail *see* entry 4126.
4150 **Montshire Museum of Science,** Montshire Rd., Norwich, VT 05055, (802) 649-2200. (IGS; MNE)
4151 **Mt. Ascutney State Park** *see* Ascutney S.P. **4094.** (MNE)
4152 **Mount Mansfield State Forest,** Rt. 1, Stowe, VT 05672, (802) 253-4014. Named trails: Hell Brook. (WCD; EGH; MNE; SNE; TVT; NET; GNA)
4153 **Mount Norris Scout Reservation,** Green Mountain Council, BSA, P.O. Box 557, Waterbury, VT 05676, (802) 244-5189. (SFC)
4154 **Mountain Trails,** Quarry Hill Rd., Rochester, VT 05767, (802) 767-3352. (WCD)
4155 **Mud Creek Wildlife Management Area,** District Wildlife Biologist, 254 N. Main St., Barre, VT 05641, (802) 828-2454. (SNE)
4156 **North Hero State Park,** US 2, South Alburg, VT 05474, (802) 372-8727 or (802) 879-6565. (WCD; MNE)
4157 **North Country Trail** (see separate entry **4955** in interstate section).
North Shore Trail *see* entry 4092.
Old Job Trail *see* entry 4092.
4158 **Old Lantern Campground,** Green Bush Rd., Charlotte, VT 05445, (802) 425-2120. (WCD)
4159 **Onion River Camping Area,** Rt. 1, Box 1205, Plainfield, VT 05667, (802) 426-3232. (WCD)
Overlook Trail *see* entry 4132.
Pico Link Trail *see* entry 4092.
Pine Cobble Trail *see* entry 4092.
4160 **Pine Hill Park Trail,** Rutland Recreation Department, Rutland, VT 05701, (802) 773-1822. 1.0 mile loop. (IGS)
4161 **Pine Mountain Wildlife Management Area,** District Wildlife Biologist, 254 N. Main St., Barre, VT 05641, (802) 828-2454. (SNE)
4162 **Pine Valley Resort Campground,** 400 Woodstock Rd., White River Junction, VT 05001, (802) 296-6711. (WCD)
4163 **Plymsbury Wildlife Management Area,** District Wildlife Biologist, Pittsford Academy, Rt. 1, Pittsford, VT 05763, (802) 483-2300. (SNE)
4164 **Putnam State Forest,** District Forester, Department of Forests, Parks and Recreation, Rt. 1, Morrisville, VT 05661, (802) 888-4607. (SNE; GNA)
4165 **Quechee Gorge State Park,** SR 4, Woodstock, VT 05091, (802) 295-2990. (WCD; IGS; SNE; TVT; GNA)
Railroad Bed Trail *see* entry 4132.
Ravine Trail *see* entry 4167.
Reading Pond Trail *see* entry 4106.
Robert Frost Wayside Trail *see* entry 4124.
4166 **Roxbury State Forest,** District Forester, Department of Forests, Parks and Recreation, Rt. 1, Morrisville, VT 05661, (802) 888-4607. (GNA)
4167 **Saint-Gaudens National Historic Site,** Cornish, NH 03745, (603) 675-2067. Named trails: Ravine 0.25. (VEG)
4168 **Shelburne Farms,** Harbor & Bay Rds., Shelburne, VT 05482, (802) 985-8442. (MNE)
Shrewsbury Peak Trail *see* entry 4092.
Silver Lake Trail *see* entry 4100.
Skyline Trail *see* entry 4091.
Slack Hill Trail *see* entry 4106.
South Trail *see* entry 4105.
4169 **Spruce Mountain Trail,** The Green Mountain Club, 43 State St., Montpelier, VT 05602, (802) 223-3463. 3 hours. (VEG)
Stratton Mountain Trail *see* entry 4092.
4170 **Stratton Mountain Tree Farm,** Woodlands and Wood Products Operations, Region VI, International Paper Company, Jay, ME 04239, Attn: Administrator, Public Relations. (GNA)
4171 **Thompson Nature Trail,** Mt. Snow, West Dover, VT 95356, (802) 464-3333. (IGS)
4172 **Tinker Brook Natural Area,** Agency of Environmental Conservation, Department of Forests, Parks and Recreation, Montpelier, VT 05602, (802) 828-3375. (ANI)
4173 **Townshend State Forest,** SR 30, Newfane, VT 05345, (802) 365-7500 or (802) 886-2215. (WCD; MNE)

VERMONT *Index* 271

4174 **Townshend State Park**, Rt. 1, Box 299, Newfane, VT 05345, (802) 365-7500. Named trails: Townshend 2.5. (FNE; IGS; SNE; TVT; GNA)
   Townshend Trail *see* entry 4174.
4175 **Tundra Trail**, The Stowe Area Association, P.O. Box 1230, Stowe, VT 05672, (802) 253-7321. 0.5 mile. (VEG)
4176 **Vermont Institute of Natural Science**, Church Hill Rd., Woodstock, VT 05091, (802) 457-2779. (FNE; IGS; MNE)
4177 **Vermont Village Walks**, Anne Mausolff, Rt. 1, Chester, VT 05143, (802) 875-3631. (VEG)
4178 **Victory Basin Wildlife Management Area**, District Wildlife Biologist, 180 Portland St., St. Johnsbury, VT 05819, (802) 748-8787. (SNE)
4179 **Victory State Forest**, District Forester, Department of Forests, Parks and Recreation, 180 Portland St., St. Johnsbury, VT 05819, (802) 748-4890. (GNA)
   Weathersfield Trail *see* entry 4094.
4180 **Wenlock Wildlife Management Area**, District Wildlife Biologist, 180 Portland St., St. Johnsbury, VT 05819, (802) 748-8787. (SNE)
   West Ridge Trail *see* entry 4092.
   West River Trail *see* entry 4097.
4181 **White Rocks**, SR 140, Wallingford, VT 05773. (TVT)

4182 **Wilgus State Park**, SR 5, Ascutney, VT 05030, (802) 674-5422 or (802) 886-2215. (WCD; IGS; MNE; TVT)
   William Tucker Trail *see* entry 4092.
4183 **Willoughby State Forest**, District Forester, Department of Forests, Parks and Recreation, 180 Portland St., St. Johnsbury, VT 05819, (802) 748-4890. (SNE)
   Windsor Trail *see* entry 4094.
4184 **Winhall Brook Campground**, Winhall Brook Campground and Ball Mountain Dam Recreation Area, SR 100, South Londonderry, VT 05155, (802) 824-9509. (WCD; IGS)
4185 **Woodford State Park**, Rt. 1, Bennington, VT 05201, (802) 447-4169. (WCD; FNE; MNE; SNE; GNA)

Generally:
Commissioner, Department of Forests, Parks and Recreation, State Office Bldg., Montpelier, VT 05602, (802) 828-3375. (SFC)
U.S. Army Corps of Engineers, New England Division, 424 Trapelo Rd., Waltham, MA 02254. (GFC)
Vermont Department of Forests, Parks and Recreation, 103 S. Main St., Waterbury, VT 05676, (802) 244-8711. (EGH)

Index (by city)

Andover: Horseshoe Acres 4129
Ascutney: Wilgus State Park 4182
Barre: Linehurst Lake Campground 4141; Mud Creek Wildlife Management Area 4155; Pine Mountain Wildlife Management Area 4161
Bennington: Greenwood Lodge and Campsites 4125; Woodford State Park 4185
Brandon: Branbury State Park 4100
Brattleboro: Fort Drummer State Park 4119
Bristol: Elephant Mountain Camping Area 4116
Brookfield: Allis State Park 4090
Burlington: Burlington Waterfront Bikeway 4103; Green Mountain Audubon Nature Center 4123
Charlotte: Old Lantern Campground 4158
Chester: Vermont Village Walks 4177
Cornish: Saint-Gaudens National Historic Site 4167
East Burke: Darling State Park 4112
East Dorset: Emerald Lake State Park 4118
East Lyndon: Victory State Forest 4179
Essex Junction: Alburg Rail-Trail 4089; Central Vermont Trail 4109
Guildhall: Maidstone State Park 4146
Hartford: Hurricane Hill Refuge Area 4131
Hewetts Corners: Amity Pond Natural Area 4091

Hubbardton: Bomoseen State Park 4099; Half Moon State Park 4127
Island Pond: Brighton State Park 4101; Hurricane Brook Wildlife Management Area 4130; Maidstone State Forest 4145
Jamaica: Jamaica State Park 4132
Jay: Jay State Forest 4133
Killington: Deer Leap Trail 4114
Kimball: Willoughby State Forest 4183
Lake Elmore: Elmore State Park 4117
Lyndonville: Lake Willoughby 4139
Manchester Center: Bromley Mountain 4102; Green Mountain National Forest 4124
Marshfield: Groton State Forest 4126
Middlebury: Green Mountain National Forest 4124; Lake Dunmore Kampersville 4136
Montpelier: Spruce Mountain Trail 4169; Tinker Brook Natural Area 4172
Newfane: Kenolie Camping Village 4134; Townshend State Forest 4173; Townshend State Park 4174
North Duxbury: Camel's Hump Forest Reserve 4107
North Sheldon: Lake Carmi State Park 4135
Norwich: Montshire Museum of Science 4150
Perkinsville: Crown Point Camping Area 4111
Pittsford: Delaware and Hudson Recreation Trail 4115; Plymsbury Wildlife Management Area 4163
Plainfield: Onion River Camping Area 4159
Plymouth: Calvin Coolidge State Forest 4106; Camp Plymouth State Park 4108; Hawk Inn and Mountain Resort 4128
Poultney: Lake St. Catherine State Park 4137
Rochester: Green Mountain National Forest 4124; Mountain Trails 4154
Roxbury: Roxbury State Forest 4166
Rupert: Merck Forest 4147
Rutland: Green Mountain National Forest 4124; Lye Brook Wilderness Trail 4144; Pine Hill Park Trail 4160

St. Albans Bay: Burton Island State Park 4104
St. Johnsbury: Bill Sladyk Wildlife Management Area 4098; Victory Basin Wildlife Management Area 4178; Wenlock Wildlife Management Area 4180
Shaftsbury: Lake Shaftsbury State Park 4138
Shelburne: Shelburne Farms 4168
Sherburne Center: Gifford Woods State Park 4120
South Alburg: North Hero State Park 4156
South Hero: Grand Isle State Park 4121
South Londonderry: Winhall Brook Campground 4184
Starksboro: Lewis Creek Wildlife Management Area 4140
Stowe: Mount Mansfield State Forest 4152; Tundra Trail 4175
Stratton: Stratton Mountain Tree Farm 4170
Swanton: Missisquoi National Wildlife Refuge 4148
Townshend: Bald Mountain Campground 4096
Vergennes: Button Bay State Park 4105; Dead Creek Waterfowl Area 4113
Wallingford: White Rocks 4181
Waltham: Ball Mountain Lake 4097
Warren: Granville Gulf State Reservation 4122
Waterbury: Cornwall Swamp Wildlife Management Area 4110; Mount Norris Scout Reservation 4153
Waterbury Center: Long Trail 4143
West Dover: Thompson Nature Trail 4171
White River Junction: Pine Valley Resort Campground 4162
Wilmington: Molly Stark State Park 4149
Windsor: Ascutney State Park 4094; Mt. Ascutney State Park 4151
Woodstock: Quechee Gorge State Park 4165; Vermont Institute of Natural Science 4176
Worcester: Putnam State Forest 4164

Virginia

4186 **A. Willis Robertson Park**, Rt. 2, Box 208-A, Lexington, VA 24450, (703) 463-4164. Named trails: Branch 1.0(s), Lake, North Boundary 1.1(s), Ridge 1.5(s), South Boundary 1.1(s). (HOD)

Abbot Lake Loop Trail see entry 4205.

Accotink Trail see entry 4324.

Acorn Ridge Trail see entry 4360.

4187 **Algonkian Regional Park**, Northern Virginia Regional Park Authority, 5400 Ox Rd., Fairfax Station, VA 22039, (703) 631-0550. (NWA)

Allegheny Trail see entry 4316.

Alpine Trail see entry 4338.

4188 **Amelia Family Campground Nature Trail**, Rt. 5, Box 3065, Amelia, VA 23002, (804) 561-3011. (WCD; VCD)

4189 **Amelia Wildlife Management Area**, Rt. 4, Amelia, VA 23002, (804) 561-3350. Named trails: Bunny 0.7(s), Fire, Lake 3.2(l), Marsh Point 2.0(l), Woodcock 4.0(l). (HOD)

Animal Walk see entry 4345.

Anthony Knobs Trail see entry 4279.

4190 **Appalachian Trail** (see separate entry **4948** in interstate section).

Apple Orchard Falls/East Trail see entry 4205.

Apple Orchard Falls/West Trail see entry 4316.

4191 **Appomattox Courthouse Historical Trail**, Appomattox Courthouse National Historical Park, Appomattox, VA 24522, (804) 352-8987; information on medal available from Blue Ridge Mountain Council, BSA, 2131 Valley View Blvd., N.W., Roanoke, VA 24012-2031, (703) 265-0656; or Ronald G. Wilson, Historian, P.O. Box 218, Appomattox, VA 24522. 6.0 miles loop. Awards available. (SAR 1992)

4192 **Appomattox-Buckingham State Forest**, c/o Cumberland State Forest, Rt. 1, Box 139, Cumberland, VA 23040, (804) 492-4121. (GNA)

Aqueduct Trail see entry 4375.

Arlington County Bicycle Trail see entry 4193.

4193 **Arlington County Parks and Recreation**, 300 N. Park Dr., Arlington, VA 22203, (703) 558-2426. Named trails: Arlington County Bicycle 8.0, Glencarlyn Park, Gulf Branch Nature 1.3, Long Branch Nature, Lubber Run 0.6, Windy Run Nature 1.4. (HOD)

Arrowhead Trail see entry 4385.

Ashton Creek Trail see entry 4227.

4194 **Assateague Island National Seashore**, National Park Service, Rt. 2, Box 294, Berlin, MD 21811, (804) 336-6577. 34.5 miles. (FTS; DMV; GFC; MMA; AGW; GNA)

Austin Mountain Trail see entry 4404.

Awareness Trail see entry 4377.

4195 **Back Bay National Wildlife Refuge**, 287 Pembroke Office Park, Virginia Beach, VA 23462, (804) 490-0505. Named trails: Back Bay 17.2(l), Eagle 0.5(l). (AMC; HOD; GNA)

Back Bay Trail see entry 4195.

Back Creek Gorge Trail see entry 4279.

Back Draft Trail see entry 4279.

Backway Hollow Trail see entry 4251.

Balcony Falls Trail see entry 4205.

Balcony Falls Trail see entry 4316.

Bald Cypress Nature Trail see entry 4400.

Bald Mountain Trail see entry 4205.

Bald Mountain Trail see entry 4279.

Bald Ridge Trail *see* entry 4279.
4196 Ballou Park Nature Trail, Danville Parks and Recreation, P.O. Box 3300, Danville, VA 24541, (804) 799-4212. 0.5 mile loop. (HOD)
4197 Barcroft Park, 4100 S. Four Mile Run Dr., Arlington, VA 22206, (703) 558-2426. (GPW)
Bark Camp Lake Trail *see* entry 4316.
4198 Barn Wharf Trail, Director, Gunston Hall, Lorton, VA 22079, (703) 550-9220. 1.7 miles loop. (HOD)
Battery 5 Spur Trail *see* entry 4372.
Battery 7 Trail *see* entry 4372.
Bayberry Nature Trail *see* entry 4438.
Beach Trail *see* entry 4430.
4199 Bear Creek Lake State Park, Rt. 1, Box 253, Cumberland, VA 23040, (804) 492-4410. Named trails: Lakeside, Pine Knob, Running Creek Cedar 1.7(l). (WCD; ATM; MMA; HOD; GNA)
Bear Draft Trail *see* entry 4279.
Bear Rock Trail *see* entry 4279.
Bear Wallow Spur Trail *see* entry 4279.
Beards Gap Hollow Trail *see* entry 4251.
Beards Gap Trail *see* entry 4251.
Beards Mountain Trail *see* entry 4279.
Bearfence Hut Trail *see* entry 4404.
Bearfence Trail *see* entry 4404.
Beartree Gap Trail *see* entry 4316.
Bearwallow Run Trail *see* entry 4279.
Beaver Cove Nature Trail *see* entry 4214.
Beaver Dam Trail *see* entry 4430.
Beaver Lake Nature Trail *see* entry 4377.
Beech Grove Trail *see* entry 4316.
Beecher Trail *see* entry 4404.
Beldor Ridge Trail *see* entry 4404.
Belfast Creek Trail *see* entry 4205.
Belfast Trail *see* entry 4316.
Belle Cove Trail *see* entry 4279.
Belle Isle Loop Trail *see* entry 4393.
Berry Hollow Trail *see* entry 4404.
4200 Best Holiday Trav-L-Park, 1075 General Booth Blvd., Virginia Beach, VA 23451, (804) 425-0249. (VCD)
Betty's Rock Trail *see* entry 4404.
Big Bend Trail *see* entry 4404.
4201 Big Blue Trail, Potomac Appalachian Trail Club, 1718 N St. NW, Washington, DC 20036, (202) 638-5306. 143 miles (112 in VA). (EGH; BMG; HOD)
Big Blue Trail *see* entries 4279 and 4404.
Big Blue-Bearwallow Trail *see* entry 4279.
Big Devil Stairs Trail *see* entry 4404.
Big Hollow Trail *see* entry 4279.
Big Mama Trail *see* entry 4279.
Big Meadow Trail *see* entry 4430.
Big Oak Trail *see* entry 4363.
Big Pinnacle Trail *see* entry 4287.
Big Ridge Trail *see* entry 4279.
Big Run Loop Trail *see* entry 4404.
Big Run Portal Trail *see* entry 4404.
Big Schloss Trail *see* entry 4279.
Big Survey Trail *see* entry 4349.
Bird Knob Trail *see* entry 4279.
Black Ridge Trail *see* entry 4205.
Black Rock Hut Trail *see* entry 4404.
Blackrock Spur Trail *see* entry 4404.
Blackrock Trail *see* entry 4404.
Black's Creek Trail *see* entry 4316.
4202 Blacksburg Parks, 300 S. Main St., Blacksburg, VA 24060, (703) 961-1135. Named trails: Huckleberry Line 1.0, Old Farm 0.7(s), Rocky Run 1.0(s), Turtle Ridge 1.5(s). (HOD)
4203 Blackwater Creek Natural Area, Chris Stinnett, Park Ranger, Blackwater Creek Natural Area, c/o City of Lynchburg Recreation and Parks Department, 301 Grove St., Lynchburg, VA 24501, (804) 847-1640. Named trails: Blackwater Creek Natural Area Bikeway 4.0(s), Creekside Trunk. (GRT; MMA)
Blackwater Creek Natural Area Bikeway *see* entry 4203.
Blackwater Creek Trail *see* entry 4338.
4204 Blue Ridge Campground, CR 670, Burnt Chimney, VA 24184, (703) 721-3866. (WCD)
4205 Blue Ridge Parkway, 400 BB&T Bldg., One Pack Square, Asheville, NC

28801, (704) 271-4779. Named trails: Abbot Lake Loop 1.0(l), Apple Orchard Falls/East 2.8(l), Balcony Falls, Bald Mountain 2.2(s), Belfast Creek, Black Ridge 3.0(l), Boston Knob 0.1(s), Buck Mountain 0.5(s), Buck Mountain Overlook 4,600', Cascades, Chestnut Ridge 5.4(l), Cone Park, Cotoctin 0.3(l), Crabtree Falls, Craggy Gardens, Dripping Rock, Elk Run 0.8(l), Fallingwater Cascades 1.6(l), Flat Rock, Flat Top 4.5(l), Greenstone 0.2(l), Groundhog Mountain Picnic Area Observation Tower 200'(s), Gunter Ridge, Hammond Hollow, Hardwood Cove Nature, Harkening Hill 3.3(l), Harvey's Knob, Humpback Mountain 2.1(s), Hunting Creek 2.0(s), Indian Gap 0.3(l), James River 0.4(s), Johnson Farm Loop 1.0(l), Linville Falls, Little Cove Mountain, Little Rocky Row, Lovington Spring, Mabry Mill, Mau-Har, Montvale Overlook, Mountain Farm Self-Guiding 0.4(s), Mountain Industry 0.4(l), Onion Mountain Loop 0.2(l), Onion Mountain Overlook, Otter Creek 3.0(s), Otter Lake 0.8(s), Pakes Mill Pond Overlook 0.5(l), Peaks of Otter Picnic Area 0.35(s), The Priest Overlook 0.2(l), Puckett Cabin Walk 75'(s), Ravens Roost Overlook, Rennett Bag, Richland Balsam, Roanoke Mountain Summit 0.3(l), Roanoke River 0.8(s), Roanoke Valley Horse 18.5(l), Rock Castle Gorge 10.6(l), Rocky Knob Picnic Loop 1.3(l), Rocky Knob Self-Guiding 0.2(s), Round Meadow Creek 0.5(l), Saddle Gap, Sharp Top 3.0(l), Sharp Top Mountain Overlook, Slacks Overlook 2.2(s), Smart View Loop 2.6(l), Spec Mine 2.9(s), Stewarts Knob 88 yards(s), Sulphur Spring, Sunset Field Overlook, Taylors Mountain Overlook, Three Ridge Overlook, Thunder Ridge 0.1(s), Torry Ridge 1.9(s), Trail of the Trees 0.6(s), White Oak Flats 0.1(s), White Rock Falls I 2.5(s), White Rock Falls II 2.5(s), Woodland 0.8(s), Yankee Horse Overlook 0.2(s). (WCD; WBR; AYH; GFC; HOD)

Blue Suck Trail *see* entry 4251.
Blue Suck Trail *see* entry 4279.
Blue Trail *see* entry 4379.

Blue Trail *see* entry 4384.
Bluebell Trail *see* entry 4213.
Blueberry Trail *see* entry 4279.

4206 **Bluemont Junction Trail**, Ritch Viola, Planner, Arlington County Department of Public Works, 2100 Clarendon Blvd., Suite 717, Arlington, VA 22201, (703) 358-3699. 1.3 miles straight. (GRT)

Bluff Trail *see* entry 4404.
Boardwalk Trail *see* entry 4249.
Bobcat Ridge Trail *see* entry 4388.
Bogan Run Trail *see* entry 4279.
Bolshers Run Trail *see* entry 4279.

4207 **Booker T. Washington National Monument**, Resources Manager, Rt. 1, Box 195, Hardy, VA 24101, (703) 721-2094. Named trails: Jack-O-Lantern Branch 2.0(s), Plantation 0.5(l). (ATM; GNM; MMA; NPS; NPV; NPE; OTB; CGA; HOD; GNA; YNP; ANP)

Boone Run Trail *see* entry 4279.
Boston Knob Trail *see* entry 4205.
Braddock Road Park Service Trail *see* entry 4258.
Braley Branch Trail *see* entry 4279.
Braley Pond Loop Trail *see* entry 4279.
Branch Trail *see* entry 4186.
Branch Trail *see* entry 4316.
Branch Trail *see* entry 4372.

4208 **Breaks Interstate Park**, Breaks, VA 24607, (703) 865-4414. Named trails: Center Creek, Chestnut Ridge, Cold Spring, Geological, Grassy Overlook, Lake, Laurel Branch, Loop, Overlook, Prospectors, River, Tower Tunnel, Towers. (WCD; VCD; ATM; MMA; HOD; GNA)

Breakthrough Point Trail *see* entry 4392.

Bridle Trail *see* entry 4379.

4209 **Briery Creek**, Virginia Commission of Game and Inland Fisheries, 4010 W. Broad St., Richmond, VA 23230, (804) 367-0939. (GFC)

Broad Hollow Trail *see* entry 4404.

4210 **Brookneal Recreation Park**, Director, Campbell County Department of Recreation, P.O. Box 369, Rustburg, VA 24588, (804) 847-0961. Named trails: Falling River 2.6(l), Lake 0.5(l). (HOD)

VIRGINIA

Brown Gap Trail *see* entry 4404.
Brown Mountain-Rocky Mountain Trail *see* entry 4404.
Browntown Trail *see* entry 4404.
Brumley Creek Trail *see* entry 4298.
Brumley Run Trail *see* entry 4298.
Brushy Ridge Trail *see* entry 4279.
Buchanan Trail *see* entry 4316.
Buck Hollow Trail *see* entry 4404.
Buck Mountain Overlook Trail *see* entry 4205.
Buck Mountain Trail *see* entry 4205.
Buck Ridge Trail *see* entry 4404.
Buck Run Spur Trail *see* entry 4279.
Buck Run Trail *see* entry 4279.
Bucks Elbow Mountain Fire Road *see* entry 4404.
Buckwheat Mountain Jeep Trail *see* entry 4279.

4211 **Buffalo Creek Trail**, Westvaco Timberland Division, P.O. Box WV, Appomattox, VA 24522, (804) 846-5291. (AMI; HOD)

4212 **Bull Run Marina**, Old Yates Ford Rd., Clifton, VA 22024, (703) 631-0549. (GPW)

4213 **Bull Run Regional Park**, c/o Northern Virginia Regional Park Authority, 5400 Ox Rd., Fairfax Station, VA 22039, (703) 631-0550. 40.0 miles. Named trails: Bluebell 1.5(l), Bull Run-Occoquan Creek, Bull Run, Cub Run 1.6(s), Nature 14.0. (WCD; VCD; ATM; MMA; NAT; GPW; AMI; NWA; PTB)

Bull Run Trail *see* entry 4213.
Bull Run-Occoquan Creek Trail *see* entry 4213.
Bull Run-Occoquan Trail *see* entry 4361.
Bullpasture Mountain Trail *see* entry 4300.
Bunny Trail *see* entry 4189.

4214 **Burke Lake Park**, 7315 Ox Rd., Fairfax Station, VA 22039, (703) 323-6600. 5.0 miles. Named trails: Beaver Cove Nature 0.75. (ATM; MMA; GPW; NWA)

4215 **Bush Park Camping Resort**, CR 702, Deltaville, VA 23043, (804) 776-6750. (WCD)

Buttermilk Trail *see* entry 4393.
Butterwood Branch Trail *see* entry 4404.
Buzzard Rock Trail *see* entry 4279.

4216 **C.F. Phelps Area**, Virginia Commission of Game and Inland Fisheries, 4010 W. Broad St., Richmond, VA 23230, (804) 367-0939. (GFC)

Cabin Creek Nature Trail *see* entry 4287.
California Ridge Trail *see* entry 4279.
Camp Hoover Trail *see* entry 4404.

4217 **Camp Roland**, Appalachian Council, BSA, P.O. Box 1498, Bluefield, WV 24701, (304) 327-5517; or Camp Roland, Bastian, VA 24314, (703) 688-3568. (SFC)

4218 **Camp Shenandoah**, Stonewall Jackson Area Council, BSA, P.O. Box 813, Waynesboro, VA 22980, (703) 943-6675; or Camp Shenandoah, Rt. 1, Swoope, VA 24479, (703) 866-7513. (SFC)

Campground Trail *see* entry 4409.
Captain Staunton's Loop Trail *see* entry 4409.
Cascades Trail *see* entry 4205.
Cascades Trail *see* entry 4316.
Cat Knob Trail *see* entry 4404.
Catlett Mountain Trail *see* entry 4404.
Catlett Spur Trail *see* entry 4404.

4219 **Cattail Creek RV Park & Campground**, 3901 Moore's Ferry Rd., Skippers, VA 23879, (804) 634-9935. (WCD)

Cave Circle Trail *see* entry 4390.
Cave Springs Nature Trail *see* entry 4397.
CCC Fire Trail *see* entry 4300.
CCC Trail *see* entry 4306.
Cedar Creek Trail *see* entry 4279.

4220 **Cedar Path Nature Trail**, Director, Stafford County Parks and Recreation Department, Rt. 6, Box 451, Hartwood, VA 22471, (703) 752-5611. 0.4 mile loop. (HOD)

Cedar Rim Trail *see* entry 4404.
Cedar Run Trail *see* entry 4404.
Cedar Run/Whiteoak Link Trail *see* entry 4404.
Cellar Mountain Trail *see* entry 4279.
Center Creek Trail *see* entry 4208.

Center Trail *see* entry 4258.
Charcoal-Passage Creek Trail *see* entry 4279.
4221 Charlottesville KOA, Rt. 1, Box 144, Charlottesville, VA 22903, (804) 296-9881. (WCD)
4222 Chatham and Old Towne Falmouth Historical Trail, Troop 849 BSA, P.O. Box 193, Thornburg, VA 22565. 8.0 miles loop. Awards available. (SAR 1993)
4223 Cherrystone Campground, P.O. Box 545, Cheriton, VA 23316, (804) 331-3063. (WCD; VCD)
4224 Chesapeake (a/k/a Chessie) Nature Trail, Public Relations Office, The Chesapeake Corp., West Point, VA 23181, (804) 843-5000. 1.5 miles loop. (PGS; HOD)
4225 Chesapeake Area, City of Chesapeake, Department of Parks and Civic Center, P.O. Box 15225, Chesapeake, VA 23320, (804) 547-6411. Named trails: Deer Island 2.2(s), Fragrance 210 yards, Indian Creek 4.2(l), Molly Mitchell 1.3(s), Shuttle, Wood Duck Slough 0.3(s). (HOD)
4226 Chessie Nature Trail, VMI Foundation, Inc., Virginia Military Institute, P.O. Box 932, Lexington, VA 24450, (703) 463-6287; or Lexington Visitor Center, 102 E. Washington St., Lexington, VA 24450, (703) 463-3777. 7.5 miles straight. (AA 1992)
4227 Chesterfield County, Director, Chesterfield County Parks and Recreation Department, P.O. Box 40, Chesterfield, VA 23832, (804) 748-1623. Named trails: Ashton Creek, Cobb's Wharf, Physical Fitness, Rockwood Nature 3.4, Woodthrush. (HOD)
Chestnut Flat Spring Trail *see* entry 4279.
Chestnut Ridge Trail *see* entry 4205.
Chestnut Ridge Trail *see* entry 4208.
Chestnut Ridge Trail *see* entry 4279.
Chestnut Ridge Trail *see* entry 4316.
4228 Chickahominy Area, Virginia Commission of Game and Inland Fisheries, 4010 W. Broad St., Richmond, VA 23830, (804) 367-0939. (GFC)
4229 Chickahominy Recreational Park, Rt. 2, Box 380, 1951 Allen Rd., Lanexa, VA 23089, (804) 966-2582. (VCD)
Chimney Hollow Trail *see* entry 4279.
4230 Chincoteague National Wildlife Refuge, P.O. Box 62, Chincoteague, VA 23336, (804) 336-6122. Named trails: Lighthouse 0.3(l), Pony 1.6(l), Sensitivity, Toms Cove Nature 0.6(l), Wildlife 3.5(l). (ATM; DMV; AMC; HOD; GNA)
4231 Chinquapin Park, 3210 King St., Alexandria, VA 22302, (703) 838-4838. (GPW)
Chippokes Plantation Loop Trail *see* entry 4232.
4232 Chippokes Plantation State Park, Rt. 1, Box 213, Surry, VA 23883, (804) 294-3625. Named trails: Chippokes Plantation Loop 2.2(l), Lower Chippokes Creek 1.0(s). (ATM; MMA; OTB; AMC; HOD)
Christian Run Trail *see* entry 4279.
4233 Christopher Run Campground, Rt. 1, Box 326, Mineral, VA 23117, (800) 582-1707 or (703) 894-4744. (WCD; VCD)
4234 Circle H Campground, P.O. Box 101, Clifton Forge, VA 24422, (703) 862-5454. (VCD)
4235 Claytor Lake State Park, SR 660, Redford, VA 24141, (703) 674-5492. Named trails: Claytor Lake 2.0(s), Deer 0.9(l), Overlook 1.5(s). (WCD; ATM; MMA; HOD)
Claytor Lake Trail *see* entry 4235.
Cliff Trail *see* entry 4279.
Cliffside Trail *see* entry 4316.
Clinch Mountain Trail *see* entry 4236.
4236 Clinch Mountain Wildlife Management Area, Rt. 2, Box 218, Saltville, VA 24370, (703) 944-3434. Named trails: Clinch Mountain 2.4(s), Fire 8.0(s), Laurel Bed Creek 8.0(l), Little Tumbling Creek 7.4(s), Red Branch 8.4(l). (GFC; HOD; GNA)
Cobb's Wharf Trail *see* entry 4227.
Cock's Comb Trail *see* entry 4279.
Cold Harbor Trail *see* entry 4392.
Cold Spring Trail *see* entry 4208.
Cold Spring Trail *see* entry 4279.

Cold Springs Run Trail *see* entry 4279.
Comers Creek Trail *see* entry 4316.
Compton Gap Trail *see* entry 4404.
Compton Peak East Trail *see* entry 4404.
Compton Peak West Trail *see* entry 4404.
Cone Park Trail *see* entry 4205.
Conway Trail *see* entry 4404.
4237 Copper Trail, Robert Old, 721 Fentress Rd., Chesapeake, VA 23320, (804) 482-1132. 0.8 mile loop. (HOD)
Corbin Cabin Cutoff Trail *see* entry 4404.
Corbin Hollow Trail *see* entry 4404.
Corbin Mountain Trail *see* entry 4404.
Cornelius Trail *see* entry 4316.
Cotoctin Trail *see* entry 4205.
4238 The Cove Campground, SR 704, Gore, VA 22637, (703) 858-2882. (VCD)
Cove Mountain Trail *see* entry 4316.
4239 Crabtree Falls Campground, SR 56, Crabtree Falls, VA 24464, (703) 377-2066. (WCD)
Crabtree Falls Trail *see* entry 4205.
Crabtree Falls Trail *see* entry 4279.
Craggy Gardens Trail *see* entry 4205.
Craig Creek Trail *see* entry 4316.
Crane Trail *see* entry 4279.
4240 Cranenest Campsite, Corps of Engineers—John W. Flannagan Reservoir, SR 83, Clintwood, VA 24228. (WCD)
Crater Spur Trail *see* entry 4372.
Crawford Knob Trail *see* entry 4279.
Crawford Mountain Trail *see* entry 4279.
Creasy Hollow Trail *see* entry 4316.
Creek Loop Trail *see* entry 4338.
Creekside Trunk Trail *see* entry 4203.
Crescent Rock Trail *see* entry 4404.
4241 Crooked Creek, Virginia Commission of Game and Inland Fisheries, 4010 W. Broad St., Richmond, VA 23230, (804) 367-0939. (GFC)
Crooms Ridge Trail *see* entry 4279.
Crow's Nest Trail *see* entry 4409.
Crusher Ridge Trail *see* entry 4404.

Cub Run Trail *see* entry 4213.
4242 Cumberland Gap National Historical Park, Chief of Interpretation, P.O. Box 840, Middleboro, KY 40965, (606) 248-2817. 50.0 miles. Named trails: Gibson Gap 2.6(s), Green Leaf Nature 0.9(l), Honey Tree Spur 0.9(l), Lewis Hollow (a/k/a Skylight Cave) 10.0(l), Ridge 17.0(s), Tri-State, Wilderness Road, Woodson Gap (a/k/a Mischa Moka). (EGH; ATM; HOD; GNA)
4243 Cumberland State Forest, Forest Resource Planner, Department of Conservation and Economic Development, Division of Forestry, P.O. Box 3758, Charlottesville, VA 22903, (804) 977-6555; or Cumberland State Forest, Rt. 1, Box 139, Cumberland, VA 23040, (804) 492-4121. Named trails: Forest Trail 24, Willis River 10.4(s). (HOD; GNA)
Curry Creek Trail *see* entry 4316.
4244 Daddy Rabbit's Campground, SR 727, Willis, VA 24380, (703) 789-4150. (WCD)
Dam Spillway Trail *see* entry 4260.
Dark Hollow Falls Trail *see* entry 4404.
4245 Davis Lakes & Campground, Byrd St., Suffolk, VA 23434, (804) 539-1191. (WCD)
Deadening Nature Trail *see* entry 4404.
Deep Cut Trail *see* entry 4342.
Deer Island Trail *see* entry 4225.
Deer Ridge Trail *see* entry 4388.
4246 Deer Run Campground, SR 622, Woolwine, VA 24185, (703) 930-2354. (WCD)
Deer Trail *see* entry 4235.
Deer Trail *see* entry 4316.
4247 Deer Trail Park, SR 686, Wytheville, VA 24382, (703) 228-3636. (WCD)
Dickey Gap Trail *see* entry 4316.
Dickey Hill Trail *see* entry 4404.
Dickey Knob Trail *see* entry 4316.
Dickey Ridge Trail *see* entry 4404.
4248 Difficult Run, Del-Mar-Va Council, BSA, 8th and Washington Sts., Wilmington, DE 19801. 5.0 miles. (DMV; HOD)
Dike Road Trail *see* entry 4340.
4249 Dismal Swamp National Wildlife

VIRGINIA

Refuge, P.O. Box 349, Suffolk, VA 23434, (804) 539-7479. 80.0 miles. Boardwalk 0.8(s), Jericho Ditch 9.5(s), RR Ditch 2.0(s), Washington Ditch 6.0(s). (OTB; AMC; HOD; GNA; GNW)

Divide Trail *see* entry 4316.
Dogwood Trail *see* entry 4385.
Dogwood Trail *see* entry 4438.
Donaldson Run Trail *see* entry 4384.

4250 **Dora Kelly Nature Trail**, Director, Ramsay Nature Center, 5700 Sanger Ave., Alexandria, VA 22311, (703) 838-4829. 1.0 mile loop. (HOD)

4251 **Douthat State Park**, Rt. 1, Box 212, Millboro, VA 24460, (703) 862-7200. 100 miles. Named trails: Backway Hollow 0.7, Beards Gap 1.1(s), Beards Gap Hollow, Blue Suck 3.0(s), Brushy Hollow, Buck Hollow 1.0(s), Buck Lick 0.3(s), Guest Lodge, Huffs 1.2(s), Locust Gap, Middle Hollow, Middle Mountain, Mountain Side 1.4(s), Mountain Top 1.8(s), Pine Tree, Ross Camp Hollow, Salt Stump, Stony Run, Tobacco House Ridge, Tuscarora Overlook, Wilson Creek. (WCD; EGH; ATM; MMA; HOD; GNA)

Dowell's Draft Trail *see* entry 4279.

4252 **Downtown Richmond Trail**, Virginia Trails Association, 13 W. Maple St., Alexandria, VA 22301, (703) 548-7490. 9.5 miles loop. (HOD)

Doyle River Cabin Trail *see* entry 4404.
Doyle River Trail *see* entry 4404.
Dragon's Tooth Trail *see* entry 4316.

4253 **Dranesville Area**, Public Affairs Office, Fairfax County Park Authority, 4030 Hummer Rd., Annandale, VA 22003, (703) 941-5008. 3.0 miles. (NAT; AMI; NWA)

Dripping Rock Trail *see* entry 4205.
Dry Run Falls Fire Road *see* entry 4404.
Dry Run Trail *see* entry 4279.
Dry Run Trail *see* entry 4404.

4254 **Dublfun Campground**, CR 605, Saluda, VA 23149, (804) 758-5432. (WCD)

Duff and Stuff Trail *see* entry 4258.
Duncan Hollow Trail *see* entry 4279.
Eagle Trail *see* entry 4195.

Eastern National Children's Forest Trail *see* entry 4279.

4255 **Ed Allen's Chickahominy Recreational Park** *see* Chickahominy Recreational Park **4229**. (WCD)

Elephant Man Trail *see* entry 4279.
Elk Run Trail *see* entry 4205.
Elkwallow Trail *see* entry 4404.

4256 **Elm Hill**, Virginia Commission of Game and Inland Fisheries, 4010 W. Broad St., Richmond, VA 23230, (804) 367-0939. (GFC)

Elmore Trail *see* entry 4316.
Encampment Trail *see* entry 4372.
Exercise Trail *see* entry 4357.

4257 **Fair Oaks Nature Trail**, Fair Oaks at the Pottery Holiday Travel Park, 901 Lightfoot Rd., Williamsburg, VA 23185, (804) 565-2101. (VCD)

4258 **Fairfax County Parks**, 4030 Hummer Rd., Annandale, VA 22003, (703) 941-5000. Named trails: Braddock Road Park Service 3.2, Center 0.3(s), Duff and Stuff 0.2(l), Holmes Run Stream Valley I 1.3, Holmes Run Stream Valley III 1.2, Old Oak Nature 0.3(l), Paw Paw Passage 1.2(l), Potomac Heritage 1.7(s), Scott Run 2.9(l), Upland, Wakefield-Accotink 6.1(s), Waverly-Wolftrap (a/k/a Wolfstream Valley) 1.0(s). (DMV)

4259 **Fairview Trail**, Fredericksburg and Spotsylvania National Military Park, P.O. Box 679, Fredericksburg, VA 22401, (703) 373-4461. (HOD)

4260 **Fairy Stone State Park**, Rt. 2, Box 134, Stuart, VA 24171, (703) 930-2424. 15.0 miles. Named trails: Dam Spillway 1.0(l), Handicapped 0.1(s), Iron Mine 1.0(l), Oak Hickory 1.3(l), Stuart's Knob 1.7(l), Whiskey Run 2.0(l). (WCD; ATM; MMA; HOD; GNA)

Falling River Trail *see* entry 4210.
Fallingwater Cascades Trail *see* entry 4205.
Falls Hollow Trail *see* entry 4279.
Falls Ridge Trail *see* entry 4279.

4261 **False Cape State Park**, P.O. Box 6273, Virginia Beach, VA 23456, (804) 426-7128. 7.0 miles. (ATM; AMC; HOD)

Farm to Forest Trail *see* entry 4388.
Fat Pat Trail *see* entry 4279.

VIRGINIA

Feathercamp Branch Trail *see* entry 4316.
Feathercamp Ridge Trail *see* entry 4316.
Federal Line Trail *see* entry 4270.
Fenwick Nature Trail *see* entry 4316.
Fern Pass Trail *see* entry 4344.
Ferrier Trail *see* entry 4316.
Ferris Hollow Trail *see* entry 4279.
Fescue Trail *see* entry 4385.
Fire Pink Trail *see* entry 4422.
Fire Trail *see* entry 4189.
Fire Trail *see* entry 4236.
Fire Trail *see* entry 4349.
4262 **First Settlers' Campground of Williamsburg**, P.O. Box 3507, Williamsburg, VA 23187, (804) 229-4900. (VCD)
Fishing Barge Trail *see* entry 4373.
Flat Rock Trail *see* entry 4205.
Flat Top Trail *see* entry 4205.
Florida Maple Trail *see* entry 4411.
Fore Mountain Trail *see* entry 4279.
Forest Trail *see* entry 4393.
Forest Trail 24 *see* entry 4243.
Fork Mountain Road *see* entry 4404.
Fork Mountain Trail *see* entry 4404.
4263 **Fort A.P. Hill Nature Trail**, Adjutant, Hqs U.S. Army Garrison, Fort A.P. Hill, Bowling Green, VA 22427, (804) 633-5041. 0.5 mile. (HOD)
4264 **Fort Chiswell RV Campground**, Rt. 2, Box 426A, Fort Chiswell, VA 24360, (703) 637-6868 or (800) 972-3345. (WCD; VCD)
Fort Darling Trail *see* entry 4392.
Fort Harrison Trail *see* entry 4392.
4265 **Fountainhead Regional Park**, Hampton Rd., Lorton, VA 22079, (703) 250-9124. 3.0 miles. (GPW)
Fox Hollow Nature Trail *see* entry 4404.
Fox Run Trail *see* entry 4400.
4266 **Fox Trail Campground**, SR 683, Fancy Gap, VA 24328, (703) 728-7776. (WCD)
Fragrance Garden Trail *see* entry 4359.
Fragrance Trail *see* entry 4225.
4267 **Franklin County Nature Trail**, Franklin County Recreation Department, Rt. 2, Box 98-A, Rocky Mount, VA 24151, (703) 483-9293. 1.2 miles loop. (HOD)
Franklin Trail *see* entry 4385.
4268 **Fraser Preserve Nature Trail**, 2636 Marcey Rd., Arlington, VA 22207, (703) 528-5547. 1.0 mile. (NWA)
4269 **Fredericksburg Historic Trail**, Fredericksburg Department of Tourism, 706 Caroline St., Fredericksburg, VA 22401. 7.0 miles loop. Awards available. (SAR 1993)
4270 **Fredericksburg and Spotsylvania National Military Park**, Scout Troop 847, c/o Tabernacle United Methodist Church, 7310-A Old Plank Rd., Fredericksburg, VA 22401. Named trails: Federal Line 2.5(s), Hazel Grove 1.0(l), Lee Drive 5.0(s), Spotsylvania Court House 7.0(l), Sunken Road 0.2(l). Awards available. (SAR 1993)
4271 **Fredericksburg Parks**, Fredericksburg Department of Parks and Recreation, 408 Canal St., Fredericksburg, VA 22401, (703) 373-9411. Named trails: Motts Run 2.0(l), Rappahannock River 14.0(s). (HOD)
Fridley Gap Trail *see* entry 4279.
4272 **Front Royal KOA**, P.O. Box 274, Front Royal, VA 22630, (703) 635-2741 or (800) 248-0828. (VCD)
Furnace Mountain Summit Trail *see* entry 4404.
Furnace Mountain Trail *see* entry 4404.
Furnace Spring Trail *see* entry 4404.
4273 **G.R. Thompson Area**, Virginia Commission of Game and Inland Fisheries, 4010 W. Broad St., Richmond, VA 23230, (804) 367-0939. (GFC)
Gap Creek Trail *see* entry 4279.
Gap Run Trail *see* entry 4404.
Garden Walk *see* entry 4345.
Gasline Road Trail *see* entry 4404.
4274 **Gatewood Park**, P.O. Box 660, Pulaski, VA 24301. (VCD)
4275 **Gathright Lake Project**, P.O. Box 432, Covington, VA 24426, (703) 962-1138. (GNA)
4276 **Gathright Wildlife Management Area**, U.S. Forest Service, Warm Springs

Ranger District, Rt. 2 Box 30, Hot Springs, VA 24445, (540) 839-2521. (GNA) **Geological Trail** *see* entry 4208. **Geology Interpretive Trail** *see* entry 4393.

4277 George Washington Birthplace National Monument, Rt. 1, Box 717, Washington's Birthplace, VA 22575. (NPS)

4278 George Washington Memorial Parkway, Turkey Run Park, McLean, VA 22101, (804) 285-2591. Named trails: Mount Vernon 17.0(s), Old Carriage 4.1(s), Patowmack Canal 0.8(s), Ridge 3.3(s), River 3.8(s). (SAR 1993)

4279 George Washington National Forest, Deerfield Ranger District, 2304 Beverley St., P.O. Box 419, Staunton, VA 24401, (703) 885-8028; Named trails: Back Draft 3.2, Bald Ridge 8.3(s), Bolshers Run, Braley Branch 1.9(s), Braley Pond Loop 0.6(l), Brushy Ridge 0.9(s), Chestnut Flat Spring 0.3(s), Chimney Hollow 3.5(s), Cold Spring 2.2(s), Crawford Knob 3.2(s), Crawford Mountain 7.8(s), Dowell's Draft 4.5(s), Falls Hollow 6.0(l), Ferris Hollow 1.7(s), Hardscrabble Knob 0.4(s), Jerkemtight Creek 4.2(s), Jerry's Run 3.8(s), Marshall Draft 1.3(s), Mill Mountain 8.3(s), Nelson Draft 1.0(s), North Mountain/North 14.5(s), Ramsey's Draft 13.0(l), Ramsey's Draft Nature 1.0(l), Shaw's Ridge 6.3(s), Shenandoah Mountain 14.2(l), Shenandoah Mountain/South 23.6(s), Signal Corps Knob 1.9(s), Sinclair Hollow 1.6(s), Taylor Hollow, Walker Mountain 13.7(s), White Oak, White Oak Draft 7.5(s). Dry River Ranger District, 510 N. Main St., Bridgewater, VA 22812, (703) 828-2591; Named trails: Bear Draft 3.0(s), Big Hollow 1.7(s), Blueberry 3.0(s), Buckwheat Mountain Jeep, California Ridge 4.6(s), Crooms Ridge (a/k/a Big Ridge) 4.0(s), Hone Quarry Ridge 8.0(s), Mines Run 3.0, Mud Pond Gap 2.0(s), North River Gorge 5.0(s), Rocky Run Jeep, Sand Spring Mountain 3.0(s), Slate Springs Circuit 12.0(l) & 15.0(l), Slate Springs Mountain, Springhouse Ridge 1.3(s), Timber Ridge 7.0(s), Todd Lake 0.5(s), Trimble Mountain 3.8(l), Wild Oak (f/k/a Chestnut Ridge, Hankey Mountain, and Lookout Mountain) 25.6(l), Wolf Ridge 5.0(s). James River Ranger District, 313 S. Monroe St., Covington, VA 22426, (703) 962-2214; Named trails: Anthony Knobs 1.5(s), Big Mama, Blue Suck 1.5(s), Cock's Comb 0.5(s), Dry Run 3.4(s), Eastern National Children's Forest 0.3(l), Fat Pat, Fore Mountain 14.8(s), Jingling Rocks 3.0(l), Middle Mountain 8.8(s), Morning Knob Tower 3.4(l), North Mountain/Central 11.0(s), Oliver Mountain 2.5 & 7.5, Rich Hole 5.7(s), White Rock Tower 3.7(s), YACC's Run 1.8(s). Lee Ranger District, Windsor Knit Rd., Rt. 1, Box 31-A, Edinburg, VA 22824, (703) 984-4101; Named trails: Bear Wallow Spur 0.5(s), Big Blue (a/k/a Pond Run), Big Blue-Bearwallow 4.4(s), Big Schloss 0.3(s), Bird Knob 2.2(s), Boone Run 1.7(s), Buzzard Rock 1.6(s), Cedar Creek 2.8(s), Charcoal-Passage Creek 0.6(l), Duncan Hollow 9.1(s), Falls Ridge, Fridley Gap 2.8(s), Gap Creek 2.0(s), Glass House, Habron Gap 1.4(s), Hunkerson Gap 3.1(s), Indian Grave Ridge 2.5(s), Kennedy Peak 0.3(s), Laurel Run 3.2(s), Laurel Spur 2.6(s), Lion's Tail 0.3(l), Little Sluice 4.8(s), Little Stony Creek, Massanutten East 23.1(s), Massanutten Mountain West (a/k/a Powell's Mountain) 11.5(s), Massanutten South 16.4(s), Milford Gap 4.7(s), Morgan Run 1.4(s), Orkney Springs 3.7(s), Pig Iron 0.2(l), Pitt Spring Lookout 0.3(s), Roaring Run 5.9(s), Scothorn Gap 1.5(s), Shawl Gap 2.4(s), Shelton, Signal Knob, Snyder 1.3(s), Stack Rock 1.5(s), Stephens, Taskers Gap 4.5(s), Tibbet Knob 3.3(s), Tolliver 2.3(s), Veach Gap 0.9(s), Wagon Road 1.3(l), Waterfall Mountain 1.3(s). Pedlar Ranger District, 2424 Magnolia Ave., Buena Vista, VA 24416, (703) 261-6105; Named trails: Bald Mountain 2.5(s), Beards Mountain, Belle Cove 9.2(l), Cellar Mountain 5.8(l), Cliff 0.7(s), Crabtree Falls 2.9(s), Elephant Man 2.4(l), Indian Gap 2.6(s), Kennedy Ridge, Lakeside 1.0(s), Little Rocky Row Run 2.7(s), Mills Creek 7.1(s), Mills Creek Spur 0.8(s), Mine Bank 2.0(s), Mount Pleasant 5.7(l), Mountain Top, Pompey Loop 1.0(l), Reservoir

Hollow 2.3(s), Saddle Gap 1.5(s), St. Mary's 1.4(s), St. Mary's Falls 3.6(s), Slacks Overlook 2.6(s), Stony Hill Loop 0.2(l), Stony Run Jeep 0.6(s), Torry Ridge 3.1(s), Torry Ridge Spur 0.6(s), Upper Lake 0.6(l), White Rocks Gap 2.5(s). Warm Springs Ranger District, Rt. 2, Box 30, Hot Springs, VA 24445, (703) 839-2521; Named trails: Back Creek Gorge 2.4(l), Bear Rock 1.4(s), Bearwallow Run 1.4(s), Bogan Run 0.3(s), Brushy Ridge 3.9(s), Buck Run, Buck Run Spur 0.6(s), Christian Run 1.5(s), Cold Springs Run 1.3(s), Crane 3.0(l), Gilliam Run 2.0(s), Hidden Valley 6.2(s), Laurel Fork, Little Mare Mountain 6.0(s), Little Mare Mountain Spur 0.7(s), Locust Spring Run 3.1(s), Locust Spring Run Spur, Middle Mountain 5.5(s), Mill Mountain 1.0(s), Muddy Run 1.1(s), Ore Bank 1.2(s), Paddy Knob 4.7(s), Paddy Knob Spur 1.2(s), Piney Mountain 3.0(s), Rock Shelter 2.6(s), Salt Pond Ridge 3.3(s), Salt Stump, Sandy Gap 3.4(s), Slabcamp Run 3.0(s), Stony Run 4.5(s), Tower Hill Mountain 2.4(s), Warm Springs Mountain 10.0(s). (LGU; WCD; EGH; ATM; GOP; GFC; MMA; AMI; FGU; HOD; GNA; NFG; SAP)

Gibson Gap Trail *see* entry 4242.
Gilliam Run Trail *see* entry 4279.
Glass House Trail *see* entry 4279.
Glen Cove Nature Trail *see* entry 4397.
Glen Maury Nature Trail *see* entry 4280.

4280 **Glen Maury Park**, Buena Vista, VA 24416, (703) 261-7321. Named trails: Glen Maury Nature 2.2(l). (WCD; HOD)

Glencarlyn Park Trail *see* entry 4193.
Glenvar Nature Preservation Trail *see* entry 4397.
Goodwin Lake Trail *see* entry 4281.

4281 **Goodwin Lake-Prince Edward State Park**, Rt. 2, Box 70, Green Bay, VA 23942, (804) 392-3435. Named trails: Goodwin Lake 1.0(l), Otter's Path 2.4(l), Twin Beech 0.5. (HOD)

4282 **Goose Dam Campground**, SR 724, Sydnorsville, VA 24151, (703) 483-2100. (WCD)

Goose Point Trail *see* entry 4373.

4283 **Goshen-Little North Mountain Wildlife Management Area**, P.O. Box 32, Swoope, VA 24479, (703) 885-1702. Named trails: Guys Run 7.8(s), Laurel Run 4.2(l), Little North Mountain 11.4(s), Meadow Ground 2.1(s), Piney Mountain 2.0(s). (GFC; HOD)

Grand Cavern Nature Trail *see* entry 4284.

4284 **Grand Caverns Regional Park**, Grottoes, VA 24441, (703) 249-5705. Named trails: Grand Cavern Nature 0.8(l). (ATM; HOD)

4285 **Grandview Preserve Trail**, Department of Recreation, City Hall, Hampton, VA 23369, (804) 727-6197. 4.5 miles loop. (HOD)

Grassy Branch Trail *see* entry 4316.
Grassy Overlook Trail *see* entry 4208.
Gravel Springs Hut Trail *see* entry 4404.
Graves Mill Trail *see* entry 4404.

4286 **Grayson County Nature Trail**, Grayson County Recreation Department, P.O. Box 358, Independence, VA 24348, (703) 773-2471. 0.8 mile loop. (HOD)

4287 **Grayson Highlands State Park**, Rt. 2, Box 141, Mouth of Wilson, VA 24363, (703) 579-7092. Named trails: Big Pinnacle, Cabin Creek Nature 1.9(l), Listening Rock 1.8(l), Rhododendron, Rock House Ridge 1.8(l), Stampers Branch, Twin Pinnacles, Wilson Creek 4.4(s). (WCD; ATM; MMA; HOD; GNA)

4288 **Great Falls Park**, 9200 Old Dominion Dr., Great Falls, VA 22066, (703) 759-2915. 6.0 miles. Named trails: Ridge, River. (ATM; NPS; CGA; AMI; GNA; NWA)

Green Leaf Nature Trail *see* entry 4242.
Green Trail *see* entry 4384.
Greenstone Trail *see* entry 4205.
Ground Pine Nature Trail *see* entry 4377.
Groundhog Mountain Picnic Area Observation Tower Trail *see* entry 4205.

4289 **Groundhog Trail**, Kanawha Trail

Club, c/o Natural Bridge Appalachian Trail Club, P.O. Box 3012, Lynchburg, VA 24503. (BMG)
Grouse Trail see entry 4316.
Guest Lodge Trail see entry 4251.
4290 Gulf Branch Nature Center, 3608 N. Military Rd., Arlington, VA 22207, (703) 558-2340. Named trails: Stream Valley 0.75, Woodland 0.5. (NWA)
Gulf Branch Nature Trail see entry 4193.
Gunter Ridge Trail see entry 4205.
Gunter Ridge Trail see entry 4316.
Guys Run Trail see entry 4283.
Habron Gap Trail see entry 4279.
Hale Lake Trail see entry 4316.
Hammond Hollow Trail see entry 4205.
Hammond Hollow Trail see entry 4316.
Handicapped Trail see entry 4260.
Hankey Mountain Trail see entry 4279.
Hannah Run Trail see entry 4404.
4291 Hanover County, Director of Parks and Recreation, Hanover Courthouse, Hanover, VA 23069, (804) 798-6091. Named trails: NRM Nature, Patrick Henry Cross-Country. (HOD)
Hardscrabble Knob Trail see entry 4279.
4292 Hardware River, Virginia Commission of Game and Inland Fisheries, 4010 W. Broad St., Richmond, VA 23230, (804) 367-0939. (GFC)
Hardwood Cove Nature Trail see entry 4205.
Harkening Hill Trail see entry 4205.
4293 Harpers Ferry Camp Resort, Rt. 3, Box 1300, Harpers Ferry, WV 25425, (304) 535-6895. (VCD)
Harris Hollow Trail see entry 4404.
Harrison Creek Trail see entry 4372.
4294 Harrisonburg Newmarket KOA, Rt. 3, Box 133-1A, Broadway, VA 22815, (703) 896-8929. (VCD)
Harvey's Knob Trail see entry 4205.
4295 Havens Wildlife Management Area, Virginia Commission of Game and Inland Fisheries, 4010 W. Broad St., Richmond, VA 23230, (804) 367-0939. (GFC)

Hawksbill Mountain Trail see entry 4404.
Hazel Grove Trail see entry 4270.
Hazel Mountain Trail see entry 4404.
Hazel River Trail see entry 4404.
Hazel Spur Trail see entry 4404.
Heiskell Hollow Trail see entry 4404.
Helms Trail see entry 4316.
Helton Creek Loop Trail see entry 4316.
Hemlock Overlook Trail see entry 4361.
Hemlock Trail see entry 4361.
Henley Hollow Trail see entry 4316.
Henry Hill Trail see entry 4342.
Hensley Church Trail see entry 4404.
4296 Hiawatha Nature Trail, Area Supervisor, WMA, Rt. 1, Box 76-G, Chatham, VA 24531, (804) 432-1377. 1.1 miles loop. (HOD)
Hickerson Hollow Trail see entry 4404.
4297 Hickory Hollow Trail, Parks and Recreation Department, P.O. Box 167, Lancaster, VA 22503, (804) 462-5220. 4.0 miles loop. (HOD)
Hickory Pass Trail see entry 4344.
Hidden Valley Trail see entry 4279.
4298 Hidden Valley Wildlife Management Area, Rt. E, Box 25, Monterey, VA 24465, (703) 468-2419. Named trails: Brumley Creek 6.0(l), Brumley Rim 3.0(s), Long Arm Hollow 9.5(l). (GFC; HOD)
High Dune Trail see entry 4400.
High Knob Lake Shore Trail see entry 4316.
High Knob Trail see entry 4316.
4299 High Top Fire Trail, Area Supervisor, WMA, Bacova, VA 24412, (703) 839-2635. (HOD)
4300 Highland Wildlife Management Area, Rt. E, Box 25, Monterey, VA 24465, (703) 468-2419. Named trails: Bullpasture Mountain 7.0(l), CCC Fire 10.0(l). (HOD)
Hightop Hut Trail see entry 4404.
Hightop Road Trail see entry 4404.
Historic Walk see entry 4345.

4301 **Hog Island Wildlife Management Area**, c/o Virginia Commission of Game and Inland Fisheries, 4010 W. Broad St., Richmond, VA 23230, (804) 367-0939. (GFC; AMC)

Hogback Spur Trail see entry 4404.

4302 **Holiday Lake State Park**, Rt. 2, Box 230, Appomattox, VA 24522, (804) 248-6308. Named trails: Lake Shore Nature 4.7(l). (WCD; ATM; MMA; HOD; GNA)

4303 **Holiday Trav-L-Park** see entry 4200. (WCD)

4304 **Hollins College Historical Walk**, Hollins College Information Office, Hollins College, VA 24020, (703) 362-6000. 1.4 miles loop. (HOD)

Hollow Trail see entry 4349.

Holly Trail see entry 4385.

Holmes Run Stream Valley I & III Trails see entry 4258.

Hone Quarry Ridge Trail see entry 4279.

Honey Tree Spur Trail see entry 4242.

Hoop Hole Trail see entry 4316.

Hopkins Branch Trail see entry 4360.

Horse Heaven Trail see entry 4316.

4305 **Horseshoe Campground**, SR 658, Draper, VA 24324, (703) 980-0278. (WCD)

Hot Mountain-Short Mountain Trail see entry 4404.

Huckleberry Line Trail see entry 4202.

Huckleberry Ridge Trail see entry 4316.

Huffs Trail see entry 4251.

Huguenot Bridge Trail see entry 4393.

Hull School Trail see entry 4404.

Humpback Mountain Trail see entry 4205.

4306 **Hungry Mother State Park**, Rt. 5, Box 109, Marion, VA 24354, (703) 783-3422. 15.0 miles. Named trails: CCC 3.1(s), Lake, Molly's Knob, Molly's Pioneer 0.6(l), Old Shawnee 0.4(l), Raider's Run 1.1(l), Ridge 0.7(s), Spillway 1.1(s). (ATM; MMA; HOD; GNA)

Hunkerson Gap Trail see entry 4279.

Hunting Creek Trail see entry 4205.

Hunting Creek Trail see entry 4316.

4307 **Huntley Meadows State Park**, Public Information Officer, Fairfax County Park Authority, 4030 Hummer Rd., Annandale, VA 22003, (703) 941-5008; or Huntley Meadows State Park, 3701 Lockheed Blvd., Alexandria, VA 22310, (703) 768-2525. (NWA)

Hurricane Creek Trail see entry 4316.

Indian Creek Trail see entry 4225.

Indian Gap Trail see entry 4205.

Indian Gap Trail see entry 4279.

Indian Grave Ridge Trail see entry 4279.

Indian Run PATC Maintenance Hut Trail see entry 4404.

Indian Run Trail see entry 4404.

4308 **Indiantown Nature Trail**, Director, Northampton County Parks and Recreation Department, P.O. Box 847, Eastville, VA 23347, (804) 678-5179. 1.5 miles loop. (HOD)

Iron Mine Trail see entry 4260.

Iron Mountain Trail see entry 4316.

Iron Ore Trail see entry 4316.

4309 **Ivy Creek Natural Area**, Ivy Creek Foundation, P.O. Box 956, Charlottesville, VA 22902, (804) 973-7772. Named trails: White. (AMI)

Ivy Creek PATC Maintenance Trail see entry 4404.

Jack-O-Lantern Branch Trail see entry 4207.

4310 **Jackson Trail**, Fredericksburg and Spotsylvania National Military Park, P.O. Box 679, Fredericksburg, VA 22401, (703) 373-4461. 10.9 miles straight. (HOD)

4311 **James Monroe Historical Trail**, American Historical Trails, Inc., P.O. Box 769, Monroe, NC 28111-0769, (704) 547-1854; or Ash Lawn-Highland, Rt. 6, Box 37, Charlottesville, VA 22901, (804) 293-9539. 2.0-4.0 miles loop. Awards available. (SAR 1993)

4312 **James River Park**, W. 22nd St. and Riverside Dr., Richmond, VA 23225; or Virginia Commission of Game and Inland

Fisheries, 4010 W. Broad St., Richmond, VA 23230, (804) 367-0939. (GFC)

4313 **James River Recreation Area**, P.O. Box 266, Natural Bridge Station, VA 24579, (703) 291-2727. (WCD; VCD)

James River Trail see entry 4205.

4314 **Jamestown Beach Nature Trail**, Jamestown Beach Campsites, P.O. Box CB, Williamsburg, VA 23187, (804) 229-7609. (VCD)

4315 **Jamestown Colony Trail**, Peninsula Council, BSA, 11725 Jefferson Ave., Newport News, VA 23606, (804) 595-3356 or (804) 877-5085. 5.5 miles loop. Awards available. (SAR 1993)

Jamison Mill Trail see entry 4373.

4316 **Jefferson National Forest.** 600 miles. Blacksburg Ranger District, Rt. 1, Box 404, Blacksburg, VA 24060, (703) 552-4641; Named trails: Allegheny 12.0(s), Cascades 3.8(s), Huckleberry Ridge 8.0(l), John's Creek 6.0(l), John's Creek Mountain 3.5(s), Old Chestnut 2.6(s), Pandapas Pond 1.0(l), Potts Mountain 6.8(s), Ribble 2.5(s), Virginia's Nature 1.5(l), War Spur 1.8(s). Clinch Ranger District, Rt. 1, Box 320-H, Wise, VA 24293, (703) 328-2931; Named trails: Bark Camp Lake 3.2(l), High Knob 3.0(l), High Knob Lake Shore 0.5(s), Keokee 1.0(s), Kitchen Rock 0.5(l), Little Stony Creek 2.8(s), Mountain Fork 2.0(s), Olinger 3.0(s), Pine Mountain 22.8(s), Stone Mountain 15.0(s). Glenwood Ranger District, P.O. Box 8, Natural Bridge Station, VA 24579, (703) 291-2189; Named trails: Apple Orchard Falls/West 3.4(s), Balcony Falls 4.1(s), Belfast 5.6(s), Black's Creek 3.0(l), Buchanan 1.6(s), Cornelius 5.8(s), Cove Mountain 1.8(s), Curry Creek 6.2(l), Gunter Ridge 9.2(s), Hammond Hollow 2.0(s), Hunting Creek 3.5(s), Little Cove Mountain 2.8(s), North Mountain 5.0(s), Piney Ridge 7.0(s), Spec Mines 2.8(s), Sulphur Spring 6.6(s), Wildcat Mountain 3.8(l). Mt. Rogers National Recreation Area, Rt. 1, Box 303, Marion, VA 24354, (703) 783-5196; Named trails: Beartree Gap 1.2(l), Beech Grove 3.4(s), Chestnut Ridge 1.8(s), Cliffside, Comers Creek 8.3(l), Creasy Hollow 3.5(s), Dickey Gap 0.5(s), Dickey Knob 4.0(l), Divide 1.0(s), Feathercamp Branch 2.5(s), Feathercamp Ridge 0.2(s), Grassy Branch, Hale Lake 0.4(s), Helton Creek Loop 4.0(l), Henley Hollow, Horse Heaven 3.3(s), Hurricane Creek 0.6(s), Iron Mountain 9.7(s), Lewis Fork 3.5(s), Little Dry Run 3.0(s), Little Mountain 2.5(s), Lum Martin 1.1(s), Mount Rogers National Recreation 4.0(s), Mullins Branch 2.4(s), Perkins Knob, Raccoon Branch 3.3(s), Rhododendron, Rush 1.5(l), Shaw Gap 1.6(l), Straight Branch 1.5(s), Sugar Maple Loop 4.5(l), Virginia Creeper 4.2(s), Virginia Highlands Horse 1.8(s), Whispering Water 0.5(l), Wright 3.4(s). New Castle Ranger District, P.O. Box 246, New Castle, VA 24127, (703) 864-5195; Named trails: Branch, Craig Creek 2.1(l), Deer 1.6(s), Dragon's Tooth 1.2(s), Elmore 1.5(s), Fenwick Nature 0.7(l), Ferrier 2.6(s), Grouse 1.0(s), Helms 0.5(s), Hoop Hole 3.4(s), Iron Ore 5.2(l), Kelly 1.6(s), Lick Branch 5.0(s), Lignite 7.6(l), North Mountain/South 13.2(s), Patterson Mountain 4.8(l), Potts Mountain/East 6.8(s), Potts Mountain/West 11.5(s), Price Mountain 6.5(s), Price-Broad Mountain 4.8(s), Roaring Run 1.4(l), Sulphur Ridge 2.1(s), Tucker 1.0(s), Turkey 1.6(s), Unaka Nature 1.0(l). Wythe Ranger District, Rt. 4, Wytheville, VA 24382, (703) 228-5551; Named trails: Punch and Judy Creek 10.0(l), Stony Fork 1.5(l). Other trails: Whitetop-Laurel Creek Circuit 11.5(l). (EGH; ATM; FTS; GFC; MMA; GFA; FGU; HOD; GNA; NFG)

Jenkins Gap Trail see entry 4404.

Jeremys Run Trail see entry 4404.

Jericho Ditch Trail see entry 4249.

Jerkemtight Creek Trail see entry 4279.

Jerry's Run Trail see entry 4279.

Jingling Rocks Trail see entry 4279.

4317 **John H. Kerr Reservoir**, Rt. 1, Box 76, Boydston, VA 23917, (804) 738-6662. Named trails: Liberty Hill 0.7(l). (HOD; GNA)

4318 **John W. Flannagan Reservoir**, Public Affairs Officer, U.S. Army Engineer, Huntington District, P.O. Box 2127, Huntington, WV 25721; or John W. Flannagan

Reservoir, Rt. 1, Box 268, Haysi, VA 24256, (703) 835-9544. 8.0 miles. (GNA; LRA)
John's Creek Mountain Trail *see* entry 4316.
John's Creek Trail *see* entry 4316.
Johnson Farm Loop Trail *see* entry 4205.
Jones Mountain Cabin Trail *see* entry 4404.
Jones Mountain Trail *see* entry 4404.
Jordan River Trail *see* entry 4404.
Kelly Trail *see* entry 4316.
Kemp Hollow Trail *see* entry 4404.
Kennedy Peak Trail *see* entry 4279.
Kennedy Ridge Trail *see* entry 4279.
Keokee Trail *see* entry 4316.
Keyser Run (Fire Rd.) Trail *see* entry 4404.
4319 **Kin Kaid Kampground**, 559 Rochambeau Dr., Williamsburg, VA 23188, (804) 565-2010. (VCD)
King Fisher Trail *see* entry 4400.
4320 **Kiptopeke State Park**, SR 13, Cape Charles, VA 23310, (804) 331-2267. (WCD)
Kitchen Rock Trail *see* entry 4316.
Knob Mountain Cutoff Trail *see* entry 4404.
Knob Mountain Trail *see* entry 4404.
4321 **KOA-Harrisonburg/New Market**, SR 608, New Market, VA 22844, (703) 896-8929. (WCD)
4322 **KOA-Shenandoah Valley**, P.O. Box 98, Verona, VA 24482, (703) 248-2746. (WCD)
4323 **KOA-Woodburne**, SR 619, Talleysville, VA 23124, (804) 932-4776. (WCD)
Lagoon Trail *see* entry 4400.
4324 **Lake Accotink Park**, Kirk Kincannon, Park Specialist III, Lake Accotink Park, c/o Fairfax County Park Authority, 3701 Pender Dr., Fairfax, VA 22030, (703) 569-0285. Named trails: Accotink 3.75(s). (GRT; ATM)
4325 **Lake Anna State Park**, SR 108, Fredericksburg, VA 22404. (ATM)
4326 **Lake Fairfax Park**, 1400 Lake Fairfax Dr., Reston, VA 22090, (703) 471-5414. (MMA; NWA)
4327 **Lake Maury Trail**, Superintendent of Buildings and Grounds, Mariners Museum, Museum Dr., Newport News, VA 23601, (804) 595-0368. 7.0 miles. (HOD)
4328 **Lake Nelson Campground**, Rt. 1, Box 146, Arrington, VA 22922, (804) 263-4345. (VCD)
Lake Shore Nature Trail *see* entry 4302.
Lake Trail *see* entry 4186.
Lake Trail *see* entry 4189.
Lake Trail *see* entry 4208.
Lake Trail *see* entry 4210.
Lake Trail *see* entry 4306.
Lakeside Trail *see* entry 4199.
Lakeside Trail *see* entry 4279.
Lakeside Trail *see* entry 4360.
Lands Run (Fire Rd.) Trail *see* entry 4404.
Laurel Bed Creek Trail *see* entry 4236.
Laurel Branch Trail *see* entry 4208.
Laurel Fork Trail *see* entry 4279.
Laurel Fork Trail *see* entry 4360.
Laurel Point Trail *see* entry 4430.
Laurel Prong Trail *see* entry 4404.
4329 **Laurel Run Trail**, Parks and Recreation, Washington Bldg., 8th and Franklin Sts., Richmond, VA 23219, (804) 786-1405. 4.0 miles loop. (HOD)
Laurel Run Trail *see* entry 4279.
Laurel Run Trail *see* entry 4283.
Laurel Spur Trail *see* entry 4279.
Leading Ridge Trail *see* entry 4404.
4330 **Lee District Park**, 6601 Telegraph Rd., Alexandria, VA 22210, (703) 922-9840. (GPW)
Lee Drive Trail *see* entry 4270.
4331 **Lengland Camping**, Rt. 2, Stuart, VA 24171, (703) 930-2739. (VCD)
Lewis Falls Spur Trail *see* entry 4404.
Lewis Fork Trail *see* entry 4316.
Lewis Hollow Trail *see* entry 4242.
Lewis Mountain East Trail *see* entry 4404.
Lewis Mountain West Trail *see* entry 4404.
Lewis Peak Trail *see* entry 4404.
Lewis Spring Falls Trail *see* entry 4404.

4332 **Lexington Area**, Visitor Information Center, 102 E. Washington St., Lexington, VA 24450, (703) 463-3777. Named trails: Lee-Jackson and VMI-Marshall Tour 2.0(l), Woods Creek Park 1.3(s). (HOD)

4333 **Lexington Historic Trail**, Boy Scout Troop 122, c/o Hebron Presbyterian Church, Rt. 1, Box 58, Staunton, VA 24401; or Lexington Visitor Center, 102 E. Washington St., Lexington, VA 24450, (703) 463-3777. 4.0 miles loop. Awards available. (SAR 1993)

Liberty Hill Trail *see* entry 4317.
Lick Branch Trail *see* entry 4316.
Lighthouse Trail *see* entry 4230.
Lignite Trail *see* entry 4316.
Limberlost Trail *see* entry 4404.
Linville Falls Trail *see* entry 4205.
Lion's Tail Trail *see* entry 4279.
Listening Rock Trail *see* entry 4287.
Little Cove Mountain Trail *see* entry 4205.
Little Cove Mountain Trail *see* entry 4316.
Little Devil Stairs Trail *see* entry 4404.
Little Dry Run Trail *see* entry 4316.
Little Mare Mountain Spur Trail *see* entry 4279.
Little Mountain Trail *see* entry 4316.
Little North Mountain Trail *see* entry 4283.
Little Rocky Row Run Trail *see* entry 4279.
Little Rocky Row Trail *see* entry 4205.
Little Sluice Trail *see* entry 4279.
Little Stony Creek Trail *see* entry 4279.
Little Stony Creek Trail *see* entry 4316.
Little Stony Man Trail *see* entry 4404.
Little Tumbling Creek Trail *see* entry 4236.
Living Forest Trail *see* entry 4388.
Loblolly Trail *see* entry 4409.
Locust Gap Trail *see* entry 4251.
Locust Spring Run Spur Trail *see* entry 4279.
Locust Spring Run Trail *see* entry 4279.
Lone Star Lakes Nature Trail *see* entry 4411.
Long Arm Hollow Trail *see* entry 4298.

4334 **Long Branch Nature Center**, 625 S. Carlyn Springs Rd., Arlington, VA 22204, (703) 558-2742. (NWA)

Long Branch Nature Trail *see* entry 4193.
Long Creek Trail *see* entry 4400.
Lookout Mountain Trail *see* entry 4279.
Lookout Tower Trail *see* entry 4438.
Loop Trail *see* entry 4208.
Lovington Spring Trail *see* entry 4205.
Lower Chippokes Creek Trail *see* entry 4232.
Lower Trail *see* entry 4353.

4335 **Lower Twin Campground**, Corps of Engineers—John W. Flannagan Reservoir, SR 611, Haysi, VA 24256. (WCD)

4336 **Lubber Run Park**, N. Columbus and Second Sts., Arlington, VA 22203, (703) 558-2426. (GPW)

Lubber Run Trail *see* entry 4193.
Lum Martin Trail *see* entry 4316.

4337 **Lunga Park**, MCB 4, Quantico, VA 22134, (703) 640-5270. (WCD)

4338 **Lynchburg Area**, Lynchburg Department of Recreation and Parks, P.O. Box 60, Lynchburg, VA 24505, (704) 847-1484. Named trails: Alpine 0.25, Blackwater Creek 8.6(s), Creek Loop 1.0(l), Upper Loop 1.2(l). (HOD)

4339 **Lynchburg College Botanical Trail**, Biology Department, Lynchburg College, Lynchburg, VA 24501, (804) 845-9071. 0.3 mile loop. (HOD)

Mabry Hill Trail *see* entry 4205.

4340 **MacKay Island National Wildlife Refuge**, P.O. Box 31, Knotts Island, NC 27950, (919) 429-3100. Named trails: Dike Road 8.0(l), Nature 1.0(l), Wildlife 0.5(l). (AMC; HOD)

Madison County Rte 649 Trail *see* entry 4404.
Madison Run Trail *see* entry 4404.
Main Trail *see* entry 4400.

4341 **Manassas Battlefield Historical Trails**, American Historical Trails, Inc., P.O. Box 769,. Monroe, NC 28110, (704) 289-1604. 7.75 and 9.1 miles loops. Awards available. (AA 1992)

4342 **Manassas National Battlefield Park**, P.O. Box 1830, Manassas, VA 22110, (703) 754-7107. Named trails: Deep Cut 1.0(l), Henry Hill 1.2(l), Stone Bridge-Van Pelt 1.4(l), Sudley Springs 1.0(l). (NPS; HOD)

Marsh Point Trail see entry 4189.
Marsh Trail see entry 4381.
Marshall Draft Trail see entry 4279.

4343 **Mason District Park**, 6621 Columbia Pike, Annandale, VA 22003, (703) 941-1730. (GPW; NWA)

4344 **Mason Neck National Wildlife Refuge**, 9502 Richmond Hwy., Suite A, Lorton, VA 22079, (703) 339-5278. Named trails: Fern Pass, Hickory Pass, Woodmarsh. (ATM; NAT; AMC; HOD; GNA; GNW)

Massanutten East Trail see entry 4279.
Massanutten Mountain West Trail see entry 4279.
Massanutten South Trail see entry 4279.
Matthews Arm Trail see entry 4404.
Mau-Har Trail see entry 4205.

4345 **Maymont Park**, Maymont Foundation, 1700 Hampton St., Richmond, VA 23220, (804) 358-7166. 4.0 miles. Named trails: Animal Walk, Garden Walk, Historic Walk, Tree Walk. (HOD)

McDaniel Hollow Trail see entry 4404.

4346 **Meadow Farm Museum/Crump Park**, Mountain Rd., Richmond, VA 23225, (804) 672-5106. (ATM)

Meadow Ground Trail see entry 4283.
Meadow School Trail see entry 4404.
Meadow Trail see entry 4393.

4347 **Meadowlark Gardens Regional Park**, 1625 Beulah Rd., Emporia, VA 23847, (804) 255-3631. (MMA)

Middle Hollow Trail see entry 4251.
Middle Mountain Trail see entry 4251.
Middle Mountain Trail see entry 4279.

Milford Gap Trail see entry 4279.
Mill Mountain Trail see entry 4279.
Mill Prong Horse Spur Trail see entry 4404.
Mill Prong Trail see entry 4404.
Millers Head Trail see entry 4404.
Mills Creek Spur Trail see entry 4279.
Mills Creek Trail see entry 4279.
Mine Bank Trail see entry 4279.

4348 **Mineral Ridge Trail**, J.T. Lewis Dickinson, Jr., 2253 Maple Ave., Buena Vista, VA 24416, (703) 261- 3495. 1.2 miles loop. (HOD)

Mines Run Trail see entry 4279.

4349 **Mint Springs Valley Park**, Albemarle County Parks and Recreation, 401 McIveire Rd., Charlottesville, VA 22901-4596, (804) 296-5845. Named trails: Big Survey 0.8(l), Fire, Hollow 0.5(s), Lake. (HOD)

Mischa Moka Trail see entry 4242.
Molly Mitchell Trail see entry 4225.
Molly's Knob Trail see entry 4306.
Molly's Pioneer Trail see entry 4306.

4350 **Monroe Bay Campground**, 551 Lafayette St., Colonial Beach, VA 22443, (804) 224-7418. (VCD)

Montvale Overlook Trail see entry 4205.
Moormans River Fire Road see entry 4404.
Moormans River Trail see entry 4404.
Morgan Run Trail see entry 4279.
Morning Knob Tower Trail see entry 4279.
Mossy Creek Trail see entry 4363.
Motts Run Trail see entry 4271.
Mount Marshall Trail see entry 4404.
Mount Pleasant Trail see entry 4279.
Mount Rogers National Recreation Trail see entry 4316.

4351 **Mount Vernon Historical Trail**, The Mount Vernon Ladies' Association, Mount Vernon, VA 22121, (703) 780-2000. 1.5 miles loop. Awards available. (SAR 1993)

Mount Vernon Trail see entry 4278.
Mountain Farm Self-Guiding Trail see entry 4205.
Mountain Fork Trail see entry 4316.

Mountain Industry Trail *see* entry 4205.
Mountain Side Trail *see* entry 4251.
Mountain Spring Trail *see* entry 4390.
Mountain Top Trail *see* entry 4251.
Mountain Top Trail *see* entry 4279.
Mud Pond Gap Trail *see* entry 4279.
Muddy Run Trail *see* entry 4279.
Mullins Branch Trail *see* entry 4316.
Muskrat Run Trail *see* entry 4446.
Naked Top Trail *see* entry 4404.
Natural Chimneys Nature Trail *see* entry 4352.
4352 **Natural Chimneys Regional Park**, SR 42, Mt. Solon, VA 22843, (703) 350-2510. Named trails: Natural Chimneys Nature 3.0(l). (WCD; VCD; ATM; MMA; OTB; HOD)
4353 **Natural Tunnel State Park**, Rt. 3, Clinchport, VA 24244, (703) 940-2674. Named trails: Lower, Tunnel Hill, Upper 0.3(s). (WCD; ATM; MMA; HOD)
Nature Trail *see* entry 4213.
Nature Trail *see* entry 4340.
Neighbor Mountain Trail *see* entry 4404.
Nelson Draft Trail *see* entry 4279.
4354 **New Point Campground**, SR 14E, New Point, VA 23145, (804) 725-5120. (WCD)
4355 **New River Community College Trail**, Information Officer, New River Community College, P.O. Box 1127, Dublin, VA 24084, (703) 674-4121. 0.8 mile loop. (HOD)
4356 **New River Trail State Park**, Anthony Slate, Chief Ranger, Rt. 1, Box 81X, Austinville, VA 24312, (703) 699-6778. 57.0 miles straight planned, current as to 40.0 miles. (GRT)
4357 **Newport News Park**, 13564 Jefferson Ave., Newport News, VA 23603, (804) 877-5211. Named trails: Exercise 0.8, Twin Forts Loop 0.7(l), White Oak Nature 4.6(l), Wynn's Mill Loop 1.1(l). (VCD; ATM; MMA; AMC; HOD)
Nicholson Hollow Trail *see* entry 4404.
Nicholson Moonshine Trail *see* entry 4404.

4358 **Nike Park**, Carrollton Nike Park, Rt. 1, Box 4, Carrollton, VA 23314, (804) 357-2291. Named trails: Nike Park Nature 0.8(l). (HOD)
Nike Park Nature Trail *see* entry 4358.
4359 **Norfolk Area**, Norfolk Department of Parks and Recreation, East Wing, City Hall, Norfolk, VA 23501, (804) 441-2400. Named trails: Fragrance Garden, R.W. Cross Nature. (HOD)
North Boundary Trail *see* entry 4186.
4360 **North Fork of Pound**, Resource Manager, North Fork of Pound Reservoir, Rt. 1, Box 369, Pound, VA 24279, (703) 796-5775. Named trails: Acorn Ridge 1.5(l), Hopkins Branch 6.6(l), Lakeside 0.5(l), Laurel Fork 0.5(s), Pine Mountain 2.3(s). (GFC; HOD)
North Mountain Trail *see* entry 4316.
North Mountain/Central Trail *see* entry 4279.
North Mountain/North Trail *see* entry 4279.
North Mountain/South Trail *see* entry 4316.
North River Gorge Trail *see* entry 4279.
4361 **Northern Virginia Regional Park Authority Trails** (not listed elsewhere), 5400 Ox Rd., Fairfax Station, VA 22039, (703) 631-0550. Named trails: Bull Run-Occoquan 17.5(s), Hemlock, Hemlock Overlook 3.0, Sweetbay. (HOD)
4362 **Northwest River Park Nature Trail**, Northwest River City Park, 1733 Indian Creek Rd., Chesapeake, VA 23322, (804) 421-3145. 6.0 miles. (WCD; VCD)
NRM Nature Trail *see* entry 4291.
Oak Hickory Trail *see* entry 4260.
4363 **Occoneechee State Park**, P.O. Box 818, US 58, Clarksville, VA 23927, (804) 374-2210. Named trails: Big Oak 1.1(l), Mossy Creek 0.7(s), Old Plantation 0.8(l), Warrior Path 0.2(s). (WCD; ATM; MMA; HOD)
Old Appalachian Trail *see* entry 4375.
Old Carriage Trail *see* entry 4278.
Old Chestnut Trail *see* entry 4316.

VIRGINIA

4364 **Old Dominion Trail**, Robert E. Lee Council, BSA, 4075 Fitzhugh Ave., Richmond, VA 23230-3935, (804) 355-4306. 7.5 miles straight. Awards available. (SAR 1992)
    Old Farm Trail see entry 4202.
    Old Hazel Trail see entry 4404.
    Old Oak Nature Trail see entry 4258.
    Old Plantation Trail see entry 4363.
    Old Rag Trail see entry 4404.
    Old Shawnee Trail see entry 4306.
    Old Skyland Road Trail see entry 4404.

4365 **"Old Town" Alexandria Historical Trail**, American Historical Trails, Inc., P.O. Box 769, Monroe, NC 28110, (704) 289-1604. 8.0 miles loop. Awards available. (SAR 1991)
    Olinger Trail see entry 4316.
    Oliver Mountain Trail see entry 4279.
    One-Mile Run Trail see entry 4404.
    Onion Mountain Loop Trail see entry 4205.

4366 **Orange and Alexandria Historical Trail**, Kirk Kincannon, Park Specialist III, Lake Accotink Park, Fairfax County Park Authority, 3701 Pender Dr., Fairfax, VA 22030, (703) 569-0285. 3.0 miles straight. (GRT)
    Ore Bank Trail see entry 4279.

4367 **Orkney Springs Campground**, P.O. Box 1, Orkney Springs, VA 22845, (703) 856-2585. (VCD)
    Orkney Springs Trail see entry 4279.
    Osmanthus Trail see entry 4400.
    Otter Creek Trail see entry 4205.
    Otter Lake Trail see entry 4205.
    Otter's Path see entry 4281.

4368 **Outdoor World Williamsburg**, 4301 Rochambeau Dr., Williamsburg, VA 23188, (804) 564-9808. (VCD)
    Oventop Mountain Trail see entry 4404.
    Overall Run Trail see entry 4404.
    Overall-Beecher Ridge Connector Trail see entry 4404.
    Overlook Trail see entry 4208.
    Overlook Trail see entry 4235.

4369 **Overmountain Victory National Historic Trail** (see separate entry **4956** in interstate section).

    Paddy Knob Spur Trail see entry 4279.
    Paddy Knob Trail see entry 4279.
    Paine Run Trail see entry 4404.
    Pakes Mill Pond Overlook Trail see entry 4205.
    Pandapas Pond Trail see entry 4316.

4370 **Park Connector Bikeway**, Travis Campbell or Steve White, Department of Planning, Operations Bldg., Room 115, 2405 Courthouse Dr., Virginia Beach, VA 23456, (804) 427-4621. 4.9 miles straight. (GRT)
    Pass Mountain Hut Trail see entry 4404.
    Pass Mountain Trail see entry 4404.
    Patowmack Canal Trail see entry 4278.
    Patrick Henry Cross-County Trail see entry 4291.
    Patterson Mountain Trail see entry 4316.
    Patterson Ridge Trail see entry 4404.
    Paw Paw Passage Trail see entry 4258.
    The Peak Trail see entry 4404.
    Peaks of Otter Picnic Area Trail see entry 4205.
    Perkins Knob Trail see entry 4316.
    Petersburg Battlefield National Recreation Trail see entry 4372.

4371 **Petersburg National Battlefield Historic Trail**, Robert E. Lee Council, BSA, 4075 Fitzhugh Ave., Richmond, VA 23230-3935, (804) 355-4306. (NHT)

4372 **Petersburg National Battlefield Park**, P.O. Box 549, Petersburg, VA 23803, (804) 732-3531. Named trails: Battery 5 Spur 1.7(l), Battery 7 1.3(l), Branch, Crater Spur 1.3(l), Encampment, Harrison Creek 0.6(s), Petersburg Battlefield National Recreation 7.0(l). (PGF; NPS; NPE; CGA; HOD)

4373 **Philpott Lake and Park**, Rt. 6, Box 140, Bassett, VA 24055, (703) 629-2703. Named trails: Fishing Barge 1.6(l), Goose Point 0.5(s), Jamison Mill 0.7(l), Salthouse Branch Nature 0.5(l), Smith River 1.4(l). (GFC; MMA; HOD; GNA; LRA)
    Physical Fitness Trail see entry 4227.

4374 **Picture Lake Campground**, US 1,

Petersburg, VA 23804, (804) 861-0174. (WCD)
Pig Iron Trail *see* entry 4279.
Pine Grove Forest Trail *see* entry 4388.
Pine Hill Gap Trail *see* entry 4404.
Pine Knob Trail *see* entry 4199.
Pine Mountain Trail *see* entry 4316.
Pine Mountain Trail *see* entry 4360.
Pine Ridge Trail *see* entry 4390.
Pine Ridge Trail *see* entry 4397.
Pine Trail *see* entry 4385.
Pine Tree Trail *see* entry 4251.
Pinefield Hut Trail *see* entry 4404.
Piney Branch Trail *see* entry 4404.
Piney Mountain Trail *see* entry 4279.
Piney Mountain Trail *see* entry 4283.
Piney Ridge Trail *see* entry 4316.
Piney Ridge Trail *see* entry 4404.
Pinnacle Trail *see* entry 4375.

4375 **Pinnacles Hydro Development**, Rt. 1, Box K33, Ararat, VA 24053, (703) 251-5141. Named trails: Aqueduct 6.0(l), Old Appalachian, Pinnacle 2.8(s). (HOD)

4376 **Pipsico Scout Reservation**, Tidewater Council, BSA, 1032 Heatherwood Dr., Virginia Beach, VA 23455-6675; or Pipsico Scout Reservation, Rt. 1, Box 290, Spring Grove, VA 23881, (804) 294-3912. (SFC)
Pitt Spring Lookout Trail *see* entry 4279.
Plantation Trail *see* entry 4207.
Pleasant Creek Trail *see* entry 4393.

4377 **Pocahontas State Forest and Park**, 10300 Beach Rd., Chesterfield, VA 23832, (804) 796-4255. Named trails: Awareness 0.3, Beaver Lake Nature 2.6(l), Ground Pine Nature, Third Branch. (ATM; MMA; HOD; GNA)

4378 **Pocahontas-Trojan Wildlife Management Area**, Virginia Commission of Game and Inland Fisheries, 4010 W. Broad St., Richmond, VA 23230, (804) 367-0939. (ATM; MMA; HOD; GNA)
Pocosin Cabin Trail *see* entry 4404.
Pocosin Fire Road Trail *see* entry 4404.
Pocosin Hollow Trail *see* entry 4404.
Pocosin Horse Trail *see* entry 4404.
Pocosin Trail *see* entry 4404.

4379 **Pohick Bay Regional Park**, SR 242, Woodbridge, VA 22191, (703) 339-6104; or Northern Virginia Regional Park Authority, 5400 Ox Rd., Fairfax Station, VA 22039, (703) 339-6104 or (703) 339-6100. 12.0 miles. Named trails: Blue 1.5, Bridle 3.0, Yellow 1.5. (WCD; VCD; ATM; NAT; GPW; GNA; NWA)
Pole Bridge Link Trail *see* entry 4404.
Pompey Loop Trail *see* entry 4279.
Pond Run Trail *see* entry 4279.
Pony Trail *see* entry 4230.

4380 **Poquoson Nature Trail**, Poquoson Parks and Recreation, 830 Poquoson Ave., Poquoson, VA 23662, (804) 868-7151. 0.5 mile loop. (HOD)

4381 **Portsmouth Area**, Portsmouth Parks and Recreation Department, 430 High St., Portsmouth, VA 23704, (804) 397-9403. Named trails: Marsh, Special Population 0.2. (HOD)

4382 **Portsmouth Sleepy Hole Park**, 4700 Sleepy Hole Rd., Suffolk, VA 23435. (VCD)
Possums Rest Trail *see* entry 4404.

4383 **Potomac Heritage National Scenic Trail** (see separate entry **4957** in interstate section).
Potomac Heritage Trail *see* entry 4258.

4384 **Potomac Overlook Regional Park**, Marcey Rd., Arlington, VA 22207, (703) 528-5406. Named trails: Blue 2.0, Donaldson Run 1.1, Green. (GPW; NWA)
Potts Mountain Trail *see* entry 4316.
Potts Mountain/East Trail *see* entry 4316.
Potts Mountain/West Trail *see* entry 4316.
Powell Mountain Trail *see* entry 4404.
Powell's Mountain Trail *see* entry 4279.
Power Line Trail *see* entry 4385.

4385 **Powhatan Wildlife Management Area**, Rt. 3, Box 150, Powhatan, VA 23139, (804) 598-3706. Named trails: Arrowhead, Dogwood, Fescue 2.1(s), Franklin, Holly, Pine, Power Line, Red Oak 0.7(s), Redbud, Squirrel Ridge, White Oak 0.7(s). (GFC; HOD)

4386 **Presquile National Wildlife Refuge**, P.O. Box 620, Hopewell, VA 23860, (804) 458-7541. Named trails: Presquile Nature 1.0. (AMC; HOD; GNA; GNW)
  Presquile Nature Trail *see* entry 4386.
  Price Mountain Trail *see* entry 4316.
  Price-Broad Mountain Trail *see* entry 4316.
  The Priest Overlook Trail *see* entry 4205.
4387 **Prince Edward-Gallion State Forest**, Goodwin Lake-Prince Edward State Park, Rt. 2, Box 70, Green Bay, VA 23942, (804) 392-3435. (GNA)
4388 **Prince William Forest Park**, P.O. Box 209, Triangle, VA 22172, (703) 221-7181. 35.0 miles. Named trails: Bobcat Ridge 0.9(s), Deer Ridge 0.7(s), Farm to Forest 3.2(l), Living Forest 0.3(l), Pine Grove Forest, T-Trail #1 1.0(l), T-Trail #3 1.0(s), T-Trail #7, T-Trail #8 9.1(l), T-Trail #10, T-Trail #11. (WCD; EGH; PGF; ATM; GFC; MMA; NAT; NPS; NPE; GCA; GPW; HOD; GNA; NWA; YNP; PTB)
4389 **Prince William Travel Trailer Village**, 16058 Dumfries Rd., Dumfries, VA 22026, (703) 221-2474 or (703) 670-4706. (VCD)
  Prospectors Trail *see* entry 4208.
  Puckett Cabin Walk *see* entry 4205.
  Punch and Judy Creek Trail *see* entry 4316.
  Quiet Woods Trail *see* entry 4393.
  R.W. Cross Nature Trail *see* entry 4359.
  Rabbit Run Trail *see* entry 4390.
  Raccoon Branch Trail *see* entry 4316.
4390 **Radford Parks**, Radford Department of Parks and Recreation, 29 1st St., Radford, VA 24141, (703) 639-4452. 4.5 miles. Named trails: Cave Circle, Mountain Spring, Pine Ridge, Rabbit Run. (HOD)
  Raider's Run Trail *see* entry 4306.
  Ramsey's Draft Nature Trail *see* entry 4279.
  Ranger Station Trail *see* entry 4404.
  Rapidan Trail *see* entry 4404.
4391 **Rappahannock Community College Nature Trail**, Recreation Department, Rappahannock Community College, South, Saluda, VA 23149, (804) 758-5324. 0.9 mile loop. (HOD)
  Rappahannock River Trail *see* entry 4271.
  Ravens Roost Overlook Trail *see* entry 4205.
  Red Branch Trail *see* entry 4236.
  Red Gate Trail *see* entry 4404.
  Red Oak Trail *see* entry 4385.
  Redbud Trail *see* entry 4385.
  Rennett Bag Trail *see* entry 4205.
  Reservoir Hollow Trail *see* entry 4279.
  Rhododendron Trail *see* entry 4287.
  Rhododendron Trail *see* entry 4316.
  Ribble Trail *see* entry 4316.
  Rich Hole Trail *see* entry 4279.
  Richland Balsam Trail *see* entry 4205.
4392 **Richmond National Battlefield Park**, 3215 E. Broad St., Richmond, VA 23223, (804) 226-1981. Named trails: Breakthrough Point 0.2(l), Cold Harbor 1.1(l), Fort Darling 0.5(l), Fort Harrison 1.4(l), River 0.4(l). (ATM; CGA; HOD)
4393 **Richmond Parks**, Richmond Department of Recreation and Parks, City Hall, 900 E. Broad St., Richmond, VA 23219, (804) 780-3930. Named trails: Belle Isle Loop 1.7(l), Buttermilk 1.4(s), Forest, Geology Interpretive 0.8(l), Huguenot Bridge 1.5, Meadow, Pleasant Creek 0.7(s), Quiet Woods, River Access, Riverside 1.4(s). (HOD)
4394 **Richwood Golf Club & Campground**, Rt. 2, Box 109, Bluefield, VA 24605, (703) 322-4575. (WCD)
  Ridge Trail *see* entry 4186.
  Ridge Trail *see* entry 4242.
  Ridge Trail *see* entry 4278.
  Ridge Trail *see* entry 4288.
  Ridge Trail *see* entry 4306.
  Ridge Trail *see* entry 4404.
  Riprap Trail *see* entry 4404.
  River Access Trail *see* entry 4393.
  River Bank Trail *see* entry 4409.
  River Trail *see* entry 4208.
  River Trail *see* entry 4278.
  River Trail *see* entry 4288.
  River Trail *see* entry 4392.

River Trail *see* entry 4430.

4395 **Riverbend Park**, 8814 Jeffery Rd., Great Falls, VA 22066, (703) 759-9018; or Riverbend Information Center, Potomac Hills St., Great Falls, VA 22066. 5.0 miles. (ATM; NAT; GPW; AMI; NWA)

4396 **Riverside Park**, Rivermont Ave., Lynchburg, VA 24503, (804) 847-1459. (MMA)

Riverside Trail *see* entry 4393.

4397 **Roanoke County Parks**, Roanoke County Parks and Recreation Department, 5929 Cove Rd. NW, Roanoke, VA 24019, (703) 366-3481. Named trails: Cave Springs Nature 0.5, Glen Cove Nature 0.5(l), Glenvar Nature Preservation 1.5, Pine Ridge, Six Oaks. (HOD)

Roanoke Mountain Loop Trail *see* entry 4205.

Roanoke River Trail *see* entry 4205.

Roanoke Valley Horse Trail *see* entry 4205.

Roaring Run Trail *see* entry 4279.

Roaring Run Trail *see* entry 4316.

Robertson Mountain Trail *see* entry 4404.

Robin's Roost Trail *see* entry 4409.

Rock Castle Gorge Trail *see* entry 4205.

Rock House Ridge Trail *see* entry 4287.

Rock Shelter Trail *see* entry 4279.

Rock Springs Cabin Trail *see* entry 4404.

Rocks Mountain Trail *see* entry 4404.

Rockwood Nature Trail *see* entry 4227.

Rocky Branch Trail *see* entry 4404.

Rocky Knob Picnic Loop Trail *see* entry 4205.

Rocky Knob Self-Guiding Trail *see* entry 4205.

Rocky Mount Trail *see* entry 4404.

Rocky Mountain-Brown Mountain Trail *see* entry 4404.

Rocky Mountain Run Trail *see* entry 4404.

Rocky Run Jeep Trail *see* entry 4279.

Rocky Run Trail *see* entry 4202.

Rockytop Trail *see* entry 4404.

Rose River Loop Trail *see* entry 4404.

Rose River Trail *see* entry 4404.

Ross Camp Hollow Trail *see* entry 4251.

Round Meadow Creek Trail *see* entry 4205.

RR Ditch Trail *see* entry 4249.

Running Creek Cedar Trail *see* entry 4199.

4398 **Rural Retreat Lake Campground**, SR 677, Rural Retreat, VA 24368, (703) 686-4331. (WCD; ATM)

Rush Trail *see* entry 4316.

4399 **S.A.F. Nature Trail**, Appomattox Courthouse National Historical Park, Appomattox, VA 24522, (804) 352-8987. (SAR 1992)

Saddle Gap Trail *see* entry 4205.

Saddle Gap Trail *see* entry 4279.

Saddle Trail *see* entry 4404.

Saddleback Mountain Trail *see* entry 4404.

St. Mary's Falls Trail *see* entry 4279.

St. Mary's Trail *see* entry 4279.

Salt Pond Ridge Trail *see* entry 4279.

Salt Stump Trail *see* entry 4251.

Salt Stump Trail *see* entry 4279.

Salthouse Branch Nature Trail *see* entry 4373.

Sams Ridge Trail *see* entry 4404.

Sand Spring Mountain Trail *see* entry 4279.

Sandy Gap Trail *see* entry 4279.

Scothorn Gap Trail *see* entry 4279.

Scott Run Trail *see* entry 4258.

4400 **Seashore State Park Natural Area**, 2500 Shore Dr., Virginia Beach, VA 23451, (804) 481-2131. 30.0 miles. Named trails: Bald Cypress Nature 2.0(l), Fox Run 0.5(s), High Dune 0.3(s), King Fisher 0.7(s), Lagoon 1.7(s), Long Creek 8.0(l), Main 10.0(l), Osmanthus 1.5(s), White Lake 2.0(s). (WCD; ATM; MMA; AMC; HOD; GNA)

Sensitivity Trail *see* entry 4230.

Sharp Top Mountain Overlook Trail *see* entry 4205.

Sharp Top Trail *see* entry 4205.

Shaw Gap Trail *see* entry 4316.

Shawl Gap Trail *see* entry 4279.

Shaw's Ridge Trail *see* entry 4279.

Shelton Trail *see* entry 4279.

4401 **Shenandoah Acres Resort,** P.O. Box 300-F, Stuarts Draft, VA 24477, (703) 337-1911. (WCD; VCD)

4402 **Shenandoah Hills Campground,** Rt. 1, Box 7, Madison, VA 22727, (800) 321-4186. (WCD; VCD)

4403 **Shenandoah KOA,** P.O. Box 98, Vienna, VA 22482, (703) 248-2746. (VCD)

Shenandoah Mountain Trail *see* entry 4279.

Shenandoah Mountain/South Trail *see* entry 4279.

4404 **Shenandoah National Park,** P.O. Box 348, Luray, VA 28235, (703) 999-2243. 500 miles. Named trails: North District: Beecher Ridge 2.2(s), Big Blue 6.2(s), Big Devil Stairs 1.3(s), Bluff 4.6(s), Browntown 2.3(s), Butterwood Branch 0.5(s), Compton Gap 2.2(s), Compton Peak East 0.2(s), Compton Peak West 0.2(s), Dickey Hill 0.5(s), Dickey Ridge 9.2(s), Elkwallow 2.0(s), Fork Mountain 1.1(s), Gravel Springs Hut 0.2(s), Harris Hollow 1.0(s), Heiskell Hollow 3.3(s), Hickerson Hollow 1.2(s), Hogback Spur 0.3(s), Hull School 4.4(s), Indian Run PATC Maintenance Hut 0.5(s), Jenkins Gap 0.8(s), Jeremys Run 5.3(s), Jordan River 1.2(s), Kemp Hollow 0.4(s), Keyser Run (Fire Rd.) 4.4(s), Knob Mountain 7.6(s), Knob Mountain Cutoff 0.5(s), Lands Run (Fire Rd.) 2.0(s), Little Devil Stairs 2.0(s), Matthews Arm 4.7(s), Mount Marshall 5.4(s), Neighbor Mountain 4.7(s), Oventop Mountain 5.3(s), Overall Run 1.2(s), Overall-Beecher Ridge Connector 0.7(s), Pass Mountain 3.0(s), Pass Mountain Hut 0.2(s), The Peak 1.9(s), Piney Branch 4.2(s), Piney Ridge 3.2(s), Pole Bridge Link 1.0(s), Possums Rest 0.1(s), Rocky Branch 3.2(s), Snead Farm Loop 0.7(l), Snead Farm Road 0.6(s), Spring House Road 0.5(s), Thompson Hollow 0.4(s), Thornton Hollow 5.2(s), Thornton River 4.0(s), Weddlewood 0.5(s). Central District: Bearfence Hut 0.2(s), Bearfence 0.8(s), Berry Hollow 0.8(s), Betty's Rock 0.4(s), Big Bend 4.2(s), Blackrock 0.2(s), Broad Hollow 2.2(s), Buck Hollow 3.7(s), Buck Ridge 2.4(s), Camp Hoover 1.0(s), Cat Knob 0.5(s), Catlett Mountain 1.2(s), Catlett Spur 1.1(s), Cedar Rim 3.5(s), Cedar Run 3.1(s), Cedar Run/Whiteoak Link 0.8(s), Conway 1.4(s), Corbin Cabin Cutoff 1.5(s), Corbin Hollow 2.0(s), Corbin Mountain 2.6(s), Crescent Rock 1.1(s), Crusher Ridge 1.8(s), Dark Hollow Falls 0.9(s), Dry Run 1.9(s), Dry Run Falls Fire Road 2.8(s), Fork Mountain 1.3(s), Fork Mountain Road 2.8(s), Furnace Spring 0.5(s), Graves Mill 0.5(s), Hannah Run 3.7(s), Hawksbill Mountain 1.8(s), Hazel Mountain 5.2(s), Hazel River 2.8(s), Hazel Spur 0.8(s), Hensley Church 1.0(s), Hot Mountain-Short Mountain 2.1(s), Indian Run 1.6(s), Jones Mountain 4.8(s), Jones Mountain Cabin 0.3(s), Laurel Prong 2.2(s), Leading Ridge 1.1(s), Lewis Falls Spur 0.1(s), Lewis Mountain East 2.5(s), Lewis Mountain West 2.5(s), Lewis Spring Falls 1.8(s), Limberlost 1.3(s), Little Stony Man 1.0(s), Madison County Rte 649 1.8(s), McDaniel Hollow 0.5(s), Meadow School 1.0(s), Mill Prong 1.0(s), Mill Prong Horse Spur 2.2(s), Millers Head 0.8(s), Naked Top 0.8(s), Nicholson Hollow 5.5(s), Nicholson Moonshine 1.3(s), Old Hazel 1.4(s), Old Rag 5.1(s), Old Skyland Road 3.2(s), Pine Hill Gap 1.7(s), Pocosin 1.3(s), Pocosin Cabin 0.1(s), Pocosin Fire Road 2.5(s), Pocosin Hollow 2.6(s), Pocosin Horse 1.6(s), Powell Mountain 2.9(s), Rapidan 7.4(s), Red Gate 4.8(s), Ridge 3.1(s), Robertson Mountain 2.4(s), Rock Springs Cabin 0.2(s), Rose River 6.5(s), Rose River Loop 1.8(l), Saddle 1.1(s), Saddleback Mountain 1.1(s), Sams Ridge 1.6(s), Skyland 3.2(s), Skyland-Big Meadows Horse 11.2, Slaughter 3.8(s), South River 1.4(s), South River Falls 1.6(s), Staunton River 4.6(s), Stony Man Horse 1.5(s), Stony Mountain 1.1(s), Tanners Ridge 1.4(s), Tanners Ridge Horse 2.5(l), Upper Dark Hollow 2.0(s), Weakley Hollow 2.4(s), West Naked Creek Road 1.8(s), White Rocks 1.7(s), Whiteoak 5.0(s), Whiteoak Canyon 1.8(s), Whiteoak Ranger Station 0.1(s). South District: Austin Mountain 3.2(s), Beldor Ridge 3.9(s), Big Run Loop 2.1(l), Big Run Portal 4.2(s),

Black Rock Hut 0.3(s), Blackrock Spur 0.1(s), Brown Gap 3.0(s), Brown Mountain-Rocky Mountain 5.3(s), Bucks Elbow Mountain Fire Road 0.6(s), Doyle River 4.7(s), Doyle River Cabin 0.1(s), Furnace Mountain 3.4(s), Furnace Mountain Summit 0.5(s), Gap Run 2.2(s), Gasline Road 2.0(s), Hightop Hut 0.1(s), Hightop Road 0.2(s), Ivy Creek PATC Maintenance 0.2(s), Lewis Peak 2.6(s), Madison Run 5.6(s), Moormans River 6.9(s), Moormans River Fire Road 9.5(s), One-Mile Run 3.7(s), Paine Run 3.7(s), Patterson Ridge 3.1(s), Pinefield Hut 0.1(s), Ranger Station 0.2(s), Riprap 4.4(s), Rocks Mountain 3.0(s), Rocky Mount 5.4(s), Rocky Mountain-Brown Mountain 5.3(s), Rocky Mountain Run 2.7(s), Rockytop 6.0(s), Simmons Gap-E/W 3.7(s), Smith Roach Gap 1.4(s), Stull Run 3.6(s), Trayfoot Mountain 5.4(s), Turk Branch 2.1(s), Turk Gap 1.6(s), Turk Mountain 1.1(s), Wildcat Ridge 2.5(s). Unblazed Nature Trails: Deadening 1.3(l), Fox Hollow 1.0(l), Stony Man 1.0(l), Story of the Forest 1.8(s), Traces Interpretive 1.7(l). (LGU; WCD; EGH; PGF; ATM; FFV; GFC; MMA; BMG; GNP; NPS; NPV; NPE; PGS; ATG #7; AMI; HOD; GNA; SAP; IFT)

4405 **Shot Tower Historical Park**, US 52, Wytheville, VA 24382, (703) 699-1791. (ATM; MMA; OTB; HOD)

Shuttle Trail see entry 4225.
Signal Corps Knob Trail see entry 4279.
Signal Knob Trail see entry 4279.
Simmons Gap-E/W Trail see entry 4404.
Sinclair Hollow Trail see entry 4279.
Six Oaks Trail see entry 4397.

4406 **Sky Meadows State Park**, SR 17, Front Royal, VA 22630, (703) 592-3556; or Potomac Appalachian Trail Club, 1718 N St., N.W., Washington, DC 20036, (202) 638-5306. 4.93 miles. (ATM; MMA; ATG #6)

Skyland Trail see entry 4404.
Skyland-Big Meadows Horse Trail see entry 4404.
Skylight Cave Trail see entry 4242.
Slabcamp Run Trail see entry 4279.
Slacks Overlook Trail see entry 4205.
Slacks Overlook Trail see entry 4279.
Slate Springs Circuit Trails see entry 4279.
Slate Springs Mountain Trail see entry 4279.
Slaughter Trail see entry 4404.

4407 **Small Country Camping Ground**, SR 649, Louisa, VA 23093, (703) 967-2431. (WCD)

Smart View Loop Trail see entry 4205.

4408 **Smith Mountain Lake State Park**, SR 626, Huddleston, VA 24104, (703) 297-6066. (WCD; ATM)

Smith River Trail see entry 4373.
Smith Roach Gap Trail see entry 4404.
Snead Farm Loop Trail see entry 4404.
Snead Farm Road see entry 4404.
Snyder Trail see entry 4279.
South Boundary Trail see entry 4186.
South River Falls Trail see entry 4404.
South River Trail see entry 4404.
Spec Mine Trail see entry 4205.
Spec Mines Trail see entry 4316.
Special Population Trail see entry 4381.
Spillway Trail see entry 4306.
Spotsylvania Court House Trail see entry 4270.
Spring House Road Trail see entry 4404.
Springhouse Ridge Trail see entry 4279.
Squirrel Ridge Trail see entry 4385.
Stack Rock Trail see entry 4279.
Stampers Branch Trail see entry 4287.

4409 **Staunton River State Park**, Rt. 2, Box 295, Scottsburg, VA 24589, (804) 572-4623. 10.0 miles. Named trails: Campground 0.1(s), Captain Staunton's Loop 0.5(l), Crow's Nest 0.4(s), Loblolly 0.6(s), River Bank 7.3(l), Robin's Roost 0.5(s), Tutelo 0.1(s). (WCD; ATM; MMA; HOD; GNA)

Staunton River Trail see entry 4404.
Stephens Trail see entry 4279.

VIRGINIA

Stewarts Knob Trail *see* entry 4205.
4410 Stokesville Park, Rt. 2, Box 125, Mt. Solon, VA 22843, (703) 350-2343. (WCD; VCD)
Stone Bridge-Van Pelt Trail *see* entry 4342.
Stone Mountain Trail *see* entry 4316.
Stony Fork Trail *see* entry 4316.
Stony Hill Loop Trail *see* entry 4279.
Stony Man Horse Trail *see* entry 4404.
Stony Man Nature Trail *see* entry 4404.
Stony Mountain Trail *see* entry 4404.
Stony Run Jeep Trail *see* entry 4279.
Stony Run Trail *see* entry 4251.
Stony Run Trail *see* entry 4279.
Story of the Forest Nature Trail *see* entry 4404.
Straight Branch Trail *see* entry 4316.
Stream Valley Trail *see* entry 4290.
Stuart's Knob Trail *see* entry 4260.
Stull Run Trail *see* entry 4404.
4411 Suffolk Parks, Suffolk Department of Parks and Recreation, Room 203, 441 Market St., Suffolk, VA 23434, (804) 484-3984 ext. 322. Named trails: Florida Maple 0.9(l), Lone Star Lakes Nature 0.5(l). (HOD)
4412 Sugar Hollow City Park, Robert E. Lee Hwy., Bristol, VA 24201. (WCD)
Sugar Maple Loop Trail *see* entry 4316.
4413 Sugarland Run Trail, Town of Herndon, Parks and Recreation, 703 Elder St., P.O. Box 427, Herndon, VA 22070, (703) 437-1000. 0.7 mile. (HOD)
Sulphur Ridge Overlook Trail *see* entry 4205.
Sulphur Ridge Trail *see* entry 4316.
Sulphur Spring Trail *see* entry 4316.
Sunken Road Trail *see* entry 4270.
Sunset Field Overlook Trail *see* entry 4205.
4414 Surfside at Sandbridge, 3665 S. Sandpiper Rd., Virginia Beach, VA 23456, (804) 426-2911 or (800) 568-7873. (VCD)
4415 Sweet Pepperbush Trail, Owners, 104 Nina Ct., Mechanicsville, VA 23111. 0.3 mile loop. (HOD)
Sweetbay Trail *see* entry 4361.

4416 **T.M. Gaithright Area**, Virginia Commission of Game and Inland Fisheries, 4010 W. Broad St., Richmond, VA 23230, (804) 367-9369. (GFC)
T-Trails #1, 3, 7, 8, 10 and 11 *see* entry 4388.
Tanners Ridge Horse Trail *see* entry 4404.
Tanners Ridge Trail *see* entry 4404.
Taskers Gap Trail *see* entry 4279.
Taskinas Creek Trail *see* entry 4446.
Taylor Hollow Trail *see* entry 4279.
Taylors Mountain Overlook Trail *see* entry 4205.
Third Branch Trail *see* entry 4377.
Thompson Hollow Trail *see* entry 4404.
Thornton Hollow Trail *see* entry 4404.
Thornton River Trail *see* entry 4404.
Three Ridge Overlook Trail *see* entry 4205.
Thunder Ridge Trail *see* entry 4205.
Tibbet Knob Trail *see* entry 4279.
Timber Ridge Trail *see* entry 4279.
4417 **Tindall's Point Park Nature Trail**, Gloucester County Parks and Recreation Department, P.O. Box 157, Gloucester, VA 23601, (804) 693-2355. 0.5 mile loop. (HOD)
Tobacco House Ridge Trail *see* entry 4251.
Todd Lake Trail *see* entry 4279.
Tolliver Trail *see* entry 4279.
Toms Cove Nature Trail *see* entry 4230.
Torry Ridge Spur Trail *see* entry 4279.
Torry Ridge Trail *see* entry 4205.
Torry Ridge Trail *see* entry 4279.
Tower Hill Mountain Trail *see* entry 4279.
Tower Tunnel Trail *see* entry 4208.
Towers Trail *see* entry 4208.
Traces Interpretive Nature Trail *see* entry 4404.
Trail of the Trees *see* entry 4205.
Trayfoot Mountain Trail *see* entry 4404.
Tree Walk *see* entry 4345.
Trimble Mountain Trail *see* entry 4279.

VIRGINIA

Tri-State Trail *see* entry 4242.
Tucker Trail *see* entry 4316.
Tunnel Hill Trail *see* entry 4353.
Turk Branch Trail *see* entry 4404.
Turk Gap Trail *see* entry 4404.
Turk Mountain Trail *see* entry 4404.
Turkey Neck Trail *see* entry 4430.

4418 **Turkey Run Farm Trail**, Superintendent, George Washington Memorial Pkwy., Turkey Run Park, McLean, VA 22101, (703) 557-8991. (NWA)

Turkey Trail *see* entry 4316.
Turtle Ridge Trail *see* entry 4202.
Tuscarora Overlook Trail *see* entry 4251.
Tutelo Trail *see* entry 4409.
Twin Beech Trail *see* entry 4281.
Twin Forts Loop Trail *see* entry 4357.

4419 **Twin Lakes State Park**, SR 621, Keysville, VA 23947, (804) 392-3435. (WCD; ATM; MMA)

Twin Pinnacles Trail *see* entry 4287.
Unaka Nature Trail *see* entry 4316.

4420 **University of Virginia Academic Walk**, Director of Information Services, University of Virginia, Charlottesville, VA 22903, (703) 924-0311. 0.6 mile. (HOD)

Upland Trail *see* entry 4258.
Upper Dark Hollow Trail *see* entry 4404.
Upper Lake Trail *see* entry 4279.
Upper Loop Trail *see* entry 4338.
Upper Trail *see* entry 4353.

4421 **Upton Hill Regional Park**, Wilson Blvd., Arlington, VA 22205, (703) 534-3437. Named trails: Upton Hill 1.0. (GPW)

Upton Hill Trail *see* entry 4421.
Veach Gap Trail *see* entry 4279.

4422 **Vesta Trails**, Mr. and Mrs. Arthur Belcher, Rt. 4, Box 183, Stuart, VA 24171, (703) 930-2285. Named trails: Fire Pink 0.8(l), Wildwood 2.5(s). (HOD)

4423 **Veterans' Memorial Park Nature Trail**, Prince William County Park Authority, 12249 Bristow Rd., Bristow, VA 22013; or Veterans' Memorial Park, 14300 Featherstone Rd., Woodbridge, VA 22191, (703) 491-2183. 0.8 mile loop. (HOD)

4424 **Virginia Coast Reserve**, Gerard Hennessey, Brownsville, Nassawadox, VA 23413, (804) 442-3049. 50.0 miles. (GNA)

4425 **Virginia Creeper National Recreation Trail**, Tina Counts, Abingdon Convention and Visitors Bureau, 208 W. Main St., Abingdon, VA 24210, (703) 676-2282; or Area Ranger, Mt. Rogers National Recreation Area, Rt. 1, Box 303, Marion, VA 24354, (703) 783-5196. 34.1 miles straight. (GRT)

Virginia Highlands Horse Trail *see* entry 4316.
Virginia's Nature Trail *see* entry 4316.
Wagon Road Trail *see* entry 4279.
Wakefield-Accotink Trail *see* entry 4258.
Walker Mountain Trail *see* entry 4279.

4426 **Wallops Park Nature Trail**, Accomack County Parks and Recreation Department, Accomack, VA 23301, (804) 787-3900. 0.5 mile loop. (HOD)

War Spur Trail *see* entry 4316.
Warm Springs Mountain Trail *see* entry 4279.
Warner Mill Park Physical Fitness Trail *see* entry 4438.
Warrior Path *see* entry 4363.

4427 **Washington and Lee Trail**, National Capital Area Council, BSA, 9190 Wisconsin Ave., Bethesda, MD 20814, (301) 530-9360. 22.0 miles straight. Awards available. (SAR 1993)

4428 **Washington and Old Dominion (W&OD) Railroad Regional Park Trail**, Paul McCray, Park Manager, Northern Virginia Regional Park Authority, 5400 Ox Rd., Fairfax Station, VA 22039, (703) 729-0596. 45.0 miles straight. (GRT)

Waterfall Mountain Trail *see* entry 4279.
Waverly-Wolftrap Trail *see* entry 4258.

4429 **Waynesboro Historic Trail**, P.O. Box 221, Waynesboro, VA 22980; or Stonewall Jackson Area Council, BSA, 801 Hopeman Pkwy., P.O. Box 813, Waynesboro, VA 22980, (703) 943-6675.

3.0 miles loop. Awards available. (SAR 1992)
Weakley Hollow Trail *see* entry 4404.
Weddlewood Trail *see* entry 4404.
West Naked Creek Road *see* entry 4404.
4430 **Westmoreland State Park**, Rt. 1, Box 53-H, Montross, VA 22520, (804) 493-8821. 17.0 miles. Named trails: Beach 1.0(l), Beaver Dam 0.3(s), Big Meadow 4.0(l), Laurel Point 3.2(l), River 0.4(s), Turkey Neck Trail. (WCD; ATM; MMA; NAT; AMC; HOD; GNA; PTB)
Whiskey Run Trail *see* entry 4260.
Whispering Water Trail *see* entry 4316.
White Lake Trail *see* entry 4400.
White Oak Draft Trail *see* entry 4279.
White Oak Flats Trail *see* entry 4205.
White Oak Nature Trail *see* entry 4357.
White Oak Trail *see* entry 4279.
White Oak Trail *see* entry 4385.
White Rock Falls Trails I & II *see* entry 4205.
White Rock Tower Trail *see* 4279.
White Rocks Gap Trail *see* entry 4279.
4431 **White Rocks Recreation Area**, SR 613, Perisburg, VA 24134, (703) 552-4641. (MMA)
White Rocks Trail *see* entry 4404.
White Trail *see* entry 4309.
Whiteoak Canyon Trail *see* entry 4404.
Whiteoak Ranger Station Trail *see* entry 4404.
Whiteoak Trail *see* entry 4404.
Whitetop-Laurel Creek Circuit Trail *see* entry 4316.
Wild Oak Trail *see* entry 4279.
4432 **Wildcat Mountain Natural Area**, Mrs. Ord Alexander, Chairman, Wildcat Mountain Preservation Committee, 2323 Porter St., N.W., Washington, DC 20008, (202) 966-7471; or Nature Conservancy, 619 High St., Charlottesville, VA 22901, (804) 295-6106. (AMI; NWA)
Wildcat Mountain Trail *see* entry 4316.

Wildcat Ridge Trail *see* entry 4404.
4433 **Wilderness Nature Trail**, Mrs. J.D. Killinger, 522 E. Main St., Marion, VA 23454, (703) 783-4303. 0.6 mile straight. (HOD)
Wilderness Road Trail *see* entry 4242.
Wildlife Trail *see* entry 4230.
Wildlife Trail *see* entry 4340.
4434 **Wildwood Campground**, Rt. 2, Box 400, Naola, VA 24574, (804) 299-5228. (WCD; VCD)
Wildwood Trail *see* entry 4422.
4435 **Williamsburg Busch Gardens KOA Kampground**, 5210 Lightfoot Rd., Williamsburg, VA 23188, (804) 565-2907 or (800) 635-2717. (VCD)
4436 **Williamsburg Campsites**, 6967 Richmond Rd., Williamsburg, VA 23185, (804) 564-3101. (VCD)
4437 **Williamsburg Colonial Trail**, Peninsula Council, BSA, 11725 Jefferson Ave., Newport News, VA 23606-1935, (804) 595-3356 or (804) 877-5085. 5.0 miles loop. Awards available. (SAR 1992)
4438 **Williamsburg Parks**, Department of Parks and Recreation, 412 N. Boundary St., Williamsburg, VA 23185, (804) 229-4821. Named trails: Bayberry Nature 1.6(l), Dogwood 3.5(l), Lookout Tower 3.6(l), Warner Mill Park Physical Fitness 0.8. (HOD)
4439 **Williamsburg Pottery Fairoaks Campground**, 901 Lightfoot Rd., Williamsburg, VA 23188, (800) 892-0320. (WCD)
Willis River Trail *see* entry 4243.
Wilson Creek Trail *see* entry 4251.
Wilson Creek Trail *see* entry 4287.
4440 **Winchester Historic Trail**, Stonewall Jackson Area Council, BSA, 2300 Roosevelt Blvd., Winchester, VA 22601; or Winchester Frederick County Visitors' Center, 1360 S. Pleasant Valley Rd., Winchester, VA 22601, (703) 662-4135. 2.5-5.5 miles straight. Awards available. (SAR 1993)
Windy Run Trail *see* entry 4193.
Wolf Ridge Trail *see* entry 4279.
Wolfstream Valley Trail *see* entry 4258.

VIRGINIA *Index* 299

Wood Duck Slough Trail *see* entry 4225.
Woodcock Trail *see* entry 4189.
4441 Woodland Ecology Trail, Peninsula Nature and Science Center, 524 Clyde Morris Blvd., Newport News, VA 23601, (804) 595-1900. 0.8 mile. (HOD)
Woodland Trail *see* entry 4205.
Woodland Trail *see* entry 4290.
Woodmarsh Trail *see* entry 4344.
Woodson Gap Trail *see* entry 4242.
Woodthrush Trail *see* entry 4227.
Wright Trail *see* entry 4316.
Wynn's Mill Loop Trail *see* entry 4357.
4442 Wytheville KOA, Rt. 2, Box 122, Wytheville, VA 24382, (703) 228-2601 or (800) 328-1824. (VCD)
YACC's Run Trail *see* entry 4279.
Yankee Horse Overlook Trail *see* entry 4205.
Yellow Trail *see* entry 4379.
4443 Yogi Bear's Jellystone Park, Rt. 1, Box 275, Greenwood, VA 22943, (703) 456-6409. (WCD)
4444 Yogi Bear's Jellystone Park, 14004 Shelter Ln., Haymarket, VA 22069, (703) 754-7944. (WCD; VCD)
4445 Yogi Bear's Jellystone Park Camp Resort, Luray, VA 22835, (703) 743-4002. (VCD)
4446 York River State Park, Rt. 4, Box 329-F, Williamsburg, VA 23185, (804) 564-9057. Named trails: Muskrat Run 0.4(l), Taskinas Creek 1.6(l). (ATM; MMA; AMC; HOD)
4447 Yorktown Battlefield Trail, Peninsula Council, BSA, 11725 Jefferson Ave., Newport News, VA 23606-1935, (804) 595-3356 or (804) 877-5085. 9.0-12.5 miles loop. Awards available. (SAR 1992)
4448 Zuni Pine Barrens Natural Area, J.A. Minetree, Union Camp Corp., Franklin, VA 23851, (804) 569-4276. (AMC)

Generally:
U.S. Army Corps of Engineers, Huntington District, P.O. Box 2127, Huntington, WV 25721. (LRA)
Virginia Commission of Game and Inland Fisheries, 4010 W. Broad St., Richmond, VA 23230, (804) 367-0939. (GFC)
Virginia Trails Association, 13 W. Maple St., Alexandria, VA 22301, (703) 548-7490. (AA 1992)

Index (by city)

Abingdon: Virginia Creeper National Recreation Trail 4425
Accomack: Wallops Park Nature Trail 4426
Alexandria: Chinquapin Park 4231; Dora Kelly Nature Trail 4250; Huntley Meadows State Park 4307; Lee District Park 4330; "Old Town" Alexandria Historical Trail 4365; Washington and Lee Trail 4427
Amelia: Amelia Family Campground Nature Trail 4188; Amelia Wildlife Management Area 4189
Annandale: Dranesville Area 4253; Fairfax County Parks 4258
Appomattox: Appomattox Courthouse Historical Trail 4191; Buffalo Creek Trail 4211; Holiday Lake State Park 4302; S.A.F. Nature Trail 4399

Ararat: Pinnacles Hydro Development 4375
Arlington: Arlington County Parks and Recreation 4193; Barcroft Park 4197; Bluemont Junction Trail 4206; Fraser Preserve Nature Trail 4268; Gulf Branch Nature Center 4290; Long Branch Nature Center 4334; Lubber Run Park 4336; Potomac Overlook Regional Park 4384; Upton Hill Regional Park 4421
Arrington: Lake Nelson Campground 4328
Asheville, NC: Blue Ridge Parkway 4205
Austinville: New River Trail State Park 4356
Bacova: High Top Fire Trail 4299
Bassett: Philpott Lake and Park 4373
Bastian: Camp Roland 4217
Berlin: Assateague Island National Seashore 4194

Blacksburg: Blacksburg Parks 4202; Jefferson National Forest 4316
Bluefield: Richwood Golf Club & Campground 4394
Bowling Green: Fort A.P. Hill Nature Trail 4263
Boydston: John H. Kerr Reservoir 4317
Breaks: Breaks Interstate Park 4208
Bridgewater: George Washington National Forest 4279
Bristol: Sugar Hollow City Park 4412
Bristow: Veterans' Memorial Park Nature Trail 4423
Broadway: Harrisonburg Newmarket KOA 4294
Buena Vista: George Washington National Forest 4279; Glen Maury Park 4280; Mineral Ridge Trail 4348
Burnt Chimney: Blue Ridge Campground 4204
Cape Charles: Kiptopeke State Park 4320
Carrollton: Nike Park 4358
Charlottesville: Charlottesville KOA 4221; Ivy Creek Natural Area 4309; James Monroe Historical Trail 4311; Mint Springs Valley Park 4349; University of Virginia Academic Walk 4420; Wildcat Mountain Natural Area 4432
Chatham: Hiawatha Nature Trail 4296
Cheriton: Cherrystone Campground 4223
Chesapeake: Chesapeake Area 4225; Copper Trail 4237; Northwest River Park Nature Trail 4362
Chesterfield: Chesterfield County 4227; Pocahontas State Forest and Park 4377
Chincoteague: Chincoteague National Wildlife Refuge 4230
Clarksville: Occoneechee State Park 4363
Clifton: Bull Run Marina 4212
Clifton Forge: Circle H Campground 4234
Clinchport: Natural Tunnel State Park 4353
Clintwood: Cranenest Campsite 4240
Colonial Beach: Monroe Bay Campground 4350
Covington: Gathright Lake Project 4275; Gathright Wildlife Management Area 4276; George Washington National Forest 4279; T.M. Gaithright Area 4416
Crabtree Falls: Crabtree Falls Campground 4239

Cumberland: Appomattox-Buckingham State Forest 4192; Bear Creek Lake State Park 4199; Cumberland State Forest 4243
Danville: Ballou Park Nature Trail 4196
Deltaville: Bush Park Camping Resort 4215
Draper: Horseshoe Campground 4305
Dublin: New River Community College Trail 4355
Dumfries: Prince William Travel Trailer Village 4389
Eastville: Indiantown Nature Trail 4308
Edinburg: George Washington National Forest 4279
Emporia: Meadowlark Gardens Regional Park 4347
Fairfax: Lake Accotink Park 4324; Orange and Alexandria Historical Trail 4366
Fairfax Station: Algonkian Regional Park 4187; Bull Run Regional Park 4213; Burke Lake Park 4214; Northern Virginia Regional Park Authority Trails 4361; Washington and Old Dominion (W&OD) Railroad Regional Park Trail 4428
Falmouth: Chatham and Old Towne Falmouth Historical Trail 4222
Fancy Gap: Fox Trail Campground 4266
Fort Chiswell: Fort Chiswell RV Campground 4264
Franklin: Zuni Pine Barrens Natural Area 4448
Fredericksburg: Fairview Trail 4259; Fredericksburg and Spotsylvania National Military Park 4270; Fredericksburg Historic Trail 4269; Fredericksburg Parks 4271; Jackson Trail 4310; Lake Anna State Park 4325
Front Royal: Front Royal KOA 4272; Sky Meadows State Park 4406
Gloucester: Tindall's Point Park Nature Trail 4417
Gore: The Cove Campground 4238
Great Falls: Difficult Run 4248; Great Falls Park 4288; Riverbend Park 4395
Green Bay: Goodwin Lake-Prince Edward State Park 4281; Prince Edward-Gallion State Forest 4387
Greenwood: Yogi Bear's Jellystone Park 4443
Grottoes: Grand Caverns Regional Park 4284

VIRGINIA Index

Hampton: Grandview Preserve Trail 4285
Hanover: Hanover County 4291
Hardy: Booker T. Washington National Monument 4207
Harpers Ferry, WV: Harpers Ferry Camp Resort 4293
Hartwood: Cedar Path Nature Trail 4220
Haymarket: Yogi Bear's Jellystone Park 4444
Haysi: John W. Flannagan Reservoir 4318; Lower Twin Campground 4335
Herndon: Sugarland Run Trail 4413
Hollins College: Hollins College Historical Walk 4304
Hopewell: Presquile National Wildlife Refuge 4386
Hot Springs: George Washington National Forest 4279
Huddleston: Smith Mountain Lake State Park 4408
Independence: Grayson County Nature Trail 4286
Jamestown: Jamestown Colony Trail 4315
Keysville: Twin Lakes State Park 4419
Knotts Island: MacKay Island National Wildlife Refuge 4340
Lancaster: Hickory Hollow Trail 4297
Lanexa: Chickahominy Recreational Park 4229; Ed Allen's Chickahominy Recreational Park 4255
Lexington: A. Willis Robertson Park 4186; Chessie Nature Trail 4226; Lexington Area 4332; Lexington Historic Trail 4333
Lorton: Barn Wharf Trail 4198; Fountainhead Regional Park 4265; Mason Neck National Wildlife Refuge 4344
Louisa: Small Country Camping Ground 4407
Lovington: James River Park 4312
Luray: Shenandoah National Park 4404; Yogi Bear's Jellystone Park Camp Resort 4445
Lynchburg: Blackwater Creek Natural Area 4203; Groundhog Trail 4289; Lynchburg Area 4338; Lynchburg College Botanical Trail 4339
Madison: Shenandoah Hills Campground 4402
Manassas: Manassas Battlefield Historical Trails 4341; Manassas National Battlefield Park 4342

Marion: Hungry Mother State Park 4306; Jefferson National Forest 4316; Wilderness Nature Trail 4433
McLean: George Washington Memorial Parkway 4278; Turkey Run Farm Trail 4418
Mechanicsville: Sweet Pepperbush Trail 4415
Middleboro: Cumberland Gap National Historical Park 4242
Millboro: Douthat State Park 4251
Mineral: Christopher Run Campground 4233
Monterey: Hidden Valley Wildlife Management Area 4298; Highland Wildlife Management Area 4300
Montross: Westmoreland State Park 4430
Mt. Solon: Natural Chimneys Regional Park 4352; Stokesville Park 4410
Mount Vernon: Mount Vernon Historical Trail 4351
Mouth of Wilson: Grayson Highlands State Park 4287
Naola: Wildwood Campground 4434
Nassawadox: Virginia Coast Reserve 4424
Natural Bridge Station: James River Recreation Area 4313; Jefferson National Forest 4316
New Castle: Jefferson National Forest 4316
New Market: KOA-Harrisonburg/New Market 4321
New Point: New Point Campground 4354
Newport News: Lake Maury Trail 4327; Newport News Park 4357; Woodland Ecology Trail 4441
Norfolk: Norfolk Area 4359
Orkney Springs: Orkney Springs Campground 4367
Perisburg: White Rocks Recreation Area 4431
Petersburg: Petersburg National Battlefield Historic Trail 4371; Petersburg National Battlefield Park 4372; Picture Lake Campground 4374
Poquoson: Poquoson Nature Trail 4380
Portsmouth: Portsmouth Area 4381
Pound: North Fork of Pound 4360
Powhatan: Powhatan Wildlife Management Area 4385
Pulaski: Gatewood Park 4274
Quantico: Lunga Park 4337

Radford: Radford Parks 4390
Redford: Claytor Lake State Park 4235
Reston: Lake Fairfax Park 4326
Richmond: Briery Creek 4209; C.F. Phelps Area 4216; Chickahominy Area 4228; Downtown Richmond Trail 4252; Hog Island Wildlife Management Area 4301; Laurel Run Trail 4329; Maymont Park 4345; Meadow Farm Museum/Crump Park 4346; Old Dominion Trail 4364; Richmond National Battlefield Park 4392; Richmond Parks 4393
Roanoke: Havens Wildlife Management Area 4295; Roanoke County Parks 4397
Rocky Mount: Franklin County Nature Trail 4267
Rural Retreat: Rural Retreat Lake Campground 4398
Rustburg: Brookneal Recreation Park 4210
Saltville: Clinch Mountain Wildlife Management Area 4236
Saluda: Dublfun Campground 4254; Rappahannock Community College Nature Trail 4391
Scottsburg: Staunton River State Park 4409
Scottsville: Hardware River 4292
Skippers: Cattail Creek RV Park & Campground 4219
South Hill: Elm Hill 4256
Spring Grove: Pipsico Scout Reservation 4376
Staunton: George Washington National Forest 4279
Stuart: Fairy Stone State Park 4260; Lengland Camping 4331; Vesta Trails 4422
Stuarts Draft: Shenandoah Acres Resort 4401
Suffolk: Davis Lakes & Campground 4245; Dismal Swamp National Wildlife Refuge 4249; Portsmouth Sleepy Hole Park 4382; Suffolk Parks 4411
Surry: Chippokes Plantation State Park 4232

Swoope: Camp Shenandoah 4218; Goshen-Little North Mountain Wildlife Management Area 4283
Sydnorsville: Goose Dam Campground 4282
Talleysville: KOA-Woodburne 4323
Triangle: Prince William Forest Park 4388
Verona: Shenandoah KOA 4403
Virginia Beach: Back Bay National Wildlife Refuge 4195; Best Holiday Trav-L-Park 4200; False Cape State Park 4261; Holiday Trav-L-Park 4303; Park Connector Bikeway 4370; Seashore State Park Natural Area 4400; Surfside at Sandbridge 4414
Washington, DC: Big Blue Trail 4201
Washington's Birthplace: George Washington Birthplace National Monument 4277
Waynesboro: Waynesboro Historic Trail 4429
West Point: Chesapeake Nature Trail 4224
Williamsburg: Fair Oaks Nature Trail 4257; First Settlers' Campground of Williamsburg 4262; Jamestown Beach Nature Trail 4314; Kin Kaid Kampground 4319; Outdoor World Williamsburg 4368; Williamsburg Busch Gardens KOA Kampground 4435; Williamsburg Campsites 4436; Williamsburg Colonial Trail 4437; Williamsburg Parks 4438; Williamsburg Pottery Fairoaks Campground 4439; York River State Park 4446
Willis: Daddy Rabbit's Campground 4244
Winchester: G.R. Thompson Area 4273; Winchester Historic Trail 4440
Wise: Jefferson National Forest 4316
Woodbridge: Pohick Bay Regional Park 4379
Woolwine: Deer Run Campground 4246
Wytheville: Deer Trail Park 4247; Jefferson National Forest 4316; Shot Tower Historical Park 4405; Wytheville KOA 4442
Yorktown: Yorktown Battlefield Trail 4447

West Virginia

4449 **Adahi Trail**, Tri-State Area Council, BSA, 733 Seventh Ave., Huntington, WV 25701-2199, (304) 523-3408. 20.4 miles. Awards available. (NHT; HTA)
Adkins Rockhouse Trail see entry 4522.
Allegheny Mountain Trail see entry 4522.
4450 **Allegheny Trail**, West Virginia Scenic Trails Association, P.O. Box 4042, Charleston, WV 25304. 300 miles planned, current as to 270 miles. (EGH; HMS)
Allegheny Trail see entry 4522.
Allegheny Trail see entry 4566.
Alligator Rock Trail see entry 4509.
4451 **Alpine Shores Campground**, US 33, Elkins, WV 26241, (304) 636-4311. (WCD)
Alum Cave Trail see entry 4454.
Anthony Creek Trail see entry 4522.
4452 **Appalachian Side Trails** (not listed elsewhere), Appalachian Trail Conference, Inc., P.O. Box 807, Washington & Jackson Sts., Harpers Ferry, WV 25425-0807, (304) 535-6331. Named trails: Ground Hog 1.8. (HMS)
4453 **Appalachian Trail** (see separate entry 4948 in interstate section).
Arboretum Trail see entry 4528.
Arbutus Trail see entry 4517.
Arrowhead Trail see entry 4566.
Ash Branch Trail see entry 4466.
4454 **Audra State Park**, SR 4 and US 33, Buckhannon, WV 26201, (304) 457-1162. Named trails: Alum Cave 2.7. (WCD; ATM; MMA; HMS)
4455 **Babcock State Park**, SR 41, Clifftop, WV 25822, (304) 438-5662 or (304) 438-6205. 20.0 miles. Named trails: Fisherman's 2.0, Island in the Sky 0.4, Lake View 1.2, Rocky 1.0, Skyline 2.0, Wilderness 2.0. (WCD; ATM; MMA; HMS; GNA)
Back Ridge Trail see entry 4522.
Backbone Trail see entry 4478.
Baker Sods Trail see entry 4522.
Balanced Rock Trail see entry 4461.
Bald Knob Trail see entry 4472.
Ballard Trail see entry 4509.
Bar Ford Trail see entry 4522.
Barranshe Trail see entry 4522.
Bays Fork Trail see entry 4509.
Bear Hunter Trail see entry 4522.
Beartown Boardwalk Trail see entry 4456.
4456 **Beartown State Park**, US 219, Hillsboro, WV 24946, (304) 653-4254. Named trails: Beartown Boardwalk 0.4(l). (MMA; OTB; HMS)
Beaver Bog Trail see entry 4566.
Beaver Creek Trail see entry 4522.
Beaver Trail see entry 4522.
Beaver's Tale Trail see entry 4522.
Bee Trail see entry 4522.
4457 **Beech Fork Lake**, Resource Manager, U.S. Army Corps of Engineers, P.O. Box 600, Lavalette, WV 25535, (304) 525-4831. Named trails: Rock Hollow 0.5. (HMS)
4458 **Beech Fork State Park**, Hughes Branch Rd., Huntington, WV 25701, (304) 522-0303. Named trails: Hiking 1.1, Lost 2.7, Overlook 1.5. (WCD; ATM; MMA; HMS)
Beech Glen Nature Trail see entry 4509.
Beech Trail see entry 4528.
Beech Trail see entry 4559.
Bennett Rock Trail see entry 4522.
Beulah Trail see entry 4522.
Big Beechy Trail see entry 4522.
4459 **Big Blue Trail**, Potomac Appalachian

Trail Club, 1718 N St., N.W., Washington, DC 20036. 66.0 miles. (EGH; HMS)
  Big Blue Trail *see* entry 4550.
  Big Buck Trail *see* entry 4497.
  Big Foot Trail *see* entry 4559.
  Big Pine Trail *see* entry 4464.
  Big Ridge Trail *see* entry 4517.
  Big Run Trail *see* entry 4522.
  Big Schloss Cutoff Trail *see* entry 4494.
  Big Schloss Trail *see* entry 4494.
  Big Spring Gap Trail *see* entry 4530.
  Big Stonecoal Trail *see* entry 4486.
4460 **Big Ugly Public Hunting and Fishing Area**, District Game Biologist, Rt. 1, Box 125, Point Pleasant, WV 25550, (304) 675-4380. 35.0 miles. (GNA)
  Billy Linger Trail *see* entry 4489.
  Birch Log Trail *see* entry 4484.
  Bird Run Trail *see* entry 4522.
  Black Bear Trail *see* entry 4500.
  Black Oak Trail *see* entry 4547.
  Blackbird Knob Trail *see* entry 4486.
4461 **Blackwater Falls State Park**, SR 32, Davis, WV 26260, (304) 259-5216. Named trails: Balanced Rock 1.0, Elakala 0.4, Falls View 1.5, Gentle 100 yards, Hemlock 0.5, Rhododendron 0.4. (WCD; MMA; GNA)
  Blackwater River Trail *see* entry 4472.
  Blue Bend Loop Trail *see* entry 4522.
4462 **Blue Bend Recreation Area**, Alvon, WV 24986. (ATM)
  Blue Blazed Trail *see* entry 4504.
  Blue Line Trail *see* entry 4522.
  Blue Trail *see* entry 4480.
  Blue-Orange Trail *see* entry 4480.
  Blue-Red Trail *see* entry 4480.
4463 **Bluestone Public Hunting and Fishing Area**, Department of Natural Resources, District IV, General Delivery, MacArthur, WV 25873, (304) 252-8585. (GNA)
4464 **Bluestone State Park**, Athens Star Route, Box 3, Hinton, WV 25951, (304) 466-1922. 4.0 miles. Named trails: Big Pine 1.7, Boundary 1.9, Rhododendron 0.8, Riverview 1.6. (WCD; ATM; MMA; HMS; GNA)
  Boar's Nest Trail *see* entry 4486.
  Bolivar Heights Trail *see* entry 4504.
  Bother Ridge Trail *see* entry 4494.
  Boundary Trail *see* entry 4464.
  Boundary Trail *see* entry 4522.
  Bowers Trail *see* entry 4509.
  Bowles Hemlock Trail *see* entry 4528.
  Breathed Mountain Trail *see* entry 4486.
  Bridge Trail *see* entry 4497.
  Brooks Trail *see* entry 4528.
  Brown Trail *see* entry 4483.
  Brushy Hollow Trail *see* entry 4494.
  Brushy Mountain Trail *see* entry 4522.
  Buck Lick Run Trail *see* entry 4494.
  Buckhorn Trail *see* entry 4566.
  Buffalo Fork Lake Trail *see* entry 4522.
  Buffalo Trail *see* entry 4478.
  Bulltown Battlefield Trail *see* entry 4465.
  Bulltown Historic Overlook Trail *see* entry 4465.
  Burner Mountain Trail *see* entry 4522.
4465 **Burnsville Lake**, P.O. Box 347, Burnsville, WV 26335, (304) 853-2371. Named trails: Bulltown Battlefield 0.3, Bulltown Historic Overlook 1.0. (ATM; HMS; GNA)
  Cabin Mountain Trail *see* entry 4486.
  Cabin Trail *see* entry 4496.
4466 **Cabwaylingo State Forest**, SR 152, Wilsondale, WV 25699, (304) 385-4255. 25.0 miles. Named trails: Ash Branch 2.3, Long Branch 1.9, Martin Ridge 1.6, Sleepy Hollow 1.0, Spruce Creek 2.8. (WCD; ATM; MMA; HMS; GNA)
4467 **Cacapon State Park**, US 522, Berkeley Springs, WV 25411, (304) 258-1022. 25.0 miles. Named trails: Central 5.0, Laurel 1.8, Ridge 0.9, Ziler 2.3, Ziler Loop 5.1(l). (ATM; MMA; HMS; GNA)
4468 **Calvin Price State Forest**, c/o Watoga State Park, Star Route 1, Box 252, Marlinton, WV 24954, (304) 799-4087. (MMA; GNA)
4469 **Camp Buckskin**, Buckskin Council, BSA, 2829 Kanawha Blvd., Charleston, WV 25311, (304) 752-4428; or Camp Buckskin, (304) 855-4621. (SFC)

4470 **Camp Chief Logan**, Chief Cornstalk Council, BSA, P.O. Box 1710, Logan, WV 25601, (304) 925-0319; or Camp Chief Logan, Dunmore, WV 24934, (304) 799-6126. (SFC)

4471 **Camp Creek State Forest**, Camp Creek, WV 25820, (304) 425-9481. 20.0 miles. Named trails: Farley Branch 2.3. (ATM; HMS; GNA)

    Camp Five Trail see entry 4522.
    Camp Wood Trail see entry 4522.
    Canaan Mountain Trail see entry 4472.

4472 **Canaan Valley State Park**, P.O. Box 22, Davis, WV 26260, (304) 866-4111. 9.0 miles. Named trails: Bald Knob 1.2, Blackwater River 0.8, Canaan Mountain 1.2, Chimney Rock 1.4, Club Run 1.3, Deer Run 1.3, Middle Ridge 2.3, Railroad Grade 1.6, Ridge 0.1, Weiss Knob 1.1. (WCD; ATM; MMA; HMS; GNA)

    Canoe River Trail see entry 4489.
    Canyon Rim Trail see entry 4497.
    Canyon Rim Trail see entry 4522.
    Canyon Rim Trail see entry 4535.

4473 **Carnifex Ferry Battlefield State Park**, Keslers Cross Lanes, WV 26675, (304) 872-3772. Named trails: Carnifex Ferry 1.2, Fishermen's 0.6, Laurel 0.2, Nature 0.3, Patteson 1.7, Pierson Hollow 0.8. (HMS)

    Carnifex Ferry Trail see entry 4473.
    Castle Rock Trail see entry 4497.
    Castle Rock Trail see entry 4527.

4474 **Cathedral State Park**, US 50, Aurora, WV 26705, (304) 735-3771. Named trails: Cathedral 1.3, Giant Hemlock 0.2, Partridge Berry 0.2, Trillium 0.1, Wood Thrush 0.5. (MMA; OTB; GNA)

    Cathedral Trail see entry 4474.
    Caves and Tunnel Trail see entry 4497.

4475 **Cedar Creek State Park**, Rt. 1, Box 9, Glenville, WV 26351, (304) 462-7158. 10.0 miles. Named trails: Fishermen's 0.9, North Boundary 1.0, Park View 1.7, Stone Trough 2.5, Two Run 2.2. (WCD; ATM; MMA; HMS; GNA)

    Central Trail see entry 4467.

4476 **Chestnut Ridge County Park**, Sand Springs Rd., Bruceton Mills, WV 26525, (304) 594-1773. (WCD)

    Chestnut Ridge Trail see entry 4522.

4477 **Chief Cornstalk Public Hunting and Fishing Area**, Nine Mile Rd., Southside, WV 25187, (304) 675-1846; or Division of Wildlife Resources, Department of Natural Resources, District V, P.O. Box 608, Milton, WV 25441, (304) 743-6186. 8.0 miles. (WCD; GNA)

    Chief Logan Fitness Trail see entry 4478.

4478 **Chief Logan State Park**, SR 10, Logan, WV 25601, (304) 752-8558. 9.0 miles. Named trails: Backbone 2.2, Buffalo 1.4, Chief Logan Fitness 1.0, Cliffside 0.6, Lake Shore 0.8, Nature 1.0, Woodpecker 1.5. (WCD; ATM; HMS; GNA)

    Chimney Rock Trail see entry 4472.
    Chimney Rock Trail see entry 4494.
    Circular Trail see entry 4483.
    Civil War Trail see entry 4522.
    Clay Furnace Hiking Trail see entry 4482.
    Clay Run Furnace Trail see entry 4482.
    Cliff Trail see entry 4504.
    Cliffside Trail see entry 4478.
    Cliffside Trail see entry 4561.

4479 **Clifton F. McClintic Wildlife Station**, District Wildlife Biologist, Rt. 1, Box 125, Point Pleasant, WV 25550, (304) 675-4380. 15.0 miles. (GNA)

    Clover Trail see entry 4522.
    Club Run Trail see entry 4472.
    Coles Mountain Trail see entry 4522.

4480 **Coolfont Resort Campground**, Cool Run Valley Rd., P.O. Box 613, Berkeley Springs, WV 25411, (800) 296-8768. Named trails: Blue 1.0, Blue-Orange 0.8, Blue-Red 0.6, Green 2.5, Green-Orange 1.3, White 1.8, Yellow 2.1, Yellow-Orange 1.1, Yellow-Red 1.1. (WCD; HMS)

    Coonskin Nature Trail see entry 4481.

4481 **Coonskin Park**, Coonskin Dr., Charleston, WV 25301, (304) 341-8000. Named trails: Coonskin Nature 1.0. (MMA; HMS)

4482 **Coopers Rock State Forest**, Rt. 1, Box 270, Bruceton Mills, WV 26525, (304)

594-1561. 30.0 miles. Named trails: Clay Furnace Hiking 2.0, Clay Run Furnace 3.6, Raven Rock 3.6, Rock City 1.2, Scott Run 1.6. (WCD; EGH; ATM; MMA; HMS; GNA)
  Copse Cove Trail *see* entry 4517.
4483 **The Core Arboretum**, Department of Biology, Brooks Hall, West Virginia University, Monongahela Blvd., Morgantown, WV 26505, (304) 293-5201. Named trails: Brown, Circular, Granville Island, Nuttall, Rumsey, Sheldon, Strausbaugh, Taylor. (ATM; HMS)
  Couch Ridge Trail *see* entry 4522.
  County Line Trail *see* entry 4494.
  County Line Trail *see* entry 4522.
  County Line Trail *see* entry 4535.
  Covey Cove Trail *see* entry 4517.
  Cow Pasture Trail *see* entry 4522.
4484 **Cranberry Back Country**, District Ranger, Gauley Ranger District, Monongahela National Forest, Richwood, WV 26261, (304) 846-6558. 75.0 miles. Named trails: Birch Log 2.9, Lick Branch 2.1, North-South 22.0. (ATM; OTB; WPS; IFT)
  Cranberry Overlook Trail *see* entry 4522.
  Cranberry Ridge Trail *see* entry 4522.
  Cranberry Trail *see* entry 4487.
  Crane Branch Trail *see* entry 4531.
  Crestline Trail *see* entry 4547.
  Critz Trail *see* entry 4509.
4485 **Dallas Pike Campground**, Rt. 1, Box 231, Triadelphia, WV 26059, (304) 547-0940. (WCD)
  Darnell Hollow Trail *see* entry 4568.
  Davis Trail *see* entry 4522.
  Deer Run Trail *see* entry 4472.
  Dilley Trail *see* entry 4522.
  District Line Trail *see* entry 4509.
  District Line Trail *see* entry 4522.
  Dock Trail *see* entry 4522.
  Dogwood Trail *see* entry 4567.
4486 **Dolly Sods Scenic Area**, Potomac Ranger District, Monongahela National Forest, Rt. 3, Box 240, Petersburg, WV 26847, (304) 257-4488. 30.0 miles. Named trails: Big Stonecoal 4.0, Blackbird Knob 2.0, Boar's Nest 2.7, Breathed Mountain 2.5, Cabin Mountain 2.5, Dunkenbarger Run 1.25, Fisher Spring Run 2.0, Flatrock Run 5.1, High Water 0.8, Little Stonecoal 1.75, Red Creek 6.75, Roaring Plains 3.3, Rocky Point 2.0, Rohrbrough Plains 3.0, South Prong 5.9, Wildlife 1.2. (AMI; WPS; BHT)
  Dorman Ridge Trail *see* entry 4522.
  Dragon Draft Trail *see* entry 4566.
  Drift Branch Trail *see* entry 4531.
4487 **Droop Mountain Battlefield State Park**, US 219, Hillsboro, WV 24946, (304) 653-4254. Named trails: Cranberry 0.7, Horse Haven 0.3, Minnie Ball 0.2, Old Musket 0.5, Overlook 0.4. (ATM; MMA; HMS)
  Dunkenbarger Run Trail *see* entry 4486.
  Dynamite Trail *see* entry 4489.
  Eagle Camp Trail *see* entry 4522.
  East Fork Trail *see* entry 4522.
4488 **East Lynn Lake**, U.S. Army Corps of Engineers, Star Route, Box 35-C, East Lynn, WV 25512, (304) 849-2355 or (304) 849-3641 or (304) 849-5000. 5.6 miles. Named trails: Lakeside 1.7. (WCD; ATM; HMS; GNA)
  East Ridge Trail *see* entry 4517.
  Elakala Trail *see* entry 4461.
4489 **Elk River Public Hunting and Fishing Area**, Department of Natural Resources, District III, P.O. Box 38, French Creek, WV 26218, (304) 924-6211. 26.0 miles. Named trails: Billy Linger 4.4, Canoe River 3.6, Dynamite 1.0, Gibson 0.9, Hickory Flats 4.8, Tower Falls 0.8, Woodell 2.2. (HMS; GNA)
4490 **The Elk River Trail**, Tom Raker, Director, Kanawha County Parks and Recreation Commission, 2000 Coonskin Dr., Charleston, WV 25311-1087, (304) 341-8000. 1.0 mile straight. (GRT)
  Elza Trail *see* entry 4522.
4491 **Exhibition Coal Mine City Park**, P.O. Drawer AJ, Beckley, WV 25802, (304) 256-1747. (WCD)
  Extra Mile Trail *see* entry 4527.
  Falls of Hill Creek Trail *see* entry 4522.
  Falls Trail *see* entry 4561.
  Falls View Trail *see* entry 4461.
  Fansler Trail *see* entry 4522.

WEST VIRGINIA

Farley Branch Trail *see* entry 4471.
Farley Ridge Trail *see* entry 4535.
Fern Trail *see* entry 4559.
Fisher Spring Run Trail *see* entry 4486.
Fisherman Trail *see* entry 4522.
Fisherman's Trail *see* entry 4455.
Fishermen's Trail *see* entry 4473.
Fishermen's Trail *see* entry 4475.
Fishermen's Trail *see* entry 4494.
Flatrock Run Trail *see* entry 4486.

4492 **Fork Creek Public Hunting and Fishing Area**, Department of Natural Resources, District V, Box 608, Milton, WV 25441, (304) 743-6186. 75.0 miles. (MMA; GNA)

Fork Mountain Trail *see* entry 4522.
Forks of Cranberry Trail *see* entry 4522.
Forks Trail *see* entry 4522.

4493 **Fox Fire Camping Resort**, Rt. 2, Box 655, Milton, WV 25541, (304) 743-5622. Named trails: Fox Fire Nature 1.1. (WCD; HMS)

Fox Fire Nature Trail *see* entry 4493.
Frosty Gap Trail *see* entry 4522.
Gauley Mountain Trail *see* entry 4522.
Gentle Trail *see* entry 4461.

4494 **George Washington National Forest**, P.O. Box 233, Rm. 210, Federal Bldg., Harrisonburg, WV 22801, (703) 433-2491; or Dry River Ranger District, 510 N. Main St., Bridgewater, VA 22812, (703) 828-2591; or Lee Ranger District, Windsor Knit Rd., Rt. 1, Box 31-A, Edinburg, VA 22824, (703) 984-4101. Named trails: Big Schloss Cutoff 1.3, Big Schloss 0.3, Bother Ridge 3.1, Brushy Hollow 3.0, Buck Lick Run 2.2, Chimney Rock 0.8, County Line 8.6, Fishermen's 0.4, Gerhard 0.6, Half Moon Lookout 0.8, Half Moon 3.2, Hawk 5.2, High Knob 5.4, Long Mountain 7.8, Mill Mountain 6.0, Miller Run 4.6, North Mountain 6.5, Peer 3.2, Pond Run 3.9, Road Run 2.8, Rock Cliff 1.0, Saw Mill 4.3, Squirrel Gap 2.2, Sugar Run 4.5, Trout Pond 2.5, Vances Cove 6.3. (WCD; EGH; GFC; HMS; GNA)

Gerhard Trail *see* entry 4494.

Giant Hemlock Trail *see* entry 4474.
Giant Tree Trail *see* entry 4527.
Gibbons Nature Trail *see* entry 4527.
Gibson Trail *see* entry 4489.

4495 **Glade Creek Trail**, Pat Esmond, National Park Service, New River Gorge National River, P.O. Box 246, Glen Jean, WV 25846, (304) 465-8883. 5.0 miles straight. (GRT)

Glade Run Trail *see* entry 4568.
Goodspeed's Highway Trail *see* entry 4568.
Gordon Trail of the Five Senses *see* entry 4555.

4496 **Grand Vue Park**, P.O. Box 523, Moundsville, WV 26041, (304) 845-9810. Named trails: Cabin 1.8. (HMS)

4497 **Grandview State Park**, Rt. 9, Beaver, WV 25813, (304) 763-3145. Named trails: Big Buck 0.8, Bridge 0.6, Canyon Rim 1.6, Castle Rock 0.7, Caves and Tunnel 0.6. (MMA; HTS)

Grant Conway National Historical Trail of Maryland Heights *see* entry 4504.

Granville Island Trail *see* entry 4483.

4498 **Grave Creek Mound State Park**, Moundsville, WV 26041. (OTB)

Green Mountain Trail *see* entry 4530.
Green Trail *see* entry 4480.

4499 **Greenbrier River Trail**, Greenbrier River Trail Association, P.O. Box 125, Caldwell, WV 24925, (304) 536-3771. 75.0 miles straight. (EGH; ATM; MMA; HMS; GNA)

4500 **Greenbrier State Forest**, Star Route, Box 125, Caldwell, WV 24925, (304) 536-1944. Named trails: Black Bear 2.4, Old Road 1.5, Rocky Ridge 2.0, Young's Nature 3.5. (EGH; ATM; MMA; HMS; GNA)

Green-Orange Trail *see* entry 4480.
Ground Hog Trail *see* entry 4452.
Half Moon Lookout Trail *see* entry 4494.
Half Moon Trail *see* entry 4494.

4501 **Handley Public Hunting and Fishing Area**, Rt. 1, Box 157E, Marlinton, WV 24954, (304) 799-4205. (GNA)

4502 **Harpers Ferry Camp Resort**, Rt. 3,

Box 1300, Harpers Ferry, WV 25425, (304) 535-6895. (WCD)

4503 Harpers Ferry Heritage Trail, Harpers Ferry Historical Association and Bookshop, P.O. Box 197, Shenandoah St., Harpers Ferry, WV 25425. 3.0 miles loop. Awards available. (SAR 1993)

4504 Harpers Ferry National Historical Park, P.O. Box 65, Harpers Ferry, WV 25425, (304) 535-6517. 12.0 miles. Named trails: Bolivar Heights 1.3, Cliff (Jefferson Rock) 0.8, Grant Conway National Historical Trail of Maryland Heights (f/k/a Blue Blazed) 4.0, Loudon Heights 1.3, Virginius Island 1.5. (SAR 1993)

4505 Harrison County Parks and Recreation Bike and Hike Trail, Michael J. Book, Director, Harrison County Parks and Recreation Commission, 301 W. Main St., Clarksburg, WV 26301, (304) 624-8619. 6.9 miles straight. (GRT)

Hart Ridge Trail see entry 4515.
Hawk Trail see entry 4494.

4506 Hawk's Nest State Park, US 60, Ansted, WV 25085, (304) 658-5212 or (800) CALL-WVA. Named trails: Hawks Nest 0.5. (ATM; MMA; HMS)

Hawk's Nest Trail see entry 4506.
Hedrick Camp Trail see entry 4522.
Hemlock Trail see entry 4461.
Hemlock Trail see entry 4561.
Hickory Flats Trail see entry 4489.
High Falls Trail see entry 4522.
High Knob Trail see entry 4494.
High Knob Trail see entry 4515.
High Rock Trail see entry 4507.
High Rock Trail see entry 4522.
High Water Trail see entry 4486.
Hiking Trail see entry 4458.
Hiking Trail see entry 4509.
Hiles Run Trail see entry 4515.
Hill Top Trail see entry 4547.
Hinkle Branch Trail see entry 4522.

4507 Holly River State Park, P.O. Box 70, Hacker Valley, WV 26222, (304) 493-6353. 33.0 miles. Named trails: High Rock 1.3, Oak Ridge 1.8, Potato Knob 2.2, Railroad Grade 1.3, Reverie 2.5, Salt Lick 1.2, Tramontane 2.3, Wilderness 4.0. (WCD; EGH; ATM; MMA; HMS; GNA)

Honeybee Trail see entry 4566.
Honeymoon Trail see entry 4566.
Horse Haven Trail see entry 4487.
Horse Run Trail see entry 4515.
Horseshoe Run Trail see entry 4522.
Horseshoe Trail see entry 4547.
Horton-Horserock Trail see entry 4522.
Howards Lick Run Trail see entry 4517.
Huckleberry Trail see entry 4522.
Huckleberry Trail see entry 4561.

4508 Huntington Galleries, Nature Coordinator, Park Hills, Huntington, WV 25701, (704) 529-2701. Named trails: Sculpture 0.2, Spicebush 0.3, Tulip Tree 1.0. (HMS)

Huss Pen Trail see entry 4515.
Island in the Sky Trail see entry 4455.
Jacob's Well Trail see entry 4566.
Jefferson Rock Trail see entry 4504.
Jesse's Cove Trail see entry 4566.
Johns Camp Run Trail see entry 4522.
Johnson Hollow Trail see entry 4509.
Johnson Hollow Trail see entry 4568.
Judy Springs Trail see entry 4522.

4509 Kanawha State Forest, Rt. 2, Box 285, Charleston, WV 25314, (304) 346-5654. 21.0 miles. Named trails: Alligator Rock 0.6, Ballard 0.7, Bays Fork 2.1, Beech Glen Nature 3.2, Bowers 2.1, Critz 0.6, District Line 1.5, Hiking 2.4, Johnson Hollow 1.6, Left Fork 0.7, Lindy 0.6, Lookout 0.8, Martin 0.3, North-South 0.7, Pigeon Roost 2.2, Rock Camp 1.1. (EGH; MMA; GNA)

4510 Kanawha Trace, Tri-State Area Council, BSA, 733 Seventh Ave., Huntington, WV 25701-2199, (304) 523-3408. 31.7 miles. Awards available. (NHT; HTA)

Kennison Mountain Trail see entry 4522.
Ken's Run Trail see entry 4568.

4511 Kumbrabow State Forest, P.O. Box 65, Huttonsville, WV 26273, (304) 335-2219. 26.0 miles. Named trails: Meatbox Run 1.4, Potato Hole Run 1.5, Raven Rocks 1.2, Rich Mountain Fire 3.1. (ATM; MMA; HMS; GNA)

4512 Lake Sherwood, Neola, WV 24961. (ATM)

Lake Sherwood Trail *see* entry 4522.
Lake Shore Trail *see* entry 4478.
4513 Lake Stephens, SR 3, Beckley, WV 25801. (ATM)
  Lake Trail *see* entry 4562.
  Lake Trail *see* entry 4566.
  Lake View Trail *see* entry 4455.
  Lakeside Trail *see* entry 4488.
  Landes Trail *see* entry 4522.
  Laurel Creek Trail *see* entry 4522.
4514 Laurel Lake Public Hunting and Fishing Area, Rt. 1, Box 626, Lenore, WV 25676, (304) 475-2823. 40.0 miles. (GNA)
  Laurel Ridge Trail *see* entry 4566.
  Laurel River Trail *see* entry 4522.
  Laurel Run Trail *see* entry 4522.
  Laurel Trail *see* entry 4467.
  Laurel Trail *see* entry 4473.
  Laurel Trail *see* entry 4517.
  Laurel Trail *see* entry 4544.
  Laurel Trail *see* entry 4559.
  Laurelly Branch Trail *see* entry 4522.
  Leading Ridge Trail *see* entry 4522.
  Leatherwood Trail *see* entry 4522.
  Lee Trail *see* entry 4517.
  Left Fork Trail *see* entry 4509.
  Lesin Run Trail *see* entry 4515.
4515 Lewis Wetzel Public Hunting and Fishing Area, Division of Wildlife Resources, District I, 1304 Goose Run Rd., Fairmont, WV 26554, (304) 366-5880. 35.0 miles. Named trails: Hart Ridge 1.0, High Knob 3.3, Hiles Run 0.7, Horse Run 0.9, Huss Pen 0.9, Lesin Run 1.1, Nettle Run 1.4. (HMS; GNA)
  Lick Branch Trail *see* entry 4484.
  Lick Hollow Trail *see* entry 4535.
  Lick Run Trail *see* entry 4568.
  Light Horse Harry Lee Trail *see* entry 4517.
  Limerock Trail *see* entry 4522.
  Lindy Run Trail *see* entry 4522.
  Lindy Trail *see* entry 4509.
  Little Allegheny Mountain Trail *see* entry 4522.
  Little Allegheny Trail *see* entry 4522.
  Little Black Fork Trail *see* entry 4522.
  Little Fork Trail *see* entry 4522.
  Little Mountain Trail *see* entry 4547.
  Little Stonecoal Trail *see* entry 4486.

4516 Lizard Mound State Park, Hartford, WV 25247. (GFA)
  Loblolly Trail *see* entry 4517.
  Lockridge Mountain Trail *see* entry 4522.
  Lonesome Pine Trail *see* entry 4527.
  Long Branch Trail *see* entry 4466.
  Long Mountain Trail *see* entry 4494.
  Lookout Trail *see* entry 4509.
  Losh Run Trail *see* entry 4522.
4517 Lost River State Park, Rt. 2, Box 24, Mathias, WV 26812, (304) 897-5372. 35.0 miles. Named trails: Arbutus 0.7, Big Ridge 2.0, Copse Cove 1.8, Covey Cove 0.5, East Ridge 2.5, Howards Lick Run 1.2, Laurel 0.5, Lee 0.5, Light Horse Harry Lee 1.3, Loblolly 0.8, Miller's Rock 3.7, Razor Ridge 1.0, Red Fox 0.3, Shingle Mill Lake 1.0, Staghorn 1.0, White Oak 1.8, Wood Thrush 0.4. (EGH; ATM; MMA; HMS; GNA)
  Lost Trail *see* entry 4458.
  Loudon Heights Trail *see* entry 4504.
  Lumberjack Trail *see* entry 4522.
  Lynn Knob Trail *see* entry 4522.
  Mail Route Trail *see* entry 4522.
4518 Marion County Trail, Ralph S. LaRue, Director, Marion County Parks and Recreation Commission, P.O. Box 1258, Fairmont, WV 26554, (304) 363-7037. 2.0 miles straight. (GRT)
  Martin Ridge Trail *see* entry 4466.
  Martin Trail *see* entry 4509.
4519 Mary Ingles Trail, Mary Ingles Chapter, West Virginia Scenic Trails Association, P.O. Box 813, Fayetteville, WV 25840, (304) 574-0225 or (304) 743-3968. 500 miles. (HMS)
  Maxwell Run Trail *see* entry 4522.
  McCray Ridge Trail *see* entry 4522.
  McGowan Mountain Trail *see* entry 4530.
  McKinley Run Trail *see* entry 4522.
  Meadow Mountain Trail *see* entry 4522.
  Meatbox Run Trail *see* entry 4511.
  Middle Fork Trail *see* entry 4522.
  Middle Mountain Trail *see* entry 4522.
  Middle Point Trail *see* entry 4522.
  Middle Ridge Trail *see* entry 4472.

Mill Mountain Trail *see* entry 4494.
Miller Run Trail *see* entry 4494.
Miller's Rock Trail *see* entry 4517.
Minnie Ball Trail *see* entry 4487.

4520 **Moncove Lake Public Hunting and Fishing Area**, Department of Natural Resources, District IV, MacArthur, WV 25873, (304) 252-1173. Named trails: Moncove Lake 1.2. (HMS)

4521 **Moncove Lake State Park**, SR 8, Gap Mills, WV 24941, (304) 772-3450. (WCD)

Moncove Lake Trail *see* entry 4520.

4522 **Monongahela National Forest**, USDA Bldg., 200 Sycamore St., Elkins, WV 26241-3962, (304) 636-1800. 850 miles. Named trails: West Fork 26.0. Cheat Ranger District, P.O. Box 368, Parsons, WV 26287, (304) 478-3251; Named trails: Allegheny (Davis) 5.2, Baker Sods 3.0, Bennett Rock 0.7, Boundary 3.5, Canyon Rim 3.0, Clover 2.0, Dorman Ridge 1.3, Fansler 1.0, Hedrick Camp 1.0, Horseshoe Run 0.5, Limerock 4.0, Lindy Run 2.0, Little Black Fork 4.0, Losh Run 2.3, Mail Route 1.7, Maxwell Run 2.1, McKinley Run 1.0, Middle Point 1.6, Mountainside 4.1, Pheasant Mountain 3.3, Plantation 8.4, Pointy Knob 4.2, Possession Camp 3.2, Railroad Grade 3.1, Ridge 0.8, Shingletree 4.5, South Haddix 4.5, Stonelick 3.4, Tablerock Overlook 1.1. Gauley Ranger District, P.O. Box 110, Richwood, WV 26261, (304) 846-2695; Named trails: Adkins Rockhouse 2.1, Barranshe 4.5, Big Beechy 5.4, Big Run 1.0, County Line 11.2, Cow Pasture 6.7, Cranberry Ridge 5.8, District Line 2.8, Eagle Camp 1.0, Falls of Hill Creek 0.8, Fisherman 1.2, Fork Mountain 21.4, Forks of Cranberry 5.7, Frosty Gap 5.2, Hinkle Branch 2.4, Kennison Mountain 9.7, Laurelly Branch 3.4, Little Fork 3.7, Middle Fork 10.0, North Fork 6.6, Pocahontas 20.2, Rough Run 3.2, Summit Lake 1.8, Tumbling Rock 2.6, Turkey Mountain 20.5, Twin Branch 1.5. Greenbrier Ranger District, Bartow, WV 24920, (304) 456-3335; Named trails: Bar Ford 1.5, Beulah 4.2, Buffalo Fork Lake 1.1, Burner Mountain 3.6, Camp Five 1.6, Chestnut Ridge 5.5, Couch Ridge 3.6, East Fork 7.9, Forks 1.1, High Falls 5.0, Johns Camp Run 0.8, Laurel River 17.2, Lynn Knob 3.9, McCray Ridge 4.7, North Fork 2.9, Peters Mountain 5.5, Rattlesnake 2.5, Smoke Camp 2.6, Span Oak 3.7, Stone Camp 1.2, Stonecoal Ridge 3.8, Whitemeadow Ridge 4.6, Yokum Ridge 1.4, Yokum Ridge Spur 0.8. Marlinton Ranger District, Marlinton, WV 24954, (304) 799-4334; Named trails: Beaver 2.8, Beaver Creek 0.4, Bird Run 4.0, Cranberry Overlook 0.5, Gauley Mountain 5.4, High Rock 3.2, Laurel Creek 8.0, Leatherwood 19.0, Lockridge Mountain 6.7, Middle Mountain 4.6, Sugar Camp 4.1, Tea Creek Mountain 4.6, Two Lick 4.3, Williams River 3.0. Potomac Ranger District, Rt. 3, Box 240, Petersburg, WV 26847, (304) 257-4488; Named trails: Allegheny Mountain 7.9, Back Ridge 4.6, Bear Hunter 1.0, Bee 1.9, Big Run 3.1, Elza 2.0, Horton-Horserock 6.2, Huckleberry 3.2, Judy Springs 0.7, Landes 1.4, Leading Ridge 5.2, Little Allegheny Mountain 4.5, Lumberjack 3.3, North Fork Mountain 23.8, North Prong 2.8, Redman Run 1.6, Seneca Creek 5.0, Seneca Rocks West Side 1.7, South Branch 3.5, Spring Ridge 3.2, Swallow Rock 3.2, Tom Lick 1.1, Whispering Spruce 0.5. White Sulphur Ranger District, P.O. Box 520, Federal Bldg., 90 E. Main St., White Sulphur Springs, WV 24986, (304) 536-2144; Named trails: Anthony Creek 3.8, Beaver's Tale 0.3, Blue Bend Loop 5.0, Blue Line 0.7, Brushy Mountain 2.1, Camp Wood 1.7, Civil War 6.3, Coles Mountain 1.2, Dilley 1.0, Dock 2.0, Lake Sherwood 3.7, Laurel Run 5.5, Little Allegheny 4.2, Meadow Mountain 9.7, Middle Mountain 13.2, Peach Orchard 4.1, Slab Camp 5.0, Snake Valley 3.6, South Boundary 4.8, Spice Ridge 12.4, Upper Meadow 1.2, Virginia 0.6, Wild Meadow 6.2. (GRT; LGU; WCD; EGH; ATM; GFC; MMA; FGU; GNA; NFG)

Monongaseneka Trail *see* entry 4566.
Moore Run Trail *see* entry 4530.

4523 **Mountain Lake Campground**, P.O. Box 486, Summersville, WV 26651, (304) 872-4220 or (800) 624-0440. (WCD)

Mountainside Trail *see* entry 4522.
Mountwood Lake Trail *see* entry 4524.
4524 **Mountwood Park**, Volcano Rd., Parkersburg, WV 26101, (304) 679-3611. Named trails: Mountwood Lake 2.2. (MMA; HMS)
Mylius Trail *see* entry 4530.
4525 **Nathaniel Mountain Public Hunting and Fishing Area**, Division of Wildlife Resources, District II, P.O. Drawer C, Romney, WV 26757, (304) 822-3551. (GNA)
Nature Trail *see* entry 4473.
Nature Trail *see* entry 4478.
Nature Trail *see* entry 4527.
Nature Trail *see* entry 4561.
Nettle Run Trail *see* entry 4515.
4526 **New River Gorge Campgrounds**, Milroy Grose Rd., Fayetteville, WV 25840, (304) 658-9926. (WCD)
4527 **North Bend State Park**, Cairo, WV 26337, (304) 643-2931 or (800) CALL-WVA. Named trails: Castle Rock 0.2, Extra Mile (Woodland), Giant Tree 0.2, Gibbons Nature 0.4, Lonesome Pine 0.1, Nature 3.0, North Bend State Park Rail-Trail 61.0, Overhanging Rock 0.5, River 1.0. (GRT; WCD; ATM; OTB; HMS; GNA)
North Bend State Park Rail-Trail *see* entry 4527.
North Boundary Trail *see* entry 4475.
North Fork Mountain Trail *see* entry 4522.
North Fork Trail *see* entry 4522.
North Mountain Trail *see* entry 4494.
North Prong Trail *see* entry 4522.
Northside Nature Trail *see* entry 4535.
North-South Trail *see* entry 4484.
North-South Trail *see* entry 4509.
Nuttall Trail *see* entry 4483.
Oak Ridge Trail *see* entry 4507.
4528 **Oglebay Park**, Wheeling, WV 26003, (304) 242-3000. Named trails: Arboretum 2.8, Beech 0.7, Bowles Hemlock 0.4, Brooks 0.4, Thoreau 0.8. (ATM; HMS)
Old Musket Trail *see* entry 4487.
Old Road Trail *see* entry 4500.
4529 **Oldtown Campground**, Rt. 1, Box 662, Point Pleasant, WV 25550, (304) 675-3095. (WCD)
4530 **Otter Creek Area**, Monongahela National Forest, Federal Bldg., Elkins, WV 26241, (304) 636-1800; or Cheat Ranger District, Post Office Bldg., Parsons, WV 26287, (304) 478-3251. 50.0 miles. Named trails: Big Spring Gap 1.0, Green Mountain 5.0, McGowan Mountain 2.67, Moore Run 4.0, Mylius, Otter Creek 11.0, Shavers Mountain 13.0, Turkey Run 2.0, Yellow Creek 3.0. (WPS; BHT; IFT)
Otter Creek Trail *see* entry 4530.
Overhanging Rock Trail *see* entry 4527.
Overlook Trail *see* entry 4458.
4531 **Panther State Forest**, US 52, P.O. Box 287, Panther, WV 24872, (304) 938-2252. Named trails: Crane Branch Nature 1.3, Drift Branch 1.3, Twin Rocks 0.6. (ATM; MMA; HMS; GNA)
Park View Trail *see* entry 4475.
Partridge Berry Trail *see* entry 4474.
Patteson Trail *see* entry 4473.
Peach Orchard Trail *see* entry 4522.
Peer Trail *see* entry 4494.
Peters Mountain Trail *see* entry 4522.
Pheasant Mountain Trail *see* entry 4522.
Pierson Hollow Trail *see* entry 4473.
Pigeon Roost Trail *see* entry 4509.
4532 **Pine Hill Campground & Cabins**, Hazelton Rd., Hazelton, WV 26535, (304) 379-4612. (WCD; HMS)
4533 **Pinnacle Rock State Park**, US 52, Bluefield, WV 27401, (304) 248-8362. (MMA; HMS)
4534 **Pioneer Campground**, Alexander Rd., French Creek, WV 26218, (304) 924-5810. (WCD)
Pipestem Knob Tower Trail *see* entry 4535.
4535 **Pipestem Resort State Park**, SR 20, Pipestem, WV 25979, (304) 466-1800. 29.0 miles. Named trails: Canyon Rim 0.7, County Line 4.2, Farley Ridge 0.7, Lick Hollow 1.1, Northside Nature 0.7, Pipestem Knob Tower 0.6, River 6.5. (WCD; EGH; ATM; MMA; HMS; GNA)
Plantation Trail *see* entry 4522.

4536 **Pleasant Creek Public Hunting and Fishing Area**, CR 10, Philippi, WV 26416, (304) 457-4336. (WCD)

4537 **Plum Orchard Lake State Wildlife Management Area**, CR 23/11, Pax, WV 25904, (304) 469-9905. (WCD; ATM)

4538 **Plum Orchard Public Hunting and Fishing Area**, Division of Wildlife Resources, District IV, MacArthur, WV 25873, (304) 252-1173. (GNA)

Pocahontas Trail see entry 4522.
Pointy Knob Trail see entry 4522.
Pond Run Trail see entry 4494.

4539 **Ponderosa Pond Park**, M.F. Kennedy, Rt. 10, Box 158, Morgantown, WV 26505, (304) 292-9174. Named trails: Ponderosa Pond. (HMS)

Ponderosa Pond Trail see entry 4539.
Possession Camp Trail see entry 4522.
Potato Hole Run Trail see entry 4511.
Potato Knob Trail see entry 4507.

4540 **Pricketts Fort State Park**, US 250, Fairmont, WV 26554, (304) 363-3030 or (800) CALL-WVA. (ATM)

4541 **Princeton Holiday Trav-L-Park**, CR 14, Princeton, WV 24740, (304) 384-9880. (WCD)

Railroad Grade Trail see entry 4472.
Railroad Grade Trail see entry 4507.
Railroad Grade Trail see entry 4522.
Rattlesnake Trail see entry 4522.
Raven Rock Trail see entry 4482.
Raven Rocks Trail see entry 4511.
Razor Ridge Trail see entry 4517.
Red Creek Trail see entry 4486.
Red Fox Trail see entry 4517.
Redman Run Trail see entry 4522.
Reverie Trail see entry 4507.
Rhododendron Trail see entry 4461.
Rhododendron Trail see entry 4464.
Rich Mountain Fire Trail see entry 4511.
Ridenour Lake Trail see entry 4542.

4542 **Ridenour Park**, Nitro Parks and Recreation Department, City Hall, Nitro, WV 25143, (304) 753-0701. Named trails: Ridenour Lake 1.0. (HMS)

Ridge Trail see entry 4472.
Ridge Trail see entry 4522.
Ridge Trail see entry 4562.

4543 **Rippling Waters Church of God Campground**, Rt. 3, Box 177, Romance, WV 25248, (304) 988-2607. (WCD)

River Trail see entry 4527.
River Trail see entry 4535.

4544 **The Riverman Campground**, P.O. Box 360, Fayetteville, WV 25850, (304) 574-0515. Named trails: Laurel 0.7. (HMS)

Riverview Trail see entry 4464.
Road Run Trail see entry 4494.
Roaring Plains Trail see entry 4486.
Rock Camp Trail see entry 4509.
Rock City Trail see entry 4482.
Rock Cliff Trail see entry 4494.
Rock Hollow Trail see entry 4457.
Rocky Point Trail see entry 4486.
Rocky Ridge Trail see entry 4500.
Rocky Trail see entry 4455.
Rohrbrough Plains Trail see entry 4486.
Rough Run Trail see entry 4522.
Rumsey Trail see entry 4483.
Ryan Nature Trail see entry 4568.

4545 **Saint Albans City Park**, St. Albans Parks and Recreation Department, 500 Washington St., St. Albans, WV 25177, (304) 727-2101. Named trails: Saint Albans Nature 0.5. (HMS)

St. Albans Nature Trail see entry 4545.
Salt Lick Trail see entry 4507.
Saltpeter Cave Trail see entry 4552.
Saw Mill Trail see entry 4494.
Scarlet Oak Trail see entry 4547.
Scott Run Trail see entry 4482.
Sculpture Trail see entry 4508.
Seneca Creek Trail see entry 4522.

4546 **Seneca Rocks National Recreation Area**, SR 28, Seneca Rocks, WV 26884, (304) 567-2827. (ATM; MMA)

Seneca Rocks West Side Trail see entry 4522.

4547 **Seneca State Forest**, SR 28, Marlinton, WV 24954, (304) 799-6213. Named trails: Black Oak 1.2, Crestline 5.4, Hill Top 1.5, Horseshoe 1.1, Little Mountain 0.6, Scarlet Oak 1.0, Thorny Creek 3.9. (ATM; MMA; HMS; GNA)

Shavers Mountain Trail see entry 4530.

4548 **Shaw Mi-Del-Eca Resort**, US 60,

WEST VIRGINIA 313

Caldwell, WV 24925, (304) 645-6316. (WCD)
    Sheldon Trail *see* entry 4483.
    Shingle Mill Lake Trail *see* entry 4517.
    Shingletree Trail *see* entry 4522.

4549 **Short Mountain Public Hunting and Fishing Area**, Division of Wildlife Resources, District II, P.O. Drawer C, Romney, WV 26757, (304) 822-3551. (GNA)
    Sinks of Gandy Trail *see* entry 4552.
    Skyline Trail *see* entry 4455.
    Slab Camp Trail *see* entry 4522.

4550 **Sleepy Creek Public Hunting and Fishing Area**, US 522, Berkeley Springs, WV 25411, (304) 822-3551. 70.0 miles. Named trails: Big Blue 20.8. (MMA; HMS; GNA)
    Sleepy Hollow Trail *see* entry 4466.
    Smoke Camp Trail *see* entry 4522.
    Snake Valley Trail *see* entry 4522.
    South Boundary Trail *see* entry 4522.
    South Branch Trail *see* entry 4522.
    South Haddix Trail *see* entry 4522.
    South Prong Trail *see* entry 4486.

4551 **Southside Junction to Brooklyn Trail**, Pat Esmond, National Park Service, New River Gorge National River, P.O. Box 246, Glen Jean, WV 25846, (304) 465-8883. 6.4 miles straight. (GRT)
    Span Oak Trail *see* entry 4522.

4552 **Speleology Trails**, West Virginia Speleological Survey, P.O. Box 200, Barrackville, WV 26559. Named trails: Saltpeter Cave 0.6, Sinks of Gandy 0.6. (HMS)
    Spice Ridge Trail *see* entry 4522.
    Spicebush Trail *see* entry 4508.
    Spring Ridge Trail *see* entry 4522.
    Spruce Creek Trail *see* entry 4466.
    Squirrel Gap Trail *see* entry 4494.
    Staghorn Trail *see* entry 4517.
    Stone Camp Trail *see* entry 4522.
    Stone Trough Trail *see* entry 4475.
    Stonecoal Ridge Trail *see* entry 4522.
    Stonelick Trail *see* entry 4522.

4553 **Stonewall Jackson Lake State Park**, US 19, Weston, WV 26452, (304) 269-0523. (WCD)
    Strausbaugh Trail *see* entry 4483.
    Sugar Camp Trail *see* entry 4522.
    Sugar Run Trail *see* entry 4494.

4554 **Summersville Lake**, Rt. 2, Box 470, Summersville, WV 26651, (304) 872-3459 or (304) 872-3412. (MMA)
    Summit Lake Trail *see* entry 4522.
    Sunrise Carriage Trail *see* entry 4555.

4555 **Sunrise Museums**, 746 Myrtle Rd., Charleston, WV 25314, (304) 344-8035. Named trails: Gordon Trail of the Five Senses 86 yards, Sunrise Carriage 0.7. (HMS)

4556 **Sutton Lake**, c/o U.S. Army Corps of Engineers, Sutton, WV 26601. (ATM)
    Swallow Rock Trail *see* entry 4522.
    Tablerock Overlook Trail *see* entry 4522.
    Taylor Trail *see* entry 4483.
    Tea Creek Mountain Trail *see* entry 4522.
    Ten Acre Trail *see* entry 4566.

4557 **Teter Creek Lake State Wildlife Management Area**, SR 92, Belington, WV 26250, (304) 457-1162. (WCD)
    Thoreau Trail *see* entry 4528.
    Thorny Creek Trail *see* entry 4547.

4558 **Thurmond-Minden Trail**, Pat Esmond, National Park Service, New River Gorge National River, P.O. Box 246, Glen Jean, WV 25846, (304) 465-8883. 3.2 miles straight. (GRT)
    Tom Lick Trail *see* entry 4522.

4559 **Tomlinson Run State Park**, P.O. Box 97, New Manchester, WV 26056, (304) 564-3651 or (304) 564-3787. Named trails: Beech 1.1, Big Foot 1.2, Fern 0.5, Laurel 2.5. (WCD; ATM; MMA; HMS; GNA)
    Tower Falls Trail *see* entry 4489.
    Tramontane Trail *see* entry 4507.

4560 **Tri-Lake Park Campground**, 1 Tri-Lake Park, Berkeley Springs, WV 25411, (304) 258-4816. (WCD)
    Trillium Trail *see* entry 4474.
    Trout Pond Trail *see* entry 4494.
    Tulip Tree Trail *see* entry 4508.
    Tumbling Rock Trail *see* entry 4522.
    Turkey Mountain Trail *see* entry 4522.
    Turkey Run Trail *see* entry 4530.
    Turkey Spur Trail *see* entry 4566.

Twin Branch Trail *see* entry 4522.
4561 **Twin Falls State Park**, P.O. Box 236, Mullens, WV 25882, (304) 294-4000. Named trails: Cliffside 2.8, Falls 1.5, Hemlock 1.2, Huckleberry 1.4, Nature 1.2, Twin Oaks Braille 0.375. (WCD; ATM; MMA; OTB; GNA)
    Twin Oaks Braille Trail *see* entry 4561.
    Twin Rocks Trail *see* entry 4531.
    Two Lick Trail *see* entry 4522.
    Two Run Trail *see* entry 4475.
4562 **Tygart Lake State Park**, Rt. 1, Box 260, Grafton, WV 26354, (304) 265-3383. 13.0 miles. Named trails: Lake 0.4, Ridge 1.0. (WCD)
4563 **Tygart River Camping Area**, SR 310, Grafton, WV 26354, (304) 265-1282. (WCD)
    Upper Meadow Trail *see* entry 4522.
4564 **Valley Falls State Park**, Rt. 6, Box 244, Fairmont, WV 26554, (304) 363-3319. (ATM; OTB; HMS; GNA)
    Vances Cove Trail *see* entry 4494.
    Virgin Hemlock Trail *see* entry 4568.
    Virginia Trail *see* entry 4522.
    Virginius Island Trail *see* entry 4504.
4565 **Warrior Trail**, Warrior Trail Association, 313 County Office Bldg., Waynesburg, PA 15370, (412) 627-5030 or (412) 627-5039. 22.0 miles straight. (HMS)
4566 **Watoga State Park**, Star Route 1, Box 252, Marlinton, WV 24954, (304) 799-4087. 40.0 miles. Named trails: Allegheny 4.5, Arrowhead 1.0, Beaver Bog 0.3, Buckhorn 0.8, Dragon Draft 1.4, Honeybee 4.7, Honeymoon 3.5, Jacob's Well 1.3, Jesse's Cove 2.4, Lake 1.1, Laurel Ridge 1.3, Monongaseneka 8.0, Ten Acre 0.2, Turkey Spur 0.4. (WCD; EGH; ATM; MMA; HMS; GNA)
4567 **Watters Smith Memorial State Park**, US 19, West Milford, WV 26451, (304) 745-3081. Named trails: Dogwood 0.8, White Oak 2.0. (ATM; MMA; HMS)
    Weiss Knob Trail *see* entry 4472.
4568 **West Virginia University Forest**, Forest Manager, WVU Forest, Rt. 1, Box 269, Bruceton Mills, WV 26526, (304) 292-6003. Named trails: Darnell Hollow 2.4, Glade Run 1.4, Goodspeed's Highway 2.7, Johnson Hollow 3.5, Ken's Run 6.3, Lick Run 1.7, Ryan Nature 1.7, Virgin Hemlock 1.2. (HMS)
4569 **Wheeling Bicycle/Jogging Path**, Paul T. McIntire, Sr., Director, Department of Development, City of Wheeling, City-County Bldg., Wheeling, WV 26003, (304) 234-3701. 5.0 miles. (GRT)
4570 **Whisper Mountain Campground**, 3 Lick Rd., Weston, WV 26452, (304) 452-8847. (WCD)
    Whispering Spruce Trail *see* entry 4522.
    White Oak Trail *see* entry 4517.
    White Oak Trail *see* entry 4567.
    White Trail *see* entry 4480.
    Whitemeadow Ridge Trail *see* entry 4522.
    Wild Meadow Trail *see* entry 4522.
    Wilderness Trail *see* entry 4455.
    Wilderness Trail *see* entry 4507.
4571 **Wilderness Waterpark & Campground**, Rt. 1, Box 141-G, Wolf Summit, WV 26462, (304) 622-7528. (WCD)
    Wildlife Trail *see* entry 4486.
    Williams River Trail *see* entry 4522.
4572 **Wine Cellar Park**, Park Manager, City of Dunbar, Dunbar, WV 25604, (304) 766-0223. Named trails: Wine Cellar Park Nature 0.6. (HMS)
    Wine Cellar Park Nature Trail *see* entry 4572.
    Wood Thrush Trail *see* entry 4474.
    Wood Thrush Trail *see* entry 4517.
    Woodell Trail *see* entry 4489.
    Woodland Trail *see* entry 4527.
    Woodpecker Trail *see* entry 4478.
    Yellow Creek Trail *see* entry 4530.
    Yellow Trail *see* entry 4480.
    Yellow-Orange Trail *see* entry 4480.
    Yellow-Red Trail *see* entry 4480.
    Yokum Ridge Spur Trail *see* entry 4522.
    Yokum Ridge Trail *see* entry 4522.
4573 **Yokum's Vacationland**, SR 28, Seneca Rocks, WV 26884, (800) 772-8342. (WCD)
    Young's Nature Trail *see* entry 4500.

WEST VIRGINIA Index 315

Generally:
Appalachian Trail Conference, Inc., P.O. Box 807, Washington & Jackson Sts., Harpers Ferry, WV 25425-0807, (304) 535-6331. (SAR 1993)
Travel, Department of Commerce, Charleston, WV 25305, (800) 225-5982. (SFC)

Potomac Appalachian Trail Club, 1718 N St., N.W., Washington, DC 20036. (EGH)
West Virginia Scenic Trails Association, P.O. Box 4042, Charleston, WV 25304. (EGH)

Index (by city)

Alvon: Blue Bend Recreation Area 4462
Ansted: Hawk's Nest State Park 4506
Augusta: Short Mountain Public Hunting and Fishing Area 4549
Aurora: Cathedral State Park 4474
Barrackville: Speleology Trails 4552
Bartow: Monongahela National Forest 4522
Beaver: Grandview State Park 4497
Beckley: Exhibition Coal Mine City Park 4491; Lake Stephens 4513
Belington: Teter Creek Lake State Wildlife Management Area 4557
Berkeley Springs: Cacapon State Park 4467; Coolfont Resort Campground 4480; Sleepy Creek Public Hunting and Fishing Area 4550; Tri-Lake Park Campground 4560
Bluefield: Pinnacle Rock State Park 4533
Bruceton Mills: Chestnut Ridge County Park 4476; Coopers Rock State Forest 4482; West Virginia University Forest 4568
Buckhannon: Audra State Park 4454
Burnsville: Burnsville Lake 4465
Cairo: North Bend State Park 4527
Caldwell: Greenbrier State Forest 4500; Shaw Mi-Del-Eca Resort 4548
Camp Creek: Camp Creek State Forest 4471
Charleston: Allegheny Trail 4450; Camp Buckskin 4469; Coonskin Park 4481; The Elk River Trail 4490; Kanawha State Forest 4509; Kanawha Trace 4510; Sunrise Museums 4555
Clarksburg: Harrison County Parks and Recreation Bike and Hike Trail 4505
Clifftop: Babcock State Park 4455
Davis: Blackwater Falls State Park 4461; Canaan Valley State Park 4472

Dunbar: Wine Cellar Park 4572
Dunmore: Camp Chief Logan 4470
East Lynn: East Lynn Lake 4488
Elkins: Alpine Shores Campground 4451; Monongahela National Forest 4522; Otter Creek Area 4530
Fairmont: Lewis Wetzel Public Hunting and Fishing Area 4515; Marion County Trail 4518; Pricketts Fort State Park 4540; Valley Falls State Park 4564
Fayetteville: Mary Ingles Trail 4519; New River Gorge Campgrounds 4526; The Riverman Campground 4544
French Creek: Elk River Public Hunting and Fishing Area 4489; Pioneer Campground 4534
Gap Mills: Moncove Lake Public Hunting and Fishing Area 4520; Moncove Lake State Park 4521
Glen Jean: Glade Creek Trail 4495; Southside Junction to Brooklyn Trail 4551; Thurmond-Minden Trail 4558
Glenville: Cedar Creek State Park 4475
Grafton: Tygart Lake State Park 4562; Tygart River Camping Area 4563
Hacker Valley: Holly River State Park 4507
Harpers Ferry: Harpers Ferry Camp Resort 4502; Harpers Ferry Heritage Trail 4503; Harpers Ferry National Historical Park 4504
Harrisonburg: George Washington National Forest 4494
Hartford: Lizard Mound State Park 4516
Hazelton: Pine Hill Campground & Cabins 4532
Hillsboro: Beartown State Park 4456; Droop Mountain Battlefield State Park 4487
Hinton: Bluestone Public Hunting and

Fishing Area 4463; Bluestone State Park 4464
Huntington: Adahi Trail 4449; Beech Fork State Park 4458; Huntington Galleries 4508
Huttonsville: Kumbrabow State Forest 4511
Keslers Cross Lanes: Carnifex Ferry Battlefield State Park 4473
Lavalette: Beech Fork Lake 4457
Lenore: Laurel Lake Public Hunting and Fishing Area 4514
Logan: Chief Logan State Park 4478
Marlinton: Calvin Price State Forest 4468; Handley Public Hunting and Fishing Area 4501; Monongahela National Forest 4522; Seneca State Forest 4547; Watoga State Park 4566
Mathias: Lost River State Park 4517
Milton: Fox Fire Camping Resort 4493
Morgantown: The Core Arboretum 4483; Ponderosa Pond Park 4539
Moundsville: Grand Vue Park 4496; Grave Creek Mound State Park 4498
Mullens: Twin Falls State Park 4561
Nellis: Fork Creek Public Hunting and Fishing Area 4492
Neola: Lake Sherwood 4512
New Manchester: Tomlinson Run State Park 4559
Nitro: Ridenour Park 4542
Panther: Panther State Forest 4531
Parkersburg: Mountwood Park 4524
Parsons: Monongahela National Forest 4522; Otter Creek Area 4530
Pax: Plum Orchard Lake State Wildlife Management Area 4537; Plum Orchard Public Hunting and Fishing Area 4538
Petersburg: Dolly Sods Scenic Area 4486; Monongahela National Forest 4522

Philippi: Pleasant Creek Public Hunting and Fishing Area 4536
Pipestem: Pipestem Resort State Park 4535
Point Pleasant: Big Ugly Public Hunting and Fishing Area 4460; Clifton F. McClintic Wildlife Station 4479; Oldtown Campground 4529
Princeton: Princeton Holiday Trav-L-Park 4541
Richwood: Cranberry Back Country 4484; Monongahela National Forest 4522
Romance: Rippling Waters Church of God Campground 4543
Romney: Nathaniel Mountain Public Hunting and Fishing Area 4525
St. Albans: Saint Albans City Park 4545
Seneca Rocks: Seneca Rocks National Recreation Area 4546; Yokum's Vacationland 4573
Southside: Chief Cornstalk Public Hunting and Fishing Area 4477
Summersville: Mountain Lake Campground 4523; Summersville Lake 4554
Sutton: Sutton Lake 4556
Triadelphia: Dallas Pike Campground 4485
Washington, DC: Big Blue Trail 4459
Waynesburg, PA: Warrior Trail 4565
West Milford: Watters Smith Memorial State Park 4567
Weston: Stonewall Jackson Lake State Park 4553; Whisper Mountain Campground 4570
Wheeling: Oglebay Park 4528; Wheeling Bicycle/Jogging Path 4569
White Sulphur Springs: Monongahela National Forest 4522
Wilsondale: Cabwaylingo State Forest 4466
Wolf Summit: Wilderness Waterpark & Campground 4571

Wisconsin

4574 **Adventureland**, CR Y, Gordon, WI 54838, (715) 376-4528. (WCD)

4575 **Ahnapee River Trails Campground**, Wilson Rd., Algoma, WI 54201, (414) 487-5777. (WCD)

4576 **Ahnapee State Park Trail**, Arnie Lindauer, c/o Potawatomi State Park, 3740 Park Dr., Sturgeon Bay, WI 54235, (414) 746-2890. 15.2 miles straight. (GRT)

4577 **Alfred L. Boerner Botanical Gardens**, Whitnall Park, 5879 S. 92nd St., Hales Corners, WI 53130, (414) 425-1130. (GFA)

4578 **American Adventure Camping**, SR 13, Wisconsin Dells, WI 53965, (608) 254-6485. (WCD)

4579 **Amnicon Falls State Park**, SR 2, Superior, WI 54880, (715) 398-3000 or (715) 398-8073. (ATW; WCD; MGL; OTB)

Anvil Trails see entry 4792.

4580 **Apostle Islands National Lakeshore**, Rt. 1, Box 4, Bayfield, WI 54814, (715) 779-3397. (ATW; WCD; GFC; MGL; RTR; NPS; NPV; OTB; CGA; YNP; ANP)

4581 **Apple River Campground**, SR 35, Somerset, WI 54025, (715) 247-3378. (WCD)

4582 **Apple River Campground North**, 165th Ave., Balsam Lake, WI 54810, (715) 268-8980. (WCD)

4583 **Arbor Vitae Trailer Resort & Camping Park**, Big Arbor Dr., Woodruff, WI 54568, (715) 356-5146. (WCD)

4584 **Arrowhead Campground**, P.O. Box 295, Wisconsin Dells, WI 53965, (608) 254-7344. (WCD)

Arrowhead Trail see entry 4660.

Balanced Rock Trail see entry 4654.

4585 **Barbican Woods Campground**, 2650 10th Ave., Adams, WI 53910, (608) 584-5343. (WCD)

4586 **Bark River Campgrounds**, Hanson Rd., Jefferson, WI 53549, (414) 593-2421. (WCD)

4587 **Bass Lake Campground**, N. 1497 Southern Rd., Lyndon Station, WI 53944, (608) 666-2311. (WCD)

4588 **Bay Park Resort & Campground**, Rt. 2, Box 2140A, Trego, WI 54888, (715) 635-2840. (WCD)

4589 **Bayshore County Park**, Green Bay, WI 54303, (414) 448-4466. (WCD)

4590 **Bear Paw Resort Campground**, Town Hall Rd., Hayward, WI 54893, (715) 462-3684. (WCD)

4591 **Bearskin State Park Trail**, Bill Eldred, Superintendent, 4125 CR M, Boulder Junction, WI 54512, (715) 385-2727. 18.4 miles straight. (GRT)

4592 **Benoit Lake Campground**, CR G, Spooner, WI 54801, (715) 635-2421. (WCD)

4593 **Benson's Century Camping Resort**, SR 67, Campbellsport, WI 53010, (414) 533-8597. (WCD)

4594 **Big Bay State Park**, CR H, Bayfield, WI 54814, (715) 779-3346. (ATW; WCD)

4595 **Big Foot Beach State Park**, SR 120, Lake Geneva, WI 53147, (414) 248-2528. (ATW; WCD)

4596 **Big Lake Campground**, SR 42, Algoma, WI 54201, (414) 487-2726. (WCD)

Birch Grove Trail see entry 4637.

4597 **Birchwood Beach Resort, Campground & Stable**, Spirit Lake Rd., Frederic, WI 54837, (715) 327-8965. (WCD)

4598 **Birchwood Campground**, Lucas Ln., Boulder Junction, WI 54512, (715) 385-2882. (WCD)

4599 **Birkensee Resort & Camping**, CR H, Tomahawk, WI 54487, (715) 453-5103. (WCD)

4600 **Black River Falls State Forest**, SR 54, Black River Falls, WI 54615, (715) 284-5301 or (715) 284-4103. (ATW; WCD; MGL)

4601 **Blackhawk Campground**, Blackhawk Rd., Milton, WI 53563, (608) 868-2586. (WCD)

4602 **Blackhawk Lake Recreation Area**, CR BH, Highland, WI 53543, (608) 623-2707. (ATW; WCD)

4603 **Blackhawk Ridge Recreation Area**, P.O. Box 516, Sauk City, WI 53583, (608) 643-3775. (MGL)

Blackhawk Trail see entry 4660.

4604 **Blue Lake Campground**, CR G, Wisconsin Dells, WI 53965, (608) 586-4376. (WCD)

4605 **Blue Mound State Park**, P.O. Box 98, Mounds Rd., Blue Mounds, WI 53517, (608) 437-5711. (ATW; WCD; MGL)

4606 **Bluebird Springs Recreation Area**, Smith Valley Rd., LaCrosse, WI 54601, (608) 781-CAMP. (WCD)

4607 **Bong State Recreation Area**, 26313 Burlington Rd., Kansasville, WI 53139, (414) 878-4416 or (414) 878-5600. (ATW; WCD; MGL)

4608 **Bosley's Upper Webb Lake Campground**, SR 77, Webb Lake, WI 54830, (715) 259-3363. (WCD)

4609 **Brian's Campground**, Bluebird Rd., Lake Tomahawk, WI 54539, (715) 277-2626. (WCD)

4610 **Broken Bow Campground**, 14855 Deer Trail Rd., Lac Du Flambeau, WI 54538, (715) 588-3844. (WCD)

4611 **Browntown-Cadiz Springs State Park**, SR 11, Browntown, WI 53522. (ATW)

4612 **Brule River State Forest**, P.O. Box 125, Superior, WI 54880, (715) 372-4866. (ATW; WCD; MGL)

4613 **Brunet Island State Park**, Rt. 2, Box 158, Park Rd., Cornell, WI 54732, (715) 239-6888. (ATW; WCD; MGL)

4614 **Brush Creek Campground**, 17th Ave., Ontario, WI 54651, (608) 337-4344. (WCD)

4615 **Buckatabon Lodge & Lighthouse Inn**, Rush Rd., Conover, WI 54519, (715) 479-4660. (WCD)

4616 **Buckhorn State Park**, Rt. 2, Box 720, Necedah, WI 54646, (608) 565-2789 or (608) 565-2425. (ATW; WCD; MGL)

4617 **Buffalo River State Park Trail**, Philip Palzkill, Perrot State Park, Rt. 1, Box 407, Trempealeau, WI 54661, (608) 534-6409. 36.4 miles straight. (GRT)

4618 **Bugline Trail**, Dave Burch, Senior Landscape Architect, Waukesha County Parks and Planning Commission, 500 Riverview Ave., Waukesha, WI 53188, (414) 548-7790. 13.0 miles straight. (GRT)

4619 **Burlington Trail**, Tom Statz, Racine County Department of Public Works, 14200 Washington Ave., Sturtevant, WI 53177, (414) 886-8457. 4.0 miles straight. (GRT)

Burma Road see entry 4654.

Butternut Lake Forest Trail see entry 4792.

4620 **Callahan Lake Resort & Campground**, Callahan Lake Rd., Hayward, WI 54843, (715) 462-3244. (WCD)

4621 **Calumet County Park**, N. 6150 CR EE, Hilbert, WI 54129, (414) 439-1008. (WCD)

4622 **Camp Holiday**, Rudolph Lake Ln., Boulder Junction, WI 54512, (715) 385-2264. (WCD)

4623 **Camp Indian Head Campground**, SR 70, Stone Lake, WI 54876, (715) 865-3911. (WCD)

4624 **Camp Lefeber Northwoods**, Milwaukee County Council, BSA, 330 S. 84th St., Milwaukee, WI 53214, (414) 774-1776; or Camp Lefeber, Hardwood Lake, Laona, WI 54541, (715) 674-2054. (SFC)

4625 **Camp Ma-Ka-Ja-Wah**, Northeast Illinois Council, BSA, 2745 Skokie Valley Rd., Highland Park, IL 60035, (312) 433-1813; or Camp Ma-Ka-Ja-Wah, Pearson, WI 54462, (715) 484-2346. (SFC)

4626 **Camp Napowan**, Northwest Suburban Council, BSA, 1300 E. Rand Rd., Arlington Heights, IL 60004, (312) 394-5050; or Camp Napowan, Rt. 2, Box 625, Wild Rose, WI 54984, (414) 622-3680. (SFC)

4627 **Camp Phillips**, Chippewa Valley Council, BSA, 710 S. Hastings Way, Eau Claire, WI 54701, (715) 832-6671; or Camp Phillips, Haugen, WI 54841. (SFC)

4628 **Camp Shin-Go-Beek**, Thatcher Woods Area Council, BSA, 855 Madison St., Oak Park, IL 60302, (312) 345-1444; or Camp Shin-Go-Beek, Rt. 2, Waupaca, WI 54981, (715) 258-2271. (SFC)

4629 **Camp Tesomas**, Samoset Council, BSA, 720 Grant St., Wausau, WI 54401, (715) 845-2195; or Camp Tesomas, 5403 Spiderlake Rd., Rhinelander, WI 54501, (715) 369-1461. (SFC)

4630 **Castle Rock County Park**, CR Z, Friendship, WI 53934, (608) 339-7713. (WCD)

4631 **Castle Rock County Park**, CR G, Mauston, WI 53948, (608) 847-9389. (WCD)

CCC Trail see entry 4654.

4632 **Cedar Falls Camp Resort**, Cedar Falls Rd., Hazelhurst, WI 54531, (715) 356-4953. (WCD)

4633 **Cedar Hills Campground**, Dunlap Hollow Rd., Sauk City, WI 53583, (608) 795-2606. (WCD)

4634 **Cedar Valley Campground**, Cedar Valley Rd., Kewaunee, WI 54216, (414) 388-4983. (WCD)

4635 **Charlie Brown's Campground**, N. Flowage Dr., Gordon, WI 54838, (715) 376-4422. (WCD)

4636 **Cheese Country Recreation Trail**, Stephen Hubner, Project Coordinator, Ag Center, Darlington, WI 53530, (608) 776-4830. 47.0 miles straight. (GRT)

4637 **Chequamegon National Forest**, 157 N. 5th Ave., Park Falls, WI 54552, (715) 762-2461 or (715) 373-2667. 200 miles. Named trails: Birch Grove, Eastwood, Long Lake, Pigeon Lake, Two Lakes. (ATW; WCD; EGH; MGL; FGU; NFG)

4638 **Chetek River Campground**, River Rd., Chetek, WI 54728, (715) 924-2440. (WCD)

4639 **Chutte Pond County Park**, SR 32/64, Mountain, WI 54149, (715) 276-6261. (WCD)

4640 **Circle K Campground**, Island Rd., Palmyra, WI 53156, (414) 495-2896. (WCD)

4641 **Circus Heritage Trail**, Baraboo Circus Heritage, Four Lakes Council, BSA, 34 Schroeder Ct., Madison, WI 53711, (608) 273-1005 or fax (608) 273-8686. Awards available. (AA 1995)

4642 **Clam Lake Resort & Campground**, 24755 Clam Lake Dr., Siren, WI 54872, (715) 349-5185. (WCD)

4643 **Clover Creek Trail**, Kay Getting, Recreation Planner, 1170 4th Ave. S., Park Falls, WI 54552, (715) 762-2461. 15.8 miles straight. (GRT)

4644 **Comfort Cove Campground**, Solberg Lake Rd., Phillips, WI 54555, (715) 339-3360. (WCD)

Compass Trails see entry 4660.

4645 **Concord Center Campground**, W. 901 Concord Center Dr., Sullivan, WI 53178, (414) 593-2707. (WCD)

4646 **Copper Falls State Park**, SR 169, Mellen, WI 54546, (715) 274-5123. (ATW; WCD; MGL)

4647 **Council Grounds State Park**, SR 107, Merrill, WI 54452, (715) 536-8773. (ATW; WCD)

4648 **Crazy Horse Campground**, CR F, Brodhead, WI 53520, (608) 897-2207. (WCD)

4649 **Creekview Campground**, Albion Rd., Edgerton, WI 53534, (608) 884-3288. (WCD)

4650 **Crex Meadows Wildlife Area**, P.O. Box 367, Grantsburg, WI 54840, (715) 463-2899. (MGL)

4651 **Deer Trail Park Campground**, CR Z, Nekoosa, WI 54457, (715) 886-3871. (WCD)

4652 **Dell Boo Campground**, P.O. Box 407, Wisconsin Dells, WI 53965, (608) 356-5898. (WCD)

4653 **Dells Timberland Campground**, US 12/16, Wisconsin Dells, WI 53965, (608) 254-2429. (WCD)

Devil's Doorway Trail see entry 4654.

4654 **Devil's Lake State Park**, S. 5975 Park Rd., Baraboo, WI 53913, (608) 356-8301. Named trails: Balanced Rock, Burma Road, CCC, Devil's Doorway, East Bluff, East Bluff Woods, Grottos, Koshawago

Spring, Landmarks Nature, Moraine, Pine Tree Nature, Potholes, Trail to Group Camp, Tumbled Rocks, West Bluff. (ATW; WCD; WOB; CGD)

4655 **Devil's Lake Trail**, Badger Trails, Inc., P.O. Box 10266, Milwaukee, WI 53210. 14.0 miles. Awards available. (HTA)

4656 **Devils River Campers Park**, CR R, Maribel, WI 54227, (414) 863-2812. (WCD)

Devil's Run Trail see entry 4792.

4657 **Dexter County Park**, SR 54, Pittsville, WI 54466, (715) 421-8422. (WCD)

4658 **Door County Kamping Resort**, Court Rd., Egg Harbor, WI 54209, (414) 868-3151. (WCD)

4659 **Double K-D Ranch**, CR W, Baraboo, WI 53913, (608) 356-4622. (WCD)

4660 **Eagle Cave Natural Park**, Rt. 2, Box 107, Blue River, WI 53518, (608) 537-2988. Named trails: Arrowhead 4.0, Blackhawk 3.0, Compass Trails, Eagle Cave 5.0, Gold Nugget 2.0, Mountain Goat 2.5, Old Stage Line 10.0. (AA 1994)

Eagle Cave Trail see entry 4660.

4661 **Eagle Flats Campground**, CR J, Wisconsin Dells, WI 53965, (608) 254-2764. (WCD)

East Bluff Trail see entry 4654.

East Bluff Woods Trail see entry 4654.

Eastwood Trail see entry 4637.

4662 **Eau Galle Lake Park**, Van Buren Rd., Spring Valley, WI 54767. (ATW)

4663 **Echo Valley Resort & Campground**, CR T, White Lake, WI 54491, (715) 276-7272. (WCD)

4664 **Eden Valley Camping & Par 3 Golf**, US 14, Richland Center, WI 53581, (608) 647-8450. (WCD)

4665 **Elroy-Sparta National Recreation Trail**, Sparta Area Chamber of Commerce, P.O. Box 26, Sparta, WI 54656; or Elroy-Sparta State Trail, P.O. Box 153, Kendall, WI 54638, (608) 463-7109 or (608) 337-4775; or Wisconsin Department of Natural Resources, P.O. Box 450, Madison, WI 53701; or Ron Nelson, Superintendent, Wildcat Mountain State Park, P.O. Box 99, Ontario, WI 54651, (608) 337-4775. 32.5 miles straight. (GRT; MGL; WOB; OTB; NFG; HTM)

4666 **Emma Carlin Hiking Trail**, County Trunk Z, Palmyra, WI 53156. (WOB)

4667 **Enchanted Inn Campground & Resort**, CR Y, Gordon, WI 54838, (715) 795-2517. (WCD)

4668 **Evergreen Acres Campground**, US 2, Ashland, WI 54806, (715) 682-4658. (WCD)

4669 **Evergreen Campsites**, Archer Ln., Wild Rose, WI 54984, (414) 622-3498. (WCD)

4670 **Family Frontier Campground**, CR A, Amherst, WI 54406, (715) 824-3614. (WCD)

4671 **Fischer's Campground**, SR 80, New Lisbon, WI 53950, (608) 562-5355. (WCD)

4672 **Fischer's Crooked River Campground**, Rt. 3, Box 52, Montello, WI 53949, (608) 297-7307. (WCD)

4673 **Flambeau River State Forest**, P.O. Box 51, CR W, Winter, WI 54896, (715) 332-5271. 72.8 miles. (ATW; WCD; MGL; BHT; HTM)

4674 **Flanagan's Pearl Lake Campsites**, Pearl Lake Rd., Redgranite, WI 54970, (414) 566-2758. (WCD)

4675 **Flying J Campground**, US 14, Lone Rock, WI 53556, (608) 583-5111. (WCD)

4676 **Fond du Lac County Park**, CR MMM, Waupun, WI 53963, (414) 324-2769. (WCD)

4677 **Forest County Veterans Memorial Park**, East Shore Rd., Crandon, WI 54520, (715) 478-3475. (WCD)

4678 **Fort Flambeau Resort & Campground**, Turtle Flambeau Dam Rd., Butternut, WI 54514, (715) 476-2510. (WCD)

4679 **The "400" State Trail**, Ron Nelson, Superintendent, Wildcat Work Unit, P.O. Box 99, Ontario, WI 54651, (608) 337-4775; or Jerry Trumm, Superintendent, Mirror Lake State Park, E. 10320 Fern Dell Rd., Baraboo, WI 53913, (608) 254-2333. 22.0 miles straight. (GRT)

4680 **Fox Hill Campground**, Reedsburg Rd., Baraboo, WI 53913, (608) 356-5890. (WCD)

4681 **Frontier Bar & Campground**, US 2, Saxon, WI 54559, (715) 893-2461. (WCD)
4682 **Gandy Dancer Trail**, Mike Luedeke, Burnett County Forest Administrator, Burnett County Forest and Parks Department, 7410 CR K, P.O. Box 106, Siren, WI 54872, (715) 349-2157; or Bob Wilson, Parks and Recreation Director, Polk County Parks Department, P.O. Box 623, Balsam Lake, WI 54810, (715) 485-3161; or Mark Schroeder, Assistant Parks and Recreation Department, P.O. Box 211, Solon Springs, WI 54873, (715) 378-2219. 67.0 miles straight planned, current as to 55.0 miles. (GRT)
4683 **George W. Mead Wildlife Area**, CR S, Milladore, WI 54454. (MGL)
4684 **Glacial Drumlin State Park Trail**, Dana White, Glacial Drumlin Trail, West, 1213 S. Main St., Lake Mills, WI 53551, (414) 648-8774; or Paul Sandgren, Glacial Drumlin Trail, East, N. 846 W. 329, C.T.H. C, Delafield, WI 53018, (414) 646-3025. 47.2 miles straight. (GRT)
4685 **Glacial Hiking Trail**, Ice Age National Scientific Reserve, c/o Department of Natural Resources, Division of Tourism and Information, P.O. Box 450, Madison, WI 53701; or Wisconsin Department of Natural Resources, P.O. Box 7921, Madison, WI 53707, (608) 266-2181. 30.0 miles. (PGF; CGA)
4686 **Glacier Hills Park**, Freiss Lake Rd., Richfield, WI 53076. (ATW)
4687 **Glacier Wilderness Campground**, SR 64, Elton, WI 54430, (715) 882-4781. (WCD)
  Gold Nugget Trail see entry 4660.
4688 **Good Turn Trail**, 2374 N. 65th St., Wauwatosa, WI 53213. 12.0 miles. Awards available. (HTA)
4689 **Goose Island County Park**, CR GI, LaCrosse, WI 54601, (608) 785-7018. (ATW; WCD; MGL)
4690 **Gordon Bubolz Nature Preserve**, CR A, Appleton, WI 54915, (414) 731-6041. (ATW)
4691 **Governor Dodge State Park**, Rt. 1, Box 42, Dodgeville, WI 53533, (608) 935-2315. (ATW; WCD; MGL)
4692 **Governor Knowles State Forest**, P.O. Box 367, Grantsburg, WI 54840, (715) 463-2898. 44.0 miles. (EGH; MGL)
4693 **Grand Valley Campground**, CR B, Kingston, WI 53939, (414) 394-3643. (WCD)
4694 **Grandpa's Bluff Campground**, CR EE, Baileys Harbor, WI 54202, (414) 839-2109. (WCD)
4695 **Granger's Campground**, CR PP, Oakdale, WI 54649, (608) 372-4511. (WCD)
4696 **Great River State Park Trail**, Philip Palzkill, Perrot State Park, Rt. 1, Box 407, Trempealeau, WI 54661, (608) 534-6409. 22.5 miles straight. (GRT)
4697 **Green Lake Conference Center**, American Baptist Assembly, Green Lake, WI 54991, (414) 294-3323 or (800) 558-8898. (MGL)
4698 **Grotto Pilgrimage Trail**, 1930 Lincoln St., Wisconsin Rapids, WI 54494. (MVC)
  Grottos Trail see entry 4654.
4699 **Hager's Hilly Haven Campground**, SR 28, Cascade, WI 53011, (414) 528-8966. (WCD)
4700 **Ham Lake Campground**, SR 32, Laona, WI 54541, (715) 674-2201. (WCD)
4701 **Happy Acres Kampground**, CR NN, Bristol, WI 53104, (414) 857-7373. (WCD)
4702 **Harrington Beach State Park**, CR O, Belgium, WI 53004. (ATW)
4703 **Hartman Creek State Park**, N. 2480 Hartman Creek Rd., Waupaca, WI 54981, (715) 258-2372. (ATW; WCD; MGL)
4704 **Havenwoods Environmental Awareness Center**, 6141 N. Hopkins St., Milwaukee, WI 53209, (414) 527-0232. 3.0 mile. (WOB)
4705 **Hayward-KOA**, Rt. 3, Hayward, WI 54843, (715) 634-2331. (WCD)
4706 **Hiawatha Trail**, Lincoln County Forestry Land and Parks, Courthouse Bldg., Merrill, WI 54452, (715) 536-0327. 6.6 miles straight. (GRT)
4707 **Hiawatha Trailer Resort**, Balsam St., Woodruff, WI 54568, (715) 356-6111. (WCD)
4708 **Hickory Hills Campground**, 856 Hillside Rd., Edgerton, WI 53534, (608) 884-6327. (WCD)

4709 **Hideaway Acres**, CR Z, Dodgeville, WI 53533, (608) 935-5019. (WCD)
4710 **High Cliff State Park**, N. 7475 High Cliff Rd., Menasha, WI 54952, (414) 989-1106. (ATW; WCD; MGL)
4711 **Hoeft's Resort & Campground**, W. 9070 Crooked Lake Dr., Cascade, WI 53011, (414) 626-2221. (WCD)
4712 **Holiday Shores Campground & Resort**, 3900 River Rd., Wisconsin Dells, WI 53965, (608) 254-2717. (WCD)
4713 **Homestead Hollow Park**, US 41, Milwaukee, WI 53201. (ATW)
4714 **Horicon Marsh Wildlife Area**, 1210 N. Palmatory St., Horicon, WI 53032, (414) 485-3000. (ATW)
4715 **Horicon National Wildlife Refuge**, W4279 Headquarters Rd., Mayville, WI 53050, (414) 387-2658. 6.0 miles. (ATW; MGL; OTB; GNW)
4716 **Hortonville to Oshkosh Recreation Trail**, Christopher Brandt, Director, Outagamie County Parks, Rt. 3, Plamann Park, Appleton, WI 54915, (414) 733-3019; or Jeffrey A. Christensen, Parks Director, Winnebago County Department of Parks, 500 E. CR Y, Oshkosh, WI 54901, (414) 424-0042. 20.3 miles straight. (GRT)
4717 **Ice Age National Scenic Trail**, National Park Service, 7818 Big Sky Dr., Madison, WI 53719; or Wisconsin Department of Natural Resources, P.O. Box 7921, Madison, WI 53707, (608) 266-2181; or Ice Age National Scenic Trail, c/o Midwest Regional Office, National Park Service, 1709 Jackson St., Omaha, NE 68102, (402) 221-3481. 1000 miles straight. (EGH; PGF; GOP; NPF; NPE; CGA; CGD; NFG)
4718 **Indian Shores**, SR 47, Woodruff, WI 54568, (715) 356-5552. (WCD)
4719 **Indian Trails Campground**, Rt. 1, Pardeeville, WI 53954, (608) 429-3244. (WCD)
4720 **Interstate State Park**, P.O. Box 703, St. Croix Falls, WI 54024, (715) 483-3747. (ATW; WCD; MGL)
4721 **Iodine Snowmobile Trail**, Kay Getting, Recreation Planner, 1170 4th Ave. S., Park Falls, WI 54552, (715) 762-2461. 4.0 miles straight. (GRT)

4722 **Irish Brothers River of Lakes Resort**, Willow Ln., Bagley, WI 53801, (608) 996-2275. (WCD)
4723 **Irvine Park**, SR 124, Chippewa Falls, WI 54729, (715) 723-3890 or (715) 723-0051. (ATW)
4724 **Island Camping & Recreation**, East Side Rd., Washington Island, WI 54246, (414) 847-2622. (WCD)
4725 **Jordan County Park**, CR Y, Stevens Point, WI 54481, (715) 346-1433. (WCD)
4726 **Kamp Dakota**, Tritz Rd., Portage, WI 53901, (608) 742-5599. (WCD)
4727 **Kamp Kegonsa Camping Resort**, Circle Dr., Stoughton, WI 53589, (608) 873-5800. (WCD)
4728 **Kastle Kampground**, Kinney Lake Rd., Marion, WI 54950, (715) 754-5900. (WCD)
4729 **Kenosha County Bike Trail**, Domenick Ventura or Ric Ladine, Kenosha County Parks, 761 Green Bay Rd., Kenosha, WI 53144, (414) 552-8500. 14.2 miles straight. (GRT)
4730 **Kettle Moraine Glacial Trail**, Badger Trails, Inc., P.O. Box 10266, Milwaukee, WI 53210. 18.0 miles. Awards available. (MVC; HTA)
4731 **Kettle Moraine State Forest** (Northern Unit), P.O. Box 410, Campbellsport, WI 53010, (414) 626-2116. 70.0 miles. (ATW; WCD; EGH; MGL)
4732 **Kettle Moraine State Forest** (Southern Unit), SR 59, Eagle, WI 53119, (414) 594-2135. 75.0 miles. (ATW; EGH; MGL)
4733 **Keyes Lake Campground**, SR 101, Florence, WI 54121, (715) 528-5320. (WCD)
    Kimball Creek Trail *see* entry 4792.
4734 **Klondyke Secluded Acres**, Pine Knob Rd., Lancaster, WI 53813, (800) 858-9477. (WCD)
4735 **KOA-Alma Center**, SR 95, Alma Center, WI 54611, (715) 964-2508. (WCD)
4736 **KOA-Fond du Lac**, CR B, Fond du Lac, WI 54935, (414) 477-2300. (WCD)
4737 **Kohler Andrae State Park** *see* entry 4893. (ATW)
    Koshawago Spring Trail *see* entry 4654.

WISCONSIN

4738 **Kosir's Rapid Rafts, Campground & Restaurant**, CR C, Crivitz, WI 54114, (715) 757-3431. (WCD)

4739 **LaBarre's Shady Bay Resort & Campground**, Nelson Lake Rd., Hayward, WI 54843, (715) 634-2097. (WCD)

4740 **LaCrosse River State Park Trail**, Ron Nelson, Superintendent, LaCrosse River State Park Trail, c/o Wildcat Mountain State Park, P.O. Box 99, Ontario, WI 54651, (608) 337-4775. 21.5 miles straight. (GRT)

4741 **Lake Chippewa Campground**, CR CC, Hayward, WI 54843, (715) 462-3672. (WCD)

4742 **Lake Dubay Shores Campground & RV Park**, 1713 Dubay Dr., Mosinee, WI 54455, (715) 457-2484. (WCD)

4743 **Lake Emilee County Park**, Old US 18, Amherst Junction, WI 54407, (715) 346-1433. (WCD)

4744 **Lake George Campsite**, Bus. US 8, Rhinelander, WI 54501, (715) 362-6152. (WCD)

4745 **Lake Joy Campground**, Bethel Grove Rd., Belmont, WI 53510, (608) 762-5150. (WCD)

4746 **Lake Kegonsa State Park**, Door Creek Rd., Stoughton, WI 53589, (608) 873-9695. (ATW; WCD; MGL)

4747 **Lake Lenwood Campground**, Wallace Lake Rd., West Bend, WI 53095, (414) 334-1335. (WCD)

4748 **Lake Mason Campground**, 1st Ln., Briggsville, WI 53920, (608) 981-2444. (WCD)

4749 **Lake of the Woods Campground**, 14th Ave., Wautoma, WI 54982, (414) 787-3601. (WCD)

4750 **Lake Wissota State Park**, Rt. 8, Box 360, CR K, Chippewa Falls, WI 54729, (715) 382-4574. (ATW; WCD; MGL)

4751 **Lakeland Camping Resort**, SR 59, Milton, WI 53563, (608) 868-4700. (WCD)

Landmarks Nature Trail *see* entry 4654.

4752 **Laursen's Campground**, Town Line Rd., Whitewater, WI 53190, (608) 883-2920. (WCD)

Lauterman National Recreation Trail *see* entry 4792.

4753 **Lazy Acres Ranch Campground**, Ellingson Rd., Northfield, WI 54635, (715) 964-8400. (WCD)

4754 **Lazy Days Campground**, Lakeview Rd., West Bend, WI 53095, (414) 675-6511. (WCD)

4755 **Lighthouse Rock Campground**, N. Walnut St., Reedsburg, WI 53959, (608) 524-4203. (WCD)

4756 **Little Bluff Campground**, N. 4003 Traut Rd., Rio, WI 53960, (414) 992-5157. (WCD)

4757 **Lizard Mound County Park**, SR 144, Port Washington, WI 53074, (414) 338-4445. (ATW; MGL)

4758 **Lofty Pines RV Park**, Big St. Germain Dr., St. Germain, WI 54558, (715) 542-3100. (WCD)

Long Lake Trail *see* entry 4637.

4759 **Lucius Woods County Park**, Marion Ave., Solon Springs, WI 54873, (715) 378-4528. (WCD; OTB)

4760 **MacKenzie Environmental Educational Center**, CR CS/Q, Poynette, WI 53955, (608) 635-4498. (ATW; MGL; GFA)

4761 **Manitou Valley Campground**, SR 35, Superior, WI 54880, (715) 399-8696. (WCD)

4762 **Mann's Harbor Campground**, SR 32, Three Lakes, WI 54562, (715) 546-3520. (WCD)

4763 **Maple Heights Campground**, P.O. Box 201, Lakewood, WI 54138-0201, (715) 276-6441. (WCD)

4764 **Maple View Campground**, N. 1267 Norman Rd., Kewaunee, WI 54216, (414) 776-1588. (WCD)

4765 **Marquette Trail**, The Optimist Club, P.O. Box 602, Portage, WI 53901; or Joseph A. Halasz, 104 E. Washington, Portage, WI 53901. 11.0 miles. Awards available. (AA 1992)

4766 **McCaslin Mountain Campground**, CR F, Athelstane, WI 54104, (715) 757-3734. (WCD)

4767 **Meadowlark Acres Campground**, North Rd., Burlington, WI 53105, (414) 763-7200. (WCD)

4768 **Memory Lake City Park**, Grantsburg, WI 54840, (715) 463-2405. (WCD)

4769 **Menominee River Campground**, US 2/141, Florence, WI 54121, (715) 696-3772. (WCD)

4770 **Merlin Lambert County Park**, McKenna Rd., Black River Falls, WI 54615. (WCD)

4771 **Merrick State Park**, SR 35, Galesville, WI 54630, (608) 687-4936. (ATW; WCD; MGL)

4772 **Merry Mac's Camp'n**, E. 12540 Hallweg Rd., Merrimac, WI 53561, (608) 493-2367. (WCD)

4773 **Military Ridge State Park Trail**, Gregory J. Pittz, Trail Manager, Military Ridge State Park Trail, Rt. 1, Box 42, Dodgeville, WI 53533, (608) 935-2315. 39.6 miles straight planned, current as to 37.9 miles. (GRT)

4774 **Mill Bluff State Park**, US 12/SR 16, Camp Douglas, WI 54637, (608) 337-4773. (ATW; WCD)

4775 **Milwaukee History Trail**, Milwaukee County Council, BSA, 330 S. 84th St., Milwaukee, WI 53214, (414) 774-1776; or Milwaukee History Trail, 9711 W. Metcalf Pl., Milwaukee, WI 53222, (414) 461-7107. 10.0 miles loop. Awards available. (AA 1992)

4776 **Mirror Lake State Park**, Rt. 1, Box 283, Baraboo, WI 53913, (608) 254-2333. (ATW; WCD; MGL)

4777 **Monster Hall Campground**, CR 7, Unity, WI 54488, (715) 223-4336. (WCD)

4778 **Moose Jaw Lodge & Resort**, FR 144, Park Falls, WI 54552, (715) 762-3028. (WCD)

Moraine Trail see entry 4654.

4779 **Mt. Valhalla Trail**, Wisconsin Department of Natural Resources, P.O. Box 450, Madison, WI 53701; or Forest Service Office, Park Falls, WI 54552. 17.0 miles. (BHT; HTM)

Mountain Goat Trail see entry 4660.

4780 **MRK Trail**, Tom Statz, Racine County Department of Public Works, 14200 Washington Ave., Sturtevant, WI 53177, (414) 886-8457. 5.0 miles straight. (GRT)

4781 **Muskego County Park**, Janesville Rd., Muskego, WI 53150, (414) 679-0310. (WCD)

4782 **Muskey Blvd. Resort & Campground**, Sissabagama Rd., Stone Lake, WI 54876, (715) 865-4545. (WCD)

4783 **Musky Tale Resort & RV Park**, CR B, Hayward, WI 54843, (715) 462-3672. (WCD)

4784 **Namekagon Outfitters-Canoes-Campground-Cabins**, S. River Rd., Trego, WI 54888, (800) 547-9028. (WCD)

4785 **Necedah National Wildlife Refuge**, Star Route W., Necedah, WI 54646, (608) 565-2551. (MGL; GNW)

4786 **Nelson Dewey State Park**, CR VV, Cassville, WI 53806, (608) 725-5374. (ATW; WCD)

4787 **Nelson Lake Landing RV Park & Motel**, Rt. 3, Hayward, WI 54843, (715) 634-4175. (WCD)

4788 **Nelson Lake Lodge**, Rt. 3, Box 3100, Hayward, WI 54843, (715) 634-3750. (WCD)

4789 **New Berlin Trail**, Dave Burch, Senior Landscape Architect, Waukesha County Parks and Planning Commission, 500 Riverview Ave., Waukesha, WI 53188, (414) 548-7790. 6.0 miles straight. (GRT)

4790 **New Glarus Woods State Park**, CR N, New Glarus, WI 53574, (608) 527-2335. (ATW; WCD)

4791 **Newport State Park**, 475 S. Newport Ln., Ellison Bay, WI 54210, (414) 854-2500. 28.0 miles. (ATW; LGU; EGH; MGL; OTB)

4792 **Nicolet National Forest**, Federal Bldg., 68 S. Stevens, Rhinelander, WI 54501, (715) 362-3415; or Eagle River Ranger District, P.O. Box 1809, Eagle River, WI 54521, (715) 479-2827. 1000 miles. Named trails: Anvil 6.0, Butternut Lake Forest 1.0, Devil's Run, Kimball Creek 12.0(s), Lauterman National Recreation 8.0(l). (ATW; GRT; WCD; EGH; GFC; MGL; FGU)

4793 **Nine Eagles Resort**, Cliff House Rd., Lyndon Station, WI 53944, (608) 666-2412. (WCD)

4794 **Nordic Pines**, CR DL, Baraboo, WI 53913, (608) 356-5810. (WCD)

4795 **Norm & Ann's Campground**, SR

10, Neillsville, WI 54456, (715) 743-3620. (WCD)

4796 **North Country Trail** (*see* separate entry **4955** in interstate section).

4797 **North Lake Campground**, CR G, Cumberland, WI 54829, (715) 822-2440. (WCD)

4798 **North Shore Trail**, Tom Statz, Racine County Department of Public Works, 14200 Washington Ave., Sturtevant, WI 53177, (414) 886-8457. 3.0 miles straight. (GRT)

4799 **Northern Highland-American Legion State Forest**, DNR Area Headquarters, P.O. Box 440, Woodruff, WI 54568, (715) 356-5211. (ATW; MGL)

4800 **Northforests Campgrounds**, Pickerel Rd., Tomahawk, WI 54487, (715) 453-2522. (WCD)

4801 **Novotny's Little Lake Campsites**, SR 27, Cadott, WI 54727, (715) 289-3355. (WCD)

4802 **Nugget Lake County Park**, CR HH, Plum City, WI 54761, (715) 639-5611. (WCD)

Old Stage Line Trail *see* entry **4660**.

4803 **Old World Wisconsin Trail**, Old World Wisconsin, SR 67, Eagle, WI 53119. 3.0 miles. (RTH)

4804 **Omaha Trail**, Dale Dorow, Rm. 16, Courthouse Annex, Mauston, WI 53948, (608) 847-9389. 12.5 miles straight. (GRT)

4805 **O'Neil Creek Camp Campground & Game Farm**, O'Neil Camp Dr., Chippewa Falls, WI 54729, (715) 723-6581. (WCD)

4806 **Osseo Camping Resort**, US 10, Osseo, WI 54758, (715) 597-2102. (WCD)

4807 **Otter Lake Recreation Area**, Otter Lake Rd., Tomahawk, WI 54487. (WCD)

4808 **The Outpost**, CR N, Tomahawk, WI 54487, (715) 453-3468. (WCD)

4809 **Ozaukee Historic 76 Bike Trail**, Thomas E. Weigend, 11511 N.E. Gate Dr., 52W, Mequon, WI 53092, (414) 242-3759. 76.0 miles loop. (AA 1994)

4810 **Parkland Village Campground**, Oasis Rd., Black River Falls, WI 54615, (715) 284-9700. (WCD)

4811 **Path of Pines Campground**, CR F, Fish Creek, WI 54212, (414) 868-3332. (WCD)

4812 **Patricia Lake Campground**, Camp Pinemere Rd., Minocqua, WI 54548, (715) 356-3198. (WCD)

4813 **Pattison State Park**, Rt. 2, Box 435, Superior, WI 54880, (715) 399-8073. (ATW; WCD; MGL)

4814 **Patzer's Last Resort and Campground**, Archer Ln., Wild Rose, WI 54984, (414) 622-3490. (WCD)

4815 **Pecatonica State Park Trail**, David Cline, Yellowstone Lake State Park, 7896 Lake Rd., Blanchardville, WI 53516, (608) 523-4427. 17.0 miles straight planned, current as to 9.6 miles. (GRT)

4816 **Peninsula State Park**, P.O. Box 218, Shore Rd., Fish Creek, WI 54212, (608) 868-3258. 17.0 miles. (LGU; WCD; MGL)

4817 **Perrot State Park**, River Rd., Trempealeau, WI 54661, (608) 534-6409. (WCD; MGL)

4818 **Peshtigo River Campground**, Airport Rd., Crivitz, WI 54114, (715) 854-2986. (WCD)

4819 **Petenwell County Park**, Bighorn Dr., Friendship, WI 53934, (608) 564-7513. (WCD)

4820 **Pettibone Park Resort**, US 14/61, LaCrosse, WI 54601, (608) 782-5858. (WCD)

Pigeon Lake Trail *see* entry **4637**.

4821 **Pike Lake State Park**, SR 60, Hartford, WI 53027, (414) 644-5248. (ATW; WCD)

4822 **Pine Aire Resort & Campground**, Chain-O-Lakes Rd., Eagle River, WI 54521, (715) 479-9208. (WCD)

4823 **Pine Grove Campground**, Campground Rd., Shawano, WI 54166, (715) 787-4555. (WCD)

4824 **Pine Harbors Campsites**, Pine Harbor Dr., Chippewa Falls, WI 54729, (715) 723-9865. (WCD)

4825 **Pine Line**, Robert P. Rusch, Secretary, Medford to Prentice Rail Trail Association, 111 E. Division St., P.O. Box 339, Medford, WI 54451-0339, (715) 748-2030. 26.2 miles straight. (GRT)

Pine Tree Nature Trail *see* entry **4654**.

4826 **Pine-Aire Trailer Park**, Trailer Park Rd., Hayward, WI 54843, (715) 634-4455. (WCD)

4827 **Pineland Camping Park**, SR 13, Big Flats, WI 53934, (608) 564-7818. (WCD)

4828 **Piney Woods Campground**, Clear Lake Rd., Elcho, WI 54428, (715) 275-3212. (WCD)

4829 **The Playful Goose**, Main St., Horicon, WI 53032, (414) 485-4744. (WCD)

4830 **Plymouth Rock Camping Resort**, P.O. Box 445W, Elkhart Lake, WI 53020, (414) 892-4252. (WCD)

4831 **Point Beach State Park**, 9400 CTH O, Two Rivers, WI 54241, (414) 794-7480. (ATW; WCD; MGL)

4832 **Poplar Golf Course Resort & Campground**, Rt. 1, Box 796, Poplar, WI 54864, (715) 364-2689. (WCD)

4833 **Potawatomi State Park**, 3740 Park Dr., Sturgeon Bay, WI 54235, (414) 743-5123. (ATW; WCD; MGL)

Potholes Trail *see* entry 4654.

4834 **Pow Wow Campground**, Pow Wow Ln., Galesville, WI 54630, (608) 582-2995. (WCD)

4835 **Prentice Municipal Park**, US 2, Ashland, WI 54806, (715) 682-7071. (WCD)

4836 **Presque Isle Campground**, Pomeroy Lake Rd., Presque Isle, WI 54557, (715) 686-7408. (WCD)

4837 **Quietwoods North Camping Resort**, 3668 Grondin Rd., Sturgeon Bay, WI 54235, (414) 743-7115. (WCD)

4838 **Quietwoods South Camping Resort**, Lovers Ln., Brussels, WI 54204, (414) 825-7065. (WCD)

4839 **Red Barn Campground**, CR B, Shell Lake, WI 54871, (715) 468-2575. (WCD)

4840 **Red Cedar State Trail**, James Janowak, Superintendent, Rt. 6, Box 1, Menomonie, WI 54751, (715) 232-1242. 14.5 miles straight. (GRT)

4841 **Reel Livin' Resort and Trailer Park**, Neumaier's Rd., Hayward, WI 54843, (715) 462-3822. (WCD)

4842 **Revelle's Landing Resort & Campground**, Nelson Lake Rd., Hayward, WI 54843, (715) 634-4216. (WCD)

4843 **Rib Mountain State Park**, CR N, Wausau, WI 54401, (715) 359-4522. (ATW; WCD; MGL)

4844 **Rib Mountain Trail**, Samoset Council, BSA, 210 Washington St., Wausau, WI 54401. (MVC)

4845 **Rice Lake-Haugen KOA**, P.O. Box 3, Haugen, WI 54841, (715) 234-2360. (WCD)

4846 **Ridge Run Park**, University Dr., West Bend, WI 53095. (ATW)

4847 **The Ridges Campground**, Griffith Ave., Wisconsin Rapids, WI 54494, (715) 421-1611. (WCD)

4848 **Ridges Sanctuary**, CR Q, Baileys Harbor, WI 54202. (LGU)

4849 **Riley Lake Snowmobile Trail**, Kay Ketting, Recreation Planner, 1170 4th Ave. S., Park Falls, WI 54552, (715) 762-2461. 23.0 miles straight. (GRT)

4850 **River Forest Rafts & Campground**, SR 55, White Lake, WI 54491, (715) 882-3351. (WCD)

4851 **Riverside Municipal Park**, N. Washington St., Janesville, WI 53545, (608) 754-2289. (MGL)

4852 **Roche A Cri State Park**, SR 13, Friendship, WI 53934, (608) 339-3385. (ATW; WCD)

4853 **Rock Island State Park**, Washington Island Tourist Bureau, Washington Island, WI 54246, (414) 847-2235. 8.0 miles. (ATW; WCD; MGL; HTM)

4854 **Rockport Municipal Park**, 2800 Rockport Rd., Janesville, WI 53545, (608) 754-2289. (MGL)

4855 **Rocky Arbor State Park**, US 12, Wisconsin Dells, WI 53965, (608) 254-2333. (ATW; WCD)

4856 **Rome Riverside Campground**, Water St., Rome, WI 53178, (414) 593-8663. (WCD)

4857 **Root River Trail**, 2467 Root River Pkwy., West Allis, WI 53227. 15.5 miles. Awards available. (HTA)

4858 **Rush Lake Trail**, Jeffrey A. Christensen, Parks Director, Winnebago County Department of Parks, 500 E. CR Y, Oshkosh, WI 54901, (414) 424-0042. 5.3 miles straight. (GRT)

4859 **Rustic Woods Campground**, E.

2585 Southwood Dr., Waupaca, WI 54981, (715) 258-2442. (WCD)

4860 **St. Croix National Scenic Waterway**, P.O. Box 708, St. Croix Falls, WI 54024, (715) 483-2184. (ATW; GFC; NPS; NPV; NPE; CGA)

4861 **Sand Lake Pines Resort & Campground**, SR 70, Stone Lake, WI 54876, (715) 865-2309. (WCD)

4862 **Sanders County Park**, 14200 Washington Ave., Sturtevant, WI 53177, (414) 886-8457. (WCD)

4863 **Sandhill Wildlife Area**, CR X, Wisconsin Rapids, WI 54494, (715) 884-2437. (ATW)

4864 **Sandman's Campground**, US 53, Holmen, WI 54636, (608) 526-4956. (WCD)

4865 **Sandy Knoll Park**, Wallace Lake Rd., West Bend, WI 53095. (ATW)

4866 **Sawmill Lake County Forest**, Town Rd., Spooner, WI 54801. (WCD)

4867 **Scenic View Campground**, SR 70, Spooner, WI 54801, (715) 468-2510. (WCD)

4868 **Schlitz Audubon Center**, 1111 E. Brown Deer Rd., Milwaukee, WI 53217, (414) 352-2880. 6.0 miles. (ATW)

4869 **Shangri-La Lodge Campground & Resort**, Rt. 1, Box 1253, Trego, WI 54888, (715) 466-2728 or (800) 352-1984. (WCD)

4870 **Sheboygan Indian Mound Park**, Panther Ave., Sheboygan, WI 53081, (414) 457-9495. (ATW)

4871 **Sherwood Forest Campground**, S. 352 W. US 12/16, Wisconsin Dells, WI 53955, (608) 254-7080. (WCD)

4872 **Silver Springs Campsites**, N. 5048 Ludwig Rd., Rio, WI 53960, (414) 992-3537. (WCD)

4873 **Sky High Camping & Canoeing Resort**, Rowley Rd., Portage, WI 53901, (608) 742-2572. (WCD)

4874 **Smokey Hollow Campground**, McGowan Rd., Lodi, WI 53555, (608) 635-4806. (WCD)

4875 **Snug Harbor Inn Resort**, P.O. Box 883, Richmond, WI 53115, (608) 883-6999 or fax (414) 728-2875. (WCD)

4876 **Solberg Lake County Park**, Solberg Lake Rd., Phillips, WI 54555, (715) 339-4505. (WCD)

4877 **Spider Lake Resort & Campground**, CR T, Birchwood, WI 54817, (715) 354-3723. (WCD)

4878 **Spike Horn Campground**, Cana Island Rd., Baileys Harbor, WI 54202, (414) 839-2430. (WCD)

4879 **Spring Brook Campground**, P.O. Box 235, Wisconsin Dells, WI 53965, (608) 254-4343. (WCD)

4880 **Spring Valley Trails Campground**, Spring Valley Rd., Dodgeville, WI 53533, (608) 935-5725. (WCD)

4881 **Stand Rock Campground**, N. 570 W. CR N, Wisconsin Dells, WI 53965, (608) 253-2169. (WCD)

4882 **Stonefield**, CR VV, Cassville, WI 53806. (OTB)

4883 **Sugar River State Park Trail**, Reynold Zeller, Superintendent, P.O. Box 781, New Glarus, WI 53574, (608) 527-2334. 23.5 miles. (GRT; MGL; WOB)

4884 **Sugarbush Lodge & Campground**, CR V, Turtle Lake, WI 54889, (715) 986-2484. (WCD)

4885 **Sun Valley Campground**, Duck Creek Ave., Neshkoro, WI 54960, (414) 293-4924. (WCD)

4886 **Sundance Campground**, Pease Rd., Hayward, WI 54843, (715) 795-2698. (WCD)

4887 **Sunrise Bay Campgrounds & RV Park**, Rt. 3, Hayward, WI 54843, (715) 634-2213. (WCD)

4888 **Sunset Municipal Park**, US 2, Ashland, WI 54806, (715) 682-7071. (WCD)

4889 **Superior Municipal Forest**, N. 28th St. & Billings Dr., Superior, WI 54880. (MGL)

4890 **Swanson's Campground & Motel**, SR 53, Solon Springs, WI 54873, (715) 378-2215. (WCD)

4891 **Tepee Park Campground**, E. 10096 W. Trout Rd., Wisconsin Dells, WI 53965, (608) 253-3122. (WCD)

4892 **Terrace View Campsites**, Wolf Rd., Tomahawk, WI 54487, (715) 453-8352. (WCD)

4893 **Terry Andrae-John M. Kohler State**

Park, CR KK, Sheboygan, WI 53081, (414) 452-3457. (WCD; MGL)
4894 **Terrytown Campground**, Terry Town Rd., Baraboo, WI 53913, (608) 356-8505. (WCD)
4895 **Thornapple River Campground**, SR 27, Ladysmith, WI 54848, (715) 532-7034. (WCD)
4896 **1000 Islands Environmental Center**, 700 Dodge St., Kaukauna, WI 54130, (414) 766-4733. (ATW)
4897 **Tilleda Falls Campground**, CR KK, Sheboygan, WI 53081, (715) 524-4986. (WCD)
4898 **Timber Trail Campground**, CR M, Algoma, WI 54201, (414) 487-3707. (WCD)
4899 **Token Creek County Park**, US 51, Madison, WI 53704, (608) 246-3896. (WCD)
4900 **Toland Springs Camping Resort**, Washington Rd., Hartford, WI 53027, (414) 474-4860. (WCD)
4901 **Tomahawk Scout Reservation**, Indianhead Council, BSA, 393 Marshall Ave., St. Paul, MN 55102, (612) 224-1891; or Tomahawk Scout Reservation, Rt. 2, Birchwood, WI 54817, (715) 354-3841. (SFC)
4902 **Tower Hill State Park**, SR 23, Spring Green, WI 53588, (608) 588-2116. (ATW; WCD)
Trail to Group Camp see entry 4654.
4903 **Tranquil Vista Campground**, Town Corner Lake Rd., Pembine, WI 54156, (715) 324-6430. (WCD)
4904 **Trees For Tomorrow Natural Resources Education Center**, 611 Sheridan St., Eagle River, WI 54521, (715) 479-6456. (MGL)
4905 **Trego Lake Park**, US 63, Trego, WI 54881, (715) 635-2091. (MGL)
4906 **Trempealeau National Wildlife Refuge**, Rt. 1, Trempealeau, WI 54661. (GNW)
4907 **Tri-County Corridor**, Roy Lindquist, Rt. 2, Box 48, Iron River, WI 54847, (715) 372-4580. 60.0 miles straight. (GRT)
4908 **Tri-Lake Timbers Campground & Resort**, FR 242, Iron River, WI 54847, (715) 372-4627. (WCD)

Tumbled Rocks Trail see entry 4654.
4909 **Tunnel Trail Campground**, SR 71, Wilton, WI 54670, (608) 435-6829. (WCD)
4910 **Turtle Creek Campsite**, CR S, Beloit, WI 53511, (608) 362-7768. (WCD)
4911 **Tuscobia State Park Trail**, Raymond E. Larsen, Superintendent, P.O. Box 187, Winter, WI 54896, (715) 634-6513. 74.0 miles straight. (GRT)
4912 **Twin Springs Campground & Cabins**, 3010 Cedar Falls Rd., Menomonie, WI 54751, (715) 235-9321. (WCD)
Two Lakes Trail see entry 4637.
4913 **Veterans Memorial County Park**, CR J, Summit Lake, WI 54485, (715) 623-6214. (WCD)
4914 **Veterans Memorial County Park**, SR 16, West Salem, WI 54669, (608) 786-3496. (WCD)
4915 **Vista Royalle Campground**, Rt. 1, Box 109, Bancroft, WI 54921, (715) 335-6860. (WCD)
4916 **Wabeno Lumberjack Trail**, Badger Trails, Inc., P.O. Box 10266, Milwaukee, WI 53210. 18.0 miles. Awards available. (HTA)
4917 **Wagon Trail Campground**, 1190 CR ZZ, Ellison Bay, WI 54210, (800) 323-8899. (WCD)
4918 **Wasco's Lakeshore Campground**, Rt. 1, Box 718, Lake Nebagamon, WI 54849, (715) 374-3514. (WCD)
4919 **Waterford-Wind Lake Trail**, Tom Statz, Racine County Department of Public Works, 14200 Washington Ave., Sturtevant, WI 53177, (414) 886-8457. 5.0 miles straight. (GRT)
4920 **Wehr Nature Center**, 9701 W. College Ave., Milwaukee, WI 53221, (414) 425-8550. (ATW)
West Bluff Trail see entry 4654.
4921 **West End Municipal Park**, 18th Ave., Washburn, WI 54891, (715) 373-6174. (WCD)
4922 **Westwood Ho Camp Resort**, Rt. 1, Glenbeulah, WI 53023, (414) 526-3407. (WCD)
4923 **Wheeler's Campground**, SR 159, Baraboo, WI 53913, (608) 356-4877. (WCD)

WISCONSIN

4924 **Whitefish Dunes State Park**, SR 57, Sturgeon Bay, WI 54235. (ATW)
4925 **Whitemound County Park**, Lake Rd., Plain, WI 53577, (608) 546-5011. (WCD)
4926 **Whitnall Park**, S. 92nd St. & Whitnall Park Dr., Milwaukee, WI 53228, (414) 425-1130. (MGL)
4927 **Wi Do To Campground**, Busse Rd., Hayward, WI 54843, (715) 462-3807. (WCD)
4928 **Wild Goose State Trail**, Pamela Kober, Planner, Dodge County Planning and Development Department, Administrative Bldg., Juneau, WI 53039, (414) 386-3700; or Sam Tobia, City-County Government Center, 160 S. Macy St., Fond du Lac, WI 54935, (414) 929-3135. 29.6 miles straight. (GRT)
4929 **Wildcat Mountain State Park**, P.O. Box 99, Ontario, WI 54651, (608) 337-4775. (ATW; WCD; MGL)
4930 **Wilderness Campground**, SR 22, Montello, WI 53949, (608) 297-2002. (WCD)
4931 **Wilderness County Park**, 9th St., Necedah, WI 54646, (608) 847-9389. (WCD)
4932 **Wildwood Park Trail**, Wildwood Park and Zoo, Roddis Ave., Marshfield, WI 54449, (715) 384-3606. (MGL)
4933 **Williams Campground**, Mary Lake Ln., Townsend, WI 54175, (715) 276-6591. (WCD)
4934 **Willow Mill Campsites**, CR SS, Rio, WI 53960, (414) 992-5355. (WCD)
4935 **Willow River State Park**, CR A, Hudson, WI 54016, (715) 386-5931. (ATW; WCD)
4936 **Wolf River Campgrounds**, CR X, New London, WI 54961, (414) 982-2458. (WCD)
4937 **Woodlake Trails**, Gannon Rd., Lodi, WI 53555, (608) 592-5607. (WCD)
4938 **Wyalusing State Park**, 13342 CR C, Bagley, WI 53801, (608) 996-2261. 18.0 miles. (ATW; WCD; MGL)
4939 **Yellowstone Lake State Park**, Rt. 2, Box 48B, 7896 Lake Rd., Blanchardville, WI 53516, (608) 523-4427. (ATW; MGL)
4940 **Yogi Bear Jellystone Campground**, P.O. Box 67, Warrens, WI 54666, (800) 322-YOGI. (WCD)
4941 **Yogi Bear Jellystone Camp-Resort**, 8425 SR 38, Caledonia, WI 53108, (414) 835-2565. (WCD)
4942 **Yogi Bear Jellystone Camp-Resort**, US 10, Fremont, WI 54940, (414) 446-3420. (WCD)
4943 **Yogi Bear Jellystone Park**, CR X, Bagley, WI 53801, (608) 996-2201. (WCD)
4944 **Yogi Bear Jellystone Park**, May Rd., Sturgeon Bay, WI 54235, (414) 743-9001. (WCD)
4945 **Yogi Bear Jellystone Park**, P.O. Box 510, Wisconsin Dells, WI 53965, (608) 254-2568. (WCD)
4946 **Yogi Bear Jellystone Park/Fort Atkinson**, Wishing Well Rd., Fort Atkinson, WI 53538, (414) 563-5714. (WCD)
4947 **Yukon Trails Camping**, CR HH, Lyndon Station, WI 53944, (800) 423-9577. (WCD)

Generally:
Department of Natural Resources, Division of Tourism and Information, P.O. Box 450, Madison, WI 53701. (PGF)
Wisconsin Department of Natural Resources, Bureau of Parks and Recreation, P.O. Box 7921, Madison, WI 53707, (608) 266-2621. (EGH)

Index (by city)

Adams: Barbican Woods Campground 4585
Algoma: Ahnapee River Trails Campground 4575; Big Lake Campground 4596; Timber Trail Campground 4898
Alma Center: KOA-Alma Center 4735
Amherst: Family Frontier Campground 4670

WISCONSIN

Amherst Junction: Lake Emilee County Park 4743
Appleton: Gordon Bubolz Nature Preserve 4690
Ashland: Evergreen Acres Campground 4668; Prentice Municipal Park 4835; Sunset Municipal Park 4888
Athelstane: McCaslin Mountain Campground 4766
Bagley: Irish Brothers River of Lakes Resort 4722; Wyalusing State Park 4938; Yogi Bear Jellystone Park 4943
Baileys Harbor: Grandpa's Bluff Campground 4694; Ridges Sanctuary 4848; Spike Horn Campground 4878
Balsam Lake: Apple River Campground North 4582
Bancroft: Vista Royalle Campground 4915
Baraboo: Circus Heritage Trail 4641; Devil's Lake State Park 4654; Double K-D Ranch 4659; Fox Hill Campground 4680; Mirror Lake State Park 4776; Nordic Pines 4794; Terrytown Campground 4894; Wheeler's Campground 4923
Bayfield: Apostle Islands National Lakeshore 4580; Big Bay State Park 4594
Belgium: Harrington Beach State Park 4702
Belmont: Lake Joy Campground 4745
Beloit: Turtle Creek Campsite 4910
Birchwood: Spider Lake Resort & Campground 4877; Tomahawk Scout Reservation 4901
Black River Falls: Black River Falls State Forest 4600; Merlin Lambert County Park 4770; Parkland Village Campground 4810
Blanchardville: Pecatonica State Park Trail 4815; Yellowstone Lake State Park 4939
Blue Mounds: Blue Mound State Park 4605
Blue River: Eagle Cave Natural Park 4660
Boulder Junction: Bearskin State Park Trail 4591; Birchwood Campground 4598; Camp Holiday 4622
Briggsville: Lake Mason Campground 4748
Bristol: Happy Acres Kampground 4701
Brodhead: Crazy Horse Campground 4648
Browntown: Browntown-Cadiz Springs State Park 4611
Brussels: Quietwoods South Camping Resort 4838

Burlington: Meadowlark Acres Campground 4767
Butternut: Fort Flambeau Resort & Campground 4678
Cadott: Novotny's Little Lake Campsites 4801
Caledonia: Yogi Bear Jellystone Camp-Resort 4941
Camp Douglas: Mill Bluff State Park 4774
Campbellsport: Benson's Century Camping Resort 4593; Kettle Moraine State Forest 4731
Cascade: Hager's Hilly Haven Campground 4699; Hoeft's Resort & Campground 4711
Cassville: Nelson Dewey State Park 4786; Stonefield 4882
Chetek: Chetek River Campground 4638
Chippewa Falls: Irvine Park 4723; Lake Wissota State Park 4750; O'Neil Creek Camp Campground & Game Farm 4805; Pine Harbors Campsites 4824
Conover: Buckatabon Lodge & Lighthouse Inn 4615
Cornell: Brunet Island State Park 4613
Crandon: Forest County Veterans Memorial Park 4677
Crivitz: Kosir's Rapid Rafts, Campground & Restaurant 4738; Peshtigo River Campground 4818
Cumberland: North Lake Campground 4797
Darlington: Cheese Country Recreation Trail 4636
Dodgeville: Governor Dodge State Park 4691; Hideaway Acres 4709; Military Ridge State Park Trail 4773; Spring Valley Trails Campground 4880
Eagle: Kettle Moraine State Forest 4732; Old World Wisconsin Trail 4803
Eagle River: Nicolet National Forest 4792; Pine Aire Resort & Campground 4822; Trees For Tomorrow Natural Resources Education Center 4904
Edgerton: Creekview Campground 4649; Hickory Hills Campground 4708
Egg Harbor: Door County Kamping Resort 4658
Elcho: Piney Woods Campground 4828
Elkhart Lake: Plymouth Rock Camping Resort 4830

WISCONSIN   **Index**   331

Ellison Bay: Newport State Park 4791; Wagon Trail Campground 4917
Elton: Glacier Wilderness Campground 4687
Fish Creek: Path of Pines Campground 4811; Peninsula State Park 4816
Florence: Keyes Lake Campground 4733; Menominee River Campground 4769
Fond du Lac: KOA-Fond du Lac 4736
Fort Atkinson: Yogi Bear Jellystone Park/Fort Atkinson 4946
Frederic: Birchwood Beach Resort, Campground and Stable 4597
Fremont: Yogi Bear Jellystone Camp-Resort 4942
Friendship: Castle Rock County Park 4630; Petenwell County Park 4819; Roche A Cri State Park 4852
Galesville: Merrick State Park 4771; Pow Wow Campground 4834
Glenbeulah: Westwood Ho Camp Resort 4922
Gordon: Adventureland 4574; Charlie Brown's Campground 4635; Enchanted Inn Campground & Resort 4667
Grantsburg: Crex Meadows Wildlife Area 4650; Governor Knowles State Forest 4692; Memory Lake City Park 4768
Green Bay: Bayshore County Park 4589
Green Lake: Green Lake Conference Center 4697
Hales Corners: Alfred L. Boerner Botanical Gardens 4577
Hartford: Pike Lake State Park 4821; Toland Springs Camping Resort 4900
Haugen: Camp Phillips 4627; Rice Lake-Haugen KOA 4845
Hayward: Bear Paw Resort Campground 4590; Callahan Lake Resort & Campground 4620; Hayward-KOA 4705; La-Barre's Shady Bay Resort & Campground 4739; Lake Chippewa Campground 4741; Musky Tale Resort & RV Park 4783; Nelson Lake Landing RV Park & Motel 4787; Nelson Lake Lodge 4788; Pine-Aire Trailer Park 4827; Reel Livin' Resort and Trailer Park 4841; Revelle's Landing Resort & Campground 4842; Sundance Campground 4886; Sunrise Bay Campgrounds & RV Park 4887; Wi Do To Campground 4927

Hazelhurst: Cedar Falls Camp Resort 4632
Highland: Blackhawk Lake Recreation Area 4602
Hilbert: Calumet County Park 4621
Holmen: Sandman's Campground 4864
Horicon: Horicon Marsh Wildlife Area 4714; The Playful Goose 4829
Hudson: Willow River State Park 4935
Iron River: Tri-County Corridor 4907; Tri-Lake Timbers Campground & Resort 4908
Janesville: Riverside Municipal Park 4851; Rockport Municipal Park 4854
Jefferson: Bark River Campgrounds 4586
Juneau: Wild Goose State Trail 4928
Kansasville: Bong State Recreation Area 4607
Kaukauna: 1000 Islands Environmental Center 4896
Kenosha: Kenosha County Bike Trail 4729
Kewaunee: Cedar Valley Campground 4634; Maple View Campground 4764
Kingston: Grand Valley Campground 4693
Lac Du Flambeau: Broken Bow Campground 4610
LaCrosse: Bluebird Springs Recreation Area 4606; Goose Island County Park 4689; Pettibone Park Resort 4820
Ladysmith: Thornapple River Campground 4895
Lake Geneva: Big Foot Beach State Park 4595
Lake Mills: Glacial Drumlin State Park Trail 4684
Lake Nebagamon: Wasco's Lakeshore Campground 4918
Lake Tomahawk: Brian's Campground 4609
Lakewood: Maple Heights Campground 4763
Lancaster: Klondyke Secluded Acres 4734
Laona: Camp Lefeber Northwoods 4624; Ham Lake Campground 4700
Lodi: Smokey Hollow Campground 4874; Woodlake Trails 4937
Lone Rock: Flying J Campground 4675
Lyndon Station: Bass Lake Campground 4587; Nine Eagles Resort 4793; Yukon Trails Camping 4947
Madison: Glacial Hiking Trail 4685; Ice Age National Scenic Trail 4717; Token Creek County Park 4899

Maribel: Devils River Campers Park 4656
Marion: Kastle Kampground 4728
Marshfield: Wildwood Park and Zoo 4932
Mauston: Castle Rock County Park 4631; Omaha Trail 4804
Mayville: Horicon National Wildlife Refuge 4715
Medford: Pine Line 4825
Mellen: Copper Falls State Park 4646
Menasha: High Cliff State Park 4710
Menomonie: Red Cedar State Trail 4840; Twin Springs Campground & Cabins 4912
Mequon: Ozaukee Historic 76 Bike Trail 4809
Merrill: Council Grounds State Park 4647; Hiawatha Trail 4706
Merrimac: Merry Mac's Camp'n 4772
Milladore: George W. Mead Wildlife Area 4683
Milton: Blackhawk Campground 4601; Lakeland Camping Resort 4751
Milwaukee: Devil's Lake Trail 4655; Havenwoods Environmental Awareness Center 4704; Homestead Hollow Park 4713; Kettle Moraine Glacial Trail 4730; Milwaukee History Trail 4775; Schlitz Audubon Center 4868; Wabeno Lumberjack Trail 4916; Wehr Nature Center 4920; Whitnall Park 4926
Minocqua: Patricia Lake Campground 4812
Montello: Fischer's Crooked River Campground 4672; Wilderness Campground 4930
Mosinee: Lake Dubay Shores Campground & RV Park 4742
Mountain: Chutte Pond County Park 4639
Muskego: Muskego County Park 4781
Necedah: Buckhorn State Park 4616; Necedah National Wildlife Refuge 4785; Wilderness County Park 4931
Neillsville: Norm & Ann's Campground 4795
Nekoosa: Deer Trail Park Campground 4651
Neshkoro: Sun Valley Campground 4885
New Glarus: New Glarus Woods State Park 4790; Sugar River State Trail 4883
New Lisbon: Fischer's Campground 4671
New London: Wolf River Campgrounds 4936

Northfield: Lazy Acres Ranch Campground 4753
Oakdale: Granger's Campground 4695
Ontario: Brush Creek Campground 4614; The "400" State Trail 4679; LaCrosse River State Park Trail 4740; Wildcat Mountain State Park 4929
Oshkosh: Hortonville to Oshkosh Recreation Trail 4716; Rush Lake Trail 4858
Osseo: Osseo Camping Resort 4806
Palmyra: Circle K Campground 4640; Emma Carlin Hiking Trail 4666
Pardeeville: Indian Trails Campground 4719
Park Falls: Chequamegon National Forest 4637; Clover Creek Trail 4643; Iodine Snowmobile Trail 4721; Moose Jaw Lodge & Resort 4778; Mt. Valhalla Trail 4779; Riley Lake Snowmobile Trail 4849
Pearson: Camp Ma-Ka-Ja-Wah 4625
Pembine: Tranquil Vista Campground 4903
Phillips: Comfort Cove Campground 4644; Solberg Lake County Park 4876
Pittsville: Dexter County Park 4657
Plain: Whitemound County Park 4925
Plum City: Nugget Lake County Park 4802
Poplar: Poplar Golf Course Resort & Campground 4832
Port Washington: Lizard Mound County Park 4757
Portage: Kamp Dakota 4726; Marquette Trail 4765; Sky High Camping & Canoeing Resort 4873
Poynette: MacKenzie Environmental Educational Center 4760
Presque Isle: Presque Isle Campground 4836
Redgranite: Flanagan's Pearl Lake Campsites 4674
Reedsburg: Lighthouse Rock Campground 4755
Rhinelander: Camp Tesomas 4629; Lake George Campsite 4744; Nicolet National Forest 4792
Richfield: Glacier Hills Park 4686
Richland Center: Eden Valley Camping & Par 3 Golf 4664
Richmond: Snug Harbor Inn Resort 4875
Rio: Little Bluff Campground 4756; Silver Springs Campsites 4872; Willow Mill Campsites 4934

WISCONSIN Index

Rome: Rome Riverside Campground 4856
St. Croix Falls: Interstate State Park 4720; St. Croix National Scenic Waterway 4860
St. Germain: Lofty Pines RV Park 4758
Sauk City: Blackhawk Ridge Recreation Area 4603; Cedar Hills Campground 4633
Saxon: Frontier Bar & Campground 4681
Shawano: Pine Grove Campground 4823
Sheboygan: Kohler Andrae State Park 4737; Sheboygan Indian Mound Park 4870; Terry Andrae-John M. Kohler State Park 4893; Tilleda Falls Campground 4897
Shell Lake: Red Barn Campground 4839
Siren: Clam Lake Resort & Campground 4642; Gandy Dancer Trail 4682
Solon Springs: Lucius Woods County Park 4759; Swanson's Campground & Motel 4890
Somerset: Apple River Campground 4581
Sparta: Elroy-Sparta National Recreation Trail 4665
Spooner: Benoit Lake Campground 4592; Sawmill Lake County Forest 4866; Scenic View Campground 4867
Spring Green: Tower Hill State Park 4902
Spring Valley: Eau Galle Lake Park 4662
Stevens Point: Jordan County Park 4725
Stone Lake: Camp Indian Head Campground 4623; Muskey Blvd. Resort & Campground 4782; Sand Lake Pines Resort & Campground 4861
Stoughton: Kamp Kegonsa Camping Resort 4727; Lake Kegonsa State Park 4746
Sturgeon Bay: Ahnapee State Park Trail 4576; Potawatomi State Park 4833; Quietwoods North Camping Resort 4837; Whitefish Dunes State Park 4924; Yogi Bear Jellystone Park 4944
Sturtevant: Burlington Trail 4619; MRK Trail 4780; North Shore Trail 4798; Sanders County Park 4862; Waterford-Wind Lake Trail 4919
Sullivan: Concord Center Campground 4645
Summit Lake: Veterans Memorial County Park 4913
Superior: Amnicon Falls State Park 4579; Brule River State Forest 4612; Manitou Valley Campground 4761; Pattison State Park 4813; Superior Municipal Forest 4889
Three Lakes: Mann's Harbor Campground 4762
Tomahawk: Birkensee Resort & Camping 4599; Northforests Campgrounds 4800; The Outpost 4808; Terrace View Campsites 4892
Townsend: Williams Campground 4933
Trego: Bay Park Resort & Campground 4588; Namekagon Outfitters-Canoes-Campground-Cabins 4784; Shangri-La Lodge Campground & Resort 4869; Trego Lake Park 4905
Trempealeau: Buffalo River State Park Trail 4617; Great River State Park Trail 4696; Perrot State Park 4817; Trempealeau National Wildlife Refuge 4906
Turtle Lake: Sugarbush Lodge & Campground 4884
Two Rivers: Point Beach State Park 4831
Unity: Monster Hall Campground 4777
Warrens: Yogi Bear Jellystone Campground 4940
Washburn: West End Municipal Park 4921
Washington Island: Island Camping & Recreation 4724; Rock Island State Park 4853
Waukesha: Bugline Trail 4618; New Berlin Trail 4789
Waupaca: Camp Shin-Go-Beek 4628; Hartman Creek State Park 4703; Rustic Woods Campground 4859
Waupun: Fond du Lac County Park 4676
Wausau: Rib Mountain State Park 4843; Rib Mountain Trail 4844
Wautoma: Lake of the Woods Campground 4749
Wauwatosa: Good Turn Trail 4688
Webb Lake: Bosley's Upper Webb Lake Campground 4608
West Allis: Root River Trail 4857
West Bend: Lake Lenwood Campground 4747; Lazy Days Campground 4754; Ridge Run Park 4846; Sandy Knoll Park 4865
West Salem: Veterans Memorial County Park 4914
White Lake: Echo Valley Resort & Camp-

ground 4663; River Forest Rafts & Campground 4850
Whitewater: Laursen's Campground 4752
Wild Rose: Camp Napowan 4626; Evergreen Campsites 4669; Patzer's Last Resort and Campground 4814
Wilton: Tunnel Trail Campground 4909
Winter: Flambeau River State Forest 4673; Tuscobia State Park Trail 4911
Wisconsin Dells: American Adventure Camping 4578; Arrowhead Campground 4584; Blue Lake Campground 4604; Dell Boo Campground 4652; Dells Timberland Campground 4653; Eagle Flats Campground 4661; Holiday Shores Campground & Resort 4712; Rocky Arbor State Park 4855; Sherwood Forest Campground 4871; Spring Brook Campground 4879; Tepee Park Campground 4891; Yogi Bear Jellystone Park 4945
Wisconsin Rapids: Grotto Pilgrimage Trail 4698; The Ridges Campground 4847; Sandhill Wildlife Area 4863
Woodruff: Arbor Vitae Trailer Resort & Camping Park 4583; Indian Shores 4718; Northern Highland-American Legion State Forest 4799

INTERSTATE TRAILS

4948 **Appalachian National Scenic Trail** (GA, NC, TN, VA, WV, PA, NJ, NY, CT, MA, VT, NH, ME), Appalachian Trail Conference, Inc., P.O. Box 807, Washington & Jackson Sts., Harpers Ferry, WV 25425-0807, (304) 535-6331; or Potomac Appalachian Trail Club, 1718 N St., N.W., Washington, DC 20036, (202) 638-5306; or Keystone Trails Association, P.O. Box 251, Cogan Station, PA 17728; or New York-New Jersey Trail Conference, 232 Madison Ave., Rm. 908, New York, NY 10116, (212) 685-9699; or Appalachian Mountain Club, 5 Joy St., Boston, MA 02108; or Maine Appalachian Trail Club, P.O. Box 283, Augusta, ME 04330; or New England Regional Office, Appalachian Trail Conference, P.O. Box 381, Boiling Springs, PA 17007; or Southern Regional Office, Appalachian Trail Conference, P.O. Box 738, Blacksburg, VA 24060; or Southern Regional Office, Appalachian Trail Conference, 100 Otis St., P.O. Box 2750, Asheville, NC 28802. 2135 miles straight. Awards available. (SAR 1993)

4949 **Bartram Trail** (FL, AL, GA, MS, SC, NC, TN), Georgia Bartram Trail Society, 6688 Marsh Ave., Lithia Springs, GA 30057, (404) 948-3871; or The Bartram Trail Conference, 431 E. 63rd St., Savannah, GA 31405; or Bartram Trail Conference, 3815 Interstate Ct., Suite 202A, Montgomery, AL 36109, (205) 277-7050; or North Carolina Bartram Trail Society, Rt. 3, Box 406, Sylva, NC 28723, (704) 293-9661. 2550 miles straight. (SAR 1991)

4950 **Benton MacKaye Trail** (GA, TN), Benton MacKaye Trail Association, P.O. Box 53271, Atlanta, GA 30305. 250 miles straight. Awards available. (AA 1994)

4951 **Lewis and Clark National Historic Trail** (IL, MO, KS, NE, IA, SD, ND, MT, ID, OR, WA), National Park Service, Midwest Region, 1709 Jackson St., Omaha, NE 68102, (402) 221-3482; or Lewis and Clark Trail Heritage Foundation, P.O. Box 3434, Great Falls, MT 59403. 4500 miles straight. (AA 1994)

4952 **Metacomet-Monadnock Trail** (CT, MA, NH), Forrest E. House, 33 Knollwood Dr., East Longmeadow, MA 01028; or Appalachian Mountain Club, 5 Joy St., Boston, MA 02108. 300 miles straight. Awards available. (AA 1994)

4953 **Mormon Pioneer National Historic Trail** (IL, IA, NE, WY, UT), National Park Service, Rocky Mountain Regional Office, 655 Parfet St., P.O. Box 25287, Denver, CO 80225, (303) 236-8720. 1300 miles straight. (AA 1994)

4954 **Natchez Trace National Scenic Trail** (TN, AL, MS), Southeast Region, National Park Service, Richard B. Russell Bldg., 75 Spring St. SW, Atlanta, GA 30303; or Natchez Trace Parkway, Rt. 1, NT-143, Tupelo, MS 38801, (601) 842-1572. 449 miles straight. (AA 1994)

4955 **North Country National Scenic Trail** (NY, PA, OH, MI, WI, MN, ND), National Park Service, Midwest Region, 1709 Jackson St., Omaha, NE 68102; or North County Trail Association, P.O. Box 311, White Cloud, MI 49349. 3170 miles straight. Awards available. (AA 1994)

4956 **Overmountian Victory National Historic Trail** (VA, TN, NC, SC), Southeast Region, National Park Service, 75 Spring St., SW, Atlanta, GA 30303. 220 miles straight. (AA 1994)

4957 **Potomac Heritage National Scenic Trail** (VA, MD, WV, DC, PA), National Capital Region, 1100 Ohio Dr., SW, Washington, DC 20242, (202) 426-6700. Completed distances are 184 miles along the C & O Canal Towpath, the 17-mile Mount Vernon Trail, and the 70-mile Laurel Highlands National Recreation Trail. (AA 1994)

4958 **Trail of Tears National Historic Trail** (AL, NC, GA, TN, KY, IL, MO, AR, OK), Southeast Region, National Park Service, 75 Spring St., SW, Atlanta, GA 30303. 2200 miles straight. (AA 1994)

List of Sources Used

AA Above Address—Source is flier provided directly from hike sponsor or area administrator in year shown

AAC *Around Atlanta with Children*, by Denise Black & Janet Schwartz, Sigma Publications, Inc. (1990)

AFW *Away for the Weekend—New England*, by Eleanor Berman, Clarkson N. Potter, Inc. (1985)

AGW *America's Greatest Walks*, by Gary Yanker and Carol Tarlow, Addison-Wesley Publishing Company, Inc. (1986)

AIF *Adventuring in Florida*, by Allen de Hart, Sierra Club Books (1991)

AMC *Audubon Society Field Guide to the Natural Places of the Mid-Atlantic: Coastal*, by Susannah Laurence, Pantheon Books (1984)

AMI *Audubon Society Field Guide to the Natural Places of the Mid-Atlantic: Inland*, by Susannah Laurence and Barbara Gross, Pantheon Books (1984)

ANB *America's National Battlefield Parks*, by Joseph E. Stephens, University of Oklahoma Press (1990)

ANC *AAA Tour Book—North Central*, American Automobile Association (1993)

ANI *Audubon Society Field Guide to the Natural Places of the Northeast: Inland*, by Stephen Kulik, Pete Salmansohn, Matthew Schmidt, and Heidi Welch, Pantheon Books (1984)

ANP *Access National Parks—A Guide for Handicapped Visitors*, National Park Service (1978)

ANY *AAA Tour Book—New York*, American Automobile Association (1993)

AOB *Alabama Off the Beaten Path*, by Gay Martin, The Globe Pequot Press (1992)

ARA *AAA Road Atlas*, AAA Travel Publishing (1993)

ATA *AAA Tour Book—Alabama/Louisiana/Mississippi*, American Automobile Association (1990)

ATF *AAA Tour Book—Florida*, American Automobile Association (1993)

ATG *Appalachian Trail Guide*, The Appalachian Trail Conference, Volume 1—Maine (1983); Volume 2—New Hampshire-Vermont (1988); Volume 3—Massachusetts-Connecticut (1988); Volume 4—New York-New Jersey (1988); Volume 5—Pennsylvania (1985); Volume 6—Maryland and Northern Virginia (1986); Volume 7—Shenandoah National Park (1986); Volume 8—Southern Virginia (1988); Volume 9—Tennessee-North Carolina (1983); Volume 10—North Carolina-Georgia (1985 with 1988 addendum)

ATI *AAA Tour Book—Illinois/Indiana/Ohio*, American Automobile Association (1991)

ATK *AAA Tour Book—Kentucky/Tennessee*, American Automobile Association (1991)

ATL *AAA CitiBook—Miami/Miami Beach/Ft. Lauderdale*, American Automobile Association (1984)

ATM *AAA Tour Book—Mid-Atlantic*, American Automobile Association (1991)

ATN *AAA Tour Book—Georgia/North*

LIST OF SOURCES USED

      Carolina/South Carolina, American Automobile Association (1991)
- **ATP** AAA Tour Book—New Jersey/Pennsylvania, American Automobile Association (1992)
- **ATW** AAA Tour Book—Michigan, Wisconsin, American Automobile Association (1993)
- **AWB** The American Walk Book, by Jean Craghead George, E.P. Dutton (1978)
- **AYH** American Youth Hostels Handbook 1990-91, American Youth Hostels (1990)
- **BGG** Brown's Guide to the Georgia Outdoors, ed. by John W. English, Cherokee Publishing Co. (1986)
- **BGI** Brunswick and the Golden Isles of Georgia Visitors Guide, Brunswick & the Golden Isles Visitors Bureau (1991)
- **BHT** Best Hiking Trails in the United States, by Dorothy Deer, Greatlakes Living Press (1977)
- **BMG** Backpacker Magazine's Guide to the Appalachian Trail, by Jim Chase, Stackpole Books (1989)
- **BPM** Backpacker, Magazine by Rodale Press, Inc. (1993)
- **BRM** Blue Ridge Mountain Pleasures, by Donald C. Wenberg, The East Woods Press (1985)
- **CBP** Exploring from Chesapeake Bay to the Poconos, by Annette Carter, J.B. Lippincott Company (1975)
- **CFC** Central Florida Camping, by Tipisa Lodge, Order of the Arrow, Central Florida Council, BSA (1992)
- **CGA** The Complete Guide to America's National Parks, National Park Foundation (1986)
- **COC** Ohio Hiking Trails, leaflet by Central Ohio Council, BSA, Columbus, OH (1991)
- **CPH** Central Park—A History and a Guide, by Henry Hope Reed and Sophia Duckworth, Clarkson N. Potter, Inc. (1972)
- **DBV** Daytrips, Getaway Weekends, and Budget Vacations, by Patricia & Robert Foulke, The Globe Pequot Press (1989)
- **DGW** Daytrips, Getaway Weekends, and Vacations in New England, by Patricia & Robert Foulke, The Globe Pequot Press (1988)
- **DIF** 22 Days in Florida, by Richard Harris, John Muir Publications (1988)
- **DMA** Daytrips, Getaway Weekends, and Vacations in the Mid-Atlantic States, by Patricia & Robert Foulke, The Globe Pequot Press (1983)
- **DMP** Frommer's Delaware, Maryland, Pennsylvania & the New Jersey Shore, by Patricia Tunison Preston and John J. Preston, Prentice Hall (1991)
- **DMV** Hiking Trails, pamphlet by DelMar-Va Council, BSA, Wilmington, DE (1990)
- **DNJ** Discovering New Jersey, by Thomas R. Radko, Rutgers University Press (1986)
- **EAN** Easy Access to National Parks, by Wendy Roth and Michael Tompane, Sierra Club Books (1992)
- **EGH** The Essential Guide to Hiking in the United States, by Charles Cook, Michael Kesend Publishing (1992)
- **EMW** The Sierra Club Guides to the National Parks—East and Middle West, Stewart, Tabori & Chang (1986)
- **FDN** Favorite Daytrips in New England, by Michael Schuman, Yankee Publishing Incorporated (1985)
- **FEI** Florida's Enchanting Islands—Sanibel & Captiva, by Linda Firestone and Whit Morse, Good Life Publishers (1980)
- **FGU** The Field Guide to U.S. National Forests, by Robert H. Mohlenbrock, Congdon & Weed, Inc. (1984)
- **FHA** Fifty Hikes in the Adirondacks, by Barbara McMartin, Backcountry Publications (1988)
- **FHO** Fifty Hikes in Ohio, Ralph Ramey, The Countryman Press, Inc. (1990)

LIST OF SOURCES USED

FIF   *Free in Florida*, by Dorothy B. Maxwell, Ariel Publishing (1988)

FMV   *Fodor's Maine, Vermont, New Hampshire*, Fodor's Travel Publications, Inc. (1991)

FNE   *Fodor's 92 New England*, Fodor's Travel Publications, Inc. (1992)

FNS   *Fodor's Nova Scotia, Prince Edward Island and New Brunswick*, Fodor's Travel Publications, Inc. (1991)

FNY   *Frommer's New York State '92-'93*, by John Foreman, Prentice Hall Travel (1992)

FOB   *Florida Off the Beaten Path*, by Diana and Bill Gleasner, The Globe Pequot Press (1990)

FRN   *Frommer's New England*, by Tom Brosnahan, Prentice Hall (1990)

FTA   *Walking the Florida Trail*, by John M. Keller and Ernest A. Baldini, Florida Trail Association, Inc. (1989)

FTG   *52 Great Getaways Throughout Florida and the Keys*, by Robert Tolf and Russell Buchan, Clarkson N. Potter, Inc. (1990)

FTS   *Fodor's 91 The South*, Fodor's Travel Publications, Inc. (1991)

FWM   *Florida Wildlife Magazine*, Florida Game and Fresh Water Fish Commission (various dates)

GAG   *A Guide to America's Greatest Historic Places*, American Heritage Magazine (1985)

GAT   *Guide to Adirondack Trails*, The Adirondack Mountain Club, Inc. Volume V—West-Central Region, by Arthur W. Haberl (1987); Volume VII—Southern Region, by Linda Laing (1988)

GBD   *A Guide to the Backpacking and Day-Hiking Trails of Kentucky*, by Arthur B. Lander, Jr., Thomas Press (1979)

GBP   *Greater Boston Park and Recreation Guide*, by Mark L. Primack, The Globe Pequot Press (1983)

GBR   *Camper's and Hiker's Guide to the Blue Ridge Parkway*, by Donald H. Robinson, The Chatham Press, Inc. (1971)

GCN   *Florida Parks—A Guide to Camping in Nature*, by Gerald Grow, Longleaf Publications (1989)

GFA   *Guide to Free Attractions*, by Don & Pam Wright, Cottage Publications (1990)

GFC   *Guide to Free Campgrounds*, by Don Wright, Cottage Publications (1990)

GGB   *The Guide to Gifts and Bequests—New York/Florida 1991-93*, The Institutions Press, Inc. (1991)

GGC   *A Guide to the Georgia Coast*, The Georgia Conservancy (1988)

GKO   *A Guide to Kentucky Outdoors*, by Arthur B. Lander, Jr., Thomas Press (1978)

GMG   *Guidebook to Mountain Getaways in Georgia, North Carolina and Tennessee*, by Rusty Hoffland, On the Road Publishing (1990)

GNC   *A Guide to North Carolina Outdoors*, by Pat Taylor, Terraqua Publications (1983)

GNA   *The Random House Guide to Natural Areas of the Eastern United States*, by John Perry and Jane Greverus Perry, Random House (1980)

GNM   *A Guide to National Monuments and Historic Sites*, by Jill MacNeice, Prentice Hall (1990)

GNP   *National Geographic's Guide to the National Parks of the United States*, National Geographic Society (1989)

GNW   *Guide to the National Wildlife Refuges*, by Laura and William Riley, Anchor Press Doubleday (1979)

GOB   *Georgia Off the Beaten Path*, by William Schemmel, The Globe Pequot Press (1989)

GOG   *The Bantam Great Outdoors Guide*, by Val Vandi, Bantam Books (1978)

GOP   *Going Off the Beaten Path*, by Mary Dymond Davis, The Noble Press, Inc. (1991)

GPW   *Going Places with Children in Washington*, by Salley Shannon

and Ruth Ann Phang, Green Acres School (1985)
GRT *500 Great Rail-Trails*, by Rails-to-Trails Conservancy, Living Planet Press (1993)
GTB *Guide to Backpacking in the United States*, by Eric Meves, Macmillan Publishing Co., Inc. (1977)
GTF *A Hiking Guide to the Trails of Florida*, by Elizabeth F. Cantor, Menasha Ridge Press (1987)
HAC *Hiking—A Celebration of the Sport and the World's Best Places to Enjoy It*, by Cindy Ross, Richard Ballantine/Byron Preiss Book (1992)
HBF *Hiking and Backpacking in Florida*, by Robert Anderson, Erwin Lampert, Vols. 1-3 (1990)
HFI *Hiking from Inn to Inn*, by David and Kathleen MacInnes, East Woods Press Books (1984)
HFK *Hidden Florida Keys and Everglades*, by Candace Leslie, Ulysses Press (1990)
HFL *Hidden Florida—The Adventurer's Guide*, by Stacy Ritz et al., Ulysses Press (1991)
HGS *Hiker's Guide to the Smokies*, by Dick Murlless and Constance Stallings, Sierra Club Books (1973)
HMS *Hiking the Mountain State—The Trails of West Virginia*, by Allen de Hart, Appalachian Mountain Club (1986)
HOD *Hiking the Old Dominion: The Trails of Virginia*, by Allen de Hart, Sierra Club Books (1984)
HTA *Hiking Trails of America*, Edition No. 16, by Shiloh Military Trail, Inc. (1984-85); Edition No. 17 was prepared by American Historical Trails (1992)
HTM *Hiking Trails in the Midwest*, by Jerry Sullivan and Glenda Daniel, Contemporary Books, Inc. (1974)
HTN *Hiking Trails in the Northeast*, by Thomas A. Henley and Neesa Sweet, Greatlakes Living Press (1976)

HUN *Horizons Unlimited*, Boy Scouts of America (publication no. 83-108) (1987)
IBP *Indiana Off the Beaten Path*, by Bill and Phyllis Thomas, The East Woods Press (1985)
IFT *Introduction to Foot Trails in America*, by Robert Colwell, Stackpole Books (1972)
IGC *Indispensable Guide to Cincinnati*, by Pay Kayser, Pat Kayser Books, Inc. (1986)
IGS *An Insider's Guide to Southern Vermont*, by Margaret Bucholt, Penguin Books, Ltd. (1991)
IGT *Insider's Guide to the Triangle*, by J. Barlow Herget and Dee Reid, Storie/McOwen Publishers (1989)
IOB *Illinois Off the Beaten Path*, by Rod Fensom & Julie Foreman, The Globe Pequot Press (1987)
IRN *Isle Royale National Park*, by Jim DuFresne, The Mountaineers (1984)
LBE *The Long Blue Edge of Summer*, by Doris Scharfenberg, William B. Eerdmans Publishing Company (1982)
LGU *Let's Go: USA*, ed. by Joseph M. Rainsbury, St. Martin's Press (1993)
LRA *Lakeside Recreation Areas*, by Bill and Phyllis Thomas, Stackpole Books (1977)
MEG *Maine—An Explorer's Guide*, by Christina Tree and Mimi Steadman, The Countryman Press, Inc. (1989)
MGL *Mobil Travel Guide—Great Lakes Area*, Prentice Hall (1990)
MGV *Maine: A Guide to the Vacation State*, by Ray Bearse, Houghton Mifflin Company (1969)
MMA *Mobil Travel Guide—Middle Atlantic*, Prentice Hall (1990)
MNE *Mobil Travel Guide—Northeast*, Prentice Hall (1990)
MOB *Michigan Off the Beaten Path*, by Jim Dufresne, The Globe Pequot Press (1988)

LIST OF SOURCES USED 341

MSE *Mobil Travel Guide—Southeast,* Prentice Hall (1990)
MSO *Mountain South,* by Dana Facaros and Michael Pauls, Hippocrene Books (1986)
MVC *Historic Trails of the United States,* leaflet by Miami Valley Council, BSA, Dayton, OH (1991)
NAT *Nature Nearby,* by Bill McMillon, John Wiley & Sons (1990)
NEO *New England Off the Beaten Path,* by Corinne Madden Ross & Ralph Woodward, East Woods Press (1981)
NET *New England Tourist Guide,* Michelin Tire Company (1986)
NFG *National Forest Guide,* by Len Hilts, Rand McNally & Company (1976)
NGC *The Naturalist's Guide to Cedar Key, Florida,* by Harriet Smith, Rife's Printing, Inc. (1987)
NHG *The Official New Hampshire Guidebook,* by New Hampshire Department of Resources and Economic Development (1994)
NHH *New Hampshire Highway Map & Parklands Guide,* by New Hampshire Office of Travel and Tourism Development (1993)
NHT *Nationally Approved Historic Trails,* Boy Scouts of America (publication no. 20-135) (1989 & 1993)
NJD *New Jersey Day Trips,* by Barbara Hudgins, The Woodmont Press (1991)
NJO *New Jersey Off the Beaten Path,* by William F. Scheller, The Globe Pequot Press (1988)
NNY *Natural New York,* by Bill and Phyllis Thomas, Holt, Rinehart and Winston (1983)
NPE *Guide to the National Park Areas: Eastern States,* by David L. Scott and Kay W. Scott, The Globe Pequot Press (1987)
NPF *National Parks—The Family Guide,* by Dave Robertson and Dr. June Francis, On Site! Publications (1991)
NPG *National Park Guide for the Handicapped,* National Park Service (1978)
NPI *The National Parks: Index 1985,* U.S. Government Printing Office (1985)
NPA *Map and Guide,* flyer by National Park Service (1989)
NPV *Great National Park Vacations,* Allstate Motor Club, Prentice Hall Trade Division (1989)
NSS *The National Seashores,* by Ruth and Walt Wolverton, Woodbine House (1988)
NWA *Natural Washington,* by Bill and Phyllis Thomas, Holt, Rinehart and Winston (1980)
NYO *New York Off the Beaten Path,* by William G. Scheller, The Globe Pequot Press (1987)
NYW *New York Walk Book,* New York-New Jersey Trail Conference, Inc., Doubleday/Natural History Press (1971)
OCS *Orange County: The Source,* Office of the Orange County Chairman (1993)
ODT *150 Day Trips—North East Florida,* by Joan Lundquist Scalpone, Let's Go Somewhere Books (1985)
OJP *Outbound Journeys in Pennsylvania,* by Marcia Bonta, Keystone Books (1987)
OMS *Outdoor Mississippi,* by Carolyn Newton, University and College Press of Mississippi (1974)
OOB *Ohio Off the Beaten Path,* by George Zimmermann, The East Woods Press (1985)
ORL *Orlando Sentinel,* newspaper (various dates)
OSG *Off-Season—A Guide to Visiting the National Parks Without the Crowds,* by Joseph E. Brown, Harcourt Brace Jovanovich (1988)
OTB *Off the Beaten Path,* The Reader's Digest Association, Inc. (1987)
PEI *Prince Edward Island 1994 Visitors Guide,* Prince Edward Island Tourism Marketing Council (1994)

PGF   *National Park Guide*, by Michael Frome, Prentice Hall Travel (1992)
PGS   *The Pelican Guide to the Shenandoah*, by Regina H. Pierce and Sharon G. Yackso, Pelican Publishing Company (1987)
PNC   *State Parks of North Carolina*, by Walter C. Biggs, Jr., and James F. Parnell, John F. Blair, Publisher (1989)
POB   *Pennsylvania Off the Beaten Path*, by Sara Pitzer, The Globe Pequot Press (1989)
POG   *Paths of Gold*, by Margot Patterson Doss, Chronicle Books (1974)
PSP   *Pennsylvania State Parks*, leaflet by Pennsylvania Department of Natural Resources (1989)
PTB   *Potomac Trail Book*, by Robert Shosteck, Potomac Books, Inc. (1968)
PTD   *Pathways to Discovery—Exploring America's National Trails*, National Geographic Society (1991)
PTG   *Places to Go with Children in Orlando and Central Florida*, by Deborah Ann Johnson and Cheryl Lani Juarez, Chronicle Books (1992)
RTH   *Restored Towns and Historic Districts of America*, by Alice Cromie, E.P. Dutton (1979)
RTR   *Thirteen National Parks with Room to Roam*, by Ruth and Walt Wolverton, BookCrafters, Inc. (1990)
SAP   *The Southern Appalachians*, by Charlton Ogburn, William Morrow & Company, Inc. (1975)
SAR   These are the author's initials, with the year indicating when he visited the area or hiked at least a portion of the trail.
SCP   *South Carolina State Parks—Cabins/Camping and Other Facilities*, leaflet by South Carolina State Parks (1990)
SCT   *South Carolina Hiking Trails*, by Allen de Hart, The East Woods Press (1984)

SFC   *Scouting Family Camping Directory*, Boy Scouts of America (publication no. 3680A) (1986)
SFL   *Sierra Club Guide to the Natural Areas of Florida*, by John Perry and Jane Greverus Perry, Sierra Club Books (1992)
SNE   *Sierra Club Guide to the Natural Areas of New England*, by John Perry and Jane Greverus Perry, Sierra Club Books (1990)
SRI   *South County, Rhode Island Trail Map & Guide*, South County Tourism Council, Inc. (1993)
SSI   *Sacred Sites—A Traveler's Guide to North America's Most Powerful, Mystical Landmarks*, by Natasha Peterson, Contemporary Books (1988)
SWC   *Short Walks on Cape Cod and the Vineyard*, by Paul and Ruth Sadlier, The Pequot Press (1976)
TBB   *The Berkshire Book*, by Jonathan Sternfield, Berkshire House (1986)
TIT   *1000 Islands Travel Guide*, 1000 Islands International Council (1993)
TNG   *The Hiking Trails of North Georgia*, by Tim Homan, Peachtree Publishers, Ltd. (1987)
TNP   *The National Parks*, by Freeman Tilden, Alfred A. Knopf (1986)
TOT   *Trail of Tears National Historic Trail—Comprehensive Management and Use Plan*, United States Department of the Interior (1992)
TOV   *The Ohio Valley*, by George Laycock and Ellen Laycock, Dolphin Books (1983)
TTN   *Travel Tennessee*, Tennessee Department of Tourist Development (1994)
TTR   *Tennessee Trails*, by Evan Means, The East Woods Press (1984)
TVT   *Travel Vermont*, by Andrew L. Nemethy, Vermont Life Magazine (1988)
VCD   *Virginia Campground Directory*, pamphlet by Virginia Travel Council (1992)

LIST OF SOURCES USED

VEG *Vermont—An Explorer's Guide,* by Christine Tree and Peter Jennison, The Countryman Press (1985)

VFM *Valley Forge & Montgomery County Visitors Guide & Calendar of Events,* Valley Forge Convention & Visitors Bureau (1994)

VOB *Virginia Off the Beaten Path,* by Judy and Ed Colbert, The Globe Pequot Press (1986)

WAF *Washington Free,* by Kiki Canniff, Ki2 Enterprises (1984)

WAT *1980 Worldwide Adventure Travelguide,* American Adventurers Association (1980)

WBR *Walking the Blue Ridge,* by Leonard M. Adkins, University of North Carolina Press (1991)

WCD *Woodall's Campground Directory,* by Woodall Publishing Company (1992 & 1993)

WCG *Washington, D.C.—The Complete Guide,* by Judy Duffield, William Kramer & Cynthia Sheppard, Vintage Books (1988)

WDC *Washington, D.C. at Its Best,* by Robert S. Kane, Passport Books (1991)

WGS *Walks in the Great Smokies,* by Rodney and Priscilla Albright, Fast & McMillan Publishers, Inc. (1984)

WIC *Walks in the Catskills,* by John Bennett and Seth Masia, The East Woods Press (1974)

WNE *Weekending in New England,* by Betsy Wittemann and Nancy Webster, Wood Pond Press (1989)

WOB *Wisconsin Off the Beaten Path,* by Martin Hintz and Dan Hintz, The Globe Pequot Press (1989)

WON *Walks of New England,* by Gary Ferguson, Prentice Hall Press (1989)

WPS *Wild Places of the South,* by Steve Price, The East Woods Press (1980)

WTN *Walks Through New England,* by Kenneth Winchester and David Dunbar, Doubleday & Company, Inc. (1980)

WTW *Walking the Wetlands,* by Janet Lyons and Sandra Jordan, John Wiley & Sons, Inc. (1989)

YNP *Your National Parks,* by George Hornby, Crown Publishers, Inc. (1980)